News from Fox's Gap

Curtis Lynn Older

HERITAGE BOOKS
2018

HERITAGE BOOKS
AN IMPRINT OF HERITAGE BOOKS, INC.

Books, CDs, and more—Worldwide

For our listing of thousands of titles see our website
at
www.HeritageBooks.com

Published 2018 by
HERITAGE BOOKS, INC.
Publishing Division
5810 Ruatan Street
Berwyn Heights, Md. 20740

Heritage Books by the author:

The Braddock Expedition and Fox's Gap in Maryland

The Land Tracts of the Battlefield of South Mountain: Including Many Other Tracts near the Area from Land Records of Frederick County, Washington County and the Maryland Archives

News from Fox's Gap

Cover: Photographs by John Gensor

The Fox Inn, Reno Monument, War Correspondents Memorial Arch,
Mountain House, Dahlgren Chapel

Cover Design: Keke Chien

International Standard Book Number
Paperbound: 978-0-7884-5842-2

In Memory of

Truxton James Older

(28 September 1911 to 06 April 2009)

Introduction

Curtis Lynn Older, President of The Society of the Descendants of Frederick Fox of Fox's Gap in Maryland, published *News from Fox's Gap* each June 1st and December 1st from 1996 through 2006. The newsletter was published only on December 1st for the years 2007 through 2010. The organization stopped accepting new members and discontinued the newsletter in 2011.

All twenty-six newsletters published by the Society are included in this publication. Some of the information included in these newsletters cannot be found anywhere else at this time. This publication is an effort to preserve this information for future generations.

May 2018

Partial Table of Contents

The Society of the Descendants of
Frederick Fox of Fox's Gap in Maryland

News from Fox's Gap

all 26 newsletters published by the Society
Volumes 1 through 4
June 1, 1996 through December 1, 2010

Remember Freedom!

The Society of the Descendants
of
Frederick Fox of Fox's Gap in Maryland

News from Fox's Gap

Volume 1

Issues 1 thru 10

June 1, 1996 through December 1, 2000

Remember Freedom!

Introduction

The Society of the Descendants of Frederick Fox of Fox's Gap in Maryland issues *"News from Fox's Gap"* each June 1 and December 1. Volume One of the newsletter includes Issues One through Ten and covers the period of 1996 through 2000, the first five years of existence for the organization.

An **Index** for each Issue of the newsletter is included at the end of each Issue included in this document.

All individuals who have joined **The Society of the Descendants of Frederick Fox of Fox's Gap in Maryland** from its inception on October 20, 1995, through December 1, 2001, are listed along with their first four ancestor lines after Frederick Fox of Fox's Gap in Maryland after Issue Ten at the end of Volume 1.

****

News from Fox's Gap

Published June 1 and December 1 of each year by

The Society of the Descendants of Frederick Fox of Fox's Gap in Maryland

Membership dues are $6.00 per year. President of the Society is Curtis L. Older.

Make Society related inquiries by the following means:

Curtis L. Older
618 Tryon Place
Gastonia, NC 28054-6066

e-mail: curtolder@earthlink.net
home phone: 704-864-3879

****

Table of Contents

(an Index for each issue is Included as the last page in that Issue)

News from Fox's Gap

The Society of the Descendants of Frederick Fox of Fox's Gap in Maryland

Volume 1, Number 1 June 1, 1996

New Society Formed - First Newsletter

The Society of the Descendants of Frederick Fox of Fox's Gap in Maryland was founded in October 1995 by Curtis Lynn Older of Gastonia, N. C. Membership in the Society is open to all individuals who are descendants of Frederick Fox. A member must only trace their ancestry to an individual listed in *The Fox Genealogy* by Daniel Gebhart Fox, published in 1924. The membership fee is $5.00 per year. The primary obligation of each member is to make a concerted effort to obtain the membership of at least one individual per year who has not previously been a member of the Society

Membership in the Society at May 31, 1996, was fifteen and there was one Honorary Member. Present members trace their lineage to three children of Frederick Fox: Mary Magdelena, George, and Daniel Booker. Members of the Society receive an 8 and 1/2 inch by 11 inch Membership Certificate, a copy of the Bylaws of the Society, and a wallet sized membership card upon receipt by the Society of their membership application form.

Objectives of the Society, among others, are: 1) To archive records that document the descendants of Frederick Fox of Fox's Gap in Maryland; 2) To archive records that document the history of Fox's Gap in Maryland; 3) To promote research related to Frederick Fox and Fox's Gap in Maryland, including the ancestors of Frederick Fox, his brothers and sisters, ancestors of his wife, and ancestors of any of the descendants of Frederick Fox; 4) To support those organizations that have a relationship to the heritage of Frederick Fox and Fox's Gap in Maryland.

Curtis L. Older is president of the Society for 1996. An election to determine a President, Vice-president, Archivist, and Secretary - Treasurer will be held December 1, 1996. The new officers will hold their positions for the calendar years of 1997 and 1998.

First Fox Reunion in Hagerstown

The first Fox Reunion to be held in Hagerstown, Maryland, will be July 4 through 6, 1996. During the Reunion, presentations will be made by Doug Bast of Boonsboro, Maryland; by Steve Stotelmyer of Sharpsburg, Maryland; and by Curtis Older of Gastonia, N. C.

Steve is the author of *Bivouacs of the Dead,* a member of the Central Maryland Heritage League, Inc., of Middletown, Maryland, and has done extensive research on Fox's Gap. Doug is the owner of the Boonsborough Museum of History and has done much research on the history of early western Maryland. Curt is the author of *The Braddock Expedition and Fox's Gap in Maryland* and President of The Society of the Descendants of Frederick Fox of Fox's Gap in Maryland.

Credit is to be given to Ellen (Mrs. James) Fox of San Antonio, Texas, for the idea to hold a Fox Reunion in Maryland.

First Honorary Member of The Society

Doug Bast of the Boonsborough Museum of History in Boonsboro, Maryland, is the Society's first Honorary Member. Doug was selected because he has been helpful and supportive of the efforts of Curtis Older, as well as others, to research the history of the Fox's Gap area in Maryland.

President's Message
by Curtis Lynn Older

As president of the Society, I recommend to the membership that we consider supporting each of the following three organizations with an annual contribution paid to them by the Society at the first of each calendar year in the amount of $25.00:

Central Maryland Heritage League, Inc.
P. O. Box 721
Middletown, MD 21759

Potomac Appalachian Trail Club
118 Park Street, SE
Vienna, VA 22180

Washington County Free Library
100 South Potomac Street
Hagerstown, MD 21740

Our support for these organizations, all of which are important to the preservation of Fox's Gap in Maryland, can increase over the years as our membership grows. The membership will vote upon the above proposal by a separate ballot at the time of the next election of Society officers.

The following organization has some relationship to the objectives of our Society and may be worthy of our support at some point in the future. Members of our Society may desire to obtain a membership in this organization:

Friends of Fort Frederick
11115 Fort Frederick Road
Big Pool, MD 21711

As a descendant of Frederick Fox of Fox's Gap in Maryland, an individual qualifies for membership in the following organizations:

Society of the Descendants of Washington's Army at Valley Forge
P. O. Box 915
Valley Forge, PA 19482-0915

Sons of the American Revolution
1000 South Fourth St.
Louisville, Ky 40203

or

Daughters of the American Revolution
1776 D Street N.W.
Washington, D.C. 20006

Concerning the election of officers at December 1, 1996, for terms of two calendar years beginning January 1, 1997, I include the following from the Bylaws of the Society:

* Any member nominated for any officer position in the Society shall appear on the election ballot.
* Nominations shall be made by any member by communicating such nomination to the President of the Society.
* Any member may nominate only one member for each officer position each year.
* A member may nominate himself or herself for an officer position.

Members should submit their nominations to me by November 1. Ballots will be mailed to members at December 1. Ballots must be returned to a designated vote counter before January 1, 1997, to be counted. Please consult your Society Bylaws for the duties of each Officer.

Members should consult their copy of the Bylaws concerning any proposed changes they wish to make to the Bylaws of the Society.

The Mary Magdelena Fox Benner Line
by William Goudy Benner

The following members of the Society are descended from Mary Magdelena Fox Benner, daughter of Frederick Fox:

William Goudy Benner - Society #0005
Laurel Ann Benner- Society #0006
Brenda Carol Saunders - Society #0007

I am the great-great-greatgrandson of Frederick Fox through his third child Mary Magdelena Fox. She was married to Jacob Benner Sr. who was born in Pennsylvania and moved to Maryland and later to Ohio. In the fall of 1807, Jacob and Mary Fox Benner came to Warren County, Ohio, along with Frederick Fox and three other families and established themselves in this new land. It had been just four short years since Ohio had become the 17th state in the Union.

Dallas, Texas, is my place of birth, however, I have grown up in the Montgomery County, Ohio, Townships of Miami and Washington where I still reside. The homesteads of Frederick Fox and his second wife Susannah Schutt Young Fox, together with the other four families; Benner, Metherd, Brininger, and Leiter who all came to Ohio with him in the fall of 1807, are practically within a "stones throw' of where I now live. Direct descendants of the original Benner/Fox line have resided in this area of Ohio for the last 190 years.

The old St. Johns, or Gebhart, Church Cemetery, as it is now known, just outside Miamisburg, is also just around the corner from here. For me, as it is for many others, visiting this old churchyard is as if you are standing in the midst of a giant "family reunion". From one spot and within a radius of fifty feet you see the names of Fox, Benner, Metherd, Leiter; all of the names familiar to us who have read and re-read the pages of D. B. Fox's book, *The Fox Genealogy*. Nowhere to my knowledge, with the exception of the Hillgrove Cemetery in nearby Miamisburg, is there a greater number of my deceased relatives than in "Gebhart Church". New home development in the past several years has practically made an island out of the lonesome old cemetery. Seemingly few people visit, but on each Memorial Day or "Decoration Day" as it was known in the past, flowers appear on many graves just as they have for more than a century and a half. Still an indication that friends and relatives haven't forgotten the ties to their ancestors.

Next time in this column . . . visiting the estate packets of some of our ancestors.

The George Fox Line

by Curtis L. Older

The following members of the Society are descended from George Fox, son of Frederick Fox:

Elizabeth Jane Bucholz - Society #0008
Dellie Jean Craig - Society #0009
Patricia Jo Edwards - Society #0011
Richard Dale Fox Sr. - Society #0015
Reva Winfried Fox - Society #0003
Robert Claude Fox - Society #0004
William Ernest Fox - Society #0002
Wilma Marion Gose - Society #0010
Curtis Lynn Older - Society #0001

All of the above are descended from John L. Fox, son of George Fox, and from Daniel Alexander Fox, son of John L. Fox. The wife of George Fox was Elizabeth Ann Link, daughter of John Adam Link II and Jane Ogle. Material on George Fox appears on page 82 of *The Fox Genealogy* by Daniel Gebhart Fox. The wife of John L. Fox was Susannah Hilligass. Material on John L. Fox appears on page 94 of *The Fox Genealogy*. The wife of Daniel Alexander Fox was Elizabeth Jane Ricketts. The listing for Daniel Alexander Fox and his children appears on page 96 of *The Fox Genealogy*.

Daniel Alexander Fox was the youngest child of John L. Fox and Sussanah Hilligas. He lived from January 13, 1860 to July 29, 1932. His wife, Elizabeth Jane Ricketts, lived from October 18, 1861 to February 28, 1922. They were united in marriage April 1, 1880. The children of Daniel Alexander Fox and Elizabeth Jane (Ricketts) Fox were:

(1) Kenneth B. Fox
(2) Ernest Daniel Fox
(3) William Edward Fox
(4) Ethel Belle Fox (Gouty)
(5) Ruby Dale Fox (Hines)

Descendants of (2) Ernest Daniel Fox include:
Claude Ernest Fox, father of:
Robert Claude Fox - Society #0004
William Ernest Fox - Society #0002

Descendants of (3) William Edward Fox include:
Elizabeth Jane Bucholz - Society #0008
Reva Winfried Fox - Society #0003
Wilma Marion Gose - Society #0010
Evelyn L. Fox Switzer, mother of
Patricia Jo Edwards - Society #0011
Richard Dale Fox Sr.- Society #0015, father of:
Dellie Jean Craig - Society #0009

Descendants of (4) Ethel Belle Fox Gouty include:
Mavis Lorene Gouty Older, mother of:
Curtis Lynn Older - Society #0001

Proposed future articles for this column, not necessarily in the sequence in which they will appear, include:

1) The Descendants of Ernest Daniel Fox, son of Daniel Alexander Fox
2) Link Ancestors of Elizabeth Ann Link, wife of George Fox
3) Ogle Ancestors of Elizabeth Ann Link, wife of George Fox

The Daniel Booker Fox Line

by Curtis Lynn Older

The following members of the Society are descended from Daniel Booker Fox, son of Frederick Fox:

James Joseph Fox - Society #0012
Raphael Henry John Fox - Society #0013
Judith Fox Smith - Society #0014

No material was submitted for this issue.

Descendants of William Edward Fox

by Dellie Jean (Fox) Craig, daughter of Richard Fox Sr., and grand-daughter of William Edward Fox

The following members of the Society are descended from William Edward Fox, a son of Daniel Alexander Fox and Elizabeth Jane (Ricketts) Fox:

Reva Winfried Fox - Society #0003;
Elizabeth Jane Bucholz - Society #0008
Wilma Marion Gose - Society #0010;
Evelyn L. Fox Switzer, mother of Patricia Jo Edwards - Society #0011
Richard Dale Fox Sr.- Society #0015, father of: Dellie Jean Craig - Society #0009

William Edward Fox was born on 05 January 1888, in Gessie, Highland Township, Vermillion County, Indiana. He was the 3rd child of Daniel Alexander Fox and Elizabeth Jane (Ricketts) Fox. William died on Tuesday 16 April 1974 at his residence in Mound Township and was buried next to his wife at Lower Mound Cemetery, Vermillion County, Indiana. Age 86y 3m 14d.

He was united in marriage to Marguerite Clem on 10 February 1909 at Danville, Vermilion County, Illinois by Henry J. Hall, Justice of Peace. James E. Hughes and Ethel Belle Fox were the witnesses. Marguerite Clem was born 09 March 1894 in Mound Township, Warren County, Indiana, the daughter of Augustus Elmer Clem and Melinda Lloyd (Cunningham) Clem. Marguerite died on 25 January 1970 in Danville, Vermilion County, Illinois. Age 75y 9m 16d. William and Marguerite lived most of their married life around the Gessie and Foster, Indiana, areas. Around Foster they resided on 30 acres in Mound Township on Section 32, T 20N, and Range 9. This was land she inherited from her mother. The land originally belonged to Marguerite's grandfather, Cyrus Cunningham, an early Warren County landowner.

William Fox had been a carpenter for many years and employed at the Neal Gravel Co. and the Indiana State Highway Dept. before retiring in 1950. He enjoyed his garden, sheep, and chicks. After his wife's death he lived in their house until 16 August 1973 when he had a stroke. After he got out of the hospital he resided with his daughter Evelyn and son-in-law Jesse Switzer. Their residence was located next door to William and Margueite's home. He died in his house in his favorite chair with the radio on.

To this union were born nine children:
1) Reva Winfred Fox born 23 May 1910
2) Evelyn Louise Fox born 15 September 1913
3) Glenn William Fox born 01 February 1916
4) Daniel Augustus Fox born 10 December 1917
5) Melinda Lloyd Fox born 19 Jan 1919, died 03 Feb 1919
6) Elizabeth Jane Fox born 14 April 19227)
7) Wilma Marion Fox born 11 October 1928
8) Richard Dale Fox born 20 July 1933
9) James Herbert Fox born 22 January 1937

a) Birth recorded for William Edward Fox - Vermillion County, Indiana.
b) Marriage certificate for William Edward Fox and Marguerite Clem recorded at Vermilion County, Illinois.
c) Both death certificates recorded at Warren County, Indiana.
d. Birth dates listed from family bible of William Fox and Marguerite (Clem) Fox.
e) Obituaries for William Edward Fox and Marguerite (Clem) Fox.
f) Land location off of land records recorded at Warren County, Indiana, courthouse

Proposed future articles for this column include:

1) The Descendants of William Edward Fox, a son of Daniel Alexander Fox
2) The Ancestors of William Edward Fox, a son of Daniel Alexander Fox
3) The Ancestors of Marguerite Clem, wife of William Edward Fox

Frederick Fox and Fox's Gap in Maryland Section

by Curtis Lynn Older

Family Line Publications of Westminster, Maryland, published in September 1995, *The Braddock Expedition and Fox's Gap in Maryland* by Curtis Lynn Older. The book documents the passage of General Braddock, George Washington, and Governor Horatio Sharpe through Fox's Gap on their way from Frederick Town in Maryland to Swearingen's Ferry at Sheperdstown, Virginia, on May 2, 1755. The earliest land tracts for the territory from Middletown to Boonsboro and Keedysville are shown. Material on Turner's Gap, one mile north of Fox's Gap, supports the creation of the road through Turner's Gap after 1755 and before 1760. Information also appears for Crampton's Gap and Orr's Gap.

Two hundred copies of the book were made. The author acquired one hundred copies and Family Line Publications acquired the other one hundred copies. The author had sold about 50 copies of the book at May 31 and Family Line Publications had sold about 50 copies. **The book will not be reprinted.** The toll-free number for ordering a catalogue or book from Family Line Publications is 1-800-876-6103. Family Line Publications has a large assortment of genealogical related books. They have many general reference books as well as books on the early records of the states of Delaware, Maryland, New Jersey, Pennsylvania, Virginia, Kentucky, West Virginia, and Washington, D. C.

As President of the Society, I would like to recommend for the consideration of the membership, the setting of an objective by the Society to reprint *The Fox Genealogy* by Daniel Gebhart Fox. Few copies of the original book by D. G. Fox are known to be in existence. The few that exist are not in good condition. The Society probably could obtain 100 paperback copies of the book for about $500, or $5.00 per book. I recommend we acquire only 100 copies. The fewer copies printed, however, leads to a higher per unit cost. If the Society membership reaches 50 members and each member commits to purchase two copies of the book at $5.00 each, it should enable us to reprint the book. I submit this proposal as a long-range goal of the Society.

Those members desiring to obtain a copy of *The Land Tracts of Fox's Gap including material on Crampton's, Orr's, and Turner's Gaps*, can obtain a loose-leaf copy from me for the sum of $50.00, which includes postage. The present version available is the 1996 version. The next version will not be produced until 1998. I continue to work on, and add to, this self-published work.

Utilizing the services of Applied CD Technology in Charlotte, N. C., I can supply Kodak Photo CD-Rom discs at $10.00 per disc plus 60 cents per image added to the disc. Each disc will hold 100 items. Your attention is directed to the **Photographs Available through the Society** section of this newsletter. I can supply members those items selected from the said list at the above indicated cost. You can access the images on the disc using Windows 95 or Macintosh Operating System 7.0 on a computer with a CD-Rom drive.

I am in the process of creating another self-published book, *Documentation Related to Frederick Fox including material on his Descendants*. This book will include all the images on the Kodak Photo CD-Rom disc entitled "Fox's Gap in Maryland." I hope to have this available for distribution in late 1997.

The following quarterly publication is very useful in researching the western Maryland area:

Western Maryland Genealogy
P. O. Box 505
New Market, MD 21774-0505

An annual subscription is $19.00.

Archives Section

** The following organizations have a copy of *The Fox Genealogy* by Daniel Gebhart Fox:

Washington County Free Library
100 South Potomac Street
Hagerstown, MD 21740

Maryland State Law Library
Courts of Appeal Building
361 Rowe Blvd.
Annapolis, MD 21401

Family History Library
35 North West Temple Street
Salt Lake City, Utah 84150

Sons of the American Revolution
1000 South Fourth St.
Louisville, Kentucky 40203

Daughters of the American Revolution
1776 D Street N.W.
Washington, D.C. 20006

** *The Land Tracts of Fox's Gap including material on Crampton's, Orr's, and Turner's Gaps*, self-published by Curtis Lynn Older, has been presented to the following organizations:

Washington County Free Library
100 South Potomac Street
Hagerstown, MD 21740

Frederick County Historical Society
24 East Church St.
Frederick, MD 20701

** A Kodak Photo CD-Rom Disc entitled "Fox's Gap in Maryland" has been presented to:

Family History Library
35 North West Temple Street
Salt Lake City, Utah 84150

Washington County Free Library
100 South Potomac Street
Hagerstown, MD 21740

** The following organizations have a copy of *The Braddock Expedition and Fox's Gap in Maryland* by Curtis Lynn Older:

Washington County Free Library
100 South Potomac Street
Hagerstown, MD 21740

Frederick County Historical Society
24 East Church St.
Frederick, MD 20701

Washington County Historical Society
P. O. Box 1281
135 W. Washington St.
Hagerstown, MD 21740

Maryland State Archives
Hall of Records
350 Rowe Blvd.
Annapolis, MD 21401

Historical Society of Western Pennsylvania
4338 Bigelow Blvd.
Pittsburgh, PA 15213

Fort Necessity National Battlefield
The National Pike
RD 2-Box 528
Farmington, PA 15437

Antietam National Battlefield
P. O. Box 158
Sharpsburg, MD 21782

Potomac Appalachian Trail Club
118 Park Street, SE
Vienna, VA 22180

Family History Library
35 North West Temple Street
Salt Lake City, Utah 84150

** An objective of the Society is to place on a microfilm roll at December 31, 1997, the following materials:

The Fox Genealogy by Daniel Gebhart Fox
The Braddock Expedition and Fox's Gap in Maryland by Curtis Lynn Older

The Land Tracts of Fox's Gap including material on Crampton's, Orr's, and Turner's Gaps by Curtis Lynn Older

Documentation Related to Frederick Fox including material on his Descendants by Curtis Lynn Older

The *Index* to "Fox's Gap in Maryland" Kodak Photo CD-Rom Disc by Curtis Lynn Older

The following material held by The Society of the Descendants of Frederick Fox of Fox's Gap in Maryland:

all Society Membership Application Forms through Dec. 31, 1997

all photos and genealogical information presented to the Society by Dec. 31, 1997

the Society Membership Roster at Dec. 31, 1997

the Society Newsletters

other material held by the Society deemed necessary to archive

Questions and Answers

(Members may submit questions and/or answers to the Society President for inclusion in this column of the newsletter.)

Question. (by Curtis Lynn Older) How do we know our Frederick Fox who lived near Miamisburg, Ohio, was the same one who lived at one time at Fox's Gap in Maryland?

Answer. (by Curtis Lynn Older) Beyond any doubt they were one and the same for the following reasons. Land records and marriage records indicate the following individuals and families lived in the immediate area of Fox's Gap in Maryland: Frederick Fox, George Fox, Jacob and Mary Magdalena (Fox) Benner, and George and Christena (Fox) Mettard. George Mettard owned 10 acres near the Reno Monument at Fox's Gap. All of these individuals are buried in the St. John or Gebhart Cemetery in Miamisburg, Ohio. The tombstone of George Fox indicates he was "born March 10, 1781 in the State of Md." The tombstone of John Liter indicates, "from Frederick County Md." The tombstone of Daniel B. Fox, a son of Frederick also buried in the Gebhart Cemetery, indicates, "born in Frederick Co. Md." A land tract record exists for Out Lot to Lot #1 in Sharpsburg, Maryland. The deed was between Frederick Fox of Warren County, State of Ohio, and Peter Ham of Washington County in Maryland.

> "This indenture made this twelfth day of September in the year of our Lord one thousand eight hundred and ten between Frederick Fox of Warren County - - - in the state of Ohio of the one part and Peter Ham of Washington County state of Maryland of the other part."

A copy of this deed was obtained from Doug Bast of the Boonesborough Museum of History in Boonsboro, Maryland. The deed contains the following section: "Received Sept. 12th 1810 to be recorded and same day receipted in Liber W folios 285 & 286 one of the land records of Wasshington County."

There is a copy of an 1812 letter from Jacob Reel of Sharpsburg to Frederick and Michael Fox of Warren County, Ohio, that discusses the death of their mother Christiana. A copy of the letter was obtained from Robert H. Fox of Cincinnati, Ohio. The letter mentions a "Mr. Widmeyer and wife." A William Widmyer sold a tract of land to Frederick Fox while Frederick lived in Maryland. The deed was for part of two tracts, I Hope It Is Well Done and Shettle. The deed was recorded 21 August 1795 in

Frederick County, Maryland, Land Records. The relationship of Jacob Reel to Michael and Frederick Fox is unknown. Perhaps a sister of Jacob Reel was married to Michael Fox, Frederick's brother.

Question. (by Curtis Lynn Older) Was Frederick Fox of Fox's Gap in Maryland a member of the Tenth Pennsylvania Regiment, Continental Line, during the American Revolution?

Answer. (by Curtis Lynn Older) We do not know conclusively the answer to this question. There is nothing I have found to refute that Frederick Fox of Fox's Gap in Maryland was the same Frederick Fox as the one in the Tenth Pennsylvania Regiment, Continental Line. On the other hand, it does not seem possible, with the information available to me, to prove beyond any question that they were one and the same Frederick Fox. We should state at the outset that it was not uncommon for men from one state to serve in the Continental Line of another state. The State of Pennsylvania probably had more out-of-state troops in its units than any other state.

In *The Fox Genealogy*, D. G. Fox states, "During the Revolution, Frederick Fox served as a drummer in Lieutenant Colonel Hay's Company, Tenth Pennsylvania Regiment, from 1777 to 1781." Perhaps Daniel Gebhart Fox relied upon, and had available, information besides material in the Pennsylvania Archives. If he did, his source is unknown to me at this time. Perhaps Daniel Gebhart Fox simply went to the Pennsylvania Archives and came across the name of Frederick Fox listed under the entries for the 10th Pennsylvania Regiment, Continental Line. If he merely assumed that the one listed was our Frederick Fox, he could have been wrong in his statement in his book.

There are three Frederick Fox listed in the Pennsylvania Archives as serving during the American Revolution. One was in the 10th Pennsylvania Regiment, Continental Line, one was in Von Heer's Dragoons, and one was in the Bedford County Militia:

1) Pennsylvania Archives, Series 5, Volume 3, page 921
Names of Soldiers of Von Heer's Dragoons, Taken from Pension Papers (a)

Fox, Andrew, resided in Berks county in 1835.
Fox, [Fuchs], David, Reading, 1778, trumpeter, resided in Berks county in 1835, aged sixty-nine.
Fox [Fuchs], Jacob, Reading, 1778; resided in Pleasant township, Fairfield county, Ohio in 1834.
Fox [Fuchs], Frederick, 1779; brother of the former, resided in Shenandoah county, Virginia, in 1829.

2) The Third Company of the First Battalion of the Bedford County Commanded by Capt. Evan Cissna. (c.) Page 110, probably the Pennsylvania Archives, Associators and Militia.

3. Frederick Fox

We know our Frederick Fox was not the Frederick Fox listed in Von Heer's Dragoons because our Frederick Fox did not reside in Shenandoah county, Virginia, in 1829 and did not have a brother named Jacob. We know our Frederick Fox was not the one listed under the Bedford County troops because he did not live in Bedford County, Pennsyvlania, at that time. The Bedford unit would have consisted of local residents.

The Frederick Fox of the 10th Pennsylvania Regiment, Continental Line, enlisted April 20, 1777, and served until January 1, 1781. He was a drummer for his unit from early 1777 until his discharge at January 1, 1781. It is very unlikely he could have held the position of drummer throughout his enlistment if he had not obeyed orders and had not been present with the troops when he was supposed to be with them.

Available records of the period that relate to our Frederick Fox do not enable us to disprove he was in the 10th Pennsylvania Regiment, Continental Line. Our Frederick Fox must have been the Frederick Fox who served as a member of Joseph Chapline's Company of Militia, probably between

1775 and 1777.[1] Our Frederick Fox must have been the Frederick Fox who signed the Patriot's Oath of Fidelity and Support, probably in 1777 or 1778.[2] We also must consider that Mary Magdalena Fox, daughter of Frederick, was born Dec 17, 1778. Let us address these three issues.

The dates of membership of Frederick Fox in Joseph Chapline's Company of Militia are not on record. The muster roll listed in the Maryland Archives does not give a date. The muster roll on which the name of Frederick Fox appears probably was similar to others that included the statement, "do enroll ourselves into a Company of Militia agreeable to the Resolves of the Provincial Convention held at the City of Annapolis this 26th Day of July 1775." Similar muster rolls usually have dates from 1775 to 1777. Even though our Frederick Fox was in a Maryland Militia unit for some period during 1775 to 1777, it does not prohibit him from being the Frederick Fox who joined the Tenth Pennsylvania Regiment, Continental Line, in April 1777.

The list of men who signed the Patriot's Oath of Fidelity and Support did so as, "Directed by an Act of the General Assembly of the State of Maryland Passed the 5th day of Feb. 1777." The list was signed as follows, "Witness my hand and Seal the 2d Day of March, 1778." It is probable our Frederick Fox signed this oath between Feb. 5, 1777, and March 2, 1778. Therefore, either he signed the oath before joining the Tenth Pennsylvania Regiment, Continental Line, or while he was in the unit.

The Tenth Pennsylvania Regiment, Continental Line, was at Valley Forge from December 1777 to May 1778. During this critical period, many troops were not present at Valley Forge for the entire period the army encamped there. It is entirely possible Frederick Fox signed the Patriot's Oath when he was on leave from his unit or when he was in the Fox's Gap area conducting some type of business related to the Pennsylvania Line. Such business might have related to the transportation or requisition of food or supplies. Thus, it is entirely possible Frederick Fox could have signed the oath while he was away from Valley Forge.

This brings us to the last issue. Mary Magdalena Fox, daughter of Frederick, was born Dec. 17, 1778. Doesn't this indicate Frederick Fox was not at Valley Forge with his unit during March or April of 1778? Again, there is no conflict here because many troops were sent out to find food and other materials during the Valley Forge encampment. The troops at the Valley Forge encampment did not spend their entire time sitting around camp freezing to death.

Ohio D.A.R. records indicate our Frederick Fox was in the 10th Pennsylvania Regiment, Continental Line. The Ohio D.A.R. records could have been submitted by Daniel Gebhart Fox. These records, therefore, do not help us solve the issue before us. Daniel Gebhart Fox may have had other sources of material unknown to us. Such sources might have been the Daniel Booker Fox family Bible or the granddaughter of Frederick Fox he identifes in one of the Appendix to his book. It is possible this unknown source substantiated that our Frederick Fox was the one who served in the 10th Pennsylvania Regiment, Continental Line.

Both our Frederick Fox, in various land records of Frederick County in Maryland, and the Frederick Fox of the Tenth Pennsylvania Regiment, Continental Line, signed an "X" for their name. Our Frederick Fox was not in any other Maryland military organization during the years of 1777 through 1781. The force of the American Revolution was so strong, it seems unimaginable Frederick Fox did not continue to serve in some military unit after he served in Joseph Chapline's militia unit at the start of the war. In conclusion, I believe our Frederick Fox of Fox's Gap in Maryland was the Frederick Fox of the Tenth Pennsylvania Regiment, Continental Line. Daniel Gebhart Fox probably had some information connecting Frederick Fox of Fox's Gap in Maryland to the Tenth Pennsylvania Regiment. He probably went to the Pennsylvania Archives to substantiate this information that was passed down to him.

Photographs Available through the Society

Photographs / Individuals

1. **Daniel Booker Fox**, circa 1860, retouched.
2. **Daniel Alexander Fox and Elizabeth Jane Ricketts**, wedding day, April 1, 1880.
3. **Daniel Alexander Fox and Elizabeth Jane Ricketts Fox Family**, circa 1900.
4. **Robert William Gouty, Ethel Belle Fox Gouty, Mavis Lorene Gouty Older**, circa 1920.
5. **Ethel Belle Fox Gouty, Ruby Dale Fox Hines, William Edward Fox, Kenneth B. Fox**, circa 1960.
6. **Reva Winfried Fox**, daughter of William Edward Fox, 1988.
7. **Curtis Lynn Older, Linda Sue Osborn Older, and Rachael Lynn Older**, 1995.

Photographs / Maps

101. **Winslows Map of 1736, also known as The "Mayo" Map of 1736-7.** "Messrs. Wm. May, Robert Brook, --- Winslow, and --- Savage appointed surveyors in 1736. The party which performed this work consisted of the four surveyors with thirteen assistants, six of them chain-carriers, employed at three shillings per day. Among the names employed to describe features of Maryland territory may be noticed the following variations from present usage: Monokasy [Monocacy], Kittokton [Catoctin], Conigochego [Conococheague]." Library of Congress, Benj. Winslow. "A Plan of the upper Part of Patomack River called Cohongoroot Survey'd in the year 1736. Geography & Map Div. Collection contains a reproduction, the original map is owned by Enoch Pratt Free Library of Baltimore, MD. [U.S. Potomac River (reg.). . 1736 . . Winslow].

102. **Fry and Jefferson Map of 1751, 1755, and 1775.** "The most important map of the Middle British Colonies published during the second half of the eighteenth century was the result of the joint labors of Professor Joshua Fry and Mr. Peter Jefferson. It is probable that the information represented on the map indicates the highest degree of knowledge of the country attainable at that time. The map apparently was completed in the year 1749, although it is dated 1751. The Maryland portion of the sheet does not adequately represent the high character of the map, since there is little indicated besides names and a few roads on the Maryland portion, while Virginia streams and roads are carefully delineated with their names attached. The roads are only such as were main thoroughfares connecting different portions of Virginia with Philadelphia." Library of Congress: Fry, Joshua. A map of the inhabited part of Virginia . . . G3880 1751 .F7 (Negative No. 2802) [1755 ed].

103. **1794 Dennis Griffith Map of Maryland.** Drawn by Dennis Griffith, a Philadelphian, and copyrighted June 20, 1794. "Map of the State of Maryland Laid down from an actual Survey of all the principal Waters, public Roads, and Divisions of the Counties therein; describing the Situation of the Cities, Towns, Villages, Houses of Worship and other public Buildings, Furnaces, Forges, Mills, and other remarkable Places." Library of Congress: [G3840 1794.G72 Vault] Scale a:308,000. size 134 x 79 1/2 cm.

104. **1808 Varle Map.** The map shows Braddock's Gap at the location where today Interstate 70 and Main Route 40 pass over South Mountain. The map shows the name *Ringer* at the location of the Fox Inn. Library of Congress: A map of Frederick and Washington Counties, State of Maryland. 1808, by Charles Varle; engraved, Francis Shallus, Phila. G3843.F7 1808 .V3 1983. 84-691291.

105. **Bond Map**. Frederick County, Maryland. Prepared under the direction of Lieut. Col. J. N. Macomb, Chf. Topl. Engr. for the use of Maj. Gen. G. B. McClellan, Commanding US Army. Drawn from I. Bond's map by E. Hergesheimer. Based on Isaac Bond's map of Frederick County, Maryland, published 1858. Library of Congress G3843 .F7 1861 .H4

Photographs / Fox's Gap Related

201. **The Wise Farmhouse at Fox's Gap.** The Wise Farmhouse on the old Sharpsburg Road at Fox's Gap, scene of fighting during the Battle of South Mountain, Maryland, September 14, 1862. U. S. Army Military History Institute, Carlisle Barracks, PA 17013, vol. 120, p. L6199 A.

202. **The Fox Inn.** Photo in 1992 by Susan Flowers.

203. **The Reno Monument at Fox's Gap.** Photo in 1992 by Susan Flowers.

204. **17th Michigan Memorial at Fox's Gap.** Photo in 1992 by Susan Flowers.

205. **The Battle of South Mountain, Md.** Library of Congress. b/w lithograph by Endicott & Co., c1864 by Joseph J. Joel, drawn on stone by A. A. Fasel. LC-USZ62-12926. Sunday, Sept. 14, 1862. The Glorious charge of the 23rd & 12th Ohio voluteers (Col. Scammon) against the 23rd & 12th North Carolina, under the rebel Gen. Garland who was killed in the charge.

206. **Society of Colonial Wars and Maryland Historical Society Marker.** General Edward Braddock. This marker is near the front of the Maryland State Police Barrack B in Frederick on Route 40 (Patrick Street). Photo by Allan Powell.

207. **Maryland Bicentennial Commission and Maryland Historical Society Marker.** Swearingen's Ferry and Pack Horse Ford. This marker is at the Rumsey Bridge on the Potomac River at Shepherdstown. Photo by Susanne Flowers.

208. **State Roads Commission Marker.** General Edward Braddock. This marker is on the square in Sharpsburg. Photo by Susanne Flowers.

209. **The Boulder at Braddock Spring**. Photo by Susanne Flowers.

210. **Letter from Jacob Reel to Frederick and Michael Fox of Warren County, State of Ohio, dated at Sharpsburg, Maryland, August 9, 1812.**

211. **Revolutionary War records for Frederick Fox, 10th Pennsylvania Regiment, Contiental Line, in the National Archives.**

Photographs / Tombstones

301. **Frederick Fox**, son of John Fox of Fox's Gap in Maryland
302. **Susannah Fox**, second wife of Frederick Fox of Fox's Gap in Maryland
303. **George Fox**, a son of Frederick Fox
304. **Elizabeth Ann Link Fox**, wife of George Fox (a son of Frederick Fox)
305. **Daniel Booker Fox**, a son of Frederick Fox
306. **Susannah Fox**, wife of Daniel Booker Fox (a son of Frederick Fox)
307. **John Liter**, husband of Elizabeth Fox (a daughter of Frederick Fox)
308. **Elizabeth Fox Liter**, a daughter of Frederick Fox
309. **George Mettard**, husband of Christena Fox (a daughter of Frederick Fox)
310. **Christena Fox Mettert**, a daughter of Frederick Fox
311. **St. John or Gebhart Cemetery, Miamisburg, Ohio, view 1**
312. **St. John or Gebhart Cemetery, Miamisburg, Ohio, view 2**
313. **John L. Fox (a son of George Fox) and his wife Susannah Hilligass Fox**, Hopewell Cemetery, Covington, Indiana
314. **Daniel Alexander Fox (a son of John L. Fox) and his wife Elizabeth Jane Ricketts Fox**, Hopewell Cemetery, Covington, Indiana
315. **Jacob Benner and Mary Magdelena Fox Benner** (a daughter of Frederick Fox)

Photographs / Wills, Birth Certificates, Death Certificates, etc.

401. **Will of John Fox** of Fox's Gap in Maryland and Sharpsburg, Maryland.
402. **Will of Frederick Fox** of Fox's Gap in Maryland and the State of Ohio.
403. **Will of Bartholomew Booker**, father-in-law of Frederick Fox
404. **Will of Margaret Booker**, mother-in-law of Frederick Fox
405. **Estate Papers of George Fox**, son of Frederick Fox
406. **Certificate of Birth of Johan Jacob Link**, great-grandfather of Elizabeth Ann Link Fox, wife of George Fox
407. **Will of John Adam Link II,** father of Elizabeth Ann Link Fox
408. **Will of John L. Fox**, son of George Fox
409. **Bible Records of Ethel Belle Fox Gouty**, daughter of Daniel Alexander Fox
410. **Death Certificate for Daniel Alexander Fox**, son of John L. Fox
411. **Death Certificate for Elizabeth Jane Ricketts Fox**, wife of Daniel Alexander Fox

Please notify
the President of the Society
regarding any errors you find in the current issue of the Newsletter.

Topics in the next issue of the Newsletter, December 1, 1996:

1. Carmen Abernathey writes her remembrances of Daniel Alexander Fox.

2. Valentine Fidler owned the Fox Inn prior to George Fox. Charles Fidler, a descendant of Valentine Fidler, writes about his ancestor.

3. Additional documentation the Road to Conococheague passed by the Fox Inn on its way from Frederick Town to Conococheague in 1754.

4. New deeds identified for several small tracts near the Mountain House at Turner's Gap.

5. Progress on the early land tracts at Crampton's Gap.

6. A visit to Valley Forge and Philadelphia.

The Society of the Descendants of Frederick Fox of Fox's Gap in Maryland

Membership Roster - May 1, 1996

Name Address	Phone	Date of Membership	Membership Number
Curtis Lynn Older 618 Tryon Place Gastonia, North Carolina 28054	704-864-3879	October 20, 1995	0001
William Ernest Fox 13071 Alger Grant, Michigan 49327		October 28, 1995	0002
Reva Winfred Fox 10226 3rd Ave. S. Seattle, Washington	206-762-3845	November 7, 1995	0003
Robert Claude Fox 10845 Edgewood Drive Demotte, Indiana 46310		November 11, 1995	0004
William Goudy Benner 1000 Hidden Ridge Lane Dayton, Ohio 45459	513-433-1365	November 15, 1995	0005
Laurel Ann Benner 112 Lower Hillside Drive Bellbrook, Ohio 45305	513-848-8107	November 20, 1995	0006
Brenda Carol Saunders 4301 Burchdale Street Kettering, Ohio 45440	513-299-3320	November 20, 1995	0007
Elizabeth Jane Bucholz 304 14th St. E. Devil's Lake, North Dakota 58301	701-662-3636	November 6, 1995	0008
Doug Bast 109 North Main Street Boonsboro, Maryland 21713	301-432-6969	December 9, 1995	0001**H**
Dellie Jean Craig 1145 Burberry Dr W Apt 5 Lafayette, Indiana 47905	317-448-9194	December 11, 1995	0009
Wilma Marion Gose P. O. Box 203 Griffith, Indiana 46319-0203	219-322-5269	December 16, 1995	0010
Patricia Jo Edwards 526 Palomino Drive	217-443-4523	January 13, 1996	0011

RR #4 Box 94C Danville, Illinois 61832			
James Joseph Fox 311 South St. Mary's Apt. 6N San Antonio, Texas 78205	210-223-6004	January 13, 1996	0012
Raphael Henry John Fox 7815 Claybrook Dallas, Texas 75231-5673	214-343-3919	January 13, 1996	0013
Judith Fox Smith 339 Stoughton Avenue Cranford, N. J. 07016-2854		January 16, 1996	0014
(membership in wife's name, Deloris Fox) Richard Dale Fox Sr. 1917 Roosevelt Drive Sellersburg, In 47172		January 24, 1996	0015

H - denotes Honorary Member

Meditation on the Divine Will

The will of God prevails. In great contests each party claims to act in accordance with the will of God. Both *may* be, and one *must* be wrong. God can not be *for*, and *against* the same thing at the same time. In the present civil war it is quite possible that God's purpose is something different from the purpose of either party--and yet the human instrumentalities, working just as they do, are of the best adaptation to effect His purpose. I am almost ready to say this is probably true--that God wills this contest, and wills that it shall not end yet. By his mere quiet power, on the minds of the now contestants, He could have either *saved* or *destroyed* the Union without a human contest. Yet the contest began. And having begun He could give the final victory to either side any day. Yet the contest proceeds.

Abraham Lincoln, *c. early September 1862*

Index

Issue 1, Volume 1

News from Fox's Gap

News from Fox's Gap

The Society of the Descendants of Frederick Fox of Fox's Gap in Maryland

Issue 2, Volume 1 December 1, 1996

The First Fox Reunion in Hagerstown

Credit goes to Ellen (Mrs. James) Fox of San Antonio, Texas, for the idea to hold a Fox Reunion in Maryland. Those in attendance at the Reunion included:

William G. and Shirly Benner of Miamisburg, Ohio; Jeffrey C. Smith (Born Fort Worth, Texas, 12-19-59) and his wife, Judith Fox Smith, born in Evansville, IN, 8-5-1960; Melissa Mae Smith, born San Antonio, Texas, 9-19-1990; Lindsey Elizabeth Smith, born Summit, NJ, 5-10-1995; James Joseph Fox, born Detroit, Michigan, 8-23-1921; Teresa Rose Fox, (Tessie), born in White Plains, NY, 7-4-1962; Curtis, Linda, and Rachael Older of Gastonia, N. C.

A presentation and discussion about the Fox Family and Fox's Gap was held at the Washington County Free Library in Hagerstown on Friday, July 5. A completed 100-image Kodak Photo CD-Rom disc *entitled Fox's Gap in Maryland* was presented to the Washington County Free Library at Hagerstown as well as the 1996 version of *The Land Tracts of Fox's Gap including material on Crampton's, Orr's, and Turner's Gaps.*

After the meeting at the library, most of the participants toured Turner's Gap, the Fox Inn, and Fox's Gap. A new monument has been added in memory of Confederate General Samuel Garland.

While I was in Maryland I was fortunate to run across the grave of Joseph Chapline Senior, the founder of Sharpsburg in 1763. He is buried about 100 feet straight in and just to the left of the entrance to the Mountain View Cemetery across the street from the Antietam National Cemetery. He was a Colonel in French and Indian War.

Also while I was in Maryland, Doug Bast and I visited the Moses Chapline Sr. Cemetery on the property of Merwin Hans, about two miles west of Fox's Gap along the old Sharpsburg Road. The cemetery is about one-fourth of a mile north of the old Sharpsburg Road.

No plans for future Reunions exist at this time. However, the possibility of holding the next Fox Family Reunion at Valley Forge, Pennsylvania, or in Miamisburg, Ohio, is under consideration. The next Reunion might be held in three to five years.

A Trip to Valley Forge and Philadelphia

The Older family traveled to Valley Forge, Pennsylvania, in late June before proceeding to Hagerstown for the First Fox Reunion. The story of Valley Forge is one of the great stories in world history. "Valley Forge was America's darkest hour - but it was also America's greatest." The camp location of the Tenth Pennsylvania Regiment, Continental Line, in which Frederick Fox served, was near the Outer Line Defenses on the south side of the Valley Forge Historical Park. The Tenth Pennsylvania was part of General Anthony Wayne's First Brigade at Valley Forge. It was under the command of Lt. Col. Adam Hubley. The National Memorial Arch pays tribute to the services of all soldiers who suffered at Valley Forge. The National Memorial Arch was under repair during our visit. The battlefields of Brandywine and Germantown are not far from Valley Forge.

A visit to Independence National Historical Park in downtown Philadelphia on Sunday, June 30, provided a wonderful learning experience. The Independence Historical Park is one of the most significant historic areas in America. It has many historic sites identified with individuals and events related to the creation and early life of the United States. The home of Benjamin Franklin was near this area.

Research Sources in Pennsylvania - A Brief List

A number of research sources are available in Pennsylvania. The David Library of the American Revolution contains a significant collection of material related to the American Revolution. Mr. Steve Zerbe at the Civil War Library and Museum in Philadelphia is a very knowledgeable researcher on Civil War topics. The U.S. Army Military History Institute at Carlisle has a large collection of Civil War material. The Pennsylvania Historical and Museum Commission sells a book entitled *The Pennsylvania Line* by John B. B. Trussell, Jr. The book is one of the best available on the history of the Pennsylvania Continental Line during the American Revolution.

David Library of the American Revolution
Route 32, River Road
P. O. Box 748
Washington's Crossing, PA 18977-0748

Pennsylvania Historical Society
1300 Locust St.
Philadelphia, PA 19107

Valley Forge Historical Society
Washington Memorial Library
P. O. Box 122
Valley Forge, PA 19481

Penn. Hist. and Museum Commission
Div. of Archives and Manuscripts
Third and Forster Streets
Harrisburg, PA 17108-1026

Germantown Historical Society
5501 Germantown Ave.
Philadelphia, PA 19144

Mr. Steve Zerbe
Civil War Library and Museum
1805 Pine Street
Philadelphia, PA 19103

Genealogical Society of Philadelphia
13th and Locust Street
Philadelphia, PA 19107

Lancaster County Historical Society
230 N. President Avenue
Lancaster, PA 17603-3125

Free Library of Philadelphia
1901 Vine Street
Philadelphia, PA 19103-1189

U.S. Army Military History Institute
Carlisle Barracks
Carlisle, PA 17013-5008

Membership Renewals

Please send your check for $5.00 for your 1997 Society membership to me by January 1, 1997. This will be the first test of how well we are doing with membership renewals as an organization. I ask for everyone's support in the coming year. We need everyone to renew their membership. It is certain we can achieve more as an organization than as individuals.

Membership Drive

The main objective of each member of the Society is to recruit at least one new member for the Society each year. The new member should not have been a previous member of the Society.

Frederick Fox and Fox's Gap Section
by Charles E. Fidler

The Fidler Family and The Fox Inn

The following material constitutes the bulk of a letter dated 6 April 1996 received by Curtis L. Older from Charles E. Fidler, 3814 Wildwood Ridge, Kingwood, Texas 77339-2613, telephone 713-358-3612.

For many years I have known my ancestor Valentine Fidler was among the early settlers in the area just east of Fox's Gap in Frederick County, MD, but was never able to determine the actual location of the property he owned there from 1767 to 1786. Needless to say, I was pleased to discover you had been able to establish the location of my ancestor's property. Since Valentine was a wheelwright by trade and no doubt dependent on wagon and coach traffic for his livelihood, I was not surprised to learn his property was located on the Great Philadelphia Wagon Road that passed through Frederick County, MD, connecting Frederick City and Sharpsburg. This road, which crossed South Mountain through nearby Fox's Gap, appears to have been heavily traveled during the years Valentine reside there, and should have provided him with enough customers to maintain a successful business.

Johann Valentine Fidler (1719-86) of Frederick Co., MD, was my 4g-grandfather. He was born in 1719 in Ilbesheim, Rheinland, Germany. The village of Ilbesheim is located west of the Rhine River, some 22 km NW of the city of Worms. Valentine emigrated to America in 1750, accompanied by his wife Elizabeth and their young son George. They arrived at Philadelphia aboard the ship Royal Union on 15 Aug 1750. I suspect Valentine resided somewhere within the German Community of Pennsylvania for several years before migrating to Maryland, but since I have been unable to confirm same, his actual whereabouts between 1750 and 1767 remain unknown.

As you are aware, Valentine Fidler purchased his land near Fox's Gap from Casper Shaff on 16 June 1767 (Liber K, Folio 1373-75). This property, located about 1.8 miles SE of Fox's Gap, actually contained 200 acres, and consisted of 150 acres from the Resurvey on Exchange Survey and 50 acres from the Buble Survey. There is no mention of the Wagon Road in the deed. Valentine subsequently sold 100 acres of same, consisting of 60 acres from the Resurvey on Exchange Survey and 40 acres from the Buble Survey, to Adam Smellser on 2 Nov. 1767 (Liber L, Folio 562-63). According to your findings, the Great Philadelphia Wagon Road passed through this 100 acres tract that was retained by Valentine Fidler. It was on this property Valentine resided and conducted his wheelwright trade for the next 19 years, and it was there he died intestate in 1786. His place of burial is unknown. Valentine and his family had been associated with the Evangelical Lutheran Church of Frederick Co., MD. He was survived by his widow Elizabeth and five children as follows: 1) George, 2) Catharina (Crepill), 3) Anna (Hehl), 4) Jacob, and 5) Elizabeth (Purgit). The oldest son George, who had migrated to Hampshire Co., VA, in 1779, administered the sale of Valentine's property (100 acres) in Frederick Co., MD, to Ludwick Layman on 8 Nov. 1786 (Liber WR-7, Folio 48-49). Following the sale, the widow, Elizabeth Fidler and her two unmarried children, Jacob and Elizabeth, accompanied George Fidler back to Hampshire Co., VA, where they joined his household. I am descended from Jacob, who later migrated to Ross Co., OH.

From your research, you have established that the Fox Inn is located on land once owned by your ancestor George Fox, that said land had been purchased by George Fox in 1805 from Peter Layman, son of Ludwick Layman, and that said land had been purchased by Ludwick Layman in 1786 from George Fidler, son of Valentine Fidler. This property had been owned by my ancestor Valentine Fidler from 1767 to 1786. On pg 98 you have indicated that evidence has been found within the Fox Inn that dates at least part of the structure back to 1777. If that is so, then George Fox may have established the Fox Inn utilizing the same structure that had once served as the residence of Valentine Fidler during the years he had conducted his wagon & coach repair business on the property. Since many of those repair jobs probably necessitated overnight stays by the customers, Valentine may have constructed his home with some extra rooms that could be used to accommodate those customers needing overnight accommodations.

Valentine's oldest son George also became a wheelwright, and evidently established his own business in the area west of Fox's Gap after he purchased 156 acres in the Seven Mountains Survey of that area from Michael Heirman on 1 March 1769 (Liber M, Folio 73-74) This property, which later became a part of Washington County when that county was created in 1776, may have been located along the Great Philadelphia Wagon Road also, but the deed does not mention the road, and I have been unable to determine the actual location of the property. Even though George Fidler moved to Hampshire Co., VA, in 1779, he did not sell this property until 1787.

The following is taken from *The Braddock Expedition and Fox's Gap in Maryland* by Curtis L. Older and is included for reference by the reader of the above article:

The Fox Inn

From Daniel Dulany Sr. (1742) to George Fox (1805)
Tract Name - The Exchange

(**Note** - The 1808 Varle Map identifies the Fox Inn by the name "Ringer")

Reference	Date	Grantee of Deed	Acres
MSA BC & GS #1, 177	10-5-1742	Daniel Dulany Esqr. - survey - The Exchange	100
MSA BY & GS #1, 177	4-29-1749	assignment to Robert Evans - The Exchange	100
MSA BY & GS #1, 177	5-20-1749	assignment to Joseph Chapline [Sr.] - The Exchange	100
FCLR, E-339	12-11-1753	Casper Shaff - The Exchange	75
MSA BY & GS #4, 585-6	5-9-1754	Joseph Chapline [Sr.] - Casper Shaff	275
MSA BC & GS #27, 578	9-29-1765	Daniel [Jr.] and Walter Dulany - patent - The Exchange	100
FCLR, K-1373	7-9--1767	**Valentine Fidler - Fidler's Purchase**	150
Probably inherited from his father.		**George Fidler**	150
FCLR, WR-7-48	11-8-1786	Ludwick Layman	100
WR-12-56	11-14-1793	Peter Layman	100
WR-27-543	10-7-1805	**George Fox**	100

The George Fox Line

by Carmen Dale Hines Abernathey

The following members of the Society are descended from George Fox, son of Frederick Fox:

Elizabeth Jane Bucholz - Society #0008
Dellie Jean Craig - Society #0009
Patricia Jo Edwards - Society #0011
Richard Dale Fox Sr. - Society #0015
Reva Winfried Fox - Society #0003
Robert Claude Fox - Society #0004
William Ernest Fox - Society #0002
Wilma Marion Gose - Society #0010
Mildred F. Metcalf - Society #00016
Curtis Lynn Older - Society #0001

All of the above members also are descended from Daniel Alexander Fox, who was a grandson of George Fox.

Daniel Alexander Fox and Elizabeth Jane (Ricketts) Fox

[The following material was provided by Carmen Dale Hines Abernathey, daughter of Ruby Dale Fox Hines. Carmen is a granddaughter of Daniel Alexander Fox and Elizabeth Jane Ricketts Fox. Ruby was a daughter of Daniel Alexander Fox and Elizabeth Jane Ricketts Fox.]

As the only grandchild to have lived with Daniel A. Fox I will attempt to give some remembrances that I have. I am the only daughter of Ruby Dale Fox Hines and Everett Hines. Ruby was the youngest of Daniel and Elizabeth's five children. My parents lived in Gessie, Vermillion County, Indiana, whereas the grandparents lived on a small farm one mile east and one mile north of Gessie. Prior to that the Fox's had resided in Covington, Fountain County, Indiana.

I have no personal recollection of Grandmother Fox - only that told me by my mother and other family members. Grandmother, Elizabeth Jane Ricketts Fox, died a tragic death. While attempting to start a fire in a cook stove early one morning the fire somehow ignited her lace collar - she ran to the back porch to call Daniel at the barn doing morning chores. I recall my mother saying the only remains she saw where the feet.

Over the years I learned from older cousins that Grandmother Fox was a very stern but lovable person. By neighbors and friends she was known as "Aunt Liz". She was the one to call when one had a sick baby or "call Aunt Liz" if the doctor wasn't available. She had a knowledge of herbs and their potential use.

It was after Grandmother's untimely death (I think in 1922 or 23) that Grandpa came to live in the Hines home. He was a carpenter by trade but a farmer at heart.

He was a very good looking gentleman. Beautiful thick coarse white, wavy hair - always neatly combed. He loved working in wood. I truly value the many hours I've spent in the wood shop at our home in Gessie. There I was allowed to whittle, talk, pound nails, saw etc. I'm sure Grandpa had infinite patience. The only time I remember him ever getting mad was an incident in which I (at about age of 10) managed to walk on a new roof on our "smoke house" - making several holes! This after Grandpa had told me not to climb the ladder and go up on the roof!

Many an hour have I spent riding through a corn field on a cultivator - a seat especially built for me - just Grandpa, me, two horses, and a brown jug of water for refreshment.

Grandpa played the violin and clarinet. The violin I still have. He would go into the south "sitting room' to practice and I, at the age of five or six, would bang on the piano to accompany him. He never scolded - he only wanted me to like music. During my life, thanks to Grandpa, I've enjoyed playing the violin, the piano, the bass viol, and the trumpet. Also I've enjoyed teaching elementary music in the Covington, Indiana, school system for twenty-eight years.

As a carpenter Daniel A Fox was well known in the community. He was the main or head one in erecting the Rileysburg Grade School, Rileysburg, Indiana; also the Perrysville, Indiana, High School. Both schools, built in the late twenties, have since been demolished, due to school consolidation. The large cornerstone from the Perrysville School is located on property in Fountain County, Indiana, formerly owned by his grandson, Richard D. Fox Senior.

Daniel was a man of the community, a neighbor for people to depend on in time of trouble or need and also one for fun. His "Fox Orchestra" played for many social functions - especially barn dances. One son, Earnest, played trumpet, son William played banjo, daughters Ethel and Ruby played violin and piano. Neighbors filled in with trombone, guitar, and saxophone.

Grandpa also, when possible, played with the Newtown, and Covington bands. Perhaps he was most proud of his oldest son, Kennie B. Fox, who worked for more than 50 years with the Starr Piano Factory in Richmond, Indiana. Kennie was especially noted for his outstanding ability as tuner on pianos and organs. he also played clarinet in the Richmond Symphonic Orchestra. His only daughter, Mildred Fox Metcalf, also became a music teacher and outstanding organist in First Presbyterian Church, Salt Lake City, Utah.

Daniel A. Fox or "Dan Fox" as he was affectionately known died an August morning 1932 after his third heart attack much to the sorrow of this granddaughter. Dan and Liz or Grandpa and Grandma are buried side by side in the Hopewell Cemetery, north of Gessie, about one mile from their beloved home. One of the greatest tributes paid to Grandpa was made by my dad, Everett Hines. Grandpa's casket was placed in our best "sitting room" for two days of mourning. Many people came to express sorrow and sympathy for "Dan". The only time I ever saw my dad cry was at the casket. He sobbed and sobbed . . . to this day that picture and sound remains with me. How many men have had that much admiration and feeling for their father-in-law.

Current Address:
Carmen Dale Hines Abernathey
321 W. Washington Street
Greenville, Michigan 48838
Phone: 1-616-225-9374

A note from Curt Older-

If you are a descendant of George Fox, son of Frederick Fox, I have available a copy of **The English Origin of John Ogle, First of the Name in Delaware**, by Francis Hamilton Hibbard, Assisted By Stephen Parks, 1967. John Ogle was the earliest Ogle ancestor of Jane Ogle, mother-in-law of George Fox, to reach America. The pamphlet is about 32 pages in length. I can provide a copy to any Society member for $3.00, that includes postage and handling. Some of the material in the pamphlet will appear in coming issues of this newsletter. The pamphlet will allow you to trace your ancestors back to King Edward I of England who lived from 1239 to 1307. King Edward I is a descendant of Alfred the Great.

Ancestors of Marguerite Clem, the wife of William Edward Fox

by Dellie Jean (Fox) Craig, daughter of Richard Fox Sr., and grand-daughter of William Edward Fox

The following members of the Society are descended from William Edward Fox, a son of Daniel Alexander Fox and Elizabeth Jane (Ricketts) Fox:

Reva Winfried Fox - Society #0003;
Elizabeth Jane Bucholz - Society #0008
Wilma Marion Gose - Society #0010;
Evelyn L. Fox Switzer, mother of Patricia Jo Edwards - Society #0011
Richard Dale Fox Sr.- Society #0015, father of Dellie Jean Craig - Society #0009

Marguerite Clem was born 09 March 1894 in a log cabin that the original settler and owner of the property was her great-grandfather, Thomas Cunningham. She was the daughter of Augustus Elmer Clem and Malinda Lloyd (Cunningham) and was born in Mound Township, Warren County, Indiana. Marguerite married William Edward Fox on 10 February 1909 in Danville, Vermilion County, Illinois. She died on 27 January 1970 at Danville, Vermilion County, Illinois. They are both buried at Lower Mound Cemetery, Highland Township, Vermillion County, Indiana.

Augustus Elmer Clem was born 11 October 1868 in Warren County, Indiana, the son of Peter Higard Clem and Phoebe (Kitchen). He married Lloyd (Cunningham) on 03 August 1890 in Warren County, Indiana. He married 2) Effie (Duerpriest). Augustus died on 13 January 1935 at age 67y 4m 2d and is buried at State Line Cemetery.

Malinda Lloyd Cunningham was born 09 December 1865 in Mound Township, Warren County, Indiana, the daughter of Cyrus Cunningham and Mary T. (Oliphant). Malinda died 11 November 1912 at age 46y 11m 2d.

Peter Higard Clem was born 05 November 1844 in Mound Township, Warren County, Indiana. He was the son of Zachariah P. D. Clem and Elsie Jane (Dixon). Peter married Phoebe (Kitchen) on 01 February 1864. He died 30 August 1906.

Phoebe Kitchen was born 26 September 1845 in Warren County, Indiana, the daughter of Thomas Kitchen and Sarah Ann (Watson). Phoebe died 07 May 1923 in Warren County, Indiana. Both are buried in Upper Mound Cemetery, Mound Township, Warren County, Indiana.

Cyrus Cunningham was born 15 December 1829 in Highland Township, Vermillion County, Indiana, the son of Thomas Cunningham and Eliza (Cunningham). They were first cousins. Cyrus married Mary T. (Oliphant) on 17 December 1855 by Esquire Elisha Rodgers at the old Cunningham house in Mound Township, Warren County, Indiana, that was her parents' home. Cyrus died 04 July 1903 at his home.

Mary T. Oliphant was born 02 January 1835 in Circleville, Pickaway County, Ohio, the daughter of Thomas Oliphant and Rhoda (Tanner). Mary died 23 January 1922 age 86y 21d. They are both buried in a private cemetery on their land called Cunningham Cemetery up on a hill over-looking their property. Also, Eliza's parents are buried there plus Malinda Lloyd (Cunningham) Fox and some of her siblings.

References:

a) Death Certificate of Marguerite (Clem) Fox - Warren County Courthouse
b) Birth - Malinda Lloyd Cunningham - page 3 - William Edward Fox Bible
c) Birth - Augustus Elmer Clem - page 3 - William Edward Fox Bible
d) Death - Malinda Lloyd Cunningham - page 3 - William Edward Fox Bible
e) Death - Augustus Elmer Clem - page 4 - William Edward Fox Bible
f) Marriage license - Augustus Clem and Lloyd Cunningham, page 497, Vol 7, Warren County, Indiana
g) Biography on Augustus Clem and family - Warren County History Book published in 1913

h) Birth information and parentage Marguerite Clem out of Wabash Valley News-Wed edit. 31 August 1977 by Mary McConnell. See article entitled "LOG CABIN TO BE MOVED, RESTORED!"
i) Cemetery tombstones, birth and death dates Peter Higard Clem and Phoebe (Kitchen)
j) Peter Clem Family also listed in book on John Clem pg 66-67
k) Birth and death dates for Cyrus Cunningham and Mary T. (Oliphant) Warren County Hist 1913
l) Marriage license - Cyrus Cunningham and Mary T. (Oliphant) Warren County Courthouse
m) Obituary - Cyrus Cunningham probably out of the Williamsport, Indiana, newspaper.
n) Obituary - Mary T. (Oliphant) Cunningham pg 1 "Covington Friend" Fri edition, January 27, 1922
o) Biography of Cyrus Cunningham in Biographical History of Tippecanoe, White, Jasper, Newton, Benton, Warren, and Pulaski Counties - IN Vol II 1899 p 949-950
p) 7 page unpublished manuscript on CUNNINGHAM GENEALOGY written by Scott Cunningham in 1903 part of info given by Cyrus Cunningham before his death
q) Some of the above information was given to me by my Aunt Wilma (Fox) Gose.

President's Message

by Curtis Lynn Older

The following listing gives the results of the September 1, 1996, Membership Survey that was mailed to all Society members. Six members returned surveys to Bill Benner. Curtis L. Older did not respond to the survey:

Issue #1. Election of officers for 1997-1998.
6 votes: all to continue current officer setup with Curtis L. Older serving in all positions.

Issue #2. Nomination of Officers.
6 votes: 2 for Curtis L. Older; 4 with no candidate nominated

Issue #3. Next Fox Family Reunion.
4 votes: 2 for Miamisburg/Cincinnati, Ohio; 1 for a central location to all members; 1 for Valley Forge; year to be held: 2 for 1998; time of year: 1 Summer and 1 Fall

Issue #4. Annual Dues.
6 votes: 4 to keep dues at $5.00 per year; 2 to raise dues to $10.00 per year

Issue #5. Donations.
6 votes: 4 for making no donations; 1 for PATC; 1 for when we have more members

Issue #6. Reprint *The Fox Genealogy*.
6 votes: 5 for a reprint; 1 for no reprint; (one of 5 yes votes suggested reprinting an expanded and updated version)

Issue #7. Proposed Bylaws.
6 left this space blank, i.e., no proposed Bylaw changes

Issue #8. Any topic you care to discuss.
1 response: gave reasons for their vote on above issues.

Continued on following page . . .

President's Message Continued . . .

My analysis and recommendations related to the member survey are as follows:

1. I will continue to serve in all Officer positions of the Society for calendar years 1997 and 1998.

2. Same as above.

3. I recommend holding a one-day Fox Family Reunion at Miamisburg, Ohio, in 1998, between Memorial Day and Labor day. Frederick Fox any many of his family members are buried in Miamisburg, not far from Dayton, Ohio. Miamisburg/Dayton, Ohio, is about as central a location as we could pick, that has some relationship to Frederick Fox.

I do not recommend Valley Forge as a Reunion site at the present time. Please see the article in the current issue on the two other men named Frederick Fox at the time of the American Revolution. I do not feel at this time, based on the information I have on these two men, that either one was in the Tenth Pennsylvania, Continental line. However, I am awaiting information on the Frederick Fox who was in the Bedford, Pennsylvania Militia during the Revolution and who owned land in Bedford County, Pa. and was on their tax rolls. Bedford is not very far northwest of Hagerstown, Maryland.

Either the Frederick Fox of Bedford, Pennsylvania, must have died before the 1790 Census (somewhat unlikely since he survived Valley Forge if indeed he was the Frederick Fox of the Tenth Pennsylvania Regiment, Continental Line) or he was the same as one of the three Frederick Fox listed in the 1790 Census. I hope to produce an article entitled, *Individuals Named Frederick Fox at the Time of the American Revolution*, for the June 1 or December 1, 1997 Newsletter.

4. Dues will remain at $5.00 per year. This seems to be about the right amount per year to cover the present printing and mailing costs of the newsletter and other Society correspondence.

5. No donations will be made by the Society or in the name of the Society to any organization. I would like for all members to be aware of the following news from the Central Maryland Heritage League in a most recent letter I received from them:

> **This July, CMHL leased and moved into the Lamar Heritage and Cultural Center . . . CMHL is establishing a Civil War museum, organizing exhibits, and developing community outreach programs in the center.**

I do not know the possibility of having material related to Frederick Fox in the museum. It is something I want to look into. I am attempting to convince individuals who are working to preserve Turner's, Fox's, and Crampton's Gaps to include the history of the gaps from their earliest days, and not just as Civil War battlefield sites.

6. I recommend the reprinting of *The Fox Genealogy* by Daniel Gebhart Fox as a long-term goal of the Society. In conjunction with the reprint of the book, I recommend that we include any documented information relevant to descendants of anyone listed in the original book by Daniel G. Fox. Inclusion of information on descendants of those individuals listed in *The Fox Genealogy* would allow us to bring forward from 1914 to the present, update if you will, *The Fox Genealogy* by Daniel G. Fox.

A reprint of *The Fox Genealogy* that included documented material on descendants of those individuals listed in the original Fox Genealogy would give the Society a reason to solicit new members. We can tell any potential new member that a benefit of joining the Society would include having their own Fox family documented information included in the reprinted version of the book.

Continued on following page . . .

President's Message Continued . . .

Each Society member need only research his or her own Fox genealogy from the present back to their latest Fox ancestor listed in *The Fox Genealogy* by Daniel Gebhart Fox. All members submitted this information on their Society membership application forms. We could include the information on each membership application form as well as include information on brothers and sisters of ancestors in the Fox line in the reprinted version of the book.

7. Since I have no Bylaw changes to recommend, the Bylaws of the Society will stand as they are.

8. The above comments cover all items included in the member survey.

Please send me any comments you might have on the member Survey results and my interpretation of those results.

Turning to other topics, I wish to pass on the following information to the membership:

As indicated above, I hope to complete, sometime in 1997, a report entitled, *Individuals Named Frederick Fox at the time of the American Revolution*. This report will be something we can send to historical societies in New York, Maryland, Pennsylvania, and Virginia, at the least, to clarify who these men were or were not. It should, I hope, resolve the issue of which Frederick Fox served in the Tenth Pennsylvania Regiment, Continental Line, during the American Revolution.

A new column in this issue of the Society newsletter contains a typed copy of a will related to Frederick Fox and his descendants, ancestors, or related family member lines. The current issue of the newsletter contains the will of John Fox, father of Frederick Fox of Fox's Gap in Maryland.

Within the next year I hope to obtain a photographic quality color printer to go with my Macintosh computer. This will allow me to include photographic quality pictures in the Society newsletter. The pictures of maps related to Fox's Gap that are included in this newsletter are not of the best quality. The maps should give all members a good idea of the location of Fox's Gap and the surrounding area in Maryland, if they are not familiar with it.

Good progress continues on my land tract research into Crampton's Gap. Within the next year or two I should have all the earliest land tracts from Crampton's Gap to Orr's Gap in Maryland. This will include all land that is part of the Battlefield of South Mountain.

Bill Benner regrets that he was unable to submit a report for the Benner Line in this issue of the newsletter.

Thanks to everyone for supporting the Society this past year. Let us continue to work toward the preservation of our family genealogies. If we don't preserve our family heritage, no one else will do it for us.

Best regards to all members and their families,

Curt Older, President

Frederick Fox Section
by Curtis Lynn Older

The following page shows the Flonham tract, between Fox's and Turner's Gaps, at the time the tract was sub-divided in 1842 upon the death of Philip Sheffer. Part #2 was "immediately south of the Mountain House". Philip Sheffer, who died in 1842, probably was the son of Philip Jacob Shafer who patented the tract in 1774.

The author is researching the area to the immediate north and west of the Mountain House. The research is being undertaken to determine where the Main Road from Frederick to Fort Frederick crossed the South Mountain. The turnpike road, built in the early 1800s, crossed South Mountain at the Mountain House. The turnpike did not follow the bed of the Main Road from Frederick to Ft. Frederick in the immediate vicinity on the east side of the Mountain House.

The Mountain House was one objective the Union Army sought to reach in the Battle of South Mountain, September 14, 1862. The structure still stands today and is known as the Old South Mountain Inn. It is owned by Russell and Judy Schwartz.

The South and East Sides of Fox's Gap

Fox's Gap and the Reno Monument are about one mile south of Zittlestown and Turner's Gap
Spoolsville is where the old Sharpsburg and old Hagerstown Roads fork at the Catoctin Creek
Route 40A is the route of the Old National Pike through Turner's Gap
The road leading south from Fox's Gap goes only to the Lamb's Knoll Look Out Tower

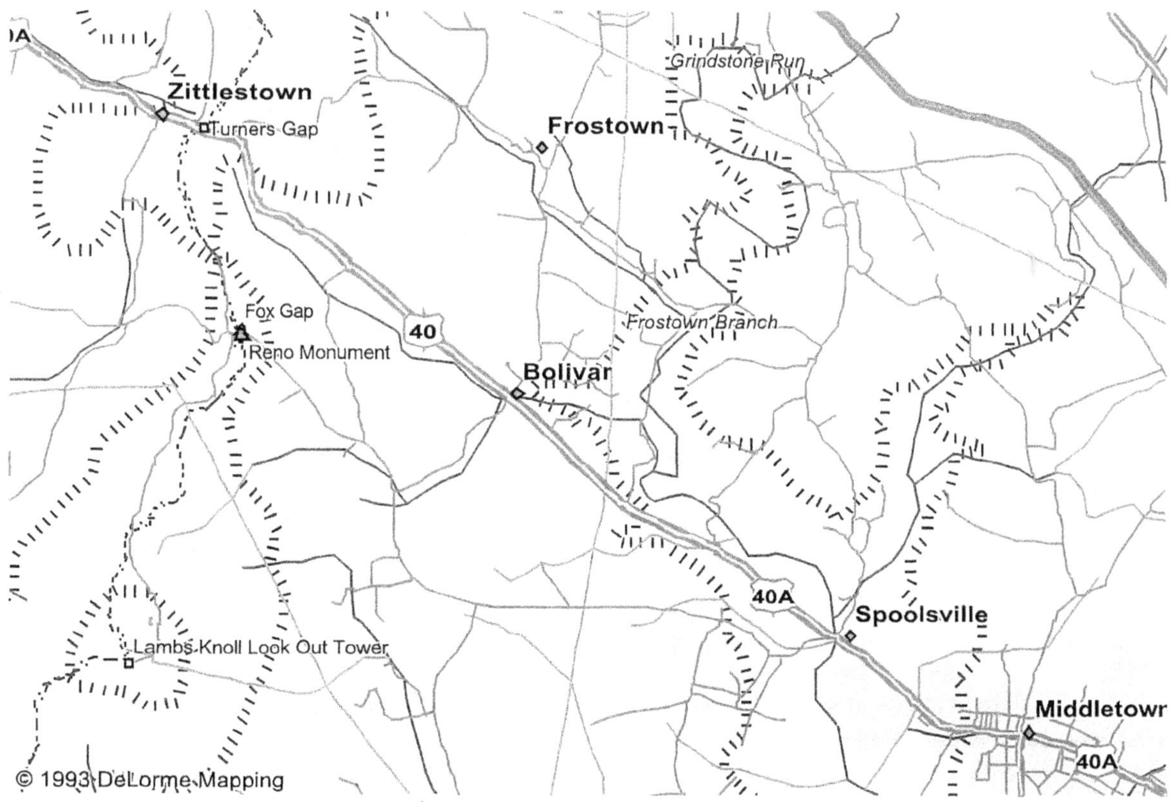

Flonham - From 1770 to 1842

Philip Jacob Shafer I surveys Flonham in 1770, MdHR 17,458, 1-23-4-12, August 27, 1770, 36 acres, and patents the tract in 1774, MdHR 17,455, 1-23-4-9, April 20, 1774, 36 acres, BC & GS #44, 439-40. The will of Philip Jacob Shafer I probably is at the Maryland Archives, in German, not translated, Will Index, GME-3-107, probably filed between Dec. 25 and 29, 1795. The entire tract of Flonham probably was left to Philip Sheffer II.

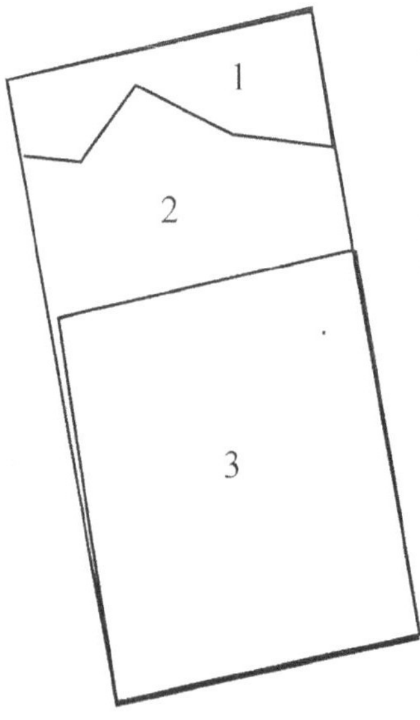

The three parts of Flonham in 1842:

1. Phillip Sheffer II to Henry Miller, 5 acres, 1826, FCLR, JS-25-372.

2. Daniel Sheffer inherits from Philip Sheffer II in 1842, 8 and 3/4 acres.

3. Philip Sheffer III inherits from Philip Sheffer II in 1842, 22 and 1/4 acres.

Flonham in 1842

Lot #2 above: (John W. Koogle from Mary Sheffer, Trustee, FCLR, DSB-1, 397.) "part of a tract of land called Flonham of which Daniel Sheffer died seized and possessed situated on south mountain in said county and immediately on the southwest side of the turnpike road leading from Middletown to Boonsborough and adjoining the lands of Daniel Beachley, William Jones and others being and lying also **immediately south of the mountain house** on said turnpike and containing eight and three quarters acres of land"

Lot #2 Above: (Madeleine V. Dahlgren from George P. and Amanda D. Sheffer, FCLR, TG-5-194.) "being on the South Mountain in said County and immediately on the south west side of the turnpike road leading from Middletown to Boonsboro and adjoining the lands of Daniel Beachley, William Jones, **the Mountain House property** on said Turnpike and others, and containing eight and three quarters acres of land"

Lot Number 2 above, from Daniel Sheffer to Madeliene Vinton Dahlgren:

1. Daniel Sheffer inherits the 8 and 3/4 acre tract from his father, Philip Sheffer II. The will of Philip Sheffer II, written in 1841, is found in GME-2-651. "I also give to my son Philip 15 acres of Mountain land lying on the south side of the Baltimore and Frederick Turnpike Road a land called Flonham . . . the residue of my mountain land called as aforesaid Flonham lying on the south side of the turnpike aforesaid I give to my son Daniel and Philip jointly . . . " Philip and Daniel split their common portion - 7 and 1/4 acres to Philip, 8 and 3/4 acres to Daniel.
2. Mary Sheffer, Trustee, transfers "part of a tract of land called Flonham of which Daniel Sheffer died seized" to John W. Koogle, FCLR, DSB-1-397, recorded May 22nd 1867.
3. John W. Koogle transfers the tract to George P. Sheffer, FCLR, TG-3-396, recorded June 1st 1875. "all those parts of tracts of land described in the deed from Mary Sheffer trustee to the said John W. Koogle bearing date on the 22nd day of april 1867 and recorded in Liber D.S.B. No. 1 folio 397"
4. George P. and Amanda D. Sheffer transfer the tract to Madeleine Vinton Dahlgren in FCLR, TG-5-194, recorded April 25, 1876.

Research Section
by Curtis Lynn Older

The Great Road to Conococheague through Fox's Gap

Additional support that the Great Road to Conococheague (Williamsport, Maryland) from Frederick Town in Maryland was the same as the road that passed the Fox Inn and went through Fox's Gap appears in the records of the Frederick County August Court of 1755:

> Richard Smith's petition for a license to operate his tavern "on the Great Road leading to Conococheague" is also granted.[3]

> James Christie state that he lives "on the Great Road that leads from Frederick Town to Conococheague" and asks for a license to keep a public house there. All these petitions are granted.[4]

A tract named Christios (or Christie's) Folly was only a short distance northeast of the Fox Inn. A Richard Smith patented the Christios Folly tract. James Christie probably had some connection to the tract, however, there are no land records for any tract in his name. The following is taken from the transfer of part of Christios Folly from Richard Smith to Peter Beaver:

> **Part of Christios Folly, Richard Smith to Peter Beaver, Frederick County, Maryland, Land Records, E-753**, recorded June 19, 1755, between **Richd Smith** of Frederick County in the Province of Maryland **Innholder** of the one part & Peter Beaver of the same county & province aforesaid of the other part . . . doth fully clearly & absolutely grant bargain & sell alien & confirm unto the said Peter Beaver his heirs or asigns all that tract or parcel of land called part of **Christios Folly** situate lying & being in the county aforsd being part of a tract of land called Christios folly patented in that name of the aforesd **Richard Smith**.

Peter Beaver owned land near the tract named Oxford, just east of the Fox Inn. This property was near the fork of the road through Turner's Gap with the road through Fox's Gap. As the road through Turner's Gap was not built until 1759 or so, the above material gives support that the Great Road to Conococheague from Frederick Town was the same as the old Sharpsburg Road in the area of the Fox Inn and must have passed through Fox's Gap.

Some historians contend the road or trail through Crampton's Gap to Conococheague was the route Dunbar's Regiment took from Frederick Town to Conococheague (Williamsport) during the Braddock Expedition of 1755. I continue to acquire the earliest land tracts in the vicinity of Crampton's Gap. Early research results indicate support for the route shown on the 1794 Dennis Griffith Map between Crampton's and Hess's on the west side of South Mountain. Hess's refers to Jacob Hess's Mill near Keedysville, a building that still stands today. Crampton's refers to Thomas Crampton's home at Crampton's Gap near Burkittsville.

A present road on the east side of South Mountain leads from Burkittsville (Crampton's Gap) and intersects the old Sharpsburg Road at the Fox Inn.

[1] Millard M. Rice, *This Was the Life excerpts from the judgment records of Frederick County, Md. 1748-1765* (Redwood City, California: Monocacy Book Company, 1979), 166.

[2] Millard M. Rice, *This Was the Life excerpts from the judgment records of Frederick County, Md. 1748-1765* (Redwood City, California: Monocacy Book Company, 1979), 166.

Archives Section

by Curtis L. Older

The Library of Congress selected *The Braddock Expedition and Fox's Gap in Maryland* by Curtis Lynn Older for inclusion in its local history holdings. Notification was received by a letter dated June 19, 1996, from Donald P. Panzera of the Library of Congress.

The Maryland State Archives in Annapolis, Maryland, added the self-published book by Curtis Lynn Older entitled, *The Land Tracts of Fox's Gap including material on Crampton's, Orr's, and Turner's Gap* to its holdings.

The book may be found under a special collection set up in the Maryland Archives under the name of Curtis Older. The book will be updated over the years as new land tracts become available. Improved master tract drawings also are in process. Current work consists of acquiring and adding those land tracts from the vicinity of Fox's Gap to Crampton's Gap.

The Palatines to America Library, Capital University, Box 101, Columbus, Ohio. 43209-2394, received a copy of *The Braddock Expedition and Fox's Gap in Maryland* .

**Please notify
the President of the Society
regarding any errors you find in the current issue of the Newsletter.**

Topics in the next issue of News from Fox's Gap, June 1, 1997:

1. Occupations of residents along the old Sharpsburg Road in the 1700s

2. Link Ancestors of Elizabeth Ann Link, wife of George Fox

3. Ancestors of William Edward Fox

4. The Frederick Fox of New York and Pennsylvania in the 1790 U. S. Census

5. Land Records Related to Crampton's Gap

6. The will of Frederick Fox of Fox's Gap in Maryland

7. The Battle of South Mountain - Some Newspaper Accounts

Proposed for 1998*: Clara Barton and the Battles of South Mountain and Antietam*

Frederick Fox in the American Revolution
by Curtis L. Older

This new section of the Newsletter will contain material related to the service of Frederick Fox in the American Revolution.

Patriot's Oaths of Fidelity and Support, 1778 - Sharpsburgh Hundred

Washington County, Maryland. Patriot's Oath, March Court, 1778.
"A List of Persons in Washington County Who Have Taken The Following Oath Before the Different Magistrates Mentioned Below; and Returned by Them to Washington County Court."
The Worshipfull Chrs. Cruso's Returns.
A True Copy of the Free Male Taxibils of Sharpsburgh and Lower Antietam Hundred. I do hereby Certify that the hereafter foloing hath Voluntarily taken and Subscribed to Oath of Allegience and Fidelity as Directed by an Act of the General Assembly of the State of Maryland Passed the 5th day of Feb. 1777.

Witness my hand and Seal the 2d Day of March, 1778.

1. Cohan, Levy
2. Reynolds, Joseph (son of John)
3. Walker, William
4. Smith, Joseph
5. Reynolds, John Jr.
6. Kupro, Philip
7. Baker, Mark
8. Wilkins, John
9. Chapline, Moses
10. Stewart, James
11. Smith, Lorance
12. Shepard, Thomas
13. Walter, William
14. Tamin, Ambroce
15. Ewart, James
16. Widmyer, William
17. Nervill, William Jr.
18. Nervill, Joseph
19. Bradford, William
20. Jackson, Hugh
21. Kuhno, Frederick
22. Read, William
23. Peek, George
24. Guselor, Phillip
25. Spang, Leonard
26. Waggoner, Phillip
27. McKoy, Thomas
28. Shop, Jacob
29. Bohrer, George
30. Chapline, James
31. Hethrick, Vernon
32. Bremick, Daniel
33. Fox, George

46. Ham, Peter
47. Meyer, Lodowick
48. Wilson, Walter
49. Hybargor, Conarod
50. Kifer, George
51. Hill, Peter
52. Kuhns, Mathias
53. Smith, George
54. Helfenstone, Nicholas
55. Deal, Philip
56. Deal, George
57. Power, Edward
58. Spangler, Mathew
59. Batos, Philip
60. Beall, Basil
61. Sam, Nicholas
62. Kiphart, John
63. Hybargor, Abraham
64. Brown, Edward
65. Dick, Peter
66. Meyer, Michl. Sr.
67. Flick, William
68. Fitch, James
69. Hoffman, Richard
70. Hill, James
71. Tussy, Jaco
72. Meyer, George
73. Brown, James
74. Chapline, Jeremiah
75. Meyer, Peter
76. Pofsenbarger, John
77. Rockenback, Jacob
78. Meyer, Jacob

34. Hyms, Andrew
35. Marker, Michael
36. Macsgemer, John
37. Steward, Thomas
38. McColough, Samuel
39. Baker, Abraham
40. Knote, John
41. Reynolds, Francis
42. **Fox, Frederick**
43. Norman, James
44. Neith, Thomas
45. Lingenfelter, Abraham
79. Meyer, Adam
80. Piper, Jacob (farmer)
81. Kretoor, Leonard
82. Pofsenbargor, Valentine
83. Hershman, Phillip
84. Flick, Adam
85. Millor, David
86. Sandman, Jacob
87. Hyms, John
88. Wise, Peter
89. Stridor, Kilian
90. Yeats, John

(Lower Antetom Hundred not included in Listing)

I do Certify that those below mentioned has solemnly, Sincerely, truely and affirm to the Oaths above mentioned. Before me CHR. CRUSO

Maryland Historical Society Records
Washington County, Maryland
A List of Officers & Men in Capt. Joseph Chapline's Company

1 Lieut. James Chapline; 2 Lieut Thomas Crampton; Ensign James Stewart
1st Class: John Norris; George Linganfelder; Lewis Wilson; Jahn Hymes; Peter Wagoner; Peter Hill; Peter Myres; Thomas McKoy; Thomas Jackson; Daniel Beall
2nd Class: Robert Cammel; William Whitemire; Frederick Cairns; Andrew Hymes; George Deale; James McNutt; James Fitch; William Roberts; William McNutt; William Patterson
3rd Class: Jacob Tussy; John Duncan; George Bower; Edward Power; William Bradford; Barnard McNutt; Robert Huflman; David Jackson; Thomas Jones
4th Class: Benadict Igonder; **Frederick Fox**; David Miller; Peter Wise; Jacob Walter; Robert McNutt; Bennona Swearengan[5]; William Reed; Frederick Mirs (Moss?)
5th Class: Henry Igonder; **Michael Fox**[6]; Jacob Sulf; William Renwick; Jacob Saintaman; Alexr. McNutt; James McKoy Junr.; John Ferguson Junr; Raymon Shanton
6th Class:Phillip Smith; Philip Deale; William Strider; Conrod Highburger; Frederick Myres; Joseph Morrison; Robert Renwick; Ozias Crampton; Henry Boyer
7th Class: Michael Marker; Ludwick Crotzinger; John Mahaman; Abraham Highbarger; John Wilkins; thomas Sheapheard; James Norman; Ignatious Thompson; George Myre
8th Class: Varner Hatnick; Teter Wise; Leonard Spong; Daniel Branch; Jacob Bruner; George Fredk. Waterbager; John McKoy; John Burroughs; Moses Chapline. [Militia Lists of Daus. of Founders and Patriots, held by Md. Hist. Soc.]

[Note: There is no date indicated on the above Muster Roll. It seems likely the roll was taken during the period of early 1775 to early 1777. A similar type of roll on page 243 of the same book contains the following inscription:

We whose names are thereunto Subscribed do enroll ourselves into a Company of Militia agreeable to the Resolves of the Provincial Convention held at the City of Annapolis this 26th Day of July 1775. We do hereby promise and Engage that we will Respectfully March to such places within this province and at such times as we shall be commanded by the Convention or Councill of Convention or Councill of Safety and there with our whole might fight against whomsoever we shall be Commanded by such Authority as aforesaid -- Witness our hands this 28th Day of August 1776.]

Footnotes for the Preceding Page

1 Probably the owner of Swearingen's Ferry after inheriting it in 1762 on the death of his father, Thomas Swearingen the Elder of the Ferry.

2 Probably the brother of Frederick Fox.

The Area on the North and West Sides of Fox's Gap

Fox's Gap and the Reno Monument appear in the lower right corner
Route 40A (Alternate 40) passes through Middletown, Turner's Gap, and Boonsboro
Route 40A was the route of the Old National Pike or National Road
The old Sharpsburg Road through Fox's Gap passes just south of Clevelandville and Keedysville
The route leading south from Fox's Gap goes only to the Lambs Knoll Look Out Tower
Fox's Gap and Turner's Gap are on the Appalachian Trail along the mountain crest
Washington Monument State Park (first monument to George Washington) is just north of Turner's Gap

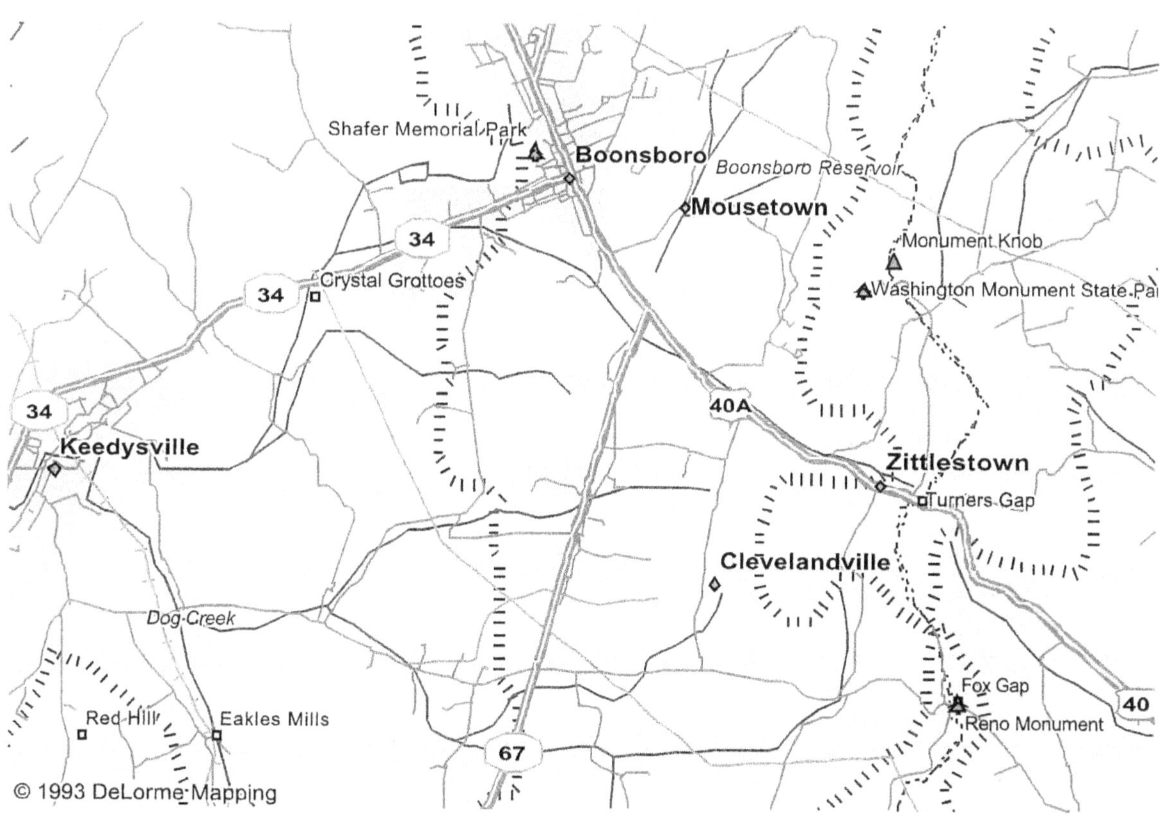

Wills

by Curtis L. Older

This new section of the Newsletter will include one typewritten version of a will that has significance to the preservation efforts of the Society. The first will to be included is the will of John Fox of Fox's Gap in Maryland, the father of Frederick Fox.

Will of John Fox Washington County, Maryland, Book A Liber 102, (probated December 4, 1784).

In the name of God Amen I John Fox of Sharpsburg Washington County and State of Maryland being very sick and weak in body but of perfect mind and memory thanks be given to God calling to mind the mortality of my body and knowing that it is appointed for all men once to die do make and ordain this my last Will and Testament, that is to say principally & first of all I give and Recommend my Soul unto the Earth to be buried in decent Christian burial at the discretion of my Executors nothing doubting but at the General Resurrection I shall receive the same again by the Almighty power of God. And as touching such worldly Estate as it has pleased God to bless me with in this life. I give devise and dispose of the Same in the following manner and (form?)

First I give and Bequeath unto my beloved Wife Christina all that I do possess of during her Natural life and at her Death it is well that my Son Frederick shall have the Clocke? and one half of the skindressing tools used my son Michael is to have the Young Mare with the Other half of the Aforesaid tools and also my Wearing Apearel Except my fine fure hat which I leave to Frederick, and the remaining and Residue of my Estate I leave and bequeath unto my Children and Grand Children Viz? as follows, Frederick, Magdelin & Michael is to have three fourth of it divided Equally amongst them and the remaining fourth part I give and Bequeath unto my live Grand Children, Elizabeth & Catherine Furtnay, and also I leave and bequeath unto my Oldest Son Daniel and my Daughter Rachel five shillings Each to be paid when demanded And also I Constitute and appoint my Wife Christina and my Son Frederick to be the Executors of this my last Will and Testament and I do hereby utterly dissalow revoke and dissamert? all and every Other Testaments Wills Legacies bequests and Executove by me in any wise before named Willed and bequesthed Ratifying and Confirming this and no other to be my last Will and Testament

In Witness whereof I have hereunto set my hand and seal this 17 day of January in the Year of our Lord Seventeen Hundred & Eighty four?

Signed Sealed published & delivered before the Said John Fox as his last Will and Testament in the presence of us who in his presence and in the presence of each other have hereto subscribed our names

John X Fox (seal)
his mark

Peter Dick Mathias Coons Christopher Cruse

Questions and Answers

(Members may submit questions to the Society President for inclusion in this column of the newsletter. Selected questions and answers, if known, will be published.)

Question: (by Curtis L. Older) How many men named Frederick Fox appear in the First Census of the United States in 1790?

Answer: (by Curtis L. Older) . The name *Frederick Fox*, while not unique, was rare in the late 1700s. Only three men named Frederick Fox appear in records that survive from the 1790 Census of the United States. Some state records for the First Census of the United States did not survive. Records for Delaware, New Jersey, Virginia, and Georgia were destroyed or lost. The 1790 Virginia Census records have been reconstructed from other sources.

There was a Frederick Fox of German Flatts Town in New York, one in Philadelphia County in Pennsylvania, and our Frederick Fox who lived in Maryland. There was no Frederick Fox listed in the 1790 Census for the following states: Connecticut, Maine, Massachusetts, New Hampshire, Rhode Island, South Carolina, North Carolina, and Vermont.

The First Census of the United States - 1790

Pennsylvania -	one Frederick Fox listed for the state on page 203, Philadelphia County
Maryland -	one Frederick Fox listed for the state on page 66, Frederick County (Frederick Fox of Fox's Gap in Maryland)
New York -	one Frederick Fox listed for the state on page 106, German Flatts Town, Montgomery County
Connecticut -	no Frederick Fox listed in the state
Delaware -	census records for 1790 no longer exist
Georgia -	included the present areas of Alabama and Mississippi, records no longer exist
Kentucky -	part of Virginia in 1790
Massachusetts -	no Frederick Fox listed in the state
New Hampshire -	no Frederick Fox listed in the state
New Jersey -	census records for 1790 no longer exist
Maine -	no Frederick Fox listed in the state (Maine was part of Massachusetts in 1790)
North Carolina -	no Frederick Fox listed in the state
Rhode Island -	no Frederick Fox listed in the state (admitted May 29, 1790, last of original 13)
Tennessee -	part of North Carolina in 1790
South Carolina -	no Frederick Fox listed in the state
Vermont -	admitted to the Union in 1791
Virginia -	no Frederick Fox listed in the state, 1790 census records have been reconstructed

The Frederick Fox listed in the 1790 New York Census, page 106, lived in German Flatts Town, Montgomery County. His household consisted of 2 males above 16 years of age, 3 males less than 16, 5 females, and 2 slaves. The Frederick Fox listed in the 1790 Pennsylvania census, page 203, lived in Philadelphia County. His household consisted of 1 male over 16 years of age and 2 females. Additional material on the men named Frederick Fox who lived in New York and Pennsylvania at the time of the 1790 Census will appear in the next Newsletter. Total United States population in 1790, exclusive of slaves, was 3,231,533.

Items for Sale Available through the Society

Members are reminded the Society has available for sale, at cost to the Society, many pictures related to Fox's Gap in Maryland as well as pictures of descendants of Frederick Fox. The items available are listed in the June 1, 1996, Newsletter and will appear again in the June 1, 1997, Newsletter.

The Society hopes to acquire within the next few months a picture of the Jacob Ricketts family. Jacob Ricketts was the father of Elizabeth Jane Ricketts, wife of Daniel Alexander Fox.

Membership Section

The Society of the Descendants of Frederick Fox of Fox's Gap in Maryland

New members since the Newsletter of June 1, 1996:

Name Address	Phone	Date of Membership	Membership Number
Mildred F. Metcalf 1819 Garfield Avenue Salt Lake City, Utah 84108	1-xxx-484-9024	June 1, 1996	0016

Mildred is the daughter of Kenneth B. Fox who is listed on page 96 of *The Fox Genealogy*.

Name Address	Phone	Date of Membership	Membership Number
Teresa Rose Fox 6168 Shadow Lane Citrus Heights, California 95621	916-722-4185	June 7, 1996	0017

Teresa is the daughter of James Joseph Fox, Society member #12, of San Antonio, Texas.

All members of the Society welcome the latest additions to our membership!

Index

Issue 2, Volume 1

News from Fox's Gap

News from Fox's Gap

The Society of the Descendants of Frederick Fox of Fox's Gap in Maryland

Issue 3, Vol. 1 **Remember Freedom!** June 1, 1997

Some Newspaper Accounts Related to the Battle of South Mountain

The following four newpaper accounts describe momentous events in September 1862, ie., the Battle of South Mountain, the Battle of Antietam, and the issuance of the Emancipation Proclamation. These articles describe some of the events that transformed Fox's Gap into hallowed ground.

In mid-September 1862, America truly held its breath. The citizens of the North were in a state of great anxiety as the Army of Northern Virginia under General Robert E. Lee invaded Maryland in early September. Until that time, the Union Army had met with many setbacks in the East. Did Lee have his eye set on capturing Philadephia, Baltimore, or perhaps Washington? Could the rebels be stopped?

The Battles of South Mountain and Antietam ended Lee's invasion. The Battle of South Mountain began at Fox's Gap about 9:00 AM on Sunday, September 14, 1862.

Chicago Tribune
Friday, September 19, 1862.
The Great Victory and the Jubilation of the People.

The news of the glorious **victories** at the East, after the long days of feverish anxiety and trembling suspense, lifted a load off the hearts of the people. The splendid aggregate-the victory, the capture of arms, of batteries, of wagon trains, of whole regiments, the death of rebel generals, the environment of the rebel hordes by the hosts of freedom-was like the bursting of the sun through a thunder cloud. It shed a whole stream of light where before had been darkness; it inspired with hope, lifted off the weight of anxiety, and filled all hearts with the buoyant joy of future safety.

The clouds had passed away-The Republic was safe-Treason was in its death throes.

Men walked more erect, breathed freer, and were filled with a calm satisfaction and thorough assurance that the storm had passed over. The old flag was flung out to the breeze again from the house tops. Eager crowds thronged about the bulletins, read the condensed statements of the victory. They spread from lip to lip, and went through the city by the human telegraph almost with the rapidity of lightning. The suddenness of the good news, and its splendid culmination, were fairly stunning, and every man for the nonce was a doubting Thomas. In the midst of all the good news, however much allowance was to be made, the fact of a great victory seemed patent beyond contradiction.

The Tribune shared in the general jubilation. It cared not what troops bore the brunt, whether Eastern or Western; it cared not what general led on those troops, so long as that general planned and those troops won a great victory. All it wanted was a fight, a telling blow at treason, and when the news came that that blow had been struck, after the long months of waiting, of suspense of disaster, it did not stop to ask who struck the blow. The Union was paramount to the General. It only knew that treason had been struck down, and that the Union was triumphant.

Therefore it felt justified in going crazy; in illuminating its windows from roof to basement; in filling the air with fire from rocket and candle. From the roof, Vaas & Dean's splendid Light Guard Band pealed forth as they never did before the national anthems, commanding the involuntary applause of the thousands below them. Our own jubilation was shared by the immense crowds in the street, who were equally confident with us, of victory. We join with them and with everybody in congratulation that we have passed through the valley of humiliation; that we are standing upon the heights of Triumph and can shout Hallelujah.

Washington Post (Front page, upper right column.)
September 18, 1865
The Battlefield

The late battle field of Sunday presents a most sickening aspect, the work of burying the dead having not yet been half finished. The field extends over an area of several miles, and a portion of it is thickly dotted with trenches and graves into which the bodies have been thrown, while other positions have not yet been reached by the working parties. Four days having past, ? ? hot ?, their condition can be better imagined than described. They lie in all manners of contortions, some of them as black as ink, and swollen up ready to burst. **At one point in a mud road to the left of the turnpike, nearly four hundred bodies are strewn thickly over less than an acre of ground, all of them in the unmistakable Rebel garb.**

The Federal? losses? ? ? ? after the fight, and were comparatively very few in number. Indeed the loss in this great battle on Sunday on our side but trifling ? as less than nine hundred wounded, including several ? ? ? to Middletown, and are now receiving attention in ? large churches and other buildings on the main street. Today fully one half of them were sent to Frederick in ambulances mostly ? with ? slight wounds in their hands and arms.

There are a large number of visitors to the battlefield, and some few ? ? ? ? close proximity to the lines. The stench, however, is so offensive, that an extensive exploration is not generally deemed very desirable.

(**Author's Note:** The mud road to the left of the turnpike undoubtedly was the old Sharpsburg Road through Fox's Gap. This article indicates the number of Confederate dead at Fox's Gap alone exceeded the number many authors give as the total Confederate death toll in the Battle of South Mountain.)

Chicago Tribune
probably Monday, September 22, 1862
The Eighth Illinois Cavalry at Boonsboro
[Correspondence N. Y. Tribune]
Boonsboro, Md, Sept. 15, 1862.
The most complete victory of the war was gained yesterday. We stormed and took the rebel Gibraltar. **Braver and more desperate fighting was never before seen on the continent.** McDowell's corps, now under the command of Gen. Hooker, fully redeemed themselves from their disaster at Bull Run. Forming the right of the army, they had the most difficult task assigned them.
The left wing under command of General Reno, fought with bravery only equal by the that of the right. Generals Cox and Willcox, commanding the divisions engaged managed their troops admirably. Both right and left wings and center slept upon the battleground. This morning as day began to break in the east, it was discovered that the enemy had gone, leaving us his dead and wounded upon the battlefield, his hospitals along the road filled with the wounded and many thousand stand of arms thrown away in their flight. The moment their retreat was discovered the 8th Illinois, Col. Farnsworth, was sent out in pursuit at the rear guard. At Boonsboro - the village in which I am now writing - he came in sight of the 4th Virginia cavalry, drawn up in the main street preparing for a charge. Col. Farnworth, at the head of his men suddenly burst upon them, and drove them through the village, killing and wounding all that remained of that once splendid regiment. One of the officers taken prisoner this moment told me "that the regiment was about gone, that we had finished them." The 8th Illinois cavalry is beyond doubt one of the best regiments in the service. Regular officers who are always slow in bestowing praise upon volunteers speak in high terms of it, and pronounce it equal to their own pet regiments, who, as yet, have done nothing but fancy duty during the war.

(**Author's Note:** This article certainly gives a positive evaluation of the Union effort in the battle. The writer's slant towards the part played by General Hooker's troops in the battle is evident.)

Chicago Tribune
Chicago, Friday, September 26, 1862
Great Ovation at Washington.
Speeches by President Lincoln, Secretary Chase, and Cassius M. Clay.
Enthusiasm of the people for Emancipation.
[Special Dispatch to the Chicago Tribune.]
Washington, Sept 24, 1862.
There was a grand popular ovation this evening, over the president's proclamation. The crowd first assembled at the executive mansion, and surrounded the president. Having been cheered and called for, he appeared at an upper window, and spoke as follows:
The Presidents's Remarks
Fellow Citizens: I appear before you to do little more than acknowledge the courtesy you pay me, and thank you for it. I have not been distinctly informed why it is you appear to do me this honor, though I suppose it is because of the proclamation. [Cries of good, and applause.] What I did, I did after a very full deliberation and under a very heavy and solemn sense of responsibility. I can only trust in God I have made no mistake. [Cries of "no mistake," "all right"] I shall make no attempt on this occasion to sustain what I have done or said, by any comment. It is now for the country and the world to pass judgement upon it, and may be take action upon it. I will say no more upon this subject.

In my position I am environed with difficulties, yet they are scarcely so great as the difficulties of those who upon the battlefield are endeavoring to purchase with their blood and their lives the future happiness and prosperity of this county. [Applause, long continued.] Let us never forget them. On the 14th and 17th of this present month, there have been battles, bravely, skillfully, and successfully fought. We do not yet know the particulars. Let us be sure that in giving praise to particular persons, we do no injustice to others. I only ask you, at the conclusion of these few remarks, to give three hearty cheers for all the good and brave officers and men who fought those successful battles."

Cheer after cheer was given, when the president bade the crowd good night, and withdrew.

(**Author's Note:** Please refer to the **Afterword** in *The Braddock Expedition and Fox's Gap in Maryland* by Curtis Lynn Older for additional material on the Battle of South Mountain and related events.)

Membership Drive

The main objective of each member of the Society is to recruit at least one new member of the Society each year. The new member should not have been a previous member of the Society.

A number of members from 1996 did not renew their membership in 1997. Please see the President's message for a new objective that he has set for the Society. The new objective is one that I hope will give motivation to everyone to help preserve and expand this organization.

President's Message

by Curtis Lynn Older

My study of history and economics has confirmed my conviction that the following is true:

**When a society has more freedom, it will have more resources;
when a society has more resources, it will have more freedom.**

I am convinced that you can have no more freedom than the freedom you can obtain under Christianity. Because God is completely free, there is nothing He cannot do. He has unlimited resources.

It was impossible for the South to have more resources than the North at the time of the Civil War. A society that is less free cannot generate the resources of a society that is more free. It is impossible to give citizens less personal freedom and thereby create more resources in the society.

The power of this statement tells us that all we have to do to defeat Communism, or any other foe, is to do what we want to do! What we do must be within the bounds of Christianity.

Although I do not have adequate data available, I am convinced that the United States, on July 4, 1776, was the most powerful nation in the world! A war cannot be won without the resources to do so.

I know of nothing illegal with teaching the above truth in the public school system. We may not be able to pray in public schools but we can teach the inevitable conclusion that comes from the study of world history. Pharaohs, kings, dictators, emperors, communists, and socialists cannot produce the resources in their society that a democracy can produce.

If the American Indians were free, why didn't they produce anything other than teepees and bows and arrows? The American Indian could not have been free. Their mind was not free. They worshiped other gods. Their society was frozen in time.

Let's start a new campaign. I would like to call it, **Remember Freedom!** If we can get across the idea of the importance of freedom, we will see a return to values in our school systems. America is great only because it is under God.

We need to remember Frederick Fox and the American Revolution. In a free market society, every job is an important job. George Washington needed a drummer. Frederick Fox was there. Abraham Lincoln needed a win over the Confederates to free the slaves. Fox's Gap was there.

The following is a proposed schedule for the proposed Fox Family Reunion in Miamisburg, Ohio, Sunday, May 31, 1998.

I would like to propose the following agenda for the Reunion:

7:00 to 8:00 PM	Saturday May 30	Check-in at local motel
8:00 to 9:30 AM	Sunday May 31	Breakfast at a local Miamisburg restaurant
11:00 AM	Sunday May 31	Attend church service at the Gebhart or St. John Church adjacent the cemetery
12:15 to 1:45 PM	Sunday May 31	Lunch at a local Miamisburg restaurant
2:00 to 3:00 PM	Sunday May 31	Visit the St. John or Gebhart Cemetery and the gravesite of Frederick Fox

continued on next page -

3:00 to 5:00 PM	Sunday May 31	A meeting of the participants in the Reunion - Discussion leader will be Curtis L. Older
5:00 PM	Sunday May 31	Depart for home

[Note: Monday, June 1 is the Memorial Day holiday, allowing everyone a day to return home]

The Reunion is scheduled for 1998, not 1997! Please advise me as early as possible if you feel you might attend. I would like some idea as to the number of possible participants.

The Daniel Booker Fox Line

by Curtis Lynn Older

A Tribute to Robert H. Fox of Cincinnati, Ohio

(from the Dayton Daily News, Dayton, Ohio, Wednesday, November 27, 1996)

Robert H. Fox, 85: A former editor of an AFL-CIO newspaper that served an organized labor audience in the Cincinnati area; Wednesday of complications from emphysema, in Cincinnati.

In 1962, Mr. Fox became editor of the *Cincinnati Chronicle*, the weekly newspaper of the Cincinnati AFL-CIO Labor Council. He left the newspaper in 1967 to become editor of the monthly publication of the Cincinnati-basedHotel and Restaurant Employees International Union. He started a career as a freelance writer in the early 1970s.

He died Wednesday at Hospice of Cincinnati. A Mass of Christian burial was Tuesday at St. Mary Church.

He is survived by a son, two daughters, three brothers, a sister and four grandchildren.

Robert H. Fox and I corresponded over two or three years during the period I researched my book, *The Braddock Expedition and Fox's Gap in Maryland*. Robert was responsible for the picture of Daniel Booker Fox that appeared in my book. The Daniel Booker Fox picture is the oldest known picture in existence of a descendant of Frederick Fox. Robert also sent me a picture of the pitcher said to have been used by George Washington at the Fox Inn.

I was fortunate to learn of Robert H. Fox through a publication entitled *Western Maryland Genealogy* and published by the Catoctin Press in Maryland. I visited with Robert one afternoon at his home in Cincinnati, probably during the summer of 1993. At that time, I took a picture of a gun he owned that belonged to Frederick Fox. Robert received the gun as a gift from Daniel Gebhart Fox, the author of *The Fox Genealogy*.

While I have studied the life and times of Frederick Fox and Fox's Gap in Maryland for the past five or six years, my study has been rather short compared to that of Robert. Robert was a student of the Fox family for many, many years. He probably dabbled in the subject for more than 60 years. He, no doubt, was the single most ardent and knowledgeable student of the John Fox and Frederick Fox families, as well as the Bartholomew Booker family. He corresponded with many individuals interested in the Fox family and related lines. I can say with complete correctness that he leaves a void that will never be filled.

The George Fox Line
by Curtis Lynn Older

The following members of the Society are descended from George Fox, son of Frederick Fox:

Toni Farol Bice - Society #0018
Elizabeth Jane Bucholz - Society #0008
Dellie Jean Craig - Society #0009
Patricia Jo Edwards - Society #0011
Richard Dale Fox Sr. - Society #0015
Richard Dale Fox Jr. - Society #0019
Reva Winfried Fox - Society #0003
William Ernest Fox - Society #0002
Wilma Marion Gose - Society #0010
Mildred F. Metcalf - Society #00016
Curtis Lynn Older - Society #0001
Rachael Lynn Older - Society #0020

All of the above members also are descended from John L. Fox, a son of George Fox, and from Daniel Alexander Fox, a son of John L. Fox.

Link Ancestors of Elizabeth Ann Link, wife of George Fox

Elizabeth Ann Link (Jan. 28, 1784 - Mar. 9, 1872) of Shepherdstown, Virginia, married George Fox, the owner of the Fox Inn and a son of Frederick Fox, on August 9, 1807.[1] She was born January 28, 1784.[2] She was the daughter of John Adam Link II and Jane Ogle. The will of John Adam Link II mentions his daughter, Elizabeth Fox. Also see the estate papers of George Fox. Elizabeth and a son, Adam, were the executors of the estate of George Fox.

The following material appears in ***The Link Family*** by Paxson Link of Paris, Illinois, published in 1951:

John Adam Link II is worthy of an especial presentation in the history of his people in America. He held high rank in character with his forefathers and moved forward in culture and living standards. While he bore the appellation of Junior in the family circle he received no special favors. Indeed, he came off short with his brothers in the father's lst testament. As he grew in years he became frugal and sagacious. On the last day in the year 1756, this fifth child was born to John Adam Link I and Elizabeth Miller in their Oley Hill home. On June 29, 1782, he was commissioned Ensign in Captain Peter Barrick's Company, the Catoctin Battalion, Militia of Frederick county, Maryland, in the home of Valentine Creager, a close neighbor of John Adam II. On April 15, 1783, John Adam Link II and Jane Ogle, accompanied by her brother and sister and his father and brother, Jacob, were married in the Frederick Lutheran Church.[3]

John Adam Link I, the first child of John Jacob Link and Anna Magdalena Neuwirth, was born in Grossgartach, Germany, October 13, 1721. John Adam I married Maria Elizabeth Miller (Muller) January 31, 1748, according to the Augustus Lutheran Church records. The Hill Church record gives the date as "Second Sunday after Epiphany" in 1748. **Maria Elizabeth Miller**, was a daughter of John Jacob Miller and Maria Magdalene Gerber. They came from Germany on Johnson's "Galley of London," Commander Davis, September 18, 1732.[4] Elizabeth was born May 17, 1728.

John Jacob Link (Hans Jacob Linck). John Jacob Link, with Anna Magdalena Neuwirth (Ana Madlena), his wife, and their four children, landed at Philadelphia, August 28, 1733. They came from Grossgartach, Germany. No children of record were born to John Jacob and his first wife, Elizabeth. John Jacob Link was an ancestor of Dwight David Eisenhower, President of the United States.

Please see the section on Items for Sale Available through the Society on page 18. Several pictures are available that relate to the Link family discussed above.

The Descent of President Dwight David Eisenhower from John Jacob Link

1. John Jacob Link and his wife were the parents of John Matthias Link.
2. John Matthias Link and Anna Mary Christina Schmit, had 10 children, one of which was Peter Link who was born in Frederick County, Maryland 26 May 1765.
3. Peter Link had a son William Link, born 24 October 1795 in Augusta County, Virginia.
4. William Link had a daughter, Elizabeth Ida (Juda) Link who married Simon P. Stover.
5. Simon P. Stover and Elizabeth Ida (Juda) Link had a daughter, Ida Elizabeth Stover who married David Jacob Eisenhower.
6. David Jacob Eisenhower and Ida Elizabeth Stover were the parents of Dwight David Eisenhower.

Letter from Dwight D. Eisenhower

Commander of American Forces in Europe during World War II; President of Columbia University; President of the United States, 1953-61.

Columbia University
in the City of New York
New York 27 N Y
Office of the President

Dear Mr. Link:

You are doing a great work in collecting and preserving for future generations the complete history of the Link family from their first arrival in America to this day. What has been accomplished by that one family through the centuries is an integral part of the American heritage and should not be forgotten. Yet family records and traditions, unless compiled in a permanent and secure form, are fatally subject to the ravages of time. Fortunately, a few men most zealous in the guardianship of our heritage have given years of their lives to the gathering and assembling of American family history. You are one of them, and I salute you for your effort.

(signed) Dwight D. Eisenhower

Mr. Paxson Link
Paris
Illinois

Descendants of Ernest Daniel Fox

by William Ernest Fox

The following members of the Society are descended from Ernest Daniel Fox, a son of Daniel Alexander Fox and Elizabeth Jane (Ricketts) Fox:

William Ernest Fox - Society #0002

Ernest Daniel Fox was born 1 December 1885 near Gessie, Vermillion County, Indiana. He was a son of Daniel Alexander Fox and his wife Elizabeth Jane Ricketts. Ernest Daniel Fox married Lola Frances Jackson on 8 January 1908 in Vermilion County, Illinois. She was born 1 January 1890 and died 28 June 1943. Ernest Daniel Fox died 3 October 1940 at Lakeview Hospital in Danville, Illinois. He is buried at Niccum Cemetery in Vermilion County, Illinois.

The children of Ernest Daniel Fox and his wife Lola Frances Jackson were:

1) Claude Ernest Fox, born 8 January 1910 in Gessie, Indiana; married 14 December 1929 in Covington, Fountain County, Indiana; died 24 June 1962 in Muskegon, Muskegon County, Michigan; buried in Restlawn Cemetery, Muskegon, Michigan. His wife was Elizabeth Pauline Pearson. She was born 6 April 1911 in Covington, Fountain County, Indiana. Her parents were Francis Marion Pearson and Martha Estel Rayphole.

2) Kenneth Leslie Fox, born 27 November 1912 in Gessie, Indiana; buried in Niccum Cemetery, Vermilion County, Illinois. His wife was Mary Frances Wichman. She was born 25 July 1915 in Danville, Illinois; died 31 August 1994. Her parents were Fred F. Wichman and Matilda Meinke.

3) Ruth Ethel Fox, born 15 June 1914 in Gessie, Indiana; married 26 November 1934 in Covington, Fountain County, Indiana; died 19 June 1987 in Danville, Illinois, buried with her husband. She married Frank Berton Moss. He was born 11 April 1913 in Vermilion County, Illinois; died 2 August 1990 in Danville, Illinois; buried in the Old Walnut Corner Cemetery near Danville, Illinois. His parents were Rolla Oliver Moss and Merle Hoover.

To be continued in the next issue of the Newsletter.

The Fork of the Roads through Turner's and Fox's Gaps

by Curtis Lynn Older

The material presented on this page and the following four pages identifies the roads and land tracts in the vicinity of the Fox Inn and to the north of the Fox Inn. Land tract records support the conclusion that the road through Turner's Gap in the 1700s, ie., the Main Road from Frederick to Fort Frederick, led out of the road through Fox's Gap, ie., the old Sharpsburg Road. The turnpike, built in the early 1800s, followed the roadbed of the Main Road from Frederick to Fort Frederick for the most part. This statement is supported by the 1792? Map of the road from Williamsport to Turner's Gap that is in the Maryland Archives.

By the time of the Civil War, the turnpike did not meet the old Sharpsburg Road just east of the Fox Inn. Sometime between 1840 and 1860, the turnpike was straightened to take its current route. At the present time, the road through Turner's Gap meets the old Sharpsburg Road through Fox's Gap near the Catoctin Creek, about one mile north of Middletown.

The following is a current map of the area of the Fox Inn.

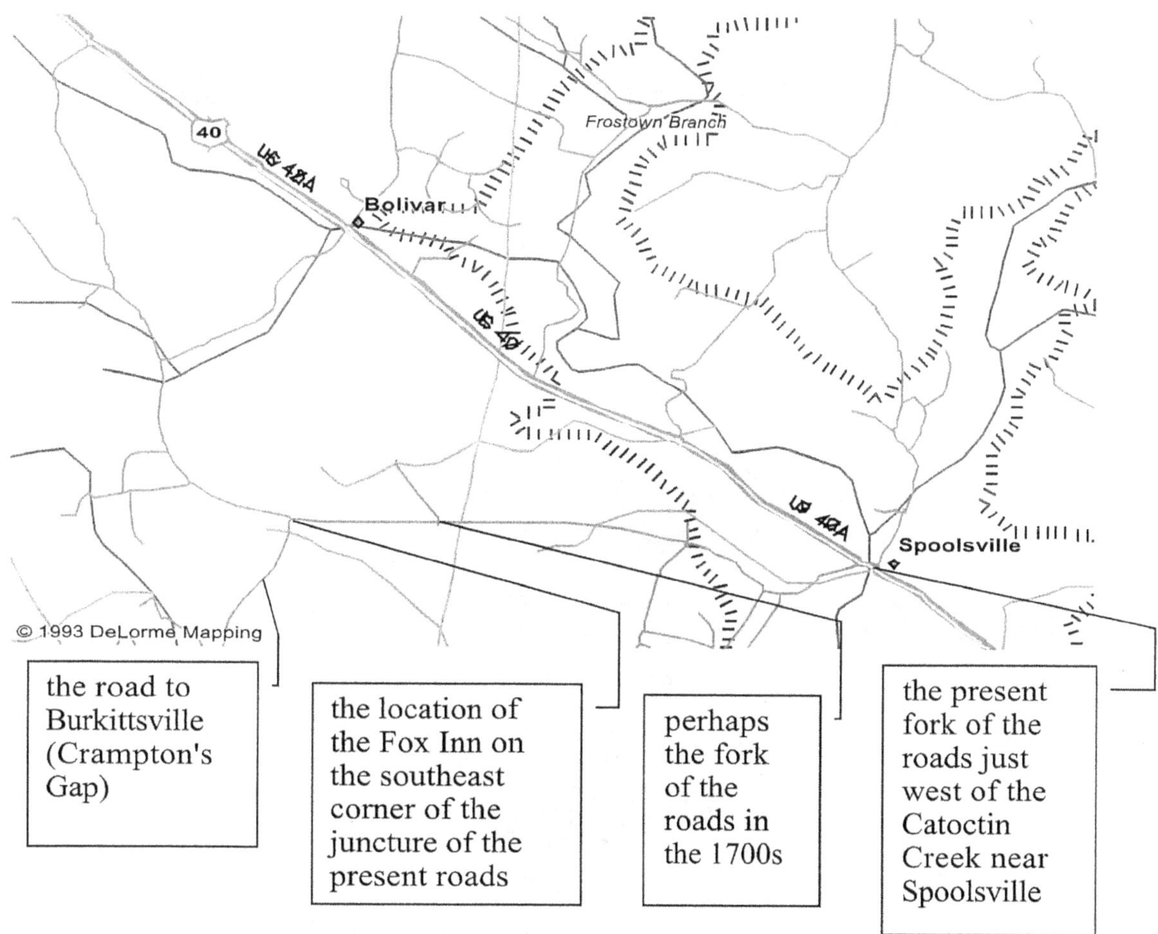

The old Sharpsburg Road through Fox's Gap meets US 40A, the route of the Turnpike after the 1840s, at the Catoctin Creek just west of Spoolsville. Before 1840, the turnpike road through Turner's Gap met the old Sharpsburg Road through Fox's Gap just east of the Fox Inn. The turnpike originally followed the bed of the Main Road from Frederick to Fort Frederick, except near the east side of Turner's Gap.

The following is the area near the Fox Inn as shown on the Varle Map of 1809.

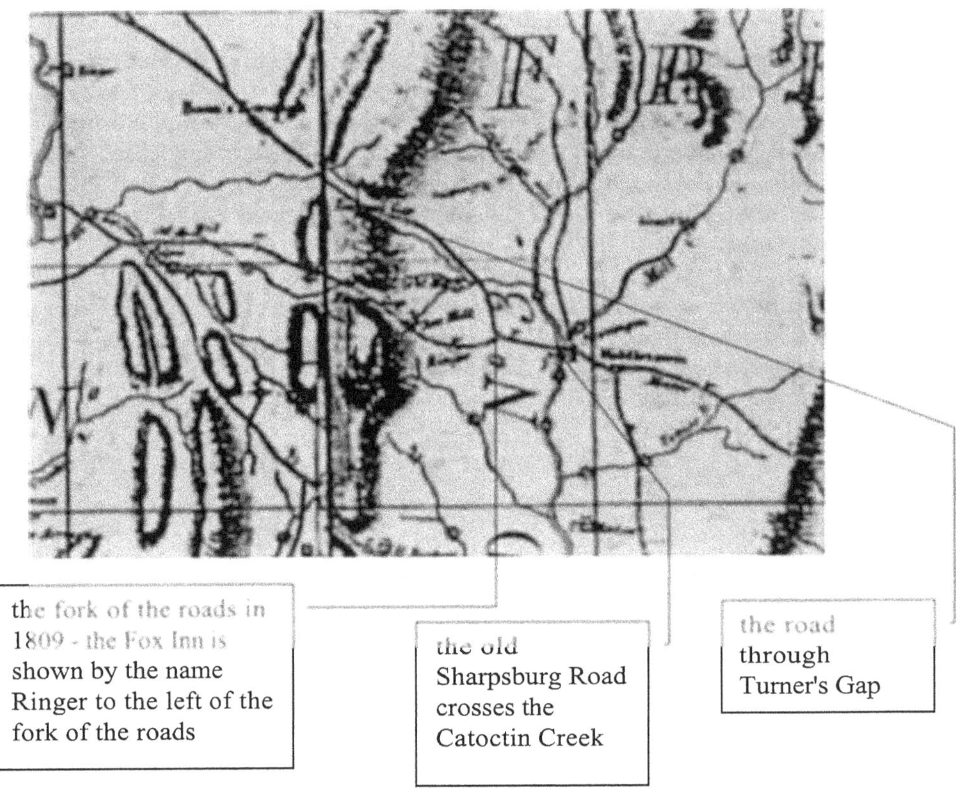

The following is from the Civil War map and shows approximately the same area as the Varle Map above.

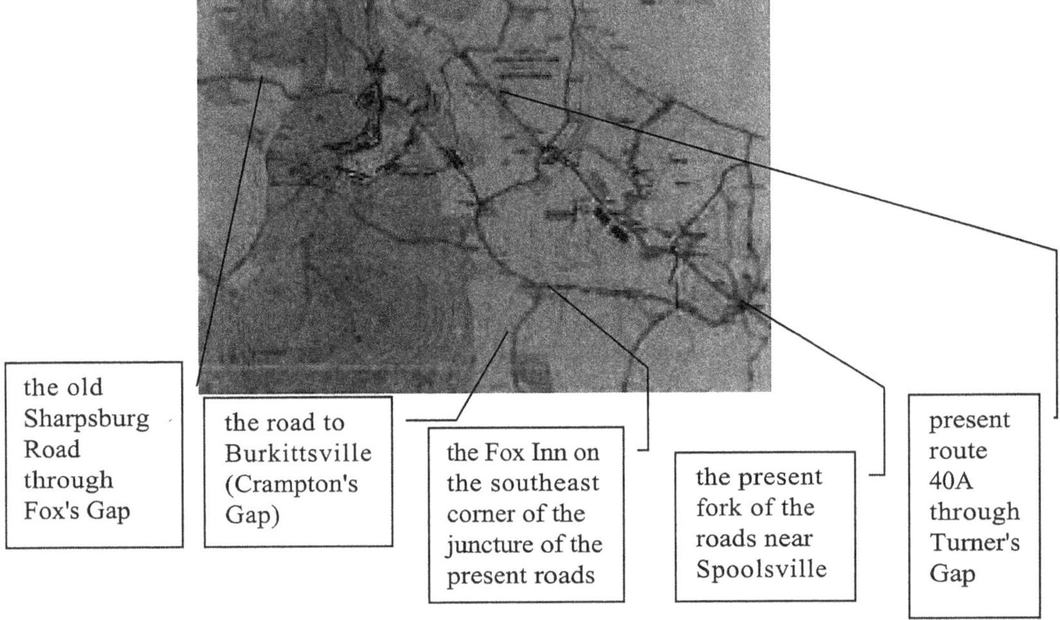

The Fox Inn Area - Selected Tracts

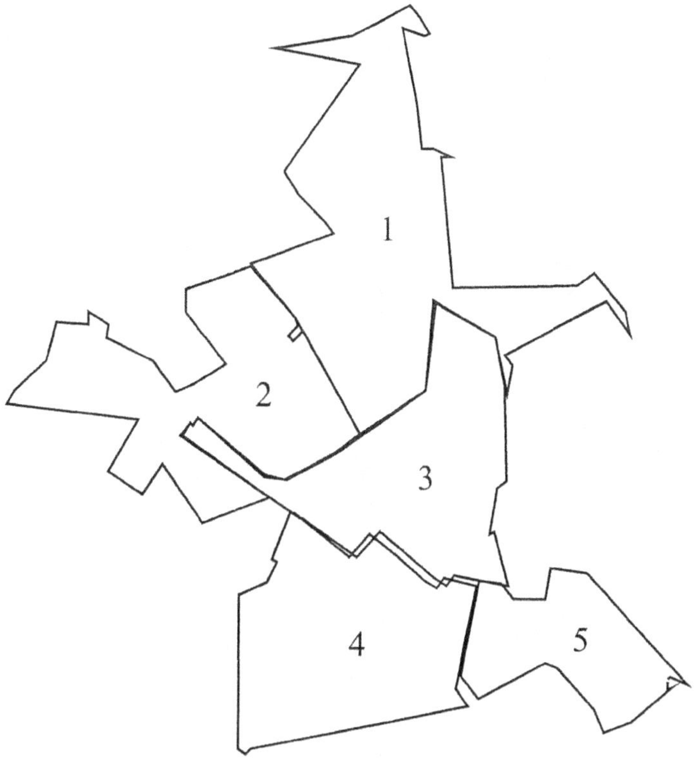

1. Bartholomew Booker Estate, Frederick County Land Records, WR-12, 358-364, recorded 19 April 1794, 304 acres, "beginning at a bounded white oak tree bounded tree of a tract of land called Johns Delight and running thence by and with the Main Road south 38 degrees East 24 perches". Newspaper notice: "on road from Frederick Town to Williamsport and Hagerstown". The author believes Bartholomew Booker's main residence was on this tract, probably not far from the beginning tree of the tract.

2. Frederick Fox to Henry Ascherman, FCLR, WR 32-63, 1807, recorded 14 October 1807, 199 and 1/2 acres, "part of the several following tracts reduced into one entire tract to wit I Hope Its Well Done, Shettle, Exchange, Piggin All, Turkey Foot, Mount Pleasant & Peters Neglect. "Beginning at stone planted near the main road leading to Sharpsburgh and the beginning of Daniel Bookers land."

3. Now I Know It, Jacob Smith, FCLR, THO-1-220, recorded 17 December 1802, 178 and 1/2 acres.

4. Vincent Sanner to Samuel Ausherman, FCLR, CM-1-582, recorded 14 April 1868, 194 and 1/2 acres, parts of Fidler's Purchase, the Resurvey on Exchange, Bubble, and Deefer Snay. Line 17: "North 22 degrees East 20 perches into the old sharpsburg road." The Fox Inn stands on this tract. The fork of the roads probably was about 130 perches or about 2800 feet east of the Fox Inn.

5. Philip Marshall and Jacob Young, FCLR, WR-6-135, recorded 28 September 1785, 100 acres. The author believes the fork of the road through Turner's Gap with the road through Fox's Gap, from the late 1750s until the 1840s, was near the west side of the Oxford tract.

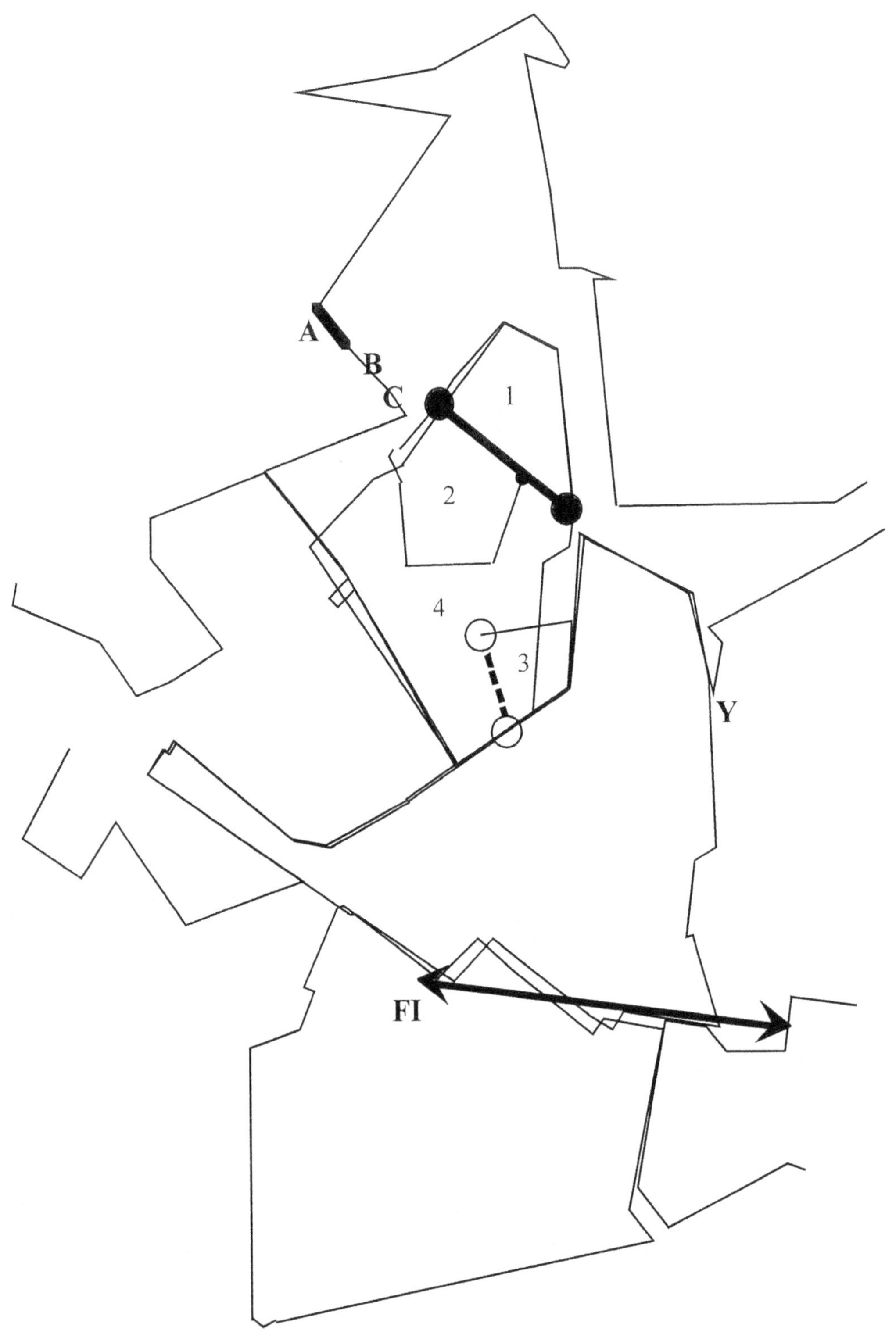
A
B
C
1
2
4
3
Y
FI

Preceding Page:

FI = Fox Inn

= Old Sharpsburg Road from Middletown through Fox's Gap to Sharpsburg

= Main Road Leading to Boonsborough (ie. the Main Road from Frederick to Ft. Frederick and the Turnpike road from the early 1800s until at least 1840)

= Turnpike Road after 1840

Tract 1 = FCLR, DSB-1, 398, W. Koogle from George Routzahn, recorded 22 April 1867, Line 4 goes to the middle of turnpike thence (line 5) along said road 84 perches (1386 feet), containing sixteen and a quarter acres, being part of a tract of land called Pickall part of a tract called the Resurvey on Mendall part of I Hope It Is Well Done and part of a tract called Shettle.

Tract 2 = FCLR, DSB-1-397, John W. Koogle from Mary Sheffer, recorded 22 May 1867, line 4 went to the middle of the turnpike road, line 5 went along road for 58 perches (957 feet), containing twenty three acres, being part of a tract of land called the resurvey on Mendall, part of a tract called Pickall part of a tract called I Hope It Is Well Done part of a tract called Shettle, and part of a tract called Martitaney.

Tract 3 = FCLR, WR-32-225, Michael Miller to Jacob Smith, I Hope It Is Well Done, recorded 30 Dec 1807, line 1 went to the middle of the main road leading to Boonsborough and with said road (line 2) 50 perches (825 feet), containing ten and one eighth acres.

Tract 4 = FCLR, WR-36-85, Michael Miller to Jacob Smith, recorded 26 December 1809, containing one hundred and twelve and a half acres of land more or less excepting thereout ten and one eight acres heretofore conveyed the said Jacob Smith.

Point Y = Near road from Bartholomew Booker's to Peter Beaver's. Resurvey on Mend All, FCLR, F-1077, Bartholomew Booker to Michael Shepfell, 100 acres, recorded 6 July 1760, "all that tract or parcel of land called Shepfell's Purchase being part of a tract of land called the Resurvey on Mend All situate lying and being in the county afsd and begining at a bounded red oak standing by the head of a little spring and near a road that leads from Bartholomew Bookers to Peter Beavers"

Line A = 24 perches or 396 feet along Main Road. "beginning at a bounded white oak tree bounded tree of a tract of land called Johns Delight and running thence by and with the Main Road south 38 degrees East 24 perches ".

Line B = 32 perches or 528 feet, perhaps along the Main Road as is Line A

Line C = 14 and 1/2 perches or 239 feet, perhaps along the Main Road as is Line A

Continued on the following page . . .

The following newspaper notice appeared after Bartholomew Booker's death:

> 101. FTM Aug 28 1792/Margaret Booker, Frederick Fox, exec, to sell farm, late the prop of Bartholomew Booker, decd, 304 a., on road from Fred Town to Williamsport, and Hager's Town, about 3 miles above Middletown/[5]

The following appear in *This Was the Life* by Millard M. Rice:

> Sundry inhabitants of the County, who are unnamed, petition the Court that they "conceive a better and nigher road might be made to Fort Frederick for the road to begin out of the road now leading thereto between the Mountains through Curry's Gap by Robert Turner's and by Joseph Holmes, by Dr. Neal's and so into the road by Joseph Volgamot's." The Court appointed Capt. Moses Chapline, Mr. James Smith and Mr. Joseph Tomlinson to lay out the road.

The material presented in this article confirms the above court minutes. The road through Turner's Gap led out of the road through Fox's Gap. It did so from the time of its creation, about 1760, until at least 1840. The fork of the road through Turner's Gap with the old Sharpsburg Road through Fox's Gap was probably one-half mile east of the Fox Inn.

Topics in the next issue of the Newsletter, December 1, 1997:

1. The War Correspondents Memorial Arch at Crampton's Gap - Tracing the deeds from the original owner all the way to the United States Government, the present owner.

2. Ancestors of Jane Ogle. Jane Ogle was the mother of Elizabeth Ann Link. Elizabeth was the wife of George Fox, the owner of the Fox Inn and a son of Frederick Fox.

3. Fredericksburg - Another land tract owned by Frederick Fox.

4. More on the descendants and ancestors of Daniel Ernest Fox.

5. The Ogle/Ogles Family Association.

6. The will of Bartholomew Booker, the father-in-law of Frederick Fox.

7. Other Frederick Fox at the time of the American Revolution.

The Land Tracts of the Battlefield of South Mountain

by Curtis L. Older

This new section of the Newsletter will contain material on the land tracts in the vicinity of Crampton's, Fox's, Turner's, or Orr's Gaps. The area included represents the Battlefield of South Mountain.

The Battle of South Mountain at Fox's and Turner's Gaps could well be called the Battle for Addition to Friendship. The tract contained 202 acres. About 125 acres were on the north and east side of Turner's Gap and about 65 acres were on the south side of the old Sharpsburg Road at Fox's Gap. The remaining 12 acres or so connected the two larger portions. The Reno Monument stands on this tract. Most of the 10 acres surrounding the Dahlgren Chapel at Turner's Gap also were part of this tract. The home of John Fox at Fox's Gap must have stood on this tract as well.

Addition to Friendship, Frederick Fox, patent, IC P, pp. 672-673, 27 May 1805, [MdHR 17,478, 1-23-4-34]. - (MdHR = Maryland Hall of Records)

Frederick Fox his patent 202 acres Addition to Friendship - - } The state of Maryland } Know ye that Whereas Frederick Fox of Frederick County on the first day of June seventeen hundred and ninety six obtained out of the western shore land office a special warrant of proclamation to resurvey and affect the vacancy included in a resurvey made for him on the eight day of June seventeen hundred and ninety five by the name of Friendship.

Beginning at the end of the first line of a tract of land called David's Will and running with said line reverse

Line No.	North South	Degrees East or West	Length
1	N	East 22	20 perches to the beginning of said land it being also the beginning of Friendship the present original and running with the original 29 courses viz
2	N	West 29 1/2	55 perches to the end of the last line of Davids Will aforesaid, still with said land reverse
3	S	West 83	63 perches to the 3rd line of Jacob Hess's Resurvey called Security and running with said resurvey 3 courses
4	N		39 perches
5	N	West 26	44 perches
6	N	West 5	66 perches
7	N	West 2	128 perches to the end of the 1st line of a tract of land called Flonham and with it reversed
8	N	East 78	56 perches to the Bounded Tree of said land and with the given line thereof reversed
9	N	West 10	108 perches
10	S	West 78	35 perches to the end of 21 perches on the 3rd line of said Flonham, then
11	N	East 20	63 perches
12	N	East 35	70 perches to the end of the 7th line of a tract of land called Knaves Good Will and with it reversed 5 courses
13	S	East 60	100 perches
14	S	East 7	56 perches
15	S	West 16	20 perches
16	S	West 66	9 perches
17	S	West 35	32 perches
18	S	West 14	12 perches
19	S	East 80	24 perches

20	S	West 15	45 perches to the 4th line of a tract of land called Turkey Ramble and with it 3 courses
21	N	West 38	27 perches
22	N	West 77	65 perches
23	S	East 18	58 perches
24	N	West 75	23 perches
25	S	West 78	41 perches
26	S	East 2	130 perches
27	S	East 45	31 perches to the end of the 3rd line of a tract of land called Bowsers Addition and with it
28	S	East 33	20 perches
29	S	East 10	5 perches
30	S	East 70	35 perches to the bounded tree of said Bowsers Addition it being the end of the tenth line of a tract of land called Friendship and with said land reverse 5 courses
31	S	East 47	62 perches
32	S	East 41	40 perches
33	S	East 44	32 perches
34	S	West 61 1/2	27 perches to a rock marked FF then
35	S	East 43	23 perches

36. then by a straight line to the first beginning containing two hundred and two acres of land bearing date the ninth day of May seventeen hundred and ninety seven, and there remaining ; together with all rights profits, benefits, and privileges thereunto belonging; To have and to hold the same unto him the said Frederick Fox his heirs and assigns forever, - given under the great seal of the state of Maryland this twenty seventh day of may eighteen hundred and five. Witness the honorable alexander contee Hanson esquire chancellor

Robt Bowie (the great seal) A C Hanson Chanr

Addition to Friendship

202 acres

Beginning at the end of the first line of a tract of land called David's Will

1. to the beginning of said land it being also the beginning of Friendship the present original
2. to the end of the last line of David's Will
3. to the 3rd line of Jacob Hess's Resurvey called Security
7. to the end of the 1st line of a trac t of land called Flonham
8. to the bounded Tree of said land
10. to the end of 21 perches on the 3rd line of said Flonham
12. to the end of the 7th line of a tract of land called Knaves Good Will
20. to the 14th? line of a tract of land called Turkey Ramble
27. to the end of the 3rd line of a tract of land called Bowsers Addition
30. to the bounded tree of said Bowsers Addition it being the end of the tenth line of a tract of land called Friendship
34. to a rock marked FF

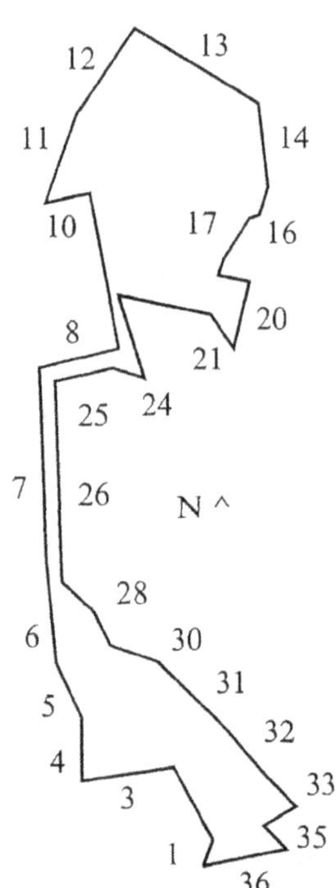

Wills

by Curtis L. Older

Each Newsletter will include one typewritten version of a will that has significance to the preservation efforts of the Society. Included in this issue is the will of Frederick Fox, the man for whom our Society is named.

Will of Frederick Fox Montgomery County, Ohio, Will Book C, case #1444. (Frederick Fox, for whom our Society is named, was a son of John Fox of Fox's Gap in Maryland).

In the name of God, Amen, I Frederick Fox of the County of Montgomery and State of Ohio, being far advanced in years but of sound mind and memory considering the certainty of death and the uncertainty of this mortal life, and as it hath pleased God to bless me with some worldly estate, and to be better prepared to leave this world, whenever it may please God to call me hence, do make and publish this to be my last will and testament, in manner following that is to say:-

First, I give and devise unto my son Joseph Fox the use and occupence of the south west quarter of Section No. Twenty two, of Township two in Range five, of the land between the Miami rivers, to my said son Joseph Fox, to have and to hold the aforesaid quarter section, except twenty five acres including a certain lease given to Mathias Wolff for payt of the said twenty five acres, to my said son Joseph to have and to hold the aforesaid quarter section except as aforesaid exceptedto him and his wife Elizabeth now living during the life of my said son Joseph and his said wife Elizabeth provided that my said son is not to commit any wast by selling or destroying any timber on the aforesaid premises more than for the use & benefit of said premises on forfature of the aforesaid devise-

2nd I give and devise unto my grand son Frederick Fox and son of the aforesaid Joseph Fox twenty five acres of land, to be laid off by said Executors herein after named to my ? ? in said twenty five acres the lease given Mathias Wolff in the greater section aforesaid to him my said grand son Frederick Fox and heirs and assigns to have and to hold the aforesaid 25 acres for ever

3rd After the death of my said son Joseph Fox and his wife Elizabeth, I give and devise the aforesaid quarter section except as above excepted to my grand children one son and seven daughters share and share equal alike all children of my son Joseph Fox-

4. It is my will and wish that after my death that my executor herein after named will make sale of the north west quarter of section fifteen of Township Two in Range five of the lands between the Miami Rivers, wherein I formerly lived and also to make sale of my house and lot in the town of Franklin in Warren County to the best advantage and the monies arising from the sale of the said premises to be equally divided between my lawful heirs share and share alike that is to say my son George and Daniel B. Fox and my four daughters to wit: Christena Meitterd, Meahany Benner, Rosannah Hogee living in Virginia near Shanodore River, and my daughter Elizabeth Lighterd and to my son Joseph Fox an equal share with all the rest of my aforesaid children to be paid to my son Joseph by my Executor herein named as he thinks the said Joseph stands in need of money at any time or times-

5. I give and bequeath to my daughter Rosannah Hoge's four children that she had by her first husband that is to say one son and three daughters receive of my estate to the amount of the ballance of my daughter Rasannah legacy ? ? the amount of my daughter Rosannah shall be equal with all ? ? ? ? as aforesaid-

And lastly I do hereby nominate & appoint my son Daniel B. Fox to this my last will and testament ? ? Sole and Sole Executor revoking and ? ? annulling all former wills by me heretofore made allowing this and none other to be my last will and testament In Witness whereof I the said Frederick Fox have hereunto set myhand and seal this tenth day of December in the year of our Lord One thousand eight hundred and thirty three

Frederick Fox (Seal)

Continued on the next page . . .

Signed, sealed and declared by the testator Frederick Fox to this will to be his last will and testament who called on us who have subscribed our names to witness the same,

John Liter
Frederick Liter
James Russell

The State of Ohio
Montgomery County ? ? Court of Common pleas, March Term 1837. Personally appeared in open Court John Liter, and Frederik Liter, who being duly sworn depose and say that the paper now before them purporting to be the last will and testament of Frederick Fox now deceased, was by the said Frederick Fox acknowledged, published and declared by him to be his last will and testament in the presence of these deponents, that the said deceased was of lawful age, that he was of sound and disposing mind and memory, and under no restraint as they verily beleive that they subscribed the same as witnesses in the presence and at the request of the testator and in thr presence of each other,
John Liter
Frederick Liter
Sworn and subscribed this 20 day of March 1837 in Open Circuit
Edward ? Daniel Clerk
The State of Ohio Montgomery Circuit Ct.

Items for Sale Available through the Society

Members are reminded the Society has available for sale, at cost to the Society, many pictures related to Fox's Gap in Maryland, as well as pictures of descendants of Frederick Fox. Recent additions to the collection of pictures available to Society members includes:

1. The home of John Adam Link II and his wife, Jane Ogle, in Shepherdstown, West Virginia. Photo taken from *The Link Family* by Paxson Link, page 81. John Adam Link II and Jane Ogle were the parents of Elizabeth Ann Link. Elizabeth was the wife of George Fox, a son of Frederick Fox.

2. The home of John Adam Link I in Frederick County, Maryland. Photo taken from *The Link Family* by Paxson Link, page 81.

3. The Commission by the State of Maryland to John Adam Link II as an Ensign in Captain Peter Barrick's Company, the Catoctin Battalion Militia of Frederick County, Maryland, June 29, 1782. Also shown is a picture of his war mess kit, shoe and knee buckles, and cuff links. Photo taken from *The Link Family* by Paxson Link, page 81.

4. The blood leeching kit of John Adam Link II and the Link Family seal. Photo taken from *The Link Family* by Paxson Link, page 81.

5. The pitcher said to have been used by George Washington at the Fox Inn. Also included is a picture of Daniel Booker Fox and two views of the Fox Inn in the 1940s.

Membership Section

I would like to welcome all new members to our Society. The following new members joined after the last Newsletter of December 1, 1996:

Name Address	Phone	Date of Membership	Membership Number
Toni Farol Bice 10626 Baker Place Crown Point, Indiana 46307	219-663-4451	December 4, 1996	0018
Richard Dale Fox, Jr. P. O. Box 301 Baggs, Wyoming 82321	none	January 1, 1997	0019
Rachael Lynn Older 618 Tryon Place Gastonia, North Carolina 28054	704-864-3879	March 20, 1997	0020

The Society of the Descendants of Frederick Fox of Fox's Gap in Maryland

Membership Roster - May 1, 1997

Name Address	Phone	Date of Membership	Membership Number
Curtis Lynn Older 618 Tryon Place Gastonia, North Carolina 28054	704-864-3879	October 20, 1995	0001
William Ernest Fox 13071 Alger Grant, Michigan 49327		October 28, 1995	0002
Reva Winfred Fox 10226 3rd Ave. S. Seattle, Washington	206-762-3845	November 7, 1995	0003
William Goudy Benner 1000 Hidden Ridge Lane Dayton, Ohio 45459	513-433-1365	November 15, 1995	0005
Elizabeth Jane Bucholz 304 14th St. E. Devil's Lake, North Dakota 58301	701-662-3636	November 6, 1995	0008

Doug Bast 109 North Main Street Boonsboro, Maryland 21713	301-432-6969	December 9, 1995	0001**H**
Dellie Jean Craig 1145 Burberry Dr W Apt 5 Lafayette, Indiana 47905	317-448-9194	December 11, 1995	0009
Wilma Marion Gose P. O. Box 203 Griffith, Indiana 46319-0203	219-322-5269	December 16, 1995	0010
Patricia Jo Edwards 526 Palomino Drive RR #4 Box 94C Danville, Illinois 61832	217-443-4523	January 13, 1996	0011
(membership in wife's name, Deloris Fox) Richard Dale Fox Sr. 1917 Roosevelt Drive Sellersburg, In 47172		January 24, 1996	0015
Mildred Fox Metcalf 1819 Garfield Avenue Salt Lake City, Utah 84108	xxx-484-9024	June 1, 1996	0016
Toni Farol Bice 10626 Baker Place Crown Point, Indiana 46307	219-663-4451	December 4, 1996	0018
Richard Dale Fox, Jr. P. O. Box 301 Baggs, Wyoming 82321	none	January 1, 1997	0019
Rachael Lynn Older 618 Tryon Place Gastonia, North Carolina 28054	704-864-3879	March 20, 1997	0020

H - denotes Honorary Member

---

1 Jefferson County, West Virginia, Marriage Records, 1807, page 286. Also see Paxson Link, *The Link Family* (Paris, Illinois: [n.p.], 1951), 81.

2 *The Fox Genealogy* indicates the date as January 28. *The Link Family* gives the date as January 29.

3 *Index to Marriage Licenses, Frederick County, 1778-1810.* Married April 14, 1783.

4 The Hill Church record, page 15 of Hinke's translation, gives the place in Germany as Niederbronn from which John Jacob Miller came to America and the year as 1738.

5 F. Edward Wright, *Western Maryland Newspaper Abstracts 1786-1798* (Silver Spring, Md.: Family Line Publications, 1985), 1:14.

Index

Issue 3, Volume 1

News from Fox's Gap

News from Fox's Gap

The Society of the Descendants of Frederick Fox of Fox's Gap in Maryland

Issue 4, Volume 1 **Remember Freedom!** December 1, 1997

The First Fox Family Reunion in Hagerstown - July 1996

Descendants of George Fox, Daniel Booker Fox, and Elizabeth Fox Benner

Front Row: Melissa Mae Smith (9-19-1990), Curtis Lynn Older, Rachael Lynn Older (3-20-1987), Judith Fox Smith, Lindsey Elizabeth Smith (5-10-1995), and Mrs. William (Shirley) Benner; **Back Row:** Jeffery C. Smith, Teresa R. Fox, James Joseph Fox, unidentified Benner from Boonsboro area, and William Goudy Benner.

Linda Older took the above photo at the Washington County Free Library in Hagerstown, Maryland, during the July 1996 Fox Family Reunion. James Joseph Fox is a descendant of Daniel Booker Fox, a son of Frederick Fox, as are his daughters, Judith and Teresa, and granddaughters Melissa Mae and Lindsey Elizabeth Smith. William G. Benner is a descendant of Elizabeth Fox Benner, a daughter of Frederick Fox. Curtis and Rachael Lynn Older are descendants of George Fox, a son of Frederick Fox.

Occupations of Residents along the Old Sharpsburg Road in the 1700s

Land tract records provide valuable information about the owners of property along the Old Sharpsburg Road in the 1700s. A review of these records provides us with the occupations of numerous residents along or near the road. Although most of the individuals living along the road in the 1700s probably made their living as farmers, many also worked, at least part time, in various skilled trades.

The various crafts practiced along the Old Sharpsburg Road imply there were enough travelers on the road to support these trades. The route must have been an important thoroughfare. The economy along the road was vibrant. The following review identifies the land tracts along or near the Old Sharpsburg Road from Shepherdstown, Virginia, to Middletown, Maryland, that give the occupation of the tract owner. The discussion attempts to use the chronological date, in the opinion of the author, that someone first occupied the various properties.

James Smith patented **Smith's Hills** for 208 acres on 17 April 1745 [MdHR 17,396, 1-23-2-30, PT 1, pp. 261-263] **[MdHR = Maryland Hall of Records in Annapolis]**. The tract had its "beginning at a bounded white oak standing on the side of a hill within a quarter of a mile of the Waggon road that crosses Anteatom". The Smith's Hills tract was not far from the Burnside Bridge on the south side of the Battlefield of Antietam. The patent states ". . . the certificate of survey aforesaid and the land & premises therein mentioned unto a certain **James Smith** of Prince Georges County **planter** . . ." Today the tract is in Washington County. Washington County was part of Frederick County until 1776. Frederick County was part of Prince Georges County until 1749.

A tract named **Shettle** was in the area of the present town of Bolivar, about one mile northeast of Fox's Gap. Daniel Dulany Esquire patented the tract on 9 September 1742 for 50 acres [MdHR 17,408, 1-23-3-1, Y & S, p. 105]. ". . . that I Daniel Dulany within named in consideration of thirty one pounds fifteen shillings and six pence current money secured to be paid to me by **Robert Marks** of Frederick County **Shomaker** have assigned and transferrd and hereby assigns set over and transfer unto him the said Robert Marks the land within mentioned . . ." Robert Marks probably was one of the earliest settlers within a mile or so of what became Fox's Gap. Traffic along the route of the Old Sharpsburg Road apparently justified the presence of a shoemaker by about 1742.

One of the most significant early deeds identifies Richard Smith as an Innholder. **Christios (Christies) Folly** was northeast of the Fox Inn. Court records identify Richard Smith as living on the **Great Road to Conococheague**. See the Newsletter of December 1, 1996, page 13, for a discussion of the Great Road to Conococheague. ". . . between **Richd Smith** of Frederick County in the Province of Maryland **Innholder** of the one part & **Peter Beaver** of the same county & province aforesaid of the other part . . . for and in consideration of the sum of forty six pounds current money . . . " [FCLR, E-753, Part of Christios Folly, Richard Smith to Peter Beaver, recorded 19 June 1755] **[FCLR = Frederick County Land Records at Frederick, Maryland]**. The year 1755 is the earliest point in time at which we can identify an innkeeper along the Old Sharpsburg Road between Shepherdstown and Middletown. Perhaps the presence of an inn was the best indicator of numerous travelers along the road.

Many craftsmen owned tracts along the Old Sharpsburg Road by 1770. Another important tract owner was Casper Shaaf, a merchant. Casper acquired The Exchange tract on which the Fox Inn stands. Casper made a resurvey on The Exchange tract. ". . . between **Casper Shaaf** of Frederick County and Province of Maryland **Merchant** of the one part and **Conrad Young** of said County and Province **farmer** of the other part witnesseth that the said Casper Shaaf for and in consideration of the sum of forty pounds current money of Maryland . . ." [FCLR, E-1026, Resurvey on Exchange, Casper Schaff to Conrad Young, 125 acres, recorded 18 March 1756].

Grim's Fancy was one half mile west of Fox's Gap and along the Old Sharpsburg Road. The record for this tract is important in the history of Fox's Gap. It identifies John Fox's house and the Road from Swearingen's Ferry to Frederick Town [FCLR, S-389, Grim's Fancy, Philip Booker from George Common, recorded 28 June 1773]. ". . . between **Philip Booker** of Fredk County and province of Maryland **Farmer** of the one part and **Geo. Common** of said County and province **Black Smith** of the other part . . ."

John Fox settled at Fox's Gap by no later than 1760. No land records for him exist, except for tracts in Sharpsburg. Perhaps John Fox was a squatter and never owned land at Fox's Gap. The will of John Fox indicates he owned skin dressing tools [Will of John Fox, Book A, Liber 102, Washington County, Maryland, 17 January 1784]. Daniel Gebhart Fox, in *The Fox Genealogy*, describes John Fox as a **tanner** by trade. The house of John Fox must have been near the site of the Reno Monument at Fox's Gap. The parcel of land on which the Reno Monument stands was part of a tract named Addition to Friendship that was patented by Frederick Fox.

The Birely Tannery Report may be of interest to those who seek additional information about the tannery craft of John Fox [Archaeological Data Recovery at the Birely Tannery (18FR575) City of Frederick, Maryland, prepared by M.A.A.R. Associates, Inc. of Newark, Delaware, 1991]. The Birely Tannery began operation in Frederick, Maryland, in the 1760s and remained in business until the 1920s! I was fortunate to learn of the report when I met Mr. Domenic A. Saguto, Master Shoemaker, at Williamsburg, Virginia. Mr. Saguto assisted in the preparation of the report, a copy of which I was able to purchase from the publisher.

A tract named **Boble (Bubble)** was just south of the Fox Inn and the Exchange tract acquired by Casper Shaaf. A transfer in 1761 between Casper Shaaf and Michael Jesserang identifies Jesserang as an Innholder [FCLR, G-17, Boble (Bubble), Michael Jesserang to Casper Schaaf, recorded 4 June 1761]. ". . . made this fifth day of May in the year of our lord one thousand seven hundred and sixty one between **Michael Jesserang** of Frederick Town in Frederick County and province of Maryland **Innholder** of the one part and **Casper Shaff** of same place **merchant** of the other part . . . in consideration of the sum of fourteen pounds ten shillings current money of Maryland . . ."

A tract named the **Resurvey on Chestnut Hill** identified Matthias Ringer as a farmer and Casper Shaaf as a merchant [FCLR, K-758, Resurvey on Chestnut Hill, Matthias Ringer to Casper Shaaf, recorded 2 October 1766]. ". . . between **Matthias Ringer** of Frederick County and province of Maryland **farmer** of the one part and **Casper Shaaff** of the same place **merchant** of the other part witnesseth that the said Matthias Ringer for and in consideration of the sum of twenty pounds current money of Maryland . . ." The Resurvey on Chestnut Hill tract is about a mile south of the Fox Inn and along the road to Burkittsville and Crampton's Gap.

The **Resurvey on Whiskey Alley** tract was north of Middletown and near the <u>fork of the Old Hagerstown Road and the Old Sharpsburg Road at the Catoctin Creek</u> [FCLR, L-588, Resurvey on Whiskey Alley, Philip Keywaughver to Nicholas Fink, recorded 28 November 1760]. ". . . between **Philip Keywaughver** of Frederick County and province of Maryland **Farmer** of the one part and **Nicholas Finck** of the county and province aforesaid **Taylor** of the other . . . for and in consideration of the sum of eighteen pounds current money . . . "

The Resurvey on Learning tract was south of the Fox Inn. A small portion of the tract came up near the old Sharpsburg Road east of the Fox Inn. Henry Lighter (Leiter) was a wheelwright. He purchased part of the Resurvey on Learning tract. A daughter of Frederick Fox married a son of Henry Lighter (Leiter) [FCLR, M-675, Resurvey on Learning, Henry Lighter to Peter Beaver, recorded 12 December 1769]. ". . . between **Henry Lighter** of <u>Hamshire County in the Province of Virginia</u> **wheelwright** of the one part and **Peter Beaver** of the same county and province aforesaid **farmer** of the other part . . ."

The **Goose Cap** tract was at the fork of the old Hagerstown and old Sharpsburg Roads at the Catoctin Creek, about one mile north of Middletown [FCLR, O-540, Goose Cap, Nicholas Fink to Thomas Welch, recorded 2 September 1771] ". . . between **Nichs Fink** of Frederick County in the province of Maryland **Taylor** of the one part & **Ths Welch** of same county & province aforesaid **Surveyor** of the other part . . . for and in consideration of the sum of ninety nine pounds current & lawful money of Maryland . . ."

Shaaff's Purchase was immediately west of the Fox Inn tract [FCLR, O-112, Shaaff's Purchase, Casper Shaaf to Peter Ruble, recorded 26 March 1771] ". . . between Casper Shaaf of Frederick Town in Frederick County and province of Maryland of the one part and **Peter Ruble** of Frederick County and province aforesaid **Clocksmith** of the other part witnesseth . . ."

The **Bray-face** tract was northeast of the Fox Inn [FCLR, WR-4-531, Bray-face, recorded 25 May 1784]. ". . . between **Peter Beaver** of Frederick County and State of Maryland **Farmer** of the one part: and **Christian Kyser** of the same county and state aforesaid **Miller** of the other Part . . . All that tract or parcel of land called Bray-face, which being part of the **Resurvey on Oxford**. Beginning at the bounded tree of said Brayface, one of the original tracts, and runing thence . . ."

The review of the preceding land records indicates the people living along the Old Sharpsburg Road in the 1700s were industrious and free-market oriented. It seems evident why there were able to unite in a common cause to oppose the British by the mid 1770s.

President's Message

by Curtis Lynn Older

* The first item of importance is to encourage every Society member to attend the **Fox Family Reunion in Miamisburg, Ohio, on May 31, 1998. Please contact me as soon as possible if you plan to attend. Proposed Reunion schedule:**

7:00 to 8:00 PM	Saturday May 30	Check-in at local motel.
8:00 to 9:30 AM	Sunday May 31	Breakfast at a local Miamisburg restaurant.
11:00 AM	Sunday May 31	Attend church service at the Gebhart or St. John Church adjacent the cemetery.
12:15 to 1:45 PM	Sunday May 31	Lunch at a local Miamisburg restaurant.
2:00 to 3:00 PM	Sunday May 31	Visit the St. John or Gebhart Cemetery and the grave of Frederick Fox.
3:00 to 5:00 PM	Sunday May 31	Meeting of the participants in the Reunion - Discussion leader will be Curtis L. Older.
5:00 PM	Sunday May 31	Depart for home.

[Note: Monday, June 1, is the Memorial Day holiday.]

* I was fortunate to receive a gift of six issues of *The Land We Love* from Aaron Boggs (deceased) of the Mecklenburg Chapter of the Sons of the American Revolution. Daniel Harvey Hill published the magazine in Charlotte, North Carolina, after the Civil War. As Major General Daniel Harvey Hill, he was the initial leader of the Confederate forces at Fox's and Turner's Gaps in the Battle of South Mountain on September 14, 1862. I donated three issues of *The Land We Love* to the University of North Carolina - Charlotte Rare Book Collection.

_ Please note the availability of a VCR tape that takes you for a ride along the Old Sharpsburg Road through Fox' Gap. The journey begins about a mile north of Middletown near the Catoctin Creek. The tape ends just west of Fox's Gap. Please refer to page 15 of this Newsletter.

_ If I am fortunate to have some spare time this next year, I should complete an abbreviated version of my work entitled, *The Land Tracts of Fox's Gap, including material on Crampton's, Orr's, and Turner's Gaps*. The shortened version will be published in a journal.

_ Less than one dozen copies of *The Braddock Expedition and Fox's Gap in Maryland* remain in my possession. Family Line Publications probably sold all 100 copies they received on publication. Members of the Rudy family of the Middletown, Maryland, area, owners of the Fox Inn, recently bought five copies from me.

_ I received a letter in mid-July from Gordon C. Baker, who had bought a copy of my Braddock book. He inquired about the tract locations of his ancestor, Peter Baker, in the late 1700s. As it turns out, Peter Baker owned Martsome, part of Raccoon, part of Addition to Middlebough, and part of the Resurvey of Well Done. These tracts are near Boonsboro, Maryland. I was able to identify the location of these tracts for Mr. Baker and was encouraged that my book assisted someone doing research on the area.

_ Our thoughts and prayers need to be with the family of James and Ellen Fox of San Antonio. One of their daughters remains disabled by a brain tumor that began more than one year ago.

* **I want your picture! Please send me a fairly recent picture of youself so that I can archive the picture of every Society member. Family photographs are acceptable substitutes. Please identify everyone in the photograph.**

_ Doug Bast, owner of the Boonesborough Museum of History in Boonsboro, Maryland, added a second floor to his museum complex. Doug is an Honorary Member of our Society.

_ A recent addition to my computer system is an Apple Color StyleWriter 2500 printer. Page 19 is a reprint of page 10 from the June 1, 1997, Newsletter. The reprint is much sharper than the prior version. Also, a new feature of the Newsletter is the inclusion of a color page. The current color print, no page number, shows the Fox Inn about 1993 along the Old Sharpsburg Road. Also shown is the circa 1885 photo of Wise's Cabin at Fox's Gap, scene of desperate fighting during the Battle of South Mountain.

_ You can now request color prints of those photographs you want from the Society collection at a much more affordable price. The enclosed color page was printed on Kodak Photo Weight Premium Glossy Paper. This type of paper is among the highest quality available and costs about 75 cents per sheet. I recommend this type of paper be used to fill any photo requests you might make. I suggest printing no more than four pictures per page using this type of paper. I can produce each page for $1.50 plus postage and handling of $.50, a total of $2.00 per page.

Topics in the next issue of the Newsletter, June 1, 1998

_ 1. The Reno School building along the Old Sharpsburg Road.

_ 2. Ancestors of Jane Ogle. Jane Ogle was the mother of Elizabeth Ann Link, the wife of George Fox.

_ 3. An evaluation of the Frederick Fox of Pennsylvania who appears in the 1790 U. S. Census.

_ 4. Estate papers of George Fox, owner of the Fox Inn and a son of Frederick Fox.

_ 5. The Pick All land tract patent of Bartholomew Booker, father-in-law of Frederick Fox.

_ 6. Ricketts ancestors of Elizabeth Jane Ricketts, the wife of Daniel Alexander Fox.

Membership Drive

The main objective of each member of the Society is to recruit at least one new member of the Society each year. The new member should not have been a previous member of the Society. The easy work is over. We now must seek to identify those individuals who are unknown to us and who qualify to join the Society.

Frederick Fox Section

by William Ernest Fox (edited by Curtis L. Older)

Rosina (Rose or Rosannah) Fox was the only child of Frederick Fox who did not move from Maryland to western Ohio in late 1807 with the other members of the Fox family. Her descendants are not published in *The Fox Genealogy* by Daniel Gebhart Fox.

Rosina (Rose or Rosannah) Fox, a daughter of Frederick Fox

The History of the Descendants of John Hottel, Immigrant from Switzerland to America, begun by Reverend W. D. Huddle, B. S., and completed by his wife, Lulu May Huddle, Westerville, Ohio. Published by Shenandoah Publishing House Inc., Strasburg, Virginia, in 1930.

The top of pages 726 and 727 in the heading of the book is entitled, History of the Descendants of John Hottel:

3x-h Daniel Hottel, son of George, b. near Mt. Olive, Va., in the seventeen hundred and fifties, and m. twice and probably three times; first, Sept. 16, 1783, Eva Hiser, daug. of Henry. Second, m. May 20, 1804, Rosina Fox, dau. of Frederick, of O., formerly of Maryland, and widow of Christian Wolgemuth, who was a flour miller by vocation and resided at Toms Brook, Va. Rosina d. in 1841. Daniel inherited from his father 220 acres in Hampshire Co., but the tract upon which he spent his life he bought of his brother Henry. It lay on the Shenandoah River near the mouth of Pughs Run, three miles northeast of Woodstock, the seat of Shenandoah county.
second m.:
2409x-e Christina Hottel, b. May 27, 1805
2409x-f Sarah Hottel, b. Feb. 6, 1807
2409x-g Lydia Hottel, b. 1809

William Ernest Fox also provides the following from Shenandoah County, Virginia, Marriage Bonds 1750-1850, the LDS Family History Center, and from Daniel G. Fox, *The Fox Genealogy*.

Rosina was born 9 Sept 1775 in Maryland and died in 1841. She was a daughter of Frederick Fox and Catherine Booker of Fox's Gap in Maryland. She married Christian Wolgemuth before 1804. Christian and Rosina (Fox) Wolgemuth were the parents of: (MBD- Marriage Bond Date)

1. Jacob Wolgemuth MBD 1. 18 Oct 1818, to Mary C. Coffman; 2. 31 July 1832, MBD Mary Shaver
2. Elizabeth Wolgemuth 30 May 1793, 14 July 1853, Va, MBD 6 Jun 1815, Shenandoah Co Va to Jonathan Zirkle
3. Catherine Wolgemuth, 1798, MBD 22 Apr 1814, Shenandoah Co Va to Samuel Gochenour

Rosina (or Rosannah) Fox, a widow of Christian Wolgemuth, next married Daniel Hottel (Huddle). Daniel Hottel was born in 1756 at Mt. Olive, Shenandoah Co Va. Daniel Hottel died 1811-1814 in Shenandoah Co Va. They married 20 May 1804, (MBD) 19 May 1804. The first wife of Daniel Hottel was Eve Hiser. Daniel's father was George Hottel and his mother was Elizabeth. Daniel and Rosina (Fox) Hottel were the parents of:

1. Christina Hottel 27 May 1805, Woodstock, Shenandoah, Va., 21 Dec 1883, MBD 11 Apr 1823, Shenandoah Co., Va., to Jacob Haun
2. Sarah Hottel 6 Feb 1807, Woodstock, Shenandoah, Va., 23 Nov 1875, 20 MBD 1824, to William Spigle (Speigle)
3. Lydia Hottel 6 Aug 1809, Woodstock, Shenandoah, Va., 7 Mar 1885, MBD 17 Jan 1826, Shenandoah Co., Va., to Joseph Borden

The George Fox Line

by Curtis Lynn Older

The following members of the Society are descended from George Fox, a son of Frederick Fox:

Elizabeth Jane Bucholz - Society #0008
Dellie Jean Craig - Society #0009
Patricia Jo Edwards - Society #0011
Richard Dale Fox Sr. - Society #0015
Reva Winfried Fox - Society #0003
Robert Claude Fox - Society #0004
William Ernest Fox - Society #0002
Wilma Marion Gose - Society #0010
Mildred F. Metcalf - Society #00016
Curtis Lynn Older - Society #0001

The above members also are descended from Daniel Alexander Fox, a grandson of George Fox.

The Ogle/Ogles Family Association, Inc.

Jane Ogle was the mother-in-law of George Fox. She was the wife of John Adam Link II and the mother of Elizabeth Ann (Link) Fox. Jane was a daughter of Alexander Ogle and grand-daughter of Thomas Ogle and his second wife, Elizabeth Graham. Jane was a great-grand-daughter of John Ogle of Delaware (1649-1683). John Ogle descended from the Ogles of Eglingham, England. He arrived in America in 1664 at age 15. The Ogles were an ancient Saxon family whose lands were on the border of Scotland. It is recorded on the monument of the Barons Ogles in the Church and Castle of Bothal in Northumberland that William the Conqueror gave to Humphry Ogle the Manor Ogle.

Wayne Ogle is President of the Ogle/Ogles Family Asociation, Inc. and resides at 4 Oceans West Blvd., Apt. 502-C, Daytona Beach Shores, FL 32118. Wayne is heading the effort to publish a comprehensive Ogle Genealogy that will contain 80,000 names of descendants of John Ogle of Delaware! I sent Wayne material on the George Fox - Elizabeth Ann Link connection to the Ogle family. The material, in a condensed version, should appear in the book that is soon to be published.

The newsletter published by the Ogle/Ogles Family Association, Inc. is entitled *Ogling for Ogles*. The publication is now on line. It is posted in the files section of the General Newsletters Genealogy Section of America On Line. The electronic version omits mailing addresses and telephone numbers of members. Email may be addressed to the Editor at JLeeO@aol.com. The organization also publishes *The Ogle Genealogist*. Back issues are available for purchase.

A recent Ogle/Ogles Family Convention was held in Salt Lake City, Utah from October 9 through 12, 1997. Previous conventions were in Indianapolis (1979), St. Louis (1988), Wilmington (1991), and Annapolis (1994). There were 73 attendees at the Annapolis event.

The Ogle/Ogles Family Association, Inc. has available to members for the fee of $63 the monumental work by Sir Henry A. Ogle, first published in 1902, *Ogle and Bothal*. This book traces the Ogle lines back to 1052.

Membership in the Ogle Family Association is $13.00 per year. Send your annual dues to: O/OFA Treasurer, Jean Godwin, 124 12th Ave., Indialantic, FL 32903. Membership includes a periodic newsletter and an annual booklet *The Ogle Genealogist*. Annual dues cover the calendar year and are payable the first day of January. The official Ogle Family Library, currently known as "The Ogle Collection," is housed in the Fulton County Museum, 27 E 375 N, Rochester, IN 46975.

Fox Family Facts

Also of interest to members of the Society may be a publication entitled FOX Family Facts, published by Sally SEAMAN-WILLIAMS, P. O. Box 1035, No. Highland CA 95660-1035. I sent Sally some information on Frederick Fox and Catherine Booker, my book on the Braddock Expedition, and *The Fox Genealogy*. The material appeared in FOX Family Facts, Issue #6, in May 1997.

Frederick Fox in the American Revolution

by Curtis L. Older

This article continues the investigation that began in the December 1, 1996, Newsletter into the men named Frederick Fox who appear in the First Census of the United States in 1790. Only three such individuals appear in the 1790 U. S. Census. One man named Frederick Fox appears under the state of New York, one under the state of Pennsylvania, and one under the state of Maryland. This article evaluates a portion of the material reviewed by the author in his attempt to prove which Frederick Fox served in the 10th Pennsylvania Regiment, Continental Line, during the American Revolution.

Question: (by Curtis L. Older) What do we know about the Frederick Fox listed under the state of New York in the First Census of the United States in 1790?

Answer: (by Curtis L. Older) The Frederick Fox of New York lived in German Flatts Town, New York, at the time of the 1790 Census and can be identified in a number of sources. The New York Historical Society provided the following information:

from *Mohawk Valley in the Revolution, Committee of Safety Papers & Genealogical Compendium*, Maryly B. Penrose, Liberty Bell Associates, Franklin Park, New Jersey, 1978.

Fox, Frederick, married Elisabeth Franck, 7/14/1763 (RDSA:172). Elisabeth, born 1746/47; died 1/20/1815, German Flats, Herkimer County, N.Y. (DRH:271). **children: Friederich, born 10/17/1764** (RDSA:51); Elisabeth, baptised 9/16/1766 (DRGF:12); Anna Elisabeth, born 9/22/1768 (RDSA:90); Lena, born 1/30/1778 (DRGF:29); James, born 3/8/1784 (DRGF:83).

Frederick was a member of the Tryon County Committee of Safety from the Germanflats & Kingsland Districts. He was a First Lieutenant in the Eighth Company, Fourth Regiment, of the Tryon County Militia. In 1791, Frederick was Supervisor in the Town of German Flats, Herkimer County, New York.

from *Early Families of Herkimer County New York, Descendants of the Burnetsfield Palatines*, by William V. H. Barker, Genealogical Publishing Co., Inc. Baltimore 1986.

3032: **Frederick Fox - born circa 1741**; **probably died by 1802**; married 1763 Elisabeth Frank (born 1747, died 1815) daughter of Capt. Conrad Frank (Comp. of Amer. Gen., vol 7, page 6) On 1790 GF Census (2-3-5) next to John Frank and John Shoemaker.

3082: **Frederick born SAR 17 Oct 1764** (John Bellingr, M. Cath. Frank)

SAR = Stone Arabia Reform Dutch Church records (Vosburgh)

from New York State Archives, *New York in the Revolution*, Albany, New York, Weed, Parsons and Company, Printers, 1887.

4th Battalion (German Flatts and Kingsland)
8th Company. 1st Lt., **Fred. Fox**

The dates of service in the 4th Battalion, 8th Company, by First Lieutenant Frederick Fox of German Flatts Town are uncertain. Changes in the membership of the 8th Company appear in the New York Archives for the year 1778. The 8th Company certainly existed as a military unit in that year. The Frederick Fox of the 8th Company in German Flatts Town was an officer, a First Lieutenant. Since he was an officer, it is very likely he could write his own name. The Frederick Fox who served in the 10th Pennsylvania Regiment signed his papers of enlistment and receipts for pay by using the mark of an "X" for his name.

The Frederick Fox of the 10th Pennsylvania Regiment, Continental Line, was a drummer. It seems unlikely the Frederick Fox of the 8th Company in German Flatts Town would leave his Militia unit where he served as an officer in order to serve as a drummer in the Pennsylvania Line.

The Pennsylvania Archives lists a Frederick Fox in the Bedford County Militia in Pennsylvania. The Frederick Fox of German Flatts Town in New York, 4th Batallion, 8th Company, should not have been the Frederick Fox of the Bedford County Militia in Pennsylvania. Bedford, in Bedford County, Pennsylvania, is about 50 miles northwest of Hagerstown, Maryland. One aspect that is interesting in the search for the identity of the Frederick Fox who served in the Bedford County Militia in Pennsylvania is the fact that Bartholomew Booker, father-in-law of Frederick Fox, owned a significant amount of land in Bedford County Pennsylvania at the time of his death

The Pennsylvania Archives also lists a Frederick Fox in Von Heer's Dragoons in Pennsylvania. The Frederick Fox of German Flatts Town in New York was not the Frederick Fox of Von Heer's Dragoons because: 1) the Frederick Fox of New York died by 1802 and the Frederick Fox of Von Heer's Dragoons was alive in 1829 and lived in Virginia according to Pennsylvania Archives records; and 2) Frederick Fox and his brother Jacob, who were both members of Von Heer's Dragoons, were from Reading, Pennsylvania, according to the Pennsylvania Archives.

The Frederick (Friederich) Fox born 17 October 1764, a son of Frederick Fox of German Flatts Town in New York, according to Stone Arabia Reform Dutch Church records (Vosburgh), was only 12 years old in April 1777. It is extremely doubtful he could have been the Frederick Fox who enlisted in the 10th Pennsylvania Regiment in April 1777 and served as a drummer. The drummer of the unit usually gave out the punishment ordered by the military against a disobedient soldier in the unit. Someone who served as a drummer must have been at least in his middle or late teens. Frederick Fox of Fox's Gap in Maryland was 26 years old in April 1777.

The above discussion leads me to rule out the Frederick Fox of German Flatts Town in New York as being the Frederick Fox who served in the 10th Pennsylvania Regiment, Continental Line. It is my opinion that the Frederick Fox of German Flatts Town, New York, served out the war as an officer in the 8th Company, German Flatts Town, New York. Additional information may be available at the Herkimer County Historical Society, 400 N. Main St., Herkimer, New York 13350. I did not attempt to access these records and do not know if any records exist there that might be of help.

In summary, none of the records related to Frederick Fox of German Flatts Town in New York lead me to believe that he was the Frederick Fox of the 10th Pennsylvania Regiment, Continental Line. Nothing in the New York records disprove that Frederick Fox of Fox's Gap in Maryland served with the 10th Pennsylvania Regiment, Continental Line, from April 1777 to January 1, 1781, during the American Revolution.

I have been unable either to locate or to obtain a copy of one document that might prove useful in this research:

Jameson, Hugh. "The Organization of the Militia of the Middle States During the War for Independence, 1775-1781." PhD dissertation, University of Michigan, 1936.

The next issue of the Newsletter will evaluate the Frederick Fox listed under the state of Pennsylvania in the 1790 United States Census.

The War Correspondents Memorial Arch at Crampton's Gap

The nation's only monument to Civil War correspondents may be better known to Appalachian Trail hikers than to the general public. According to a June 19, 1996, article in The Frederick Post, entitled "Gathland Centennial Planned," George Alfred Townsend, who covered the Civil War for the New York Herald, lived at the site until the early 1900s on his estate, Gathland, which was later purchased by the state. Townsend deeded the arch and a half-acre of land to the War Department in 1904. It was later transferred to the National Park Service and is now administered by Antietam National Battlefield.

The striking, five-story stone arch straddling the ridge of South Mountain is difficult to find by car but hard to miss from the trail, which runs past it through Gathland State Park. The arch, engraved with the names of 151 Civil War correspondents and artists from the North and the South, was completed in October 1896. The Arch was financed with $5,000 in contributions from donors including Joseph Pulitzer and Thomas Edison. Gathland was one of 18 state parks closed due to budget constraints in 1990. It is located 18 miles south of Hagerstown and about five miles south of Fox's Gap.

Names Appearing On Arch And Newspaper Affiliation Of Some Who Are Known

Finley Anderson
J. N. Ashley
Adam Badean
T. Barnard
Geo.W. Beumaw
H. Bentley
W. D. Bickham
A. H. Bodman
Geo. C. Bower
H. V. Boynton
J. H. Brown,
New York Tribune
S. T. Bulkley
A. H. Byington
S. Cadwallader
S. M. Carpenter
T. M. Cash
F. G. Chapman
F. P. Church
W. C. Church
G. W. Clarke
John A. Cockerill
C. C. Cofin,
Boston Journal
R. T. Colburn
J. Cook
T. M. Cook
E. Crapsey
Creighton
L. L. Crounse
E. Cuthbert
N. Davidson
W. E. Davis
E. F. DeNyse
J. P.Dunn
D. B. M. Eaton
C. H. Farrell
J. C. Fitzxpatrick
R. D. Francis
T. B. Glover
T. C. Grey
C. H. Griffen
Chas. G. Halpine
C. Hannem
B. Harding
G. H. Hart
J. Hasson
John Hay
S. Hayes
L. A. Hendricks
A. R. Henry
F. Henry
V. Hickox
A. S. Hill
G. W. Hosmer
E. H. House
A. Houston
W. P. Isham
D. R. Keim
W. H. Dent
Thos. W. Knox,
New York Herald
R. C. Long
P. T. McAlpin
Richard C. McCormick
Joseph B. McCullugh
W. H. Merriam
J. E. Norcross
C. S. Noyes,
Washington Star
G. H. Hosbon
B. S. Osbon,
New York World,
later Herald
B. F. Osborn
C. A. Page
Nat'l Paige
U. H. Painter
Count De Paris
A. Paul
E. A. Paul
E. Peters
Henry J. Raymond,
New York Times
Whitelaw Reid,
Cincinnati Gazette, later
New York Tribune
Albert D. Richardson,
New York Tribune
W. H. Runkle
O. G. Sawyer
W. F. G. Shanks
R. H. Shelly
Geo. W. Smalley,
Tribune, New York City

Continued on next page . . .

Henry M. Stanley
Edmund C. Stedman
Jerome B. Stillson
W. H. Stiner
William Swinton
R. H. Sylvester
Ben F. Taylor
Geo. Alfred Townsend
B. C. Truman
Henry villard,
New York Herald
J. H. Vosburg
E. W. Wallazz
J. S. Ward
Sam Ward
F. Watson
E. D. Westfall
F. B. Wilkie
Sam Wilkeson
F. Wilkison
A. W. Williams
J. C. Wilson
T. C. Wilson
John Russell Young,
Phildelphia Press
W. Young

Army Artists

J. A. Becker
F. Beard
C. E. H. Bomwill
S. S. Davis
F. Dielman
G. Ellsbury
S. Fox
C. E. Hillen
E. B. Hough
A. F. Laycock
H. Bensancon
A. Berghaus
A. McCallum
W. B. McComas
E. F. Mullen
Fred Shell
W. L. Sheppard
J. S. Trexler
G. E. Williams
W. Waud

Southern

P. W. Alexander
Durant Daponte
F. G. DeFontaine
D. C. Jenkins
Geo. W. Olney
Geo. Perry
Jas. B. Sener
W. Shepardson
Henry Watterson

Artists

M. B. Brady
W. T. Crane
F. O. C. Darley
Theo. R. Davis
Ed Forbes
J. S. Jewett
Henry Lovi
Arthur Lumley
F. H. Mason
Larkin G. Mead
Henry Mosler
Frank Shell
Dav. H. Strother
Alfred Waud
H. Vizzitelly
J. E. Taylor

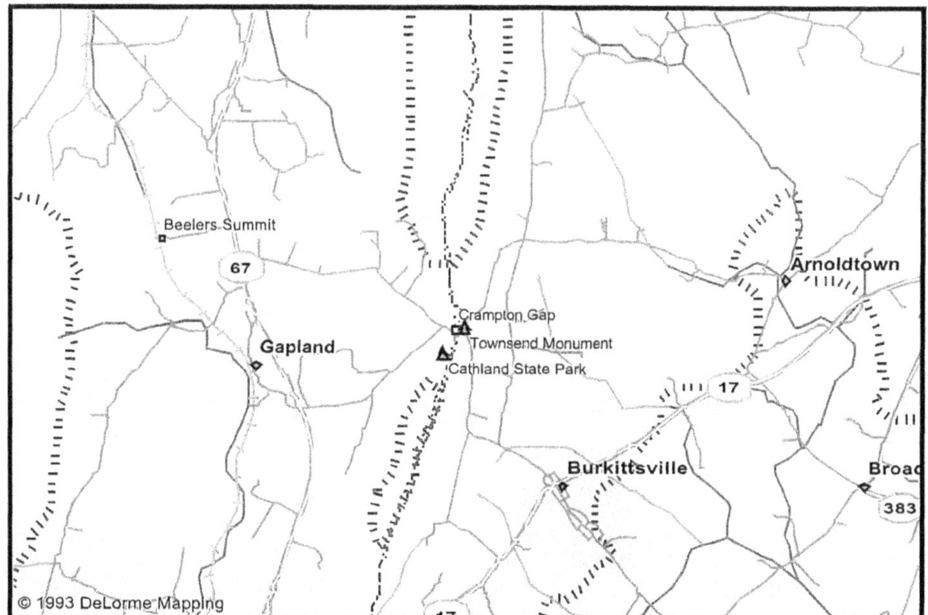

Crampton's Gap on Current Map

The War Correspondents' Memorial Arch at Crampton's Gap

From Fielder Gannt and Peter Gaver to the United States Government
Tract Name - Fielderia Manor and Gaver's Recovery

Reference	Date	Grantee of Deed	Acres
MdHR BC & GS #47, pp. 1-12	18 May 1770	Fielder Gannt - Fielderia Manor[8] (25 acres of Fielderia Manor became part of the resurvey called Gaver's Recovery)	10,471 & 1/4
MdHR IC #E pp. 702-704	8 Dec 1789	Peter Gaver - Gaver's Recovery[9]	197
Estate of Peter Gaver	Death of Peter Gaver	Michael Bruner, Daniel Booker, John Cain, David Gaver, and others[10]	195
FCLR WR-26-569	11 April 1805	Joshua Harley	195
FC Equity HS-2-92	7 Mar 1831	Equity Case #945, Ezra Slifer, Trustee[11] (Joshua Harley Sr., a lunatic)	195+
FCLR JS-44-393	1833	David Mullendore	220 1/2
(unrecorded)	about Sept 1835	Tilghman Biser and Mary Ann Biser his wife (see FCLR AF-9-541 for reference to the transfer from Mullendore to Biser)	(unrecorded)
FCLR ES-3-57, 58	12 April 1853	Ezra Williard & William Carroll, in trust	All Real Estate In Trust
FCLR ES-5-252	12 April 1853	David Arnold and John Arnold Jr.	168 & 3/4
No Deed	1856	From Trustees to William F. Gitings[12]	16
No Deed	1856	From William F. Gitings to George W. Padget	16
Estate of George Padget	Death of George Padget	Mary A. E. Koontz	16
FCLR CM-7-381	6 May 1869	William M. Feaga, Collector	16
FCLR CM-7-381	12 Oct 1871	David Arnold	16

Continued on next page . . .

Reference	Date	Grantee of Deed	Acres
FCLR AF-9-541	15 Dec 1884	George Alfred Townsend[13]	12 acres, 3 roods, and 17 square perches
FCLR STH-267-367	24 Sep 1904	United States Government[14]	28 & 1/8 square perches

(Curtis L. Older prepared the preceding documentation that gives the lineage of the land tracts of the War Correspondents' Memorial Arch at Crampton's Gap.)

An article of particular interest related to Crampton's Gap appears in *the Maryland Genealogical Society Bulletin*, Volum 29, No. 3 (Summer, 1988), pp. 252-266. Timothy J. Reese, a local authority on Crampton's Gap, wrote an article entitled, Coming Home: The Deardorff Family in Burkittsville, Frederick County, Maryland, 1769-1803. Reese identifies many of the earliest tracts in the area of Crampton's Gap.

An article on George Alfred Townsend appears in "Frederick, The Magazine for Mid-Maryland," October 1996. The magazine probably is part of the Frederick city newspaper.

Additional information on Crampton's Gap is available from:

Mrs. Marge Magruder
6516 Morningside Court
Middletown, Maryland 21769
(home phone: 301-371-6923)

The Friends of Gathland State Park
P. O. Box 192
Burkittsville, Maryland 21718

Material on Crampton's Gap also will appear in future issues of the Newsletter.

Please notify

the President of the Society

regarding any errors you find in the current issue of the Newsletter.

Land Tracts of the Battlefield of South Mountain

by Curtis L. Older

Each Newsletter includes a survey, patent, or deed related to the land tracts in the vicinity of Crampton's, Fox's, and Turner's Gaps. These three gaps in South Mountain represent the main area contested by the Union and Confederate Armies in the Battle of South Mountain on September 14, 1862.

Frederick County Land Records, HGO-1-156, Frederick Fox, Fredericks Burgh, surveyed 6 July 1792, 75 acres.

The State of Maryland to wit, By virtue of a Common Warrant for ?? Granted? out? of the land office for the western ?? to Frederck Fox of Frederick County bearing? date June the 11th 1792 being due to him by virtue of an assignment from Thos. Van Swearingen for that quantity granted him the 26th May 1791 I therefore certify that I have carefully surveyed for & in the name of him the said Frederick Fox all that tract of land lying & being in the County aforesaid beginning at the end of the 12th line of a tract of land called Pickall granted Bartholomew Booker in or about the 25th day of March 1766 and running thence

Line No.	North South	Degrees East or West	Length
1	S	East 3	180 perches
2	S	East 51	37 perches
3	S	West 40	6 1/2 perches
4	N	West 54	50 perches
5	S	West 79	30 perches
6	N	West 43	23 perches To a stone marked FF
7	N	East 61 1/2	27 perches to the main road, then with said road 3 courses
8	N	West 44	32 perches
9	N	West 41	40 perches
10	N	West 47	62 perches to the bounded? tree? of a tract of land called Bowsers Addition
11	N	East 21 1/2	11 perches
12	N	East 31 1/2	16 perches
13	N	East 88	40 perches
14	N	East 53	24 perches to a stone marked HB growing in the root of a black oak tree
15	N	East 70	14 perches
16	S	East 4	25 perches
17	S	West 81 1/2	30 perches
18	S	West 13	27 perches
19	S	East 64	8 perches
20	N	East 71	32 perches then
21	N		63 perches
22	then by a straight line to the beginning containing 75 acres of land.		

Amtg? 75 acres? of land surveyed 6th of July 1792 & called "Fredericks Burgh" Jo.? Swearingen? ??? ??? for Saml Davall? ?? ?? F County?

Continued on next page . . .

Beginning at the end of the 12th line of a tract of land called Pickall granted Bartholomew Booker in or about the 25th day of March 1766 and running thence

lines 8, 9, and 10 are along main road, "6th line of Long Dispute Ended"

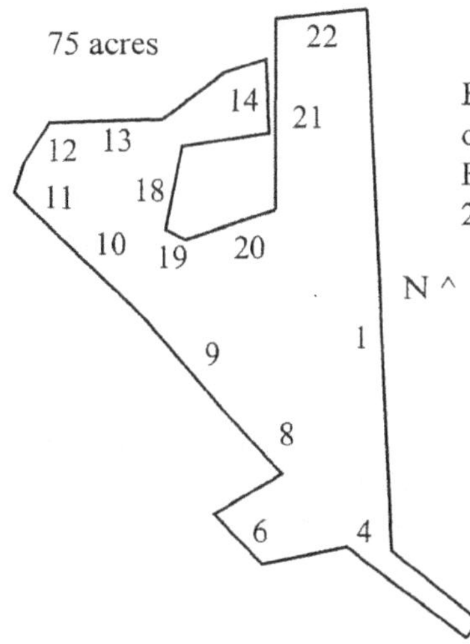

N ^

Fredericks Burgh

Beginning at the end of the 12th line of a tract of land called Pickall granted Bartholomew Booker in or about the 25th day of March 1766

6. To a stone marked FF
7. To the main road, then with said road 3 courses
10. to the bounded tree of a tract of land called Bowser's Addition

Noted on deed: "lines 8, 9, and 10 are along main road. 6th line of Long Dispute Ended."

Now Available from the Society!

"A Trip along the Old Sharpsburg Road"

Are you unable to make the trip to Fox's Gap in Maryland? Would you like to take a drive along the old Sharpsburg Road through Fox's Gap without having to leave your home? Now you can. William G. Benner of Miamisburg, Ohio, filmed a short documentary from his car while driving along the road through Fox's Gap.

The VCR tape, entitled "A Trip along the Old Sharpsburg Road", is now available for the use of members for a period of up to two months for just the price of postage. Just request a copy of the tape from Curtis Older and submit with your letter the sum of $3.00 for postage. You will receive the tape which you may use for up to two months before it must be returned at your expense.

Items for Sale Available through the Society

Members are reminded the Society has available for sale, at cost to the Society, many pictures related to Fox's Gap in Maryland as well as pictures of descendants of Frederick Fox. The photos available are listed in the June 1, 1996, Newsletter and will be listed again in the June 1, 1998, Newsletter.

Wills

by Curtis L. Older

Each Newsletter includes one typewritten version of a will that has significance to the preservation efforts of the Society. Included in this issue is the will of Bartholomew Booker, the father-in-law of Frederick Fox.

Will of Bartholomew Booker Frederick County, Maryland, Register of Wills Records, GM-2-431.

In the Name of God Amen I Bartholomew Booker of Frederick County and State of Maryland, being in sound Mind and memory, but weak in body calling to Mind all Men must die, do make this my last Will and Testament, recommending my Soul into the Hands of the Almyhty God, who gave it me and my Body to the Earth to be Buried in a Christian like manner by my Executors, and touching my Worldly Estate. I dispose of the same in the following manner and form - first, that all my Just debts be paid by me Executors; Item I give and bequeath unto my two Sons Bartholomew and Mathias their Heirs and Assigns for Ever, one Tract of land containing about the quantity of Three hundred and seventeen acres lying in Bedford County and State of Pennsylvania Know by the Name of the Yellow Spring to be equally divided Between the yeilding and Paying to my Estate or to the Executors thereof the Sum of Two hundred and Sixty pounds Lawfull money - Item I Give and Bequeath unto my Son Peter during his Natural Life one hundred and twenty acres of land lying in Bedford County and State of Pensylvania to be taken off at the lower End of my Land near Rippleogles Plantation where one Green lives and after his decease to be the Right and Estate of the Heirs of my said son Peter's for Ever he yielding and paying to my Estate or the Executors thereof the Sum of one hundred and twenty pounds Lawfull Money; Item I Give and bequeath unto my Son Daniel his Heirs and Assigns for ever, two hundred acres of land lying in Bedford County and State of Pennsylvania to be taken off my Land adjoining my Son Peters Land abvoe mentioned he yielding and paying to my Estate or the Executors thereof the sum of two hundred pounds Lawfull money Item I Give and bequeath unto my Son John his Heirs and Assigns for Ever the remaining part of the said Tract of Land lying in Bedford County and State of Pennsylvania know by the name of Rippleogles Plantation at the upper end thereof and adjoing my Son Daniel part above mentioned containing two hundred acres he yielding and paying to my Estate or the Executors thereof the sum of two hundrd pounds Lawfull money Item I give and bequesth unto my Daughter Leah her Heirs and Assigns one Feather Bed and funiture one Cow, a Heifer and a side Saddle; Item I give and Bequeath unto my Daughter Rachel heirs and assigns one feather bed and Furniture, one cow and a side saddle - Item I Give and Bequeath unto my Daughter Mary her Heirs and Assigns one Cow, one Feather Bead and Furniture, Item I Give and Bequeath unto my Daughter Salome one Feather Bead, and one Cow to her and her Heirs and assigns with the furniture to said bed, Item I Give and Bequeath unto my Daughter Hannah her Heirs and Assigns one Feather Bed and furniture and one Cow. Item I Give and Bequeath unto my Daughter Margaret, her Heirs and Assigns, one Cow, Item I Give and Bequeath my Daughter Barbara her Heirs and Assigns one Cow - Item. It is my Will that all the remaining part of my Real and Personal Estate be sold by my Executors to the best advantage, and I give and bequeath the one third part of the money so arising from the same to my beloved wife Margaret, with the one third part of all my Bills, Bonds, Notes, and Accounts. Except the money's payable from my five sons, Bartholomew, Mathias, Peter, Daniel, and John with one Feather Bead and furniture and her side saddle to her and her Heirs and assigns for ever Item I also give to said wife Margaret my House Clock during her Natural Life. then to be the right and Estate of my son John his Heirs and Assigns - Item It is also my Will that all the remaining part of my estate not heretofore Devised when sold by my Executors, and the moneys to arising with all the remaining part of all my bills, bonds, notes

Continued on next page . . .

and accounts with the different sums of monies payable from my five sons Bartholomew, Mathias, Peter, Daniel and John, be equally divided between all my sons and daughters share and share alike that is Catharine, Daniel, Peter, Margaret, Bartholomew, Leah, Matthias, Rachel, Barbara - Elisabeth, Mary, Solome, John and Hannah -
and Lastly I Nominate and Appoint my Beloved Wife Margaret and Frederick Fox my whole and sole Executors of this my last will and Testament Revoking all other Wills by me formerly made In Witness whereof I have herunto set my Hand and Affixed my Seal this Twenty first day of October In the Year of our Lord one Thousand Seven Hundred and Ninety One --
Signed Sealed Published and Declared by Bartholomew
Booker to be his last Will and Testament in the presence
of us who at his request and in his presence have subscribed
our Names as Witnesses thereto the day and year first above written
Philip Jacob ???? ???? Sfmidt Jo. Swearingin

Frederick County May the 1st 1792 then came Margaret Booker and Frederick Fox Executors of Bartholomew Booker Deceased and Solumly Affirmed and Declared that the aforegoing Instrument of Writing is the True and Whole Will and Testament of the said Bartholomew Booker late of Frederick County deceased. That hath come to their Hands an apoprfcion?? and that they doth not know of any other --

Geo. Murdoch Reg.

Frederick County ?? May 1st 1792 then came Philip Jacob Shafer and Henry Smith two of the Subscribing witnesses to the aforegoing last Will and Testament of Bartholomew Booker late of Frederick County deceased and made Oath on the Holy Evangels of Almighty God that they did see the Testator therein named sign and seal this will that they heard him publish pronouce and declare that same to be his last Will and Testament that at the time of his so doing he was to the best of their apprehension of sound and disposing mind memory and understanding that they respectively Subscribed their names as Witnesses to this Will in the presence and at the request of the Testator and that they did also see Joseph Swearingin the other Subscribing witness sign his name as a Witness thereto in the presence and at the request of the Testator and all in the presence of each other --

Geo. Murdoch Reg.

Membership Section

There are no new members of the Society since June 1, 1997.

The following are new addresses of existing members.

Name Address	New Phone
Richard Dale and Deloris Fox Sr. P. O. Box 64 Covington, In 47932	765-793-3674
Dellie Jean Craig 1624 Arlington Road Lafayette, Indiana 47904	317-448-9194

Footnotes to Pages 12 and 13

The War Correspondents' Memorial Arch at Crampton's Gap

[1] "Fielderia originally on the 6th day of September anno domini 1763 granted unto the said Fielder Gannt for 8151 acres"

[2] "Gavers Recovery by resurvey made the 8th day of December 1789." "in the following tracts or parts of tracts or parcels of land lying and being in the county aforesaid and contiguous to each other viz nineteen and a half acres part of the resurvey on Dawsons Purchase originally on the fifth day of October seventeen hundred and fifty two granted Thomas Dawson for two hundred and fifteen and three quarters acres eighty nine acres part of I Got It At Last originally on the fifth day of November seventeen hundred and fifty four granted Thomas Hawkins for one hundred acres The Mountain originally on the nineteenth day of October seventeen hundred and sixty granted Thomas Hawkins for thirty acres and twenty five acres part of a tract of land called Fielderia Manor originally on the fifteenth day of January seventeen hundred and seventy two granted Fielder Gannt for ten thousand four hundred and seventy one and a quarter acres, contiguous to which lands he has discovered some vacancy and being desirous to add the same and to reduce the whole into one entire tract"

[3] "Michael Brunner and Elizabeth Brunner his wife Daniel Booker and Catherin Booker his wife Samuel Gaver John Cain and Mary Cain his wife Henry Beeler and Hannah Beeler his wife Jacob Parson and Huldak Parson his wife Gedion Gaver David Gaver Samuel Landis and Arsenith Landis his wife John Bizer and Lydia Bizer his wife, all heirs and representatives of Peter Gaver deceased"

[4] "by a decree of Frederick county court setting as a Court of Equity bearing date the seventh day of March in the year one thousand eight hundred and thirty one the above named Ezra Slifer was appointed a trustee and authorized and empowered to sell and dispose of all the real estate of Joshua Harley Senr then a lunatic"

[5] "said Trustees in execution of said trust did about A. D. 1856 did sell said lot to William F. Gitings but did not give any deed for the same, though the purchase money was paid, & the said Gittings did about A. D. 1856, sell the same lot to one George W. Padget now deceased of the same county intestate, and whose sole child and heir is the said Mary A. E. Koontz and whereas after the death of said Padget intestate, said lot was sold at Public Sale for Taxes due thereon for the years 1866 & 7 by William A. Fenga Tax Collector for the County aforesaid on the sixth day of May A. D. 1869 to the said David Arnold"

[6] "It being part of the same land which was conveyed to said George Alfred Townsend by a deed executed by David Arnold and his wife dated December 15, 1884, and which is recorded in Liber A. F. No 9 folio 541 one of the land records of Frederick County, Maryland."

[7] "all that triangular tract or parcel of land lying in the forks of the road leading from the summit of South Mountain to Arnoldstown and Burkittsville respectively being in Frederick County state of Maryland and more particularly described, as beginning at a point near the dividing line between Frederick and Washington counties Maryland and in the middle of the road leading from Burkittsville to Gapland Station said point being S 10 degrees west 1 & 1/10 perches from a stone planted on the north side of said road and near the stone fence, and running thence with the middle of the road"

Index

Issue 4, Volume 1

News from Fox's Gap

News from Fox's Gap

The Society of the Descendants of Frederick Fox of Fox's Gap in Maryland

Issue 5, Volume 1 **Remember Freedom!** June 1, 1998

Reunion at Miamisburg, Ohio, May 31, 1998

A number of families representing descendants of Frederick Fox of Fox's Gap in Maryland will meet on Sunday, May 31, 1998, in Miamisburg, Ohio.

7:00 to 8:00 PM	Saturday May 30	Check-in at local motel.
8:00 to 9:30 AM	Sunday May 31	Breakfast at Bob Evans restaurant, Exit #44, I-75.
11:00 AM	Sunday May 31	Attend church service at the Gebhart or St. John Lutheran Church adjacent the cemetery.
12:15 to 1:45 PM	Sunday May 31	Lunch at a local Miamisburg restaurant.
2:00 to 3:00 PM	Sunday May 31	Visit the St. John or Gebhart Cemetery and the grave of Frederick Fox.
3:00 to 5:00 PM	Sunday May 31	Meeting of the participants in the Reunion - Discussion leader will be Curtis L. Older.
5:00 PM	Sunday May 31	Depart for home.

Don Smith, the newest member of the Society, probably will have the largest contingent of Fox descendants at the Reunion. Don, who lives in Indianapolis, has many relatives who live in Ohio and who descend from Frederick Fox. Those who expect to attend the Reunion include: Dellie Jean Craig, Dick and Delores Fox, Bill Benner and wife, Don Smith and wife, Curt Older and wife Linda and daughter Rachael, and perhaps up to 10 or so relatives of Don Smith.

President's Message
by Curtis Lynn Older

** Welcome to new Society member Donald Smith of Indianapolis, Indiana. Don and his wife, Joan S. Smith, plan to attend the reunion at Miamisburg, Ohio. Curt came across Don when he was reviewing the 1997 Sons of the American Revolution Directory and noticed Don's named listed under descendants of Frederick Fox.

** The Frederick County Library, Frederick, Maryland, recently purchased three copies of *The Braddock Expedition and Fox's Gap in Maryland*. The Carlyle House, also known as the Braddock House, in Alexandria, Virginia, also recently purchased a copy of the book.

** *The Land Tracts of the Battlefield of South Mountain* is almost ready to send to the publisher. Family Line Publications of Westminster, Maryland, will publish the book. The book will run about 225 pages and is an abbreviated version of my "Long Version" of the same title. I hope this book will permanently serve to identify the earliest land tracts in the battlefield area.

The George Fox Line

by Dellie Jean Craig

The following members of the Society descend from George Fox, a son of Frederick Fox:

Elizabeth Jane Bucholz - Society #0008
Dellie Jean Craig - Society #0009
Patricia Jo Edwards - Society #0011
Richard Dale Fox Sr. - Society #0015
Reva Winfried Fox - Society #0003
William Ernest Fox - Society #0002
Wilma Marion Gose - Society #0010
Mildred F. Metcalf - Society #00016
Curtis Lynn Older - Society #0001
Don Smith - Society #0021

Jacob and Melissa Ricketts, parents of Elizabeth Jane Ricketts

Dellie Jean Craig submitted the following picture of the family of Jacob and Melissa Ricketts.

Front row: Jake Ricketts, Melissa Barnard Ricketts, Jacob Ricketts, and Elizabeth Jane Ricketts. Back row: Daniel Ricketts, Frederick Ricketts, Hiram Ricketts, Joseph Ricketts, Dave Ricketts, and Abraham Lincoln Ricketts. Not in photograph: Nan Ricketts.

Jacob and Melissa Ricketts were the parents of Elizabeth Jane Ricketts. Elizabeth married Daniel Alexander Fox. Daniel and Elizabeth Fox were the parents of Kenneth, Ernest, William, Ethel, and Ruby Fox. (See Application for Letters of Administration, 23 January 1924, on the death of Melissa Ricketts. Also see the 1870 and 1880 United States Census records for Mound Township, Warren County, Indiana. Pension papers of Jacob Ricketts appear in the National Archives under Union Army, Company D, 57th Indiana Volunteer Infantry, 1864 to 1865, Certificate 703568; Pensioner: Melissa J.; Widow of Veteran: Jacob Ricketts; Can No: 561621; bundle No.: 3.)

The following list identifies records placed on a Kodak Photo CD-Rom disc by Curtis L. Older that relate to Jacob Ricketts and his wife, Melissa Jane Barnard:

1. Pension paper dated 29 February 1904, at Danville, Illinois, for Jacob Ricketts of Company D, 57th Indiana Volunteer Infantry.

2. Declaration of Pension, Jacob Ricketts, dated 25 February 1907.

3. Original Invalid Pension, Jacob Ricketts, dated 30 April 1890.

4. Application for Letters of Administration, 23 January 1924, on the death of Melissa Ricketts. Lists children as Abraham L. Ricketts, Joseph, Nancy Ricketts Dixon, Hiram, Fred, and Jacob. Lists grandchildren as Kenneth Fox, Ernest Fox, William Fox, Ethel Fox Gouty, and Ruby Fox Hines.

5. Department of Pensions, Jacob Ricketts, gives wife as Melissa Jane Ricketts, married March 20, 1860, at Danville, Illinois. Jacob Ricketts had a previous wife who died in 1850.

6, Map of Land Owners in 1872, Highland Township, Indiana, The township was between the Wabash River and the Illinois State Line.

7. Landowners of Highland Township, Indiana.

8. Marriage record that acknowledges existence of marriage license for Jacob Ricketts and Melissa J. Barnard on 21 March 1861.

The father of Jacob Ricketts was John Ricketts. (See the death certificate for Jacob Ricketts. Also see the 1840 United States Census records for Vermillion County, Highland Township, Indiana.) The father of John Ricketts was Robert Ricketts. (See January Term 1856, page 397, Ohio County, Indiana, that lists the heirs of Robert Ricketts. Robert died February 14, 1853. The first beneficiary listed for Robert Ricketts is "John Ricketts's heirs." John preceded his father, Robert, in death. John died February 23, 1843, in Highland Township, Vermillion County, Indiana.

The above chain of descent, from Robert Ricketts to John Ricketts to Jacob Ricketts to Elizabeth Jane Ricketts appears to be correct. However, additional records to prove the line of descent will be sought in the coming months. A more in-depth discussion of the ancestors of Jacob Ricketts will appear in the December 1, 1998, Newsletter.

National Archive Microfilm Publications contain information about Robert Ricketts under No. S 17,047, Pennsylvania. The material appears to be from pages 0146 through 0156 of the microfilm. Also see Pennsylvania Archives, Series III, v. 23, p. 453. Page 0156 of the National Archive microfilm consists of the following letter:

Rev. & 1812 Wars Section

May 7, 1927

Mrs. W. H. Shonts
203 E. Marion St.
South Bend, Indiana

Madam:

I have to advise you that it appears from the papers in the Revolutionary War pension claim, S. 17047, that Robert Ricketts was born January 15, 1765, near Hagerstown, Maryland. He enlisted in Cumberland County, Pennsylvania, in 1780 as a private in Captain James Johnson's Company in Colonel Piper's Pennsylvania Regiment and served three months. While living in Kishacoquillas Val ley, Pennsylvania, he enlisted in 1782 and served three months and seven days as a private in Captains Robert's Samuel's and Bowls' Pennsylvania Companies. He was allowed pension on his application executed September 18, 1832, at which time he was a resident of Dearborn County, Indiana. He died February 14, 1853, leaving a widow and eleven children, their names not stated. His widow died February 20, 1853.

Respectfully,
Winfield Scott

Commissioner

Frederick Fox in the American Revolution
by Curtis L. Older

The Frederick Fox of Pennsylvania in the 1790 U. S. Census

There is a Frederick Fox listed in *Emigrants of Pennsylvania*, Genealogical Publishing Company, Inc., 1978, Baltimore, Maryland:

> April 14, 1773, Record of servants & apprentices bound & assigned before Hon. John Gibson, Mayor of Philadelphia, Dec. 5th, 1772 - May 21, 1773.
>
> Frederick Fox with consent of his step mother Eliza Fox, apprentice to Conrad Alster of Phila Cordwainer.

Since the Frederick Fox who emigrated to Pennsylvania in 1773 was apprenticed to someone who lived in Philadelphia, it seems likely this Frederick Fox was the one who resided in Philadelphia County in the 1790 census. Because he must have been rather young, he received his step mother's consent to be an apprentice. Perhaps he did not serve in the Revolutionary War.

The 1791 Philadelphia Directory lists a "Fox Frederick, cordwainer, St. John's St. above Poplar lane, No. Lib." The Frederick Fox who appears in the following record in 1773 perhaps was the same Frederick Fox listed as a cordwainer in 1791 in Philadelphia. This is not completely certain however. There is no listing of a Frederick Fox in the 1785 MacPherson's Directory For The City and Suburbs of Philadelphia or in the 1795 Philadelphia Directory published by Edmund Hogan.[1]

This Frederick Fox cannot be ruled out as serving in the 10th Pennsylvania Regiment, Continental Line.

The following letter, dated August 16, 1996, was received from Domenic A. Saguto, Master Shoemaker, Manager, Leather Trades Programs, Department of Historic Trades, Presentations & Tours, Williamsburg, Virginia.

Dear Mr. Older:

Thank you for your letter of 5 August, and the pleasant comments about your visit to the Shoemakers' Shop last year at Thanksgiving. I am glad I was able to assist you then, and I shall try again with your latest questions.

The "Bierly Tannery" report I referred you to is: Archaeological Data Recovery at the Bierly Tannery (18FR575) City of Frederick, Maryland, 1991, by M.A.A.R. Associates, Inc., 9 Liberty Plaza, Newark, DE 19715. This is a very important site, as it began operations in the 1760s or before, and stayed in continual use until the 1920s. If you wish to actually see the shoes and other leather artifacts, they were last reported to be on display at the public library in the city of Frederick, about one hour's drive north from Washington, D. C., but I'd recommend you call them first to be certain.

Your question regarding the age of Frederick Fox in 1773 is not so simple. If he required his stepmother's permission to be apprenticed off to Conrad Alster between December 1772 and May 1773, he must have been a minor. In Virginia, at least, this would suggest he was under twenty-one. Since there is no length of apprenticeship given, we have no idea exactly how much younger than twenty-one he was.

Typically an apprenticeship ranged from five to seven years, and for males had to end upon turning twenty-one (eighteen for females in Virginia). Some "orphans" were put off to trade at a very young age, some as young as six or seven; others as late as sixteen or older. Apprenticeship was seen

---

[1] Per research of William B. Brown, III, Genealogist, in late 1996.

here, by the courts at least, as a handy way of finding foster-parents for "orphans" (which usually meant the child of a widowed mother who did not have the estate or income to support them).

Given this situation, there were "apprentices" and there were "apprentices". Some served a full term of six or seven years to become journeymen in the traditional way. Others were "apprenticed" for an abbreviated period of time and only with the intent of keeping them out of mischief until they reached their majority. One embittered New Jersey writer of the 1750s commented on the effects of such abbreviated apprenticeships -- which required no more than three years -- calling the journeymen so produced "Rather Jobbers and Cobblers than Workmen," and it is "almost incredible to think what a Number of such Insects infest this Country."

Contrary to English law, which limited the number of apprentices one master could take on to three, there were no such constraints in Virginia, and probably elsewhere in the Colonies, where masters could accept as many apprentices as they felt they could feed. This also changed the face of apprenticeship in colonial America away from the traditional Old World arrangements, and gave rise to such abuses as related above in New Jersey.

Traditionally, shoemaking apprenticeships by the later 18th-century in England had grown to a minimum of seven full years, though it is often state in several books to the young would-be apprentice shoemaker, that more like ten years was necessary to develop enough proficiency to make a good living at it.

From what we know about the shoemaking trade itself, it was always one of the largest occupations in any city. Philadelphia, in particular, where the shoemakers had been organized earlier in the 18th century into "Labor" and "Management" camps with societies for the masters and others for the journeymen, was no exception. Where numbers were high like this, competition was ferocious, and only the best journeymen could find and maintain employment. The inferior workmen drifted out of the countryside, or took up the ridiculed occupation of shoe repair as a "Cobbler."

The shoemakers of Philadelphia led the 1788 Grand Federal Procession, with the largest contingent of tradesmen and a horse-drawn float representing a shoe shop with six men actually at work on it, followed by the standard bearer and over three hundred shoemakers, marching six abreast, each wearing white leather aprons embellished with the company's arms richly painted -- such was the state and prosperity of the shoe trade in 18th century Philadelphia.

Since Fox was apprenticed off by his stepmother, not stepfather, I would suspect that his father (or stepfather) was deceased or else he would have been acting as the guardian in this case.

As to whether he served in the military during the War for Independence, that question would be even more difficult to answer with any certainly. I do not know the proportion of Loyalists, Rebels, and neutrals in Philadelphia, but what is generally thought is that only about one-third of the American population played a combative role in the conflict. Of this one-third, some joined provincial, Loyalist units, or the American Army. If Fox had only just arrived, presumably from England in 1772, and depending on the political bent of his master, Alster, there's an equally good chance he could have served in a Loyalist regiment. I wouldn't automatically assume that if he took part in the war he would have necessarily been in the Continental Army.

Furthermore, Philadelphia was, by 1770, a major center for the manufacture of boots and shoes "in this as [in] the neighboring Provinces and the West Indies which are mostly supplied from hence," producing very fine work up to London standards. During war time the shoe trade finds unparalleled prosperity in supplying footwear to the military, so another distinct possibility is that Fox road out the war making shoes. Another scenario is that Fox, if he did indeed enlist in the Continental Army, might have been assigned to work in the Continental Army She Factory established in Newark, New Jersey, with operated at least through 1777/8.

The Continental Army also organized a Corps of Artificers, and other sub-organizations of craftsmen who, while enlisted in the service, were used to support the war effort as tradesmen rather than combat soldiers.

This is all speculation in the case of your Frederick Fox, of course, but all are distinct possibilities for you to investigate. The city directories for Philadelphia are very useful, and I would suggest you start there to try and find Alster's dates of operation and reference to Fox, who may have gone on to run his own business. Rosters for several of the Pennsylvania regiments might survive too, as well as Loyalist claims, so you might want to search these out in your research.

If you want to read more about the shoemakers of 18th-century Philadelphia, I can recommend:

Quimby, Ian J., "The Cordwainers Protest: A Crisis in Labor Relations", Winterthur Portfolio, Volume III, 1967.

Smith, Billy G., The Lower Sort: Philadelphia Laboring People, (no date, but recently published).

Smith, Billy G., "The Material Lives of Laboring Philadelphians, 1750-1800," The William and Mary Quarterly, Volume XXXVIII, Number 2, April 1981.

I appreciate your kind offer to reimburse me financially for my reply, but that is not necessary, nor ethical. As a museum we are committed to research and education in the public trust, and I am glad to be able to assist your research as part of my job. If you wish to make a contribution either to the on-going work of The Colonial Williamsburg Foundation, or specifically the work of the Shoemaking Program, please feel free to either call me directly (757-229-1000, ext. 2543) or contact our Director for Development, Mr. Barry Dress (757-220-7226).

If I can be of any further assistance, don't hesitate to write or call.

Sincerely,

D. A. Saguto, Master Shoemaker
Manager, Leather Trades Programs
Department of Historic Trades,
Presentations & Tours

Records in the National Archives, Washington, DC, for Frederick Fox, 10th Pennsylvania Regiment, Continental Line

Heading Card
sent with the below mentioned cards:
Fox, Frederick
10 Pennsylvania Reg't.
(Revolutionary War.)
Drumr & fifer Drummer
Card Numbers.
1. 37404176
2. 4837
3. 37188278
4. 39144421

Card One
F 10 Pa.
Frederick Fox
Drum.
Appears as shown below in an
Account
of what Monies Received & paid by William Feltman
Lieut Paymaster. To Lieut. Col. Samuel
Hay's Company Tenth Pennsya Regt To the
Officers & Privates of said Regt
(Revolutionary War.)
Account dated
not dated, 17 .
Name, Frederick Fox drum
Sum paid, Dollers, 90ths
Sum reced for pay &
Subsistance as Pr
pay Roll. January 52, Dollars, 90ths
February & March
1780,
We the Subscribers do Acknowledge to have
reced the sums Annex'd to our Names Respectively,
Fredk. X Fox's mark
Remarks:
Number of record:
6 ??VP Ripley??
(545i) copyist

Card Two
F 10 Pa.
Frederick Fox
Drummer, 10 Regiment Pa
(Revolutionary War.)
Appears in a book*
Compiled from Rolls
of the organization named above, under the head
of "State of Pennsylvania against United
States for Depreciation on Pay of the Army."
Sum charged L91 - s7 - d8
Sum admitted
Remarks: Inlistd 26 April 77
*This book appears to have been compiled (from original rolls) in the Office of Army Accounts under the Paymaster General, U.S.A., who was authorized by Congress, July 4, 1783 to settle and finally adjust all accounts whatsoever between the United States and the officers and soldiers of the American army. (Journal American Congress, Vol. 4, page 237.)-R. & P. 436,786.
Vol. 7, page 37
(someone's name)
(575) Copyist

Card Three
F 10 Pa.
Frederic Fox
, Tenth Regiment, 1780.
Appears in a
Book*
under the following heading:
"We and each of us whose names are hereunto subscribed do acknowledge to have received from Major Thomas B. Bown and Captain Ercurius Beatty, Agents for the late Pennsylvania Line, the several sums opposite to our names, respectively, in certificates dated July 1, 1784, bearing Interest at Six Per cent. fro January 1, 1781, Signed by John Pierce, Commissioner, and described as below, being for a Balance of a settlement between the United States and us for Pay To January 1st 1781."
(Revolutionary War.)
Date of Issue , 17 .
No of Certificate 67913; Letter P.
No of voucher
Sum 36 Dollars 60 90ths.
Signer Deld??
Remarks:
*This book bears the following Certificate: "I Certify that this Book (Containing 200 hundred and eleven pages) is a correct Copy of Pay Roll Book 'B' one of the Books of pay rolls of the agents of the United States for the settlement of the pay of the Pennsylvania Line in the Revolutionary War. Witness my hand and seal of Office at Harrisburg the twenty first day of September, A.D. 1818?? - Geo. Bryan, auditor Gen. State of Pennsylvania."
Vol. 171: page 17
Riverson??
(547) copyist

Card Four
F 10 Pa.
Frederick Fox
Appears with the rank of Drumr & fifer on a
Roll
of Lieut Colo. Hubley's Company 10th Pennsyla.
Regimt Commanded by Colo Richd Humpton
Enlisted During the War-
(Revolutionary War.)
Roll dated
Sept 10, 1778.
Remarks: In the field
signed name of someone??
(555) Copyist

Frederick Fox and Fox's Gap Section
by Curtis Lynn Older

The Reno School Building along the old Sharpsburg Road

A 1996 photograph of the former Reno School building. The school was named after United States Major General Jesse Lee Reno who was killed at Fox's Gap during the Battle of South Mountain. The building probably was built in late 1865. It has been used as a house since 1924. Edna I. Toms owned the building in early 1997. Photo by Susanne Flowers.

The Reno School Building Land Tract Records

From Bartholomew Booker, 1764, to Edna I. Toms, 1997
Tract Name - Pick All

MdHR = Maryland Hall of Records at Annapolis, Maryland
FCLR = Frederick County Land Records, Frederick, Maryland

Reference	Date	Grantee of Deed	Area
MdHR BC & GS 30 pp. 214-216	3 Feb 1764	Bartholomew Booker, Patent for Pick All A Resurvey on Mendall and Small All	1224 acres
FCLR L-71	16 Oct 1767	Bartholomew Booker to George Shidler, Long Dispute (Shidler's Dispute and part of Pick All)	200 acres
FCLR P-651	22 Mar 1773	George Shidler to Henry Smith, Long Dispute (Shidler's Dispute and part of Pick All)	200 acres
FCLR WR-8-662	20 Oct 1789	Henry Smith to Peter Hutzel, Long Dispute (Shidler's Dispute and part of Pick All)	200 acres

Reference	Date	Grantee of Deed	Area
FCLR JS-17-504	7 Apr 1823	Ex of Peter Hutzel to Jacob Hutzel	160 acres
FCLR JS-19-6	1 Dec 1823	Jacob Hutzel to John Hutzel	160 acres
FCLR BFG-6-569	1 Apr 1861	John Hutzel Estate to Ezra Warenfeltz (Adam Hutzel, Samuel Hutzel, and Vincent Sanner, executors)	162 and 1/2 acres and 17 perches
FCLR BGF-6-680	7 May 1861	Ezra Warenfeltz to William J. Kepler and Anna M. Kepler, his wife	162 and 1/2 acres and 17 perches
FCLR BGF-7-561	30 June 1862	William J. Kepler and Anna M. Kepler, his wife, to John Mentzer and Martha E. Mentzer, his wife	3 acres and 66 perches
FCLR AF-11-311	27 Aug 1865	John Mentzer and Martha E. Mentzer, his wife, to County School Commissioners of Frederick County (the Reno School)	1 acre
FCLR 368-32	25 Aug 1928	Board of Education to George L. Miller (the Reno School building became a private residence)	1 acre
FCLR 421-320	12 Sep 1939	Orpha M. Miller, widow of George L. Miller, to Everett Moser (Mount Reno School Lot)	1 acre
FCLR 438-345	19 Apr 1943	Everett Moser to Murvil L. and Edna I. Toms (Reno School House Lot)	1 acre, also 5 acres

---

Topics in the next issue of the Newsletter, December 1, 1998

* 1. The deed for the transfer of the Reno Monument from the Society of the Burnside Expedition to the United States Government.
* 2. Ancestor Chart for John Ogle, First of the Name in Delaware.
* 3. Frederick Fox at Valley Forge in the winter of 1777-78.
* 4. The will of John Adam Link II.
* 5. The land record for the Bowser's Addition tract at Fox's Gap.

Membership Drive

The main objective of each member of the Society is to recruit at least one new member of the Society each year. The new member should not have been a previous member of the Society. The easy work is over. We now must seek to identify those individuals who are unknown to us and who qualify to join the Society.

Land Tracts of the Battlefield of South Mountain

by Curtis L. Older

Each Newsletter includes a survey, patent, or deed related to the land tracts in the vicinity of Crampton's, Fox's, and Turner's Gaps. These three gaps in South Mountain represent the main area contested by the Union and Confederate Armies in the Battle of South Mountain on September 14, 1862.

Maryland Hall of Records 17,441, 1-23-3-41, BC & GS 30, pp. 214-216, Bartholomew Booker, Pick All, resurveyed 3 Feb 1764, 1224 acres. "1224 acres. completed 10-2-95. .i."

Bartholomew Booker, his cert 1224 a Pickall, pattd 25th March 1764 rent ? ann 12.g sterling charged to the rent roll -- } Frederick County ? By virtue of a special warrant granted out of his lordships land office of this province to Bartholomew Booker of the county afsd bearing date by renewment the 8th September 1763 to Resurvey part of two tracts of land lying in the county afsd and contiguous to each other viz 146 acres part of a tract or parcel of land called Mendall originally on the 21st day of December 1758 granted him for 546 acres under new rent and one quarter of an acre part of a tract or parcel of land called Small-all originally on the 24th day of June 1759 granted unto the said Bartholomew Booker for 25 acres under new Rent to Resurvey the afsd land to amend all errors to add the contiguous vacancy I therefore certify as deputy surveyor under his excellency Horatio Sharpe Esquire Governor of Maryland that I have carefully resurveyed the afsd lands and find that the afsd Tract of land called Mendall that there appears to be the quantity of two hundred and four acres remaining in possession of said Booker and I also find that the other tract called Small All has been all conveyed to certain George Shidler but about one quarter of an acre which quarter lays in the first original and I have added three pieces of contiguous vacancy containing one thousand and twenty acres and have reduced the whole into one entire tract which will appear by the platts below lastly beginning for the out lines of the whole by virtue of the before mentioned warrant at the beginning tree of a tract of land called Johns Delight patented to James Wardrop which tree is a white oak standing by the side of the main road that leads from Frederick Town to Fort Frederick and running thence

Line No.	North South	Degrees East or West	Length
1	S	38 east	66 perches
2	N	70 east	80 perches
3	S	45 west	148 perches
4	S	86 west	100 perches
5	N		34 perches
6	N	69 east	140 perches
7	S	79 1/2 west	148 perches
8	N	10 west	57 perches
9	N	36 west	60 perches
10	N	51 east	52 perches
11	N	62 1/2 west	80 perches
12	S	88 west	20 perches
13	S	3 east	180 perches
14	S	51 east	98 perches
15	S	9 east	10 perches
16	S	60 west	40 perches
17	S	3 west	67 perches
18	S	33 west	28 perches
19	S	49 east	41 perches
20	N	34 east	94 perches
21	S	51 east	78 perches
22	S	81 east	64 perches
23	S	21 east	30 perches
24	N	44 east	100 perches
25	N		80 perches
26	S	80 east	75 perches
27	S	25 east	17 perches
28	N	80 east	96 perches
29	S	19 west	162 perches
30	N	76 west	36 perches
31	S	88 west	26 perches
32	N	7 west	13 perches
33	S	74 west	24 perches
34	S	8 west	27 perches
35	N	75 east	22 perches
36	S	16 east	46 perches
37	S	40 east	20 perches
38		east	40 perches
39	N	8 east	10 perches
40	N	89 east	63 perches
41	N	35 east	40 perches
42	N	11 1/2 east	154 perches

Line No.	North South	Degrees East or West	Length
43	N	80 west	13 perches
44	S	71 west	31 perches
45	N		22 perches
46	N	11 west	27 perches
47	N	39 west	40 perches
48	S	60 west	20 perches
49	N	88 1/2 west	110 perches
50	N	4 west	113 perches
51	N	88 east	147 perches
52	N	87 west	156 perches
53	N	4 west	37 perches
54	N	1 1/2 west	74 perches
55	S	32 east	20 perches
56	N	66 east	60 perches
57	S	60 east	56 perches
58	N	79 east	60 perches
59	S	54 east	40 perches
60	S	40 east	40 perches
61	S	82 east	22 perches
62	N	76 east	66 perches
63	N		28 perches
64	N	38 west	40 perches
65	N		55 perches
66	N	30 1/2 east	31 perches
67	S	72 east	30 perches
68	N	25 west	175 perches
69	S	55 west	44 perches
70	N	11 west	116 perches

Line No.	North South	Degrees East or West	Length
71	N	25 west	83 perches
72	N	46 west	88 perches
73	S	36 west	15 perches
74	S	53 east	30 perches
75	S	21 west	28 perches
76	S	40 west	12 perches
77	S	88 west	104 perches
78	N	22 west	117 perches
79	N	58 west	60 perches
80	S	28 west	106 perches
81	S	36 east	110 perches
82	S	60 east	30 perches
83	S	38 east	74 perches
84	N	41 east	19 perches
85	N	82 east	100 perches
86	S	36 east	60 perches
87	S	5 west	30 perches
88	S	44 east	60 perches
89	S		50 perches
90	S	12 west	60 perches
91	S	3 east	64 perches
92	S	43 west	17 perches
93	S	81 west	30 perches
94	N	60 west	94 perches
95	S	88 west	20 perches
96	S	64 west	99 perches
97	S	81 west	82 perches
98	S	13 east	80 perches
99	then with a straight line to the beginning		

containing and now laid out for one thousand two hundred and twenty four acres of land to be held of Conogocheigue Manor by the name of Pickall
February 22d 1764 Examined & passed Resurveyed the 3d day of February 1764.
U Scott Examr ? John Murdock

on the back of the foregoing certificate was the following receipt viz - I have received two pounds eighteen shillings for the within surplus fifty two pounds thirteen shillings for the vacancy added four shillings ? nine pence for four years ? nine months rent ? Small All to sady? day 1764 ? four pounds six? pense for improvements patent may therefore issue with his excellency's approbation Edwd Lloyd
20th February 1764 approved H Sharpe

(**Author's Note:** lines 41 and 42 are contiguous to lines 6 and 7 of Christies Folly; line 44 is the same as line 39 of the Resurvey on Oxford)

The Reno School building, as noted in the previous article, stands on part of the Pick All tract.

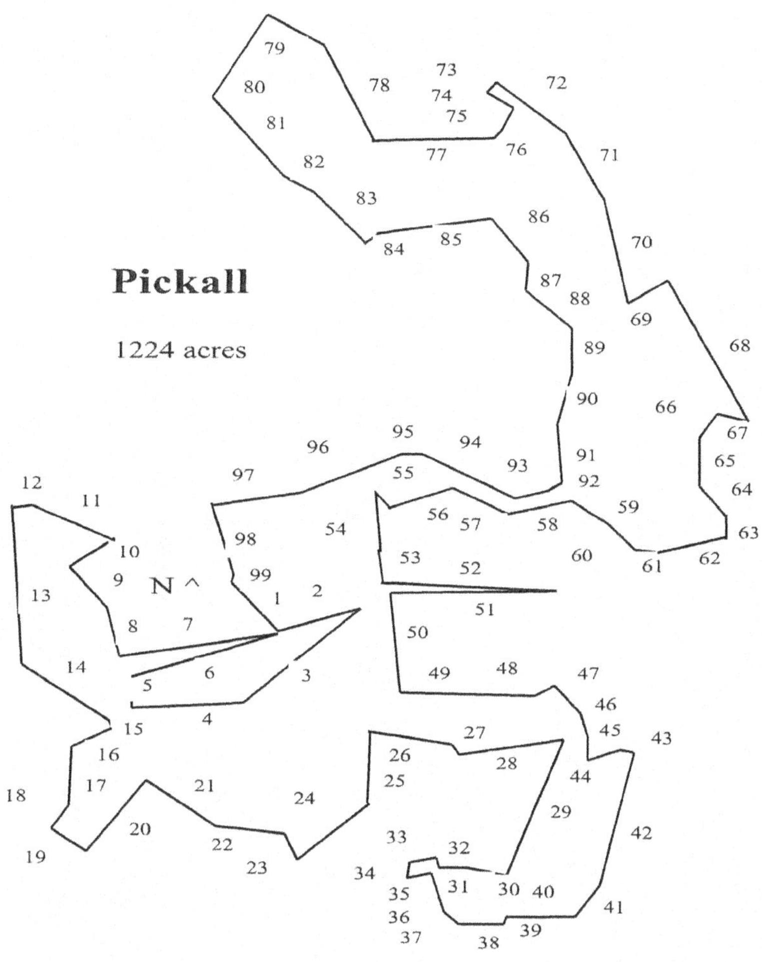

Please notify

the President of the Society

regarding any errors you find in the current issue of the Newsletter.

Wills

by Curtis L. Older

Each Newsletter includes one typewritten version of a will that is significant to the preservation efforts of the Society. Included in this issue are the Estate Papers of George Fox, a son of Frederick Fox. George Fox owned the Fox Inn along the Old Sharpsburg Road northwest of Middletown, Maryland, from 1805 to 1807.

The Estate Papers of George Fox Obtained through the Warren County Genealogical Society, 300 East Silver Street, Lebanon, Ohio 45036

Elisabeth Fox and Adam Fox Adm of George Fox Decd In acpt with the widow and Heirs of said Estate.

Debtor

Amounts found remaining in the hands of said Admrs are final settlement at the October Term 1850
$ 2591.54 1/2

Credit

Vouchers No. 1 to 7 inclusive Elisabeth Fox widow of said Decd	930.51
Vouchers No. 8 to 12 inclusive Adam Fox	184.63
Vouchers No. 13 to 17 inclusive Frederick L. Fox	184.63
Vouchers Nos. 18 to 22 inclusive Daniel L. Fox	184.63
Vouchers Nos. 23 to 28 inclusive George L. Fox	184.63
Vouchers Nos. 29 to 33 inclusive John L. Fox	184.63
Vouchers Nos. 34 to 38 inclusive Alexander Fox	184.63
Vouchers Nos. 39 to 42 inclusive Elisabeth L. Fox	184.63
Vouchers Nos. 43 to 46 inclusive Mary L. Fox (now deceased)	184.00
Vouchers No 47 John Fox guardian of Elisabeth Ann & David M. Fox	184.63

State of Ohio Warren County

Personally appeared in open court Adam Fox one of the administrators of George Fox Decd and was duly sworn according to law deposeth and saith that the foregoing accounts & vouchers therein referred to is last & correct to best of his knowledge & belief and he further saith that after they had paid out to each of the heirs at law (except the two minors entitled to one share) that Mary L. Fox died intestate and without issue and then the small balance remaining in the hands of the Adms was divided among the remaining heirs & saith he saith not

sworn to & subscribed in open court this 23rd Nov 1850 } Adam Fox

A W Stokes Clk

George Fox Estate Receipts

Received of Elisabeth Fox & Adam Fox administrators of the Estate of George Fox Decs. the sum of seventeen dollars & fifty cents part of the above named Estate.
February the 24th 1849 John L. Fox (signed)

Received of Elisabeth Fox and Adam Fox administrators of the Estate of George Fox decd the sum of fifty dollars, part of the above - named Estate
January 4th 1848 Susannah Fox for John L Fox (signed)

June 23rd 1849.
Received of Adam Fox one of the administrators of the Estate of George Fox Decd, the sum of fifty dollars part of the above named Estate due the widow.
Elisabeth Fox (signed)

Springboro June 15th 1847
The estate of George Fox deceased to C F Farr
? 1 coffin & attendance $18.00

Received of Adam Fox one of the administrators of the estate of George Fox decd the goods and chattel set off to me as the widow of said Decd by the appraisal amounting to one hundred nine dollar and ten cents also forty dollars and ninety cents in cash as a further sum set off for the same purposes in all one hundred and fifty dollar
$150 Elisabeth Fox (signed)
Oct 2nd 1847

$10.00
Rec'd Feby 7 1849 of Adam Fox admr of the Estate of Geo Fox decd. Ten dollars being the two last installments in full of the subscription to the Ev. Lutheran Seminary at Columbus O. made by sd. decd. & not pd. during his life time.
John Donley Sp. agent (signed)

$1.50
Received March 25th 1848 of Adam Fox one of the administrators of the Estate of George Fox Decd ? one dollar & fifty cents for the subscription to Rev George Tony made by the said Geo. Fox
Joseph Gottschull (signed)

Decd George For or order Eight Dollars for Boards and Cider, for value recd Miamisburg April 8 18??
John Heiser

Paid to George L. Fox the sum of fourteen dollars to buy his saddle that he was to have from his Father before his death but never got it till now not to be charged to the undersigned
Sept. 21st 1849 George L. Fox (signed)

Received of Elisabeth Fox & Adam Fox Administrators of the Estate of George Fox Dec. the sum of forty five dollars for a marble tomb stone for the grave of said George Fox decd.
La Dow & Hamilton (signed)
Jnry 8 1848

Received of Elisabeth Fox and Adam Fox administrators of the Estate of George Fox Decd the sum of one hundred and eighty four dollars & sixty three cents it being paid as the distributive share of Elisabeth Ann. & David. M. Fox minor heirs of Catharine L. Fox Decd and heirs at Law of said George Fox Decd. Also nine dollars and fifteen cents interest received thereon.

Nov 11th 1850 John Fox (signed)
Guardian of Elisabeth
Ann & David M. Fox

Received of Elizabeth Fox & Adam Fox administrators of the Estate of George Fox Decd the sum of sixteen dollars & fifty cents part of the above named Estate.

June 23rd 1849 Mary L Fox (signed)

Received of Elizabeth Fox & Adam Fox administrators of the Estate of George Fox Decd. the sum of Eighty five dollars part of the above named Estate.

Sept 4th 1848 Daniel L Fox (signed)

Received of Elisabeth Fox & Adam Fox administrators of the estate of George Fox Decd, the sum of sixteen dollars & fifty cents part of the above named estate.

June 23rd 1849 Daniel L Fox (signed)

Received of Elisabeth Fox & Adam Fox administrators of the Estate of George Fox decd., the sum of seventeen dollars & fifty cents part of the above name Estate

February 24th 1849 Elizabeth L Fox (signed)

Received of Elizabeth Fox & Adam Fox administrators of the Estate of George Fox Decd. the sum of twenty four dollars for value received

Sept the 16th 1847 George L Fox (signed)

Received of Adam Fox one of the Administrators of the Estate of George Fox dd. sum of two hundred and sixty three dollars and fifty one cents the widows third of the money on hand at this time

Sept ?nd 1848 Elisabeth Fox (signed)

Received of Adam Fox one of the administrators my note of the amount of property taken at the appraisement the sum of one hundred and eighteen dollars & forty nine cents.

Sept ?nd 1848 Elisabeth Fox (signed)

Received of Elisabeth Fox & Adam Fox administrators of the Estate of George Fox decd. the sum eighty five dollars on my sale notes part of the above named estate

Sept. 4th 1848 Frederick L. Fox (signed)

Received of Elisabeth Fox one of the administrators of the Estate of George Fox Decd the sum of seventeen dollars & fifty cents part of the above named estate.

February the 24th 1849 Adam Fox (signed)

Received of Elisabeth Fox & Adam Fox administrators of the estate of George Fox Decd. the sum of eighty five dollars part of the above named Estate

Sept 4th 1848 Alexander Fox (signed)

George Fox Estate Newspaper Notices

The State of Ohio Warren County

Personally appeared Adam Fox one of the admrs of George Fox decd and on oath says that the attached notice was published for three consecutive weeks beginning on the 27th day of August 1847 in the Sober Second Thought a newspaper of general circulation in the County of Warren where said George Fox last dwelt:-

Sworn to & subscribed before } Adam Fox
me October 28, 1847

ADMINISTRATORS NOTICE

Notice is hereby given that the undersigned have been duly appointed administrators of the estate of George Fox, decd, late of Clear Creek township, Warren County, Ohio. All persons therefore having claims against said estate are requested to present them, legally attested for settlement, and all persons indebted to said estate are requested to make immediate payment.

ELIZABETH FOX, } Administrators AUGUST 27, 1847
ADAM FOX, }

Notice

To all whom this may concern There will be an appraisment and inventory of the chattel property of George Fox Late of the County of Warren State of Ohio Decd. at his late residence two miles North of Springborough County & State aforesaid those interested may attend on the 6th of Sept Next at 9 o'clock AM if they see proper

Elizabeth Fox } Administr
Adam Fox
Monday August 30th 1847

State of Ohio Warren County}

Adam Fox one of the admins of the Estate of George Fox deceased make solemn oath that the above notice was duly served on all the heirs of said George Fox decd residing in the said County of Warren and was also set up in two of the most public places in Clear Creek Township in said County, in which the said Fox died & last resided at least five days before the taking of said inventory.

New Members of the Society since December 1, 1997.

Name Address	Phone	Date of Membership	Membership Number
Donald A. Smith 7 E. Hill Valley Drive Indianapolis, Indiana 46227	317-865-7761	10 March 1998	0021

Address Changes since December 1, 1997.

Dellie Jean Craig 406 Vandalia Court Crawfordsville, Indiana 47933	765-361-2891	11 December 1995	0009

Photographs Available through the Society

Photographs / Individuals

1. **Daniel Booker Fox**, circa 1860, retouched.
2. **Daniel Alexander Fox and Elizabeth Jane Ricketts**, wedding day, April 1, 1880.
3. **Daniel Alexander Fox and Elizabeth Jane Ricketts Fox Family**, circa 1900.
4. **Robert William Gouty, Ethel Belle Fox Gouty, Mavis Lorene Gouty Older**, circa 1920.
5. **Ethel Belle Fox Gouty, Ruby Dale Fox Hines, William E. Fox, Kenneth B. Fox**, circa 1960.
6. **Reva Winfried Fox**, daughter of William Edward Fox, 1988.
7. **Curtis Lynn Older, Linda Sue Osborn Older, and Rachael Lynn Older**, 1995.
8. **Jacob and Melissa Ricketts and Family**. Jake Ricketts, Melissa Barnard Ricketts, Jacob Ricketts, and Elizabeth Jane Ricketts. Back row: Daniel Ricketts, Frederick Ricketts, Hiram Ricketts, Joseph Ricketts, Dave Ricketts, and Abraham Lincoln Ricketts. Not in photograph: Nan Ricketts. circa 1900.

Photographs / Maps

101. **Winslows Map of 1736, also known as The "Mayo" Map of 1736-7.**
102. **Fry and Jefferson Map of 1751, 1755, and 1775.**
103. **1794 Dennis Griffith Map of Maryland.**
104. **1808 Varle Map.**
105. **Bond Map**.

Photographs / Fox's Gap Related

201. **The Wise Farmhouse at Fox's Gap.** The Wise Farmhouse on the old Sharpsburg Road at Fox's Gap, scene of fighting during the Battle of South Mountain, Maryland, September 14, 1862.
202. **The Fox Inn.** Photo in 1992 by Susan Flowers.
203. **The Reno Monument at Fox's Gap.** Photo in 1992 by Susan Flowers.
204. **17th Michigan Memorial at Fox's Gap.** Photo in 1992 by Susan Flowers.
205. **The Battle of South Mountain, Md.** Library of Congress.
206. **Society of Colonial Wars and Maryland Historical Society Marker.** General Edward Braddock. This marker is near the front of the Maryland State Police Barrack B in Frederick on Route 40 (Patrick Street). Photo by Allan Powell.
207. **Maryland Bicentennial Commission and Maryland Historical Society Marker.** Swearingen's Ferry and Pack Horse Ford. This marker is at the Rumsey Bridge on the Potomac River at Shepherdstown. Photo by Susanne Flowers.
208. **State Roads Commission Marker.** General Edward Braddock. This marker is on the square in Sharpsburg. Photo by Susanne Flowers.
209. **The Boulder at Braddock Spring**. Photo by Susanne Flowers.
210. **Letter from Jacob Reel to Frederick and Michael Fox of Warren County, State of Ohio**
211. **Revolutionary War records for Frederick Fox, 10th Regiment, Pennsylvania Continental Line, in the National Archives.**

Photographs / Tombstones

301. **Frederick Fox**, a son of John Fox of Fox's Gap in Maryland
302. **Susannah Fox**, the second wife of Frederick Fox

303. **George Fox**, a son of Frederick Fox
304. **Elizabeth Ann Link Fox**, the wife of George Fox
305. **Daniel Booker Fox**, a son of Frederick Fox
306. **Susannah Fox**, the wife of Daniel Booker Fox
307. **John Liter**
308. **Elizabeth Fox Liter**, a daughter of Frederick Fox
309. **George Mettard**
310. **Christena Fox Mettert**, a daughter of Frederick Fox
311. **St. John or Gebhart Cemetery, Miamisburg, Ohio, view 1**
312. **St. John or Gebhart Cemetery, Miamisburg, Ohio, view 2**
313. **John L. Fox, son of George Fox, and his wife Susannah Hilligass Fox**, Hopewell Cemetery, Covington, Indiana
314. **Daniel Alexander Fox, son of John L. Fox, and his wife Elizabeth Jane Ricketts Fox**, Hopewell Cemetery, Covington, Indiana
315. **Jacob Benner and Mary Magdelena Fox Benner**, a daughter of Frederick Fox

Photographs / Wills, Birth Certificates, Death Certificates, etc.

401. **Will of John Fox** of Fox's Gap in Maryland and Sharpsburg, Maryland.
402. **Will of Frederick Fox** of Fox's Gap in Maryland and the State of Ohio.
403. **Will of Bartholomew Booker**, the father-in-law of Frederick Fox
404. **Will of Margaret Booker**, the mother-in-law of Frederick Fox
405. **Estate Papers of George Fox**, a son of Frederick Fox
406. **Certificate of Birth of Johan Jacob Link**, great-grandfather of Elizabeth Ann Link Fox, wife of George Fox
407. **Will of John Adam Link II,** the father of Elizabeth Ann Link Fox
408. **Will of John L. Fox**, a son of George Fox
409. **Bible Records of Ethel Belle Fox Gouty**, a daughter of Daniel Alexander Fox
410. **Death Certificate for Daniel Alexander Fox**, a son of John L. Fox
411. **Death Certificate for Elizabeth Jane Ricketts Fox**, the wife of Daniel Alexander Fox

---

The Society of the Descendants of Frederick Fox of Fox's Gap in Maryland

Membership Roster - May 1, 1998

Name Address	Phone	Date of Membership	Membership Number
Curtis Lynn Older 618 Tryon Place Gastonia, North Carolina 28054 E-Mail: CLOLDER@AAAQA.COM	704-864-3879	20 October 1995	0001
William Ernest Fox 13071 Alger Grant, Michigan 49327	616-834-5051	28 October 1995	0002

Reva Winfred Fox 10226 3rd Ave. S. Seattle, Washington	206-762-3845	7 November 1995	0003
William Goudy Benner 1000 Hidden Ridge Lane Dayton, Ohio 45459 E-Mail: STEAM611@WORLDNET.ATT.NET also: STEAM611@AOL.COM	513-433-1365	15 November 1995	0005
Elizabeth Jane Bucholz 304 14th St. E. Devil's Lake, North Dakota 58301	701-662-3636	6 November 1995	0008
Doug Bast 109 North Main Street Boonsboro, Maryland 21713	301-432-6969	9 December 1995	0001**H**
Dellie Jean Craig 406 Vandalia Court Crawfordsville, Indiana 47933	765-361-2891	11 December 1995	0009
Wilma Marion Gose P. O. Box 203 Griffith, Indiana 46319-0203	219-322-5269	16 December 1995	0010
Patricia Jo Edwards 526 Palomino Drive RR #4 Box 94C Danville, Illinois 61832	217-443-4523	13 January 1996	0011
(membership in wife's name, Deloris Fox) Richard Dale Fox Sr. P. O. BOX 64 Covington, Indiana 47932	765-793-3674	24 January 1996	0015
Mildred Metcalf Garfield Salt Lake City, Utah	???-484-9024	1 June 1996	0016
Donald A. Smith 7 E. Hill Valley Drive Indianapolis, Indiana 46227 E-Mail: DON@LOGAL.COM	317-865-7761	10 March 1998	0021

H - denotes Honorary Member

Index

Issue 5, Volume 1

News from Fox's Gap

News from Fox's Gap

The Society of the Descendants of Frederick Fox of Fox's Gap in Maryland

Issue 6, Volume 1 **Remember Freedom!** December 1, 1998

Reunion at Miamisburg, Ohio, May 31, 1998

A rather small but enjoyable Fox Family Reunion was held on Sunday, May 31, 1998, at Miamisburg, Ohio. The participants all had a very good time discussing their backgrounds and their common bond with Frederick Fox. Four descendants of Frederick Fox attended: Bill Benner, Don Smith, Rachael Older, and Curt Older.

Frederick Fox and his second wife, Susannah, are buried at the Gebhart Church Yard Cemetery in Miamisburg, as well as George Fox and his wife, Elizabeth Link; Daniel Booker Fox and his wife, Susannah Christman; George Methard and his wife, Christiana Fox. Michael Hilligass and his wife, Anna, also are buried at the Gebhart Cemetery. They were the parents of Susannah Hilligass, who was the wife of John L. Fox. John L. Fox and Susannah Hilligass were the parents of Daniel Alexander Fox, from whom a number of Fox Society members are descendants.

The Fox tombstones, like many of the tombstones in the Gebhart Cemetery, are very large. Most of the tombstones remain in good condition, given the passage of over 150 years of time, in many cases. Some of the tombstones have been repaired at some point in the past. The tombstone of Frederick Fox appears to have been broken in half at some point in time and then been joined together again with the aid of metal bars.

From Fort Sumter to Fox's Gap

The following information about Lieutenant Colonel George Sholter James, Confederate States of America, (1829 - 1862) appears on the Internet site of the Central Maryland Heritage League, Inc.:

James was born in Laurens County, South Carolina. At age 17 he ran off to fight in the Mexican War with the Palmetto Regiment. Upon his return home he entered the South Carolina College. Unsatisfied with student life. James soon left college for the United States Army. He served in the U. S. Artillery from 1856 to 1861. When South Carolina seceded from the Union, James resigned his commission and offered his services to his native state. In April 1861, Captain James commanded two Confederate batteries of 12-in mortars at Fort Johnson on James Island in Charleston Harbor. On the morning of April 12, 1861, James received and executed orders to open fire on Fort Sumter. He had, in effect, started the American Civil War.

On September 14, 1862, Lieutenant Colonel James commanded the 3rd South Carolina Infantry Regiment at Fox's Gap. As a part of Drayton's Brigade, his severely outnumbered men made a last desperate stand that afternoon. Just as night approached and the firing began to cease, James received a fatal chest wound. His body was buried near Wise's Cabin, but the wooden headboard noting the site was missing in 1874 when South Mountain's Confederate dead were reinterred at Hagerstown, Maryland. It is assumed that James rests with the unknowns in the city's Rose Hill Confederate Cemetery.

President's Message

by Curtis Lynn Older

** Election of officers at December 1, 1998 for two year term of 1999 and 2000. Unless three or more members call for an election for the two year term of 1999 and 200, I do not intend to have a vote by members this time. I will continue serving as Society President and editor of the Newsletter. If you feel we should hold another election, please notify me promptly.

** The George Fox Section of the Newsletter contains an article on Robert Ricketts and his service in the American Revolution. Robert Ricketts probably was the grandfather of Jacob Ricketts. Jacob Ricketts was the father of Elizabeth Jane Ricketts, wife of Daniel Alexander Fox.

** Papers documenting the service of Robert Ricketts in the American Revolution, and other papers related to him, have been added to the CD-Rom collection of the Society.

** My latest book, *The Land Tracts of the Battlefield of South Mountain*, will help preserve the history of the area of Fox's Gap in Maryland. The book is almost complete. It probably will be sent to the publisher by March 1, 1999.

** The Library of Congress call number for *The Braddock Expedition and Fox's Gap in Maryland*, by Curtis L. Older, published in 1995 by Family Line Publications is: E199 .057 1995

Fox's Gap on the Internet

If you have access to the Internet, be sure to visit the Central Maryland Heritage League site:

http://www.cmhl.org/html/fox.html

The CMHL Internet site devotes two full pages of text and pictures to Fox's Gap. Photographs related to Fox's Gap show; the Reno Monument; the Garland Monument (dedicated September 11, 1993); Fox's Gap in 1912; and the Wise Cabin of Civil War fame in the early 1880s. The Internet site also contains material on Turner's Gap, the Dahlgren Chapel, the Lamar Sanitarium, Reenactments, Preservation Efforts, Unique Gifts, and other related information.

The CMHL is currently working with the Appalachian Trail Conference, the Appalachian Trail Club, and the National Park Service on a Fox's Gap management plan that will restore the area to its Civil War condition.

A Civil War Reenactment of the Battle of South Mountain took place on September 12 and 13, 1998. The Internet site provided information on Registration for the event and Rules and Regulations regarding the event.

The CMHL uses the Lamar Sanitarium, now known as the Lamar Heritage and Culture Center, for its headquarters. The Center serves as a central depository for South Mountain Battlefield materials, including regimental histories, letters, diaries, and artifacts for display to the public. The State of Maryland has pledged $100,000 to purchase the site if the community raises the same amount of funds. The Center is located at 200 West Main Street in historic Middletown, Maryland.

The E-mail address of the Central Maryland Heritage League is: INFO@CMHL.ORG

Also on the Internet:

Civil War Sites Advisory Commission Report on the Nation's Civil War Battlefields

Check out the Civil War Sites Advisory Commission Report on the Nation's Civil War Battlefields on the Internet at:

http:/www2.cr.nps.gov/abpp/battles/tvii.htm

The report was prepared for the Committee on Energy and Natural Resources, United States Senate Committee on Natural Resources, United States House of Representatives, The Secretary of the Interior. The Civil War Sites Advisory Commission was established by public law on November 28, 1990.

Some 10,500 armed conflicts occurred during the Civil War ranging from battles to minor skirmishes; 384 conflicts (3.7 percent) were identified as the principal battles and classified according to their historical significance. Class A and B battlefields represent the principal strategic operations of the war. Class C and D battlefields usually represent operations with limited tactical objectives of enforcement and occupation.

45 sites (12%) were ranked "A" (having a decisive influence on a campaign and a direct impact on the course of the war;

104 sites (27%) were ranked "B" (having a direct and decisive influence on their campaign);

128 sites (33%) were ranked "C" (having observable influence on the outcome of a campaign);

107 sites (28%) were ranked "D" (having a limited influence on the outcome of their campaign or operation but achieving or affecting important local objectives)

A unique reference number was assigned to each site. A Preservation Priority designation was made by the Commission based on the level of historical significance, the integrity of the remaining battlefield features, and the level of threat to the battlefield's existence. Fox example, IV.1 (Class D) means that the Commission determined that a particular battlefield site was Priority IV: Fragmented Battlefields, All Military Classes, Poor Integrity. (See Table 7, pages 49-53 in the Report on the Nation's Civil War Battlefields, for the preservation priority of all the battlefields studied.

The Battle Summary given in the Commission Report lists the result of the battle as a Union Victory. The Principal Commanders are given as Major General George B. McClellan [US] and General Robert E. Lee [CS]. Estimated Casualties are listed as 4,500 total.

The Preservation Priority for the Battlefield of South Mountain is I.3 (Class B). The CWSAC Reference # is: MD002. The Battlefield of South Mountain is the only battlefield on the Appalachian National Scenic Trail. This is very fortunate for Fox's Gap. With continued efforts of interested individuals and groups, the area of Fox's Gap will be preserved as a national historic site for future generations.

The Appalachian National Scenic Trail is a 2,158 mile footpath along the ridge crests and across the major valleys of the Appalachian Mountains from Katahdin in the central Maine wilderness to Springer Mountain in a designated wilderness area in north Georgia. Primary use is by weekend or short-term hikers. The Trail is managed by volunteers in 32 local clubs under Appalachian Trail Conference auspices through a cooperative agreement with the National Park Service. More than 98% of the Trail is now on public land.

Mailing address for visitor information:

Appalachian Trail Conference
P. O. Box 807
Harpers Ferry, WV 25425-0807
Telephone: 304-535-6331

Mailing Address for N.P.S. Project Office:

Appalachian National Scenic Trail NPS Project Office
c/o Harpers Ferry Center
P. O. Box 50
Harpers Ferry, WV 25425-0050
Telephone: 304-535-6278

Fox's Gap was blessed through the years to retain much of its original look and feel. The area has remained relatively undisturbed compared to many other historic sites. Let us hope the efforts of the National Park Service, The Central Maryland Heritage League, The Appalachian Trail Conference, The Appalachian Trail Club, and other interested parties continues to meet with success in preserving Fox's Gap and the Battlefield of South Mountain.

A Couple of Cemetery Locations
and
Some Library Reference Materials about Those Cemeteries

Lower Mound - The Lower Mound Cemetery, in Vermillion County, Indiana, is on Road 200 East, just south of Interstate 74. It is north of Perrysville in Highland Township. The location is west of Covington, Indiana, and not far from Gessie, Indiana. It is south of Route 136.

Jacob Ricketts and his wife Melissa, parents of Elizabeth Jane Ricketts, are buried at this cemetery. Two children of Daniel Alexander Fox and his wife Elizabeth Jane Ricketts are buried in this cemetery. The two children are Ethel Bell (Fox) Gouty, wife of Robert William Gouty, and Ruby Dale (Fox) Hines, wife of Everett Hines.

Information on this cemetery may be found under the two following library call numbers:

G pf 977.201 V526 pam no.3
GENEAL pam 977.201 Vuncat

Hopewell - The Hopewell Cemetery, in Vermillion County, Indiana, is on Road 900 West near Gessie, Indiana. It is west of Covington, Indiana, and just south of Interstate 74.

John L. Fox and wife Susannah Hilligass and Daniel Alexander Fox and wife Elizabeth Jane Ricketts are buried at this cemetery.

There are a number of cemeteries in Vermillion County, Indiana, that have Hopewell as part of their name. I believe the following reference material relates to the above Hopewell Cemetery. Information on this cemetery may be found under the three following library call numbers:

G pam 977.201 V526i p19-45
G pf 977.201 V526 v.4
G pf 977.201 V526 no.3

Information Included In Each Census
by Curtis L. Older

Each Census taken every 10 years in the United States usually collects different information than the prior census. These records are very helpful in doing genealogy research. A sample of some of the information you will find in the Census records follows:

1790
the name of the head of the family
the number of free white males 16 years and older
the number of free white males under 16 years old
the number of free white females
the number of all other free persons
the number of slaves

1860
the name, age, and sex of each individual in the household
whether each individual was white, black, or mulatto
the profession, occupation, or trade of each male over 15
the profession, occupation, or trade of each female over 15
the value of the real estate owned by each individual
the value of the personal property owned by each individual
each individual's state, territory, or country of birth
whether or not an individual married within the year
whether or not an individual attended school within the year
whether or not an individual can read and write, if over 20
whether an individual was deaf, dumb, blind, insane, idiotic, a pauper, or a convict

1900
the street name and house number in cities
then name and sex of each individual in the household
the relationship of each individual to the head of household
the color or race of each individual
the month and year of birth of each individual, and their age at their last birthday
whether an individual is single, married, widowed, or divorced
number of years that an individual has been married
number of children born to female individuals, and the number of those children still living
each individual's place of birth
each individual's mother's place of birth
each individual's father's place of birth
an individual's year of immigration to the United States
the number of years that an individual has resided in the United States
whether or not an individual is naturalized
the profession, occupation, or trade of each male over 10
the profession, occupation, or trade of each female over 10
number of months in the year that the individual was not employed
whether or not an individual attended school within the year
whether or not an individual can read and write
whether or not an individual can speak English
whether or not the family owns or rents their home, whether or note the home is mortgaged, and whether it is a farm or a house

The George Fox Line
by Curtis L. Older

Nine members of the Society descend from Daniel Alexander Fox and Elizabeth Jane Ricketts. Daniel was a grandson of George Fox. Elizabeth Jane Ricketts was a daughter of Jacob Ricketts who served in the 57th Indiana Volunteer Infantry during the Civil War.

Robert Ricketts, a grandfather of Jacob Ricketts

National Archive Microfilm Publications contain information about Robert Ricketts under No. S 17,047, Pennsylvania. The material appears to be from pages 0146 through 0156 of the microfilm. Page 0146 indicates he was issued a certificate of pension on 28 August 1833 under a Revolutionary Claim by Act of June 7, 1832. He was entitled to 20 dollars and 77 cents per annum to commence on the 4th day of March 1831. The record, filed in Dearborn County, Indiana, indicates he was a private in the company commanded by Captain Johnson of the regiment commanded by Col. Piper in Pennsylvania, serving a period of six months and seven days.

Page 0148 indicates Robert Ricketts served in 1780 for a period of three months as a private under Captain Johnson and Colonel Piper. It also indicates he served about two months in 1781 or 1782 under Capt. Robt Samuels as a private. Page 0148 gives his residence as Cumberland County, Pennsylvania, at the time he entered the service. Page 0148 gives his age as 67 at the time of the preparation of the form. Page 0148 is entitled, "Brief in the case of Robert Ricketts of Dearborn County in the State of Indiana (Act 7th June, 1832). The declarations on the form were made in a court.

Pages 0150 and 0151 consist of a number of sworn statements and answers given to questions:
In the matter of Robert Ricketts} An applicant for a pension, under the act of Congress of June 7, A. A. 1832 Recorded in Book F, page 80 Edwd Patton clerk. The state of Indiana, Switzerland county, SS: On the eighteenth day of September A. D. 1832 personally appeared in open court before the honorable the Circuit Court of the county aforesaid being a court of record, Robert Ricketts a resident of Dearborn county Indiana aged sixty seven years, who being first duly sworn according to law, doth, on his said oath, make the following declaration in order to obtain the benefit of the provision made by the act of congress, passed the 7th of June A. D. 1832 - that he, the said Robert Ricketts entered the service of the United States, during the AMERICAN REVOLUTIONARY WAR, under the following named officers, and served as herein stated -- That he, the said Robert served in 1780 in a company of Pennsylvania Militia commanded by Capt. James Johnson of Col. Pipers regiment - again in 1781 or 1782 in a company commanded by Capt. Robert Samuels of the Cumberland County, Pennsylvania Militia.

1. Where, and in what year were you born? I was born near Hagerstown, Maryland, in January 15 AD 1765.
2. Have you any record of your age, and if so, where is it? I have no record except the one I made when I went to school from my mother's information.
3. Where were you living when called into service; where have you lived since the Revolutionary war; and where do you now live? I lived in Pennsa. After the revolution I lived in Pennsylvania about ten years then I removed to Kentucky and was about 15 years - since that I lived in Indiana.
4. How were you called into service; were you drafted - did you volunteer, or were you a substitute? and if a substitute, for whom? I enlisted for three months and volunteered once.

Page 0152 gives a page long answer to question number five, State the names of some of the Regular officers, who were with the troops where you served; such Continental and Militia regiments as you can recollect, and the general circumstances of your service. Page 0153 consists of a sworn statement by Nathan Ricketts which states he knew Robert Ricketts since his birth in 1765 and served with him in 1780.

The author has not documented the accuracy of the following information:

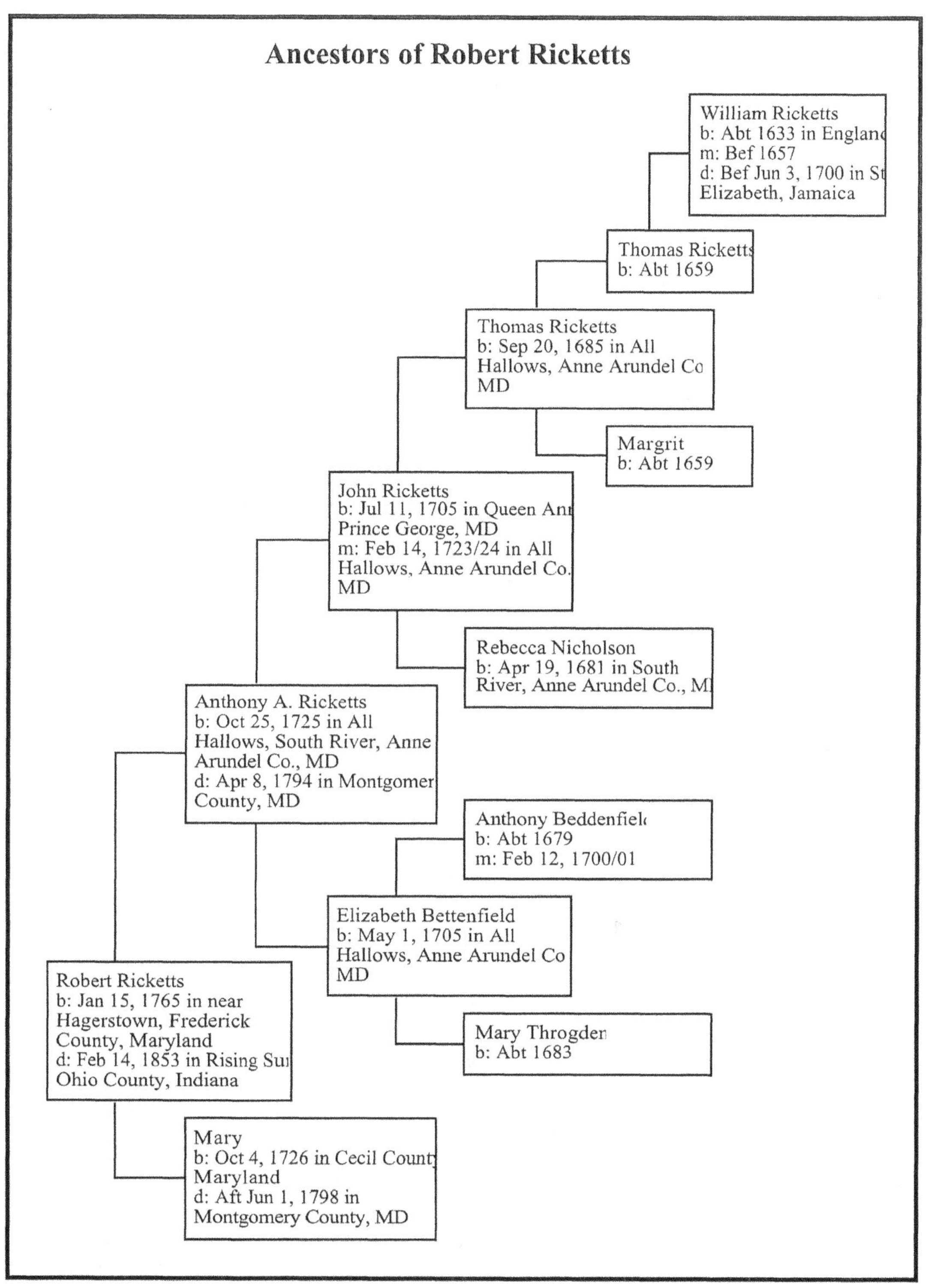
Ancestors of Robert Ricketts
William Ricketts
b: Abt 1633 in Englan
m: Bef 1657
d: Bef Jun 3, 1700 in St
Elizabeth, Jamaica
Thomas Ricketts
b: Abt 1659
Thomas Ricketts
b: Sep 20, 1685 in All
Hallows, Anne Arundel Co
MD
Margrit
b: Abt 1659
John Ricketts
b: Jul 11, 1705 in Queen An
Prince George, MD
m: Feb 14, 1723/24 in All
Hallows, Anne Arundel Co.
MD
Rebecca Nicholson
b: Apr 19, 1681 in South
River, Anne Arundel Co., M
Anthony A. Ricketts
b: Oct 25, 1725 in All
Hallows, South River, Anne
Arundel Co., MD
d: Apr 8, 1794 in Montgomer
County, MD
Anthony Beddenfiel
b: Abt 1679
m: Feb 12, 1700/01
Elizabeth Bettenfield
b: May 1, 1705 in All
Hallows, Anne Arundel Co
MD
Robert Ricketts
b: Jan 15, 1765 in near
Hagerstown, Frederick
County, Maryland
d: Feb 14, 1853 in Rising Su
Ohio County, Indiana
Mary Throgden
b: Abt 1683
Mary
b: Oct 4, 1726 in Cecil Count
Maryland
d: Aft Jun 1, 1798 in
Montgomery County, MD

Frederick Fox and Fox's Gap Section
by Curtis Lynn Older

Frederick Fox originally owned the land on which the Reno Monument stands at Fox's Gap. Fox's Gap became famous during the Battle of South Mountain, September 14, 1862. At the time of the battle, Daniel Wise owned the land in the immediate vicinity of the gap. Daniel and his two children, John and Matilda, lived in the cabin at Fox's Gap at the time of the battle. The following deed is the transfer of the Wise property at Fox's Gap from John W. Wise and his wife Lana Wise to Jonas Gross. The monument 40 foot by 40 foot square of the Reno Monument property was entrusted to the perpetual care of the United States of America in 1899.

Reference: Frederick County, MD, Land Records, John W. Wise to Jonas Gross WIP-9-149.

Ex and delivered to Grantee June 13, 1889

At the request of Jonas Gross, the following deed is received for record and recorded April 5, 1889 at 9 o'clock AM

Test, W. Irving Parsons, Clerk

This Deed made this ninth day of June in the year eighteen hundred and seventy nine by us, John W. Wise and Lana Wise his wife of Wood County in the State of West Virginia. Witnesseth that in consideration of the sum of fifty five dollars, we the said John W. Wise and Lana Wise his wife do grant unto Jonas Gross of Frederick County in the State of Maryland, all that lot and portion of ground situated in Frederick County, Maryland, and which is more particularly described in a deed from Joel Keller and wife to the said John Wise and Matilda Wise, dated on the seventh day of May in the year eighteen hundred and fifty eight, reference to said deed being had for courses and distances will fully and at large appear, excepting and reserving thereunto a road as stated in said deed and the said John W. Wise covenants that he will warrant generally the property hereby conveyed

Test

Attest R. P. Caldwell

Witness our hands and seals
John W. Wise (Seal)
her
Lana X Wise (Seal)
mark

State of West Virginia, Wood County Court
I hereby certify that on this ninth day of June in the year eighteen hundred and seventy nine before the subscriber a notary public of said county, personally appeared John W. Wise and Lana Wise his wife and did each acknowledge this foregoing deed to be their respective act.
Place In testimony whereof I have affixed my hand and seal this 9th day of June in the year eighteen hundred and seventy nine. Seal

W. T. Sensensy
Notary Public

The Reno Monument Deed

Frederick County, Maryland Land Records, page 316
Executed and delivered to Grantee February 9th 1899
At the request of the United States of America the following deed is received for record and recorded January 24th 1899 at 1 o'clock 50 minutes past. Test: Douglass H. Hazzett Clerk.

This deed, made this 11th day of Sept. in the year one thousand and ninety eight, between Orlando B. Wilcox, James Wren and W C Hansell, Trustees for the Reno Memorial of the Society of the Burnside Expedition and of the Ninth Army Corps, parties of the first part and the United States of America party of the second part.

Whereas, at a regular business meeting of the Society of the Burnside Expedition and of the Ninth Army Corps held at Niagara Falls, New York on the first day of September, one thousand eight hundred and ninety eight, it was resolved, that whereas by a resolution of the Society of the Burnside

Expedition and of the Ninth Army Corps dated the second day of July, one thousand eight hundred and ninety eight, it was resolved that the deed of the Monument site upon the? South Mountain Battlefield, then about to be purchased should be made to Orlando B. Wilcox, James Wren and H. C. Hansell, as trustees to hold said lot as said trustees until such time as they can convey said site to a custodian who shall be authorized by some competent authority to accept perpetual charge and care of said site with the Monument to be thereafter erected thereon and whereas the said lot of land was by deed of Jonas Gross conveyed to said Orlando B. Wilcox, James Wren and W. C. Hansell, as trustees of the said Society of the Burnside Expedition and of the Ninth Army Corps for the above named purpose by a deed dated the twenty third day of November, one thousand eight hundred and eighty nine, recorded on the Nineteenth day of February one thousand eight hundred and ninety in Liber W I P No. 11, Folios 8, 9 and 10, one of the land records of Frederick County, Maryland, and whereas the Monument is now erected it from said lot or site, and Whereas, The United States of America have agreed to accept perpetual charge and care of said site and the Monument thereon, Resolved, that Orlando B. Wilcox, James Wren and H. C. Hansell trustees for this Society of the Reno Memorial at South Mountain, Maryland be authorized and directed to convey by deed to the United States of America for perpetual custody and care the land with the Monument therein erected to the memory of Jesse L. Reno, under and by resolution of this Society, at a business meeting on the second day of July, one thousand eight hundred and eighty-eight, said land being described in a deed, dated the twenty third day of November, one thousand eight hundred and eight nine, of Jonas Gross, and others, to said trustees and recorded the nineteenth day of February one thousand eight hundred and ninety, in Liber W. B. P. No. 11, folios 8, 9, and 10, one of the land Records of Frederick County, Maryland. Now therefore, in consideration of the promises the said parties of the first part do hereby grant and convey unto the said party of the second part all the following real estate, etc., to wit. All the following tract or parcel of land situated in Middletown Election District in Frederick County in the State of Maryland, along the Old Sharpsburg Road leading from Sharpsburg in Washington County in the State aforesaid to the pike near Middletown in said Frederick County, said land being on the South Mountain and fronting forty feet on said Old Sharpsburg Road and running back with uniform width at right angles to said road, a distance of forty feet, being a tract of land forty feet square upon which is now erected a Monument in memory of General Reno, said Monument being near the center of said lot of ground, said land being a part of the same land that was conveyed to said Jonas Gross by John W. Wise and wife by a deed dated the 9th day of June AD 1879, and recorded in Liber W I P No. 9, folio 149, one of the land record books for said Frederick County, to which reference is hereby made, the North western corner of the land hereby conveyed being a distance of one hundred and seventeen feet (117 ft) from the beginning front of the aforesaid deed, and the North eastern corner of said lot of ground being two hundred and twenty six feet (226 ft.) from the end of the second line of said deed, together with all the rights, roads, ways, waters, privileges, appurtenances and advantages to the same in any wise appertaining, in fee simple, and together with the Monument erected on said premises, for the purpose of taking perpetual charge and care of said lot or site with the Monument erected hereon. Being the same premises which were conveyed by the aforesaid Jonas Gross and others to the aforesaid parties of the first part by deed, dated the twenty third day of November, one thousand eight hundred and eighty nine, and recorded in Liber W. I. P. No. 11, folios 8, 9 and 10, one of the land records of Frederick County, Maryland, heretofore mentioned. To have and to hold the above described premises unto the said party of the second part for the purposes herein before mentioned forever. In Witness Whereof the said parties of the first part have hereunto set their hands and seals respectively the day and year first above named.

Witness, C. I. Bundy Orlando B. Wilcox
L. J. Wyeth Trustee (seal)

Fox's Gap in Maryland

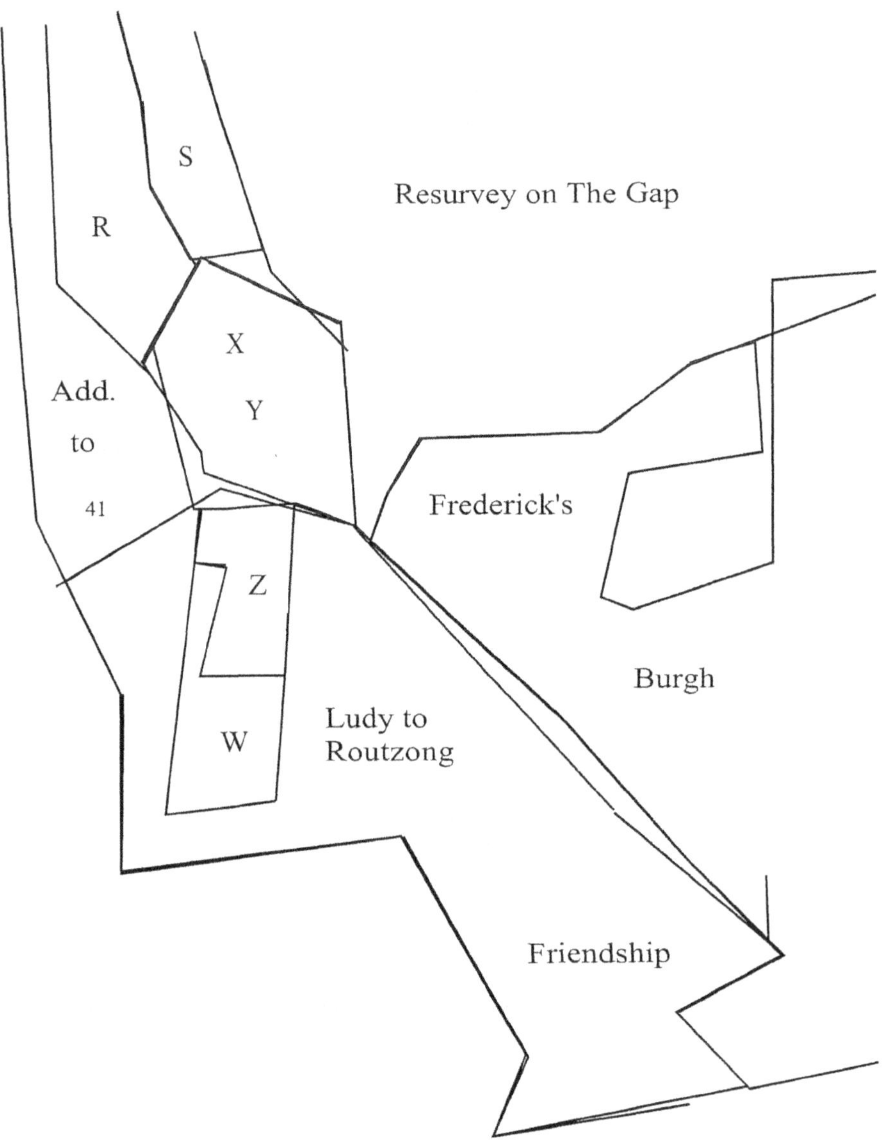

R = The Resurvey on The Gap - Henry Beakley, MSA, IC N, pp. 467-468, special warrant, examined and passed 16 Jul 1798, [MdHR 17,476, 1-23-4-32].

S = Apple Brandy - Jacob Fulwiler, ID D, p. 75, surveyed 31 Oct 1791, [MdHR 17,487- 1, 1-23-4-44].

X = Bowser's Addition - Christian Baer to Jacob Routzong, FCLR, WR-46-312.

Y = Susan Miller et al to John Miller - Bowser's Addition and three and one half acres of Addition to Friendship - FCLR, WBT-1-100.

Z = The Wise Tract of Civil War Fame - The Reno Monument stands on this tract - Joel Keller to John Wise, 7 May 1858, FCLR, WR-42-550.

W = George H. Kefauver to Jonas Gross - 13 Feb 1880, FCLR, WIP-9-148.

41 = Last line of the Road from Swearingen's Ferry to Fox's Gap - 1791 - [MSA G1427-507, B5-1-3].

Land Tracts of the Battlefield of South Mountain

by Curtis L. Older

Each Newsletter includes a survey, patent, or deed related to the land tracts in the vicinity of Crampton's, Fox's, and Turner's Gaps. These three gaps in South Mountain represent the main area contested by the Union and Confederate Armies in the Battle of South Mountain on September 14, 1862.

092. FCLR JS 38, 480-481, Peter Brengle, Sheriff to Henry Miller, Bowser's Addition, recorded 7 Apr 1832, 10 acres.

Examined and deld grantee } At the request of Henry Miller the following deed is April 19th 1833 } recorded April 7th 1832.

This Indenture made this twenty sixth day of March in the year of our Lord, one thousand eight hundred and thirty two between Peter Brengle Sheriff of Frederick county Maryland of the one part and Henry Miller of the County and State aforesaid, of the other part; witnesseth that whereas on the 25th day of May? eighteen hundred and thirty one a certain writ of the State of Maryland of Fieri Facia did ? forth and of the county court of the county aforesaid to the disputed ? that ? ? County Court begin & held at the Court House in Fredericktown in aforesaid county.

Sheriff of said County on the first Monday of August in eighteen hundred and twenty seven a certain Peter? Philip Hauptman by judgment of the same recovered against a certain Jacob Routzahn as ? the ? of six hundred & thirty nine Dolls current money a certain debt as two thousand for his damages which he has sustained as well by reason the detention of that Routzahn is convict as it appears of record. Therefore, you are hereby commanded that of the goods and chattels lands and tenements of the said Jacob Routzahn being in your bailiwick ? to the made the debt damages ? and ?

? before the judges of the next county court to be held at the court house in Frederick County and for said county on the fourth Monday of February next to render unto the said farmer & Hauptman the debt damages cost and charges aforesaid and whereas also said writ came to the hands of said Sheriff and in pursuance of the command therein contained the said Sheriff laid the same upon all the right title interest and estate of said Jacob Routzahn in and to a Tract of Land called Bowser's Addition situate lying & being in the county and state aforesaid together with all and singular the buildings improvements and appurtenances hereunto belonging or in any wise appertaining it being the same land heretofore conveyed to the said Jacob Routzahn by a certain Christian Baer? by deed bearing date on or about the 21st March 1814 duly executed recorded in Liber I.L. folio 312 & 313 and of the land records of the County aforesaid and containing Ten acres of Land more or less and whereas also after due notice being given of the same the said Sheriff did on the 19th day of January eighteen hundred and thirty two experience ? title interest and estate of him the said Jacob Routzahn of ? to the land & premises open to public sale to the highest bidder and the ? the there in before named Henry Miller be ? the highest bidder and purchases of the said Land & premises with the appurtenances The ? belonging for the sum of Twenty one Dollars fifty cents and hath since paid the said purchase money to the said Sheriff and is now desirous of obtaining title to the same in consequence thereof Now this Indenture Witnesseth that for and in consideration of the premises and of the sum of one dollar current money of the United States to the said Peter Brengle Sheriff aforesaid in hand paid at before the sealing and delivery of these presents the ? whereof is thereby acknowledged the said Peter Brengle Sheriff hath granted bargained and sold and by these presents doth grant bargain and use unto the said Henry Miller his heirs and assigns the said land & premises as aforesaid to him by virtue of the writ of Fieri Facia aforesaid and so as aforesaid enforced to sale in on ? of said write, with the appurtenances thereunto belonging to him and to hold the same unto the said Henry Miller his heirs and assigns to the ? for ? and ? of him the said Henry Miller his heirs and assigns forever . In witness whereof the said Peter Brengle Sheriff as aforesaid hath hereunto ? and affixed his seal the day & year first herein before written.

Signed sealed and delivered in presence of ? Shriver} Peter Brengle (seal) Which is thus endorsed to

with State of Maryland Frederick County to wit. Be it remembered that on this twenty sixth day of March eighteen hundred and thirty two personally appeared before me the subscribers ? of the ? judges of the fifth judicial district of the state of Maryland Peter Brengle Sheriff Fredk Cty. ? and acknowledged the foregoing instrument of writing to be his act and deed according to the due intent and meaning of the ? and the act of ? in ? ? provided
Acknowledged before ? ? Shriver

155. FCLR, WR-46-312, Christian Baer to Jacob Routzong, Bowser's Addition, 10 acres.

all that tract or lot of land called Bowser's Addition lying situate in Frederick County aforesaid beginning at a bounded white oak standing near the top of the South Mountain on the side of the main road leading from Frederick Town to Sharpsburgh and running thence

Line No.	North South	Degrees East or West	Length
1	N	4 west	46 perches
2	N	65 west	35 perches
3	S	29 west	24 perches
4	S	33 east	20 perches
5	S	10 east	5 perches

6. then by a straight line to the beginning containing ten acres more or less together with all and singular the appurtenances and described land and premises with its appurtenances

(**Author's Note:** Lines 4, 5, and 6 above are the same as lines 28, 29, and 30 of Addition to Friendship)

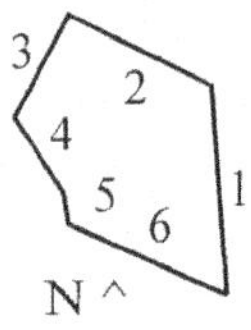

Bowser's Addition

10 acres

Beginning at a bounded white oak standing near the top of the south mountain on the side of the main road leading from Frederick Town to Sharpsburgh

185. FCLR, WBT-1-100, Susan Miller, et al, to John Miller, recorded 1 Apr 1845, 13 and 1/4 acres.

(**Author's Note:** Bowser's Addition and Addition to Friendship; - This tract is contiguous to the Wise tract of Civil War fame at Fox's Gap.)

At the request of John Miller, the following deed was recorded April 1 1845. This Indenture made this seventh day of May in the year of our lord one thousand eight hundred and forty four between Susan Miller of Washington County and state of Maryland (Widow of Henry Miller late of said County decd) John W. Derr and Elizabeth Derr his wife, Phineas Williams and Mary Ann Williams his wife, Adam Koogle and Catharine Koogle his wife, of Frederick County and State of Maryland, Henrietta Williams, Joseph Nyman and Jane Rebecca Nyman his wife of Washington County and State of Maryland, (heirs at law of the said late Henry Miller deceased) of the one part and John Miller of Frederick County and state aforesaid of the other part. Witnesseth that the said parties of the first part for and in consideration of the sum of two hundred & five dollars and thirty cents current money to them in hand paid by the said John Miller at and before the sealing and delivery of these presents the receipt whereof they do hereby acknowledge have granted bargained and sold aliened enfeoffed and confirmed and by these presents do give grant bargain and sell alien enfeoff and confirm unto the said John Miller his heirs and assigns all that of land called Bowers Addition and part of a tract called Addition to Friendship lying and being in Frederick & Washington County and state aforesaid and included within the following courses and distance metes and bounds Beginning at a large white oak tree standing on the top of the South Mountain on the north side of the main road leading from Middletown to Sharpsburg and running thence

Line No.	North South	Degrees East or West	Length
1	N	4 west	46
2	N	65 west	34
3	S	29 west	24 perches then
4	N	55 east	2 8/10 perches
5	S	13 1/2 east	37 1/2 perches to a large chestnut tree standing on the north side of the aforesaid road then by and with the said road
6		east	7
7	N	86 east	16 perches
8	S	6? east	16 perches to the place of beginning containing thirteen and one fourth acres of land more or less. ETC.

Susan Miller
John W. Derr
Elizabeth Derr
Phineas Williams
Ann M. Williams
John Miller of H

Susan Miller
Adam Koogle
Catherine Koogle
Henrietta Miller
Joseph Nyman
Jane R. Nyman

(**Author's Note:** This tract consists primarily of Bowser's Addition and is contiguous with the north side of the Wise Tract & Reno Monument. Lines 6 and 7 are the same as two lines of the Keller-Wise deed.)

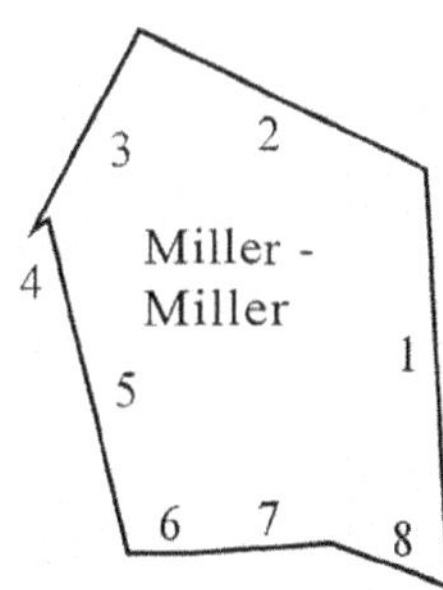

The Wise tract, upon which the Reno Monument stands, is contiguous to a 13 and 1/2 acre tract on the north side of the road, transferred from Susan Miller to John Miller, consisting of ten acres of Bowser's Addition and three and one-half acres Addition to Friendship. See Frederick County Land Records, WBT-1-100. Bowser's Addition (MdHR 17,448, 1-23-4-2, Bowser's Addition, surveyed April 10, 1765, 10 acres. MSA BC & GS #37, 138-9), "by the side of the wagon road leading from Sharpsburg to Frederick Town and on top of South Mountain," was surveyed in 1763. The Bowser's Addition tract offers proof the road through Fox's Gap crossed the mountain at the same point in 1763 as it does in 1995.

Wills
by Curtis L. Older

Each Newsletter includes one typewritten version of a will that is significant to the preservation efforts of the Society. Included in this issue is the will of John Adam Link II, the father of Elizabeth Ann Link and father-in-law of George Fox.

Will of John Adam Link II Will Book 8, pages 88, 89, and 90, Jefferson County Court House, Charles Town, West Virginia, (son of John Adam Link I), (in part), (the father-in-law of George Fox, son of Frederick Fox).

Last Will & Testament
of

In the name of God amen, I Adam Link senior. of Jefferson County Adam Link senior. decd.

& State of Virginia, being weak in body, but of sound & perfect mind & memory, blessed be Almighty God for the same, do make & publish this my last Will & Testament, in manner & form following, that is to say, First . . . And I also give & bequeath to my wife Jane two hundred dollars annually during her natural life, to be paid her by my son Adam Link Jr. as P. agreement with him, in the arrangement & division of my whole estate, made by myself and wife _

Next, **I give and bequeath to my daughter Elizabeth Fox**, a bond for one thousand dollars executed to me, by my son Adam Link Jr. with his brother Alexander Link as security.

Next, I give & bequeath to my daughter Catharine Ramspark, a bond for one thousand dollars, executed to me, by my son Adam Link Jr. with his brother Alexander Link as security.

Next, I give & bequeath to my daughter Martha Link a bond for five hundred dollars . . . Next, I give & devise to my daughter Mary Crowl a certain tract of land, the same purchased of David Hess & Anna his wife (& gave in payment therefor a bond for one thousand dollars, executed to me by my son Adam Link Jr. with his brother Alexander Link security) situate, lying & being in Sandusky, Sandusky County & state of Ohio, as will fully appear by reference to the deed now of record in said county: to have & to hold to her & her heirs & assigns forever-

Next, I give & bequeath to my daughter Rebeccah Demery, a bond for five hundred dollars . . . Next, I give & bequeath to my son Alexander Link a black boy named Aaron & Negro girl, slaves, to get the latter after the death of my wife Jane, to whom I give the girl for life, called Adaline . . .

Next, I give & bequeath to my son Adam Link Jr. . . . and I also give & bequest to my son Adam Link Jr. my eight day clock & best large family Bible-

Next, I give & bequeath to my grand daughter Ellen Link, to her heirs & assigns forever a female, child of Agnes, a twin & slave for life- & I also give & bequeath a male twin child of Agnes & slave for life, to my grand son Alexander Link to him & his heirs forever.

And next, it is my will & desire & I hereby direct the balance or residue of my estate not herein specifically bequeathed, to be equally divided among my seven children, namely Elizabeth Fox, Catharine Ramspark, Marth Link, Mary Crowe, Rebeccah Demory, Alexander Link & Adam Link jr. . . .

Lastly, I do hereby constitute & appoint my friend Edward Lucas Jr. executor of this my last will & testament: hereby revoking all other aforesaid wills or testaments by me heretofore made_In witness whereof I have hereunto set my hand seal this thirtieth day of October 1834.

Signed, sealed, published & declared by
the above named Adam Link senior. to be Adam Link senior. [seal]
his last Will & Testament in the presence
of us, who have hereunto subscribed our
names as witnesses in the presence of the testator -
Edward Lucas / Robert Lucas

Jefferson County ?:

At a court held for said county, on the 19th day of October, 1835, The foregoing Last Will and Testament of Adam Link senior. decd. was proved by the oaths of Edward Lucas & Robert Lucas, two of the subscribing witnesses and ordered to be recorded: and on the motion of Edward Lucas junior.?, the executor therein named, who made oath according to Law & with Robert Lucas, Wm. Lucas, Adam Link and Alexander Link, his securities, entered into & acknowledged a Bond, in the penalty of $15,000, conditioned according to Law, certificate is granted him for obtaining probate in due form.

Test_ Lam. J. Cramer j.c.c.?

New Additions to Photographs Available through the Society

The Battle Flag of the 57th Indiana Volunteer Infantry

Film of Road through Fox's Gap by Bill Benner

The tombstone of Michael and Anna Hilligass in the Gebhart Cemetery

Joseph P. Gouty and Luella M. Hartman

Tombstones of Jacob and Melissa Ricketts

Tombstone of Robert Ricketts

Documentation related to Robert Ricketts and Jacob Ricketts

Please notify

the President of the Society

regarding any errors you find in the current issue of the Newsletter.

Topics in the next issue of the Newsletter, June 1, 1999

* 1. The newest book by Curt Older, *The Land Tracts of the Battlefield of South Mountain*.
* 2. Jacob Ricketts and the 57th Indiana Volunteer Infantry during the Civil War.
* 3. More information on the ancestors of Elizabeth Ann Link, wife of George Fox.
* 4. The will of John L. Fox.
* 5. The land record for the tract on which the Fox Inn stands.

The proposed Table of Contents from the next book by Curtis L. Older, *The Land Tracts of the Battlefield of South Mountain*:

Contents

Index

Issue 6, Volume 1

News from Fox's Gap

News from Fox's Gap

The Society of the Descendants of Frederick Fox of Fox's Gap in Maryland

Issue 7, Volume 1 **Remember Freedom!** June 1, 1999

The Land Tracts of the Battlefield of South Mountain

My second book, *The Land Tracts of the Battlefield of South Mountain*, should be ready to go to the publisher in the next few months. The new book will preserve the land tract records of the Battlefield of South Mountain. A copy of the Table of Contents from the new book is included in this Newsletter.

The book should sell for about $30. It will be available to all members of the Society of the Descendants of Frederick Fox of Fox's Gap in Maryland at cost. Cost should be 60% of the retail price. Postage and handling will be an additional $3 or $4. Perhaps only 100 copies of the book will be printed. Therefore, if you are interested in obtaining a copy, please let me know so that I can estimate how many copies of the book to order for distribution. Presently, I plan to order 20 copies for myself and will distribute about 10 of those copies to research institutions.

The land tract book will have a Library of Congress number. The Braddock Expedition book, which is in the Library of Congress, did not have a Library of Congress number printed on it. The new book should permanently preserve the land tract history of the Battlefield of South Mountain area. Researchers will no longer have to reinvent the wheel each time they begin to study the land tracts of the area from the time of the earliest settlers.

A Short Newsletter

The current Newsletter is much shorter than my normal 20 page version. I have spent a lot of time the past few months working on my latest book and have not spent the time necessary to prepare my standard length Newsletter. Instead, I have chosen to include along with this Newsletter a copy of a brochure published by the Central Maryland Heritage League, the American Battlefield Protection Program, and the National Park Service. The Battlefield Guide is entitled "Fire on the Mountain". It represents a concise review of the Battle of South Mountain, September 14, 1862, and includes a map of the area. The guide is enclosed along with this Newsletter and consists of 13 pages.

All members of The Society of the Descendants of Frederick Fox of Fox's Gap in Maryland should be interested in this Battlefield Guide. This guide gives a vivid reason why Fox's Gap in Maryland should be preserved for the ages. Fox's Gap in Maryland is hallowed ground. As Shelby Foote, noted Civil War historian has so aptly stated, "Any understanding of this nation has to be based . . . on an understanding of the Civil War. It was the crossroads of our being, and it was a hell of a crossroads."

Land Tracts of the Battlefield of South Mountain

by Curtis L. Older

Each Newsletter includes a survey, patent, or deed related to the land tracts in the vicinity of Crampton's, Fox's, and Turner's Gaps. These three gaps in South Mountain represent the main area contested by the Union and Confederate Armies in the Battle of South Mountain on September 14, 1862.

Partnership of John Mansberger

MdHR 17,473, 1-23-4-29, IC K, pp. 343-344, John Mansberger, Partnership, resurveyed 20 Aug 1794, 685 acres. (A resurvey of Newcomer's Purchase that was a resurvey of Fox's Last Shift)

John Mansberger his Certificate 685 acres} The State of Maryland ? By
Partnership Patd ? 23 Nov 1795 } virtue of a special warrant of Resurvey bearing date the 17th day of May 1794 granted John Mansberger of Washingotn County to resurvey a tract of Land called Newcomer's Purchase lying in said county on the 16 day of May 1794 granted said Mansburger for 101 acres to amend all errors in the original and add any vacant land contiguous thereto. I hereby certify that I have carefully resurveyed for and in the name of him the said John Mansberger the aforesaid tract of land and find it lies clear of elder surveys and contains 101 acres the quantity for which it was originally granted and I have added thereto one piece of vacancy containing 584 acres and have reduced the whole into one entire tract as appears by the annexed plat. Lastly beginning for the outlines of the resurvey by virtue of the aforesaid warrant at a stone marked 1794 standing at the original beginning it being also the beginning tree of a tract of land called Swearingen's Disappointment and running thence

Line No.	**North South**	**Degrees East or West**	**Length**
1	N	43 west	30 perches to the end of the last line of said land and still with said land reversed
2	S	52 west	14 perches
3	N	36 west	56 perches
4	N	8 east	31 perches
5	N	20 east	80 perches
6	S	76 east	38 perches
7	S	14 west	21 perches
8	S	42 east	20 perches
9	S	18 east	178 perches
10	S	65 west	25 perches
11	N	65 west	40 perches
12	N	59 west	40 perches
13	N		12 perches

(Land record continued on the next page.)

Please notify

the President of the Society

regarding any errors you find in the current issue of the Newsletter.

14	N	73 east	27 perches to the beginning of the present resurvey
15	N	43 west	30 perches
16	S	50 west	173 perches to the end of the tenth line of a tract of land called Lucky Bit surveyed for Samuel Baker and running with said land reversd
17	S		62 perches to the seventh line of a tract of land called Fox's Last Shift and with said line
18	S	23 west	43 perches to the end thereof
19	S	89 east	103 perches
20	S	54 west	43 perches to the end of the third line of Lucky Bit aforesaid and with the same reversed
21	S	88 west	90 perches
22	N		77 perches to the end of the third line of a tract of land called Birds Bill and with the same reversd
23	S	45 west	48 perches
24	S	15 west	68 perches to the seventh line of Boocker's Resurvey on Well Done and with the same reversd
25	N	88 east	217 perches to the end of the sixth line of said resurvey
26	S?		100 perches to the end of the eighth line of a tract of land called Security resurveyed and with the same reversd
27	S	89 east	49 perches
28	N	16 east	80 perches
29	N	8 d east	460 perches
30		west	180 perches
31	N	14 east	128 perches to the end of the sixth line of a tract of land calld Stoney Point and with the same
32	N	79 1/2 west	74 perches to the end of the fourth line of a tract of land called Raccoon and with the same reversd
33	S	25 west	151 perches
34	S	75 west	10 perches
35	S		121 perches
36	S	80 west	69 perches tothe beginning tree of said land then
37	S	57 east	86 perches to the end of the first line of a tract of land called Boon Forrest and with the same reversed
38	S		10 perches to the beginning thereof
39	S	5 west	80 perches then
40		west	20 perches to the seventy second? line of a tract of land called the Resurvey on Well Done and with the same
41	S	16 west	35 perches to the end thereof then
42	N	72 1/2 east	70 perches to the end of the sixteenth line of this present resurvey and with the same reversed
43	N	50 east	173 perches then

44 by a straight line to the beginning containing and now laid out for six hundred and eighty five acres of land more or less to be held by the name of Partnership Resurveyed the 20th day of Augt 1794

May 14 1795 Examd & passed by Joseph Sprigg P W Coty
Wm Hansen Examr Genl

On the Back of the aforegoing certificate was the following receipt ? Recd May 14, 1795 one hundred nine pounds ten shillings ? caution and five shillings for Impts. Tho Harwood Jr.

Fox's Gap on the Internet

If you have access to the Internet, be sure to visit the Central Maryland Heritage League site:

http://www.cmhl.org/html/fox.html

The E-mail address of the Central Maryland Heritage League is: INFO@CMHL.ORG

Wills
by Curtis L. Older

Each Newsletter includes one typewritten version of a will that is significant to the preservation efforts of the Society. Included in this issue is the will of John Adam Link I.

Will of John Adam Link I - taken from pages 777 and 778 of *The Link Family* by Paxson Link. (Printed here as it appears in context, spelling, and punctuation in the Frederick County, Maryland records.)

In the Name of God Amen I Adam Link, Senior, of Frederick County & State of Maryland, being in perfect Health of Body & of Disposing mind & Memory considering the uncertainly of life's duration, the certainty of Death & the great propriety of a seasonable arrangement of our concerns temporal & Eternal Do make and publish this my last will & Testament in manner & form following Vizt:
Imprimis I Earnestly recommend my Soul to the mercy of Almighty God and my body to the Earth to be decently buried at the discretion of my Executors, hereinafter named & after my funeral charges & debts are paid I devise & bequeath as follows Vizt:
2ndly. To my daughter Elizabeth I give & bequeath the sum of thirty pounds lent by me to her first husband (Henry Stoner deceased) on the twentieth day of March Anno - - Seventeen Hundred and Seventy One together with the interest thereon & Sundry Other Articles received by her as her full portion & in full of her claim of Inheritance from me. **Item** to my son Thomas Link I give and bequeath twenty five acres of land part of the tract called The Four Friends to be laid off across the roads to Annapolis and Baltimore from Frederick Town. **Item** to my son George I Give and bequeath the like quantity of twenty five acres of land of said tract to be laid off in manner aforesaid. **Item** my wish & desire is that the remainder of the tract aforesaid fifty acres more or less be considered as appertaining to the Home Place on Israel's Creek & sold or retained therewith but of the two twenty five acre lots aforesaid my son Thomas is to have the first choice. **Item** To my grand daughter Elizabeth Boyer I give and bequeath thirty six pounds specie which I lent her father in November Seventeen Hundred & Eighty Six to be paid to her when she shall arrive at her sixteenth year on the payment whereof I acquit & release said Jacob Boyer her Father of the interest thereof & the sum of four pounds the price of a cow sold to him & the Furniture received by my daughter Catherine when first married.
Item to my youngest son Daniel I give & bequeath my feather bed, bedstead, curtains, sheets, blankets, & all appendages to it.
Item After my Decease I order my Executors, hereinafter mentioned to sell and dispose of all my real & personal property not already Devised or bequeathted Vizt: my Plantation on Israel's Creek also the remainder of my tract of land called The Four Friends herein before mentioned together with my lot in The Addition to George Town lately in the Tenure & Possession of George Murdock, Esqu.
Item to my four grand children Adam Boyer, Elizabeth Boyer, Ferdinand Boyer, and Rebecca Boyer, I give and bequeath the sum of one hundred pounds by equal shares but if any of them die without Issue their protion shall be equally divided among the survivors of them.
Item to my son Jacob I give and bequeath one hundred pounds specie to be paid by my Executor as soon as possible after the sale of my estate as aforementioned. And I will and desire that the remainder of my Estate be equally shared among my four sons Adam, Thomas, George, & Daniel. And Lastly I do constitute & appoint my Sons Daniel & Thomas Joint Executors of this my last will and Testament which alone I do ratify and confirm as such hereby revoking & disannulling all my other former Wills Legacies and Bequests by me heretofore in any wise made left or bequeathed.
In Witness whereof I have hereunto set my hand and affixed my seal this ___ day of ___ in the Year of our Lord Eighteen Hundred and Three.

Continued on the next page--

Signed Sealed Published & Declared by the Testator to be his last Will & Testament in our presence who signed the same at his request & in the presence of the Testator and in the presence of each other.

Abraham Haff, Senr.
Edw. Salmon
Saml. Cock.

Before Signing or Sealing the within mentioned Will & testament I have added the following Codicil or Schedule Vizt: That my oldest Negro boy Harry shall become the sole property of my son Daniel, the second eldest Davy the property of my son George, & the youngest Ben the property of my son Thomas. In confirmation whereof I have hereunto set my hand & affixed my seal this Twenty Sixth day of July in the year of our Lord Eighteen hundred & three.

Adam Link (Seal)

Probated May 25, 1805

John Adam Link I

John Adam Link I was born October 13, 1721, in Grossgartach, Germany. John Adam Christ from Biberach, Lorenz Flinspach, a wagonmaker, and Max Eckstein were godparents. He died April 24, 1805, in Frederick County, Maryland. He married Mary Elizabeth Miller January 31, 1748, in Berks County, Pennsylvania. Mary Elizabeth Miller was the daughter of John Jacob and Mary Magdalene (Gerber) Miller and was born May 17, 1728, in Niederbronn, Germany. She died March 18, 1786, in Frederick County, Maryland.

The birth date of John Adam Link I is from the record of the St. Lorenz Protestant Church, Grossgartach. The birth date for Mary Elizabeth Miller and death dates for John Adam Link I and Mary Elizabeth Miller are from their tombstones at the Frederick Lutheran Church in Frederick, Maryland. Both are buried under the Frederick Luthern Church building because the church building was extended over their graves.

Welcome New Members

Four new members joined the Society in the past six months! **The Society of the Descendant's of Frederick Fox of Fox's Gap in Maryland** welcomes the following new members:

Name and Address	Telephone	Join Date	Society Number
Mr. William Ernest Fox II Route 1, Box 76c Puposky, Minnesota 56667	telephone not known	January 3, 1999	0022
Alice Takase P. O. Box 6945 Fort Bliss, Texas 79906-0945	telephone not known	May 11, 1999	0023
Michael J. Fox 524 Elm Tree Court Cincinnati, Ohio 45244	telephone not known	May 17, 1999	0024
Kurt D. Graham 3448 Valley Vista Road Smyrna, Georgia 30080	telephone not known	May 20, 1999	0025

The Table of Contents from the next book by Curtis L. Older, *The Land Tracts of the Battlefield of South Mountain* follows:

Contents

Questions and Answers

William Fox of Michigan seeks answers to the following questions that he poses for our membership.

1. Does anyone have any information on the brothers or sisters of Frederick Fox, other than what appears in *The Fox Genealogy* by Daniel Gebhart Fox?

2. Is it possible that the Jacob Reel of Sharpsburg, Maryland, who wrote to Frederick Fox and Michael Fox in Ohio about the death of "our aged mother," was married to one of Frederick's sisters?

3. Does anyone have any information on Michael Fox after he went to Ohio?

Note from Curtis L. Older regarding questions by William Fox of Michigan:

1. This would be a great topic for someone to research for our society. See the will of John Fox, the father of Frederick Fox of Fox's Gap in Maryland, for the listing of his children. This will was published in a prior Newsletter. The children of John Fox who are listed in his will are: Daniel, Frederick, Magdelin, Michael, and Rachel.

2. A few years ago I obtained a copy of the will of Jacob Reel of Sharpsburg. I came to the conclusion that Jacob was not married to a sister of Frederick Fox, at least at the time he wrote the letter to Frederick and Michael in Ohio. I feel that he probably used the word "mother" in a broad context, perhaps referring to their relationship as members in the family of God.

Jacob Reel died in 1844 in Sharpsburg. His will is found in ?, pages 547-552, in Washington County Records. He mentions Christina Fox twice in his will, both times in reference to the 1/2 of Lot #6 in Sharpsburg which he purchased from her. He gives his wife's name in the will as Elizabeth. On an 1877 Map of Sharpsburg, 1/2 of Lot #66 was owned by a D. Reel. Although this property was left by Jacob Reel to his daughter, ? ? , it could have come into the hands of one of his sons, David Reel.

"Item. To my daughter Nancy Michael, wife of Adam Michael, I give and devise the half lot and premises in the town of Sharpsburg Washington County Maryland adjoining Crise and Beard and which was purchased of Christina Fox etc."

"To my beloved wife Elizabeth I give, bequeath and devise for and during her natural life the following property viz. half a lot of ground in the town of Sharpsburg Washington County Maryland adjoining Crise and Beard which was purchased of Christina Fox, also the house and lot on which I now live situate in the said town of Sharpsburg and which I purchased from Jacob Houser etc."

3. According to Robert H. Fox of Cincinnati, Ohio, Michael Fox preceded Frederick Fox and his family to western Ohio by three years. Michael Fox appears in militia records along with Frederick Fox for the militia Company of Joseph Chapline Junior in Sharpsburg, Maryland, probably in 1775 or 1776.

Index

Issue 7, Volume 1

News from Fox's Gap

News from Fox's Gap

The Society of the Descendants of Frederick Fox of Fox's Gap in Maryland

Issue 8, Volume 1 **Remember Freedom!** December 1, 1999

Significant Research Findings on The Battle of South Mountain

(Note by Curtis Older: We are honored to present for our readers the following article by Kurt Graham. I was fortunate to run across Kurt on the Internet. The following material provides new evidence regarding the battle at Fox's Gap in Maryland on September 14, 1862. In the June 1, 2000, Society Newsletter, Kurt will provide us with another significant research article on Drayton's Brigade at the Battle of South Mountain. Both of Kurt's articles are thoroughly researched and provide primary sources from which he obtained his information. Kurt retains all copyright privileges related to his articles.)

Kurt Graham retired from IBM in 1991 and lives in Vinings, Georgia with his wife, Mary, and sons Griff and Jack. His lifelong love affair with American history was fueled by a father and grandfather who "had dragged him across every Civil War battlefield by the time he was ten." Kurt is an enthusiastic supporter of battlefield preservation and collector of military art and books. He is currently researching the history of the Phillips Georgia Legion and co-authoring a book on this little known Georgia unit. He maintains a website for this unit at www.angelfire.com/tx/RandysTexas and encourages interested parties to contact him at (e-mail) kdgraha@attglobal.net.

Lost Legion
The Phillips Legion Infantry Battalion at Fox's Gap, Maryland September 14, 1862

by Kurt Graham

This story begins in a rather unusual manner back in 1996. I was getting a haircut from my barber and friend Dick Flannagan, and the subject turned to my interest in American history and the Civil War (or War for Southern Independence as it's termed here in Georgia). Dick mentioned that his wife, Regina, was an avid genealogist with an interesting Civil War mystery in her family. Her great great grandfather, Alfred Arwood, had enlisted in Company O of the Phillips Legion's Infantry Battalion during the spring of 1862 and marched off to war. His company had gone to South Carolina and had trained there until July, when they were placed in a brigade with two other Georgia units (the 50th and

51st) and two South Carolina units (the 15th and the 3rd Battalion) and sent north under Brigadier General Thomas F. Drayton to join the Army of Northern Virginia at Richmond, Virginia. That fall, Alfred's wife received word that Alfred had fallen in battle during Lee's first invasion of the north in September and that was the last ever seen or heard of Alfred Arwood. Regina had often wondered just where Alfred had fallen and been buried. Dick asked if I might like to probe the mystery.

As it turns out, I love a good mystery, and jumped on the opportunity to learn something new and possibly make someone else happy. I figured, look at a few works on the 1862 Maryland campaign to get the Legion's movements figured out, a trip to the state archives to look over Alfred's compiled service records and then some research on burials once I had the location of Alfred's death nailed down. So, move to step one and look at the reference works. What's this! The Phillips Legion Infantry does NOT exist during the 1862 Maryland campaign. All published works reviewed covering this period (including the extensive Official Records) show them present and in action on August 30, 1862, with Drayton's brigade at the battle of Second Manassas, then . . . POOF! They vanish, not to reappear until late November of 1862 when they are reassigned to T. R. R. Cobb's Georgia brigade upon the dissolution of Drayton's brigade. After some unproductive flailing around, I decided to move to step two and have a look at Alfred's compiled service record at the Georgia State Archives.

These microfilm records were done around the turn of the century by the Federal government when it was discovered that many of the original paper records were deteriorating beyond usability. A small army of "compilers" sifted through original Federal and Confederate muster rolls, pay records, hospital records, POW records, death claims, requisitions, etc. They produced a multiple card file for each soldier who fought in the war. Microfilm copies of these cards were eventually distributed to the various southern states for their respective soldiers. Sure enough, Alfred was there. His records show his enlistment in the Legion's Infantry Battalion in April of 1862 and end with a chilling notation on a December muster roll which states 'killed at Sharpsburg (southern name for Antietam) September 17, 1862.'

So now we DO have a good mystery. How does soldier get himself killed in a battle where his unit is not present? A friend suggested I take a look at the records at the Georgia Room of the Cobb County Library. Several companies of the Infantry Battalion had been recruited from Cobb County and they might have something. Sure enough, they have a Phillips Legion folder and contained in these folders were some rosters of men who had served in companies C, M, and O of the Infantry Battalion. Of immediate interest was the fact that these listings showed a number of soldiers killed or wounded at Boonsboro (the southern name for the battles at Fox's and Turner's Gaps on South Mountain, Maryland) September 14, 1862, and at Sharpsburg, Maryland, on September 17, 1862. The source of these rosters is shown as the State Archives, so back there we go. The nice folks at the Archives quickly identify these rosters for me as a work product of the 1906 Georgia Roster Commission. This Commission was formed in an attempt to have all the old surviving Confederate veterans provide information on just who was in their various units. At this point, the Federal government had not yet given copies of the captured wartime records back to the southern states. The southern states had, by the 1890s, begun providing pensions for their soldiers and were having a most difficult time sorting valid pension applicants from fraudulent ones. They had to write to Washington and wait months for someone to try to find a record of the individual applicant's military service records.

Thus it was that the Roster Commission idea came about in an attempt to build some local record of just who had served in the various Georgia units. As you would expect, some units had formed reunion groups and had very good records and others had little or no information available. When these attempts at reconstructing a 45 year old unit roster were attempted it was inevitable that clouded old memories would misspell names, show people killed in the wrong battles and often simply forget many men.

So what this told me that my new found, exciting rosters showing Phillips Legion casualties in the 1862 Maryland campaign were interesting, but not concrete evidence that they had been there. Now came a tough decision. I knew that I had found what appeared to be good solid evidence for Alfred Arwood's death during the Maryland campaign in his actual service record. Therefore, I could do the same for the entire Infantry Battalion IF I were willing to scroll through the eight or nine reels of microfilm containing copies of the untold thousands of card records for all members of the unit. Sounds easy? These card records were handwritten and the writing styles of the compilers varied widely. Many wrote in the frilly cursive of that period. Bottom line was that this was going to be a several hundred hour task.

I was almost ready to stop at that point, tell Dick and Regina that it appeared that Alfred HAD been killed in Maryland in September of 1862, and to heck with the Phillips Legion Infantry. I then figured that I should at least take a shot at finding out where Alfred had been buried and moved along to step three. I vaguely recalled that I had once seen a nice book at the Antietam National Visitor's Center which covered the subject of what had happened to those who fell at the battles of South Mountain (Boonsboro) and Antietam (Sharpsburg).

In trying to find out how I might obtain a copy, I ended up contacting it's author, Steve Stotelmyer. Steve, who lives in Sharpsburg, Maryland, patiently listened to my tale and then told me that he had something that he thought would be of interest to me. He then read me an article by one Reverend George Gilman Smith, chaplain of the Phillips Legion, that had been published in an 1886 anthology titled "Campfire Sketches and Battlefield Echoes." This article describes in very precise detail the actions of the Phillips Legion Infantry Battalion at the battle of Fox's Gap on South Mountain, September 14, 1862. The reverend makes it clear that they are there as part of Drayton's brigade, and that they took significant casualties; one of which was himself. At the climax of the fight, Smith is shot in the neck and the wound, at first thought to be mortal, cripples him for life.

I will now let Chaplain Smith speak for himself. We pick up his account on the morning of September 14 at Hagerstown, Maryland. He states that, "On the Sunday morning on which the battle of South Mountain began, we were in camp at Hagerstown. We were expecting quite a time of repose when the order came to return towards Boonsboro. I had not the remotest dream of any hot work, nor do I think any of us had, for we had no idea that the Army of the Potomac could be reorganized and mobilized so soon. We thought the assault upon our lines was merely a feint of cavalry. This was evidently General Lee's opinion, or else he would not have allowed Jackson to have crossed the Potomac; but it was soon evident from the rapid motion of the artillery and infantry that hot work was before us. My regiment had gone and I ambled off as rapidly as I could toward the front.

Somehow I got the name of "fighting chaplain" and candidly I did not like it, for it was neither just nor complimentary. I did not go to the army to fight; I did not fight after I got there. I had as little stomach for fighting as Falstaff had. I went to the army as a chaplain, and as a chaplain I did my work, and yet that day I got a bullet through my neck. I ought not to have gone where the bullets were flying, but I did go and I got hit, and this is how it came about. I found Generals Lee, Longstreet, and Jones standing at the base of the pass, and with them was one of the staff officers of our brigade, Captain Young. Inquiring of him for my regiment, he told me that it was behind a stone fence on the right of the Boonsboro and Frederick Pike, and I immediately repaired to that place. A battery of light artillery (Bondurant's) was firing overhead and we lay quietly looking toward the south (his direction was off, this should read east). Suddenly the order came to change front. We were now to face toward the west (again his direction is off, this should read south). The turnpike (Old Sharpsburg Road) was narrow, and the enemy were upon us. The change of position called for a change from line of battle to column and then from column into line. My own regiment did beautifully and for a moment we looked to the woods expecting the Federals to charge upon us, but instead we were ordered to leave the protection of the stone wall (bordering the south side of the Old Sharpsburg Road) and to charge into the woods. As we entered the woods I saw a poor fellow fall and heard him say, "Lord Jesus receive my spirit." I went to him and said, "My friend, that's a good prayer, I hope you feel it." He answered, "Stranger, I am not afraid to die; I made my peace with God over thirty years ago." Just at that moment I heard Cook (Lt. Col. Robert T. Cook), our commander say in a loud voice, "For God's sake don't fire; we are friends!" I turned and saw a body of our troops about to fire. I said, "I will go back colonel, and stop them." As I ran back to the fence, I looked down the very road we had left, and saw a body of Federals moving upon us (the 800 man 17th Michigan regiment). Something must be done and I ran to General Drayton, our commander, and told him the position. A feint certainly must be made; if the Federals should know that the stone fence was abandoned, they would sweep upon the fence and thus capture the last man. Major Gest (Major William Gist, 15th SC), when he saw how matters were, placed the few men he had in position, and I started for my regiment. As I came to the pike, I saw a soldier shooting toward the east. It took but a moment for me to see that the Federals were east, south, and west of us.

The firing was now fierce, but I felt that my regiment must be brought out of that pocket at all hazards, and I started to warn it, when I found it retreating. Poor Ellis (Ellis Williams, Co. D, KIA) a Welchman, had run the gauntlet and given them a warning, and the regiment was now retreating in a broken and confused manner. One of the boys, Gus Tomlinson, said in tears, "Parson, we've been whipped; the regiment is retreating." "And none to soon either," said I, "for we are surrounded on all sides but one." Just then I felt a strange dizziness and fell, my arm dropping lifeless by my side. I knew that I was hit, and I thought mortally wounded. But where was I hit? Was my arm torn off by a shell? No, here that is? Was I shot through the breast? Or - yes, here it was - blood gurgling from my throat. The dear boys rushed to me, laid me on a blanket and bore me off the field."

This was evidence enough to pull me deeper into the mystery, so I decided to go ahead and invest the time required to pore through the compiled service records of the Legion at the State Archives. This ended up taking several months, working as time was available. **The results were amazing. This unit, which, according to published history, wasn't even in the Maryland campaign, had managed to suffer 113 casualties at Fox's Gap on September 14, 1862. These consisted of 31 men killed or mortally wounded, 39 wounded, and 43 captured. Pretty devastating losses for a unit that is not supposed to be there!**

Further evidence supporting their presence there has continued to trickle in. One of the casualties from Company C, William Dobbins, was last seen on the battlefield, shot through the chest. His father, a moderately well-to-do planter back in Habersham County, Georgia, began a frantic letter writing campaign trying to find out what had happened to his son. The Dobbins papers are currently archived at Emory University and contain a response from Captain Alex Erwin dated December 1862 which describes young William's loss at Boonsboro (as the Confederates dubbed the battles at South Mountain on September 14) and the fact that he has not been seen or heard from since. In fact, that's the last anyone ever heard of William as he died on the field and was either buried in a shallow grave by a Federal burial detail on September 15th or was possibly one of 58 dead Confederates dumped into a well at Daniel Wise's farm at the gap.

An October 4th, 1862 letter (copy in Georgia Archives) from A. J. Reese of the Infantry Battalion states "We have heard nothing of the four boys we lost in Sunday's fight. I expect they war (sic) kill. I hope not though." The only recent Sunday fight for the Legion would have been the Sunday September 14th fight at Fox's Gap.

A short historical sketch of the Phillips Legion written by it's quartermaster, Major S. M. H. Byrd and published in the May 5-6, 1914 Cedartown Standard states, "We moved with the army into Maryland. Drayton's brigade bore a prominent part and suffered very heavily at Boonsboro Gap (the Confederate's name for Fox's Gap). The Legion lost a good many men in killed, wounded, and missing; Major Barclay, Capt. Daniel, Lieut. Col. Cook, Chaplain Smith, wounded; Lieut. A. Jones killed. The loss was so heavy in officers that the command fell upon Lieut. Price of Co. E. At Sharpsburg, the Legion was again hotly engaged. Among the wounded was Capt. Hamilton of Co. E."

I am certain that one reason for the absence of the Phillips Legion in the historical records for this campaign is the fact that neither General Drayton nor any of his regimental commanders appear to have filed after action reports. This has created a real vacuum of information relative to the strength, composition, and actions of Drayton's brigade at Fox's Gap that persists to this day. One thing that we CAN now be certain of, however, is that the Phillips Legion's Infantry Battalion was engaged in a vicious holding action at Fox's Gap on the afternoon of September 14th, 1862. Their sacrifice, and indeed that of their entire brigade, bought just enough time to hold McClellan's huge army back one additional day and this, in turn, allowed Stonewall Jackson to force the surrender of the 12,000 man garrison at Harpers Ferry on September 15. This, in turn, set the stage for the bloody battle of Antietam at Sharpsburg on September 17, 1862.

A map provided by Kurt Graham of the action involving the Phillips Legion Infantry Battalion at Fox's Gap appears on page 8.

The following list details the casualties suffered by the Phillips Legion at Fox's Gap, Maryland, September 14th, 1862, as obtained from the compiled service records and 1906 Georgia Roster Commission records at the Georgia State Archives:

Company A	Capt. Oliver Daniel	WIA
	C. H. Miller	WIA*
	Musician Joseph B. Walker	KIA
	William F. Williams	MIA later declared KIA
Company B	August Abraham	WIA/CAP
	J. A. Blanton	WIA/CAP (shoulder)
	Marcellus F. Broyles	CAP
	Lyman Chapman	CAP
	William Cowan	KIA
	J. C. Currenton	CAP
	W. R. Davis	WIA (lost arm)
	Joseph C. England	CAP
	Darling P. Glover	KIA
	James W. Hawkins	CAP
	S. J. Henderson	MIA presumed KIA
	William B. Lynch	MIA later declared KIA
	James H. Mitchell	MIA later declared KIA
	Monroe Mitchell	MIA later declared KIA
	W. P. Mitchell	CAP
	Cpl. Charles H. Quinn	CAP*
	H. L. Russell	CAP
	John W. Samples	CAP
	Richard P. Stone	KIA
	F. M. Turner	CAP
Company C	James S. Alley	CAP
	Capt. Elihu S. Barclay	WIA/CAP
	William H. Dobbins	MIA later declared KIA
	Henry W. Dodd	MWIA dies at Winchester, Va. 11/12
	Jonas Mills	MIA later declared KIA
	J. J. A. Powers	CAP*
	J. B. F. Red	WIA
	Thomas J. Roman	KIA
	J. T. Spruell	CAP
	J. N. Taylor	WIA/CAP
	Hunter Vandiver	KIA

Company D	John T. L. Baldwin	WIA (lost fingers)
	David H. P. Barton	WIA/CAP (left leg & right side)
	John A. Brooks	WIA
	R. H. Echols	WIA*
	Lt. Abraham Jones	KIA
	Frank B. Luke	WIA*
	Sgt. Major Jno. A. Mathias	WIA
	T. H. McElroy	MWIA dies at home 11/1/62
	J. M. Murphy	WIA/CAP
	John F. Murphy	MIA later declared KIA
	John A. Scott	KIA
	James W. Spratling	KIA
	John M. Steward	CAP
	W. J. Sumner	CAP
	Samuel Turner	WIA/CAP
	E. C. Williams	CAP
	Ellis E. Williams	KIA
	Sgt. Augustus Wimberly	CAP*
	James Springer Wood	CAP
Company E	James Blackwell	CAP
	Jesse Blackwell	CAP
	M. V. Collins	CAP
	James M. Dempsey	WIA (back)
	Capt. Joseph Hamilton	WIA
	James W. Roberts	CAP
	Noah White	WIA
Company F	William Carroll	WIA/CAP
	Bernard C. Conway	CAP
	Richard Deignan	CAP
	Lt. John W. Duggan	KIA
	Richard Furlong	MIA later declared KIA
	Patrick G. Gary	WIA/CAP
	Richard G. Gillespie	WIA (arm & side)
	James Lawler	CAP
	Lt. Patrick M. McGovern	CAP
	Lt. Michael S. Walsh	CAP
Company L	Andrew J. Alexander	CAP
	Henry C. Bryant	CAP
	Isaac Campbell	CAP
	William J. Eslar	CAP
	Clement J. Hunt	CAP
	Newton J. Ivey	KIA
	Capt. James M. Johnson	WIA/CAP
	Doctor L. Malone	WIA/CAP
	Ira F. McClellan	CAP
	William Pilgrim	WIA
	J. B. Richardson	WIA (lost arm)
	Solomon Sanders	CAP
	Mitchell Walraven	CAP
	Harrison Wilmoth	CAP

	Clement J. Hunt	CAP
	Newton J. Ivey	KIA
	Capt. James M. Johnson	WIA/CAP
	Doctor L. Malone	WIA/CAP
	Ira F. McClellan	CAP
	William Pilgrim	WIA
	J. B. Richardson	WIA (lost arm)
	Solomon Sanders	CAP
	Mitchell Walraven	CAP
	Harrison Wilmoth	CAP
Company M	William Bannister Sr.	WIA (lost arm)
	Cpl. William Bannister Jr.	KIA
	John Pleasant Bryan	CAP
	Charles B. Collins	CAP
	Hiram Folds	KIA
	John W. Hodge	CAP
	Andrew J. Inzer	WIA
	Henry E. McKee	WIA
	Malachi W. Pitts	CAP*
	Daniel H. Ponder	CAP
	W. H. Sauls	WIA/CAP (lost arm)
	John W. Sewell	WIA (head wound)
	James E. Smith	CAP
Company O	Thomas C. Austin	CAP
	Lt. Theophilus G. Bowie	WIA*
	Emsley J. Childers	MIA later declared KIA
	Zell Conger	WIA
	Andrew Davis	WIA/CAP
	Samuel E. Fields	MIA later declared KIA
	Hiram A. Harrison	CAP
	John Ransom Hawkins	KIA
	Charles P. Henderson	WIA
	Jesse M. Jackson	MIA later delcared KIA
	Robert Moore	WIA/CAP
	Sgt. Allen H. Summers	WIA/CAP
	William G. Taylor	WIA
	Lt. William O. Watson	KIA
	Rufus W. West	KIA
	Chaplain George G. Smith	WIA

KIA = Killed in Action
MIA = Missing in Action
WIA = Wounded in Action
MWIA = Mortally Wounded in Action
CAP = Captured
* Denotes casualty where location and date are not certain. Could be either Fox's Gap on 9/14, Sharpsburg 9/17, or in the case of captures, somewhere in between.

Map provided by Kurt Graham to accompany his article on The Phillips Legion Infantry Battalion at Fox's Gap on September 14, 1862

See the maps on pages 3, 5, 7, and 9 of Issue #9, Volume 1 of *News from Fox's Gap* and look for The Phillips Legion on each map.

South Mountain State Battlefield Initiative

by Julie Maynard, publisher: *The Citizen Newspaper*

(IN PART - from the Heritage Chronicle, Volume 9, Number 1, Summer 1999, of the Central Maryland Heritage League)

Maryland State Delegate Louise Snodgrass sees tourism in this area's future. And she sees establishing the First State Battlefield Park atop South Mountain as a way to capitalize on Maryland's assets of history and natural beauty.

Earlier this year she worked to set up a task force to study the feasibility of a new park. That task force has been signed into existence, and the next step is gathering ideas to prove a State battlefield makes sense here.

In the long run creating a battlefield park will be a matter of convincing the State legislature that the expense of a new park is justified and then convincing the tourist industry to put South Mountain on its map.

House Joint Resolution 12 By: Washington County Delegation

Introduced and read first time: February 12, 1999
Assigned to: Commerce and Government Matters

A House Join Resolution concerning South Mountain Battlefield Historic Tourism Initiative Task Force

FOR the purpose of establishing a Task Force on the South Mountain Battlefield Historic Tourism Initiative; providing for the membership of the Task Force; specifying the duties of the Task Force; requiring the Task Force to report to the General Assembly and the Governor on or before a certain day; and generally relating to the creation of a Task Force on the South Mountain Battlefield Historic Tourism Initiative.

WHEREAS, On September 14, 1862, the Union and Confederate forces fought a fierce battle over a 7 mile stretch of the South Mountain Range which was the first major Civil War battle in the State; and

WHEREAS, The results of that fateful day helped to shape the events and the outcome of the Battle of Antietam that was fought 3 days later; and

WHEREAS, The State wishes to forever remember the ultimate sacrifice made by those brave soldiers, their families, and their communities, and

WHEREAS, The Department of Natural Resources, the Central Maryland Heritage League, the Friends of Washington Monument State Park, county and municipal government, tourism offices, private landowners, and others have worked closely in protecting and managing lands and interpreting Civil War events within the historical boundaries of the South Mountain Battlefield, and

WHEREAS, It is fitting and right to provide Maryland's citizens and visitors to this State with an opportunity to see, to learn, and to appreciate the important role that the Battle of South Mountain played in this Country's history; and

WHEREAS, Promotion of this important battle in American history will encourage tourism in Frederick County and Washington County; now, therefore, be it

RESOLVED BY THE GENERAL ASSEMBLY OF MARYLAND, That the State of Maryland strongly supports the Department of Natural Resources' effort to study the establishment of a State park at South Mountain that encompasses the battlefield known as South Mountain, including Turner's Gap, Fox's Gap, and Crampton's Gap; and be it further

RESOLVED, That a Task Force on the South Mountain Battlefield Historic Tourism Initiative be established to assist the Department of Natural Resources in studying the establishment of a State park at South Mountain and to ascertain the efficacy of establishing a State park at South Mountain; be it further

RESOLVED, That the Task Force shall be composed of:

(1) Two members of the House of Delegates, appointed by the Speaker of the House, and two members of the Senate, appointed by the President of the Senate;

(2) One representative from the Department of Natural Resources, appointed by the Governor;

(3) One representative from the Department of Transportation, appointed by the Governor;

(4) One representative from the business community of Washington County; and

(5) One representative from the business community of Frederick County; and be it further

RESOLVED, That the Governor designate the chairman of the Task Force from among the members of the Task Force; and be it further

RESOLVED, That the Task Force shall be staffed by the Department of Natural Resources; and be it further

RESOLVED, That the Task Force shall report its findings to the Governor and the General Assembly on or before January 19, 2000; and be it further

RESOLVED, That a copy of this Resolution be forwarded by the Department of Legislative Services to the Honorable Parris N. Glendening, Governor of Maryland; the Honorable Thomas V. Mike Miller, Jr., President of the Senate of Maryland; the Honorable Casper R. Taylor, Jr., Speaker of the House of Delegates; the Honorable David P. Gray, President, Board of County Commissioners, Frederick County; and the Honorable Gregory I. Snook, President, Board of County Commissioners, Washington County.

Bound Copies of *The Fox Genealogy* are Available and also *The Link Family*

You may order hard-bound and soft-bound copies of *The Fox Genealogy* by Daniel Gebhart Fox and/or *The Link Family* by Paxon Link, from Blairs' Book Service. To order copies, please read this page carefully.

Internet site address: http://www.glbco.com/default/order.html

How To Order

Please read the descriptions carefully because the books differ in format, condition, etc. Some books are print-to-order and have rather long lead times. Some are from regular stock and shipped shortly after receipt of order. Please follow these instructions when ordering:

Please include $4.00 shipping and handling for each item unless the listing notes otherwise. They accept orders by credit card, check, or money order. Texas residents please add 8.25% sales tax. Faulty or damaged books may be returned within 10 days for refund.

E-Mail: You may E-Mail your order with credit card payment to: linda@glbco.com

Fax: You may fax your order with credit card payment to Blairs' Book Service at 972-783-1008.

Mail: You may mail your order with payment by any method to:

Blairs' Book Service
2503 Springpark Way
Richardson, TX 75082

Please include the following information with your order:

Books: List the Reference Number, brief title, and price.
Your Name and Address
Shipping Name and Address (If Different Than Yours.)
If paying by credit card include:
Name as it appears on the card.
Card Type (Visa, MasterCard, Amex, or Discover.)
Card Number (Please be sure to double check the digits.)
Expiration Date.

Reference Number: XR-2546

FOX Genealogy, including the Metherd, Benner * Leiter descendants, giving biographies of the first & second generation with sketches of the third generation [Frederick Fox of Prussia & Maryland & descendants], by D. G. Fox. 172 pages 1924. $27.50 This book is a quality reprint with sturdy paper binding. Hardbound is available for an additional $10. This book is print-to-order; please allow 8-12 weeks, plus an additional 2 weeks for hardbound.

Re-enactment of the Battle of South Mountain

The Central Maryland Heritage League has been instrumental in creating a re-enactment of the Battle of South Mountain the past few years. A re-enactment was held again this year on September 11 and 12.

The e-mail address of the Central Maryland Heritage League is: INFO@CMHL.ORG

If you have access to the Internet, be sure to visit the Central Maryland Heritage League site:

http://www.cmhl.org/html/fox.html

New Members

Due to the fact there are many individuals who have an interest in Fox's Gap in Maryland and the Battle of South Mountain, I have opened up membership in our Society to include anyone with an interest in joining the Society. In this way, we have the best opportunity to preserve the history and heritage of Fox's Gap in Maryland.

Kurt Graham
3448 Valley Vista Road
Smyrna, Georgia 30080

Kurt has a tremendous interest in Fox's Gap and the Battle of South Mountain.

Randy Howald
418 Kelly Court
Duncanville, Texas 75137-2511

Randy had an ancestor in the Battle of South Mountain. He maintains a Civil War website on the Internet.

George D. Fox
1308 Mound Avenue
Miamisburg, Ohio 45342

Ann Schulz Trimmer
58 Riverview Terrace
Belle Mead, New Jersey 08502
e-mail: ann@trimmer.net

A descendant of Frederick L. Fox, who was a brother of John L. Fox of Gessie, Indiana.

Change of Address

William E. Fox II
8126 W. 10 Mile Road
Bitely, MI 49309

William E. Fox of Grant, Michigan
e-mail: wefox@mail.ncats.net

President's Message
by Curtis Lynn Older

** My latest book, *The Land Tracts of the Battlefield of South Mountain*, is now available from Willow Bend Books, 65 East Main Street, Westminster, Maryland 21157-5036. Their toll free number is 1-800-876-6103. The book sells for $36.50 from the publisher. Society members may purchase the book directly from me for $18.00 plus $4.00 postage, a total of $22.00.

The book is 259 pages in length with individual drawings for 328 tracts. Two fold-out pages from the book, the "Author's Master Road Map" and the "Author's Master Tract Map", are included as pages 19 and 20 at the end of this Newsletter. Both maps are 11" by 17".

The International Standard Book Number, ISBN, for the book is: 1-58549-066-0

The Willow Bend Books website is: www.WillowBend.net

** Kodak Photo CD-Rom Disc - "Fox's Gap in Maryland" is now being distributed free to all Society Members. If you have not received your copy of the computer disc and would like to receive one, please let me know and I will be happy to send you a copy. Copies of the disc are now in the Maryland Historical Society in Baltimore, Maryland, as well as the Frederick and Washington County Historical Societies in Maryland.

** The 6th Ogle/Ogles Family Association Convention will be held in Gatlinburg, Tennessee, September 21-23, 2000. A block of 80 sleeping rooms has been reserved at the Gatlinburg Holiday Inn SunSpree Resort at discounted room rates. Call the hotel direct at 423-436-9201 and tell them you are part of the Ogle/Ogles Family Convention in order to receive the discounted room rate.

Please notify

the President of the Society

regarding any errors you find in the current issue of the Newsletter.

Topics in the next issue of the Newsletter, June 1, 2000

* 1. Drayton's Brigade at Fox's Gap in the Battle of South Mountain, by Kurt Graham.
* 2. The Third Generation of descendants of Frederick L. Fox, a son of George Fox.
* 3. How Middletown Celebrated Birthday of George Washington in 1932.
* 4. The will of John L. Fox of Gessie, Indiana, the father of Daniel Alexander Fox.
* 5. From The Bookshelf - A review of several Civil War books recently read by Curt Older.

George Fox Line

by Curtis L. Older

Nine members of the Society descend from Daniel Alexander Fox and Elizabeth Jane (Ricketts) Fox. Daniel was a son of John L. Fox of Gessie, Indiana, and a grandson of George Fox.

The following article, which appeared in *The Citizen*, December 15, 1994, is a copy of material that was from *The Valley Register*, December 14, 1894. This article seems to give the impression that the Battle of South Mountain, at least through the eyes of the writer, may have had a more significant impact on the issuance of The Emancipation Proclamation than most writers give it credit.

The Latest from the Last
* C * E * N * T * U * R * Y *

Pleasant paragraphs About Those Who Come and Those Who Go

(In part) ***From The Valley Register, December 14, 1894**

I call the attention of the people of the larger "Pleasant Valley," which extends from Beeler's summit, above Gapland Station, to Sandy Hook and Weverton, to the propriety of giving their beautiful vale a name which will not confound it with any other locality. The most obvious name for our Potomac "Pleasant Valley" is *Gapland Valley*, as well as for the creek which threads it, which is now called Israel's creek.

The chosen people have also left their name upon Solomon's Gap, which I suggest should be called *McLaws' Gap*, after the rebel general McLaws, who forced his cannon up that height by hand and opened the road out to the point over Harpers Ferry, the only event in the history of that mountain, which is misnamed 'Elk Ridge' and 'Maryland Heights,' confusingly. As it is the true Blue Ridge of Virginia, and the Northern conclusion thereof, it ought to be called *Maryland Blue Ridge*.

The tall summit of South Mountain between Bolivar and Rohrersville has no other name than the 'White Rock,' a poor name, and there is also a 'White Rock' on Catoctin Mountain. The finger-board at Gapland tollgate calls this mountain locality 'Mt. Gath,' but as President Lincoln after these battles of three days issued his emancipation proclamation, the noble promontory might be called 'Mount Emancipation.'

The great instep of Catoctin mountain, northeast of Middletown, now sometimes named High Knob, might be named in honor of General Hayes, who lay wounded in Middletown, *President mountain*.

The way to adopt these changes is in the first place, to favor them; in the next place to finger-board them on or about the places.

A finger-board society would be no injury to our hidden nooks of Western Maryland.

Frederick L. Fox Line
sent so Newsletter by Alice Takase
written by Suella Fenton, a great-granddaughter of Samuel Fox

A new member of the Society, Alice Takase, is a descendant of Frederick L. Fox. Frederick L. Fox was a son of George Fox and Elizabeth Ann (Link) Fox. He was a brother of John L. Fox of Gessie, Indiana. Alice Takase's address is: PO Box 6945, Fort Bliss, Texas 79906-0945.

Descendants of Frederick L. Fox

(A son of George Fox and a grandson of Frederick Fox of Fox's Gap in Maryland)

Generation No. 1

1. Frederick L. Fox was born February 28, 1810, in Montgomery County, Ohio, and died November 20, 1851. Buried at the St. John (or Gebhart) Church Cemetery, Miamisburg, Warren County, Ohio. He married Anna Maria Zehring March 28, 1833. She was a daughter of Johann Zehring and Frances Garst.

Frederick L. Fox was married to Maria Zehring III, by Henry Awyer, Justice of Peace. They resided one or two years in the cabin in which his parents resided prior to the erection of the brick dwelling. They then moved to Preble County, Ohio, residing there about two years, then returned to the cabin, where they resided until 1851. They then moved on the tract which was his portion of his father's estate, it being the northwest corner of his father's tract.

The seven children of Frederick L. Fox and Anna Zehring:

2. 1. Samuel Fox, born September 28, 1840, Ohio; died November 2, 1917, Warren County, Ohio.
   2. George Fox
   3. Lavinia Fox
   4. John P. Fox
3. 5. Frances A. Fox, born about 1848
   6. Elizabeth Fox
4. 7. Jacob "Job" Henry Fox, born October 9, 1851, Woodburn, Montgomery County, Ohio; died October 2, 1929, Montgomery County, Ohio.

Generation No. 2

Samual Fox (Frederick L. Fox, George Fox, Frederick Fox, John Fox) was born September 28, 1840, in Ohio, and died November 2, 1917, in Warren County, Ohio. He married Elizabeth Ware Russell October 13, 1870, in Warren County, Ohio, daughter of James Russell and Rachel Ware.

Children of Samuel Fox and Elizabeth Russell are:

5. i. Francis "Frank" Marion Fox, born March 18, 1873; died March 5, 1955, Waynesville, Ohio.
6. ii. Mary Sophia Fox, born July 7, 1874, Franklin, Warren County, Ohio; died 1956, Springboro, Warren County, Ohio.
7. iii. Elmira "Myra" R. Fox, born August 17, 1875; died April 19, 1914.
8. iv. Orissa J. Fox, born April 8, 1877, Warren County, Ohio; died January 13, 1963, Springboro, Warren County, Ohio.
9. v. Walter Scott Fox, born May 26, 1880, Warren County, Ohio; died July 8, 1917, buried in Springboro Cemetery, Warren County, Ohio.

3. Frances A. Fox (Frederick L. Fox, George Fox, Frederick Fox, John Fox) was born About 1848. She married David L. Brown.

Notes for David L. Brown:
Information on the Brown family came from notes found in my mother's effects after her death and from Becky (Brown) Coker and Barbara (Taylor) Roberts, both of Ohio.

Children of Frances Fox and David Brown are:
10. i. Clarence David Brown, born April 18, 1883, Ohio; died January 23, 1972, Carlisle, Ohio.
11. ii. Florence E. Brown
12. iii. Harriet M. Brown

4. Jacob "Job" Henry Fox (Frederick L. Fox, George Fox, Frederick Fox, John Fox) was born October 9, 1851, in Woodburn, Montgomery County, Ohio, and died October 2, 1929, in Montgomery County, Ohio. He married Phoebe Angeline Brelsford December 31, 1878, daughter of Thomas Brelsford and Anna (Brelsford).

Notes for Jacob "Job" Henry Fox:
Information for Jacob "Job" Fox family was given to me by a report given to my brother (Glenn Leis), by Melvina (Montgomery) Null of Ohio.

Children of Jacob Fox and Phoebe Brelsford are:
i. Harry Ervin Fox, born November 12, 1879, Warren County, Ohio; died June 12, 1964, Montgomery County, Ohio; married Rosa Vanderwater.
12. ii. Laura Etta Fox, born July 24, 1881, Warren County, Ohio; died May 10, 1955, Montgomery County, Ohio.
13. iii. Anna Marie Fox, born November 20, 1882, Warren County, Ohio; died 1960, Montgomery County, Ohio.
14. iv. John "Henry" Fox, born September 5, 1884, Warren County, Ohio; died 1968, Montgomery County, Ohio.
v. Copra E. Fox, born September 30, 1884, Warren County, Ohio; died September 4, 1947, Warren County, Ohio; married Elmer Sheets.
15. vi. Edwin E. Fox, born November 4, 1888, Warren County, Ohio; died November 21, 1969, Montgomery County, Ohio.
vii. Ralph "Ernest" Fox, born August 4, 1890, Warren County, Ohio; died January 9, 1975, Warren County, Ohio.
16. viii. Lucy May Fox, born April 4, 1892, Warren County, Ohio; died December 28, 1974, Pittsburgh, Pennsylvania.
17. ix. Katheryn Myrtle Fox, born October 25, 1893, Warren County, Ohio; died May 22, 1994, Warren County, Ohio.
18. x. Lydia "Liddy" Z. Fox, b. November 04, 1895, Montgomery County, Ohio; d. 1962, Montgomery County, Ohio.
19. xi. Cloyce "Wilford" Fox, b. June 04, 1899, Warren County, Ohio; d. October 30, 1976, Warren County, Ohio.

The next issue of the Fox Society Newsletter will contain information on Generation No. 4 of the Descendants of Frederick L. Fox.

Land Tracts of the Battlefield of South Mountain
by Curtis L. Older

Each Newsletter includes a survey, patent, or deed related to the land tracts in the vicinity of Crampton's, Fox's, and Turner's Gaps. These three gaps in South Mountain represent the main area contested by the Union and Confederate Armies in the Battle of South Mountain on September 14, 1862.

The following material relates to a small tract about a mile west of Fox's Gap called Mountain. This tract helps identify the route of the Old Sharpsburg Road west of Fox's Gap. The survey record for the tract bears a date of September 27, 1745.

MdHR 17,400, 1-23-2-34, TI 3, pp. 236-237, John Baley, Mountain, surveyed 27 Sep 1745, 50 acres.

John Baley's Patent 50 acres the Mountain} Charles ? Know ye that whereas Joseph Chapline of Prince Georges County in our said Province of Maryland had surveyed and laid out for him a tract of land called the mountain situate & lying and being in the county afsd containing fifty acres by virtue of a warrant for seven hundred acres granted him by renewment the ninth day of April seventeen hundred and forty five as appears in our land office but before he sued out our grant for the same he did on the twenty second day of June seventeen hundred and forty seven assign over all his right title interest claim and demand whatsoever of in and unto the certificate of survey afsd and the land and premises therein mentioned unto a certain John Baley of Prince Georges County and desired Patent might issue in his name for the same which we have thought fit to condescend unto and upon such conditions and terms as are expressed in our conditions of Plantation of our said Province - bearing date the fifth day of April sixteen hundred and eighty four & remaining upon record in our said province together with such alterations as in them are made by our father conditions bearing date the fourth day of December sixteen hundred and ninety six together also with the alterations made by our instructions bearing date at London the twelfth day of September seventeen hundred and twelve and registered in our secretary's office of our said province together with a paragraph of our instructions bearing date at London the fifteenth day of December seventeen hundred and thirty eight and registered in our land office we do therefore hereby grant unto him the said John Baley all that tract or parcel of land lying in the county afsd called the Mountain beginning at a bounded white oak tree standing on the side of an hill on the west side of Shanandore Mountain (author: South Mountain) near the road that leads from Minococie (author: Monocacy) to Teague's Ferry (author: at Shepherdstown) running thence

Line No.	North South	Degrees East or West	Length
1	S	48 east	54 perches thence
2	S	2 west	80 perches then
3	S	70 west	80 perches then
4	N	15 west	42 perches

5 then by a straight line tot he beginning tree containing and now laid out for fifty acres of land more or less according to the certificate of survey thereof taken and returned into our land office bearing date the twenty seventh day of September seventeen hundred and forty five and there remaining together with all rights profits benefits and privileges there unto belonging royal mines excepted to have and to hold the same unto him the said John Baley his heirs and assigns for ever to be holden of us and our heirs as of our manor of Conegochieg (author: Conococheague or Williamsport) in free and common soceage by fealty only for all manner of services yielding and paying therefore yearly unto us and our heirs at our receipt at our city of St. Mary's at the two most usual feasts in the year vizt. the feast of the annunciation of the blessed virgin Mary and St. Michael the arch angel ofry? even and equal portion the rent of two shillings sterling in silver or gold and for a fine upon every alienation of the said land or any part or parcel thereof one whole years rent in silver or gold or the full value thereof in such commodities as we and our heirs or such officer or officers as shall be appointed by us and our heirs from time to time to collect and receive the same shall accept in discharge thereof at the

choice of us and our heirs or such officer or officers afsd provided that if the said sum for a fine for alienation shall not be paid unto us and our heirs or such officer or officers afsd. before such alienation and the said alienation entered upon record either in the provincial court or county court where the same parcel of land both within one month next after such alienation then the said alienation shall be void and of no effect given under our great seal of our said province of Maryland this twenty second day of June anno dom seventeen hundred and forty seven witness our truly and well beloved Samuel Ogle Esq. Lieutenant General and chief governor of our said province of Maryland Chancellor and Keeper of the great seal thereof.

Sam (the great seal) Ogle Chan.

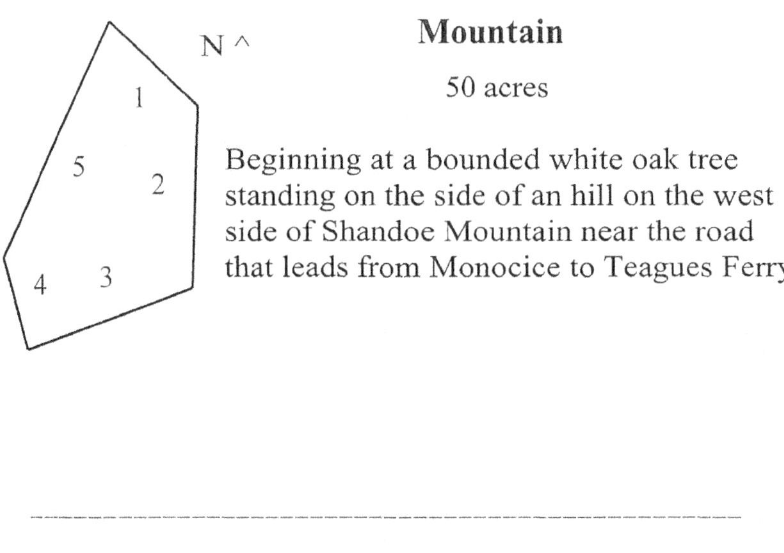
N ^
1
2
3
4
5
Mountain
50 acres
Beginning at a bounded white oak tree standing on the side of an hill on the west side of Shandoe Mountain near the road that leads from Monocice to Teagues Ferry

---

The Ogle / Ogles Family Association

Web site: www.ogles.org

An Internet Site for all Fox related genealogy

The following site on the Internet contains genealogy information and forums related to all Fox families across the United States.

http://homepages.rootsweb.com/~fox/index.html

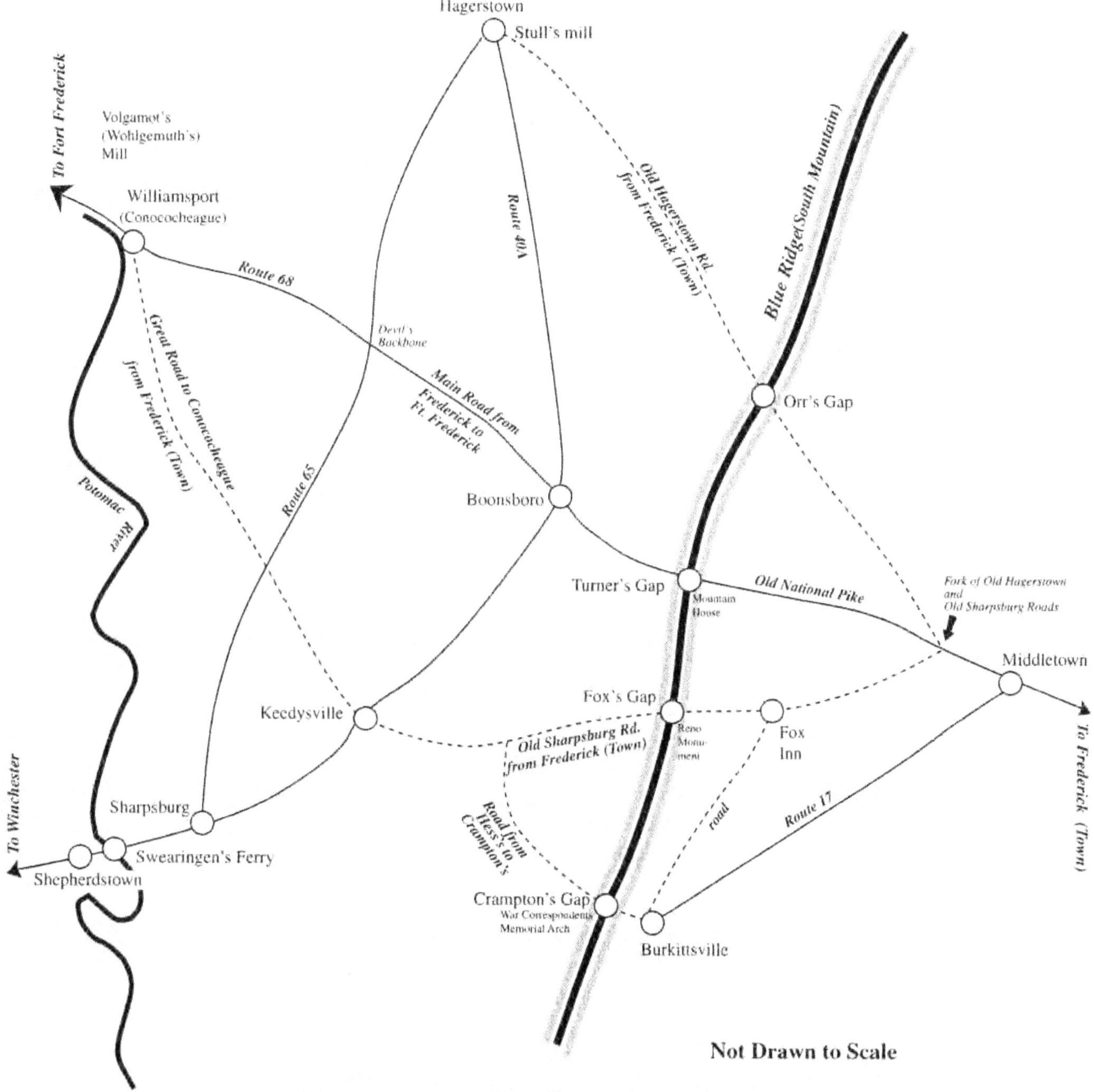

Author's Master Road Map

- **Battlefield of South Mountain** - includes the areas of Turner's, Fox's, and Crampton's Gaps
- **Key landmarks on the Battlefield of South Mountain** - Mountain House at Turner's Gap, Reno Monument at Fox's Gap, and War Correspondents Memorial Arch at Crampton's Gap

Points Along the Roads

- **Old Sharpsburg Road** – Frederick, Middletown, Fox's Gap, Sharpsburg
- **Old Hagerstown Road** – Frederick, Middletown, Orr's Gap, Hagerstown
- **Great Road to Conococheague** – Frederick, Middletown, Fox's Gap, Keedysville, Williamsport
- **Main Road from Frederick to Fort Frederick** – Frederick , Middletown, Turner's Gap, Boonsboro, Devil's Back Bone, Williamsport, Fort Frederick
- **Old National Pike** – Frederick, Middletown, Turner's Gap, Boonsboro, Hagerstown
- **Great Philadelphia Wagon Road** – Winchester, Shepherdstown, Sharpsburg, Fox's Gap, Middletown, Frederick, Philadelphia
- **Route 40A** – Frederick, Middletown, Turner's Gap, Boonsboro, Hagerstown
- **Road from Frederick Town to Swearingen's Ferry** – Frederick, Middletown, Fox's Gap, Sharpsburg, Shepherdstown

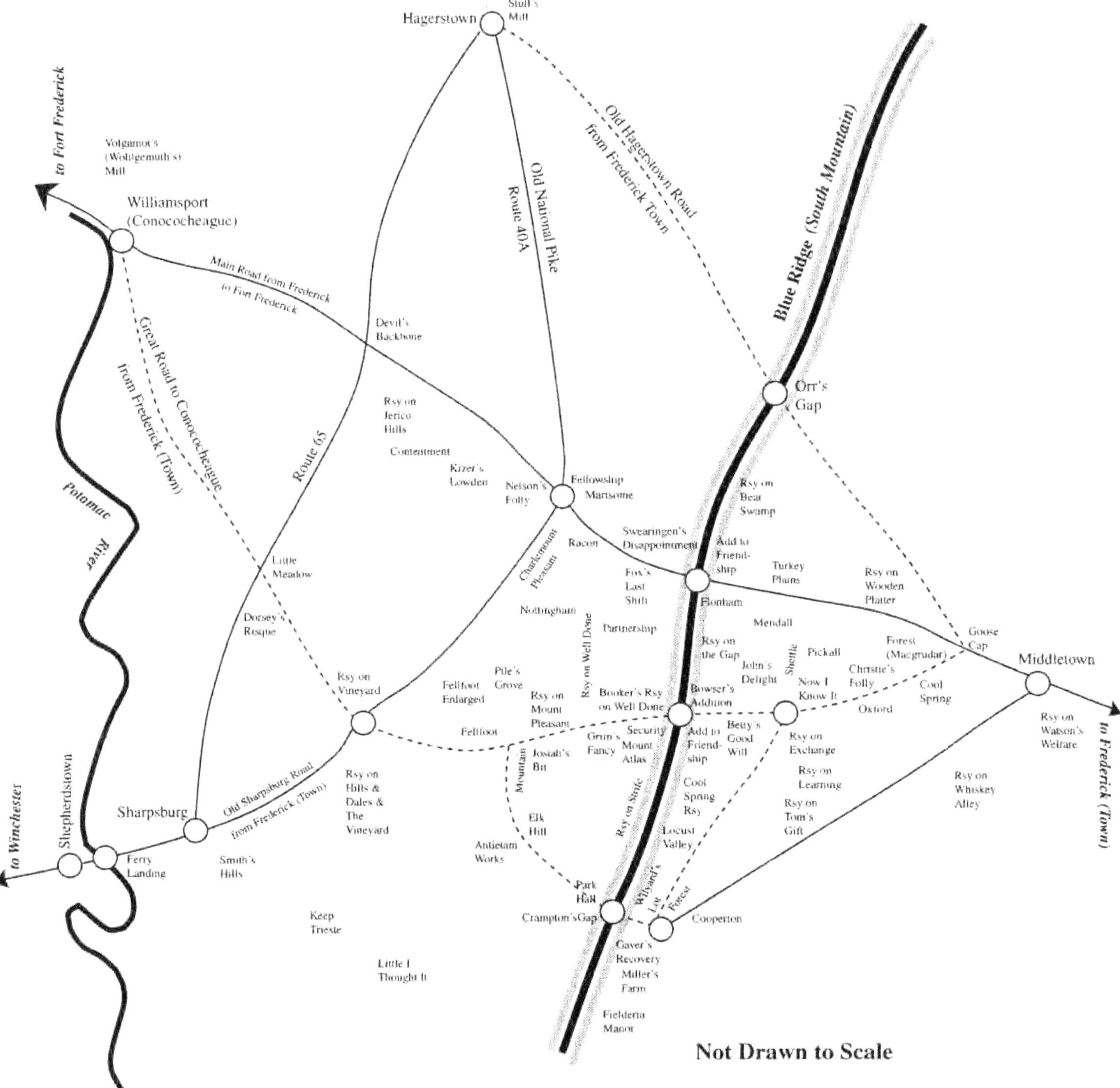

Author's Master Tract Map

1. This map is identical to the Author's Master Road Map on page three as far as the lines that show roads, towns, the Potomac River, the Blue Ridge, Swearingen's Ferry, or other locations. Comparison of the Author's Master Tract Map with the Author's Master Road Map should give the reader the ability to identify the approximate location of those tracts shown on the Author's Master Tract Map.

2. The location of tracts is only approximate on this map. Please refer to Master and Sub-Master drawings for the detail of a tract and its surrounding tracts. Only selected tracts appear on the above map.

3. Sub-Master Tract Drawings that appear on the following pages include: Fellfoot Enlarged Master; Resurvey on Hills and Dales and (The) Vineyard Master; Resurvey on (The) Gap Master; Resurvey on Well Done Master; Contentment Master; Resurvey on Oxford Area; West of Fox's Gap all the way to Crampton's Gap; Gaver's Recovery Master #1; Gaver's Recovery Master #2; Cost's Content Master; Tracts Surrounding the Mountain House at Turner's Gap; The Fox Inn Area - Selected Tracts; and Pile's Grove Master.

Index

Issue 8, Volume 1

News from Fox's Gap

News from Fox's Gap

The Society of the Descendants of Frederick Fox of Fox's Gap in Maryland

Issue 9, Volume 1 **Remember Freedom!** June 1, 2000

Significant Research Findings on the Battle of South Mountain

We are honored to present to our readers the following article by Kurt Graham. The material provides new evidence regarding the battle at Fox's Gap in Maryland on September 14, 1862. It presents documented casualty counts of Confederate forces under General Drayton during the battle. Kurt's article is thoroughly researched and provides primary sources from which he obtained his information. Kurt retains all copyright privileges related to his article.

Kurt Graham retired from IBM in 1991 and lives in Vinings, Georgia, with his wife, Mary, and sons Griff and Jack. His lifelong love affair with American history was fueled by a father and grandfather who "had dragged him across every Civil War battlefield by the time he was ten." Kurt is an enthusiastic supporter of battlefield preservation and collector of military art and books. He is currently researching the history of the Phillips Georgia Legion and co-authoring a book on this little known Georgia unit. He maintains a website for this unit at www.angelfire.com/tx/RandysTexas and encourages interested parties to contact him at (e-mail) kdgraha@attglobal.net.

****

Death of a Brigade

Drayton's Brigade at Fox's Gap September 14, 1862

by Kurt Graham

In the process of doing the research required to establish the presence of the Phillips Legion's Infantry Battalion at Fox's Gap, September 14, 1862, as part of Thomas F. Drayton's brigade (see article "Lost Legion" in the December 1999 "News from Fox's Gap"), it became evident to me that no one who has ever written about this action had a very good idea of the specific actions of Drayton's brigade in it. There is a very good reason for this "vacuum" of knowledge. Neither Drayton nor any of his five unit commanders filed after-action reports or, if they did, these have been lost to history. The only major published account of any member of Drayton's command is that of Major W. G. Rice of the 3rd South Carolina Battalion in Dickert's "History of Kershaw's Brigade". Major Rice's account concentrates solely on the actions of the 3rd and does not mention the other four units of Drayton's command. Historians apparently have taken this to mean that these four units had little or no major impact in this fight.

As an example, J. M. Priest in his book, "Before Antietam", presents a scenario where the relatively small 3rd South Carolina Battalion attacked southeast across the wise field south of the Old Sharpsburg Road while the remainder of the brigade was dug in on the Wood Road north of the Old Sharpsburg Road with their only offensive action being the impromptu charge of 50 or so rebels east from the Wood Road some 600 to 800 yards. He goes on to credit Drayton's troops with having "fought with the ferocity of a division before melting away from the double stone walls (of the Wood Road) in front of the 17th Michigan." Other authors simply lump Drayton's brigade together with those of G. T. Anderson and G. B. Anderson and state that the aggregate command fought well (with the support of two of John Hood's brigades) until nightfall. If one has an interest in their battle history at a "micro" level they are quickly disappointed in the accounts of the afternoon action at Fox's Gap.

At any rate, having established that the Phillips Legion Infantry had been there as part of Drayton's command and having come to a good understanding of their actions, I decided to take a crack at figuring out exactly what happened to and with the entire brigade.

Returning to Mr. Priest's work, one thing that he had ascertained very clearly was that Drayton's brigade was alone at the gap between 3 and 4 PM when the afternoon action exploded again into violent combat. This was the result of a conference that had taken place earlier in the afternoon between Major General D. H. Hill, commanding the South Mountain defense and the four brigade commanders at Fox's Gap. The first of these was George B. Anderson, whose command was first to arrive at the gap following the rout of Samuel Garland's brigade in the morning. The timely arrival of Anderson's North Carolinians stalled the attack of General Jacob Cox's IX Corps "Kanawha Division" just south of the gap. Cox pulled his exhausted troops back behind the woods south of Wise's four acre field and the two sides took an uneasy pause to regroup and reinforce. Next to arrive at the gap was the mixed Georgia, North Carolina brigade of Roswell Ripley. Ripley went into position to G. B. Anderson's left and Anderson extended his line down the Old Sharpsburg Road west of the gap. Longstreet's first two units to arrive at the top of the mountain at Turner's Gap were George T. Anderson's small 500 man Georgia brigade and Thomas F. Drayton's 1,300 man, mixed Georgia, South Carolina brigade. D. H. Hill had personally escorted G. T. Anderson and Drayton to Fox's Gap and planned to use their brigades (with the two brigades already there) in an attack designed to sweep the Federals off the mountain south of the gap and back down the east face.

Hill envisioned the deployment of these four brigades in a line running down the west side of the mountain. Once in position, they would charge forward in a huge left wheeling attack with Drayton's brigade at the gap serving as the "hinge". G. B. Anderson and Ripley were told to move farther west down the Old Sharpsburg Road to make room for the new arrivals. G. T. Anderson was told to file off to the west following Ripley and Drayton was instructed to deploy his men at the gap itself. Having given his orders, D. H. Hill placed the senior brigade commander, Roswell Ripley, in command and hurried back to Turner's Gap to oversee the action developing on his left.

Things went wrong almost from the moment Hill departed. The three brigades ahead of Drayton's moved too far west down the Old Sharpsburg Road and a 300 yard gap opened up between G. T. Anderson's left and Drayton's right. When Anderson heard firing erupt back at the gap he attempted to rectify this situation by moving back towards the gap, but discovered that Federals had moved into this opening. G. B. Anderson's leading brigade moved south into the tangled, rocky woods and struggled to get into position to attack. Ripley's own brigade shifted southwest completely off the mountain. When Ripley's men turned east and began to reascend the mountain, their skirmishers reported another force moving across their front. These were, in fact, G. B. Anderson's troops working southeast up the slope, but Ripley somehow decided that they were a Federal force and retreated with his men off the mountain and out of the battle.

In the meantime, Drayton had initially deployed his brigade in an inverted L shaped formation at the gap. The 550 men in his two South Carolina units were in the Old

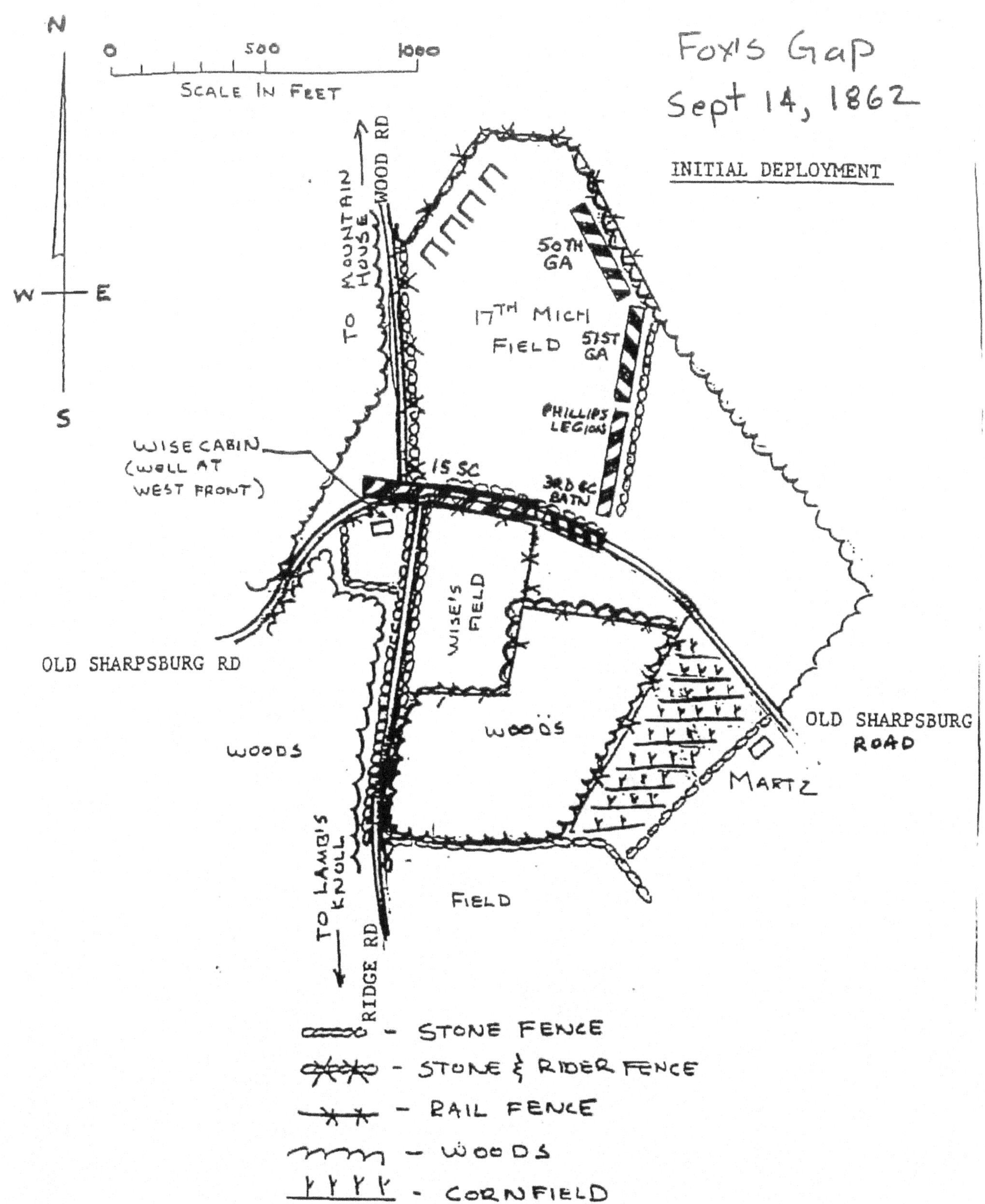

Deployment of Forces at Fox's Gap

Approximately 3:00 PM to 4:00 PM

Sharpsburg Road facing south and the 750 soldiers in the three Georgia units were posted facing east at a stone wall overlooking a deep ravine some 200 yards east of the Wood Road. This deployment made sense for a number of reasons. First, it placed Drayton's two most combat experienced units (the 15th SC on the right and the 3rd SC Battalion on the left) facing south against the perceived strength of the Federals who had been attacking from that direction earlier in the day. The most experienced of the Georgia units was the Legion and it was formed at a right angle to the 3rd SC Battalion and connecting to its left flank where the stone wall intersected the Old Sharpsburg Road. The other two "green" Georgia units (the 50th and 51st) formed along the stone wall to the Legion's left. Another reason this deployment was sound relates to the topography of the gap. The Wood Road, which runs into the Old Sharpsburg Road from the north, lies **behind** the military crest of the east side of South Mountain. The "military crest" is that point at which one can see down the face of the forward slope. If one deploys troops behind the military crest of a position, he permits an approaching enemy to get within a short distance of his position without being seen.

So, how do we know this is how Drayton initially deployed? The first clue lies in the Chaplain George Smith account. The chaplain served with the Phillips Legion and, although severely wounded in this fight, left a wonderfully detailed account of the battle. This account was presented in the "Lost Legion" article in the 12/99 Newsletter. In it he states that "a battery of light artillery (Bondurant's) was firing overhead and we lay quietly looking toward the east." Previous research by Steve Stotelmyer which is presented in the book "From Selma to Appomattox" (A history of the Jeff Davis Artillery AKA Bondurant's battery) has established that this battery had moved to a position in the north end of the field north of the Old Sharpsburg Road and east of the Wood Road by mid afternoon. Therefore, there is no way that a battery could have been firing over the heads of the Legion Infantry if they had been deployed in the Wood Road as the battery would have been in front of them. Further evidence of the lower stone wall's having been the location where Drayton's Georgians originally deployed comes from the regimental history of the 35th Massachusetts. It states that when the firing finally died out after dark, "we then marched into the field north of the sunken road (Old Sharpsburg Road) and stacked arms with orders to rest behind the stacks but be ready for action at any moment." The account goes on to describe the restless, uneasy night spent in this field adjacent the Wood Road. In the morning the tired and hungry Federals began to look around for something to eat. The account states, "Down the east side of the hill, in our rear, **WHERE THE CONFEDERATE LINE OF BATTLE HAD LAIN THE DAY BEFORE**, along a stone wall, the ground was gray with the knapsacks and blankets they had thrown off in the fight and left behind in their hasty departure."

As the gap opened between Drayton's right and G. T. Anderson's left, Drayton took action to rectify this situation by shifting his command farther west. He did this by moving the 15th SC and 3rd SC Battalion west on the Old Sharpsburg Road and moving the Legion into the Old Sharpsburg Road. Again, the Chaplain tells how it happened . . . . . "Suddenly orders came to change front. We were to now face toward the south. The turnpike (Old Sharpsburg Road) was narrow and the enemy were upon us. The change of position called for a change from line of battle into column and then from column into line. My own regiment did beautifully and for a moment we looked to the woods expecting the Federals to charge upon us.

In the meantime, Drayton had sent a company of the 3rd SC Battalion south across Wise's field south of the Old Sharpsburg Road to reconnoiter. Captain D. B. Miller's Company F spotted large numbers of Federals and scrambled back to advise Drayton. Knowing that he had orders to attack, Drayton launched his three units in the Old Sharpsburg Road southward across Wise's field with most of the 15th SC on the right, the 3rd SC Battalion in the center and the Legion on the left. How do we know this? Again to Chaplain Smith. ."We entered the pike, crossed it and entered a wood. As we did, I found the enemy were in our front." The accounts of Private Sam Puckett and Major Rice of the 3rd Battalion also confirm this

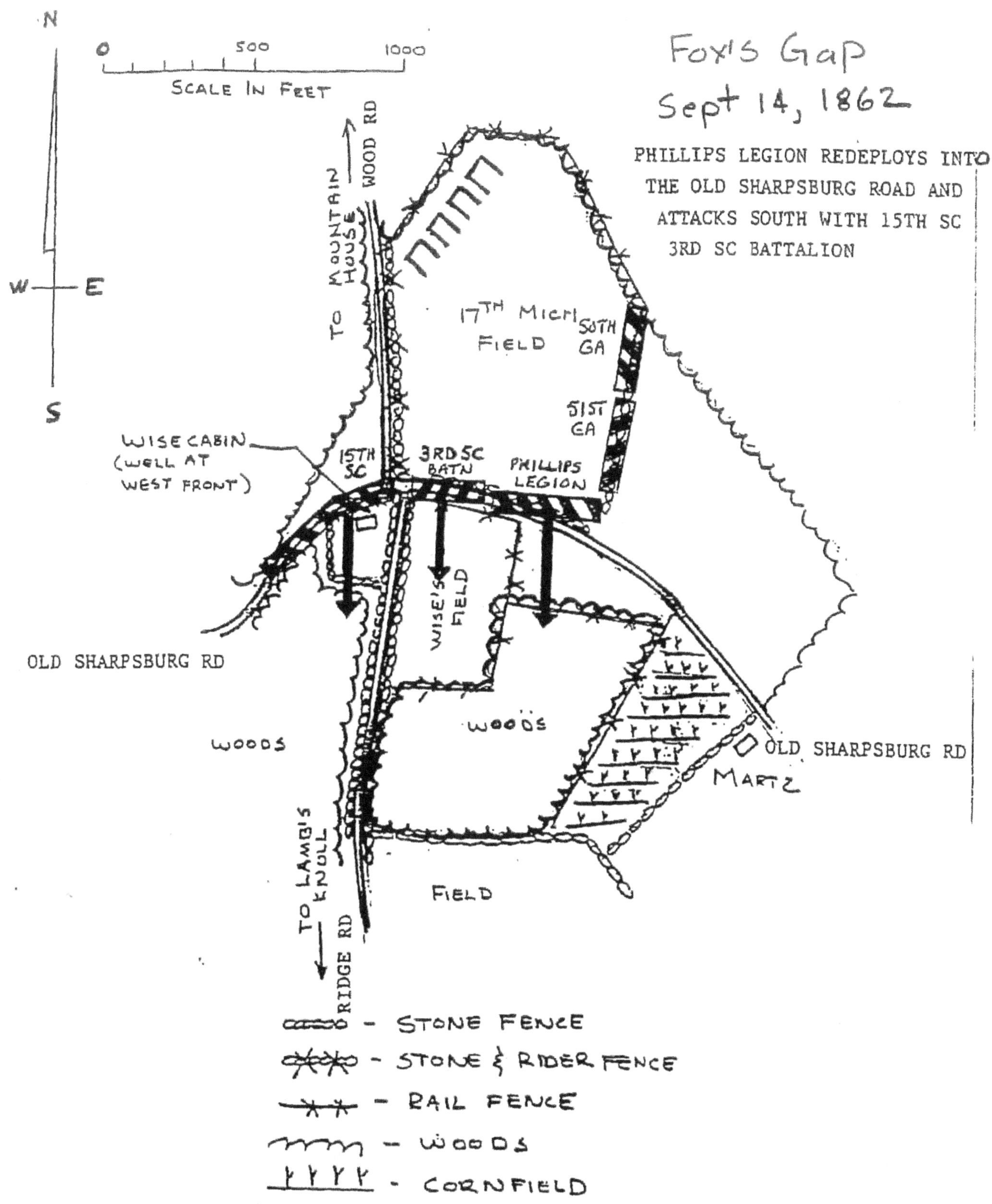

Attack South of Old Sharpsburg Road by Phillips Legion, 3rd SC and 15th SC

Approximately 4:00 PM to 4:15 PM

attack. Puckett says, "We were then ordered to vacate the cut (the Old Sharpsburg Road) and charge the enemy." Major Rice states, "General Drayton ordered the command to forward and drive them (the Federals seen by Captain Miller's recon) from the woods." The Puckett account further reinforces the fact that the initial direction of the attack was to the south as he states, "Colonel James (Lt. Col. George James), seeing the enemy to be too strong, wheeled the battalion to the right between two rock fences, where we attempted to check them." The position he describes is the rock walled Ridge Road, which runs north/south through Wise's field. If James "wheeled" his men into the Ridge Road, they had to have initially been headed south. Major Rice also confirms the direction of the attack with his statement that, "There was a low rock wall running at RIGHT ANGLES to the battle line, and behind this the battalion sought to protect itself."

As the 800 soldiers in the Old Sharpsburg Road moved south to attack, General Drayton, having observed no Federal activity to the east, ordered the 51st and 50th Georgia to execute the same movement that the Legion had previously performed; a shift from the stone wall facing east into the Old Sharpsburg Road facing south. This would provide Drayton with either a second attack wave to launch south or a defensive line should the attack of the South Carolinians and Legion infantry be repulsed. How do we know about this shift? Lt. William O. Fleming, commanding Company F of the 50th Georgia penned a superb account of this fight shortly after the battle. This account was subsequently published in the Savannah Republican during October 1862. In it, Lt. Fleming tells us that, "While forming in line of battle so as to be in position to make the assault we were exposed to a most dreadful rifle and musket fire from the enemy. The 50th Georgia who were on the extreme left towards the enemy, and the last to form on the right by file into line, were under the hottest fire. Our position was in a narrow road between an embankment eight feet in front as we were faced and a stone wall on an embankment about four feet high in the rear. The embankment in front of us gradually declined on the left, until it gave us no protection at all from the balls of the enemy. Our company (F) was the last that could take its position in line, and this took some of our men entirely from under cover. It was painful to see our men shot down while taking their positions. O. Trawick, near me on the right of the company, was shot down while about to file into his place. He was shot in reach of me. The ball passed through his thigh breaking the bone. I mention him, as he was the first one of our company shot. Many others soon shared the same fate."

Even today, one can stand in the Old Sharpsburg Road and easily locate the spot so clearly described by Lt. Fleming. The embankment to the south of the Old Sharpsburg Road drops away to the east to road level today just as it did 138 years ago. The remnant of the stone wall to their rear on the north side of the road is still there. There is simply no other place on this field that fits the Fleming description. There was initially one major problem with fitting the account to this location and it was only a stroke of luck that allowed this to be resolved. To understand this problem, we will continue with the Fleming account . . . . . "The enemy were posted behind a fence and trees, not over sixty or seventy yards from us, pouring their deadly volleys into us in comparative security. Some of the boldest of the enemy would come out into the road and fire down it. Our boys acted nobly, loading and firing as fast as they could; but I am afraid, though, they aimed when the enemy were concealed - very few of their bullets struck a Yankee."

The problem we had in completing the identification of the 50th according to Fleming lay in the fact that period maps seemed to show woods adjoining the south side of the Old Sharpsburg Road at this point yet Fleming is clearly talking about a gun battle being fought over a small field some sixty yards across from north to south. While discussing this problem with my friend Steve Stotelmyer, the preeminent expert on the Fox's Gap battlefield, he suggested that we dig through his extensive files. It was in the course of this "digging" that I came across an aerial photo of the battlefield that had been taken in 1936. Unbelievably, the small field described by Fleming was clearly visible. It even fits the 60 to 70 yard width

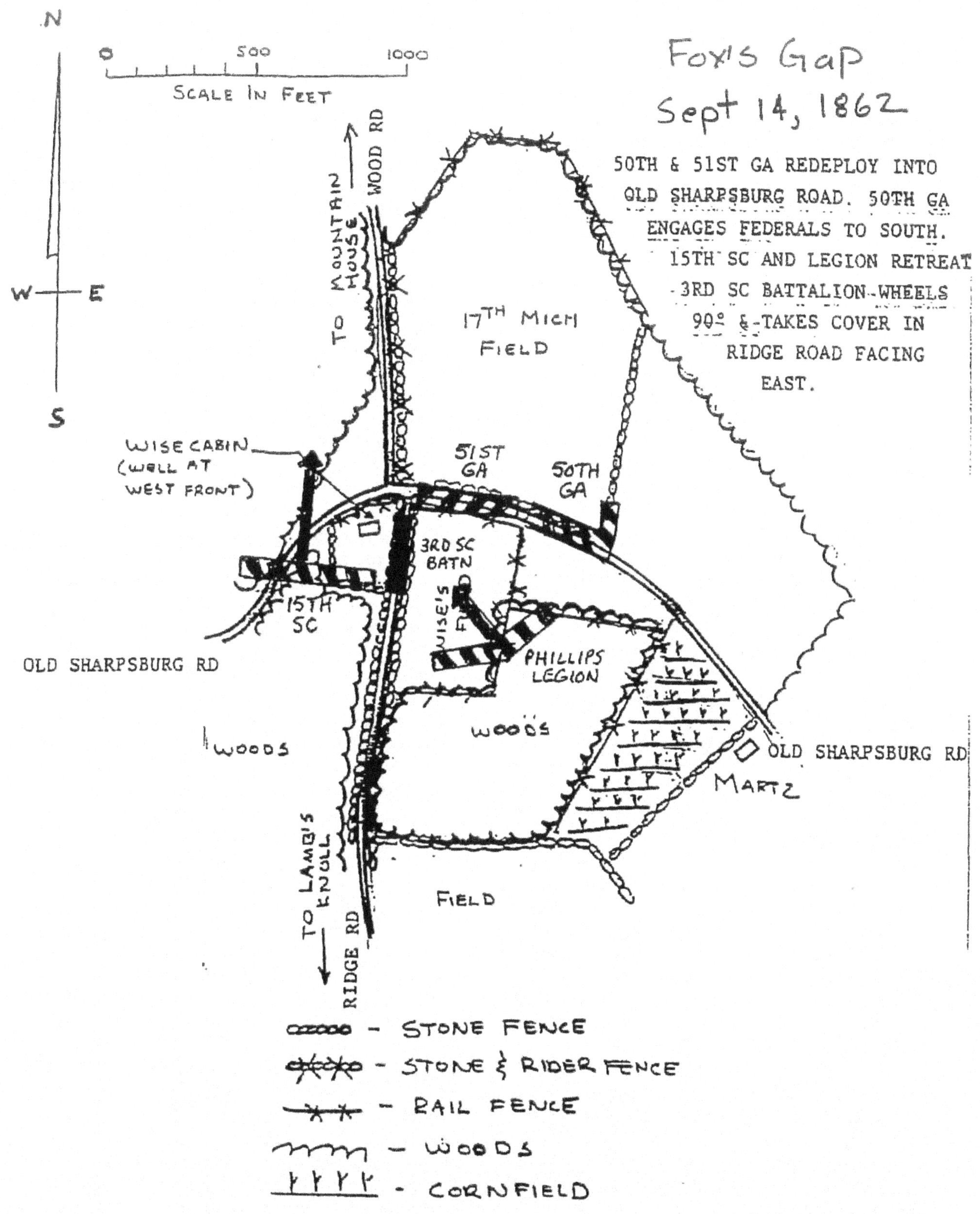

Phillips Legion and 15th SC retreat - 3rd SC wheels 90 degrees into Ridge Road

Approximately 4:15 PM to 4:45 PM

specified by Fleming perfectly. Apparently this field has grown up into forest (as has the Wise field to its west) since 1936. With this discovery, the Fleming account was now an exact match.

As one can see from looking at the maps which accompany this article, the attack launched by Drayton sent three units south down the length of Wise's field with the Legion soon entering woods on the left and the 15th SC with its right in the woods to the west of Wise's cabin. The 3rd SC Battalion in the middle went down the left center of the field. What Drayton did not know was that Orlando Willcox's 3600 man IX Corps division had arrived on the field and was massed ready to launch an attack just beyond the forest to the Legion's left front. The Federals charged northwest into the woods and pushed the Legion out of the woods into Wise's field. Willcox's Federals quickly reached the edge of the woods facing the 50th Georgia in the Old Sharpsburg Road and the fight described by Fleming ensued. The 30th Ohio of Cox's division had also charged forward south of Wise's field and, in conjunction with Willcox's troops now at the eastern edge of Wise's field, forced the 3rd SC Battalion to spin 90 degrees and drop into the "protection" of the Ridge Road.

As all this occurred, a "friendly fire" incident almost took place as the Legion emerged from the woods into Wise's field. Legion Chaplain Smith relates, "I heard Cook, my Lt. Colonel, cry out, "For God's sake, don't fire, we are friends." I saw a body of our men about to fire on us thinking we were Federals. I ran back to check them and was pointing out the position of the troops when I looked up the road we (the Legion) had abandoned, and saw a body of Federals moving behind us."

This information allows us to determine where the chaplain ran to as being at or near the Old Sharpsburg Road's intersection with the Ridge Road which ran south and formed the western boundary of the Wise field. If he had run west back to the Ridge Road, he would not have been able to look down the Old Sharpsburg Road. It is likely that the troops who almost fired at the Legion were those of the 51st Georgia who had already moved into the Old Sharpsburg Road ahead of the 50th and would have been located in that road (and possibly the Ridge Road near the intersection as well).

This body of Federals was the large, 800 man 17th Michigan regiment of Willcox's division, which had been sent by Willcox to get behind the Confederate's left (eastern) flank. Chaplain Smith continues, "I saw their line of battle was moving upon the stone fence we had left (the east facing stone wall where the three Georgia units had originally deployed), but it struck me from the way they moved that they did not know that is was abandoned. I ran to the General (Drayton) and told him about it. He ran up to the fence and said something about charging, but there was nobody to (make the) charge. Major Gest (Major William Gist, commanding a rear guard detachment of the 15th SC) when he saw how matters were, placed the few men he had in position and I started for my regiment." The flanking attack of the 17th Michigan is also part of Lt. Fleming's account. He continues his story, "We had been exposed to this fire (from across the small field to their south) about twenty minutes, when a Yankee regiment made its appearance suddenly in our rear about 80 yards distant. The command was given to charge and they came towards us at the charge bayonet about 20 or 30 yards and stopped. I directed my men to fire at them, which the few that were left did, with some effect, I know. About this time, there was a general move out of the lane, and we followed. I carried into this action with me 38 men, and brought out 10."

Federals had now almost surrounded Drayton's men. The 45th Pennsylvania and 46th New York were pouring in volleys from the east side of Wise's field. The 30th Ohio was firing from the south end of the field and elements of Cox's division were working through the woods to the west. Meanwhile the 17th Michigan had moved around behind the Confederate left (eastern) flank and was charging up the fields north of the Old Sharpsburg Road. The trap was closing fast. Chaplain Smith relates, "As I came to the Pike, (on the way back to the Legion after leaving Major Gist and General Drayton) I saw a soldier shooting toward the east. It took but a moment for me to see that the Federals were east, south, and west of us. The firing was now

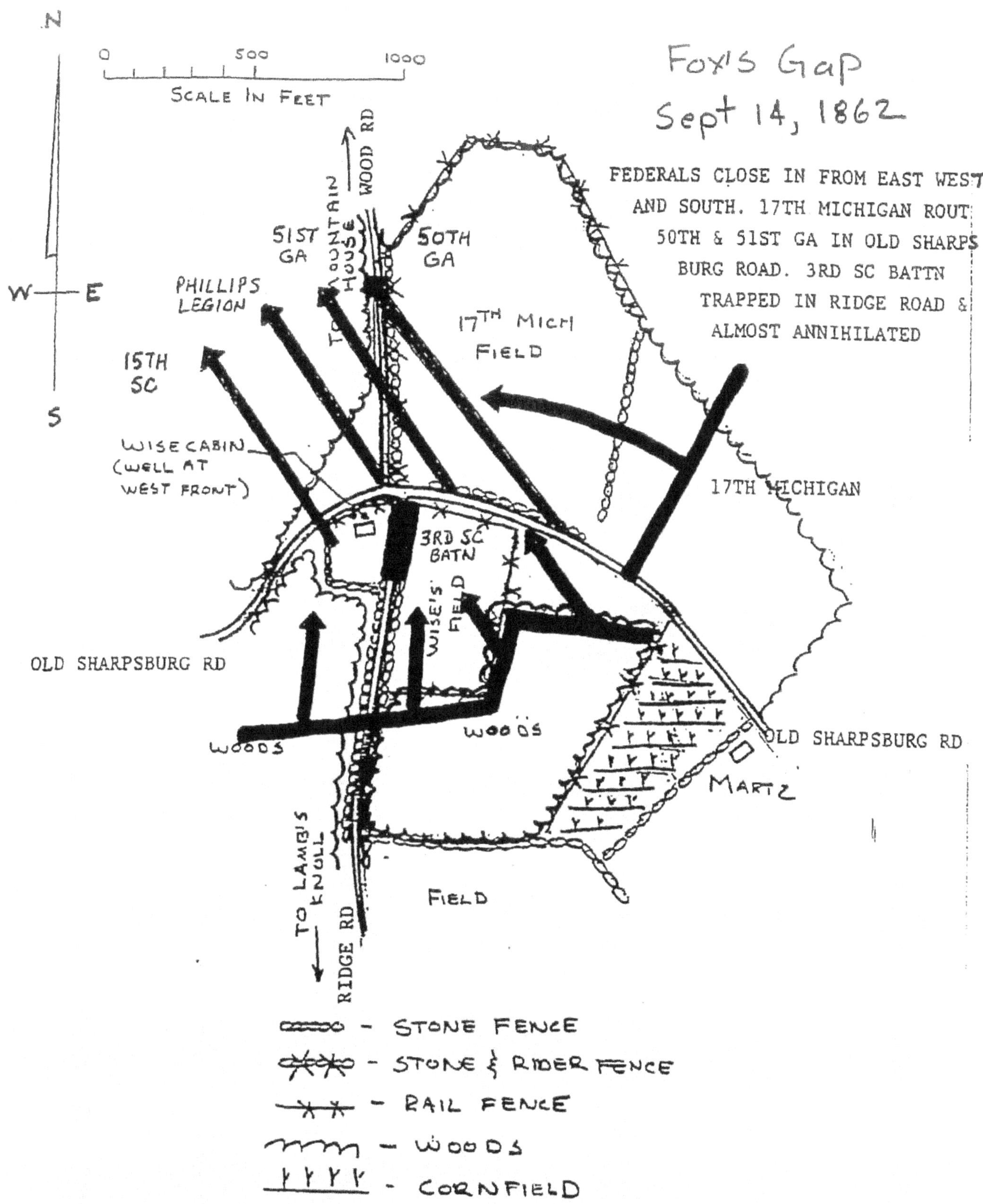

Confederate Forces Overwhelmed by Federals

Approximately 4:45 PM to 5:15 PM

fierce, but I felt that my regiment must be brought out of that pocket at all hazards and I started (forward) to warn it, when I found it retreating."

Not everyone made it out. Stubborn Lt. Colonel George James of the 3td Battalion refused to retreat and kept his unit between the stone walls of the Ridge Road. This proved to be a fatal error, as 136 of his 160-man unit became casualties. James was shot in the chest and died on the field later that evening. Many other pockets of dazed and exhausted rebels were scooped up by the victorious Federals. The "horror story" was not over for many of the wounded men of the 50th and 51st Georgia who lay in the Old Sharpsburg Road. George Hitchcock, a private in the 21st Massachusetts who came on the field just after the Confederate collapse wrote in his diary, "The sunken road (Old Sharpsburg Road) is literally packed with dead and dying rebels who had held so stubbornly the pass against our troops who have resistlessly swept up over the hill. Here the horrors of war were revealed as we see our heavy ammunition wagons go tearing up, right over the dead and dying, mangling many in their terrible course. The shrieks of the poor fellows were heartrending."

This account may help to explain the incredible ratio of wounded to killed among the Southerners in this battle. An examination of the casualties of most battles of the Civil War shows that the normal ratio of wounded to killed was in the area of four or five to one. This vicious fight produced 206 men killed or mortally wounded and 227 wounded in Drayton's brigade an almost unprecedented one to one ratio! An additional 210 men were captured unwounded. Casualties ranged from 85% of the surrounded and overwhelmed 3rd SC Battalion, 76% of Lt. Fleming's battered 50th, 60% of the 51st, 40% of the Phillips Legion, to 25% of the 15th SC (probably by virtue of its position on the far right of the command). The entire brigade suffered a staggering 51% loss.

What did this sacrifice buy the Southern army? Lt. Fleming asked his regimental commander, Colonel Manning, "Why we were left in such a place?" Manning replied "that he could not understand it." Major Rice of the 3rd Battalion criticized Drayton for ordering the attack, saying, "The road (Old Sharpsburg Road) in which the brigade was stationed was as all roads crossing hills, much washed and worn down, thus giving the troops therein stationed the advantage of first class breastworks. I do not know that the 15th SC and the other portion of the brigade were thus sheltered - have heard indeed that all were not - but within my vision the position was most admirable, now almost impregnable with good troops to defend to. To leave such a place was suicidal, especially when we were ordered to march through open ground and attack the enemy sheltered behind trees and rocks. This is my estimate at least, and the result proved most disastrous to the brigade and General Drayton himself, as he was soon afterwards relieved of his command." Of course, Major Rice ignores the fact that Drayton had orders from D. H. Hill to attack. At the battle of Second Manassas just two weeks earlier, General Drayton had delayed the ordered forward movement of his brigade to a critical point due to rumors of a Federal cavalry attack on his flank. He had been severely criticized for the delay in responding to orders and one can only surmise that he wasn't going to let this happen again.

The several hours "bought" by the sacrifice of Drayton's brigade did have the effect of allowing General Hood's two brigades to move into position north and west of the gap thus blocking any further Federal advance on the 14th. The time so dearly purchased allowed General Stonewall Jackson to force the surrender of the 12,000 man Harpers Ferry garrison on September 15th. This, in turn, set the state for the bloody battle of Antietam at Sharpsburg on September 17th, 1862.

I would like to express my appreciation and thanks to Mr. Steve Stotelmyer for providing the Fleming and Smith accounts as well as the key 1936 aerial photo of the gap. Steve was also generous with his time in spending a day with me examining the ground at the gap. **I am also indebted to Mr. Jim Clary and Mr. Sam Davis for providing the casualty figures for the 15th SC and the 3rd SC Battalion. As I have done with the three Georgia units, these figures were compiled by detailed examination of the compiled service records as well as letters, diaries, and casualty reports from period newspapers.**

President's Message
by Curtis Lynn Older

* **South Mountain becomes Maryland's first state battlefield!**

Please see the last page of this Newsletter for information on this great event in the history of Fox's Gap and the Battlefield of South Mountain.

* ***Braddock Road Chronicles, 1755*** compiled and annotated by Andrew J. Wahll. This book is from diaries and records of members of the Braddock Expedition and others arranged in a day by day chronology. Wahll mentions my book, *The Braddock Expedition and Fox's Gap in Maryland*, in his book. Published in 1999, 489 pp., illus., maps, paper, $39.00, #W034, from Heritage Books, Inc. I have not seen this book but hope to view a copy on my next trip to Maryland.

* ***The Braddock Expedition and Fox's Gap in Maryland*** by Curtis L. Older will again be available in print. Willow Bend Books in Westminster, Maryland, will schedule a reprint of the book sometime during the remainder of this year.

Kodak Photo CD-Rom Computer Disc - "Fox's Gap in Maryland"

* Several years ago I created a 100 photograph Kodak Photo CD-Rom disc entitled, "Fox's Gap in Maryland." The disc contains photos related to members of the Frederick Fox family and some of their descendants. It includes photos of the Fox Inn, the Reno Monument, copies of wills, maps related to western Maryland, and tombstone photographs, among many other items. Within the past year I have been able to obtain a CD-Rom Writer that will duplicate the disc inexpensively. During the past year, I started a campaign to distribute the disc to individuals and organizations that indicated they would like to receive a copy. I also distributed along with the disc an archive quality printout of the Index, which is included on the disc. The Index describes all the items that appear on the disc.

The following organizations or individuals received a free copy of my Kodak Photo CD-Rom Computer Disc entitled, "Fox's Gap in Maryland":

1. 8-26-99 William Fox, Grant, Michigan
2. 8-25-99 Dick Fox, Covington, Indiana
3. 8-28-99 Don Smith, Indianapolis, Indiana
4. 8-28-99 Patricia Jo Edwards, Danville, Illinois
5. 8-28-99 Alice Takase, Ft. Bliss, Texas
6. 9-2-99 James Joseph Fox, San Antonio, Texas
7. 9-7-99 Washington County Historical Society, Hagerstown, Maryland

Continued on the following page -

8.	9-7-99	Wilma M. Gose, Griffith, Indiana
9.	9-7-99	Mildred Metcalf, Salt Lake City, Utah
10.	9-9-99	Doug Bast, Boonsborough Museum of History, Boonsboro, Maryland
11.	9-13-99	Elizabeth Jane Bucholz, Devil's Lake, ND
12.	9-13-99	Bill Benner, Dayton, Ohio
13.	9-17-99	Maryland Historical Society, Baltimore, Maryland
14.	9-23-99	Waynette Brandt, Greenville, Michigan
15.	9-23-99	Michael J. Fox, Cincinnati, Ohio
16.	9-23-99	Kurt Graham, Smyrna, Georgia
17.	9-27-99	Historical Society of Frederick County, Frederick, Maryland
18.	10-07-99	Central Maryland Heritage League, Middletown, Maryland
19.	10-11-99	Reva Fox, Seattle, Washington
20.	11-1-99	William E. Fox II, Bitely, Michigan
21.	11-1-99	George D. Fox, Miamisburg, Ohio
22.	12-03-99	Ann Trimmer, Belle Mead, New Jersey
23.	12-27-99	Maryland State Archives, Annapolis, Maryland
24.	3-5-00	Terri A. Woods, Westerville, Ohio
25.	3-5-00	Gerald Robert Fox, Valparaiso, Indiana
26.	3-5-00	Suella Jane Fenton, Milpitas, California
27.	4-3-00	Peggy Ellen Gallahue, Wabash, Indiana

If you are a member of the Society and have not received a free copy of the disc and would like to receive one, please let me know. I will be happy to send one to you.

* Included within this issue of the Newsletter, beginning on page 19, is an article on "The Children of Daniel Alexander Fox and Elizabeth Jane Ricketts". The article lists all descendants of Ethel Belle Fox, Ruby Dale Fox, and Kenneth Benjamin Fox. The listings for the descendants of William Edward Fox and Ernest Daniel Fox are not complete. I hope to include the remainder of their descendants in an article in the December 2000 Newsletter.

Bound Volume of the First Ten Fox Society Newsletters to be made available in December

* After publication of the Fox Society Newsletter Issue 10, Volume 1, December 1, 2000, I will bind all of the first ten Newsletters published by the Society into a single volume. Please contact me if you would like to purchase a copy of the bound volume that will contain these first ten Newsletters. I estimate the price will be about $10.00, plus the cost of postage and packaging. I will create a Master Index for the first ten Newsletters that will be at the end of the bound volume. I am not sure at this time how the ten issues will be bound, but I am presently thinking about some type of spiral binding. The Newsletter for June 1, 2001, will be Issue 1, in Volume 2.

Six New Members Join the Society the Past Six Months!

* The year 2000 got off to a great start with the addition of six new members. See the following page for the names, addresses, and ancestors of our newest members.

Welcome New Members!

We extend a hearty welcome to six new members of the Society who joined since our last Society Newsletter on December 1, 1999. These members represent a number of new lines of descent from Frederick Fox not previously represented in the Fox Society. This is a great way to start the new year.

Robert Benner is a descendant of Mary Magdalena Fox, a daughter of Frederick Fox, who married Jacob Benner II. Information on Mary Magdalena Fox and Jacob Benner II appears on page 57 of *The Fox Genealogy* by Daniel Gebhart Fox.

Terri A. Woods is a descendant of Christiana Fox, a daughter of Frederick Fox, who married George Mettert or Metherd II. Her ancestors include Chancy Chrisman and Bertha Stiver who appear on page 22 of *The Fox Genealogy* by Daniel Gebhart Fox.

Gerald Robert Fox is a descendant of George Fox, a son of Frederick Fox. Information on George Fox and his wife, Elizabeth Ann Link, appears on page 82 of *The Fox Genealogy* by Daniel Gebhart Fox.

Suella Jane Fenton is a descendant of George Fox, a son of Frederick Fox. Her ancestors include Frederick L. Fox, a brother of John L. Fox of Vermillion County, Indiana.

Peggy Ellen Gallahue is the mother of Terri A. Woods and descends from Christiana Fox, a daughter of Frederick Fox, who married George Mettert or Metherd II.

Anne Elizabeth Edgecombe is a descendant of Elizabeth Fox, a daughter of Frederick Fox, who married John Leiter. Information on John Leiter and Elizabeth Fox appears on page 138 of *The Fox Genealogy* by Daniel Gebhart Fox.

Name and Address	Telephone	Date Joined	Member #
Robert Eugene Benner 8677 Cook Street Montague, Michigan 49437	xxx-894-6651	December 1, 1999	0029
Terri A. Woods 970 E. College Ave. Westerville, OH 43081-2509	xxx-xxx-xxxx	February 18, 2000	0030
Gerald Robert Fox 506 N 300 E Valparaiso, IN 46383	219-531-2852	February 22, 2000	0031
Suella Jane Fenton 325 San Miguel Ct. #3 Milpitas, CA 95035	408-263-8348	February 24, 2000	0032
Peggie Ellen Gallahue 1263 Richmond Drive Wabash, IN 46992	xxx-563-1459	March 24, 2000	0033
Anne Elizabeth Edgecombe 973 Buchon St. San Luis Obispo, CA 93401	xxx-594-1891	April 5, 2000	0034

Frederick L. Fox Line
Listing of descendants researched by Suella Fenton. Material submitted by Alice Takase.

Frederick L. Fox was a son of George Fox and Elizabeth Ann (Link) Fox. He was a grandson of Frederick Fox of Fox's Gap in Maryland. He was a brother of John L. Fox of Gessie, Indiana.

Descendants of Frederick L. Fox

Generation No. 3

5. Francis "Frank" Marion[6] Fox (Samuel[5], Frederick Link[4], George "1"[3], Frederick, "1"[2], John "1" Frederick[1]) was born March 18, 1873, and died March 05, 1955 in Waynesville, Ohio. He married Grace F. Johnson January 03, 1900.

Children of Francis Fox and Grace Johnson are:

20. i. Marion Johnson[7] Fox, b. January 03, 1901.
21. ii. Kenneth Lynn Fox, b. November 23, 1903.
22. iii. Leonard Orville Fox, b. June 03, 1907.
23. iv. Grace "Jeannette" Fox, b. July 12, 1910.
24. v. Harold C. "Bus" Fox, b. April 19, 1913.
vi. Verdena Arlene Fox, b. October 10, 1914; m. Jack Mardis.
25. vii. Marvin L. Fox, b. October 08, 1917.
26. viii. Lyle Scott Fox, b. June 09, 1924.

6. Mary Sophia[6] Fox (Samuel[5], Frederick Link[4], George "1"[3], Frederick, "1"[2], John "1" Frederick[1]) was born July 07, 1874 in Franklin, Warren Co., Ohio, and died 1956 in Springboro, Warren Co., Ohio. She married Rufus Hamilton Taylor April 17, 1901.

Children of Mary Fox and Rufus Taylor are:

i. Grace Eliza[7] Taylor, b. April 18, 1902,; d. September 21, 1994.
Notes for Grace Eliza Taylor:
Never married.
ii. Lawrence Hugh Taylor, b. June 30, 1903; d. February 14, 1998, Montgomery County, Ohio.
Notes for Lawrence Hugh Taylor:
Never married. Had Alzeimers, was put into a nursing home with sister Grace.
iii. Nellie Viol Taylor, b. August 16, 1904; m. Charles Hutchinson.

27. iv. Merle Rufus Taylor, b. august 20, 1905.
v. Calvin Jesse Taylor, b. December 05, 1906; d. 1907, infancy.
Notes for Calvin Jesse Taylor: Died in infancy.
vi. Lester Samuel Taylor, b. May 23, 1908; m. Helen Leiter Eyer.
vii. Roy Elmer Taylor, b. December 13, 1910; d. 1911, infancy.
Notes for Roy Elmer Taylor: Died in infancy.

7. Elmira "Myra" R.[6] Fox (Samuel[5], Frederick Link[4], George "1"[3], Frederick, "1"[2], John "1" Frederick[1]) was born August 17, 1875, and died April 19, 1914. She married James K. Wright.

Children of Elmira Fox and James Wright are:
28. i. Ruth Irene[7] Wright, b. January 01, 1908.
ii. Hazel Gladys Wright, b. February 26, 1909.

8. Orissa J.[6] Fox (Samuel[5], Frederick Link[4], George "1"[3], Frederick, "1"[2], John "1" Frederick[1]) was born April 08, 1877 in Warren County, Ohio, and died January 13, 1963 in Springboro, Warren County, Ohio. She married William Everett Hayner April 06, 1904 in Warren County, Ohio, son of John Hayner and Julia Kesling.

Notes for William Everett Hayner:

William Everton Hayner, known as Everton was born on a farm owned and built by his parents, John Puter & Julie (Kesling) Hayner. He lived there and farmed the land until his death. He went to Salem School, a one room school house, in Clearcreek Twp., Springboro, Warren County, Ohio. He helped his Uncle Asher Borden farm his land in Franklin, Ohio. There he met the neighbor, Orissa Fox, whom later became his wife. Orissa helped his Aunt Fannie with the housework and cooking. Everton had a stroke, was feeling better and got up and moved around for a short period of time, then later had another stroke and never recovered from it.

Children of Orissa Fox and William Hayner are:

i. Verna Mae Hayner, b. March 11, 1905, Springboro, Warren Co., Ohio; d. December 28, 1970, Springboro, Warren Co., Ohio; m. George Anderson Sidenstick, October 28, 1933, Lebanon, Warren Co., Ohio.

Notes for Verna Mae Hayner:

Verna went to Salem School, a one room school, through the eighth Grade. Then she went to Springboro High School and graduated in 1923. She helped her father on the farm. She worked at the Mutual Furniture Company, in Miamisburg, Ohio, 1926-1933. She married George Sidenstick at the Presbyterian Church in Lebanon, Ohio,. They lived on several farms throughout Springboro, until Verna's mother (Orissa) bought a farm on Crossley Road, from the money she received from her mother Eliza Fox's estate. George & Verna farmed this land until George got a job working for D. P. & L. Recreation Park as a grounds care-taker. At that time, 1944 - Lawrence & Ruby (Hayner) Leis, Verna's sister, moved onto the farm, which is still (1997) in the possession of their seven children. Later George bought a corner lot (across the road from Verna's parents) from Ira Kesling. They lived there until her mother died, and they moved into her house, and sold their own home. The farm built by John Puter & Julie (Kesling) Hayner on Red Lion Five-Points Road, is still (1997) in the possession of their seven great-grandchildren. Verna was a very good gardener and artist. She died with cancer, in 1970. George later married her cousin Ester Brown.

29. ii. Ruby Jeanette Hayner, b. August 07, 1906, Springboro, Warren Co., Ohio; d. December 28, 1983, Springboro, Warren Co., Ohio, buried in Springboro Cemetery.

9. Walter Scott[6] Fox (Samuel[5], Frederick Link[4], George "1"[3], Frederick, "1"[2], John "1" Frederick[1]) was born May 26, 1880 in Warren County, Ohio, and died July 08, 1917. Buried in Springboro Cemetery, Warren County, Ohio. He married Agnes Mae Voegele December 28, 1905.

Children of Walter Fox and Agnes Voegele are:

i. Walter Scott[7] Fox, Jr.

Notes for Walter Scott Fox, Jr.: Died in infancy.

30. ii. Dorethea Eliz Fox, b. July 03, 1907.
31. iii. Woodrow Wilson Fox, b. March 03, 1913.

iv. Wintella Mae Fox, b. March 03, 1913.

Notes for Wintella Mae Fox: Died in infancy.

10. Clarence David[6] Brown (Frances A.[5], Frederick Link[4], George "1"[3], Frederick, "1"[2], John "1" Frederick[1]) was born April 18, 1883 in Ohio, and died January 23, 1972 in Carlisle, Ohio. He married Ardella Mae "Della" Metherd March 09, 1909 in Luthern Church, Franklin, Ohio by Rev. C. F. Marker, daughter of Isaac Metherd and Bena Hahn.

Notes for Clarence David Brown: Clarence as the father of Goldie Metherd, born in 1912. Goldie is the daughter of Lola, a sister of Ardella, the wife of Clarence.

Children of Clarence Brown and Ardella Metherd are:

32. i. Lewis Marion[7] Brown, b. April 30, 1910, southeast of Miamisburg, Ohio; d. January 25, 1998, Ohio.
33. ii. Ada Luella Brown, b. April 14, 1912, southeast of Miamisburg, Ohio.
34. iii. Ester Esterlla Brown, b. August 30, 1913, Springboro, Warren County, Ohio.
35. iv. Ethel May Brown, b. August 30, 1913, Springboro, Warren County, Ohio.
36. v. Walter Howard Brown, b. January 23, 1918, Carlisle, Ohio.
37. vi. Lester Isaac "Ike" Brown, b. May 16, 1920, Carlisle, Ohio; d. August 09, 1967.
38. vii. Raymond Brown, b. December 28, 1924, West Carrollton, Ohio.
39. viii. Mary Kathryn Brown, b. April 08, 1926, west Carrollton, Ohio.

11. Florence E.[6] Brown (Samuel[5], Frederick Link[4], George "1"[3], Frederick, "1"[2], John "1" Frederick[1]). She married Daniel "1" Eckhart.

Children of Florence Brown and Daniel Eckhart are:

i. David[7] Eckhart.
ii. Daniel "2" Eckhart.
iii. Liddy Eckhart.
iv. Elizabeth Eckhart.

12. Laura Etta[6] Fox (Jacob "Job" Henry[5], Frederick Link[4], George "1"[3], Frederick, "1"[2], John "1" Frederick[1]) was born July 24, 1881 in Warren County, Ohio, and died May 10, 1955 in Montgomery County, Ohio. She married Herbert Weidel.

Children of Laura Fox and Herbert Weidel are:

40. i. Harry R.[7] Weidel.
41. ii. Hazel Weidel, b. 1899; d. 1965.
42. iii. Irvin Weidel.

43. iv. Carl Z. Weidel, b. December 21, 1904; d. August 14, 1980, buried Butler Memorial Park, Trenton Rt. 73, Ohio.

13. Ana Marie[6] Fox (Jacob "Job" Henry[5], Frederick Link[4], George "1"[3], Frederick, "1"[2], John "1" Frederick[1]) was born November 20, 1882 in Warren County, Ohio, and died 1960 in Montgomery County, Ohio. She married William R. "1" Chenewoth.

Children of Anna Fox and William Chenewoth are:

44. i. Reber[7] Fox, b. 1904; d. 1976.
45. ii. Jack A. Chenewoth, b. January 21, 1919.
46. iii. William R. "2" Chenewoth, b. March 15, 1928.

14. John "Henry"[6] Fox (Jacob "Job" Henry[5], Frederick Link[4], George "1"[3], Frederick, "1"[2], John "1" Frederick[1]) was born September 05, 1884 in Warren County, Ohio, and died 1968 in Montgomery County, Ohio. He married (1) Belle Montgomery. He married (2) Linnie Heelman.

Child of John Fox and Belle Montgomery is:
i. Harold[7] Fox, b. 1909; d. 1920, Drown.

15. Edwin E.[6] Fox (Jacob "Job" Henry[5], Frederick Link[4], George "1"[3], Frederick, "1"[2], John "1" Frederick[1]) was born November 04, 1888 in Warren County, Ohio, and died November 21, 1969 in Montgomery County, Ohio. He married (1) Mary (Fox). He married (2) Eva Irene Robinson April 10, 1915.

Child of Edwin Fox and Eva Robinson is:
47. i. James Norman[7] Fox, b. March 29, 1918.

16. Lucy May Fox (Jacob "Job" Henry[5], Frederick Link[4], George "1"[3], Frederick, "1"[2], John "1" Frederick[1]) was born April 04, 1892 in Warren County, Ohio, and died December 28, 1974 in Pittsburgh, Pennsylvania. She married Charles William "1" Beachler April 15, 1913, son of George Beachler and Catherine Heitman.

Notes for Lucy May Fox: Information on Lucy (Fox) Beachler family was given to me by Dorothy (Beachler) Hoskins of Arizona.

Children of Lucy Fox and Charles Beachler are:

48. i. Dorothy May[7] Beachler, b. January 26, 1914, Miamisburg, Montgomery County, Ohio.
ii. Oscar Edwin Beachler, b. June 10, 1915, Miamisburg, Montgomery County, Ohio; d. July 07, 1969, Dayton, Montgomery County, Ohio.
49. iii. Charles Monroe Beachler, b. June 24, 1917, Miamisburg, Montgomery County, Ohio; d. December 11, 1986, Sarasota, Florida.

17. Katheryn Myrtle[6] Fox (Jacob "Job" Henry[5], Frederick Link[4], George "1"[3], Frederick, "1"[2], John "1" Frederick[1]) was born October 25, 1893 in Warren County, Ohio, and died May 22, 1994 in Warren County, Ohio. She married Alpha "Harold" Montgomery May 22, 1915.

Children of Katheryn Fox and Alpha Montgomery are:
i. Gladys Angeline[7] Montgomery, b. March 08, 1916, Warren County, Ohio; d. Warren County, Ohio; m. (1) Shirl Stanton, March 18, 1939; m. (2) Frank Norton, June 21, 1973.
ii. George Glen Montgomery, b. November 20, 1918, Warren County, Ohio; d. December 08, 1918, Warren County, Ohio.

50. iii. Harold Everett Montgomery, b. May 16, 1921, Warren County, Ohio.
51. iv. Robert Eugene Montgomery, b. September 11, 1926, Warren County, Ohio.

18. Lydia "Liddy" Z.[6] Fox (Jacob "Job" Henry[5], Frederick Link[4], George "1"[3], Frederick, "1"[2], John "1" Frederick[1]) was born November 04, 1895 in Montgomery County, Ohio, and died 1962 in Montgomery County, Ohio. She married Millard Degler.

Child of Lydia Fox and Millard Degler is:
52. i. Robert Degler.

19. Cloyce "Wilford"[6] Fox (Jacob "Job" Henry[5], Frederick Link[4], George "1"[3], Frederick, "1"[2], John "1" Frederick[1]) was born June 04, 1899 in Warren County, Ohio, and died October 30, 1976 in Warren County, Ohio. He married Mary Irene Bennett April 26, 1926 in Warren County, Ohio.

Child of Cloyce Fox and Mary Bennett is:
53. i. Kenneth Wilfred[7] Fox, b. December 25, 1927.

Fox's Gap Section
by Curtis L. Older

The North Carolina South Mountain Monument

A new monument is destined for Fox's Gap. The North Carolina South Mountain Monument is well on its way toward realization. Headed by the Living History Association of Mecklenburg, Inc., the North Carolina South Mountain Monument Fund is raising $60,000 to erect a monument to the soldiers from North Carolina who fought in the Battle of South Mountain, September 14, 1862. The monument will be placed not far from the Reno Monument at Fox's Gap and will be the first monument on the battlefield that will honor Confederate troops at South Mountain. North Carolina troops at Fox's Gap included the 1st, 2nd, 3rd, 4th, 5th, 6th, 12th, 13th, 14th, 15th, 20th, 23rd, and 30th Infantry Regiments and the 1st North Carolina Artillery, Manly and Reilly Batteries.

Rex Hovey, President of the Board of Directors of the Living History Association of Mecklenburg, Inc., recently spoke to the Piedmont Civil War Round Table in Charlotte, NC. He described the Battle of South Mountain, with emphasis on the fighting at Fox's Gap, and the efforts of his organization to raise the $60,000 necessary to build the monument at Fox's Gap. The area of Fox's Gap is presently being restored to the condition it was in at the time of the battle. Few trees were in the area of what is today the Reno Monument at the time of the battle. A pathway is planned to connect the various monuments at Fox's Gap. The use of highway markers will lead visitors along a route that will enable them to tour the entire battlefield, from Turner's Gap all the way to Crampton's Gap.

George Fox Line
by Curtis L. Older

A number of Society members descend from Daniel Alexander Fox and Elizabeth Jane (Ricketts) Fox. Daniel Alexander Fox was a son of John L. Fox of Gessie, Indiana, and a grandson of George Fox. Daniel and Elizabeth Jane Fox had five children: Ruby Dale Fox, Ethel Belle Fox, Kenneth Benjamin Fox, William Edward Fox, and Ernest Daniel Fox. The following article lists all of the descendants of Ethel Belle Fox, Ruby Dale Fox, and Kenneth Benjamin Fox. The listings for the descendants of William Edward Fox and Ernest Daniel Fox are not complete. I hope to include the remainder of the descendants of William Edward Fox and Ernest Daniel Fox in an article in the December 2000 Newsletter.

The Children of Daniel Alexander Fox and Elizabeth Jane Ricketts

Ruby Dale Fox was born Dec. 13, 1896, in Highland Township, Vermillion County, Indiana, and died Nov. 12, 1990, in Grand Rapids, Michigan. She married Everett Hines on Apr. 10, 1920, in Covington, Indiana. He was born July 30, 1894, and died Apr. 5, 1963. Both are buried at Lower Mound Cemetery west of Covington, Indiana. Everett and Ruby Hines had one daughter, Carmen Dale Hines, born Apr. 21, 1921, in Gessie, Indiana. Carmen Hines married Wayne Lawson Abernathey on Nov. 16, 1940, in Louisville, Kentucky. He was the son of Harrison Abernathey and Mary Lawson. He was born Oct. 7, 1918, in Cates, Wabash Township, Fountain County, Indiana. He died April 14, 1957, in Covington, Indiana. Wayne and Carmen Abernathey adopted one daughter, Waynette Dale Abernathey, who was born July 4, 1955, in Danville, Illinois. Waynette married Michael Brandt. Waynette and Michael Brandt had one son, Carter Brandt.

Ernest Daniel Fox was born Dec. 1, 1885, near Gessie, Vermillion County, Indiana. He married Lola Frances Jackson on Jan. 8, 1908, in Vermilion County, Illinois. She was born Jan. 1, 1890, and died June 28, 1943. Ernest died Oct. 3, 1940, at Lakeview Hospital in Danville, Illinois. He is buried at Niccum Cemetery in Vermilion County, Illinois. The children of Ernest Daniel Fox and his wife Lola Frances Jackson were: Claude Ernest Fox, Kenneth Leslie Fox, and Ruth Ethel Fox.

Claude Ernest Fox, born Jan. 8, 1910, in Gessie, Indiana; He married Elizabeth Pauline Pearson on Dec. 14, 1929, in Covington, Fountain County, Indiana. Her parents were Francis Marion Pearson and Martha Estel Raypole. She was born Apr. 6, 1911, in Snoddy's Mill, Fountain County, Indiana. Claude Ernest Fox died June 24, 1962, in Muskegon, Muskegon County, Michigan. He is buried at Restlawn Cemetery, Muskegon, Michigan. Claude and Elizabeth Fox had two sons: Robert Claude Fox, born Sept. 29, 1930, in Perrysville, Indiana; and William Ernest Fox, born March 25, 1936, at Gessie, Indiana.

Kenneth Leslie Fox was born Nov. 27, 1912, in Gessie, Indiana. He is buried in Niccum Cemetery, Vermilion County, Illinois. Kenneth married Mary Frances Wichman. She was born July 25, 1915, in Danville, Illinois. She died Aug. 31, 1994. Her parents were Fred F. Wichman and Matilda Meinke. Kenneth and Mary Fox had one child, Larry Harold Fox, born Dec. 18, 1934.

Ruth Estel Fox was born June 15, 1914, in Gessie, Indiana. She married Frank Berton Moss on Nov. 26, 1934, in Covington, Indiana. She died June 19, 1987, and is buried with her husband. Frank Berton Moss was born Apr. 11, 1913, in Vermilion County, Illinois. He died Aug. 2, 1990, in Danville, Illinois, and is buried in the Old Walnut Corner Cemetery near Danville. His parents were Rolla Oliver Moss and Merle Hoover. Frank and Ruth Moss were the parents of one child: Marcia Marlene Moss, born May 3, 1937.

Continued on the following page -

William Edward Fox was born Jan. 5, 1888, and died Apr. 16, 1974. He married Marguerite Clem on Feb. 10, 1909, in Danville, Illinois. She was born Mar. 9, 1894, in Mound Township, Warren County, Indiana. She died Jan. 27, 1970, at Danville, Illinois. Her parents were Augustus Elmer Clem and Malinda Lloyd Cunningham. William and Marguerite are both buried at the Lower Mound Cemetery west of Covington, Indiana. William and Marguerite Fox had the following children: Reva Winfred Fox, Evelyn Louise Fox, Glenn Fox, Daniel Augustus Fox, Melinda Lloyd Fox, Elizabeth Jane Fox (Bucholz), Wilma Marion Fox (Gose), Richard Dale Fox, Sr., and James Hebert Fox, Sr.

Reva Winfred Fox was born May 23, 1910, in Gessie, Indiana, and did not marry.

Evelyn Louise Fox was born Sept. 15, 1913, in Mound Township, Warren County, Indiana, and died Oct. 9, 1991, at Williamsport, Warren County, Indiana. She married Jesse Frank Switzer on Aug. 13, 1933. He as born July 17, 1911, in Baltimore Maryland, and died Apr. 26, 1991. Both are buried at Lower Mound Cemetery. Children of Evelyn Fox and Jesse Switzer are: Barry Monroe Switzer, born Dec. 5, 1934; Chester Dean Switzer, born Sept. 29, 1936, and Patricia Jo Switzer, born Sept. 19, 1938.

Glenn Fox was born Feb. 1, 1916. He died Aug. 12, 1975, in Denver, Colorado. He married Betty Dune on Dec. 11, 1943, in Newfoundland. The child of Glenn Fox and Betty Dune is Glenna Joe Fox who was born June 9, 1944.

Daniel Augustus Fox was born Dec. 10, 1917, in Gessie, Indiana, and died Jan. 13, 1954, at Wallace, Fountain County, Indiana. He married Stella Marie Gooding on Jan. 17, 1939, in Covington, Indiana. She was the daughter of Monroe Gooding and Laura Sackmire. She was born Apr. 1, 1918, in Wallace, Fountain County, Indiana. The child of Daniel A. Fox and Stella Gooding is Daniel Wayne Fox, Sr., born Jan. 24, 1944, in Crawfordsville, Montgomery County, Indiana.

Melinda Lloyd Fox was born Jan. 19, 1919, and died Feb. 8, 1919.

Elizabeth Jane Fox was born Apr. 14, 1922. She married Alvin Joseph Bucholz on Nov. 17, 1944, in Rossville, Walker County, Georgia. He was the son of Ferdinand Bucholz and Mary Schubert. He was born Nov. 17, 1912, in Sarles, Dash Township, Towner County, North Dakota. Children of Elizabeth Jane Fox and Alvin Bucholz are: Jerry Lee Bucholz, born Sept. 29, 1945, at Ft. Oglethorpe, Walker County, Georgia; Bonnie Leah Bucholz, born Oct. 31, 1946, at Devils Lake, Ramsey County, North Dakota; and Larry Leo Bucholz, born Feb. 8, 1960, in Cando, Towner County, North Dakota.

Wilma Marion Fox was born Oct. 11, 1928, at Foster, Mound Township, Warren County, Indiana. She married Anton Keith Gose on Jan. 11, 1946, in Covington, Indiana. He was the son of Anton Gose and Opal Cunningham. He was born May 22, 1923, in Covington, Indiana, and died Feb. 7, 1979, in Chicago, Illinois. Children of Wilma Fox and Anton Gose are: Anton Keith Gose, Jr. born Jan. 5, 1947, in Danville, Illinois, and died July 30, 1973, in Griffith, Indiana; Toni Farol Gose, born Apr. 10, 1948, in Danville, Illinois.

Richard Dale Fox, Sr. was born July 20, 1933, in Mound Township, Warren County, Indiana. He married Deloris Mae Jinkins on Sept. 26, 1952, in Cates, Fountain County, Indiana. She was the daughter of Delbert Jinkins and Jennie Jones. She was born Aug. 7, 1933, in Catlin, Vermilion County, Illinois. Children of Richard and Deloris Fox are: Dellie Jean Fox, born Nov. 8, 1953, in Crawfordsville, Montgomery County, Indiana; and Richard Dale Fox, Jr., born Jan. 28, 1955, in Crawfordsville, Indiana.

James Herbert Fox was born Jan. 22, 1937, in Covington, Indiana, and died May 18, 1995, in Lakewood, Jefferson County, Colorado. He married Vere Joan Wynn on Aug.30, 1958. Children of James Fox and Vere Wynn are: James Herbert Fox, Jr., born Jan. 30, 1959; Carl Timothy Fox, born July 12, 1960; Kelly Joan Fox, born Nov. 28, 1961, in Danville, Illinois, died Apr. 29, 1962, in Danville, Illinois; and Brian Anthony Fox, born Dec. 31, 1963, in Illinois.

Continued on the following page -

Ethel Belle Fox was born October 6, 1892, on the Daniel Alexander Fox farm one mile north east of Gessie, Indiana. She married Robert William Gouty on February 2, 1917. Robert was the son of Joseph P. Gouty and Luella M. Hartman. Robert William Gouty was born August 26, 1889, near Gessie, Indiana. Robert and Ethel (Fox) Gouty had one child, Mavis Lorene Gouty. Mavis was born April 11, 1918, on the Daniel Alexander Fox farm. Robert William Gouty died June 4, 1949, at Lakeview Hospital in Danville, Illinois, from spinal meningitis. Ethel Belle (Fox) Gouty died January 25, 1971, after spending a number of years in a nursing home due to a stroke.

Mavis Lorene Gouty married Truxton James Older on September 1, 1938, in Danville, Illinois. Truxton was the son of Roy Burton Older and Ethel Leona (Worth) Older. He was born September 28, 1911. Truxton and Mavis (Gouty) Older had one son, Curtis Lynn Older, who was born November 5, 1947, in Danville, Illinois, at Lakeview Hospital. Mavis Lorene (Gouty) Older died August 17, 1986.

Curtis Lynn Older married Linda Sue Osborn on May 5, 1979, in Indianapolis, Indiana. Linda is the daughter of Harold Emerson Osborn and Patty Lou Pennington. She was born February 24, 1954, in Albuquerque, New Mexico. Curtis and Linda (Osborn) Older have one daughter, Rachael Lynn Older who was born March 20, 1987, in Duluth, Minnesota.

Kenneth Benjamin Fox was born Nov. 17, 1882, in Gessie, Highland Township, Vermillion County, Indiana. He died Sept. 30, 1971, in Richmond, Indiana. He married Virgie Butche on March 26, 1910. VirgieButche was born Aug. 4, 1885. She died Nov. 2, 1983, in Salt Lake City, Utah. Kenneth and Virgia Fox had one daughter, Mildred Fox, who was born Oct. 3, 1912. Mildred Fox married John Winthrop Metcalf on June 18, 1936. John Winthrop Metcalf was born Nov. 4, 1910, and died May 19, 1984. John Metcalf and Mildred Fox had two sons: Donald Warren Metcalf and Thomas James Metcalf.

Donald Warren Metcalf was born Mar. 12, 1940. He married 1st: Ramona Ortega, April 6, 1960. Divorced, 1972. Two sons from first marriage: Thomas Arthur Metcalf, born Oct. 20, 1961; John Albert Metcalf, born Dec. 15, 1963. He married 2nd: Rikki Watts, Sept. 16, 1982. One daughter: Erin Jeanne Metcalf, born Oct. 21, 1985.

Dr. Thomas James Metcalf was born Oct. 14, 1942. He married Karen Mae McClain, Sept. 21, 1968. Two sons and one daughter: Ian Todd Metcalf, born May 20, 1971; Timothy Sean Metcalf, born Oct. 11, 1972; and Sarah Lynn Metcalf, born Apr. 25, 1974, adopted from Korea on 3rd birthday in 1977. Dr. Thomas Metcalf graduated from Stanford Medical School.

Please notify

the President of the Society

regarding any errors you find in the current issue of the Newsletter.

Topics in the next issue of the Newsletter, December 1, 2000

* 1. An Index for the first 10 Society Newsletters.
* 2. From the Bookshelf - A new section devoted to book reviews.
* 3. The will of John L. Fox of Vermillion County, Indiana.
* 4. Names of Confederate casualties in Drayton's Brigade during the Battle of South Mountain.
* 5. Obituary notices from newspapers related to descendants of Frederick Fox.

South Mountain

becomes

Maryland's first state battlefield

For years, South Mountain has been regarded as one of Maryland's most unrecognized historic sites. Increasingly threatened by development, it has also been designated by the federal government as one of the country's most endangered historic sites.

Maryland lawmakers took what they hope will be the first step toward preserving the battlefield and paying tribute to the soldiers who fought there by passing a bill to make South Mountain Maryland's first state battlefield.

Most of the land to be designated a state battlefield is already owned by Maryland state government and is encompassed in Gathland State Park and Washington Monument State Park.

Members of the Washington and Frederick county delegations say they don't intend to make any major changes to the current landscape or to the Appalachian Trail, which runs through the battlefield. Instead, they hope to improve access and signage at the battlefield while increasing public awareness of South Mountain.

Delegate Louise V. Snodgrass, a Frederick/Washington County Republican, said the delegations preferred designating South Mountain as a state battlefield rather than a national battlefield or park because the two state parks encompassing most of the historic area already operate with minimal budgets.

"We wanted to keep it named a battlefield and not a park because we didn't want to conjure up images of swing sets and pools. And we wanted to keep the respect" for those who died in the battle, Snodgrass said.

Index

Issue 9, Volume 1

News from Fox's Gap

News from Fox's Gap

The Society of the Descendants of Frederick Fox of Fox's Gap in Maryland

Issue 10, Volume 1 **Remember Freedom!** December 1, 2000

North Carolina South Mountain Symposium August 17, 18, and 19, 2001 Boonsboro, Maryland

by Rex Hovey, N. C. South Mountain Monument News

(Note by Curtis Older: The North Carolina South Mountain Fund will place a $60,000 monument at Fox's Gap within a few years in memory of N. C. troops who fought in the Battle of South Mountain.)

It is with great honor that we announce the North Carolina South Mountain Symposium, August 17, 18, and 19, 2001. It will be centered at the American Legion Hall in downtown Boonsboro, Md. Proceeds go to the North Carolina South Mountain Monument Fund. The Living History Association of Mecklenburg, Inc. (Charlotte, N.C.) and The Central Maryland Heritage League is presenting it.

Friday will start with tours of the Boonsboro Museum of History; the best collection of artifacts from South Mtn. Doug Bast will have the museum open for early arrivals to the symposium. Friday night is when we honor all the ancestors at a reception in Middletown, Md. Make plans to attend this special event.

Saturday begins at the Legion Hall with a full slate of nationally known speakers and authors. The following are scheduled to speak: Ed Bearss, Scott Hartwig, Steve Stotelmeyer, John Michael Priest, Kurt Graham, Clint Johnson, Lawrence Laboda and Paul Martin, III. Others have expressed an interest. Time will be available to have books signed by the authors. After an evening break, we will be served a dinner buffet of Southern food. Mr. Stan Clardy of Statesville, NC will perform his music and play.

Sunday starts at 8:30 AM at the Legion Hall in Boonsboro as we board buses for a tour of all three Gaps (Turner's, Fox's, and Crampton's). Many of the speakers above will host the tours. You will be able to get out and walk the field at each stop. Tour is over at 1:00 PM with buses returning to the Legion Hall. You have the rest of the afternoon to return to your favorite gap.

Rooms are now blocked at two hotels in the area (there are none in Boonsboro): The Four Points Sheraton in Hagerstown and the Holiday Inn, Patrick Ave., Frederick. Ask for the special rate under LHAM at each location. More information to come.

Fox Family Reunion - August 2001

A Fox Family Reunion will be held at or near Boonsboro, Maryland, on or about Friday, August 17, or Sunday, August 19, 2001. This is the same weekend as the North Carolina South Mountain Symposium. Please contact Curt Older if you think you might be able to attend. You ideas, suggestions, and attendance are needed.

Attendance at the North Carolina South Mountain Symposium is not required in order to attend the Fox Reunion. The Symposium has an attendance fee of $175. The only cost to attend the Fox Reunion will be your expense of food, motel, and travel.

We could have a Fox Reunion luncheon and meeting on either Friday or Sunday, or even both days. If you would like to visit the Fox Inn, along the Old Sharpsburg Road, I can probably arrange a visit for you through the owner of that property.

Fox's Gap is off the beaten path. However, as part of Maryland's first State Battlefield Park, it is beginning to receive the recognition it deserves. Road signs to direct one around the Battlefield of South Mountain have been installed or are supposed to be installed. I will be happy to provide maps to help you find your way around the area.

If you have not visited Fox's Gap, the Fox Inn, and the Battlefield of South Mountain, I hope you can make your first visit in August 2001.

Welcome New Members!

We extend a warm welcome to two new members of the Society who joined since our last Society Newsletter of June 1, 2000. It has been an outstanding year with the addition of eight new members.

Homer Carr Hendrickson is a descendant of Daniel Booker Fox, a son of Frederick Fox, who married Susannah Christman. His most recent ancestor who is listed in *The Fox Genealogy* is Harry Fox Hendrickson who is buried in the North Monroe Cemetery, Monroe, Butler County, Ohio.

Beth Ellen Davis is a descendant of Mary Magdalena Fox, a daughter of Frederick Fox, who married Jacob Benner. Her most recent ancestor who is listed in *The Fox Genealogy* is Daniel Benner who is buried in Hicks Cemetery, Perrysville, Indiana.

Name and Address	Telephone	Date Joined	Member #
Homer Carr Hendrickson 876 West Turtlecreek Union Road Lebanon, Ohio 45036	513-932-6577	August 30, 2000	0035
Beth Ellen Davis 8355 Camfield Circle Colorado Springs, Colorado 80920	719-282-9741	October 7, 2000	0036

President's Message
by Curtis Lynn Older

- * Can you name the President of the United States who held the office immediately before Abraham Lincoln? If you are unsure of the events during the six months that lead up to the start of the American Civil War, I recommend that you read **Days of Defiance - Sumter, Secession, and the Coming of the Civil War** by Maury Klein. My review of this book appears on page 4. You'll find out about the battle for Washington, the battle over secession, the battle over Fort Sumter, and you'll find out who was President of the United States immediately before Lincoln.

- * We are fortunate to present, on pages 22 through 30 of this Newsletter, another great article by Kurt Graham on the Battle of South Mountain. This is the third article Kurt wrote for us. We are pleased to present his latest research findings on the battle.

- * A number of obituaries from Covington, Indiana, area newspapers are included in this Newsletter. Unfortunately, I do not know the newspaper or newspapers these obituaries appeared in nor their date of publication. They are presented because they provide published information about ancestors of some of our Society members.

- * This Newsletter, which is Issue 10, Volume 1, is the last Newsletter that will be included in Volume 1. The next Newsletter, June 1, 2001, will be Issue 1 of Volume 2. All of the first ten Newsletters that make up Volume 1 will be bound into a single volume.

  The bound volume of the first ten Fox Society Newsletters will contain a Master Index that will enable readers to find key words within any of the 10 Newsletters. I am not sure at this time how the ten issues will be bound, but I am thinking about some type of spiral binding. I estimate the price will be about $10.00, plus the cost of postage and packaging. I anticipate donating copies of the first bound volume to several libraries or historical societies in Maryland.

- * Copies of ***The Fox Genealogy*** by Daniel Gebhart Fox are available. See page twelve of this Newsletter for information on how to obtain a copy.

Table of Contents for this Newsletter

From The Bookshelf
by Curtis L. Older

Days of Defiance
Sumter, Secession, and the Coming of the Civil War
by Maury Klein

If you seek a splendid review of the key individuals and events during the six months leading up to the initiation of hostilities in the American Civil War, this is probably about as good an account as you will find. Klein reviews the period of time from the election of Abraham Lincoln to the surrender of Fort Sumter in Charleston harbor, a period of approximately 5 months. He divides his work into three major sections: The Battle for Washington, The Battle Over Secession, and The Battle Over Fort Sumter. The first section reviews events in Washington, DC, during November and December of 1860. The Battle Over Secession covers events in January and February of 1861 and The Battle Over Fort Sumter describes the events of March and April of 1861 and the outbreak of hostilities.

What is an American? *Days of Defiance* addresses this question by focusing on individuals and their beliefs at the time of the greatest crisis in American history. Klein describes in clear detail the thoughts and views of many key individuals who took part in the events leading to our national Civil War. This is a great book for anyone who wants to identify those key individuals, their beliefs, and the events that propelled the nation through the final months that led to the start of the war.

Few Americans seem to be able to name the President of the United States who served immediately prior to Abraham Lincoln. The man was James Buchanan. President Buchanan was a man of compromise at a time when the nation, both North and South, was no longer willing to compromise. The issue of slavery, which the founding fathers of the nation had tiptoed around in the late 1700s, had come front and center stage. The nation was split into two camps, one pro-slavery and the other anti-slavery. Neither section of the nation, North nor South, wanted to yield control of the United States Senate, or for that matter control of anything else, to the opposing section of the nation.

Northerners called them the "chivalry". The chivalry ruled the South. "The cult of chivalry assumed many forms: cults of manners, of women, of the military, of oratory, of medieval pageantry, and of the code duello." There was one salient point that lay at the foundation of chivalry; it always came back to race. The South had come to view itself as a nation of the right people, by the right people, and for the right people.

Ward Lamon, Lincoln's law partner in Danville, Illinois, accompanied the new president to Washington. With his inauguration, Lincoln was faced immediately with both the threat and the reality of Southern states claiming to secede from the Union. South Carolina was at the forefront of the movement. Would other border states, such as Virginia, secede?

Events of early 1861 moved the nation into the quandary of having to deal with two major issues, slavery and secession. "Negotiation could not succeed because there was nothing to negotiate, on either slavery or secession. On these intractable issues opponents remained as far apart in March as they had in November."

Major Robert Anderson, the Union commander at Fort Sumter, was thrust, like Lincoln, into the national spotlight when the South Carolina government demanded surrender of his fort. Events at Fort Sumter came to a crescendo with the firing of the first shot of the war by Captain George S. James, at 4:30 AM, Friday, April 12, 1861. (Later, on September 14, 1862, James would be killed at Fox's Gap during the Battle of South Mountain.)

Perhaps the thoughts of Abner Doubleday, second in the Union command at Ft. Sumter, represented the view of the North. "To me it was simply a contest, politically speaking, as to whether virtue or vice should rule."

The end of slavery in the United States was a monumental achievement of the war. However, a case can be made that no result of the war was more important than the destruction of the idea of secession.

Land Tracts of the Battlefield of South Mountain
by Curtis L. Older

Each Newsletter includes a survey, patent, or deed related to the land tracts in the vicinity of Crampton's, Fox's, and Turner's Gaps. These three gaps in South Mountain represent the main area contested by the Union and Confederate Armies in the Battle of South Mountain on September 14, 1862.

Previous issues of the Society Newsletter contain descriptions of the following tracts:

June 1, 1997	Addition to Friendship of Frederick Fox
December 1, 1997	Fredericksburgh of Frederick Fox
June 1, 1998	Pick All of Bartholomew Booker
December 1, 1998	Bowser's Addition of David Bowser
June 1, 1999	Partnership of John Mansberger
December 1, 1999	Mountain of John Baley
June 1, 2000	no tract included in Newsletter

The Flonham survey record and patent record are presented in this Newsletter. The Mountain House, presently known as the Old South Mountain Inn, at Turner's Gap stands on the Flonham tract.

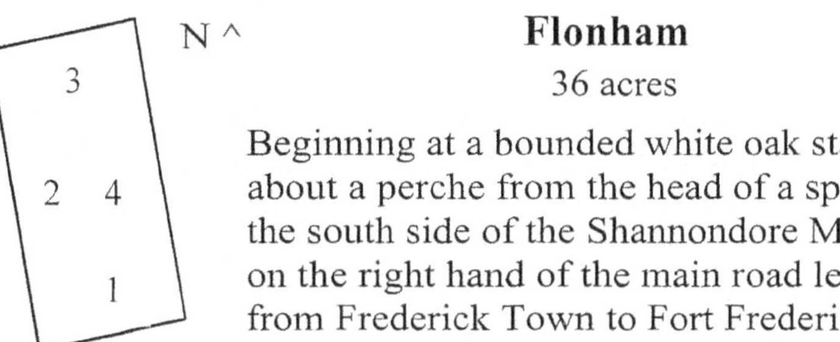
3
2 4
1
N ^
Flonham
36 acres
Beginning at a bounded white oak standing about a perche from the head of a spring on the south side of the Shannondore Mountain on the right hand of the main road leading from Frederick Town to Fort Frederick.

The Survey for Flonham - MdHR 17,458, 1-23-4-12, BC & GS 47, pp. 496-497, Philip Jacob Shafer, Flonham, surveyed 27 Aug 1770, 36 acres.

Philip Jacob Shafer his cert 36 acres Flonham patented 20th April 1774 Rent ? 1/5/2 stg charged to the rent roll} Frederick County by virtue of a warrant granted out of his lordships land office unto Philip Putman of said county for thirty six acres of land bearing date the 17th day of March 1770 and which said warrant being assigned unto Philip Jacob Shafer of the county afsd I certify as Deputy surveyor of Frederick County under George Lee? Esquire surveyor general of the western shore of Maryland that I have carefully surveyed and laid out for and in the name of the aforesaid Philip Jacob Shafer all that tract or parcel of land called Flonham lying and being in the county aforesaid beginning at a bounded white oak standing about a perch from the head of a spring on the south side of the Shannondore Mountain on the right hand of the main road leading from Frederick Town to Fort Frederick and running thence

Continued on the next page -

Continued from the prior page -

Line No.	North South	Degrees East or West	Length
1	S	78 west	56 perches
2	N	10 west	108 perches
3	N	78 east	56 perches

4 then with a straight line to the beginning containing thirty six acres more or less to be held of his lordships Manor of Monocacy surveyed 27th August 1770.

June 15th 1771 Examd & passed John Hanson Jr. A? Scott Ec?

Annexed to ? on the back of the aforegoing certi was this following afsd receipt vizt, I do hereby transfer assign and make over unto Philip Jacob Shafer of Frederick County his heirs executors administrators or assigns all my right title interest property claim and demand into or out of a common warrant granted me out of his lordships land office on the seventeenth day of March last for thirty six acres of land for value received of him as witness my hand and seal this 22nd day of August Anno Domini 1770
Witness Thomas Brooke Phillip Birude Mont. (seal)

I have received two shillings and one half penny for rent to March 1772 patent may therefore issue with his Excellency's approbation
6th April 1772 Danl of N? Thos Jenifer

The Patent for Flonham - MdHR 17,455, 1-23-4-9, BC & GS 44, pp. 439-440, Philip Jacob Shafer, Flonham, patented 20 April 1774, 36 acres.

Philip Jacob Shafer his patt 36 acres Flonham} the right honourable Henry Harford Esqr Know ye that for and in consideration that Philip Jacob Shafer of Frederick County hath due unto him thirty six acres of land within our said province by virtue of an assignment of a warrant for that quantity from Philip Putnam granted the said Putman the seventeenth day of March seventeen hundred and seventy as appears in our land office according to Charles Lord Baron of Baltimore his Instructions to Charles Carroll Esqr his then agent bearing date at London the twelfth day of September seventeen hundred and twelve and registered in our secretary's office afsd in said province together with a paragraph of our instructions bearing date at London the fifteenth day of December seventeen hundred and thirty eight and registered in our land office we do therefore hereby grant unto him the said Philip Jacob Shafer all that tract or parcel of land called Flonham lying and being in the county aforesaid beginning at a bounded white oak standing about a perch from the head of a spring on the south side of the Shannondore Mountain on the right hand of the main road leading from Frederick Town to Fort Frederick and running thence

Line No.	North South	Degrees East or West	Length
1	S	78 west	56 perches
2	N	10 west	108 perches
3	N	78 east	56 perches

4 then with a straight line to the beginning containing thirty six acres more or less

Continued on the next page -

Continued from the prior page -

according to the certificate of survey thereof taken and returned into our land office bearing date the twenty seventh day of August seventeen hundred and seventy and there remaining together with all rights profits benefits and privileges thereunto belonging royal mines excepted to have and to hold the same unto him the said Philip Jacob Shafer his heirs and assigns forever to be ? in ? of us and our heirs as of our manor of Monocacy in free and common soccage by fealty only for all manor of services yielding and paying therefore yearly unto us and our heirs at our receipt at our city of Saint Marys at the two most usual feasts in the year vizt the feast of the annunciation of the blessed Virgin Mary and Saint Michael the archangel by even and equal portions the rent of one shilling and five pence half penny sterling in silver or gold and for a fine upon every alienation of the said land or any part or parcel thereof one whole years rent in silver or gold or the full value thereof in such commodities as we and our heirs such officer or officers as shall be appointed by discharge thereof at the choice of us and our heirs or such officer or officers aforesaid provided so that if the said sum for assigns for alienation shall not be paid unto us and our heirs or such officer or officers aforesaid before such alienation and the said alienations entered upon record either in this provincial court or county court where the same parcel of land lieth within one month next after such alienation then the said alienation shall be void and of no effect and provided also and it is the true intent and meaning of these presents that the same is subject and liable to the following express conditions that is to say, that the said Philip Jacob Shafer his heirs or assigns shall well and truly pay or cause to be paid the rent herein reserved according to the tenor of these presents by the space of thirty days next after is shall become due and after demand made thereof by the former or other person who shall be appointed by us and our heirs from time to time to collect and receive the same given under our great seal of our said province of Maryland this twentieth day of April Anno Domini seventeen hundred and seventy four witness Robert Eden Esquire governor and commander in chief in and over our said province of Maryland Chancellor and Keeper of the great seal thereof -

Robt (the Great Seal) Eden

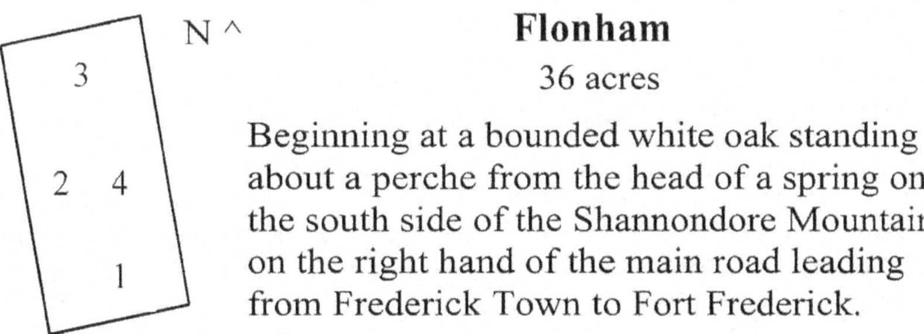

Flonham

36 acres

Beginning at a bounded white oak standing about a perche from the head of a spring on the south side of the Shannondore Mountain on the right hand of the main road leading from Frederick Town to Fort Frederick.

George Fox Line
by Curtis L. Older

The newspaper items presented on this and the following two and one-half pages are included in this Newsletter because they provide documentation for some of the ancestors of members of our Fox Society. They probably appeared in either a Danville, Illinois, or Covington, Indiana, newspaper.

Obituary of Mrs. Lola Fox (from a newspaper account)

Funeral services for Mrs. Lola Fox, 53, 613 Bensyl Ave., former resident of Union Corner vicinity, who died Monday at St. Elizabeth Hospital, were at 2 p. m. Thursday at Union Corner Church, southeast of Danville. Interment in Niccum Cemetery with Shelby Undertakers of Covington in charge.

Obituary of Claude E. Fox (from a newspaper account)

PERRYSVILLE, Ind. (CNS) - Claude E. Fox, 52, a former resident of the Perrysville and Gessie communities, died Sunday (June 24, 1962) following a heart attack at Muskegon, Mich. He had resided there for the past 21 years.

Born Jan. 8, 1910, in Gessie, Ind., he was the son of Ernest and Lola Jackson Fox. He was married at Perrysville to Pauline Pearson, who survives.

Other survivors include two sons; Robert of Muskegon and William stationed with the Army in Germany; a sister, Mrs. Frank Moss of Danville Route 3; a brother, Kenneth of Danville; and four grandchildren.

Services will be at 1 p. m. Wednesday at the Clock Funeral Home in Muskegon with burial there.

Daniel A. Fox Will Probated (from a newspaper account)

The will of the late Daniel A. Fox, life long resident of Highland township, was probated Monday. The instrument was written May 6, 1927 and was witnessed by Edgar Prather and Geo. D. Sunkel. It contained four items, which briefly, are as follows:

Item 1. - Just debts, expense of last sickness and funeral expenses to be paid by executor out of first money coming to his hands.

Item 2. - All real estate and personal property shall be sold at public or private sale. After payment of all debts as provided in item 1, the residue of the moneys left in hands of the executor shall be divided share and share alike between the following children: Ruby Hines, Ethel Gouty, Kenneth B. Fox and William Fox.

Item 3. - I make no provision in this will for my son Ernest Fox, as I have heretofore paid out for him as much or more than what I should deem to be his interest in my estate and for that reason I am giving him nothing by this will.

Item 4. - I do hereby nominate and appoint my friend, John W. Carithers, executor of this will.

Continued on the next page -

Obituary of William Edward Fox (from a newspaper account)

Covington, Ind. (CNS) - William E. Fox, 86, died Tuesday (April 16, 1974) at his home. He had been ill since August. Born Jan. 5, 1888, in Highland Township, Vermillion County, he was the son of Daniel A. and Elizabeth Ricketts Fox. He was married Feb. 10, 1909, to Marguerite Clem, who died Jan. 25, 1970.

A life resident of the Foster and Gessie communities, he had been a carpenter for many years and was employed at the Neal Gravel Co. and the Indiana State Highway before retiring in 1950.

Survivors include four daughters, Miss Reva Fox of Seattle, Wash., Mrs. Evelyn Switzer of Covington Route 2, Mrs. Elizabeth Bucholz of Rock Lake, N. D. and Mrs. Wilma Gose of Griffith; three sons, Glenn of Englewood, Colo., Richard of Covington and James of California; a sister, Mrs. Ruby Hines of Covington; 15 grandchildren; and 23 great-grandchildren.

A son, a daughter, a sister, two brothers and two grandchildren preceded him in death.

Services will be at 2 p. m. Friday at the Bodine & Shelby Funeral Home, with the Rev. Jerry Kinninger officiating. Burial will be in Lower Mound Cemetery. Visitation will be at the funeral home after 2 p. m. Thursday.

Obituary of Robert William Gouty (from a newspaper account)

Robert W. Gouty 59, Dies at Lake View, Rites Held On Monday

Funeral services for Robert William Gouty, age 59, well know farmer of the State Line neighborhood who died last Saturday morning, were held at 3 o'clock Monday afternoon at the Benson Chapel.

Mr. Gouty died at 7:30 a. m. at Lake View Hospital, Danville, Ill., where he had been a patient for the past three weeks. Death was attributed to meningitis. He had been in ill health for some time following an attack of the flu.

He was born August 26, 1889 near Gessie, Ind., the son of Joseph and Luella Hartman Gouty. He as married February 3, 1917 to Ethel Fox, who survives.

Mr. Gouty was a member of the Fountain Lodge 274, F. & A. M., of Covington and was well known in this community, having lived near here all his life.

Surviving beside the widow are: a daughter, Mrs. Mavis Lorene Older, Danville, Ill. one grandson, Curtis Lynn; two brothers, Ezra of State Line Route, and Leslie, of Covington, and three sisters, Mrs. Anna Remster, Villard, Minn., Mrs. Ida Saltsgaver, Danville, Ill., and Miss Inez Gouty of Indianapolis.

Dr. A. F. Bremicker, pastor of the Presbyterian Church in Danville, Ill., and the Rev. J. W. Knight of Perrysville officiated. The pallbearers were Earl Strawser, Russell Patton, Archie Fields, Jerd Crouch, Regan Mallett and Lawrence Vickery. Musical selections were by Clifford Martin. Burial, with Bodine & Shelby in charge, was in the Lower Mound Cemetery.

Continued on the next page -

Obituary of Ethel Belle (Fox) Gouty (Danville Commercial News)

Mrs. Ethel B. Gouty, 78, of 1705 E. Main, died at 4:50 a. m. Monday (Jan. 25, 1971) at Lake View Memorial Hospital. She had been ill three and a half years.

Born Oct. 6, 1892, near Gessie, Ind., she was the daughter of Daniel A. and Elizabeth Ricketts Fox. She was married on Feb. 3, 1917 to Robert W. Gouty, who died June 4, 1949.

Former resident of Warren County, Ind., she had resided on E. Main for 16 years. She was a member of the Howard Chapel Church and attended the First Presbyterian Church.

Survivors include a daughter, Mrs. Truxton J. Older of Danville; a sister, Mrs. Ruby Hines of Covington, Ind.; two brothers, William E. Fox of Covington, Ind. Route 2 and Kennie B. Fox of Richmond, Ind.; and a grandson, Curtis L. Older, with the Navy.

She was preceded in death by a brother.

Services will be at 10:30 a.m. EST Wednesday at the Bodine and Shelby Funeral Home in Covington, with the Rev. Oliver C. Starns officiating. Burial will be in Lower Mound Cemetery in Covington. Friends will be received at the funeral home from 2-4:30 and 7-9 p.m. EST Tuesday.

Obituary of Ernest D. Fox

Former director of the local Municipal and Moose Bands many years, Ernest D. Fox, 54, Route 5 Danville, died at 10 p. m. Thursday, Oct. 3, 1940 at Lake View Hospital where he had been two weeks.

Death resulted from a cerebral hemorrhage. Son of Mr. and Mrs. Daniel A. Fox, he was born Dec. 1, 1885 near Gessie, Ind., and was married in 1908 to Miss Lola Jackson. He was also a mechanic and had lived in the Danville and Gessie communities all his life.

Surviving are his widow; three children, Claude, of Perrysville, Kenneth of Danville and Mrs. Ruth Moss, Alvin; a brother, Kenneth, of Richmond, Ind., and William of Covington; two sisters, Mrs. Ethel Gouty, Danville, and Mrs. Ruby Hines, Perrysville.

The body is at Shelby's Funeral Home in Covington. Funeral services will be at 2 p. m. Sunday at Union Corner Church, east of Danville.

Covington Friend Newspaper, May 11, 1923:

Dan Fox who has been in Richmond for several weeks with his son Kenny Fox and family has returned.

Covington Friend newspaper, May 10, 1922:

Dan Fox Improving - Dan Fox, of North Vermillion, who was terribly burned about the hands and forearms, and who received a terrible nervous shock when Mrs. Fox was burned to death on Tuesday of last week is reported to be improving as rapidly as could be expected. The entire community surely greatly sympathizes with Mr. Fox and his family on their awful misfortune.

Reel #182072 Covington, Indiana, Covington Republican, January 1931 - December 1932:

August 5, 1932

Daniel A. Fox, age 70 yr., native of Vermillion County, passed away at the home of his daughter, Mrs. Everett Hines at Gessie, Indiana, Friday July 29th. His funeral was held at Howard Chapel, Sunday July 31st, at 2:30 o'clock. Rev. H. A. Lashbrook officiating. Interment was made at Hopewell Cemetery, with the Masonic burial service at the grave.

Continued on the next page -

Obituary Notice for Elizabeth Jane (Ricketts) Fox

(from the Covington, Indiana. Republican Newspaper, front page, column one, probably about March 1, 1922)

Mrs. Daniel Fox Meets Awful Death - Clothes Catch Fire When Kerosene Explodes, Gasoline Adds Fuel to the Flames. Clothes Burned From Body - Our people were almost paralyzed Monday morning by the announcement that Mrs. Dan Fox, the family living on a farm about one and a half miles north east of Gessie, had been burned to death at an early hour. Statements regarding the terrible affair from the family are as follows: The family had set apart Tuesday to do the butchering. Mr. Fox had arisen early, set a fire in the cook stove and under the kettles to heat the water out of doors and gone to the barn to feed and do the morning chores. Mrs. Fox arose and on going to the kitchen stove found the fire had not burned. She threw in kerosene to hasten the fire and it exploded setting her clothing on fire. In her excitement she ran out onto a back porch where she stumbled and fell upon a bottle of gasoline setting there, which broke at once enveloping her in flames. Her screams brought her husband to her aid but in her suffering and terror he could do nothing with her, nothing being at hand to wrap her in, until her clothes were practically burned from her body, death resulting before she could be removed from the porch and within a few minutes. Mr. Fox himself was also terribly burned. Mrs. Elizabeth Ricketts - Fox was sixty years old and is survived by her husband, Dan Fox, three sons, Kenneth, Earnest, and William, and two daughters, Ethel and Ruby, together with eleven grandchildren, an aged mother, living at Foster, and six brothers, High, Jos, Jacob, Dan, Fred, and Link, a twin brother, and one sister, Mrs. Frank Dixon. The funeral services, conducted by Rev. Cyrus Briles was held from the Howard M. E. Church of which she was a member at 1:30 p. m. Thursday, interment following in Hopewell Cemetery.

The Battle of Franklin Descendants Reunion

October 13, 14, and 15, 2000
The Carter House, Franklin, Tennessee

Descendants of Jacob Ricketts, the father of Elizabeth Jane Ricketts, should plan to visit the Carter House and the Battlefield of Franklin, in Franklin, Tennessee. I had the pleasure of attending this event that covered parts of three days. Several entertainers who sang Civil War style songs provided music. About 100 descendants attended the event, which was presented by The Carter House.

The Battle of Franklin, Tennessee, was one of the great battles of the Civil War. It was an overwhelming Union victory in terms of casualties suffered by the Confederates under General John Bell Hood. Hood also was in the Battle of South Mountain at Fox's Gap. General Jacob Dolson Cox, also in the Battle of South Mountain at Fox's Gap, was one of the Union commanders in the Battle of Franklin. His headquarters were at The Carter House, at the center of the battle.

A photograph hangs in the Museum at the Carter House that shows the 1909 Reunion of the 57th Indiana Volunteer Infantry. This is the unit Jacob Ricketts was in at The Battle of Franklin. I am still trying to figure out if he is in the picture which was taken in Muncie, Indiana, one year before his death in 1910. All the surviving members of the 57th Indiana were treated that day to their first automobile ride. For additional information please contact:

The Carter House — phone: 615-791-1861
1140 Columbia Ave. — fax: 615-794-1327
P. O. Box 555
Franklin, Tennessee 37065-0555

How to Obtain a Bound Copy of *The Fox Genealogy* or *The Link Family*

You may order hardbound and softbound copies of *The Fox Genealogy* by Daniel Gebhart Fox and/or *The Link Family* by Paxon Link, from Blairs' Book Service. To order copies, please read this page carefully.

Internet site address: http://www.glbco.com/default/order.html

How to Order

Please read the descriptions carefully because the books differ in format, condition, etc. Some books are print-to-order and have rather long lead times. Some are from regular stock and shipped shortly after receipt of order. Please follow these instructions when ordering:

Please include $4.00 shipping and handling for each item unless the listing notes otherwise. They accept orders by credit card, check, or money order. Texas residents please add 8.25% sales tax. Faulty or damaged books may be returned within 10 days for refund.

E-Mail: You may E-Mail your order with credit card payment to: linda@glbco.com

Fax: You may fax your order with credit card payment to Blairs' Book Service at 972-783-1008.

Mail: You may mail your order with payment by any method to:

Blairs' Book Service
2503 Springpark Way
Richardson, TX 75082

Please include the following information with your order:

Books: List the Reference Number, brief title, and price.
Your Name and Address
Shipping Name and Address (If Different Than Yours.)
If paying by credit card include:
Name as it appears on the card.
Card Type (Visa, MasterCard, Amex, or Discover.)
Card Number (Please be sure to double check the digits.)
Expiration Date.

Reference Number: XR-2546

FOX Genealogy, including the Metherd, Benner * Leiter descendants, giving biographies of the first & second generation with sketches of the third generation [Frederick Fox of Prussia & Maryland & descendants], by D. G. Fox. 172 pages 1924. $27.50 This book is a quality reprint with sturdy paper binding. Hardbound is available for an additional $10. This book is print-to-order; please allow 8-12 weeks, plus an additional 2 weeks for hardbound.

Frederick L. Fox Line
by Suella Jane Fenton
(material submitted by Alice Takase)

Suella Jane Fenton and Alice Takase are members of the Society. They are descendants of Frederick L. Fox who was a grandson of Frederick Fox of Fox's Gap in Maryland. Frederick L. Fox was a son of George Fox and Elizabeth Ann (Link) Fox. He was a brother of John L. Fox of Gessie, Indiana.

Descendants of Frederick L. Fox

A son of George Fox and a grandson of Frederick Fox of Fox's Gap in Maryland

Generation No. 4

20. Marion Johnson Fox (Francis "Frank" Marion, Samuel[5], Frederick Link[4], George "1"[3], Frederick, "1"[2], John "1" Frederick[1]) was born January 03, 1901. He married Esther P. Iversen.

Child of Marion Fox and Esther Iversen is:
54. i. Melinda Fox, b. February 08, 1939

21. Kenneth Lynn Fox (Francis "Frank" Marion, Samuel, Fredrick Link, George "1", Frederick "1", John "1", Frederick) was born November 23, 1903. He married Lillian Watkins Crane.

Child of Kenneth Fox and Lillian Crane are:
55. i. Lonnie Lee Fox, b. June 28, 1947.
56. ii. Larry Lynn Fox, b. June 28, 1947.
iii. Frances Ann Fox, b. September 14, 1949; m. Francis Ousley.
Notes for Francis Ann Fox:
Married 1st Joseph Scarpiello, 2nd Francis Ousley.

22. Leonard Orville Fox (Francis "Frank", Marion, Samuel, Frederick Link, George "1", Frederick "1", John "1", Frederick) was born June 03, 1907. He married Crystal Huston.

Children of Leonard Fox and Crystal Huston are:
57. i. Leonard Orville Fox Jr., b. August 08, 1930.
58. ii. Marion Huston Fox, b. January 14, 1932.

23. Grace "Jeannette" Fox (Francis "Frank", Marion, Samuel, Frederick Link, George "1", Frederick "1", John "1", Frederick) was born July 12, 1910. She married Harold Hutchinson.

Children of Grace Fox and Harold Hutchinson are:
i. Nancy Jean Hutchinson, b. March 21, 1939.
Notes for Nancy Jean Hutchinson:
Never married

59. ii. Charles Richard "Dick" Hutchinson, b. October 10, 1943.

Continued on the next page -

24. Harold C. "Bus" Fox (Francis "Frank", Marion, Samuel, Frederick Link, George "1", Frederick "1", John "1" Frederick) was born April 19, 1913. He married Virginia Lackey.

Children of Harold Fox and Virginia Lackey are:
60. i. Kathleen Lynn "Kitty" Fox, b. February 13, 1942.
61. ii. Jerold Curtis Fox, b. August 30, 1943.
iii. Rita Jean "Jeannie" Fox, b. January 25, 1947; m. John Cooper.

Notes for Rita Jean "Jeannie" Fox:
Married 1st, James Barney - divorced
Married 2nd, John Cooper

25. Marvin L. Fox (Francis "Frank", Marion , Samuel, Frederick Link, George "1", Frederick "1", John "1" Frederick) was born October 08, 1917. He married Naomi Bodenberg.

Children of Marvin Fox and Naomi Bodenberg are:
i. Sarah L. Fox, b. January 04, 1944; m. Martin Roth
ii. Peggy L. Fox, b. February 14, 1946.
62. iii. Michael M. Fox, b. May 04, 1951.

26. Lyle Scott Fox (Francis "Frank", Marion, Samuel, Frederick Link, George "1", Frederick "1", John "1" Frederick) was born June 09, 1924. He married Ellen West Moss.

Children of Lyle Fox and Ellen Moss are:
63. i. Karen Kay Fox, b. July 21, 1951.
ii. Jon Hartley Fox, b. June 08, 1953.

27. Merle Rufus Taylor (Mary Sophia Fox, Samuel, Frederick Link, George "1", Frederick "1", John "1" Frederick) was born August 20, 1905. He married Martha Comer.

Child of Merle Taylor and Martha Comer is:
i. Ray Taylor

28. Ruth Irene Wright (Elmira "Myra" R. Fox, Samuel, Frederick Link, George "1", Frederick "1", John "1" Frederick) was born January 01, 1908. She married Thomas Green are:

Children of Ruth Wright and Thomas Green are:
i. Susan Lee Green.
ii. Ruth Ann Green.
iii. James Green.

29. Ruby Jeanette Hayner (Orissa J. Fox, Samuel, Frederick Link, George "1", Frederick "1", John "1" Frederick) was born August 07, 1906 in Springboro Warren Co., Ohio, and died December 28, 1983 in Springboro, Warren Co., Ohio, buried in Springboro Cemetery. She married Lawrence DeWitt Leis June 10, 1936 in Springboro, Warren Co., Ohio, son of William Leis and Lillie Heistand.

Notes for Ruby Jeanette Hayner:
Ruby went to Salem School, a one room school, through the eighth Grade. Then she went to Springboro High School and graduated in 1925. She helped her mother and father on the farm. She also, like her sister Verna, worked at the Mutual Furniture company, in Miamisburg, Ohio, 1926-1936.

Continued on the next page -

She met Lawrence Leis at a dance in Germantown, in 1935. They got married at the Springboro Reformed church by Rev. Jerome Schulz, in 1936. They lived in Jackson Twp., New Lebanon, Montgomery County, Ohio until 1944 when they moved into the farm owned by her mother, Orissa (Fox) Hayner. The farm on Crossley Road is still (1997) in possession of their seven children. The oldest son, Delbert Leis, never married and still lives there.

Ruby also inherited the farm on Red Lion Fives-Points Road, upon the death of her sister, Verna, in 1970. This farm is also still (1997) in the possession of her children.

Ruby was very active in the Springboro Garden Club and the United Church of Christ (formerly the German Reformed Church), where she and Lawrence were in charge of communion. She served as leader of Springboro Eager Workers 4-H Club for 22 years. Ruby played the piano, but her hobby was drawing.

Children of Ruby Hayner and Lawrence Leis are:

i. Delbert Hayner Leis, b. October 07, 1938, New Lebanon, Montgomery Co., Ohio.
64. ii. Bernard Adam Leis, b. February 16, 1940, New Lebanon, Montgomery Co., Ohio.
65. iii. Frieda Irene Leis, b. August 24, 1941, New Lebanon, Montgomery Co., Ohio.
66. iv. Lenora Margaret Leis, b. February 16, 1943, New Lebanon, Montgomery Co., Ohio.
67. v. Glenn Ervin Leis, b. March 20, 1944, Springboro, Warren County, Ohio.
68. vi. Suella Jane Leis, b. March 18, 1946, Springboro, Warren Co., Ohio.
69. vii. Kermit Paul Leis, b. April 08, 1948, Springboro, Warren Co., Ohio.

30. Dorethea Eliza Fox (Walter Scott, Samuel, Frederick Link, George "1", Frederick "1", John "1" Frederick) was born July 03, 1907. She married Oscar Michel.

Children of Dorethea Fox and Oscar Michel are:

i. Carolyn Michel

Notes for Carolyn Michel:
Adopted

ii. Marcia Michel

Notes for Marcia Michel:
Adopted

31. Woodrow Wilson Fox (Walter Scott, Samuel, Frederick Link, George "1", Frederick "1", John "1" Frederick) was born March 03, 1913. He married Ruth (Fox).

Children of Woodrow Fox and Ruth (Fox) are:

i. David "2" Fox.
ii. Dianne Fox.

32. Lewis Marion Brown (Clarence David, Frances A. Fox, Frederick Link, George "1", Frederick "1", John "1" Frederick) was born April 30, 1910 in Southeast of Miamisburg, Ohio, and died January 25, 1998 in Ohio. He married Ruth Goodman.

Children of Lewis Brown and Ruth Goodman are:

i. Charles Brown, b. 1937.
ii. Donald Brown, b. September 1938.
iii. Mary "2" Brown, b. Abt. 1940.

Continued on the next page -

33. Ada Luella Brown (Clarence David, Fances A. Fox, Frederick Link, George "1", Frederick "1", John "1" Frederick) was born April 14, 1912 in Southeast of Miamisburg, Ohio. She married (1) William Noland. She married (2) Ralph Taylor August 30, 1930 in Kentucky, son of Edison Taylor and Ida Phol.

Children of Ada Brown and Ralph Taylor are:

72. i. Clarence Edwin Taylor, b. January 12, 1931, Franklin, Warren County, Ohio; d. March 29, 1995, Middletown, Butler County, Ohio.
73. ii. Barbara Taylor, b. May 07, 1933, Franklin, Warren County, Ohio.
iii. Larry Taylor, b. September 14, 1914, Red Lion, Warren County, Ohio; m. Barbara Davis, June 24, 1967, Middletown, Butler County, Ohio.

34. Ester Estella Brown (Clarence David, Frances A. Fox, Frederick Link, George "1", Frederick "1", John "1" Frederick) was born August 30, 1913 in Springboro, Warren County, Ohio. She married (1) Harry Berger. She married (2) George Anderson Sidenstick.

Children of Ester Brown and Harry Berger are:

i. Donald Berger.
ii. Nancy Berger, m. (1) Calvin Zinck; m. (2) (Husband) Raney.

35. Ethel May Brown (Clarence David, Frances A. Fox, Frederick Link, George "1", Frederick "1", John "1" Frederick) was born August 30, 1913 in Springboro, Warren County, Ohio. She married (1) Raymond Bullock Bef. 1936, son of Homer Bullock and Buelah (Bullock). She married (2) Robert Wetzel April 14, 1945, son of William Wetzel and Odie Greenfield.

Children of Ethel Brown and Raymond Bullock are:

i. Darrell Bullock, b. November 12, 1936; m. Marjorie Legitt, May 28, 1958.
74. ii. Robert Bullock, b. September 06, 1940, Middletown, Butler County, Ohio.

36. Walter Howard Brown (Clarence David, Frances A. Fox, Frederick Link, George "1", Frederick "1", John "1" Frederick) was born January 23, 1918 in Carlisle, Ohio. He married Florence Elisabeth Sprow September 29, 1938 in West Carrollton, Ohio.

Children of Walter Brown and Florence Sprow are:

75. i. Janet Rose Brown, b. September 03, 1939.
76. ii. Betty Lou Brown, b. October 12, 1942.
77. iii. Carolyn Sue Brown, b. April 18, 1945.
78. iv. Walter Howard Brown, Jr., b. November 04, 1950.
79. v. David Lewis Brown, b. September 30, 1952.
80. vi. Becky Lynn Brown, b. December 06, 1958.
81. v ii. Patty Ann Brown, b. September 07, 1960.
82. viii. Edward Lee Brown, b. February 08, 1962.

37. Lester Isaac "Ike" Brown (Clarence David, Frances A. Fox, Frederick Link, George "1", Frederick "1", John "1" Frederick) was born May 16, 1920 in Carlisle, Ohio, and died August 09, 1967. He married Doris Leach.

Children of Lester Brown and Doris Leach are:

i. Michael Brown.
ii. Cathy Brown, m. John W. Wahsum.
iii. Norma Brown.
iv. Brenda Brown, m. Kenneth Davis.

Continued on the next page -

38. Raymond Brown (Clarence David, Frances A. Fox, Frederick Link, George "1", Frederick "1", John "1" Frederick) was born December 28, 1924 in West Carrollton, Ohio. He married Mildere Irene Whisman, daughter of John Whisman and Goldie Cable.

Children of Raymond Brown and Mildere Whisman are:
83. i. Ricky Brown, b. July 26, 1962, Franklin, Warren County, Ohio.
84. ii. Vicki Brown, b. April 16, 1963, Franklin, Warren County, Ohio.

39. Mary Kathryn Brown (Clarence David, Frances A. Fox, Frederick Link, George "1", Frederick "1", John "1" Frederick) was born April 08, 1926 in West Carrollton, Ohio. She married Clifford Burns May 1946 in Kentucky>

Children of Mary Brown and Clifford Burns are:
i. Paul W. Burns, b. July 22, 1947, Centerville, Montgomery County, Ohio.
ii. Charlotte Burns, b. October 20, 1948, Centerville, Montgomery County, Ohio; m. Doug Berger, October 20, 1967, Carlisle, Ohio.
iii. Edward Burns, b. April 16, 1951, Franklin, Warren County, Ohio.
iv. Margaret Burns, b. December 27, 1957, Franklin, Warren County, Ohio: m. Len Rose.

40. Harry R. Weidel (Laura Etta Fox, Jacob "Job" Henry, Frederick Link, George "1", Frederick "1", John "1" Frederick).

Child of Harry R. Weidel is:
85. i. Eilen Weidel, b. 1925; d. 1993.

41. Hazel Weidel (Laura Etta Fox, Jacob "Job" Henry, Frederick Link, George "1", Frederick "1", John "1" Frederick) was born 1899, and died 1965. She married Floyd Routzahn.

Children of Hazel Weidel and Floyd Routzahn are:
i. Russell Routzahn.
ii. Elmer F. Routzahn.
iii. Mary Etta Routzahn, m. Paul Schell.
iv. Mildred Routzahn, m. Louis A. Hein.

42. Irvin Weidel (Laura Etta Fox, Jacob "Job" Henry, Frederick Link, George "1", Frederick "1", John "1" Frederick). He married (1) Mary Stamm. He married (2) Ester Elizabeth Stine.

Children of Irvin Weidel and Ester Stine are:
i. Francis Weidel.
ii. Frederick Weidel.
iii. Robert Weidel.

43. Carl Z. Weidel (Laura Etta Fox, Jacob "Job" Henry, Frederick Link, George "1", Frederick "1", John "1" Frederick) was born December 21, 1904, and died August 14, 1980. He was buried in Butler Memorial Park, Trenton Rt. 73, Ohio. He married Estella Veidt.

Children of Carl Weidel and Estella Veidt are:
i. Leroy Weidel.
86. ii. Lowell E. Weidel.
87. iii. Eugene Weidel, b. June 14, 1945.
iv. Kathy Weidel, m. Danny Philpot, July 30, 1948.

Continued on the next page -

44. Reber Fox (Anna Marie, Jacob "Job" Henry, Frederick Link, George "1", Frederick "1", John "1" Fredrick) was born in 1904, and died in 1976. He married Marguerite Hammiel.

Children of Reber Fox and Marguerite Hammiel are:
i. Mary Rose Fox.
88. ii. John Richard Reber Fox, b. May 18, 1943.

45. Jack A. Chenewoth (Anna Marie Fox, Jacob "Job" Henry, Frederick Link, George "1", Frederick "1", John "1" Frederick) was born January 21, 1919. He married Dolorbs Hartshona.

Child of Jack Chenewoth and Dolorbs Hartshona is:
89. i. Stephany Ann Chenewoth

46. William R. Chenewoth (Anna Marie Fox, Jacob "Job" Henry, Frederick Link, George "1", Frederick "1", John "1" Frederick) was born March 15, 1928. He married Martha Jeanne Harden February 23, 1952.

Child of William Chenewoth and Martha Harden is:
90. i. Steven Chenwoth, b. September 19, 1955.

47. James Norman Fox (Edwin E., Jacob "Job" Henry, Frederick Link, George "1", Frederick "1", John "1" Frederick) was born March 29, 1918. He married Dorothy Baker.

Children of James Fox and Dorothy Baker are:
91. i. Linda Christine Fox, b. 1948.
ii. John Charles Fox, b. 1953; m. Cheri Hitt.

48. Dorothy May Beachler (Lucy May Fox, Jacob "Job" Henry, Frederick Link, George "1", Frederick "1", John "1" Frederick) was born January 26, 1914 in Miamisburg, Montgomery County, Ohio. She married Courtney Joseph Hoskins February 28, 1942.

Children of Dorothy Beachler and Courtney Hoskins are:
92. i. Alice Louise Hoskins, b. October 22, 1946, Pittsburgh, Allegheny County, Pennsylvania.
93. ii. Bruce Courtney Hoskins, b. February 29, 1948 Pittsburgh, Allegheny County, Pennsylvania.
94. iii. Eugene Paul Hoskins,b. July 08, 1951, Pittsburgh, Allegheny County, Pennsylvania.

49. Charles Monroe Beachler (Lucy May Fox, Jacob "Job" Henry, Frederick Link, George "1", Frederick "1", John "1" Frederick) was born June 24, 1917 in Miamisburg, Montgomery County, Ohio, and died December 11, 1986 in Sarasota, Florida. He married Mabel Bridge August 13, 1944.

Children of Charles Beachler and Mabel Bridge are:
i. Charles William Beachler, b. October 25, 1945; m. Marjorie Gail Ferguson, October 1969.
95. ii. Jessie Luicinda "Cindi" Beachler, b. October 27, 1948.

50. Harold Everett Montgomery (Katheryn Myrtle Fox, Jacob "Job" Henry, Frederick Link, George "1", Frederick "1", John "1" Frederick) was born May 16, 1921 in Warren County, Ohio. He married Jeanette Martha Robinson June 22, 1946 in Warren County, Ohio.

Child of Harold Montgomery and Jeanette Robinson is:
96. i. Richard Harold Montgomery, b. September 10, 1947.

Continued on the next page -

51. Robert Eugene Montgomery (Katheryn Myrtle Fox, Jacob "Job" Henry, Frederick Link, George "1", Frederick "1", John "1" Frederick) was born September 11, 1926 in Warren County, Ohio. He married Melvina Null May 14, 1948.

Children of Robert Montgomery and Melvina Null are:

97. i. Ronald Eugene Montgomery, b. September 07, 1950.
98. ii. Debra Ann Montgomery, b. December 13, 1956.

52. Robert Degler (Lydia "Liddy" Z. Fox, Jacob "Job" Henry, Frederick Link, George "1", Frederick "1", John "1" Frederick). He married Yvonne (Degler).

Children of Robert Degler and Yvonne (Degler) are:

i. Roy Degler
ii. Ray Degler

53. Kenneth Wilfred Fox (Cloyce "Wilfred", Jacob "Job" Henry, Frederick Link, George "1", Frederick "1", John "1" Frederick) was born December 25, 1927. He married Barbara Jean Murphy.

Children of Kenneth Fox and Barbara Murphy are:

99. i. Kenneth Michael Fox, b. January 03, 1952.
100. ii. Timothy Wilford Fox, b. December 08, 1952.
101. iii. Patrick Alan Fox, b. October 04, 1954.
102. iv. Thomas Daniel Fox, b. December 29, 1956.
103. v. Mary Ann Fox, b. October 16, 1958.

****

News from Fox's Gap

Published June 1 and December 1 of each year by

The Society of the Descendants of Frederick Fox of Fox's Gap in Maryland

Membership dues are $5.00 per year. President of the Society is Curtis L. Older.

Make Society inquiries by the following means:

Curtis L. Older
618 Tryon Place
Gastonia, NC 28054-6066

e-mail: curtolder@earthlink.net
phone: 704-864-3879

****

Wills Section

by Curtis L. Older

Each Newsletter includes one typewritten version of a will that is significant to the preservation efforts of the Society. Included in this issue is the will of John L. Fox who was a son of George Fox and a grandson of Frederick Fox of Fox's Gap in Maryland. He was the father of Daniel Alexander Fox. The wife of John L. Fox was Susannah Hillegass. John L. and Susannah Fox are buried at Hopewell Cemetery west of Covington, Indiana.

Previous issues of the Society Newsletter contained copies of the following wills and estate papers:

December 1, 1996	will of John Fox of Fox's Gap in Maryland
June 1, 1997	will of Frederick Fox of Fox's Gap in Maryland
December 1, 1997	will of Bartholomew Booker, father-in-law of Frederick Fox
June 1, 1998	estate papers for George Fox, the oldest son of Frederick Fox
December 1, 1998	will of John Adam Link II, the father-in-law of George Fox
June 1, 1999	will of John Adam Link I, the father of John Adam Link II
December 1, 1999	no will included in newsletter
June 1, 2000	no will included in newsletter

Will of John L. Fox

John L. Fox
Vermillion County, Indiana
Court House, Newport

520 John L. Fox

WILL RECORD

In the name of God, Amen:
I John L. Fox of the County of Vermillion and State of Indiana being weak in body and of sound mind, memory and understanding but considering the uncertainly of this transitory life, do make and publish this my last Will and Testament in manner and form following, to wit:
First, - It is my Will and I do order that all my just debts and Funeral expenses be duly paid and satisfied as soon as conveniently can be after my decease,
Second, -
Item, - I give unto my Daughter Margaret Ricketts ($5.00) Dollars.
Item, - I give unto my son John A. Fox Five ($5.00) Dollars.
Item, - The balance of my Estate shall be equally divided between my Daughters Anna E. Goff, Mary Burnett and **Daniel A. Fox**.
The said Margaret Ricketts and John A. Fox have already received more of my estate than their shares.
And, lastly, I nominate, constitute and appoint W. H. Goff of Gessie Ind. To be the Executor of this, my Will, hereby revoking all other Wills, legacies and bequests by me heretofore made, and declaring this, and no other, to be my last will and testament.
In Witness Whereof I have hereunto set my hand and seal this 8 day April, in the year 1898.

John L. Fox (seal)

Continued on the following page.

Continued from the prior page -

Signed, sealed, published, and declared by the said John L. Fox as and for his last Will and Testament, in the presence of us who at his request and in his presence and in the presence of each other, have subscribed our names as witnesses thereto.

Alexander Swisher (seal)
Jacob B. Swisher (seal)

State of Indiana, Vermillion County, SS:

Before me, John T. Lowe Clerk of the Vermillion Circuit Court, personally came Jacob B. Swisher one of the subscribing witnesses to the foregoing last Will and Testament of John L. Fox late of Vermillion County, Indiana, deceased, and being duly sworn on oath says that he was present at the execution of said last will: that the same was duly executed: that said testator requested said Jacob B. Swisher and Alexander Swisher to sign said will as Witnesses thereto, which they accordingly did in the presence of said testator, and in the presence of each other as subscribing witnesses thereto.

Jacob B. Swisher
Subscribed and sworn to before me this 28th day of January 1899,

John T. Lowe clerk

521

VERMILLION COUNTY, INDIANA

State of Indiana } SS:
Vermillion County}

I John T. Lowe Clerk of the Vermillion Circuit Court do hereby certify that the above and foregoing last will and testament of John L Fox late of Vermillion County State of Indiana deceased was this day duly admitted to probate and record and the proof thereof duly made by Jacob B. Swisher one of subscribing witnesses thereto which said Will together with such proof have been duly recorded in Record of Will Lo 3 Page 520 in this office

Witness my name and the seal of said Court this 28th day of Jany 1899

John T. Lowe Clerk

Please notify the President of the Society

regarding any errors you find

in the current issue of the Newsletter!

Fox's Gap Section
By Kurt Graham

Significant Research Findings on the Battle of South Mountain

Kurt Graham honors us to present to our readers the following article. The material provides new evidence regarding the battle at Fox's Gap in Maryland on September 14, 1862. It presents documented casualty counts of Confederate forces in the 50th Georgia Regiment under General Drayton during the battle. Kurt's article is thoroughly researched and provides primary sources from which he obtained his information. Kurt retains all copyright privileges related to his article.

Kurt Graham retired from IBM in 1991 and lives in Vinings, Georgia, with his wife, Mary, and sons Griff and Jack. His lifelong love affair with American history was fueled by a father and grandfather who "had dragged him across every Civil War battlefield by the time he was ten." Kurt is an enthusiastic supporter of battlefield preservation and collector of military art and books. He is currently researching the history of the Phillips Georgia Legion and co-authoring a book on this little known Georgia unit. He maintains a website for this unit at www.angelfire.com/tx/RandysTexas and encourages interested parties to contact him at (e-mail) kdgraha@attglobal.net.

****

Casualties in the 50th Georgia Regiment at the Battle of South Mountain September 14, 1862

by Kurt Graham

The Battle of South Mountain, as it was known in the North, included the battles fought in the areas of Crampton's, Fox's, and Turner's Gaps in South Mountain west of Frederick, Maryland. The South referred to the battles at Turner's and Fox's Gaps and the area just north of Turner's Gap as the Battle of Boonsboro. The South referred to the Battle of Crampton's Gap as a separate battle under that name.

Some veterans of Drayton's brigade, who were posted at Fox's Gap, actually thought they fought at Crampton's Gap and left postwar accounts to this effect. The accounts of the battle written in the late 1800s by J. S. Wood and George Fahm state that the Phillips Legion and 50th Georgia Regiment fought at Crampton's Gap under the command of General McLaws. Their memories had gotten fuzzy because (1) McLaws did not become their division Commander until late November 1862 and (2) the only Georgians at Crampton's Gap were Howell Cobb's ill fated Cobb Legion, and the 10th, 16th, and 24th Georgia.

The Battle of South Mountain took place September 14, 1862. Three days later on September 17, 1862, the Battle of Antietam, the bloodiest single day of battle during the Civil War, took place five miles west of Fox's Gap along the Antietam Creek near Sharpsburg. The Battle of Antietam was known in the South as the Battle of Sharpsburg.

A variety of sources were used to prepare the Casualty List for the 50th Georgia Infantry at the Battle of South Mountain on September 14, 1862. The Compiled Service Records at the George State Archives are the single best source as they are a direct extract from actual wartime documents, i. e., muster rolls, POW records, hospital records, etc. These microfilm records were done around the turn of the century by the Federal government when it was discovered that many of the original paper records were deteriorating beyond usability. A small army of "compilers" sifted through original Federal and Confederate muster rolls, pay records, hospital records, POW records, death claims, requisitions, etc. They produced a multiple card file for each soldier who fought in the war.

Microfilm copies of these cards were eventually distributed to the various Southern states for their respective soldiers. The reels of microfilm contain copies of the untold thousands of card records for all members of each unit. These card records were handwritten and the writing styles of the compilers varied widely. Many wrote in the frilly cursive of that period.

The Georgia State Archives also contains the 1906 Georgia Roster Commission rolls. This Commission was formed in an attempt to have all the old surviving Confederate veterans provide information on just who was in their various units. At this point, the Federal government had not yet given copies of the captured wartime records back to the Southern states. The Southern states, by the 1890s, had begun providing pensions for their soldiers and were having a most difficult time sorting valid pension claims from fraudulent ones. They had to wait months for someone in Washington and to find a record of the applicant's military service records.

The Roster Commission idea came about in an attempt to build a local record of who had served in the various Georgia units. As you would expect, some units had formed reunion groups and had very good records while others had little or no information available. In attempting to reconstruct a 45-year-old unit roster, it was inevitable that clouded old memories would misspell names, show people killed in the wrong battles and often simply forget many men. Therefore, the 1906 Georgia Roster Commission rolls were used only as a corroborative source in preparing the Casualty List.

Other sources of information from which the Casualty List was compiled include period letters, diaries, and newspapers. The Lt. Francis L. Mobley letter that appears at the end of the Casualty List is found in the North South Trader Magazine, Vol. XXVII, #2.

Abbreviations used in the Casualty List:

ADM Admitted (to hospital)
AWOL Absent Without Leave (from 50th Georgia unit)
CAP Captured (by Union forces)
EXC Exchanged (returned by Union forces to the Confederates)
FRD Frederick, Maryland
MOC Mt. Olivet Cemetery (grave number follows)
POW Prisoner of War (held in a Union prison camp)
RH Richmond Hospital (Confederate) - a consolidated name representing various Confederate hospitals in Richmond, Virginia
USGH United States General Hospital - (a Union hospital, city follows)

Clarification of other items appearing in the Casualty List:

Mt. Olivet Cemetery - in Frederick, Maryland, was the place of burial for many Confederates
Richmond Hospital - any of a number of Confederate hospitals in Richmond, Virginia, including Chimborazo #1 and #2, GH 1-24, Winder hospital, Howard's Grove, Mayo Island, and others. The name of the specific hospital unit in Richmond may be found for each veteran in the Compiled Service Records at the Georgia State Archives.

Notes to the Casualty List for the 50th Georgia Infantry at the Battle of South Mountain

(1) Casualties fall into three categories:

(a) Men captured in Frederick, Maryland, on September 12, 1862. It is likely that these men were left behind, too sick to move with the army when it moved west on September 10th.

(b) Battle casualties from the September 14th fight at Fox's Gap

(c) Men who were captured September 15th with Longstreet's ordinance wagon train between Hagerstown and Williamsport by Federal cavalry escaping from Harpers Ferry.

(2) Status codes are abbreviated as follows:

KIA - Killed in Action
WIA - Wounded in Action
MWIA - Mortally Wounded in Action (died from wounds)
MWIA/CAP - Mortally Wounded in Action and Captured
WIA/CAP - Wounded in Action and Captured
CAP - captured
MIA - Missing in Action

(3) An **asterisk** (*) next to the Status code means that it was impossible to determine whether the casualty took place at Fox's Gap on September 14, at Sharpsburg, Maryland, on September 17, or, in the case of captures, somewhere in between.

(4) The 50th Georgia's battle casualties at Fox's Gap are as follows:

Present - Approximately 230 (per Lt. William Fleming's account)

KIA	52
MWIA	20
WIA	48
WIA/CAP	28
CAP	30
MIA	6
TOTAL	184

(5) <u>The ratio of killed to wounded (72:76, or roughly 1:1) is virtually unprecedented for any regiment in any Civil War battle.</u> Typically, there were three to five men wounded for each man killed. This gives mute testimony to the tenacity of the 50th's soldiers and the savagery of this battle. An additional contributing factor is an account from a private in the 21st Connecticut who claims that he witnessed Federal ammunition wagons being driven over wounded Confederates in the Old Sharpsburg Road. These would have been the wounded of the 50th and 51st Georgia regiments.

Name	Company	Status	Comments
Allen, George W.	A	WIA/CAP	EXC 12/18/62
Altman, Jasper S.	A	MIA/CAP	CAP in FRD 9/12/62
Altman, Samuel	A	MWIA/CAP	Died at USGH Philadelphia 10/11/62 from head wound
Collins, George W.	A	WIA	ADM to RH 9/27/62
Dowling, David A.	A	MIA/CAP	CAP 9/12/62 near FRD; EXC during Oct 1862
Dowling, Lt. Aaron	A	WIA/CAP	EXC Oct 1862; ADM to RH 10/8/62
Eddenfield, William	A	MIA/CAP	CAP at Middletown, MD; EXC during Oct 1862
Fletcher, John W.	A	WIA	Feb 1863 roll states "sent to hospital 9/14/62"; no further record
Gooding, William A.	A	WIA	
McElhaney, John T.	A	KIA	
Minshew, Sgt. Wryan F.	A	MIA/CAP	EXC during Oct 1862
Oberry, Robert G.	A	WIA	
Stone, George R.	A	KIA	
Stone, William H.	A	MIA/CAP	EXC during Oct 1862
Thomas, Jackson	A	MIA/CAP	CAP at FRD, 9/19/62; died from disease 10/8/62
Thomas, James F.	A	KIA	
Thomas, Lewis R.	A	MIA/CAP	ADM to RH 9/27/62 with gun shot wound
Thomas, Sgt. Edmund	A	MIA/CAP*	In USGH FRD 9/19/62; died from disease in prison
Tippens (Tippins) James	A	WIA	
Waldron, Benjamin D.	A	WIA/CAP	EXC 10/17/62; RH 10/23/62 with shoulder wound
Wilson, Captain John T.	A	MWIA	Not on rolls after battle; death claim filed Jan 1863
Anderson, James	B	WIA	ADM to RH 9/25/62
Bailey, Sgt. James S.	B	MIA/CAP	CAP at FRD 9/12/62; EXC in Oct 1862
Brewton (Bruton), David	B	WIA/CAP	CAP at FRD 9/12/62; USGH 9/18/62; EXC in Oct 1862
Lee, George	B	WIA	
Morgan, Isaac	B	MIA/CAP	CAP 9/15/62 at Hagerstown; EXC in Oct 1862
Music, Mills	B	MWIA/CAP	USGH FRD with elbow wound; dies Dec 1863 at Fort Delaware
Phillips, Gordon J.	B	WIA/CAP	USGH Philadelphia 9/27/62 with head wound; EXC Dec 1862
Pitman, Sgt. Noah	B	WIA*	RH 10/14/62 with wound; furloughed 10/23/62; never returns
Rowland, R. L.	B	MWIA	Died at Staunton, VA 10/31/62
Rowland, William N.	B	WIA/CAP	RH 10/62; had not returned to unit by Dec 1862
Walker, Cpl. Joel	B	WIA/CAP	EXC in Oct 1862
White, Cpl. George	B	MIA/CAP	EXC in Oct 1862
White, Van A.	B	MIA	Dec 1864 roll states "left sick on March 9/62, supposed to have died"
Carver, James A.	C	WIA/CAP	EXC 10/17/62; RH with broken arm 10/24/62
Carver, James J.	C	MWIA/CAP	Died 9/28/62 at Boonsboro, MD
Cato, William R.	C	WIA/CAP	EXC 10/19/62; RH 10/23/62 with arm wound
Dent, Cpl. John A.	C	MIA/CAP	EXC 12/18/62
Eady (Eddy), William F.	C	KIA	
Hargraves, Christopher	C	WIA/CAP	EXC in Oct 1862

Name	Company	Status	Comments
Joiner, Cpl. Jacob	C	KIA	
Joiner, Hardy Sr.	C	WIA	
Kirkland, Zean W.	C	WIA/CAP	USGH FRD 10/22/62 with leg wound. EXC Jan 1863
McCafferty, Dominic	C	MIA/CAP	EXC in Oct 1862
Merritt, Benjamin	C	KIA	
Miller, Cpl. William M.	C	KIA	
Moore, Sgt. Edward H.	C	WIA/CAP	Paroled 9/25/62
Nettles, Alexander	C	WIA	Feb 1863 roll shows him on wounded furlough
Passmore, Nathan C.	C	KIA	
Ricketson, Ivey	C	KIA	
Ruis (Rewis), James J.	C	WIA	Dec 1862 roll shows him on wounded furlough
Smith, Henry	C	KIA	
Smith, William	C	WIA	ADM RH 10/7/62; then on wounded furlough
Teston, Henry J.	C	WIA	ADM to RH 10/18/62
Teston, James	C	WIA	EXC 10/11/62; RH 10/17/62; at hospital 12/62
Thigpen, Stafford	C	KIA	
Vining, James	C	MIA/CAP	EXC 10/17/62
Ward, John F.	C	WIA	ADM to RH 9/27/62 with facial and shoulder wounds
Wooten, Simon L.	C	WIA/CAP	EXC 10/19/62 and ADM to RH
Wright, Cpl. Riley	C	WIA/CAP	USGH Philadelphia 9/27/62; took Oath of Allegiance 10/18/62
Briggs, Sgt. William H.	D	MIA/CAP	CAP 9/15/62 near Williamsport; EXC in Oct 1862
Brown, Hezekiah	D	KIA	
Bynum, Joseph	D	MIA/CAP	EXC 9/27/62
Coleman, Bernard	D	MIA/CAP	Paroled at Sharpsburg 9/27/62; rolls show as POW through Feb 1865
Hardie (Hardee), Jesse A.	D	MIA/CAP*	EXC in Oct 1862
Herndon, G. W.	D	WIA	
Hughes, E.	D	MWIA	Henderson and 1906 Roster Commission roll both indicate, "died of wounds"
Hughes, R. P.	D	MWIA/CAP	Died 11/5/62 at USGH FRD; buried MOC, #174
Lester, Simeon B.	D	MIA/CAP	CAP at FRD 9/12/62; EXC in Oct 1862
McConnell, Cpl. W. F.	D	KIA	
Nelson, William J. Sr.	D	WIA/CAP	EXC 10/17/62; RH 10/24/62, toe amputated
Newnans, A. S.	D	MIA	No Federal capture/exchange records; present on 12/62 roll
Peters, S. F.	D	MWIA/CAP	USGH Washington 9/29/62; RH 10/9/62; died 11/62 in Georgia
Rodgers, Thomas J.	D	MIA	No Federal capture/exchange records
Swilly, Jack	D	KIA	
Taylor, John W.	D	MIA/CAP	EXC in Oct 1862
Vickers, Jackson	D	KIA	
Vickers, Matthew	D	KIA	
Walker, J.	D	MIA	No Federal capture/exchange records; died Nov 1862 in Lynchburg, VA
Wilson, William	D	WIA	

Name	Company	Status	Comments
Brown, Cpl. William Ponder	E	WIA/CAP	USGH FRD 9/18/62; EXC in Oct 1862
Cooper, Jesse M.	E	WIA/CAP	USGH FRD 9/19/62, "hand shot off"
Creed, Paul M. J.	E	WIA/CAP	
Donaldson, Aaron J.	E	WIA/CAP	USGH Washington 9/21/62; RH 11/4/62
Douglass, William W.	E	WIA	RH 9/28/62 with head wound; discharged from army 1/12/63
Dunbar, Timothy S.	E	WIA	Dec 1862 roll states, "wounded at Boonsboro and now at home"
Gandy, Samuel	E	KIA	
Gill, Thomas	E	MIA/CAP*	EXC in Oct 1862
Harden, John	E	MIA	No Federal capture/exchange records
Hardy, Blythel	E	KIA	
Hicks, Moses	E	KIA	
Hurst, William E.	E	MIA/CAP	CAP 9/12/62 at FRD; EXC in Oct 1862
McCoy, Sgt. John	E	KIA	
McGlynn, John	E	MIA/CAP	EXC in Oct 1862
McPherson, Wyatt H.	E	MWIA/CAP	USGH FRD; leg amputated; died 10/27/62; buried MOC, #14
Murphey, James N.	E	KIA	
O'Rourke, James	E	KIA	
Phillips, Joshua G.	E	KIA	
Radney, Henry J.	E	MIA/CAP	CAP 9/15/62; EXC 10/6/62
Reneau, Sgt. Russell R.	E	KIA	
Sheffield, Simeon B.	E	WIA/CAP	Dec 1862 roll states, "captured, took Oath"; no further record
Shuman, Emanuel	E	MWIA/CAP	Died 9/24/62 at USGH FRD; buried MOC, #34
Stanfill, Joseph J.	E	WIA	
Vann, John	E	KIA	
Atkinson, Benjamin	F	KIA	
Bachelor, William Bennett	F	WIA	
Boyett, William T.	F	WIA	ADM to RH 9/27/62
Bryant, Daniel H.	F	WIA/CAP	USGH FRD 10/1/62; wounded in both legs
Bryant, John W.	F	KIA	
Burns, Sgt. Seaborn	F	KIA	
Cloud, Martin L.	F	MIA/CAP	EXC in Oct 1862
Cloud, Peter M.	F	WIA	ADM to RH 9/26/62
Davidson, Gideon	F	MIA/CAP	EXC in Oct 1862
Dekle, Lt. William G.	F	KIA	
Garland, Nathaniel	F	MWIA/CAP	Paroled 9/25/62; died at Boonsboro, MD, 9/30/62
Grantham, Cpl. Elijah T.	F	KIA	
Harrison, Joseph	F	MWIA/CAP*	USGH Washington 9/21/62; 12/62 roll shows absent on furlough
Herring, Elisha D.	F	KIA	
Hicks, Newton	F	WIA	ADM to RH in Oct 1862 with arm wound
Horn, John M.	F	KIA	
Mallard, George R.	F	KIA	
Maxwell, Cpl. William F.	F	WIA/CAP	EXC in early Oct 1862; ADM to RH 10/1/62

Name	Company	Status	Comments
McTyre, Sgt. Henry W.	F	MIA/CAP	EXC in Oct 1862
Metcalf, Benjamin F.	F	WIA/CAP	Paroled 9/25/62; ADM to RH 10/1/62 with leg wound
Nesmith, Elijah	F	KIA	
Nix, Clayton	F	KIA	
Nix, John T.	F	MWIA/CAP	Died 10/4/62 at FRD; buried MOC, #88
Powell, Jesse H.	F	MIA/CAP	EXC in Oct 1862; exchange record shows J. H. Powers
Powell, William J.	F	KIA	
Ricks, James W.	F	MIA/CAP	EXC in Oct 1862
Sloan, David	F	MWIA/CAP	Died 9/27/62 at FRD; buried MOC, #53
Smith, Benjamin W.	F	KIA	
Trawick, Orthwald	F	MWIA/CAP	Died 9/28/62 at FRD; buried MOC, #56
Trulock, Charles	F	MWIA/CAP	Died 9/27/62 at USGH FRD; buried MOC, #16
Wiley, William R.	F	MWIA/CAP	Died 9/23/62 at USGH FRD; buried MOC, #23
Williams, William H.	F	MIA/CAP	Present on Dec 1862 roll; no further record
Bass, David	G	KIA	
Bassd, Archibald	G	WIA	
Brack, Sgt. Augustus	G	WIA	ADM to RH 10/5/62
Buckland, ?	G	WIA	Possibly Lt. Isaac Burkholder; ADM RH 10/16/62
Clemmens, James	G	WIA	ADM to RH 9/26/62
Corbett, Manning	G	MWIA/CAP	Died 10/1/62 at USGH FRD; buried MOC, #73
Corbitt, Cpl. William B.	G	WIA	ADM to RH 9/27/62 with head wound
Corbitt, Martin	G	WIA	
Curry, Sgt. Charles W.	G	WIA/CAP	USGH Washington 9/29/62; RH 10/6/62; at home 12/31/62
Douglass, Sgt. James	G	WIA/CAP	Paroled 10/3/62; ADM to RH 10/23/62
Guthrie, William James	G	KIA	
Hargraves, James B.	G	WIA	
Henderson, Mark F.	G	MIA/CAP	CAP near Williamsport 9/15/62; EXC in Oct 1862
Jones, Abner	G	WIA	Winchester hospital 10/20/62; 1864 death claim says he died from wounds
Lastinger, David M.	G	MIA/CAP*	EXC in Oct 1862
Osteen, Captain John R.	G	MWIA/CAP	Died 9/23/62 at USGH FRD; buried MOC, #30
Register, John T.	G	WIA	ADM to RH 9/27/62 with neck wound
Roberts, Cpl. William T.	G	WIA	Feb 1863 roll states, "wounded 9/14 and furloughed home"
Roberts, John	G	KIA	
Roberts, Moses	G	WIA	At RH 10/5/62 wounded, furloughed; no further record
Sears, James	G	WIA*	At RH 9/27/62 with chin wound; no further record
Sermons (Sirmons), L. R.	G	KIA	
Strickland, Matthew T.	G	MWIA/CAP	Died 12/14/62 at USGH FRD; buried MOC, #177
Thomas, Colin	G	WIA/CAP	EXC in Oct 1862; furloughed from RH 11/16/62
Vining, Jasper H.	G	KIA	

Name	Company	Status	Comments
Allred, Jackson A.	H	WIA	ADM to RH 10/15/62 with thigh wound
Brown, Sgt. James	H	KIA	
Castleberry, Joseph	H	KIA	
Flowers, James B.	H	WIA	ADM to RH 9/26/62
Flowers, Nathan O.	H	WIA	
Gay, Matthew	H	WIA	
Giles, David A.	H	WIA	Wounded in hand; received disability discharge Apr 1863
Hancock, Cpl. Henry W.	H	MIA/CAP	Paroled 9/21/62
Hancock, Cpl. Jeremiah	H	KIA	
Hancock, Hardin	H	MIA	Feb 65 roll states, "AWOL since 9/62, dropped out on march 9/14"
Hancock, Harrison G.	H	KIA	
Hood, Cpl. James A.	H	KIA	
Kinard, Jacob	H	MIA/CAP	EXC in Oct 1862
Mercer, John	H	WIA	ADM to RH 10/29/62
Price, Willis	H	MWIA	Died 9/28/62 at Winchester
Chambers, Hugh C.	I	MIA/CAP	CAP 9/15/62 near Williamsport; EXC in Oct 1862
Gaskins, Lt. Daniel D.	I	WIA	
Hartley, William H.	I	KIA	
Hendley, Cpl. Matthew	I	KIA	
Marshall, Lewis	I	KIA	
McCranie, Josiah	I	MIA/CAP	CAP 9/15/62 near Williamsport; EXC in Oct 1862
McMillan, Randall	I	WIA	ADM to RH 10/6/62
Mobley, Lt. Francis L.	I	WIA	Ball grazed head; MWIA at Sharpsburg on 9/17/62
Purvis, Andrew J.	I	KIA	
Tison, James H.	I	KIA	
Alderman, William R.	K	MIA/CAP	EXC in Oct 1862
Daylay, (Daily), Daniel	K	MIA/CAP	EXC 10/17/62
Edwards, Seaborn A.	K	MIA/CAP	Paroled 9/25/62; RH 10/1/62; died at Winchester 10/30/62
Finch, Jimpsey B.	K	MIA/CAP	EXC in Oct 1862
Finch, Lt. James B.	K	WIA	Lost left eye
Hill, Sgt. Joseph L.	K	WIA/CAP	EXC 10/17/62; furloughed 10/25/62; no further record
Jones, Malachi Frank	K	WIA	ADM to RH 10/5/62 with gun shot wound
Rambo, Thomas, W.	K	WIA/CAP	Wounded leg, side, and arm; EXC 4/63; furloughed; never returns
Vickery, William	K	MIA/CAP	EXC 10/17/62
Manning, Colonel William R.	X	WIA	Flesh wound in hip

Letter from
Lt. Francis L. Mobley (50th Georgia, Company I)
to his wife, Rhoda

September 25th, 1862, Winchester, Va.

My Dear Wife,

I wrote you from Kedeville City (Keedysville?) in Maryland giving you an account of our march up to those places and hope you have duly received it. After leaving those places we marched about 30 miles about it was said with the intention of going into Pennsylvania. But hearing that a large force was coming in our rear we were marched back at double quick to oppose them. The (this) was on Sunday about 3 o'clock we came up to where the enemy were position(ed) in the gap of a Mountain (Fox's Gap) and our men came into a slaughter pen to our regiment. The enemy could fire at us from their front now and from our side. Early in the action our Colonel (Colonel William R. Manning) was wounded and was carried off. He is now doing very well. I also about this time I was slightly wounded on the side of my head. This was on Sunday the 14th. We then came on to a place called Sharpsburg where we had the most terrible battle of the war. The fight lasted all day. We were first sent out on Pickett, but in the evening we became engaged in the hottest of this fight. During this fight I received a wound. The bullet passed through my right breast just below the nipple. It was God's mercy that saved me from instant death, as there is not one in a thousand that could live after receiving such a wound. It is now the next day (9/26) and though I am feeble yet, I feel like I am getting much better every day. I am in good, comfortable quarters in Winchester and have Mr. Weakly to nurse me. He gives me anything done for me that is necessary. I have no doubt I will get a furlough to go home as soon as I can travel not being able to now.
I remain as ever,
Your affectionate Husband

(Note: Lt. Mobley's hoped for recovery was not to be. He passed away on October 9, 1862, at Winchester from complications (likely pneumonia) that had set in as a result of his wound. At his request the minim ball that ended up killing him was sent to his wife.)

Index

Issue 10, Volume 1

News from Fox's Gap

The Society of the Descendants of Frederick Fox of Fox's Gap in Maryland

Membership Roster with Ancestor Line through Four Generations

December 1, 2001

The children of Frederick Fox of Fox's Gap in Maryland:

Christiana Fox	(Mrs. George Metherd)
Rose Fox	(Mrs. Christian Wohlgemuth; Mrs. Daniel Hottel)
Mary Magdalena Fox	(Mrs. Jacob Benner)
George Fox	(Elizabeth Ann Link)
Daniel Booker Fox	(Susannah Christman)
Joseph Fox	(Elizabeth Unger)
Elizabeth Fox	(Mrs. John Leiter)

Name Address	Phone	Date of Membership	Membership Number
Curtis Lynn Older 618 Tryon Place Gastonia, North Carolina 28054 curtolder@earthlink.net	704-864-3879 **Ancestor Line:** George Fox, a son of Frederick Fox; John L. Fox, Daniel Alexander Fox, Ethel Belle Fox	October 20, 1995	0001
William Ernest Fox 13071 Alger Grant, Michigan 49327-9637	616-834-5051 **Ancestor Line:** George Fox, a son of Frederick Fox; John L. Fox, Daniel Alexander Fox, Ernest Daniel Fox	October 28, 1995	0002
Reva Winfred Fox 10226 3rd Ave. S. Seattle, Washington	206-762-3845 **Ancestor Line:** George Fox, a son of Frederick Fox; John L. Fox, Daniel Alexander Fox, William Edward Fox	November 7, 1995	0003
Robert Claude Fox 10845 Edgewood Drive Demotte, Indiana 46310	**Ancestor Line:** George Fox, a son of Frederick Fox; John L. Fox, Daniel Alexander Fox, Ernest Daniel Fox	November 11, 1995	0004

Name Address	Phone	Date of Membership	Membership Number
William Goudy Benner 1000 Hidden Ridge Lane Dayton, Ohio 45459	513-433-1365 **Ancestor Line:** Mary Magdalena Fox, a daughter of Frederick Fox; Jacob Benner Jr., Valentine Benner, William Goudy Benner Sr.	November 15, 1995	0005
Laurel Ann Benner 112 Lower Hillside Drive Bellbrook, Ohio 45305	513-848-8107 **Ancestor Line:** Mary Magdalena Fox, a daughter of Frederick Fox; Jacob Benner Jr., Valentine Benner, William Goudy Benner Sr.	November 20, 1995	0006
Brenda Carol Saunders 4301 Burchdale Street Kettering, Ohio 45440	513-299-3320 **Ancestor Line:** Mary Magdalena Fox, a daughter of Frederick Fox; Jacob Benner Jr., Valentine Benner, William Goudy Benner Sr.	November 20, 1995	0007
Elizabeth Jane Bucholz 304 14th St. E. Devil's Lake, North Dakota 58301	701-662-3636 **Ancestor Line:** George Fox, a son of Frederick Fox; John L. Fox, Daniel Alexander Fox, William Edward Fox	November 6, 1995	0008
Doug Bast 109 North Main Street Boonsboro, Maryland 21713	301-432-6969 **Ancestor Line:** none	December 9, 1995	0001**H**
Dellie Jean Craig 406 Vandalia Court Crawfordsville, Indiana 47933	765-361-2891 **Ancestor Line:** George Fox, a son of Frederick Fox; John L. Fox, Daniel Alexander Fox, William Edward Fox	December 11, 1995	0009
Wilma Marion Gose P. O. Box 203 Griffith, Indiana 46319-0203	219-322-5269 **Ancestor Line:** George Fox, a son of Frederick Fox; John L. Fox, Daniel Alexander Fox, William Edward Fox	December 16, 1995	0010
Patricia Jo Edwards 526 Palomino Drive RR #4 Box 94C Danville, Illinois 61832	217-443-4523 **Ancestor Line:** George Fox, a son of Frederick Fox; John L. Fox, Daniel Alexander Fox, William Edward Fox	January 13, 1996	0011
James Joseph Fox 311 South St. Mary's Apt. 6N San Antonio, Texas 78205	210-223-6004 **Ancestor Line:** Daniel Booker Fox, a son of Frederick Fox; Frederick Christman Fox, Frederick Coffman Fox, Winfield Scott Fox	January 13, 1996	0012

Name Address	Phone	Date of Membership	Membership Number
Raphael Henry John Fox 7815 Claybrook Dallas, Texas 75231-5673	214-343-3919 **Ancestor Line:** Daniel Booker Fox, a son of Frederick Fox; Frederick Christman Fox, Frederick Coffman Fox, Winfield Scott Fox	January 13, 1996	0013
Judith Fox Smith 1050 Kingscote Drive Harleysville, PA 19438	**Ancestor Line:** Daniel Booker Fox, a son of Frederick Fox; Frederick Christman Fox, Frederick Coffman Fox, Winfield Scott Fox	January 16, 1996	0014
Richard Dale Fox Sr. P. O. Box 64 Covington, In 47932	765-793-3674 **Ancestor Line:** George Fox, a son of Frederick Fox; John L. Fox, Daniel Alexander Fox, William Edward Fox	January 24, 1996	0015
Mildred Fox Metcalf 1819 Garfield Avenue Salt Lake City, Utah 84108	xxx-484-9024 **Ancestor Line:** George Fox, a son of Frederick Fox; John L. Fox, Daniel Alexander Fox, Kenneth Benjamin Fox	June 1, 1996	0016
Teresa Rose Fox 6168 Shadow Lane Citrus Heights, California 95621	916-722-4185 **Ancestor Line:** Daniel Booker Fox, a son of Frederick Fox; Frederick Christman Fox, Frederick Coffman Fox, Winfield Scott Fox	June 7, 1996	0017
Toni Farol Bice 10626 Baker Place Crown Point, Indiana 46307	219-663-4451 **Ancestor Line:** George Fox, a son of Frederick Fox; John L. Fox, Daniel Alexander Fox, William Edward Fox	December 4, 1996	0018
Richard Dale Fox, Jr. P. O. Box 301 Baggs, Wyoming 82321	none **Ancestor Line:** George Fox, a son of Frederick Fox; John L. Fox, Daniel Alexander Fox, William Edward Fox	January 1, 1997	0019
Rachael Lynn Older 618 Tryon Place Gastonia, North Carolina 28054 curtolder@earthlink.net	704-864-3879 **Ancestor Line:** George Fox, a son of Frederick Fox; John L. Fox, Daniel Alexander Fox, Ethel Belle Fox	March 20, 1997	0020
Donald A. Smith 7 E. Hill Valley Drive Indianapolis, Indiana 46227	317-865-7761 **Ancestor Line:** George Fox, a son of Frederick Fox; Alexander Fox, Elizabeth Catherine Fox, Walter Alvin Rabold	March 10, 1998	0021

Name Address	Phone	Date of Membership	Membership Number
Mr. William Ernest Fox II 8126 West 10 Mile Road Bitely, Michigan 49309	not known **Ancestor Line:** George Fox, a son of Frederick Fox; John L. Fox, Daniel Alexander Fox, Ernest Daniel Fox	January 3, 1999	0022
Alice Takase P. O. Box 6945 Fort Bliss, Texas 79906-0945	not known **Ancestor Line:** George Fox, a son of Frederick Fox; Frederick L. Fox	May 11, 1999	0023
Michael Justin Fox 524 Elm Tree Court Cincinnati, Ohio 45244	513-528-9258 **Ancestor Line:** Daniel Booker Fox, a son of Frederick Fox; Frederick Christman Fox, Frederick Coffman Fox, Winfield Scott Fox, Henry Frederick Fox, Robert Henry Fox	May 17, 1999	0024
Kurt D. Graham 3448 Valley Vista Road Smyrna, Georgia 30080	not known **Ancestor Line:** none	May 20, 1999	0025**H**
Randy Howald 418 Kelly Court Duncanville, Texas 75137-2511	not known **Ancestor Line:** none	June 8, 1999	0026
George D. Fox 1308 Mound Avenue Miamisburg, Ohio 45342	not known **Ancestor Line:** not known	November 1, 1999	0027
Ann Schulz Trimmer 58 Riverview Terrace Belle Mead, New Jersey 08502 e-mail: ann@trimmer.net	908-359-3876 **Ancestor Line:** Christiana Fox, a daughter of Frederick Fox; George F. Metherd, Benjamin Metherd, Benjamin F. Metherd	November 2, 1999	0028
Robert Eugene Benner 8677 Cook Street Montague, Michigan 49437	231-894-6651 **Ancestor Line:** Mary Magdalena Fox, a daughter of Frederick Fox; Jacob Benner Jr., Valentine Benner, Albert Benner, Robert Ray Benner	December 1, 1999	0029
Terri A. Woods 970 E. College Ave. Westerville, OH 43081-2509	not known **Ancestor Line:** Christiana Fox, a daughter of Frederick Fox; Jacob Metherd, Frederick Metherd, Eliza Ann Metherd	February 18, 2000	0030

Name Address	Phone	Date of Membership	Membership Number
Gerald Robert Fox 506 N 300 E Valparaiso, IN 46383	219-531-2852 **Ancestor Line:** George Fox, a son of Frederick Fox; John L. Fox, Daniel Alexander Fox, Ernest Daniel Fox	February 22, 2000	0031
Suella Jane Fenton 17 Sun Cloud Circle Oroville, CA 95965-9268	408-263-8348 **Ancestor Line:** George Fox, a son of Frederick Fox; Frederick L. Fox, Samuel Fox, Orissa J. Fox	February 24, 2000	0032
Peggie Ellen Gallahue 1263 Richmond Drive Wabash, IN 46992	xxx-563-1459 **Ancestor Line:** Christiana Fox, a daughter of Frederick Fox; Jacob Metherd, Frederick Metherd, Eliza Ann Metherd	March 24, 2000	0033
Anne Elizabeth Edgecombe 973 Buchon St. San Luis Obispo, CA 93401	xxx-594-1891 **Ancestor Line:** Elizabeth Fox, a daughter of Frederick Fox; Henry Leiter, John Benton Leiter, Anna Catherine Leiter	April 5, 2000	0034
Homer Carr Hendrickson 876 West Turtlecreek Union Road Lebanon, Ohio 45036	513-932-6577 **Ancestor Line:** Daniel Booker Fox, a son of Frederick Fox; Christiana Fox, William Perry Hendrickson, Harry Fox Hendrickson	August 30, 2000	0035
Beth Ellen Davis 8355 Camfield Circle Colorado Springs, Colorado 80920	719-282-9741 **Ancestor Line:** Mary Magdalena Fox, a daughter of Frederick Fox; Samuel S. Benner, Daniel Benner, Edwin Rabb Benner	October 7, 2000	0036
Bertha L. Parker 6899 E. So. Barbee Drive Pierceton, Indiana 46562-9152	219-594-5112 **Ancestor Line:** Christiana Fox, a daughter of Frederick Fox; George Metherd, Jacob Metherd, Frederick Metherd, George W. Metherd, Benjaman F. Metherd (went by Frank B. Metherd)	March 18, 2001	0037
Janice Vanderhyde 881 Ursula Street Aurora, Colorado 80011	303-738-0328 **Ancestor Line:** Mary Magdalena Fox, a daughter of Frederick Fox; Jacob Benner Jr., Valentine Benner, Albert Benner, Forrest Benner	January 26, 2001	0038
Roger Lee Benner 881 Ursula Street Aurora, Colorado 80011	303-738-0328 **Ancestor Line:** Mary Magdalena Fox, a daughter of Frederick Fox; Jacob Benner Jr., Valentine Benner, Albert Benner, Forrest Benner	March 19, 2001	0039

Name Address	Phone	Date of Membership	Membership Number
Alan K. Sentman 140 Cabrini Blvd., #129 New York, New York 10033-3434	212-740-3532 **Ancestor Line:** Daniel Booker Fox, a son of Frederick Fox; Frederick C. Fox, Caroline Fox, Ida Stansel, James Monroe Sentman, Forrest Eugene Sentman	April 20, 2001	0040
Larry W. Cole 161 Hickory Grove Rd. Leesburg, Georgia 31763-5349 e-mail: lcole@appliedfiber.com	229-432-1068 Joined under interest in Battle of South Mountain.	June 28, 2001	0041
Jon B. Barber 3733 Barmer Drive Jacksonville, Florida 32210-5023	Joined under interest in Battle of South Mountain.	June 28, 2001	0042

H - denotes Honorary Member

News from Fox's Gap

The Society of the Descendants of Frederick Fox of Fox's Gap in Maryland

Issue 1, Volume 2 **Remember Freedom!** June 1, 2001

South Mountain Symposium August 17, 18, and 19, 2001

(From a press release of The North Carolina South Mountain Fund, 9225 Surrey Road, Charlotte, NC 28227.)

The greatest gathering of historians ever for The Battle of South Mountain Symposium. In September, 1862 during General Robert E. Lee's Maryland Campaign, the Federal forces were pressing the Confederates at three gaps in Maryland's South Mountain chain, Turner's, Fox's, and Crampton's. North Carolinians fought at Fox's and Crampton's heroically and fatally. The dead were never brought home.

In October, 2000, the State of Maryland made this their first state battlefield. In honor of the North Carolinians that fought and died there, citizens are placing a monument at Fox's Gap for those brave young soldiers. Private citizens throughout the state are helping raise funds for this monument. Many prominent speakers have donated their time for this symposium, August 17, 18, 19, 2001 in Boonsboro, MD, at the American Legion Hall.

Located at the western foot of South Mountain, Boonsboro, MD, served as General D. H. Hill's base of operations. The determination of the Confederates to hold these three gaps on the 14th, gave General Stonewall Jackson the time needed to capture Harpers Ferry and General Lee time to consolidate his forces at Sharpsburg.

Schedule

Friday 17th:	Tours of Boonsboro Museum of History. Ancestors reception
and	check-in (open to all) Middletown, MD (on eastern side of Mtn.)
Saturday 18th:	Symposium on Battle of South Mountain 8:30-4:30; lunch on your own. Buffet dinner 7-8:00 PM Live auction 8-8:30 PM "Soldiers in Gray" performed by Mr. Stan Clardy 8:30-9:30 PM
Sunday 19th:	Buses depart for the Gaps from the American Legion Hall 8:30 am; Arrive back at 1:00 PM

Registration includes all of the above, lodging on your own, The Four Points Sheraton, Hagerstown, MD 301-790-3010 and the Holiday Inn, Patrick St., Frederick, MD, 301-662-5141 are the two host hotels. When making reservations mention "LHAM" for group rate. Group rates are good for 3 days prior and past.

Speaker Schedule and Cost - See Next Page

Speaker Schedule - Saturday August 18, 2001

Opening panel discussion on the importance of the Maryland Campaign politically and militarily as well as the loss of Special Order 191.

Ted Alexander Historian at Antietam National Battlefield
Ed Bearss retired Historian with National Parks Service
Paul Chiles Historian at Antietam National Battlefield

"My God Be Careful", D. Scott Hartwig Historian at Gettysburg National Battlefield

"Legend of Wise's Well" , Steve Stotelmyer

"Jeff Davis Artillery at South Mountain" Bondurant's Battery played an important part at Fox's Gap. Lawrence Laboda, Author of above and historian.

"Battlefield Ghosts of Old South Mountain" Doug Bast Curator of Boonsboro Museum of History

"Crampton's Gap" John Michael Priest Author, Historian, Teacher

"Drayton's Brigade: Afternoon Battle at Fox's Gap" Kurt Graham, Author, Historian, Researcher

"Blundering Personalities of Some of the Commanders of South Mountain" Clint Johnson, Author, Historian, Reenactor

Also appearing Paul R. Martin III, Artist and Wilmer Mumma, Author and Historian

Above schedule subject to change due to unforeseen circumstances, new speakers may be added.

Cost: $175.00 for one, $305 for two, Dinner only $30

Make checks payable to: LHAM
Mail to: LHAM
9225 Surrey Road
Charlotte, NC 28227
Contact: hovey13thnc@yahoo.com

Medal of Honor Recipient of the 16th New York Regiment

Allen, James - Rank and organization: Private, Company F, 16th New York Infantry. Place and date: At south Mountain, Md., 14 September 1862. Entered service at: Postdam, N. Y. born: 6 May 1843, Ireland. Date of issue: 11 September 1890. Citation: Single-handed and slightly wounded he accosted a squad of 14 Confederate soldiers bearing the colors of the 16th Georgia Infantry (C.S.A.). By an imaginary ruse he secured their surrender and kept them at bay when the regimental commander discovered him and rode away for assistance.

Fox Family Reunion

August 17, 18, and 19

A Fox Family Reunion will be held at or near Boonsboro, Maryland, on Friday, August 17 through Sunday, August 19, 2001. This is the weekend of the North Carolina South Mountain Symposium. Please contact Curt Older if you think you might be able to attend. Your ideas, suggestions, and attendance are needed.

Attendance at the North Carolina South Mountain Symposium is not required in order to attend the Fox Reunion. The Symposium has an attendance fee of $175. The only cost to attend the Fox Reunion will be your expense of food, motel, and travel.

Please contact me at home, 704-864-3879, or write to me no later than July 31 if you wish to meet with me in the Hagerstown, Frederick, or Fox's Gap area this August.

If you have not visited Fox's Gap, the Fox Inn, or the Battlefield of South Mountain, I hope you can make your first visit to the area in August 2001.

Table of Contents for this Newsletter

Death of Captain Glenn, 13th NC, Company I

(From the Summer 2000 issue of N. C. South Mountain News published by the Living History Association of Mecklenburg, Inc., Charlotte, North Carolina.)

From the North Carolina Troops, Chalmers Glenn resided in Rockingham County and was by occupation a lawyer prior to enlisting in Rockingham County at age 30. Elected 1st Lieutenant on April 30, 1861, to rank from may 3, 1861, and was elected Captain to rank from April 26, 1862. Present or accounted for until killed at South Mountain, Maryland, September 14, 1861. "A very gallant officer."

The Company, known as the Rockingham Ranger, was from Rockingham County and enlisted at Wentworth on May 3, 1861. The company received orders to march to Garysburg the same day and began the march on May 13,. It arrived at Garysburg on May 17. There it was assigned to the regiment as Company I.

The 13th was under command of Lt. Col. Thomas Ruffin, Jr. of Alamance County. The 13th, 5th, 12th, 20th, and 23rd made up Brigadier General Samuel Garland's Brigade which served in General D H Hill's Division. General Hill's orders were to prevent any Yankee retreat along Pleasant Valley and to guard the mountain passes. In the early hours of September 14th, 1862, General Garland received word from General Hill to march to Turner's Gap. Upon reaching the Gap at about dawn, Hill deployed Garland's brigade a mile south to Fox's Gap. Upon reaching Fox's Gap General Garland found a small force of Virginia Cavalry under Colonel Rosser, left behind by General J. E. B. Stuart.

General Garland deployed his force across a 1300 yard front, quite unusual for a brigade of just over 1000 men, with Colonel Rosser and the 5th NC on the far right and the 13th on the far left. General Garland stayed with the 13th, commanding his brigade. Lt. Col. Ruffin suggested to Garland that he might seek safer ground for himself as the battle was under way. General Garland state, " I may as well be here as yourself". At that moment, Lt. Col. Ruffin was struck in the thigh by a projectile, he turned to Garland to ask him to get someone to lead his troops, when Garland was mortally struck and killed.

Another young officer died that morning, from Rockingham County, NC. Chalmers Glenn and his faithful servant Mat had been reared together since childhood. Mat had shared in all the boyish pranks and frolics of his master, and in later life had been his constant attendant and faithful servant. On the morning of the battle, north of Boonsboro, Captain Glenn called mat to him and said: "Mat, I shall be killed in this battle. See me buried, then go home and be to your mistress and my children all that you have ever been to me."

From behind a rock the faithful fellow watched all day the form of his beloved master, as the tide of battle ebbed and flowed over that eventful field. At last he missed him, and rushing forward, found the prediction too truly verified--life was already extinct. Assisted by two members of his company, a grave was dug with bayonets, and soon the cold, silent earth held all that was dearest in the life to Mat. Slowly and sadly he turned his face homeward and delivered all the messages and valuables with which his master had entrusted him. From that time it seemed his mission on earth was accomplished.

Though constantly attending his master's children and promptly obedient to the slightest word of his mistress, he visibly declined. Finally he was taken sick, and despite the best medical attention and kindest nursing, he died February 4, 1863.

One of the children Mat helped raise was Chalmers' son Robert B. Glenn, a future governor of North Carolina.

Welcome New Members!

We welcome the following new members who joined the Society since December 1, 2000.

Bertha L. Parker is a descendant of Christiana Fox, a daughter of Frederick Fox, who married George Metherd. Information on Christiana Fox and George Metherd appears on page 19 of *The Fox Genealogy* by Daniel Gebhart Fox.

Janice Vanderhyde is a descendant of Mary Magdalena Fox, a daughter of Frederick Fox, who married Jacob Benner II. Information on Mary Magdalena Fox and Jacob Benner II appears on page 57 of *The Fox Genealogy* by Daniel Gebhart Fox.

Roger Lee Benner is a descendant of Mary Magdalena Fox, a daughter of Frederick Fox, who married Jacob Benner II. Information on Mary Magdalena Fox and Jacob Benner II appears on page 57 of *The Fox Genealogy* by Daniel Gebhart Fox.

Alan K. Sentman is a descendant of Daniel Booker Fox, a son of Frederick Fox, who married Susannah Christman. Information on Daniel Booker Fox and Susannah Christman appears on page 101, 102, and 103 of *The Fox Genealogy* by Daniel Gebhart Fox.

Name and Address	Telephone	Date Joined	Member #
Bertha L. Parker 6899 E. So. Barbee Drive Pierceton, Indiana 46562-9152	219-594-5112	March 18, 2001	0037
	Ancestor Line: Christiana Fox, a daughter of Frederick Fox; George Metherd, Jacob Metherd, Frederick Metherd, George W. Metherd, Benjaman F. Metherd (went by Frank B. Metherd)		
Janice Vanderhyde 881 Ursula Street Aurora, Colorado 80011	303-738-0328	January 26, 2001	0038
	Ancestor Line: Mary Magdalena Fox, a daughter of Frederick Fox; Jacob Benner Jr., Valentine Benner, Albert Benner, Forrest Benner		
Roger Lee Benner 881 Ursula Street Aurora, Colorado 80011	303-738-0328	March 19, 2001	0039
	Ancestor Line: Mary Magdalena Fox, a daughter of Frederick Fox; Jacob Benner Jr., Valentine Benner, Albert Benner, Forrest Benner		
Alan K. Sentman 140 Cabrini Blvd., #129 New York, New York 10033-3434	212-740-3532	April 20, 2001	0040
	Ancestor Line: Daniel Booker Fox, a son of Frederick Fox; Frederick C. Fox, Caroline Fox, Ida Stansel, James Monroe Sentman, Forrest Eugene Sentman		

Land Tracts of the Battlefield of South Mountain

by Curtis L. Older

Each Newsletter includes a survey, patent, or deed related to the land tracts in the vicinity of Crampton's, Fox's, and Turner's Gaps. These three gaps in South Mountain represent the main area contested by the Union and Confederate Armies in the Battle of South Mountain on September 14, 1862.

Previous issues of the Society Newsletter contained descriptions of the following tracts:

June 1, 1997	Addition to Friendship of Frederick Fox
December 1, 1997	Fredericksburgh of Frederick Fox
June 1, 1998	Pick All of Bartholomew Booker
December 1, 1998	Bowser's Addition of David Bowser
June 1, 1999	Partnership of John Mansberger
December 1, 1999	Mountain of John Baley
June 1, 2000	no tract included in newsletter
December 1, 2000	Flonham of Philip Jacob Shafer

The Fox Inn stands on a tract of land named Exchange that was surveyed in 1742 for Daniel Dulany.

MdHR 17,412-2, 1-23-2-37, BY & GS 1, p. 177, Daniel Dulaney, The Exchange, surveyed 5 Oct 1742, 100 acres. completed 9-30-95.

Prince Georges County By virtue of a warrant granted out of his lordship's land office of this province to Daniel Dulany of the city of Annapolis esqr for four thousand two hundred and fifty six acres of land bearing date by renewment September 9th 1742 I therefore certifie as deputy surveyor of Prince Georges County under his excellency Thomas Bladen esqr governor of Maryland I have carefully laid out for and in the name of him the said Daniel Dulany Esq all that tract of land called the Exchange beginning at t bound Red oak standing by the side of a spring called Punch Spring it being a draught of Abrams Creek and running thence

Crse No.	North South	Degrees East or West	Length
1.	N	68 west	140 perches then
2.	N	35 west	220 perches then
3.	S	56 east	333 perches

4. then by a straight line to the beginning tree containing and now laid out for one hundred acres of land to be held of Conegochieg manor surveyed the fifth day of October 1742 examd & passed B. Young exam signed ? order Peter Dent?

On the back of the aforegoing certificate was the following assignment vizt I have received the sum of one pound eight shillings ? sterling for seven years rent of the within land to ? 1749 patent may therefore issue with his excellency's approbation Sam Ogle Cha? Bend Tasker
May 1749

Know all men by these presents that I Daniel Dulany of the city of Annapolis esq in consideration of forty pounds currency received from Robert Evans of Frederick County planter have assigned set over and transferred unto the said Robert Evans a tract of land called the Exchange containing one hundred acres the certificate thereof to the end he may obtain my lords grant for the same to him and his heirs ? assigns in usual form Witness my hand and seal this 29th day of April 1749 D Dulany (seal) witness John Darnall

Know all men by these presents that I Robert Evans for a valuable consideration all ? received from Joseph Chapline of Frederick County have assigned set over and transferred unto the said Joseph Chapline a tract of land called the exchange containing one hundred acres which was assigned me by Daniel Dulany esqr and the certificate thereof to the end he may obtain his lordships grant for the same as witness my hand this 10th day of May Anno Domi 1749 Robert Evans
witness W? Jennings

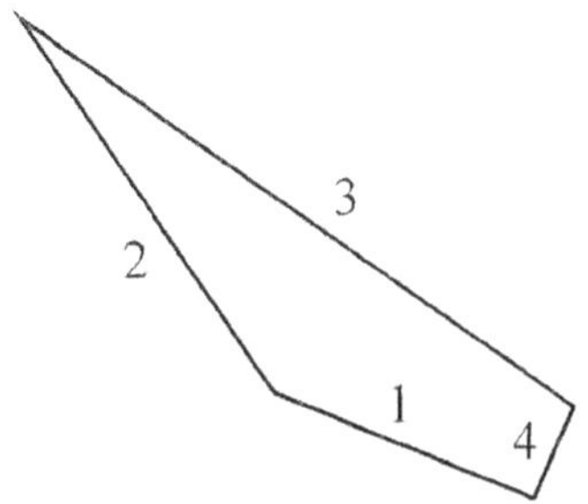

The Patent for the Exchange tract follows:

MdHR 17,438, 1-23-3-38, BC & GS 27, p. 578, Daniel Dulany, The Exchange, surveyed 5 Oct 1742, patented to Daniel and Walter Dulany, 100 acres. completed 10-1-95.

Daniel Dulany Esqr his cert 100 acres The Exchange Patd to Daniel & Walter Dulany the 29th Sept 1765 Rent ? Charged to the rent roll}

Prince Georges County By virtue of a warrant granted out of his lordship's land office of this province to Daniel Dulany Esqr. of the city of Annapolis for four thousand two hundred and fifty six acres of land bearing date by renewment September 9th 1742 I therefore certifie as deputy surveyor of Prince Georges County under his excellency Thomas Bladen esqr governor of Maryland I have carefully laid out for and in the name of him the said Daniel Dulany Esq all that tract of land called the Exchange beginning at a bounded Red oak standing by the side of a spring called Punch Spring it being a draught of Abrams Creek and running thence

Crse No.	North South	Degrees East or West	Length
1.	N	68 west	140 perches then
2.	N	35 west	220 perches then
3.	S	56 east	333 perches

4. then by a straight line to the beginning tree containing and now laid out for one hundred acres of land to be held of Conegochieg manor surveyed the fifth day of October 1742 signed ? order
Pet Dent Depty Surv

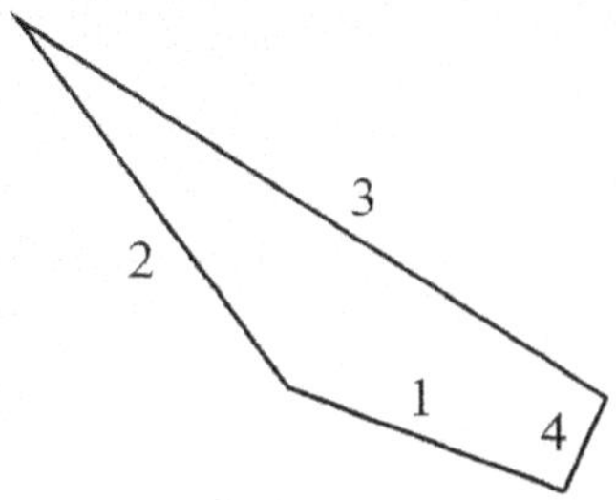

On the back of the aforegoing certificate was the following receipt vizt - I have received the sum of three pounds eight shillings for seventeen year rent of the within land to Michalmas 1759 patent may therefore issue with his excellency approbation 12 Decem 1759 Edw Lloyd

I have received the sum of one pound and four shillings for six years rent to Michas 1765 of the within land patent may therefore issue with his excellency approbation Oct 30th 1765 approved h. Sharpe Edw Lloyd

Maryland ? to the Honble Benedict Calvert and George Steuart Esqr the Lord Proprietary's chief judges in land affairs within this province The petition of Daniel and Walter Dulany Executors of the last Will & Testament of Daniel Dulany Esqr late of the city of Annapolis deceased
Humbly sheweth that Daniel Dulany Your petitioners father had in his lifetime to wit on the fifth day of October 1742 surveyed and laid out for him a tract or parcel of land called The Exchange lying and being formerly in Prince Georges but now (note: The next page, page 579, was not sent to me by the Maryland Archives in Annapolis when I ordered this document. Page 579 should contain the remaining portion of the patent document.)

President's Message

by Curtis Lynn Older

* There will be a Fox Family Reunion at Boonsboro, Maryland, on Friday, Saturday, and Sunday August 17, 18, and 19, 2001, if anyone cares to meet with me at that time and place. Please contact me as soon as possible and we will make arrangements.

* A file containing the first10 issues or Volume 1 of the Society Newsletter, "News from Fox's Gap", has not been completed by me. Most of the work is done but I still need to polish off the rough edges. The file was created using the Adobe Acrobat software and may be accessed on a computer using the "free" Adobe Acrobat Reader. If you do not have the Acrobat Reader on your computer you may download it for free from the Adobe web site. I plan to distribute the file as part of my next CD-Rom project (see next).

* A CD-Rom disc is planned by me that will contain: 1) *The Fox Genealogy* by Daniel Gebhart Fox; 2) the first 10 issues, or Volume 1, of the Fox Society Newsletter, "News from Fox's Gap"; 3) *The Braddock Expedition and Fox's Gap in Maryland* published in 1995; and 4) *The Land Tracts of the Battlefield of South Mountain* that published in 1999. The CD-Rom disc will contain the above four documents and will be created using the Adobe Acrobat software. All the files on the disc will be in the Adobe Acrobat PDF format and may be accessed with the free Adobe Acrobat Reader. I hope to complete this project in the next year or two. Rough drafts of the files already have been completed.

George Fox Line

listing of descendants by Suella Fenton (material sent in by Alice Takase)

Alice Takase, a member of the Society, is a descendant of Frederick L. Fox. Frederick L. Fox was a son of George Fox and Elizabeth Ann (Link) Fox. He was a brother of John L. Fox of Gessie, Indiana. Alice Takase's address is: PO Box 6945, Fort Bliss, Texas 79906-0945.

Descendants of Frederick L. Fox

(A son of George Fox and a grandson of Frederick Fox of Fox's Gap in Maryland)

Generation No. 5

54. Melinda Fox (Marion Johnson, Francis "Frank" Marion, Samuel, Frederick Link, George, Frederick, John Frederick) was born February 08, 1939. She married John Proctor.

Children of Melinda Fox and John Proctor are:

i. Frederick Marion Proctor, b. November 26, 1963.
ii. Allison Lynn Proctor, b. October 29, 1964.

55. Lonnie Lee Fox (Kenneth Lynn, Francis "Frank" Marion, Samuel, Frederick Link, George "1", Frederick "1", John "1" Frederick) was born June 28, 1947. He married Carol Tanner.

Children of Lonnie Fox and Carol Tanner are:

i. Stacy Michelle Fox, b. July 21, 1947.
ii. Christopher Kenneth Fox, b. November 27, 1977.
iii. Jeffrey Fox, b. Unknown.

56. Larry Lynn Fox (Kenneth Lynn, Francis "Frank" Marion, Samuel, Frederick Link, George "1", Frederick "1", John "1" Frederick) was born June 28, 1947. He married Donna D'angelo.

Child of Larry Fox and Donna D'angelo is:

i. Janet Fox, b. Unknown.

57. Leonard Orville Fox, Jr. (Leonard Orville, Francis "Frank" Marion, Samuel, Frederick Link, George "1", Frederick "1", John "1" Frederick) was born August 08, 1930. He married Martha Horlamus.

Children of Leonard Fox and Martha Horlamus are:

i. Leonard Kenneth Fox, b. October 01, 1963.
ii. Richard Fox, b. October 21, 1964.

58. Marion Huson Fox (Leonard Orville, Francis "Frank" Marion, Samuel, Frederick Link, George "1", Frederick "1", John "1" Frederick) was born on January 14, 1932. He married Leslie Calhoun.

Children of Marion Fox and Leslie Calhoun are:

i. Suzanne Marie Fox, b. March 05, 1963.
ii. Lorena Leslie Fox, b. May 25, 1964.

59. Charles Richard "Dick" Hutchinson (Grace "Jeannette" Fox, Francis "Frank" Marion, Samuel, Frederick Link, George "1", Frederick "1", John "1" Frederick) was born October 10, 1943. He married Gayette Ann Baker.

Children of Charles Hutchinson and Gayette Baker are:
i. Jill Lynn Hutchinson, b. July 17, 1969.
ii. John Richard Hutchinson, b. October 02, 1971.
iii. Jane Erin Hutchinson, b. May 24, 1973.

60. Kathleen Lynn "Kitty" Fox (Harold C. Bus, Francis "Frank" Marion, Samuel, Frederick Link, George "1", Frederick "1", John "1" Frederick) was born February 13, 1942. She married Hooper Goldsworthy.

Children of Kathleen Fox and Hooper Goldsworthy are:
i. Jenny Elizabeth Goldsworthy, b. December 26, 1966.
ii. Marcy Ellen Goldsworthy, b. February 07, 1968.

61. Jerold Curtis Fox(Harold C. "Bus", Francis "Frank" Marion, Samuel, Frederick Link, George "1", Frederick "1", John "1" Frederick) was born August 30, 1943. He married Kathleen Killworth.

Children of Jerold Fox and Kathleen Killworth are:
i. Bret Aaron Fox, b. September 30, 1969.
ii. Beth Ann Fox, b. December 05, 1971.

62. Michael M. Fox (Marvin L., Francis "Frank" Marion, Samuel, Frederick Link, George "1", Frederick "1", John "1" Frederick) was born May 04, 1951. He married Karen Shite Strawoet.

Children of Michael Fox and Karen Strawoet are:
i. Elizabeth Naomi Fox.
ii. Susanna "2" Fox.
iii. Carolyn Rachel Fox.

63. Karen Kay Fox (Lyle Scott, Francis "Frank" Marion, Samuel, Frederick Link, George "1", Frederick "1", John "1" Frederick) was born July 21, 1951. She married David Reuben.

Child of Karen Fox and David Reuben is:
i. Nicholas Vercelles Reuben, b. Unknown.

64. Bernard Adam Leis (Ruby Jeanette Hayner, Orissa J. Fox, Samuel, Frederick Link, George "1", Frederick "1", John "1" Frederick) was born February 16, 1940 in New Lebanon, Montgomery Co., Ohio. He married Doris Ann Baker June 16, 1962 in Springboro, Warren Co., Ohio, daughter of Herbert Baker and Nellie Sandlin.

Children of Bernard Leis and Doris Baker are:
104. i. Wesley Lawrence Leis, b. March 27, 1963, Middletown Butler Co., Ohio.
ii. Lesley Herbert Leis, b. March 27, 1963, Middletown Butler Co., Ohio; d. January 16, 1964, Middletown, Butler Co., Ohio.

iii. Todd Allen Leis, b. April 23, 1964, Middletown, Butler Co., Ohio; d. April 23, 1964, Middletown, Butler Co., Ohio.
iv. Darwin Dwain Leis, b. August 04, 1966.
v. Jeanell Balynda Leis, b. November 12, 1969.

65. Frieda Irene Leis (Ruby Jeanette Hayner, Orissa J. Fox, Samuel, Frederick Link, George "1", Fredrick "1", John "1" Frederick) was born August 24, 1941 in New Lebanon, Montgomery Co., Ohio. She married Arthur Raymond Hellmund, Jr. September 03, 1960 in Springboro, Warren Co., Ohio, son of Arthur Hellmund and Goldie Phillips.

Children of Frieda Leis and Arthur Hellmund are:
105. i. Clifford Eugene Hellmund, b. October 29, 1964, Dayton, Montgomery County, Ohio.
106. i. Elaine Mashel Hellmund, b. July 27, 1966, Dayton, Montgomery Co., Ohio.

66. Lenora Margaret Leis (Ruby Jeanette Hayner, Orissa J. Fox, Samuel, Frederick Link, George "1", Frederick "1", John "1" Frederick) was born February 16, 1943 in New Lebanon, Montgomery Co., Ohio. She married Bruce Lewis May 04, 1963 in Springboro, Waren Co., Ohio, son of Marcus Lewis and Alice Halcomb.

Children of Lenora Leis and Bruce Lewis are:
107. i. Leonard Bartholomew Lewis, b. May 26, 1966, Springboro, Warren Co., Ohio.
108. ii. Emmett Rodney Lewis, b. October 11, 1967, Springboro, Warren Co., Ohio.
109. iii. Nathan Uyl Lewis, b. July 26, 2969, Springboro, Warren Co., Ohio.
110. iv. Orissa Cheryleen Lewis, b. January 02, 1971, Springboro, Warren Co., Ohio.
111. v. Ryan Everett Lewis, b. January 18, 1972, Springboro, Warren Co., Ohio.
112. vi. Aaron Lyle Lewis, b. January 18, 1972, Springboro, Warren Co., Ohio.

67. Glenn Ervin Leis (Ruby Jeanette Hayner, Orissa J. Fox, Samuel, Frederick Link, George "1", Frederick "1", John "1" Frederick) was born March 20, 1944 in Springboro, Warren County, Ohio. He married Connie Sue Williams June 25, 1966 in Springboro, Warren County, Ohio, daughter of Milford Williams and Gladys Carpenter.

Children of Glenn Leis and Connie Williams are:
113. i. Glenna Sue Leis, b. July 01, 1967, Dayton, Montgomery County, Ohio.
114. ii. Patricia Lynn Leis, b. August 17, 1969, Springboro, Warren County, Ohio.
iii. Carol Marie Leis, b. April 09, 1972, Springboro, Warren County, Ohio; m. James Massingill, December 04, 1993, Springboro, Warren Co., Ohio.

68. Suella Jane Leis (Ruby Jeanette Hayner, Orissa J. Fox, Samuel, Frederick Link, George "1", Frederick "1", John "1" Frederick) was born March 18, 1946 in Springboro, Warren Co., Ohio. She married (1) Timothy Marvin Wyant October 30, 1965 in Springboro, Warren Co., Ohio, son of Jonas Wyant and Lois Clark. She married (2) Donald Frank Fenton August 24, 1996 in Sanborn Park, Saratoge, California, son of Donald Fenton and Marianna Apalategul.

Notes for Donald Frank Fenton:
Eric is a step-son of Donald Fenton. He was never adopted by Donald, just raised him since he was 1 1/2 years old.

Children of Suella Leis and Timothy Wyant are:
i. Victoria Lynn Wyant, b. January 05, 1967, Mountain View, Santa Clara Co., California; m. Kenneth Scott Breneisen, May 19, 1990, Sacramento, Sacrament Co., California.
115. ii. Pamela Sue Wyant, b. July 10, 1971, San Jose, Santa Clara Co., California.

69. Kermit Paul Leis (Ruby Jeanette Hayner, Orissa J. Fox, Samuel, Frederick Link, George "1", Frederick "1", John "1" Frederick) was born April 08, 1948 in Springboro, Warren Co., Ohio. He married Reta Fay Williams June 30, 1968 in Springboro, Warren Co., Ohio, daughter of Milford Williams and Gladys Carpenter.

Children of Kermit Leis and Reta Williams are:

116. i. Shalatta Kae Leis, b. December 28, 1969, Giessen, Germany.
ii. Eric Jason Leis, b. March 20, 1973; m. Karen Diane Peura, November 14, 1997, Troy, Ohio.

70. Donald Brown (Lewis Marion, Clarence David, Frances A. Fox, Frederick Link, George "1", Frederick "1", John "1" Frederick) was born September 1938. He married Mary Lou (Brown).

Child of Donald Brown and Mary (Brown) is:

i. Donald Brown, Jr.

71. Mary "2" Brown(Lewis Marion, Clarence David, Fraces A. Fox, Frederick Link, George "1", Frederick "1", John "1" Frederick) was born Abt. 1940. She married (Husband) Grewe.

Child of Mary Brown and (Husband) Grewe is:

i. Connie Brown.

72. Clarence Edwin Taylor (Ada Luella Brown, Clarence David, Frances A. Fox, Frederick Link, George "1", Frederick "1", John "1" Frederick) was born January 12, 1931 in Franklin, Warren County, Ohio, and died March 29, 1995 in Middletown, Butler Co., Ohio. He married (1) Charlotte Brookey December 09, 1950 in Miamisburg, Montgomery Co., Ohio, daughter of Charles Brookey and Amanda (Brookey). He married (2) Janet (Taylor) Aft. 1962.

Children of Clarence Taylor and Charlotte Brookey are:

i. Velena Taylor, b. January 21, 1953, Dayton, Montgomery Co., Ohio; m. Wendell Perkins, November 03, 1978, Middletown, Butler Co., Ohio.
ii. Susan Louise Taylor, b. May 31, 1956, Middletown, Butler Co., Ohio.
iii. Clarence Taylor, b. November 22, 1959, Middletown, Butler Co., Ohio.
iv. Keith Taylor, b. February 21, 1961, Middletown, Butler Co., Ohio.

73. Barbara Taylor (Ada Luella Brown, Clarence David, Frances A. Fox, Frederick Link, George "1", Frederick "1", John "1" Frederick) was born May 07, 1933 in Franklin, Warren Co., Ohio. She married (1) James "1" Dalton July 06, 1950 in Richmond, Indianna, son of Lloyd Dalton and Catherine Cox. She married (2) Winfred M. Roberts June 26, 1976 in Farmersville, Montgomery Co., Ohio, son of Ostle Roberts and Mary (Roberts).

Children of Barbara Taylor and James Dalton are:

117. i. Penny Dalton, b. November 20, 1953, Germantown, Montgomery Co., Ohio.
118. ii. James "2" Dalton, b. October 31, 1951, Franklin, Warren Co., Ohio.
iii. Jerry Edison Dalton, b. November 26, 1957, Germantown, Montgomery Co., Ohio.
iv. Kelly Ann Dalton, b. August 20, 1960, Germantown, Montgomery Co., Ohio.

74. Robert Bullock (Ethel May Brown, Clarence David, Frances A. Fox, Frederick Link, George "1", Frederick "1", John "1" Frederick) was born September 06, 1940 in Middletown, Butler Co., Ohio. He married Carol Stiver March 06, 1965 in Middletown, Butler County, Ohio.

Child of Robert Bullock and Carol Stiver is:
120. i. Rachel Bullock, b. September 28, 1971.

75. Janet Rose Brown (Walter Howard, Clarence David, Frances A. Fox, Frederick Link, George "1", Frederick "1", John "1" Fredrick) was born September 03, 1939. She married James Wilson Payne.

Children of Janet Brown and James Payne are:
121. i. Sharon Payne, b. 1962.
ii. Diane Payne, b. 1963; m. Jim Price.

76. Betty Lou Brown (Walter Howard, Clarence David, Frances A. Fox, Frederick Link, George "1", Frederick "1", John "1" Frederick) was born October 12, 1942. She married Don Petticrew.

Child of Betty Brown and Don Petticrew is:
122. i. Donna Petticrew.

77. Carolyn Sue Brown (Walter Howard, Clarence David, Fraces A. Fox, Frederick Link, George "1", Frederick "1", John "1"Frederick) was born April 18, 1945. She married Larry Eugene Hofer.

Children of Carolyn Brown and Larry Hofer are:
123. i. Thomas Lee Hofer, b. 1969.
ii. Keith Wayne Hofer, b. 1973; m. Missy (Hofer).
iii. Mark Allen Hofer, b. 1989.

78. Walter Howard Brown Jr. (Walter Howard, Clarence David, Fraces A. Fox, Frederick Link, George "1", Frederick "1", John "1" Frederick) was born November 04, 1950. He married Vicki Lee Demons.

Children of Walter Brown and Vicki Demons are:
i. Julie Elizabeth Brown, b. 1979.
ii. Walter Howard Brown III, b. 1982; d 1982.
iii. James Alexander Brown, b. 1990; d. 1990.
iv. Justin Andrew Brown, b. 1991.

79. David Lewis Brown (Walter Howard, Clarence David, Frances A. Fox, Frederick Link, George "1", Frederick "1", John "1" Frederick) was born September 30, 1952. He married Kathy Sue Burns.

Children of David Brown and Kathy Burns are:
i. David Michael Brown, b. 1976.
ii. Kolby Rae Brown, b. 1984.
iii. Sammatha Jo Brown, b. 1986.

80. Becky Lynn Brown (Walter Howard, Clarence David, Fraces A. Fox, Frederick Link, George "1", Frederick "1", John "1" Frederick) was born December 06, 1958. She married Harold Lee Coker.

Children of Becky Brown and Harold Coker are:
i. Harold Lee Coker, Jr., b. 1978.
ii. Randy H. Reddick, b. 1983
iii. David Lee Coker, b. 1987.
iv. Richard Lee Coker, b. 1989.

Remainder of Generation Five to be concluded in next issue of this Newsletter.

Wills Section

Each Newsletter includes one typewritten version of a will that is significant to the preservation efforts of the Society. Included in this issue is the will of Jacob Benner. The wife of Jacob Benner was Mary Magdalena Fox, a daughter of Frederick Fox of Fox's Gap in Maryland. Jacob Benner was born in Pennsylvania on July 3, 1765. He died July 7, 1852 and is buried in the St. John or Gebhart church yard in Miamisburg, Ohio.

Previous issues of the Society Newsletter contained copies of the following wills and estate papers:

December 1, 1996	will of John Fox of Fox's Gap in Maryland
June 1, 1997	will of Frederick Fox of Fox's Gap in Maryland
December 1, 1997	will of Bartholomew Booker, father-in-law of Frederick Fox
June 1, 1998	estate papers for George Fox, the oldest son of Frederick Fox
December 1, 1998	will of John Adam Link II, the father-in-law of George Fox
June 1, 1999	will of John Adam Link I, the father of John Adam Link II
December 1, 1999	no will included in newsletter
June 1, 2000	no will inlcuded in newsletter
December 1, 2000	will of John L. Fox, a grandson of Frederick Fox of Fox's Gap in Maryland

---

Will of Jacob Benner

(Note: Jacob Benner was the husband of Mary Magdelana Fox, a daughter of Frederick Fox of Fox's Gap in Maryland.)

In the name of the Benevolent Father of all, I, Jacob Benner of the County of Montgomery and State of Ohio, do make and publish this my last will and testament.

Item first, I give and bequest to my beloved wife Mary Benner all the house hold and kitchen furniture that she may chose to take for her own use, and one third of the net proceeds of all my real and personal estate that I may be possessd of at my death, in money after the same shall have been reduced to money by my executor as hereinafter provided.

It is my will and desire that my executor shall in a reasonable time after my decease, sell at public veue all my personal propert, and within one year after my decease also to sell all the real estate that I may be posessed of at public sale to the highest bidder on such terms as he may think best for the interest of my heirs.

And the money arrisingfrom my personal assets and from the sale of the real estate, after first paying my just debts and expenses, shall be divided as follows:

First, I give and bequest to my beloved wife Mary Benner as above stated one third of the net proceeds of my real and personal estate in money, and the remaining two thirds to be divided into eight equal shares. To my children as follows: one share to eaqch of my sons, Jacob Benner, Samuel Benner, Daniel Benner, and Trederick Benner, and one share to each of my daughters Mary intermarried with Sampson Strader, and Elizabeth intermarried with Jona Gebhart and Catherine intermarried with Wm Akin, deceased, and the remaining one share to my daughter Sarah intermarried with James Ryon, except one hundred dollars of her share, which I give and bequeath to her daughter Mariah Friberger now about twelve years of age said one hundred dollars I hereby authorize my executor to put on interest for the use of said Mariah Friberger until she arrives at the age of eighteen years and then to pay the same over together with the interest to the said Mariah Friberger.

Continued on the following page.

(Will of Jacob Benner - continued)

Item 2nd, I do hereby nominate and appoint John Conley my executor of this my last will and testament hereby empowering him to settle up my estate, to collect all my just dues and to convey all my real estate as herein before named by good and sufficient deed or deeds to the pruchasers.

It is further my will and desire that my son Frederick shall have the use of the farm on which I now live from the term of one year from the time of my decease, at the same rate of rent that he now pays for the same provided he desires to remain on it.

In testimony whereof I have hereunto set my hand and seal this twelth day of April AD 1852 Signed and acknowledged by said Jacob Benner his last will and testament in our presence, and signed by us in hi presence, Thomas (Roberts?) his
George Liter Jacob X Benner (seal)
Mark

Please notify

the President of the Society

regarding any errors you find in the current issue of the

Newsletter.

Topics in the next issue of the Newsletter, December 1, 2001

* 1. The 3rd South Carolina Battalion under Lt. Col. James at Fox's Gap
* 2. The will of Daniel Alexander Fox
* 3. Report on the North Carolina South Mountain Symposium
* 4. Report on the Fox Family Reunion in August 2001
* 5. Land Tracts of the South Mountain Battlefield - Betty's Good Will
* 6. Descendants of Frederick L. Fox - completion of Generation #5

Fox's Gap Section

By Kurt Graham

Casualties in the 51st Georgia Regiment during the Maryland Campaign

September 1862

Significant Research Findings related to the Battle of South Mountain

We again have the privilege of presenting an article by Kurt Graham. The article provides new evidence regarding the battle at Fox's Gap in Maryland on September 14, 1862. It presents documented casualty counts of Confederate forces in the 51st Georgia Regiment during the Maryland Campaign. Kurt retains all copyright privileges related to his article.

Kurt Graham retired from IBM in 1991 and lives in Vinings, Georgia, with his wife, Mary, and sons Griff and Jack. He is currently researching the history of the Phillips Georgia Legion and co-authoring a book on this little known Georgia unit. He maintains a website for this unit at:

www.angelfire.com/tx/RandysTexas

He encourages interested parties to contact him at (e-mail): galegion@bellsouth.net

---

The 51st Georgia Volunteer Infantry Regiment was formed during the spring of 1862. Its men came from the rural counties of southwest Georgia. During the winter of 1861/62, the Confederacy came to the realization that the war would last much longer than originally expected and that great numbers of new soldiers would be needed to carry on the fight.

The 51st was one of many new units formed that spring to fill this need. Initially the unit was sent to South Carolina to train and to guard against Federal raids from the coast. The 51st was placed in a brigade with the 50th Georgia, 15th South Carolina, 3rd South Carolina Battalion and Phillips Georgia Legion in July 1862 and was ordered to report to Richmond, Virginia. Command of this brigade was assigned to Brigadier General Thomas F Drayton, a West Point classmate of President Jefferson Davis.

Drayton's brigade became part of Longstreet's wing of the Army of Northern Virginia and headed north to join Stonewall Jackson's wing near Gordonsville, Virginia in mid August 1862. The 51st was involved in two skirmishes on the upper Rappahannock River on August 23rd (Beverlys Ford) and August 25th (Waterloo Bridge) and sustained a number of casualties in each of these actions.

At Second Manassas on August 29th and 30th, the 51st was held in reserve and suffered no casualties. They would not be so fortunate in the upcoming Maryland Campaign. On September 14, 1862, GT Anderson's brigade and Drayton's brigade led D R Jones division as they hurried back south from Hagerstown, Maryland to reinforce D H Hill's hard pressed division holding Turner's and Fox's Gaps on South Mountain against the attacks of two full Federal Corps. Upon arriving at Turner's Gap around noon, Major General Daniel Harvey Hill hurriedly led Anderson's and Drayton's 1900 men south along the ridge of the South Mountain to Fox's Gap.

It was at Fox's Gap where the Federals routed Samuel Garland's North Carolina brigade earlier in the day and threatened to break through into Pleasant Valley beyond the gap. Hill already had forwarded G B Anderson's and Roswell Ripley's brigades from his own division to Fox's Gap and now planned to employ the 4000+ men of these four brigades to counterattack the Federals and drive them back down the east side of the mountain.

Ordering an alignment of the four brigades in the Old Sharpsburg Road, Hill envisioned a huge left wheeling attack that would flank the Federals on their left. Drayton's brigade was positioned at the Gap itself and was to form the hinge or pivot point for the attack. Things went wrong almost immediately.

G T Anderson's brigade shifted too far down the Old Sharpsburg Road opening a 300-yard gap between it's left and Drayton's right. Nonetheless, Drayton had his attack orders and with the Phillips Legion, 3rd SC Battalion and most of the 15th SC aligned left to right in the Old Sharpsburg Road, he launched these 900 troops forward into the open field and woods to the south. Meanwhile, the 50th and 51st Georgia, which had been aligned behind a stone wall facing east to guard the brigade's left flank, were now ordered to shift into the Old Sharpsburg Road and face south.

Unbeknownst to General Drayton, two fresh Federal divisions arrived just beyond the woods to the southeast at about the same time his troops reached the gap. The Federals were poised to unleash their own attack just as Drayton launched his. As the 300 man Phillips Legion penetrated the woods on the left flank of the attack they ran into two thousand attacking Federals. The two South Carolina units to the Legion's right were also hit by thousands of additional Federals pouring in from the south. The situation quickly became hopeless and the three attacking Confederate units were pushed backwards through the woods and across Wise's field.

As the Phillips Legion came out of the woods, the 51st Georgia, located in the Old Sharpsburg Road, almost mistook the Legion men for Federals and would have opened fire had not Chaplain George Smith of the Legion ran back to tell them not to fire. The 3rd South Carolina Battalion rotated 90 degrees and dove behind a stone wall bordering the Ridge Road south of the gap and began firing at the Federals now coming out of the woods to the south and east.

Although this gallant action provided the retreating Legion with covering fire and caused the pursuing Federals to pause at the line of woods bordering the east side of the field, it eventually proved to be fatal. Other Federals began to enfilade the 3rd's position from the south and even began to penetrate the woods to the west behind the 3rd. Meanwhile the 50th and 51st Georgia in the Old Sharpsburg Road (with the 50th on the left) slugged it out with Federals on the other side of Wise's field and another small field to the east. Their resistance did not last long as the 800 man 17th Michigan regiment moved north under cover of a ravine and came in behind the exposed flank of the 50th. Now taking fire from front, flank and rear the two regiments were shot to pieces, finally breaking and fleeing into the woods to the northwest of the gap.

The 50th Georgia on the left suffered the most damage, losing 80% of its men, with a high percentage of killed and wounded. Nonetheless, the 51st still was very severely handled, losing 60% of its men. Unlike the 50th, though, half of the 51st's casualties were made up of men who were captured. Almost all were exchanged within a month and would rejoin their unit to fight again.

Sgt. Isaac Domingos of the 51st's Company G observed in a letter to his family, "at Boones Burrow (sic), or South Mountain, I was in the fight and was color bearer, carrying the flag for the regiment. In that fight we did not have more than 15,000 to 20,000 men while the enemy had all 100,000; so you can see they soon flanked and whipped us, and captured a great many. Here I was captured with my flag and carried to Fort Delaware but was released in three weeks and three days afterwards." While Sgt. Domingos is well off the mark in his estimate of the troops engaged, the 800 Georgians of Drayton's command must have felt that they had been attacked by 100,000!

Abbreviations used in the Casualty List:

(1) Status codes are abbreviated as follows:

KIA - Killed in Action
WIA - Wounded in Action
MIA/CAP - Missing in Action and Captured
MWIA - Mortally Wounded in Action (died from wounds)
MWIA/CAP - Mortally Wounded in Action and Captured
WIA/CAP - Wounded in Action and Captured

(2) Comments include the following abbreviations:

ADM	Admitted (to hospital)
AWOL	Absent Without Leave (from 51st Georgia unit)
Bo/Sh	Boonsboro or Sharpsburg (either The Battle of South Mountain or the Battle of Antietam as the battles were called by the Union)
Boons	Boonsboro (or the Battle of South Mountain as it was called by the Union)
Bur	buried
CAP	Captured (by Union forces)
CEXC	Considered Exchanged
CSR	Compiled Service Record
EXC	Exchanged (returned by Union forces to the Confederates)
Fred	Frederick, Maryland
GSW	Gun Shot Wound
Hosp	Hospital
MOC	Mt. Olivet Cemetery (grave number follows)
NCL	Newspaper Casualty Listing
PAR	Paroled
POW	Prisoner of War (held in a Union prison camp)
PWR	Post War Roll
Rappa	Rappahanock
RH	Richmond Hospital (Confederate) - a consolidated name representing various Confederate hospitals in Richmond, Virginia
Sharp	Sharpsburg (or the Battle of Antietam as it was called by the Union)
USGH	United States General Hospital - (a Union hospital, city follows)
Wash	Washington, D.C.
Willi	Williamsport, Maryland
2nd Ma	Second Manassas
?????	battle not known

Clarification of other items appearing in the Casualty List:

Mt. Olivet Cemetery - in Frederick, Maryland, was the place of burial for many Confederates
Richmond Hospital - any of a number of Confederate hospitals in Richmond, Virginia, including Chimborazo #1 and #2, GH 1-24, Winder hospital, Howard's Grove, Mayo Island, and others. The name of the specific hospital unit in Richmond may be found for each veteran in the Compiled Service Records at the Georgia State Archives.

Name	Status	Battle	Comments

Company - A

Name	Status	Battle	Comments
Alexander, Asa W	MWIA	Boons	NCL, died Winchester 10/16/62
Allen, James R	MIA/CAP	Boons	CEXC 11/10/62
Bailey, William Riley	MIA/CAP	Boons	CEXC 11/10/62
Barnard, William H	WIA	Boons	on Jan/Feb 1863 roll as WIA Boonsboro on furlough
Culpepper, James T	MIA/CAP	Boons	CEXC 11/10/62
Daugherty, John (A or R)	KIA	Boons	
Ford, James L	WIA/CAP	Boons	wounded hips/bowels, USGHs until EXC 2/63
Gray, Gabriel W	MIA/CAP	Boons	EXC 10/6/62, RH 10/21/62 with variola
Gray, Hosea C	MIA/CAP	Boons	RH 10/20/62, CEXC 11/10/62
Grier, Thomas M	WIA	?????	PWR says wounded in hand August 1862
Harrison, Thomas	MIA/CAP	Boons	CEXC 11/10/62
Johnson, James W	MWIA	Bo/Sh	MWIA per 1862 NCL, death claim filed 1/16/63
McCann, Charles	MIA/CAP	Boons	CEXC 11/10/62
McDonald, Cpl Robert	WIA/CAP	Sharp	Ft. Monroe for EXC 10/2/62, WIA Sharp per PWR
McLendon, James Dennis	MIA/CAP	Boons	CEXC 11/10/62
Philmon, William F	KIA	Bo/Sh?	on NCL, death claim filed 2/23/63
Ritchie, James D	KIA	Boons	
Simmons, Charles W	MIA/CAP	Sharp	to Fort Monroe for EXC 10/17/62
Smith, Daniel	MIA/CAP	Boons	to Fort Monroe for EXC 12/15/62

Company - B

Name	Status	Battle	Comments
Barefield, William T	KIA	Boons	
Batten, Bryan	KIA	Boons	
Calhoun, Lt Joel	KIA	Boons	
Gurr, Sgt Thomas J	MIA/CAP	Boons	CEXC 11/10/62
Howell, Thomas	KIA	Boons	
Hudson, Beasly	KIA	Boons	
Kendrick, James A	MIA/CAP	Boons	Ft Monroe for EXC 12/15/62
Laramore, James A	KIA	Boons	
Leverett, John	MWIA/CAP	Boons	died 10/11/62 USGH Fred, Bur MOC #103 as J L Evans
Marsh, Solomon Archibald	KIA	Boons	
Moore, Edward J N	MIA/CAP	Boons	CEXC 11/10/62
Parker, Gabriel M	MIA/CAP	Boons	CEXC 11/10/62
Parker, William J	WIA/CAP	Boons	Ft Monroe for EXC 10/13/62, RH thigh wound
Perkins, Sgt Henry C	WIA	Boons	arm wound
Powell, Abraham	MIA/CAP	Sharp	Ft Monroe for EXC 10/17/62
Ware, Capt William C	KIA	Rappa	hit by shell 8/23/62 at Beverly's Ford

Name	Status	Battle	Comments
Company - C			
Ackridge, Sgt James T	MIA/CAP	Fred	CAP 9/12/62, CEXC 11/10/62
Ackridge, William M	WIA	Boons	Chimborazo Hosp 9/27/62 facial wound
Faircloth, Thomas	MIA/CAP	?????	PAR 9/26/62, USGH Fred until 10/22/62, WIA?
Griner, Richard C	WIA/CAP	Boons	USGH Fred 9/18, RH 11/9/62 GSW right thigh
Hudson, Daniel	MIA/CAP	Boons	CEXC 11/10/62
Ott, George W	MIA/CAP	Fred	USGH Fred 9/18/62, CEXC 11/10/62
Sapp, Sgt Harmon D	MIA/CAP	Boons	CEXC 11/10/62
Sawyer, Lemuel P	MIA/CAP	Boons	CEXC 11/10/62
Shirah, Charles	WIA	?????	ADM to RH 9/30/62 GSW
Simpson, John D	MIA/CAP	Boons	CEXC 11/10/62
Smith, L H	MIA/CAP	Boons	CEXC 11/10/62
Stewart, Sgt James L	MIA/CAP	Boons	CEXC 11/10/62
West, Henry O	MIA/CAP	Boons	to Aiken's Landing for EXC 10/2/62
West, Lt George W	KIA	Boons	
West, Sgt Jeremiah C	MIA/CAP	Boons	CEXC 11/10/62
West, William L	MIA/CAP	Fred	CAP 9/12/62, USGH Fred 9/18/62, Aiken's Landing for EXC 10/6/62
West, William P	MWIA/CAP	Sharp	died USGH Fred 10/14/62, Bur MOC #121
Whigham, John W	WIA	?????	ADM to RH 9/27/62 GSW
Whitley, Allen	KIA	Bo/Sh	MIA on 1862 NCL, widow's pension application says KIA Maryland
Company - D			
Glass, James	WIA	Boons	AWOL Jan/Feb 1863 roll, never returns, MWIA?
Glass, Robert	MWIA/CAP	?????	USGH Wash 9/21/62, died 10/22/62
Grimsley, William J	MWIA	Rappa	PWR says WIA 8/26/62, died 9/15/62
Hammond, Francis Marion	WIA	Rappa	wounded in thigh 8/25/62 at Waterloo Bridge
Hare(Hair), Franklin C	KIA	Rappa	Waterloo Bridge 8/25/62 per NCL
Ingram, A J	MIA/CAP	?????	USGH Wash 9/2x/62, no EXC record but present 2/63
Johnson, H W	MIA/CAP	?????	PAR 9/21/62, no EXC record but present 2/63
Kinney, Daniel	KIA	Bo/Sh	per NCL
Pate, Richard	WIA	2nd Ma	went home wounded, never returned
Willis, Daniel M	MIA/CAP	Willi	CAP 9/15/62, to Aiken's Landing for EXC 10/6/62

Name	Status	Battle	Comments

Company - E

Name	Status	Battle	Comments
Bartlett, Legrand B	KIA	Boons	
Bell, Marion A	WIA/CAP	Boons	USGH Wash 9/21/62, Winder Hosp 10/4/62
Clower(Glover), George W	KIA	Boons	
Clower(Glover), William	WIA	2nd Ma	ADM to Charlottesville Hosp with GSW
Crawford, William	MIA/CAP	Boons	CEXC 11/10/62
Davis, Francis E	WIA/CAP	Boons	EXC 11/15/62, RH 11/9?/62 GSW right arm
Dickey, Capt James	MIA/CAP	Fred	EXC 10/24/62, PWR says CAP at Frederick
Everett, Jordan	MIA/CAP	Boons	CEXC 11/10/62, PWR says Boonsboro 9/14/62
Hainsley, Lt Lewis G	KIA	Boons	CSR says Sharp but PWR roll says Boons 9/14/62
Jones, David G	MWIA/CAP	Sharp	died 10/6/62 at USGH Fred, Bur MOC #93
King, Lt William L	MIA/CAP	Boons	CEXC 11/10/62
Martin, Joseph P	MWIA	Rappa	wounded in face at Waterloo Bridge 8/25/62, died at home
Maury, Benjamin F	MWIA/CAP	Boons	brother to John Maury, Bur near Middletown Academy
Maury, John R	KIA	Boons	brother to Benjamin F Maury
Moore, John H	MIA/CAP	Boons	Aikens Landing for EXC 10/6/62, present 2/63 roll
Reeves, Andrew J	MIA/CAP	Boons	CEXC 11/10/62
Rimes, Virgil P	MIA/CAP	Boons	CEXC 11/10/62
Sauls, Richard C	MIA/CAP	Boons	CEXC 11/10/62
Thompson, James M	WIA/CAP	Boons	ADM to RH with wound to lower jaw

Company - F

Name	Status	Battle	Comments
Baird, Robert A	MIA/CAP	Boons	CEXC 11/10/62
Bellflower, Sgt Joseph R	WIA/CAP	Sharp	PAR 9/27/62, RH 9/27/62 with thigh wound
Bradley, J S	MIA/CAP	Boons	CEXC 11/10, died at Richmond 11/8/62 of anemia/dys
Dyson, Robert A	MIA/CAP	Boons	CEXC 11/10/62
Felder, A A	KIA	Rappa	in artillery duel Beverly's Ford 8/25/62 (Waterloo Bridge)
Grice, Benjamin F	KIA	Rappa	Waterloo Bridge 8/25/62
Harper, Sgt W J	MIA/CAP	Fred	CAP 9/12/62, USGH Fred 9/18/62, EXC 3/63
Haynes, Thomas S	MIA/CAP	Fred	CAP 9/12/62, CEXC 11/10/62
Huff, Frank	WIA	Rappa	Severe arm & leg wounds at Beverly's Ford 8/23/62
Huff, Vincent	WIA	Boons	Jan/Feb 63 roll states "absent since wounded 9/14/62"
Knight, Jacob E	WIA	Rappa	wounded slightly per 1862 NCL
Land, William H	MIA/CAP	?????	PAR 9/27/62, no EXC record but present 2/63

Name	Status	Battle	Comments

Company - F continued

Name	Status	Battle	Comments
Lang, David A	MIA/CAP	Boons	CEXC 11/10/62
Lang, William D	KIA	Boons	
Lawhorn, John P	WIA	Rappa	Jan/Feb 63 roll states absent WIA since 8/23/62, retired 12/64
Lee, Robert T	KIA	Rappa	in artillery duel at Beverly's Ford 8/23/62
Odom, Cpl George W	MIA/CAP	Boons	CEXC 11/10/62
Price, Joseph	MWIA	Rappa	severe knee wound at Beverly's Ford 8/23/62, died 9/5/62
Sessions, William E	WIA	Rappa	wounded thigh & hand Beverly's Ford 8/23/62
Shine, James	MWIA/CAP	?????	USGH Fred GSW, died 9/27/62, Bur MOC #52
Simpson, Lt William G	WIA	Rappa	wounded slightly per 1862 NCL
Smith, John J	MIA/CAP	Boons	CEXC 11/10/62
Vinson, Isaac	MIA/CAP	Boons	died at Fort Delaware 10/7/62
Wainwright, John R	KIA	Boons	
Whitaker, Sgt James E	MIA/CAP	Boons	CEXC 11/10/62
Wimberly, W M	KIA	Boons	
Wright, Robert E	MIA/CAP	Boons	CEXC 11/10/62

Company - G

Name	Status	Battle	Comments
Collins, Leroy G	WIA	Boons	per NCL
Craft, W J	MWIA	Boons	per PWR (died in hospital) & NCL
Crawford, William M	WIA/CAP	Boons	per NCL, CEXC 11/10/62
Domingos, Sgt Isaac	WIA/CAP	Boons	per NCL, CEXC 11/10/62
Findley, Stephen D	MIA/CAP	Boons	CEXC 11/10/62
Harrell, Wade H	MIA/CAP	Boons	CEXC 11/10/62
Hooker, Charles W	MIA/CAP	Willi	teamster CAP 9/15/62, transported for EXC 10/6/62
Mann, Sgt Joel J	WIA/CAP	Boons	per NCL, CEXC 11/10/62
McDaniel, Jonathan O	MIA/CAP	Boons	CEXC 11/10/62
McKinney, C C	KIA	Sharp	per NCL and PWR
Mercer, J	WIA	Bo/Sh	per NCL
Mitchell, J M	MIA/CAP	Fred	CAP 9/11/62, USGH Fred 9/19/62, present on 2/63 roll
Moore, Sgt Ezekiel	MIA/CAP	Boons	CEXC 11/10/62
Murdock, Sgt A W	WIA	Bo/Sh	per NCL, RH 10/62
Peterson, William	WIA	Bo/Sh	ADM RH 9/26/62
Rains, Frederick G	WIA	Bo/Sh	ADM RH 9/28/62
Ray, William H	WIA	Bo/Sh	ADM RH 9/26/62
Rentz, Peter	MIA/CAP	Boons	CEXC 11/10/62

Name	Status	Battle	Comments
Company - G continued			
Rentz, William	KIA	Bo/Sh	on NCL, death claim filed 1/12/63
Sharp, Sherod L	MIA/CAP	Boons	CEXC 11/10/62
Thomas, Daniel	KIA	Bo/Sh	on NCL, death claim filed 2/20/63
Thomas, Edwin	KIA	Bo/Sh	on NCL, death claim filed 12/24/62
Touchstone, Henry H	MIA/CAP	Boons	CEXC 11/10/62
Touchstone, Jesse	KIA	Sharp	
Tye, Henry M	MIA/CAP	Boons	CEXC 11/10/62
Company - H			
Anderson, J P	MIA/CAP	Sharp	CAP 9/28/62, PAR 10/11/62
Andrews, James F	MIA/CAP	Sharp	CAP 9/28/62, PAR 10/1/62
Arrington, William S	MIA/CAP	?????	PAR 9/21/62
Blue, Henry J	MIA/CAP	Sharp	PAR 10/1/62
Cheshire, James T	KIA	Boons	on NCL, death claim filed 1/63
Cox, James R	MIA/CAP	Boons	PAR 9/21/62
DuBose, Joseph A	KIA	Boons	
Ethridge, William A	WIA	Rappa	hit by shell 8/23/62 Beverly's Ford, lost left leg
Sheffield, W H C	WIA	Rappa	8/23/62 Beverly's Ford, leg amputated
Stephens, James	KIA	Bo/Sh	per NCL
Strickland, Jesse	MIA/CAP	?????	PAR 9/21/62, died 11/10/62 in RH
Company - I			
Bruner, Cpl John H	KIA	Rappa	Waterloo Bridge 8/25/62
Burnett, Capt William L	MIA/CAP	Boons	CEXC 11/10/62
Fullwood, Sgt John W	MIA/CAP	Boons	CEXC 11/10/62
Killingsworth, Cpl James	WIA/CAP	Boons	CEXC 11/10/62
Lee, William D	MIA/CAP	?????	PAR 9/21/62, no EXC record but present 2/63
McElroy, William H	MIA/CAP	Boons	CEXC 11/10/62, died 11/13/62 of hemorrhoids
McLendon, Cpl Silas	MWIA	Boons	died Boonsboro, Bur Disciples Church Cemetery
Mills, Cpl John F	MIA/CAP	Boons	CEXC 11/10/62
Peterson, Oclious	MIA/CAP	?????	PAR at Keedysville 9/19/62, present 2/63
Reynold, Jackson	MIA/CAP	Boons	CEXC 11/10/62
Sanderlin, E D	WIA	?????	ADM to RH 10/4/62
Shivers, George Oscar	WIA/CAP	Boons	PAR 10/1 at USGH Fred; RH with GSW
Todd, James H	MIA/CAP	Fred	CAP 9/12/62, CEXC 11/10/62
Wood, Sgt Edward	MIA/CAP	Boons	CEXC 11/10/62

Name	Status	Battle	Comments
Company - K			
Cannon, Henry C	WIA	Sharp	Jan 65 letter requests retirement based on Sharpsburg arm wound
Cook, Cpl Lewis M	WIA/CAP	Sharp	shoulder wound, PAR 10/1/62, RH 10/23/62
Cooper, James B	MIA/CAP	?????	PAR 9/21/62
Ethridge, John D	WIA/CAP	?????	EXC 11/10/62; Petersburg Hosp 11/18/62 GSW right leg
Gilbert, Richard T	MIA/CAP	Boons	EXC 10/17/62
Hobbs, Capt Richard	WIA	Boons	resignation letter 11/20/62 "lost left arm 9/14/62 at Boonsboro"
Hood, S L	WIA	?????	ADM Charlottesville Hosp 9/26/62 GSW chest
Houston, Stephen	WIA	Boons	per NCL
Johnson, J W	MIA/CAP	Fred	CAP 9/12/62, CEXC 11/10/62
Jordan, J W	MIA/CAP	Boons	at USGH Fred 10/62; no further record
Laseter, William M	WIA	2nd Ma	per PWR
Meads, David S	WIA/CAP	Sharp	Ft Monroe 10/17/62 for EXC; RH 11/21/62 GSW leg
O'Sullivan, Cornelius	KIA	Bo/Sh	per NCL
Quick, Robert	WIA/CAP	Sharp	no capture date, Ft Monroe for EXC 10/17/62, GSW leg
Rawson, Edmund P	MIA/CAP	Willi	CAP 9/15/62, CEXC 11/10/62
Smith, Appleton M	MIA/CAP	?????	9/30/62
Spitz, Charles A	MIA/CAP	Boons	CEXC 11/10/62

****

News from Fox's Gap

Published June 1 and December 1 of each year by

The Society of the Descendants of Frederick Fox of Fox's Gap in Maryland

Membership dues are $5.00 per year. President of the Society is Curtis L. Older.

Make Society inquiries by the following means:

Curtis L. Older
618 Tryon Place
Gastonia, NC 28054-6066

e-mail: curtolder@earthlink.net
phone: 704-864-3879

****

News from Fox's Gap

The Society of the Descendants of Frederick Fox of Fox's Gap in Maryland

Issue 2, Volume 2 **Remember Freedom!** December 1, 2001

The North Carolina South Mountain Symposium and Tour

Saturday, August 18th, 2001

The 18th of August, 2001, was a special day for those who have sought to preserve the history of the Battle of South Mountain in Maryland during America's Civil War. The greatest gathering of historians of the Battle of South Mountain met in Boonsboro, Maryland, to help raise funds for a $70,000 monument. The monument will be erected at Fox's Gap in about two years to commemorate the North Carolina troops who fought in the battle there on September 14, 1862.

Kurt Graham, who has written several articles for *News from Fox's Gap*, and I had corresponded from a distance on numerous occasions. The symposium gave us the opportunity to meet in person. My friend Doug Bast, who helped me produce my two books, one on the Braddock Expedition and the other on the land tracts of the Battlefield of South Mountain, owns the Boonesborough Museum of History. Doug attended the event and was one of the speakers. Both Kurt and Doug are honorary members of the Society of the Descendants of Frederick Fox of Fox's Gap in Maryland.

The Central Maryland Heritage League had a number of items for sale related to the Battle of South Mountain and I couldn't resist acquiring several items. One person I was fortunate to make the acquaintance of was Paul Martin, III. Paul has produced for sale two outstanding pictures, one of General Jesse Lee Reno and the other of General Samuel Garland. Both generals were killed at Fox's Gap during the Battle of South Mountain.

The program for the symposium consisted of the following:

8:30 AM - Opening Remarks and Welcome
9:00 AM - Panel Discussion with Ed Bearss, Paul Chiles, *The Maryland Campaign and Special Order 191*
9:45 AM - Break
9:55 AM - Scott Hartwig - "My God Be Careful"
10:40 AM - Larry Laboda - "Jeff Davis Artillery at South Mountain"
11:20 AM - Paul R. Martin, III - "General Jesse Reno and General Samuel Garland"
Lunch
1:00 PM - Wilmer Mumma, - Doug Bast "Ghosts of South Mountain"

1:40 PM - John Michael Priest - "Crampton's Gap"
2:20 PM - Kurt Graham - "Afternoon Battle at Fox's Gap"
3:20 PM - Break
3:30 PM - Clint Johnson - "Blunders of the Battles"
4:40 PM - Gary Casteel - "Sculpturing the Monument"
7:00 PM - Dinner, Live Auction, Mr. Stan Clardy - "Soldiers in Gray"

The following provides some brief background on the various speakers:

Ed Bearss - National Park Service Historian emeritus and Board member of the Civil War Preservation Trust. Ed presented with the first Edwin C. Bearss Lifetime Achievement Award earlier this year.

D. Scott Hartwig - Ranger and Historian at Gettysburg National Military Park. Author of *A Killer Angels Companion* and numerous other stories.

Wilmur Mumma - Sharpsburg Historian whose great grandfather's farm was burned before the battle of Sharpsburg (Antietam) by Confederates who thought it would be a Union sharpshooters haven. Author of *Ghosts of Antietam, Antietam the Aftermath, Out of the Past I and II.*

Clint Johnson - Historian and re-enactor, author of *Touring the Carolinas' Civil War Sites, Blunders, Touring West Virginia and Virginia Civil War Sites.*

Doug Bast - Historian and curator and owner of the Boonsborough Museum of History.

Kurt Graham - Leading historian on the afternoon battle at Fox's Gap has done extensive research in the Georgia Archives compiling the Phillips Legion legacy which was not even listed as being at South Mountain.

John Michael Priest - Historian and author of *The Soldiers' Battle, Before Antietam: The Battle for South Mountain, John T. Mcmahon's: Diary of the 136th New York*

Paul Chiles - Historian and Ranger at Antietam National Battlefield. Very knowledgeable of the tactics and artillery of the War Between the States.

Larry Laboda - Historian and author of *Jeff Davis Artillery and Alfred Lives on Bentonville Battlefield.*

Paul R. Martin, III - Artist and school teacher owner of Silent Sentinal Studios, Friend of the NC South Mountain Monument Fund. His official print of the monument is one of our leading fund raisers. Last year he had an exhibit at the Gettysburg Cyclorama and this year from August 20th through October 6th he had an exhibition at West Point, which conincides with the Academy's Bicentennial.

Gary Casteel - Owner of Four Winds Studio in Gettyburg and sculptur of the North Carolina South Mountain Monument. He is an accomplished sculptur of many fine pieces including the *Longstreet Monument at Gettysburg.*

President's Message
by Curtis Lynn Older

* Volume 1, the first ten issues of the Fox Society Newsletter, "News from Fox's Gap", has been put into Adobe Acrobat Reader format and is available on CD-Rom computer disc for $5.00. The price includes all postage and handling costs.

* My daughter, Rachael, is typing *The Fox Genealogy* by Daniel Gebhart Fox into my computer using Microsoft Word. The Microsoft Word version of the book will be converted into Adobe Acrobat Reader format and made available on a CD-Rom computer disc for $5.00. The project should be completed in 2002.

* Please be sure to read the great article by Sam B. Davis on the Third South Carolina Battalion in the battle at Fox's Gap. The article provides new evidence on the casualties suffered during the battle.

* Fox Society dues will increase to $6.00 for calendar year 2002. This is the first dues increase since the Society began.

Table of Contents for this Newsletter

Page

Welcome New Members!

No new members to report since June 1, 2001.

From The Bookshelf

by Curtis L. Older

To the Gates of Richmond
The Peninsula Campaign
by Stephen W. Sears

Perhaps you already know the chain of events during the American Civil War that led up to the Battle of South Mountain on September 14, 1862. If not, may I suggest you read Stephen Sears excellent book, *"To the Gates of Richmond, the Peninsula Campaign."* Sears covers the events in which the participants of the Battle of South Mountain were engaged from mid-March 1862 up to August 16, 1862. The events of this five month period, for the Army of the Potomac under General George B. McClellan and the Army of Northern Virginia under General Robert E. Lee, have come to be known as the Peninsula Campaign.

The Peninsula Campaign included the Siege of Yorktown, the Battle of Williamsburg, the Battle of Hanover Court House, the Battle of Seven Pines, and the Battle of the Seven Days. Within the conflict known as the Battle of the Seven Days were the following battles: the Battle of Oak Grove, the Battle of Mechanicsville, the Battle of Gaines's Mill, the Battle of Savage's Station, the Battle of Glendale, and the Battle of Malvern Hill.

"The Peninsula campaign of 1862 was the largest campaign of the Civil War and also one of the bloodiest. Of the 250,000 men who fought in it, only a fraction had ever been in battle before, and one in four was killed, wounded, or missing by the time the fighting ended. The operation was General George McClellan's grand scheme to march up the Virginia Peninsula and take the Confederate capital. For three months Mcclellan battled his way toward Richmond, but then Robert E. Lee took command of the Confederate forces. In seven days, by splitting his army, Lee drove the cautious McClellan out, thereby changing the course, if not the outcome, of the war."

One quote contained in Sears's book seems to stick in my mind. During the Federal retreat from the outskirts of Richmond, Union General "Phil Kearny sardonically informed his men they were 'the rear guard of all God's creation'."

McClellan's failure in the Peninsula Campaign led Robert E. Lee to look north toward Maryland and Pennsylvania. After McClellan's retreat from the peninsula in mid August 1862, the Union Army of the Potomac would meet the Confederate Army of Northern Virginia at Manassas. The Confederate victory at Second Manassas or Second Bull Run convinced Lee to cross the Potomac in early September and embark on what has been called the Maryland Campaign. Lee's failure at Crampton's, Fox's, and Turner's Gaps in the Battle of South Mountain forced him to fall back to the Antietam Creek and end any chance of a Pennsylvania invasion in 1862.

Anyone interested in the battles of South Mountain and Antietam during the Maryland Campaign should read another of Sears' books, *Landscape Turned Red: The Battle of Antietam*. Sears provides a complete account of the Battle of South Mountain and devotes much attention to the battle at Fox's Gap. For those without much knowledge of the Battle of South Mountain , Sears' *Landscape Turned Red* is the place to begin your inquiry into that battle and related events.

In 1863, we again see a scenario similar to what was seen 1862. The Union failure in the battle of Chancellorsville in May of 1863 would give Lee the impetus to again look northward. Lee would move his Army of Northern Virginia into Pennsylvania for a fight on Northern soil, at what would turn out to take place at a small village called Gettysburg. For those who wish to learn about the fascinating events leading up to and including the Battle of Chancellorsville, I suggest another excellent book by Sears, *Chancellorsville*.

Land Tracts of the Battlefield of South Mountain
by Curtis L. Older

Each Newsletter includes a survey, patent, or deed related to the land tracts in the vicinity of Crampton's, Fox's, and Turner's Gaps. These three gaps in South Mountain represent the main area contested by the Union and Confederate Armies in the Battle of South Mountain on September 14, 1862.

Previous issues of the Society Newsletter contained descriptions of the following tracts:

June 1, 1997	Addition to Friendship of Frederick Fox
December 1, 1997	Fredericksburgh of Frederick Fox
June 1, 1998	Pick All of Bartholomew Booker
December 1, 1998	Bowser's Addition of David Bowser
June 1, 1999	Partnership of John Mansberger
December 1, 1999	Mountain of John Baley
June 1, 2000	no tract included in newsletter
December 1, 2000	Flonham of Philip Jacob Shafer
June 1, 2001	The Exchange of Daniel Dulaney

Betty's Good Will is one of the very oldest tracts in the Battlefield of South Mountain area. It is a key tract because it mentions the earliest road through Fox's Gap and it is not far from the Fox Inn.

The Survey for Betty's Good Will, Maryland Hall of Records 17,415, 1-23-3-9, BC & GS 4, pp. 195-196, Robert Evans, 15 October 1747, 50 acres.

Robert Evans Cert. 50a Betty's Good Will pat 29? Sept 1754 to Edwd Grimes rent ? ann? 2/0 sterling Chad to the Rent Roll} Prince Georges County ? By virtue of a warrant granted out of his lordships land office of this province unto Daniel Oneal of Prince Georges county for three hundred acres of land bearing date by renewment the 22d day of April 1747 assigned unto John Mills by the said Oneal and by the said Mills assigned unto Rober Evans of Prince Georges County.

Therefore certifie as Deputy Surveyor of Prince Georges county under his excellency Samuel Ogle Esquire Governor of Maryland I have carefully laid out for and in the name of him the said Robert Evans all that tract or parcel of land called Betty's Good Will, lying in the said County beginning at a bounded white oak standing at the foot of Shannandore Mountain near the waggon road that goes from Teagues Ferry to Minonocee Town running thence

Line No.	North South	Degrees East or West	Length
1	N	6 east	36 perches
2	N	34 east	94 perches
3	S	51 east	130 perches

4 then by a straight line to the beginning tree containing and now laid out for fifty acres of land to be held of Calverton or Conegocheige Manor, surveyed this 15 day of October anno domini 1747. Thomas Cresap D. S. of P. G. County

18 august 1749 examined & passed Ross examiner

on the back of the foregoing certificate was the following receipt ? I have received the sum of fourteen shillings sterling for seven years rent of the within land to Michaelmas next patent may therefore issue with his excellency approbation 25 July 1754 Edwd Lloyd

(**Author's Note:** See MdHR 17,415, 1-23-3-9, GS 2, pp. 12-13, record for Betty's Good Will that gives a survey date of 20 Oct 1727.)

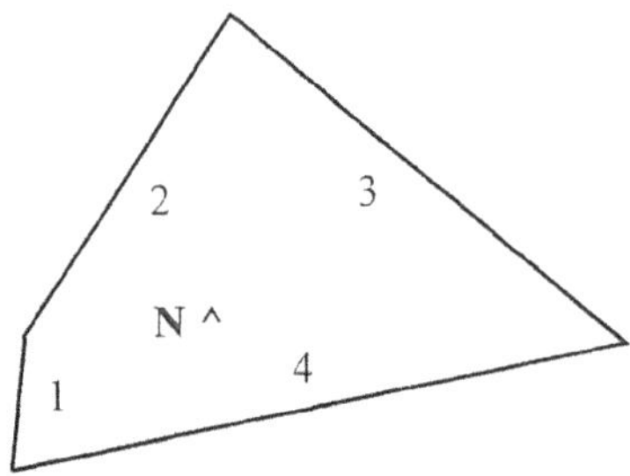

The Patent for Betty's Good Will, Maryland Hall of Records 17,415, 1-23-3-9, GS 2, pp. 12-13, patent, Edward Grimes, 29 September 1754, 50 acres.

Edward Grimes Patent 50 Betty's Good Will} Examd Frederick ? Know ye that whereas Robert Evans of Frederick County had on the twentieth day of October seventeen hundred & twenty seven surveyed & laid out for him a tract or parcel of land called Betty's Good Will lying and being formerly in Prince Georges but now in Frederick County containing fifty acres by virtue of so much part of an assignment of a warrant for three hundred acres from John Mills who was assignee of Daniel Oneal by renewment the twenty second day of April seventeen hundred & forty seven but before the said Evans laid? out our grant thereon he did on the fourth day of May seventeen hundred and forty nine assign over all his right title and interest thereto unto Edward Grimes of the County aforesaid and desired our grant might issue unto him thereon which we have thought fit to condescend unto as appears on our land office and upon such conditions and terms as are expressed in our conditions of plantation of our said province bearing date the fifth day of April sixteen hundred and eighty four and remaining upon record in our said Province together with such alterations as in them are made by our further conditions bearing date the fourth day of December sixteen hundred and ninety six together also with the alterations made by our instructions bearing date at London the twelfth day of September seventeen hundred and twelve and registered? in our Srot? Office aforesaid? ? together with paragraph of our instructions bearing date at London the fifteenth day of December seventeen hundred and thirty eight registered in our land office we do therefore hereby grant unto him the said Edward Grimes all that Tract or Parcel of Land called Bettys Good will lying in the said county beginning at a bounded white oak standing at the foot of Shanandore Mountain near the Waggon Road that goes from Teagues Ferry to Monococy Town running thence

Line No.	**North South**	**Degrees East or West**	**Length**
1	N	6 east	36 perches
2	N	34 east	94 perches
3	S	51 east	130 perches

4. then by a straight line to the beginning tree containing and now laid out for fifty acres of land more or less according to the certificate of survey thereof taken and returned into our land office bearing date the sixteenth day of October seventeen hundred forty seven

... given under our great seal of our said province of Maryland this twenty ninth day of September Anno Domini seventeen hundred fifty four witness our trusty and well beloved Horatio Sharpe Esquire Lieutenant General & chief Governor of our said Province of Maryland Chancellor and Keeper of the great seal thereof. Horo (the great seal) Sharpe.

George Fox Line

listing of descendants by Suella Fenton (material sent in by Alice Takase)

Alice Takase, a member of the Society, is a descendant of Frederick L. Fox. Frederick L. Fox was a son of George Fox and Elizabeth Ann (Link) Fox. He was a brother of John L. Fox of Gessie, Indiana. Alice Takase's address is: PO Box 6945, Fort Bliss, Texas 79906-0945.

Descendants of Frederick L. Fox

(A son of George Fox and a grandson of Frederick Fox of Fox's Gap in Maryland)

Conclusion of Generation No. 5

(The first portion of Generation No. 5 was in the June 1, 2001 Newsletter)

81. Patty Ann Brown (Walter Howard, Clarence David, Frances A. Fox, Frederick Link, George "1", Frederick "1", John "1" Frederick) was born September 07, 1960. She married Chip ?.

Children of Patty Brown and Chip ? are:

i. Chipper ?, b. 1979.
ii. Shannon Crystal Rudicil ?, b. 1984; d. 1985.

82. Edward Lee Brown (Walter Howard, Clarence David, Frances A. Fox, Freerick Link, George "1", Frederick "1", John "1" Frederick) was born February 08, 1962. He married Judy Metcalf.

Children of Edward Brown and Judy Metcalf are:

i. Edward Lee Brown II, b. 1990.
ii. Nora Askley Brown, b. 1994.

83. Ricky Brown (Raymond, Clarence David, Frances A. Fox, Frederick Link, George "1", Frederick "1", John "1" Frederick) was born July 26, 1962 in Franklin, Warren County, Ohio. He married (1) Lora Barton Bef. 1980. He married (2) Nancy Smith July 26, 1980 in Franklin, Warren County, Ohio.

Children of Ricky Brown and Nancy Smith are:

i. Jennifer Marie Brown, b. July 12, 1979, Dayton, Montgomery County, Ohio.
ii. Stephanie Irene Brown, b. July 10, 1980, Dayton, Montgomery County, Ohio.

84. Vicki Brown (Raymond, Clarence David, Frances A. Fox, Frederick Link, George "1", Frederick "1" John "1" Frederick) was born April 16, 1953 in Franklin, Warren County, Ohio. She married Randy Church August 02, 1970 in Franklin, Warren County, Ohio.

Children of Vicki Brown and Randy Church are:

i. Dennis Church, b. June 15, 1971, Franklin, Warren County, Ohio; m. Stacy (Church).
ii. Wendy Church, b. February 27, 1973, Franklin, Warren County, Ohio.
iii. Timothy Church, b. November 14, 1977, Fraklin, Warren County, Ohio.

85. Eilen Weidel (Harry R., Laura Etta Fox, Jacob "Job" Henry, Frederick Link, George "1", Frederick "1", John "1" Fredrick) was born 1925, and died 1993. She married James A. Roney I.

Children of Eilen Weidel and James Roney are:

i. James A. Roney II.
ii. Alan R. Roney.
iii. Sarah R. Roney.
iv. Carol E. Roney.

86. Lowell E. Weidel (Carl Z., Laura Etta Fox, Jacob "Job" Henry, Frederick Link, George "1", Frederick "1", John "1" Frederick). He married Mary Kathleen Jackson.

Childeren of Lowell Weidel and Mary Jackson are:

124. i. Joseph Allen Weidel, b. April 17, 1963.
125. ii. Lawrence Andrew Weidel, b. September 28, 1964.
iii. John Gregory Weidel, b. July 02, 1969.
iv. Mary Anne Weidel, b. December 02, 1972.
v. Lori Elane Weidel, b. June 25, 1974.
vi. Susan Elizabeth Weidel, b. August 24, 1975.

87. Eugenie Weidel (Carl Z., Laura Etta Fox, Jacob "Job" Henry, Frederick Link, George "1", Frederick "1", John "1" Frederick) was born June 14, 1945. She married (1) David Blanton. She married (2) James Shelton.

Children of Eugenie Weidel and David Blanton are:

126. i. Scott Blanton, b. May 04, 1961.
127. ii. Suzanne Blanton, b. June 23,1964.
128. iii. Douglas Blanton, b. August 23, 1965.

88. John Richard Reber Fox(Reber, Anna Marie, Jacob "Job" Henry, Frederick Link, George "1", Frederick "1", John "1" Frederick) was born May 18, 1943. She married Janet L. Fisher June 09, 1960.

Children of John Fox and Janet Fisher are:

129. i. Joy Kay Fox, b. October 07, 1961.
130. ii. Jeannie Marie Fox, b. May 20, 1963.

89. Stephany Ann Chenewoth(Jack A., Anna Marie Fox, Jacob "Job" Henry, Frederick Link, George "1", Frederick "1", John "1" Frederick) was born August 11, 1941, and died August 27, 1993. She married Remo "Ray" Prosperl June 06, 1964.

Children of Stephany Ann Chenewoth and Remo Prosperl are:

131. i. Caryoln Prosperl, b. March 26, 1966.
ii. Christine Prosperl, b. March 11, 1968.

90. Steven Chenewoth(William R., Anna Marie Fox, Jacob "Job" Henry, Frederick Link, George "1", Frederick "1", John "1" Frederick) was born September 19, 1955.

Children of Steven Chenewoth are:

132. i. Amanda Chenewoth, b. 1976.
ii. Jason Chenewoth, b. August 16, 1984.

91. Linda Christine Fox(James Norman, Edwin E., Jacob "Job" Henry, Frederick Link, George "1", Frederick "1", John "1" Frederick) was born 1948. She married Thomas Pate.

Child of Linda Fox and Thomas Pate is:

i. Jason Pate, b. 1978.

92. Alice Louise Hoskins(Dorothy May Beachler, Lucy May Fox, Jacob "Job" Henry, Frederick Link, George "1", Frederick "1", John "1" Frederick) was born October 22, 1946 in Pittsburgh, Allegheny County, Pennsylvania. She married Francis K. Takase April 12, 1969 in Pittsburgh, Allegheny County, Pennyslvania.

Child of Alice Hoskins and Francis Takase is:

i. Jason Grant Takase, b. November 19, 1970.

93. Bruce Courtney Hoskins (Dorothy may Beachler, Lucy May Fox, Jacob "Job" Henry, Frederick Link, George "1", Frederick "1", John "1" Frederick) was born February 29, 1948 in Pittsburgh, Allegheny County, Pennsylvania. He married Karen Louise Geyer September 17, 1984, daughter of Rodney Geyer and Margaret Appell.

Children of Bruce Hoskins and Karen Geyer are:

i. Tyler Courtney Hoskins, b. July 03, 1986, Oregon City, Oregon.
ii. Andrew Koskins, b. October 12, 1988, Portland, Oregon.
iii. Keluz Marie "Kelsey" Hoskins, b. March 08, 1990, Seoul, Korea.

94. Eugene Paul Hoskins (Dorothy May Beachler, Lucy May Fox, Jacob "Job" Henry, Frederick Link, George "1", Frederick "1", John "1" Frederick) was born July 08, 1951 in Pittsburgh, Allegheny County, Pennsylvania. He married Nancy Brenton June 12, 1970.

Children of Eugene Hoskins and Nancy Brenton are:

i. Lindsey Hoskins, b. April 09, 1981.
ii. Matthey Brenton Hoskins, b. October 11, 1982.

95. Jessie Lucinda "Cindi" Beachler (Charles Monroe, Lucy May Fox, Jacob "Job" Henry, Frederick Link, George "1", Frederick "1", John "1" Frederick) was born October 27, 1948. She married (1) Robert "1" Nancarrow. She married (2) Rodney Bellamy.

Children of Jessie Beachler and Robert Nancarrow are:

i. (Child) Nancarrow.
ii. Robert "2" Nancarrow, b. Februay 1970.

96. Richard Harold Montgomery (Harold Everett, Katheryn Myrtle Fox, Jacob "Job" Henry, Frederick Link, George "1", Frederick "1", John "1" Frederick) was born September 10, 1947. He married Patricia Scearce May 21, 1969.

Child of Richard Montgomery and Patricia Scearce is:

i. Stephen Wayne Montgomery, b. May 31, 1975.

97. Ronald Eugene Montgomery (Robert Eugene, Katheryn Myrtle Fox, Jacob "Job" Henry, Frederick Link, George "1", Frederick "1", John "1" Frederick) was born September 07, 1950. He married (1) Teresa Ann Martin August 17, 1973. He married (2) Kelly Sherritt July 04, 1981.

Children of Ronald Montgomery and Kelly Sherritt are:

i. Angela Marie Montgomery, b. March 20, 1982.

ii. Ryan Eugene Montgoemry, b. June 17, 1985.

98. Debra Ann Montgomery (Robert Eugene, Katheryn Myrtle Fox, Jacob "Job" Henry, Frederick Link, George "1", Frederick "1", John "1" Frederick) was born December 13, 1956. She married (1) David Ratliff. She married (2) Jeffery Linn Trick May 17, 1978.

Children of Debra Montgomery and Jeffery Trick are:

i. Jamie Nicole Trick, b. August 18, 1979.

ii. Benjamin Matthew Trick, b. June 03, 1982.

99. Kenneth Michael Fox (Kenneth Wilfred, Cloyce "Wilford", Jacob "Job" Henry, Frederick Link, George "1", Frederick "1", John "1" Frederick) was born January 03, 1952. He married (1) Kathleen Wilhoite June 16, 1972. He married (2) Shelly Mae Wasmuth November 27, 1977.

Children of Kenneth Fox and Shelly Wasmuth are:

i. Emily Michele Fox, b. June 12, 1978; d. June 12, 1978.

ii. Teresa Michele Fox, b. March 15, 1981.

iii. Allice Danielle Fox, b. May 07, 1984.

100. Timothy Wilford Fox (Kenneth Wilfred, Cloyce "Wilford", Jacob "Job" Henry, Frederick Link, George "1", Frederick "1", John "1" Frederick) was born December 08, 1952. He married (1) Jill Chapman July 20, 1973. He married (2) Darlene Marie Jones 1977. He married (3) Sandy Smith June 02, 1989.

Child of Timothy Fox and Sandy Smith is:

i. Jessica Fox, b. October 29, 1980.

101. Patrick Alan Fox (Kenneth Wilfred, Cloyce "Wilford", Jacob "Job" Henry, Frederick Link, George "1", Frederick "1", John "1" Frederick) was born October 04, 1954. He married Cherie Denise Gay July 29, 1978.

Children of Patrick Fox and Cherie Gay are:

i. Ryan Patrick Fox, b. January 11, 1980.

ii. Jason Matthew Fox, b. October 02, 1981.

iii. Bethany Cherilece Fox, b. November 16, 1984.

102. Thomas Daniel Fox (Kenneth Wilfred, Cloyce "Wilford", Jacob "Job" Henry, Frederick Link, George "1", Frederick "1", John "1" Frederick) was born December 29, 1956. He married (1) Susan Elyane Tackis September 02, 1978. He married (2) Penny Linn Bloom August 20, 1983.

Children of Thomas Fox and Penny Bloom are:

i. Danielle Renei Fox, b. July 31, 1984.

ii. Christopher Thomas Fox, b. December 12, 1986.

103. Mary Ann Fox (Kenneth Wilfred, Cloyce "Wilford", Jacob "Job" Henry, Frederick Link, George "1", Frederick "1", John "1" Frederick "1", John "1" Frederick) was born October 16, 1958. She married William Joseph Kerstanski April 07, 1979.

Child of Mary Fox and William Kerstanski is:

i. Tanya Marie Kerstanski, b. December 26, 1979.

Reprint from the Middletown Valley Register of 1932

How Middletown Celebrated Birthday of Washington in '32

The nation-wide Bicentennial Celebration of George Washington's birthday was inaugurated unofficially in Middletown at the various church services on Sunday morning February 21, 1932, at which time the pastors paid tribute to the Father of His Country in their sermons.

In some sections of the country, the religious services got under way 3 days preceding Washington's Birthday, and it was the aim to make a celebration never paralleled in all history - a celebration in which those who participated would honor themselves in doing honor to the nation's founder.

The Valley Register ran a large advertisement on February 5, 1932, on which was printed the George M. Cohan song "Father Of The Land We Love" composed especially for the George Washington Bicentennial Celebration. A limited number of copies of the song were available and would be sent upon request. The ad also showed sketches of the Wakefield, Virginia, birthplace of George Washington, as well as his Mt. Vernon home.

In the search for forgotten or neglected bits of history of the life of George Washington in preparation for the 200th celebration of his birth, it was found that Washington visited Middletown Valley upon several occasions.

The Maryland Bicentennial Commission found that Washington had visited Maryland at least 127 times between 1748 and 1798, and upon each of his visits he stopped to sleep, or at least to eat and drink at approximately 100 public and private houses and traveled over 500 miles of the State's roads of that day.

According to the history of the Fox family of Montgomery County, Ohio, which descended from Frederick Fox, who at one time resided on the outskirts of Middletown, Washington passed through Middletown shortly after the Revolutionary War, on a trip to western Maryland.

The Fox family history states that Washington was once an honored guest at a tavern conducted by Frederick Fox, along the Sharpsburg Road, near Fox's Gap, which was built around the end of the Revolution.

This old tavern, known as the John H. Routzahn place, is one of the oldest stands in the country. Long before the National Pike (which Washington is said to have laid out) was built, the tavern was the stopping place for hundreds of travelers. The National Pike was built between 1804 and 1809. Frederick Fox sold the tavern to John Ringer in 1807, and moved his family to Montgomery County, Ohio.

Land records show that the old Sharpsburg road was a traders' pass long before the National Highway was laid out and traffic at that time was heavy through to Sharpsburg and on to the West Virginia mountains. Thousands of cattle were driven over the route and would be stopped at Fox's overnight.

Records show further that Washington visited the southern section of Middletown Valley, where he was entertained by Governor Thomas Simm Lee, who lived at Needwood Forest, near Burkittsville. Washington visited Lee in order to suggest to the Governor that he become a member of the Commission for laying out the new District of Columbia. Governor Lee was said to have been a close friend of Washington, and received a number of letters from him, some of which told of his movements and suggested which route he would take on his trips because he had received reports that the roads were bad between certain points.

The Maryland Bicentennial Commission also had data which showed that Washington had visited Knoxville, which was then known as Smith's Ferry, and it is presumed that Knoxville was one of his stopping places on his way through Harper's Ferry into West Virginia.

Wills Section

Each Newsletter includes one typewritten version of a will that is significant to the preservation efforts of the Society. Included in this issue is the will of Daniel Alexander Fox. Daniel was a son of John L. Fox and a great-grandson of Frederick Fox of Fox's Gap in Maryland. He was a great-grandfather of Curtis L. Older. Daniel Alexander Fox was born January 13, 1860, in Vermillion County, Indiana and died July 29, 1932, in Covington, Indiana. He is buried next to his wife and his parents in the Hopewell Cemetery west of Covington, Indiana.

Will of Daniel Alexander Fox

Will of Daniel Alexander Fox Vermillion County, Indiana, Newport Court House, (a son of John L. Fox and a great-grandson of Frederick Fox of Fox's Gap in Maryland).

218

WILL OF
Daniel A Fox

I, Daniel A. Fox of Highland Township, in Vermillion County, State of Indiana, being of sound and disposing mind and memory, do hereby make ordain and publish this my last will and testament hereby revoking any and all other wills heretofore made by me.

Item I It is my will that all my just debts including funeral expenses and expenses of last sickness, or m? a first charge upon my estate, and be paid by my ? Executor out of the first-moneys coming into his hands.

Item II It is my wil that all my real and personal property, shall as soon after my death as is practical be sold either at public or private sale as my executor shall deem most advisable and in the manner he believe in it will sell for the most money, and after the paymetns of my debts and funeral expenses as set out in Item I of this will the residue of the moneys left in the hands of my executor shall be divided share and share alike between my following named children, to-wit Ruby Hines, Ethel Gouty, Kenneth B. Fox and William E. Fox. In event that any or either of my above named children should die before the time they or either of them would inherit hereunder, then the share which would have gone to such child living shall go to his or her children in equal shares.

Item III I make no provision in this will for my son Ernest E. Fox, as I have heretofore paid out for him, as much or more than what I would deem to be his interest in my Estate and for that ? I am giving him nothing by this will.

Item IV I do hereby nominate and appoint my ??? John W. Carithers?, Executor of this Will.

In testimony? ????, I Daniel A. Fox, have here unto set my hand and seal at Newport, Vermillion County Indiana, this 6th day of May 1927

Daniel A Fox

The above and foregoing instrument was signed by the said Daniel A Fox in our presence and declared by ?? to be his last will and testament and at his request and in hsi presence and in the presence of each other we now subscribed our names hereto as witnesses this 6th day of May - 1927

Edgar Prather
witnesses Geo D. Sunkel

Proof of Will
State of Indiana
County of VErmillion

Edgar Prather personally appeared before the Clerk of Vermillion Circuit Court, and being duly sworn says that Daniel A Fox signed his name to the above writing of date of May 6 - 1927 as and for his last will and that the same was attested and subscribed by said offiant and Geo D Sunkel as witnesses hereunto in the presence of said Testator and by his request and in the presence of each other that said Testator declared to same to be his last Will and that said Testator was not at the time of executing said will an infant or of unsound mind, or under coercion

Edgar Prather

Certificate of Probate
State of Indiana
County of Vermillion
Court I J N Jones, Clerk of the Vermillion Circuit Curt Certified the within last Will of Daniel A Fox late of said County, deceased has been duly admitted to probate: that its due execution was this day proofed? by Edgar Prather whose proofs together with such Will, have been duly recorded on page 218 of Record No 6 of Wills in my office

In witness whereof I have hereunto set my hand and offixed the seal of said Court this 1st Day of August 1932

J N Jones clerk (seal)

Please notify the President of the Society

regarding any errors you find in the current issue of the Newsletter

---

****

News from Fox's Gap

Published June 1 and December 1 of each year by

The Society of the Descendants of Frederick Fox of Fox's Gap in Maryland

Membership dues are $6.00 per year. President of the Society is Curtis L. Older.

Make Society related inquiries by the following means:

Curtis L. Older
618 Tryon Place
Gastonia, NC 28054-6066

e-mail: curtolder@earthlink.net
home phone: 704-864-3879

****

Fox's Gap Section
By Sam Davis

The Third (James) South Carolina Infantry Battalion Takes a Licking at Fox's Gap September 14, 1862

Sam B. Davis

We are fortunate to present this article by Sam Davis of Greenwood, South Carolina. He is Assistant Professor of Mass Communications at Lander University.

(e-mail: sdavis@lander.edu)

Given a family history pretty well saturated with the Civil War and its aftereffects, perhaps it is not surprising that my own interest seems to have developed naturally. As usual in such cases, the more I learned the more I wanted to know. Some of my ancestors had been members of regiments and battalions whose records have been well documented. Mac Wyckoff's excellent history of the Third South Carolina Regiment, for example, provided information on several of my great-great grandfathers, but there was one unit—the Third South Carolina Infantry Battalion—whose record seems to have been almost completely ignored by historians. I had found some little information in D. A. Dickert's History of Kershaw's Brigade, *but not nearly enough to satisfy my curiosity about the unit in which two of my great-great-grandfathers had served.*

I met Wyckoff one December day in 1997 while searching for a personal copy of his book in the visitors center at Chancellorsville and told him of my ambition to research the unit and write something about it myself. He referred me to Jim Clary in Cary, North Carolina, who was then in the process of writing a history of the Fifteenth South Carolina, a unit closely tied to the one that interested me. Clary was enthusiastic and extremely helpful; it was he who suggested that the two of us co-author a history of the battalion. Though I was a little skeptical at first, both Wyckoff and Clary encouraged me to begin the process by developing a biographical roster covering every soldier in the unit. I set to work and by the time the chore was finished, about a year later, I was firmly committed to the goal of a published history of the Third South Carolina Infantry Battalion. I tackled the first chapter at the suggestion of my collaborators, and when Clary found his own research and writing as much as he could handle, I simply kept going. As the year 2001 draws to a close, the work goes on. The history is about 65% complete at this writing, and it now seems entirely possible that a published volume will be a reality in the not too distant future.

My initial research established what seemed to me unusually high losses for the small battalion at Boonsboro, Maryland. It was there, in fact, that the unit sustained its highest casualty rate of the entire war, though it participated in a number of hot spots, among them Gettysburg, Chickamauga, the Wilderness, and Spotsylvania. As time went on, accounts of the fighting at Fox's Gap near Boonsboro began to capture my imagination. I read any number of versions of the action but frankly made little progress, either in understanding exactly how it developed or the precise involvement of the battalion. But that was before Jim Clary put me in touch with a fellow in Smyrna, Georgia, named Kurt Graham. His interpretation of the battle made real sense to me, and I, along with others who have studied his views and his research have grown to respect his knowledge and judgment. I am pleased to acknowledge a debt of gratitude for Graham's friendship and help with my project.

I also want to thank Steve Stotelmyer of Sharpsburg, Maryland, who took me on a step-by-step tour of the battleground one day. When one is trying to visualize something that happened more than a hundred years ago, there is no substitute for actually walking the terrain. An added advantage of the tour was that it strongly reinforced Graham's view of what really happened with the Third South Carolina Battalion that day. I came away convinced.

The South Carolina Battalion consisted of seven companies on the fateful afternoon of September 14, 1862, at Fox's Gap, Maryland. Five of the companies were made up predominately of men from Laurens District, while one consisted of enlistees from Fairfield District, and another was made up of men from in and around Columbia. The action at Fox's Gap marked the first and last time the battalion's commander, Lieutenant Colonel George Strother James, would lead his troops into battle. James was born in Laurens, South Carolina, in 1828. His first military service came in the Mexican War; he was commissioned a Sergeant Major for meritorious conduct in the Palmetto regiment. Following the war and several fruitless attempts at academic pursuits, James headed west and was commissioned an artillery officer in 1856. Like many other southerners, he resigned his federal commission and offered his services to his native state when war seemed inevitable in early 1861. Mid-April of that year found him in command of two South Carolina artillery batteries on James Island in Charleston harbor. One of James's batteries - with James himself at the lanyard - actually fired the warning shot that burst over Fort Sumter on April 12.

Continuing his service with the state troops along the coast, James was placed in command of the Third South Carolina Battalion in December. The men quickly adopted a new name – the James Battalion – no doubt in recognition of their commander's actions in the Fort Sumter barrage. Though it guarded the railroad near Adams Run between Charleston and Savannah, the battalion's battle experience was quite limited during this period. It had marched to Secessionville but did not arrive in time to take part in that action. The following month saw guard duty around Charleston, but orders soon came to join the Fiftieth and Fifty-First Georgia, the Phillips Georgia Legion, and the Fifteenth South Carolina, all under the command of Brigadier General Thomas Fenwick Drayton, for a move to Richmond. With their enemies limited thus far to typhoid fever and measles, the 300-man battalion arrived in the Confederate capital as the greenest of the green insofar as actual combat was concerned. Within the short span of six weeks, however, the battalion would participate in a battle that would virtually destroy it.

It seems reasonable that, because of its small size and lack of experience, the Third Battalion may have been assigned to the Fifteenth South Carolina Regiment, commanded by Colonel William Davie DeSaussure, upon its arrival at Richmond. Such a move would have made sense for several reasons, among them the logistical and administrative makeup of the combined unit structure employed at the time. Research has thus far failed to uncover details of the exact command structure relationship between the Fifteenth and the Third Battalion during the period before the battle at Fox's Gap.

The battalion sustained minimal damage at Second Manassas, and its casualties in other operations of Drayton's Brigade can also be considered light. But, after Manassas, as Lee's army headed toward Leesburg on September 3, the divisions under the command of General Longstreet were reduced considerably, not because of casualties but as the result of an order issued by the general himself. All shoeless, sick, and combat "inefficients" were ordered to proceed to Winchester, Virginia, from which place they would rejoin the army at a later date. This order was reported to have affected as many as 5,000 men and did cover a hundred members of the James Battalion who were declared ineffective for one reason or another.

This order reduced the battalion's strength to approximately 175 men, the number who moved out on September 6 to cross the Potomac River and invade Maryland. Evidence of an intriguing confrontation between DeSaussure and James crops up at this point. It seems that when DeSaussure balked at the idea of crossing the river, on the grounds that the Fifteenth had enlisted to defend the South and not to invade the North, the ever volatile James rushed to the front, accused the colonel of cowardice, and personally led the entire regiment across the Potomac.

A short stay in Frederick was followed by a march to Middletown, over South Mountain, through Turner's Gap to Boonsboro, and on to a spot near Hagerstown, where the brigade arrived on Friday, September 12. A planned respite for the men would prove of short duration when the troops were rushed back to Boonsboro on Sunday morning in response to a call for assistance from Major General Daniel Harvey Hill. Hill's division of 5,000 men was attempting to impede the progress of General George B. McClellan's Army of the Potomac as its lead elements attacked Fox's Gap. McClellan had determined the whereabouts of Lee's scattered forces from intelligence contained in Lee's General Order No. 191. A copy of the order had been retrieved from an abandoned Confederate campsite, its authenticity quickly verified, and the information passed on to McClellan. The general was pushing the bulk of his army toward Boonsboro in order to cut Lee's forces in half, troops he knew were scattered from Harper's Ferry all the way to Hagerstown.

The battalion left Hagerstown at daylight on the morning of September 14 and joined the march back along the same roads they had covered two days before. Longstreet wrote that "the day was hot and the roads dry and beaten down into impalpable powder, that rose in clouds of dust from under our feet as we marched." The tired, dusty, and footsore men reached the hamlet of Boonsboro, nestled at the western base of South Mountain, about noon but barely had time to catch their breath. The road behind them to Hagerstown was littered with men who had dropped by the wayside from sheer exhaustion. The remaining South Carolinians marched through the town and quickly reached the point where the road began its steep incline up the mountain to Turner's Gap. The battalion at this point probably numbered no more than 160 men.

Fighting was already underway at the top of the mountain as the battalion began its ascent on the National Pike. General Samuel Garland's North Carolinians had been pushed back into the woods north of the Old Sharpsburg Road at Fox's Gap, a mile to the south of the battalion's destination. Hill's forces were in grave danger of being flanked by a superior force. The battalion reached the summit and found that Hill had already sent G. B. Anderson's and Roswell Ripley's brigades toward Fox's Gap to try to stem the tide of advancing bluecoats now moving north toward his position. The Federals had not managed to follow up on their repulse of Garland's troops by the time of Anderson's arrival, but Hill still faced a desperate situation on his right.

Garland's brigade of 1,100 men had bought some precious time during the three-hour morning fight south of Fox's Gap as they held off General Jacob Cox's IX Corps "Kanawha Division." The time turned out to be dearly bought indeed – Garland was killed during the battle. Hill's right flank at Fox's Gap was turned by noon, and Cox's division pulled back into a strategic position in the woods southeast of the gap to wait for other IX Corps divisions to arrive. Anderson's Confederate brigade, which had already arrived at the gap, managed to stall Cox's troops as Garland's routed forces continued pulling back.

The South Carolinians and Georgians under Drayton and G. T. Anderson arrived at the Mountain House at Turner's Gap around 2 PM and were immediately ordered to march along the Wood Road toward Fox's Gap a mile to the south where the booming of artillery could now be heard clearly. Prior to the marching order, Roswell Ripley's brigade had been sent toward the action to support G. B. Anderson, whose forces were already deployed along the western face of the mountain down the Old Sharpsburg Road.

Ripley fell into line on Anderson's left, but the lines of both brigades shifted too far down the western face to make much difference in the critical onslaught that awaited the trailing brigades, especially Drayton's, a little later that afternoon.

The small South Carolina battalion and the larger South Carolina and Georgia regiments fell in on the narrow, tree-lined road that curled its way a short distance around the eastern crest of the mountain, by the Hartz farm, and then gently ascended to the plateau of the mountain ridge. This one -mile stretch represented the first time since leaving Boonsboro that the haggard men had been able to march on fairly level terrain. Drayton's exhausted brigade arrived at Fox's Gap around 3 PM. The fighting had taken a toll on both sides. By early afternoon the Ohioans were resting in the woods south of Daniel Wise's four-acre field, tending the wounded, and replenishing their ammunition. In addition, Captain James Bondurant's Confederate artillery battery (aka Jeff Davis Artillery) was pelting the woods where Cox lay waiting for Federal reinforcements.

About two hundred yards before entering the Old Sharpsburg Road, the Carolinians could see a large field just beyond a stone wall on their left. That field offered a view to the east along the winding road, which descended in the same direction toward the distant valley around Middletown. In the northern sector of this field, Bondurant's four guns were wreaking havoc, raining shell and canister on Cox's position beyond Wise's Field and cabin to the south of the Old Sharpsburg Road. Holding Fox's Gap was absolutely essential if the Yankees were to be foiled in their attempt to flank Hill's forces at Turner's Gap to the north, where everything was being done to fight off the approaching mass of Federals ascending toward that spot.

The Third South Carolina Battalion was ordered to the far southern end of the large field, later to become known as the Seventeenth Michigan Field, and deployed into the Old Sharpsburg Road which bordered it. Their position offered little in the way of a good view down the curling mountain pass road to the east. To the battalion's right and west, and occupying the entire distance to the Wise Cabin and just beyond, was the Fifteenth South Carolina. In the immediate front of the battalion lay the open Wise Field. Along the battalion's left rear were aligned in order from right to left, the Phillips' Legion, and the Fifty-first and Fiftieth Georgia behind a stone wall. Facing east, the Georgia men had a deep gully to their front. It is clear that Drayton's Brigade did, in fact, deploy initially in a militarily advantageous position at Fox's Gap. What went wrong, and why was this strategically sound position changed?

Linking up with G. T. Anderson's brigade deployed to Drayton's right along the Old Sharpsburg Road was crucial, but a dangerous gap opened between Anderson and Drayton. This gap had to be joined if the brigades of both Andersons (G. T. and G. B.), Ripley, and Drayton were to execute an ordered and difficult left wheeling attack. D. H. Hill stated that his strategy was for all the brigades to coordinate their attacks with the objective of driving the Yankees back down the east side of the mountain. Drayton's position was to be the hinge on which the four brigades would turn in a sweeping movement back over the mountain to the east and possibly roll up the Federals' left flank saddling the crest. Potentially, this might have been good strategy and seems on the surface quite logical, but a combination of terrain and circumstances defeated the purpose that day. As a matter of fact, the idea of such a movement at such a time causes modern-day strategists to view the generalship at Fox's Gap as a problem on a par with the topography.

As it played out, Drayton's forces were left isolated at the relatively unobstructed gap as the other brigades attempted to initiate the complicated wheeling movement. While the commanders were struggling to implement the ill-fated maneuver, which never really got started and wound up in total disarray, Drayton found himself confronted head on by a superior force.

For some insane reason, Drayton decided to send a company - the Third Battalion's Company F - southeast across Wise's Field to ascertain the position of the enemy who, he surely knew, were already there. This reconnaissance move makes little sense unless Drayton was acting on orders from a superior since, apart from that action, his deployment from his arrival had been militarily sound.

Soon, even before he knew the position of the remaining Confederate brigades to his west, Drayton ordered the Phillips Legion, the Third South Carolina Battalion, and the Fifteenth South Carolina Regiment to attack toward the woods at the south end of the field. The Legion gained some protection in the woods lining the left edge of the field, but the battalion found itself facing a storm of lead in the open. The Fifteenth, though also somewhat protected by woods on the right, charged by Daniel Wise's Cabin and along a road leading south. This road, called the Ridge Road (a southerly extension of the Wood Road at the intersection of the Old Sharpsburg Road) was lined with rock walls which offered some protection as well. Even so, it was almost immediately apparent that there was no possibility the three units would be able to gain the woods at the southern end of Wise's Field. The battalion, fighting alongside the Legion, held on desperately for about fifteen minutes while the Fifteenth faced the opposition in its front down the Ridge Road to the south. At the height of the melee, the remaining Georgia regiments, initially deployed facing east in the Seventeenth Michigan Field, were moved into vacated positions left by the battalion and the Legion along the Old Sharpsburg Road.

James's men could not possibly remain where they were. The dead were piling up, and the smoky air along the mountain ridge was filled with the sounds of wounded men. The ghastly affair grew even worse as more Federals emerged from the southern edge of the field and headed toward the shattered battalion. To make matters worse, Yankees slammed into the Legion's left flank in the woods, and the Georgians were pushed out of the woods and across Wise's Field. Even the Georgia regiments trailing in the Old Sharpsburg Road were flanked and forced to retreat to the west; no help from that sector would be forthcoming. James had no recourse but to withdraw to the protection of the rock wall of the Ridge Road near Wise's Cabin. As they shot it out with Federals across the field, the battalion was ripped to shreds and its thinning ranks fell in heaps. The unit was now completely isolated by virtue of its position at a forward point in the Ridge Road.

The high toll of casualties can be explained in part by the tenuous position assigned to the battalion during the battle. Its final position – caught between the rock walls of the Ridge Road – became even more vulnerable as the Georgians and the Fifteenth South Carolina fell back northwest of Wise's Cabin. Left completely unsupported and facing hordes of the enemy converging from the east and south, the battalion found itself virtually helpless. At some point in these final moments, Lieutenant Colonel James went down with a mortal wound and expired on the field before morning. All alone, the battalion continued to defend its Ridge Road position as the afternoon advanced. Meanwhile, the Seventeenth Michigan Regiment assailed the Georgians from the northeast and gained a flanking position from which it was able to inflict heavy casualties on the Georgia units as they retreated. Thus buffeted themselves, the Georgians could offer no assistance to the beleaguered and isolated Carolinians. In all probability, the Seventeenth, after dispersing the fleeing Confederates, turned their weapons on the almost annihilated battalion and finished it off. There was plenty of courage and bravery that day, but little common sense seemed to prevail.

Brigadier General Roswell Ripley, left in command of the attack, led his brigade off the mountain to the west and completely out of the fight. Brigadier General G. T. Anderson moved his brigade too far west, opening up a 300-yard gap between his left and Drayton's right. Finally, Drayton, who had been criticized for delaying an attack at Second Manassas just two weeks earlier, chose to regard his orders as non-discretionary and attacked several thousand Federals with 800 Confederates. In retrospect, he should have dug in behind the stone walls at the gap and forced the enemy to come to him.

Several factors might account for the terrific casualty rate suffered by the Third South Carolina Battalion at Fox's Gap. One has to be, simply, poor overall generalship at the brigade level. Another is that the terrain did not lend itself to the action that was planned, a clear example of inadequate reconnaissance by D. H. Hill and his staff. The four Southern brigadiers had just over 4,000 men near the gap, but only 1,300 of these were actually there. The Federals, on the other hand had over 5,000 men at the gap.

Delving deeper into the realm of speculation, could it be that Lieutenant Colonel James expected more of his battalion than it was capable of delivering? It should be remembered that his troops had never really fought a battle; was he perhaps trying to impress his own men and those around him with his ability to lead even green troops to a glorious victory? Might he have been trying to make amends for his haughty attitude toward DeSaussure at the Potomac crossing? Or, conversely, could he have been paying the price for that attitude by having his men placed in the most perilous position of all during the battle? Perhaps, in spite of everything, James was simply a good soldier. He died doing his duty and holding on as best he could until that duty was done. We shall probably never have a complete answer to any of these questions. We do know, however, that his battalion suffered 132 casualties at Fox's Gap – a full 82% of its members were killed in action, mortally wounded, wounded, and captured. Clearly, this little band of about 160 warriors, green though they undoubtedly were at the start of the battle, paid a terrible price in the late afternoon of September 14, 1862.

Down, but not yet defeated, the battalion was transferred to Kershaw's Brigade before Fredericksburg. It would be restored to a full compound infantry battalion, but never again during the war would it suffer as it did on that bloody Sabbath on a mountaintop in Maryland.

Lt. Col. George Strother James

**Courtesy of the South Carolina
Confederate Relic Room and Museum, Columbia, SC**

Casualty List of the Third South Carolina Infantry Battalion at The Battle of Fox's Gap September 14, 1862

CIA = Captured in Action	41
KIA = Killed in Action	38
WIA = Wounded in Action	20
WIA & CIA = Wounded in Action and Captured in Action	31
MIA = Missing in Action	2
Total =	132

Aiken, Hugh W. - Company G - CIA
Anderson, James J. - Company A - KIA
Anderson, John Stennis - Company C - CIA
Armstrong, Dempsy - Company D - KIA
Austin, Isaac G. - Company B - WIA
Austin, L. Samuel - Company B - KIA
Avery, Joseph J. - Company C - KIA
Babb, Doctor Anderson "Dock" - Company ? - KIA
Baldwin, James E. - Company C - WIA
Baruch, Simon. - Assistant Surgeon - CIA
Boyd, J.W. - Company G - WIA and CIA
Bramlett, Lewis Robert - Company E. - CIA
Brown, G.W. - Company G. - WIA
Brownlee, Joseph R. - Company D - WIA and CIA
Bryant, John Wesley - Company E - CIA
Burdette, George R. - Company D - WIA
Calhoun, James - Company A - KIA
Calhoun, John William Jr. - Company A - KIA
Calhoun, Thomas Harrison - Company B - CIA
Campbell, James Richard - Company F. - CIA
Cannon, Capers Bowman - Company A - WIA and CIA
Cannon, William N. - Company C - KIA
Claffey, Patrick - Company F - CIA
Clardy, Reuben Stacey - Company A - WIA
Coleman, Thomas J. - Company B - WIA and CIA
Cook, Henry H. - Company A - WIA and CIA
Cooper, Thomas Porter - Company C - WIA and CIA
Crawford, John W. - Company B - KIA
Curry, Henry Linden - Company D - CIA
Dagnall, William - Company C - WIA
Davis, James W. - Company B - WIA and CIA
Elmore, Logan C. - Company A - WIA
Finley, James Henry - Company A - WIA
Fleming, Alexander Hamilton - Company F - WIA and CIA
Fooshe, James D. - Company A - WIA
Fooshe, John Coleman - Company A - CIA
Fowler, James Wiley - Company E - WIA
Freideberg, Joseph F. - Company F - Mortally wounded
Fuller, Adolphus A. - Company B - WIA and CIA
Fuller, Edwin T. - Company B - KIA
Fuller, John Cook - Company B - WIA and CIA
Fuller, Pressley A. - Company B - KIA
Fuller, William Benton - Company B - WIA
Fulmer, William E.C. - Company F - CIA
Glaze, John - Company F - CIA
Griffin, Elihu Clayton - Company B - KIA
Griffin, Elihu Watts - Company A - CIA
Grumbles, William Winston - Company E - WIA and CIA
Haigood, R.M. - Company G - WIA and CIA
Hand, William H. - Company B - CIA
Hanvey, Wright Joshua - Company B - CIA
Henderson, Masten W. - Company C - KIA
Henry, Robert Leland - Company E - WIA
Hines, George W. - Company A - CIA
Hitt, Henry Lewis - Company B - CIA
Hollingsworth, Abraham, Jr. - Company B - KIA
Hudgens, Ambrose Watts - Company C - WIA
Irby, Waddy Thompson - Company B - KIA
James, George Strother - Lieutenant Colonel - KIA

Johnson, Benjamin F. - Company C - KIA
Jones, James A. - Company B - WIA & CIA
Kelly, William Franklin - Company D - WIA & CIA
Keough, P.H. - Company F - KIA
Langston, Henry L. - Company D - MIA
Ligon, George Anderson - Company B - CIA
Lindley, William T. - Company C - KIA
Loyd, J. Thomas - Company D - WIA & CIA
McCawley, J.B. - Company F - MIA
McCluney, James - Company D - WIA & CIA
McConnell, A.C. - Company G - CIA
McKnight, William Downs - Company D - KIA
McNeely, John O. - Company E - CIA
Madden, Charles Simmons - Company D - WIA and CIA
Madden, E. Decatur - Company D - CIA
Madden, William Cunningham - Company B - KIA
Martin, David R. - Company G - KIA
Martin, Jasper Ray - Company E - WIA and CIA
Mason, Washington N. - Company G - WIA
Miller, Daniel Byrd - Company F - CIA
Monroe, J.L. Wesley - Company D - KIA
Moore, George W. - Company A - WIA and CIA
Morgan, J.S. - Company E - WIA & CIA
Motes, A. Tolen - Company C - KIA
Nelson, James Franklin - Company B - CIA
Nelson, John M. - Company A - CIA
Nickels, John Henry - Company A - WIA and CIA
North, Samuel R. - Company F - WIA
Owens, Elias N. - Company A - KIA
Owens, Mancil - Company E - CIA
Owings, Richard Leander - Company D - CIA
Patterson, William Preston - Company E - WIA & CIA
Paul, John F. - Company G - WIA & CIA
Pitts, John S. - Company C - WIA
Puckett, Cason Keels - Company A - KIA
Puckett, Samuel David - Company A - CIA
Ramage, Joseph Franklin - Company D - WIA
Rampy, Joseph M. - Company A - WIA & CIA
Ramsey, James - Company A - CIA
Rembert, John - Company F - WIA & CIA
Rice, William George Washington - Major - WIA
Riddle, Drury Boyce - Company E - KIA
Riddle, James Andrew - Company E - CIA
Riddle, Martin - Company E - CIA
Riddle, W. Drayton - Company E - KIA
Riddle, Willis Marion - Company E - CIA
Robinson, W.H. - Company G - WIA and CIA
Senn, Dederick - Company F - KIA
Shedd, James P. - Company G - KIA
Shockley, Robert T. - Company D - KIA
Simpson, William Wade - Company D - KIA
Smith, Maxwell - Company B - KIA
Smith, Thomas McLaughlin - Company F - KIA
Snow, Andrew J. - Company B - WIA
Speake, John L. - Company D - CIA
Spears, Robert S. - Company D - CIA
Stewart, Joseph Warren - Company E - WIA
Stokes, Elwood R. - Company F - WIA & CIA
Sumerel, Martin - Company E - KIA
Sumerel, Toliver - Company E - WIA & CIA
Sumerel, William W. - Company E - WIA & CIA
Thrift, Robert - Company F - CIA
Tinkler, George S. - Company G - CIA
Todd, Robert James - Company E - CIA
Townsend, Joshua Milton - Company A - CIA
Trapp, Labon H. - Company G - CIA
Waldrop, William Ephram (Ephraim) - Company B - KIA
Walker, Francis Marion - Company B - WIA and CIA
Walker, John M. - Company C - CIA
Watkins, Lawson - Company C - KIA
Watson, James Ewell - Company B - CIA
Watts, B.F. - Company G - CIA
Wilson, John Newton - Company C - WIA & CIA

Bibliography for the Sam Davis Article

Calhoun, C. M. *Liberty Dethroned.* Publisher unknown, 1903.
Charleston (SC) Daily Courier
Compiled Service Records of Confederate Soldiers Who Served in Organizations From the State of South Carolina. Microfilm Copy 267, Roll 179. Washington, DC: Government Printing Office, 1958.

Dickert, D. August. *A History of Kershaw's Brigade*. Newberry, SC: Elbert H Aull Company, 1899.

Emory University , Woodruff Library, Atlanta Ga: "Letters of Lieutenant Alex Erwin."

Graham, Kurt. "The Death of a Brigade: Drayton's Brigade at Fox's Gap September 14, 1862." NC South Mountain Monument News. Fall, 2000.

Johnson, Robert Underwood, and Buel, Clarence Clough, Editors. *Battles and Leaders of the Civil War*. Reprint Edition. Four Volumes. New York: Thomas Yoseloff, 1956.

Library of Congress, Washington DC: John Evans Edings Diary.

Longstreet, James. *From Manassas To Appomattox: Memoirs of the Civil War in America*. Philadelphia: Lippencott Company, 1896.

Stotelmyer, Steven R. *The Bivouacs of the Dead: The Story of Those Who Died at Antietam and South Mountain: With histories and rosters of Antietam, Washington, Mt. Olivet and Elmwood Cemeteries*. Linthicum, Maryland: Tommey Press, 1992.

The War of the Rebellion: A Compilation of the Official Records in the Confederate and Union Armies. Four Series, Seventy Volumes in 128 Parts. Washington, DC. Government Printing Office, 1880-1901.

Frederick Fox and Fox's Gap Section

Books related to Fox's Gap, Fox genealogy, the Battle of South Mountain, etc. Inquire online at the Barnes and Noble website: barnesandnoblez.com

The Braddock Expedition and Fox's Gap in Maryland by Curtis L. Older
The Land Tracts of the Battlefield of South Mountain by Curtis L. Older
both available at Willow Bend Books, 65 E. Main Street, Westminster, MD 21157-5026, www.willowbendbooks.com, 1-800-876-6102, e-mail: bookorder@willowbend.net

The Fox Genealogy by Daniel Gebhart Fox
available from Blairs' Book Service, 2503 Springpark Way, Richardson, Texas 75082, reference number XR-2546, e-mail: linda@glbco.com, fax: 972-783-1008

Before Antietam, the Battle for South Mountain by John Michael Priest, 206 Weldon Drive, Boonsboro, MD 21713, 301-432-8720

Landscape Turned Red, The Battle of Antietam by Stephen W. Sears

The Pennsylvania Line, Regimental Organization And Operations, 1776-1783, by John B. B. Trussell, Jr., Pennsylvania Historical and Museum Commission

Related Family Lines:
The Link Family by Paxson Link, available from Blair's Book Service, see above
Sir Henry A. Ogle, first published in 1902, *Ogle and Bothal*
The official Ogle Family Library, currently known as "The Ogle Collection," is housed in the Fulton County Museum, 27 E 375 N, Rochester, IN 46975

News from Fox's Gap

The Society of the Descendants of Frederick Fox of Fox's Gap in Maryland

Issue 3, Volume 2 **Remember Freedom!** June 1, 2002

Michael Fox of Fox's Gap in Maryland

By Lois Ann Baker

We are extremely fortunate and pleased to publish for the first time an article about Michael Fox, a brother of Frederick Fox. Michael and Frederick were sons of John Fox of Fox's Gap in Maryland. Michael preceded Frederick in moving to near Dayton, Ohio, in the early 1800s.

The author of this article is Lois Baker of Versailles, Ohio, who is a descendant of Michael Fox. She has done extensive genealogical research into the descendants of Michael Fox and has graciously submitted the following article.

Lois assisted in marking the grave of Michael Fox as a soldier of the American Revolution. We anticipate Lois will submit a second article on Michael Fox and his descendants that will appear in the December 1, 2002 newsletter.

In 1966 after surgery, the doctor grounded me. I was to do nothing at all. No newspapers, no television, and no traveling. Relax and rest. Go camping and lay in a hammock. I am not a camper, I can't put up a tent, and never saw a hammock put up either. Do what? Nothing. Boring! I found a book published in 1964 about the history of Versailles and its early settlers. Several cousins had written about some of the branches of our family. My mother never wrote an article for the book. So I asked her, Why hadn't she written one? So I asked my mother questions. What a memory and knowledge she had about our family.

I searched the local area in Versailles for any and all research material available that would shed light on the whereabouts of my family. My mother gave me the names of Nischwitz, Davidson, English, Mendenhall, Pittsenbarger, DeFligne, Radabaugh, and Brandon for a start. As research developed, so did more names.

While working on the family history and searching for the next lead that would uncover some forgotten clue to my family's whereabouts, I would try my mother for more information.

Her father was Charles Nischwitz and her mother was Rachel Davidson, were the parents of seven children - William Nischwitz, Marjorie Nischwitz Miller, Anna Nischwitz Schrader, Lawrence Nischwitz, Calvin Nischwitz, Myrtle Nischwitz Bryson, and Ellen Nischwitz. My mother was the youngest child and spent a lot of time traveling in the buggy or car with her father.

My mother related that she remembered visits made by her father when she was quite young to Butler Township, Montgomery County, Ohio, to visit relatives. She recalled the surnames of Waymire and Coover. Now when searching for family evidence, my mother, Ellen Nischwitz Judy, and I visited the area searching for family ties. I interviewed people living in Butler Township, Montgomery County, who cited me to Popular Hill Cemetery. After finding the tombstones and the death dates, I then found and copied death certificates and obituaries. This led to marriage records of Montgomery County, Ohio, producing more family ties.

Interviews revealed family traditions and legends and close associations with other unknown relatives who lived or had lived in nearby counties. Obituaries indicated a search was needed in nearby counties in Ohio and research in Pennsylvania and Maryland.

Charles Nischwitz was the son of George Nischwitz and Mary Louisa DeFligne. George Nischwitz was the son of Jacob Nischwitz and Elizabeth Beard. Elizabeth Beard was the daughter of John Beard and Elizabeth Fox. Elizabeth Fox was the daughter of Michael Fox and Susanna.

The death entry in Probate Court stated that Elizabeth Fox Beard was born in Sharpsburg, Maryland, on April 10, 1778, and died on February 13, 1879, in Butler Township. She married John Beard on April 9, 1809, in Warren County, Ohio. John Beard and Elizabeth Fox were the parents of Sarah Beard Wilhelm, Mary Beard Wolaver, Elizabeth Beard Nischwitz, Susannah Beard Kenney, Eve Beard Coover, Samuel Beard, John Beard, Jacob Beard, George Beard, and Nancy Beard Maxton.

The obituary of Elizabeth Fox Beard stated she was born in Sharpsburg, Maryland. The family sketch that was written in a Montgomery County History suggested Warren County, Ohio, for research as well as searching for a locally written family genealogy. I found the Ohio Fox Genealogy which indicated that this family and my family had roots in the same area of Ohio and Maryland.

After three months of research, I was back to the Revolutionary War period. I was curious. Was Michael Fox a Patriot or Loyalist? So this demanded more research. It took years to make the connection between Michael Fox and Frederick Fox. In John Fox's will, probated in Washington County, Maryland, it lists the children of John Fox as Daniel, Frederick, Magdeline, Michael, and Rachael.

The next big clue that I found was in the local newspaper of Versailles, The Versailles Policy. I saw a notice where William Ware of Versailles had died and left his wife Mary Fox Ware as a survivor. They lived in Versailles, Ohio, where I live. I remembered seeing the article in The Fox Genealogy by D. G. Fox announcing that Mary Fox married William Ware.

William and Mary Fox Ware's daughter Thelma married Henry Peschke and lived in Versailles. They even attended the same Lutheran Church that my family did. My grandpa Charles Nischwitz and Henry Peschke were great friends but never mentioned a relationship. My grandfather died in 1937. My mother did not recall that her father ever mentioned any family ties.

I had found on the 1830 Ohio Census for Warren County that Michael Fox resided there. I made a visit to the cemetery of Franklin, Ohio. I searched the cemetery register books but could not find the burials listed for Michael or Susannah Fox.

Several years later Marsha Fitzgerald and I found we were in several families that were related to one another. So she and I made a trip to Franklin, Warren County, Ohio. The cemetery register books were large and heavy. The cemetery sexton provided us with a table and chairs and wished us "Happy Hunting".

We divided the register books and each took sheets of paper to write down family information that we found on families that were related to us. That way, we each had only several books to lift and check for information.

After the third book we were getting tired. Marsha's thumb got caught in the back cover of her book. Instead of pulling her thumb out, she opened the book to the back cover and let out a squeal of delight. Handwritten in the back of the register was written 77 persons buried from the old Franklin Cemetery and reburied in the new cemetery. Among the 77 names listed were Michael Fox and Susanna Fox. What a find!

You know, I think I would have pulled my thumb out and not have opened to the back cover. We now had dates for Michael and Susannah Fox. I copied the entire list of 77 burials. This list was published by Anita Short's publication called Gateway to the West. We also found a sort story in the newspaper of Franklin that stated railroad wanted to go through Franklin and the old cemetery was to be dug up and reburied in the new Franklin Cemetery.

These 77 stones were relocated on different hillsides of the new Franklin Cemetery. Some of the bodies and stones were re-interred in other cemeteries. Frederick Fox and family were reburied in the Gephart Cemetery. Michael Fox and wife were re-interred in the new Franklin Cemetery. Thus, the two brothers buried together in the same cemetery were later buried in different cemeteries.

The other clue that proved that Frederick and Michael Fox were brothers came about when Robert H. Fox of Cincinnati, Ohio, showed me the envelope and letter that was addressed in 1812 to Misters Frederick and Michael Fox, Warren County, Franklin Township, Ohio, from Jacob Reel in Sharpsburg, Maryland stating that their mother, Christiana Fox, had died. This conclusive evidence to me provided proof of family relationship between Frederick and Michael Fox.

A second letter from Jacob Reel, dated July 6, 1806, from Sharpsburg, Maryland, also exists. There is no addressee in this letter but it appears to have been sent to Frederick Fox and informed him of the health of his mother. Copies of both these letters, as transcribed from the originals, are available from the Society.

Michael Fox, a brother of Frederick Fox of Fox's Gap in Maryland, was born on January 6, 1760 and died in Franklin, Warren County, Ohio, on August 23, 1837, aged 77 years, 7 months, and 17 days. He and his wife Susannah Fox, 1761 - 1836, are both buried in Woodhill Cemetery in Franklin, Warren County, Ohio.

Michael Fox served in the Revolutionary War. Washington County Committee of Observation lists Michael Fox as a member of a company of militia raised in Washington County on January 6, 1776, with Joseph Chapline as Captain published in Maryland Historical Magazine.

Michael Fox also is listed among those who enlisted in the upper district of Frederick County at Elizabethtown - now Hagerstown - as the first militia company organized for the Revolutionary War in Hagerstown subscribed to the obligations as published in Scharf's History of Western Maryland.

After the Northwest Territory was opened for settlement and statehood was being planned for Ohio and after the death of his father, John Frederick Fox who died in Washington County, Maryland in 1784, Michael Fox moved his family settling near Cincinnati, Ohio, in the 1790s. Michael and Susannah Fox were the parents of Elizabeth, Eve, Jacob, Daniel, and Michael. They later moved to Franklin, Warren County, Ohio.

John Frederick Fox was a 5th great-grandfather of Lois Ann Baker. The lineage of Lois Ann Baker back to John Fox would be: Lois Ann Baker was a daughter of Ellen Nischwitz and Cleatus Judy. Ellen Nischwitz was the daughter of Charles Nischwitz and Rachel Davidson. Charles Nischwitz was the son of George Nischwitz and Mary Louisa DeFligne. George Nischwitz was the son of Elizabeth Beard and Jacob Nischwitz. Elizabeth Beard was the daughter of Michael Fox and Susannah (last name unknown). Michael Fox was the son of John Frederick Fox and Christena (last name unknown).

From The Bookshelf

By Curtis L. Older

Burnside

By William Marvel

Published by The University of North Carolina Press

Commanding Union General George B. McClellan placed his Army into three Wings as they departed Washington, DC, and marched toward the Catoctin and South Mountains in Maryland in pursuit of General Robert E. Lee and the Army of Northern Virginia during September 1862. The Right Wing, the largest of the three, was under the command of Major General Ambrose Burnside.

Burnside's Right Wing consisted of the 9th Corp under Major General Jesse Lee Reno and the 1st Corp under Major General Joseph Hooker. Burnside soon became familiar with the generals of the 9th Corp at South Mountain: Rodman Wilcox, Sturgis, Cox, and Crook. Wilcox was a West Point classmate of Burnside and was with him from the start of the Maryland Campaign in 1862 and remained with him until the end of his service.

It was Burnside who led the Right Wing of the Union Army at South Mountain and Antietam. Burnside commanded about 20,000 men as they marched through Fox's Gap after the Battle of South Mountain. The Old Sharpsburg Road through Fox's Gap led to the banks of the Antietam Creek near Sharpsburg, Maryland, where Burnside's men would face America's bloodiest day.

A picture included by author William Marvel in his book on Burnside is one of Fox's Gap in 1922, showing The Old Sharpsburg Road in the foreground. The caption states that Reno was mortally wounded at the crest, just above the house at the right of the picture. The photo is from the collection of Jim Clifford and Jack Burke.

Ambrose Burnside was a graduate of the U. S. Military Academy where he graduated 18th in a class of 38. He was an early friend of George McClellan. The main periods of Burnside's military service include: 1) the Burnside Expedition to North Carolina; 2) the Maryland Campaign; 3) Head of the Army of the Potomac; 4) Service in the mid-west and at the Battle of Knoxville; 5) the summer of 1864 serving under General Grant.

Burnside was in First Bull Run in 1861, where he led a brigade, the 1st Rhode Island. However, it was the Burnside Expedition and the battles at New Bern and Roanoke in North Carolina that made Burnside one of the earliest Union heroes of the Civil War. And yes, the term "sideburns" does come from General Burnside, who could always be easily distinguished by his beard.

After the Battle of Antietam and the ouster of McClellan by Lincoln, Burnside was placed in charge of the Army of the Potomac. He led the Army of the Potomac at the Battle of Fredericksburg, which is regarded as a significant Union defeat or setback.

Burnside's departure from command of the Army of the Potomac led to his placement in Kentucky and Tennessee. He played a key role in the Battle of Knoxville, which was significant for its impact on the Battle of Chattanooga. Burnside was sent back East in 1864, where he served under Grant in the campaigns of the Wilderness and Spotsylvania as well as at Richmond and the Battle of the Crater.

After the Civil War, Burnside served as governor of Rhode Island and later as United States senator from that state. It is not easy to pigeonhole Burnside as incompetent, as many portray him to have been. He certainly served his country throughout the entire period of the Civil War and was later elected to political offices. While Burnside had his detractors, he certainly had many supporters.

President's Message

by Curtis Lynn Older

* Michael Fox – a brother of Frederick Fox. A breakthrough seems to have been made in discovering information about the brothers and sisters of Frederick Fox. Please read the article about Michael that begins on page one.

* Volume 1 of the Fox Society Newsletter, "News from Fox's Gap" has been re-worked to add a few pages of pictures that were not previously included in the Adobe Acrobat version.

* The Fox Genealogy by Daniel Gebhart Fox has been placed in typewritten format on my computer thanks in great part to my daughter, Rachael. From the typewritten version I created an Adobe Acrobat Reader version that I intend to distribute free, if it is small enough to send via e-mail. Otherwise, it will be placed on a cd-rom disc and distributed with other Fox Society items at a nominal charge. We will need a couple more months to complete our review of the typewritten material.

* May 2005 will be the 250th anniversary of the Braddock Expedition

* My 2 year and 3 month old Apple computer went down in March and could not be repaired. Fortunately, Apple Computer exchanged it for a brand new iMac under my 3-year warranty. However, I was without a computer for almost 8 weeks.

* The North Carolina South Mountain Monument at Fox's Gap continues toward realization as much the goal of $70,000 has been reached.

* Please, if at all possible, respond to the call for donations to the Civil War Preservation Trust to help preserve the hallowed ground at Fox's Gap. See pages 12 and 13.

Table of Contents for this Newsletter

Page

Welcome New Members!

I apologize for failing to report two new members of the Fox Society for the six months ending December 1, 2001. The two new members are:

Name Address	Phone	Date of Membership	Membership Number
Larry W. Cole 161 Hickory Grove Rd. Leesburg, Georgia 31763-5349 e-mail: lcole@appliedfiber.com	229-432-1068 Joined under interest in Battle of South Mountain.	June 28, 2001	0041
Jon B. Barber 3733 Barmer Drive Jacksonville, Florida 32210-5023	Joined under interest in Battle of South Mountain.	June 28, 2001	0042

Both Larry and Jon had an ancestor who was killed in the Battle of South Mountain at Fox's Gap.

New members since December 1, 2001:

Lois Ann Baker 330 East Main Versailles, Ohio 45380	937-526-5493 **Ancestor Line:** Michael Fox, a brother of Frederick Fox; Elizabeth Fox, Elizabeth Beard, George Nischwitz, Charles Nischwitz, Ellen Nischwitz	March 10, 2002	0043

Lois is a descendant of John Fox of Fox's Gap in Maryland and one of his sons, Michael Fox. Michael was a brother of Frederick Fox of Fox's Gap in Maryland and preceded Frederick to the area near Dayton, Ohio. Lois is the author of the article about Michael Fox that appears on page one of this newsletter

News from Fox's Gap

Published June 1 and December 1 of each year by
The Society of the Descendants of Frederick Fox of Fox's Gap in Maryland
Membership dues are $6.00 per year. President of the Society is Curtis L. Older.
Make Society inquiries by the following means:

Curtis L. Older
618 Tryon Place
Gastonia, NC 28054-6066
e-mail: curtolder@earthlink.net
phone: 704-864-3879

Land Tracts of the Battlefield of South Mountain
By Curtis L. Older

Each Newsletter includes a survey, patent, or deed related to the land tracts in the vicinity of Crampton's, Fox's, and Turner's Gaps. These three gaps in South Mountain represent the main area contested by the Union and Confederate Armies in the Battle of South Mountain on September 14, 1862. Previous issues of the Society Newsletter contained descriptions of the following tracts:

June 1, 1997	Addition to Friendship of Frederick Fox
December 1, 1997	Fredericksburgh of Frederick Fox
June 1, 1998	Pick All of Bartholomew Booker
December 1, 1998	Bowser's Addition of David Bowser
June 1, 1999	Partnership of John Mansberger
December 1, 1999	Mountain of John Baley
June 1, 2000	no tract included in newsletter
December 1, 2000	Flonham of Philip Jacob Shafer
June 1, 2001	The Exchange of Daniel Dulaney
December 1, 2001	Betty's Good Will

This issue of the newsletter includes a list of all the land records I found for Bartholomew Booker, father-in-law of Frederick Fox, in Frederick County, Maryland. One complete land record is included after the Frederick County list. The record given in its entirety is for the land tract owned by Bartholomew Booker at his death.

Booker, Bartholomew (Probably born in 1720. Died in 1791 or 1792.), was age "71 years or thereabouts" on December 26, 1790. Bartholomew and Peter Booker arrived in Philadelphia, September 3, 1739, on the Loyal Judith from Rotterdam. Robert H. Fox of Cincinnati indicates the first land record for Bartholomew was August 1748 for 100 acres of land in Lancaster [now Franklin] county, Pennsylvania. Bartholomew married Margaret. They were the parents of 14 children. Bartholomew arrived in the Fox's Gap area by 1754, when he acquired a tract named Mendall (Mindall) from Joseph Chapline Sr. Bartholomew owned Pickall, patented February 22, 1764, a tract stretching from the forks of the roads at the Catoctin Creek just north of Middletown all the way to Orr's and Fox's Gaps. Bartholomew was the father-in-law of Frederick Fox. According to Robert H. Fox of Cincinnati, Ohio, a desk of Bartholomew Booker passed to his widow, Margaret, and then to Frederick Fox. Robert viewed the desk in the 1930s when he visited Daniel Gebhart Fox, author of *The Fox Genealogy*, who owned the desk at that time. Margaret Booker died in 1796.

Bartholomew Booker Land Records in Frederick County, Maryland

Ref No	Date	To-From	Other Party	Name of Tract	Acres
Tracey	12-4-54	F	Joseph Chapline	Mindall	66
F-1020	6-14-60	T	Christian Everhart	Resurvey on Mendall	100

Continued on the following page -

Ref No	Date	To-From	Other Party	Name of Tract	Acres
F-1023	6-17-60	T	George Yeast	Resurvey on Mendall	52
F-1054	6-20-60	T	Edward Grimes	Grimes Purchase*	50
F-1064	6-25-60	T	George Shitler	Shitler's Dispute*	100
F-1077	7-5-60	T	Michael Shepfell	Shepfell's Purchase*	100
BC&GS #30	2-22-64	T	Patent - B. Booker	Pickall	1224
L-69	10-6-67	F	George Shitler	Mendall, Small All	100
L-71	10-6-67	T	George Shitler	Long Dispute**	?
N-57	4-11-70	T	Christian Kizer	Pickall	485
N-517	12-15-70	T	Peter Beaver	Pickall	53
N-560	1-23-72	F	Jacob Smith	Resurvey on Mendall	100
N-625	3-14-72	T	Christian Kizer	Pickall	51+
BC&GS #47	4-3-72	T	Survey - B. Booker	I Hope It's Well Done	575+
P-387	10-1-72	F	Daniel Dulaney	Shettle	50
T-19	6-28-73	T	Peter Booker	Resurvey on Mendall I Hope It's Well Done	81+ 5+
WR-6-111	9-3-85	T	Peter Smeltzer	I Hope It's Well Done	4+
WR-6-113	9-3-85	T	Peter Smeltzer	I Hope It's Well Done	4+
WR 6-133	9-27-85	F	Peter Smeltzer	Resurvey on Martitany	5+
WR 7-213	4-11-87	T	Frederick Fox	I Hope It's Well Done	
WR-7-214	4-14-87	T	Jacob Smith	Pickall & Mendall	111
WR-9-607	2-1-91	T	Samuel Buzzard et. al.	Resurvey on Wooden Platter	
WR10-708	4-30-91	T	Jacob Everhart	I Hope It's Well Done	7+

Continued on the following page -

Ref No	Date	To-From	Other Party	Name of Tract	Acres

The following by the Executors of Bartholomew Booker Estate:
All remaining properties - 6 pages

WR12-355	4-19-93	T	John Routzahn		
WR12-359	4-19-93	T	Peter Layman		
WR12-360	4-19-93	T	William Widmeyer		
WR12-362	4-19-93	T	Christian Coogh		
WR12-363	4-19-93	T	Daniel Boocher (Booker)		

* Part of Resurvey on Mendall
**Part of Pickall

Bartholomew Booker Estate

Part of Pickall, recorded 19 April 1794, 304 acres

FCLR, WR-12, 358-364, Bartholomew Booker Estate, recorded 19 Apr 1794, 304 acres, on road from Frederick Town to Williamsport and Hagerstown, see newspaper notice. (Pick All)
Examd & delv grantee 25th Mar 1795 At the request of John Routzahn the following deed was recorded 19th April 1794. to wit
This indenture made this nineteenth day of April in the year of our lord seventeen hundred and ninety four between Margaret Booker and Frederick Fox of Frederick County and State of Maryland of the one part and John Routzahn of same place of the other part whereas Bartholomew Booker late of Frederick county deceased by his last will and testament in writing bearing date on or about the twenty first day of October in the year of our lord one thousand seven hundred and ninety one amongst other things did devise and direct that the remaining part of the Estate both real and personal should be sold by his executors to the best advantage which same will the same Bartholomew Booker appointed his wife Margaret and Frederick Fox to be his executors who have caused the same will to be duly posted and recorded and have taken on themselves the Burden of the execution thereof by which means a sale of the Estate both real and personal of the said Bartholomew Booker is necessary - and that on the twenty fourth day of November in the year of our lord one thousand seven hundred and ninety three on the premises the aforesaid John Routzahn because the best purchaser of Lot Number one part of five several tracts of land the resurvey on Mend all Pick All I Hope Its Well Done Shettle and Martitany lying in Frederick County aforesaid all and for the sum of thirteen hundred and sixty eight pounds in good and lawful money of Maryland - the said Lot Number One containing three hundred and four acres of land more or less Now this Indenture witnesseth that the said Margaret Booker and Frederick Fox for and in consideration of the sum of thirteen hundred and sixty eight pounds good and lawful money of Maryland - the said Lot Number One containing three hundred and four acres of land more or less Now this indenture witnesseth that the said Margaret Booker and Frederick Fox for and in Consideration of

Continued on the following page -

the sum of thirteen hundred and sixty eight pounds good and lawful money of Maryland to him in hand paid before the sealing and delivery of these presents the receipt whereof the said Margaret Booker and Frederick Fox doth hereby acknowledge and thereof and therefrom every part and parcel thereof doth fully clearly and absolutely acquit exonerate and discharge the said John Routzahn his heirs executors Administrators and assigns and every of them by these presents hath given granted bargained and sold aliened released enfeoffed and confirmed and by these presents doth give grant bargain and sell alien release enfeoff and confirm unto the said John Routzahn all that tract or parcel of land called Lot Number One lying in the county and state aforesaid and being part of the five tracts of land hereinbefore mentioned beginning at a bounded white oak tree bounded tree of a tract of land called Johns Delight and running thence by and with the Main Road

Line No.	North South	Degrees East or West	Length
1	S	38 East	24 perches then
2	S	44 east	32 perches then
3.	S	34 east	4 1/2 perches to the end of 141 perches on the third line of the aforesaid land called Shettle then reversing said land
4.	S	70 west	77 3/4 perches to a stone planted
5.	S	40 east	61 perches to a stone planted at the bounded tree of said Shettle then
6.	S	31 east	117 perches to a stone standing at the end of 30 perches on the 13th line of Jacob Smith's part of the aforesaid land called I Hope It Is Well Done and running with said Smith's lines thence
7.	N	56 1/2 east	70 perches to a stone planted then
8.	N	4 1/2 east	75 1/2 perches to a white oak sapling then
9.	S	61 east	62 perches then
10.	S	14 east	50 perches to the bounded tree of the said Smith land then
11.	N	10 east	24 3/4 perches to the bounded tree of a tract of land called Last Shift formerly Peter Booker's land then
12.	N	38 west	10 perches to the end of the 15th line of said Peter Bookers Land then reversing it three courses
13.	N	62 1/2 east	82 perches to a locust post
14.	N	60 east	20 perches to a locust post
15.	S	39 east	35 1/2 perches to the 7th line of the Resurvey on Wooden Platter then with said land two courses
16.	N	12 west	19 perches
17.	N	41 west	44 perches to the end of the 4th line of Jacob Everhart's part of the Resurvey on Mendall deed for 100 acres then with said land three courses
18.	S	58 west	20 perches
19	S	89 1/2 west	110 perches
20.	N	6 west	113 perches then
21.	N	87 1/2 east	8 1/2 perches
22.	N	71 west	16 perches to the end of 45 and 1/2 perches on the third line of the aforesaid Jacob Everhart's 50 acres part of the aforesaid Resurvey on Mendall then with it two courses
23.	N	89 west	10 1/2 perches
24.	N	6 west	37 perches
25.	N	10 1/2 west	69 perches to the bounded tree of Mendall then
26.	S	69 1/2 east	21 perches to the end of the 12 line of the aforesaid Resurvey on Wooden Platter then

Continued on the following page -

Line No.	North South	Degrees East or West	Length
27.	N	39 east	4 perches to a stone the beginning of Christian Coogle's part of the aforesaid land called I Hope Its Well Done and with the given line reversed
28.	N	33 west	14 perches then
29.	N	39 west	14 perches to a black oak tree marked with 11 notches then end of the last line of the aforesaid Bartholomew Booker's part of Martitany thence with the given line
30.	S	62 1/2 west	58 perches to the 31st line of the aforesaid Resurvey on Mendall thence with it reversed
31.	S	81 west	72 perches still reversing said land
32.	S	81 east	80 perches

33. thence with a straight line to the beginning containing 304 acres of land more or less together with all and singular the buildings improvements conveniences and advantages whatsoever to the aforesaid lot of land and premises belonging or in any manner of way appertaining to have and to hold the lot of land and all and singular the other premises herein mentioned and intended to be hereby granted with the appurtenances thereunto belonging unto the said John Routzahn his heirs and assigns forever and to and for no other use intent or purpose whatsoever. And the said Margaret Booker and Frederick Fox for themselves their Heirs executors and Administrators the said lot of land and all and singular the other premises with the appurtenances unto the said John Routzahn his heirs and assigns shall and will warrant and forever defend by these presents against all persons claiming under them or any or them in Witness whereof the said Margaret Booker and Frederick Fox hath hereto subscribed their names and affixed their seals the day and year first herein before written Margaret Booker Frederick Fox

Signed sealed and delivered Jacob Young in the presence of WM Beale

Which was then endorsed to wit: Frederick County to wit Be it remembered that on the 19th day of April 1794 Margaret Booker and Frederick Fox appeared before us the subscribers two of the justices of the peace for the county aforesaid and acknowledged the within instrument of writing to be their act and deed and land and premises therein described to be the right and estate of the within John Routzahn his heirs and assigns forever At the same time the aforesaid Margaret wife of the said Bartholomew Booker ? relinquished her right of Dower as the law directs in such cases Jacob Young W M Beale

Lot Number One part of five several tracts of land the Resurvey on Mend All, Pick All, I Hope Its Well Done. Shettle, and Martitany

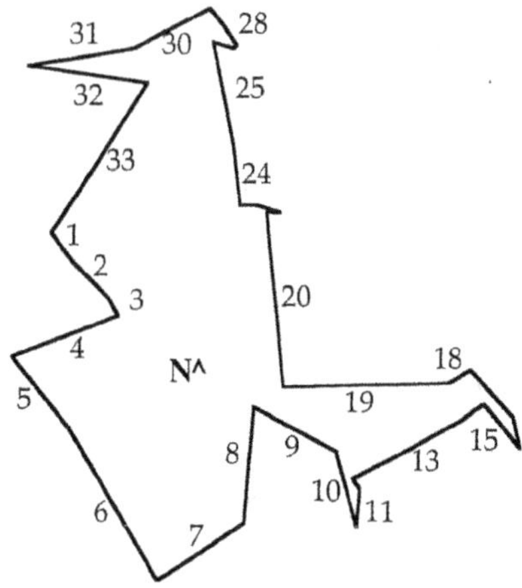

News from the Civil War Preservation Trust

The Civil War Preservation Trust sent Curt Older a letter about the end of February of this year. The letter, in part, read as follows:

Membership Center:
11 Public Square
Suite 200
Hagerstown, MD 21740

President: James Lighthizer
1-888-606-1400
e-mail: civilwartrust@civilwar.org
www.civilwar.org

One hundred forty years ago, Confederate General Robert E. Lee began his Maryland Campaign, which culminated with the Battle of Antietam, the bloodiest day in American history. Today, you and I can embark on our own "Maryland Campaign" to save a whopping 552 acres at three battlefields, including one of the largest tracts of unprotected land remaining at Antietam!

Working with officials from the Maryland Department of Natural Resources, The Conservation Fund and the American Battlefield Protection Program of the National Park Service, we have put together a project that preserves 200 acres at Antietam, another 107 acres of core battlefield at South Mountain/Fox's Gap, and an additional 245 acres at Monocacy.

What's more, as part of this 552-acre deal, any support you and other CWPT members provide today is matched and will be multiplied by a factor of eight! Every $25 becomes $200 instantly, $50 becomes $400, $100 becomes $800 and so on.

Trust me. . . we will need every dollar of that leveraging power, as the price for preserving these 552 acres is $1.8 million!

Here for your review are the nuts and bolts of this landmark campaign:

This project (which I am calling our "2002 Maryland Campaign") will utilize approximately $500,000 of the $11 million for battlefield preservation that was passed by Congress last year. . .

. . . plus approximately $1,000,000 put in by the State of Maryland's "Program Open Space". . .

. . . plus an extremely generous $100,000 donation from one of your fellow CWPT members who has requested that his gift be used where the Army of Northern Virginia fought-and Antietam and Fox's Gap certainly meet that criteria.

You can do the math. We've already got $1.6 million of the $1.8 million on the table. All that remains is for CWPT to raise the final $200,000 to leverage that million-six, and the deal is done.

Now I don't think for a minute that raising $200,000 will be a walk in the park. Far from it...it will be a huge challenge, especially when we hope to close the deal in 120 days.

Continued on the following page -

Now, let me quickly tell you what happened on this hallowed ground:

South Mountain/Fox's Gap: September 14, 1862. The Ninth Corps of the Union Army under command of Major General Jesse Reno engaged Confederate troops under Brigadier General Samuel Garland, Jr., on and around this historic property. Both Generals were killed that day, near the property.

This land was also the site of some of the most intense fighting by troops under Union commanders Cox, Sturgis and Willcox, and is also the site where then-Lieutenant Colonel and later-President Rutherford B. Hayes was wounded.

Officials at Maryland's Department of Natural Resources call this land "one of the most important visual and historic elements of the Battle of South Mountain."

Determined Southern resistance held off Union attempts to force their way through the South Mountain gaps, allowing Robert E. Lee to consolidate his widely scattered forces at Sharpsburg, Maryland, and set the stage for a battle that will forever by synonymous with enormous combat casualties: Antietam.

Please join me in taking advantage of this historic 8 to 1 match, and help save another 552 acres of the most important Civil War ground at any battlefield anywhere.

Awaiting your reply,
James Lighthizer
President

See Battle of South Mountain Map, September 14, 1862, included in Civil War Preservation Trust letter to CWPT members. Permission to print map not granted by CWPT.

(Map included with the letter from the Civil War Preservation Trust.)

Wills Section

Each Newsletter includes one typewritten version of a will that is significant to the preservation efforts of the Society.

Previous issues of the Society Newsletter contained copies of the following wills and estate papers:

December 1, 1996	will of John Fox of Fox's Gap in Maryland
June 1, 1997	will of Frederick Fox of Fox's Gap in Maryland
December 1, 1997	will of Bartholomew Booker, father-in-law of Frederick Fox
June 1, 1998	estate papers for George Fox, the oldest son of Frederick Fox
December 1, 1998	will of John Adam Link II, the father-in-law of George Fox
June 1, 1999	will of John Adam Link I, the father of John Adam Link II
December 1, 1999	no will included in newsletter
June 1, 2000	no will included in newsletter
December 1, 2000	will of John L. Fox, a grandson of Frederick Fox of Fox's Gap in Maryland
June 1, 2002	will of Jacob Benner, the husband of Mary Magdalena Fox and a son-in-law of Frederick Fox of Fox's Gap in Maryland
December 1, 2001	will of Daniel Alexander Fox, a son of John L. Fox, a grandson of George Fox, and a great-grandson of Frederick Fox of Fox's Gap in Maryland

---

Included in this issue of the newsletter is the will of Samuel Benner. Samuel was a son of Jacob Benner (1765-1852) and Mary Magdalena Fox (1778-1856). Mary Magdalena Fox was a daughter of Frederick Fox of Fox's Gap in Maryland.

Jacob Benner and Mary Magdalena Fox were the parents of nine children: Mary (Mrs. Samson P. Strader), Jacob, Samuel, Elizabeth (Mrs. Jonathan Gebhart), Daniel, Catherine (Mrs. William Akin), Frederick, Sarah (Mrs. George Fryberger and James Ryan) and David.

Samuel Benner was born in Maryland, April 21, 1800; died December 19, 1854, aged 54 years, 7 months, 28 days; buried in Mound Hill cemetery, Eaton, Ohio. He was united in marriage July 21, 1827, by John Folkerth, J. P., with Susanna Dunkerly, who was born in England, April 23, 1808; died June 15, 1856; aged 48 years, 1 month, 22 days; buried beside her husband. They located on a tract of land near Campbellstown, Preble County, Ohio. They were the parents of seven children.

Will of Samuel Benner

The State of Ohio Preble County

Be it remembered thus heretofore to wit before the Probate Court within and for the County of Preble and State of Ohio held at the Court House in Eaton on the third day of January AD eighteen hundred and fifty five, by John Campbell Judge of said court the last will and testament of Samuel Benner late of Jackson Township, Preble County, deceased was this day brought before the Court and was proved by the oath of Frederick Wumdhen? and John Mish? whose examination were reduced to writing and is appearing to the satisfaction of the Court thus the said Samuel Benner as the time of executing said will was of full age and of sound mind and memory and not under any ? it is ordered this said will and the proof so reduced to writing as recorded and thereupon on motion of Susannah? Benner

Continued on the following page -

and Jacob Benner the executors in said will named it is ordered that ? testamentary be wanted to the said Susannah Benner and Jacob Benner who thereupon gave an under ? with Frederick Numdhenk and Jacob Weish security to the acceptance of the court in the penalty of four thousand dollars conditioned according to law whereupon it is ordered by the court that Jacob Val, Thomas McHinney, and John Weist appraise the personal property of said estate, and thereupon Susannah Benner widow of the said Samuel Benner deceased appeared in open Court and made here election to take under the provisions of her said husband's will in lieu of her dower. Said will is in the ? and ? following to wit, "In the name of the Benevolent Father of all, I Samuel Benner of the Township of Jackson and County of Preble Ohio do make and publish this my last will and testament

Item 1st. I give and devise to my beloved wife in lieu of her dower the farm on which we now reside in Jackson Township Preble County Ohio containing one hundred seventy five and a half acres of land during her natural life, and all the stock, household goods furniture provisions and other goods and chattels which may be thence at my decease during her natural life aforesaid the however selling so much thereof as may be necessary and sufficient to pay my last debts at the death of my said wife the real estate aforesaid and such part of the said personal property in the proceeds thereof as may then remain ? ? and unexpended I give and devise to my children Samuel Benner, Jr. Daniel Benner, Jacob Benner, James Benner, John Benner, David Benner and Mary Ann Benner and their heirs to be equally divided among? them.

2nd I give and devise to my sons Samuel Benner Jr., David Benner, Jacob Benner James Benner John Benner and Daniel Benner and my daughter Mary Ann Benner each Four Hundred Dollars in money to be paid to them by my wife as then? reported? become of lawful age. If my wife cannot pay the said Four Hundred Dollars at the time children arise? at lawful age, the said child? is to draw Interest at the rate of ? percent per annum until my said wife is able to pay it, or until her decease then to be deducted out of the Real Estate of Chattel property ? named? ?

3rd I do hereby nominate and appoint my beloved wife Guardian of my heirs James Benner, John Benner, and David Benner until they arrive at the age of twenty one years and also of my daughter Mary Ann Benner until she arrives at the age of Twenty One years or ?

Item 4th I do hereby authorize and request my beloved wife to keep and support all of my minor children out of the proceeds of the Farm in which we now live during their minority -

Item 5th I do hereby Nominate and appoint my beloved wife and my son Jacob Benner Executors of this my last will and Testament hereby authorizing and empowering them to compromise adjust release and discharge in such manner as they may deem proper the debts and claims due me. I do also authorized and empower them to make such arrangements for the settlements of my debts as they may deem best (provided there should be any) It is also my request and desire that my beloved wife and son Jacob should settle my indebtedness or business that may be unsettled at my decease without having my personal or chattel property offered at public Venue if consistent with the requirements of law. I do hereby revoke all former wills made by me.

In Testimony whereof I have thereunto set my hand and seal this 22nd day of November AD 1871 Samuel Benner (Seal) Signed and acknowledged by Samuel Benner as his last will and testament in our presence and signed by us in his presence Frederick Wundburk?and John Weist of lawful age, who being duly sworn depose and say that the paper writing now exhibited in Court is the last will and testament of Samuel Benner late of Preble County deceased That they saw him sign and heard him acknowledge the same that they signed the same as witnesses in his presence and at his request and at the time of executing the same he was of full age of sound mind and memory and not under any restraint. Sworn to and subscribed in Preble County this third day of January AD 1855 Frederick Wundburk John Weist John V. Campbell Probate Judge.

(signed) W V Campbell PJ

The Braddock Expedition

By Curtis L. Older

Carlyle House Historic Park - Alexandria, Virginia

(Excerpts from a pamphlet on the Carlyle House)

One result of the French and Indian War was supremacy over the North American continent for the English and the largest land transfer in the history of the world. The French and Indian War provided military training to the men who would lead both the American and British forces in the American Revolution. It was a struggle with worldwide implications. One of the most important chapters in this struggle was . . . the Braddock Expedition of 1755.

The role of Maryland and Fox's Gap in the Braddock Expedition has become lost to both visitor and area resident. Indeed, many a hiker on the Appalachian Trail has come to Fox's Gap unaware of its long history. It is the history of the American journey, from early settlers and founding fathers to the agony of civil strife and reconstruction. It is this history the author seeks to preserve.

Colonial governors in 1755 included Robert Dinwiddie of Virginia, Horatio Sharpe of Maryland, Arthur Dobbs of North Carolina, William Shirley of Massachusetts, James De Lancey of New York, and Robert Hunter Morris of Pennsylvania. Until the arrival of General Braddock, Governor Sharpe of Maryland was the Commander-in-Chief of British forces in North America.

Governor Sharpe, in company with some of the other governors, departed Annapolis for Alexandria on April 12. The Governors, as well as Colonel Johnston, arrived at Alexandria on the 13th. General Braddock, Commodore Keppel, and Governors Shirley, Delancy, Dinwiddie, Sharpe, and Morris held their conference on the 14th in the Carlyle House, often called the Braddock House.

On August 15, 1755, John Carlyle wrote to his brother George "there was the Grandest Congress held at my home ever known on this Continent." This legendary conference of five colonial governors was called together by General Edward Braddock, the Commander-in-Chief of His Majesty's Forces in North America. Sent to the colonies to oversee the escalating French and Indian War, Braddock chose Carlyle House as his headquarters upon his arrival in Alexandria with 1200 British troops.

Throughout this period, Great Britain and France fought over land claims in the trans-Allegheny region. Braddock convened the colonial governors to discuss the financing of an upcoming campaign against the French. Braddock asked the governors to collect funds from the colonial assemblies for the expedition. The ensuing debate over the financing of the campaign was one of the earliest examples of the friction between Britain and her American colonies, which would eventually result in the American Revolution.

When the lots for the new city of Alexandria were auctioned in 1749, John Carlyle purchased two of the most expensive, numbers 41 and 42. The site, between the Potomac River and Market Square, was an ideal location for Carlyle's merchant business, providing easy access to customers and trade routes.

Carlyle began construction of the house in 1751, using indentured servants and slave labor and built his home with public and private concerns in mind. The home itself, designed in the Georgian Palladian style, provides both public spaces for entertaining and private areas for family and servant use. He also arranged the surrounding dependencies and landscaping according to the needs of both his household and his business. The outbuildings serviced both the family lifestyle (necessary, smokehouse, etc.) and his merchant business (office, warehouses). Although construction took almost three years, Carlyle's completed home signified both his status as a gentleman and his business enterprises.

Following Carlyle's death, his oldest daughter Sarah lived in the house with her family. By 1827, the house was no longer owned by the family, and over the next century and a half, passed through many hands. The site served a variety of purposes including a hospital during the Civil War, a hotel and a private residence. In 1970, the Northern Virginia Regional Park Authority acquired the property. After six years of restoration, the house and gardens were open to the public as a museum.

John Carlyle was born the second son of a landed Scottish family in 1720. As a young man, he apprenticed with an English merchant firm and by 1741, he emigrated to Virginia as a factor, or representative, for William Hicks, an English Merchant. Like many other emigrants to the colonies, John Carlyle came to Virginia hopeful of making "a fortune sufficient . . . to live independent."

Carlyle's ensuing financial success was matched by his good fortune in winning the hand of Sarah Fairfax, a young lady from one of the most influential families in colonial Virginia. Through his growing business and social ties, Carlyle emerged as one of the leading figures in Northern Virginia and counted such luminaries as George Washington among his friends. Carlyle owned thousands of acres of land, including three working plantation. He served as one of the original trustees of Alexandria, the commissary for the Virginia militia during the French and Indian War and the Revolutionary War, and a justice of the peace for Fairfax County.

Carlyle House Historic Park
121 North Fairfax Street
Alexandria, Virginia 22314

703-549-2997

Open Tuesday through Saturday
10:00 AM - 4:30 PM
Sunday 12 Noon - 4:30 PM
Northern Virginia Regional Par Authority
Participating Jurisdictions: Arlington,
Fairfax, Loudoun, Alexandria, City of Fairfax,
Falls Church

Books related to Fox genealogy, Fox's Gap, the Braddock Expedition, and the Battle of South Mountain

The Braddock Expedition and Fox's Gap in Maryland by Curtis L. Older
available at Will Bend Books, 65 E. Main Street, Westminster, MD 21157-5026, www.willowbendbooks.com, 1-800-876-6102, e-mail: bookorder@willowbend.net

The Land Tracts of the Battlefield of South Mountain by Curtis L. Older
available at Will Bend Books, 65 E. Main Street, Westminster, MD 21157-5026, www.willowbendbooks.com, 1-800-876-6102, e-mail: bookorder@willowbend.net

The Fox Genealogy by Daniel Gebhart Fox
available from Blair's' Book Service, 2503 Springpark Way, Richardson, Texas 75082, reference number XR-2546, e-mail: linda@glbco.com, fax: 972-783-1008

Before Antietam, the Battle for South Mountain by John Michael Priest, 206 Weldon Drive, Boonsboro, MD 21713, 301-432-8720

Landscape Turned Red, The Battle of Antietam by Stephen W. Sears

The Pennsylvania Line, Regimental Organization And Operations, 1776-1783, by John B. B. Trussell, Jr., Pennsylvania Historical and Museum Commission

Related Family Lines:

The Link Family by Paxson Link, available from Blair's Book Service, see above

Sir Henry A. Ogle, first published in 1902, *Ogle and Bothal*

The official Ogle Family Library, currently known as "The Ogle Collection," is housed in the Fulton County Museum, 27 E 375 N, Rochester, IN 46975

The Society of the Descendants of Frederick Fox of Fox's Gap in Maryland

Membership Roster
With Ancestor Line through Four Generations
June 1, 2002

The children of Frederick Fox of Fox's Gap in Maryland:

Christiana Fox	(Mrs. George Metherd)
Rose Fox	(Mrs. Christian Wohlgemuth; Mrs. Daniel Hottel)
Mary Magdalena Fox	(Mrs. Jacob Benner)
George Fox	(Elizabeth Ann Link)
Daniel Booker Fox	(Susannah Christman)
Joseph Fox	(Elizabeth Unger)
Elizabeth Fox	(Mrs. John Leiter)

Name Address	Phone	Date of Membership	Membership Number
Curtis Lynn Older 618 Tryon Place Gastonia, North Carolina 28054 curtolder@earthlink.net	704-864-3879 **Ancestor Line:** George Fox, a son of Frederick Fox; John L. Fox, Daniel Alexander Fox, Ethel Belle Fox, Mavis Lorene (Gouty) Older	October 20, 1995	0001
William Ernest Fox 13071 Alger Grant, Michigan 49327-9637	616-834-5051 **Ancestor Line:** George Fox, a son of Frederick Fox; John L. Fox, Daniel Alexander Fox, Ernest Daniel Fox	October 28, 1995	0002
Reva Winfred Fox 10226 3rd Ave. S. Seattle, Washington	206-762-3845 **Ancestor Line:** George Fox, a son of Frederick Fox; John L. Fox, Daniel Alexander Fox, William Edward Fox	November 7, 1995	0003
Robert Claude Fox 10845 Edgewood Drive Demotte, Indiana 46310	**Ancestor Line:** George Fox, a son of Frederick Fox; John L. Fox, Daniel Alexander Fox, Ernest Daniel Fox	November 11, 1995	0004
William Goudy Benner 1000 Hidden Ridge Lane Dayton, Ohio 45459	513-433-1365 **Ancestor Line:** Mary Magdalena Fox, a daughter of Frederick Fox; Jacob Benner Jr., Valentine Benner, William Goudy Benner Sr.	November 15, 1995	0005

Name Address	Phone	Date of Membership	Membership Number
Laurel Ann Benner 112 Lower Hillside Drive Bellbrook, Ohio 45305	513-848-8107 **Ancestor Line:** Mary Magdalena Fox, a daughter of Frederick Fox; Jacob Benner Jr., Valentine Benner, William Goudy Benner Sr.	November 20, 1995	0006
Brenda Carol Saunders 4301 Burchdale Street Kettering, Ohio 45440	513-299-3320 **Ancestor Line:** Mary Magdalena Fox, a daughter of Frederick Fox; Jacob Benner Jr., Valentine Benner, William Goudy Benner Sr.	November 20, 1995	0007
Elizabeth Jane Bucholz 304 14th St. E. Devil's Lake, North Dakota 58301	701-662-3636 **Ancestor Line:** George Fox, a son of Frederick Fox; John L. Fox, Daniel Alexander Fox, William Edward Fox	November 6, 1995	0008
Doug Bast 109 North Main Street Boonsboro, Maryland 21713	301-432-6969 Joined under interest in Battle of South Mountain.	December 9, 1995	0001H
Dellie Jean Craig 406 Vandalia Court Crawfordsville, Indiana 47933	765-361-2891 **Ancestor Line:** George Fox, a son of Frederick Fox; John L. Fox, Daniel Alexander Fox, William Edward Fox	December 11, 1995	0009
Wilma Marion Gose P. O. Box 203 Griffith, Indiana 46319-0203	219-322-5269 **Ancestor Line:** George Fox, a son of Frederick Fox; John L. Fox, Daniel Alexander Fox, William Edward Fox	December 16, 1995	0010
Patricia Jo Edwards 526 Palomino Drive RR #4 Box 94C Danville, Illinois 61832	217-443-4523 **Ancestor Line:** George Fox, a son of Frederick Fox; John L. Fox, Daniel Alexander Fox, William Edward Fox	January 13, 1996	0011
James Joseph Fox 311 South St. Mary's Apt. 6N San Antonio, Texas 78205	210-223-6004 **Ancestor Line:** Daniel Booker Fox, a son of Frederick Fox; Frederick Christman Fox, Frederick Coffman Fox, Winfield Scott Fox	January 13, 1996	0012
Raphael Henry John Fox 7815 Claybrook Dallas, Texas 75231-5673	214-343-3919 **Ancestor Line:** Daniel Booker Fox, a son of Frederick Fox; Frederick Christman Fox, Frederick Coffman Fox, Winfield Scott Fox	January 13, 1996	0013
Judith Fox Smith 1050 Kingscote Drive Harleysville, Pennsylvania 19438	**Ancestor Line:** Daniel Booker Fox, a son of Frederick Fox; Frederick Christman Fox, Frederick Coffman Fox, Winfield Scott Fox	January 16, 1996	0014

Name Address	Phone	Date of Membership	Membership Number
Richard Dale Fox Sr. 106 A. Edgewood Drive Attica, Indiana 47918	765-793-3674 **Ancestor Line:** George Fox, a son of Frederick Fox; John L. Fox, Daniel Alexander Fox, William Edward Fox	January 24, 1996	0015
Mildred Fox Metcalf 1819 Garfield Avenue Salt Lake City, Utah 84108	xxx-484-9024 **Ancestor Line:** George Fox, a son of Frederick Fox; John L. Fox, Daniel Alexander Fox, Kenneth Benjamin Fox	June 1, 1996	0016
Teresa Rose Fox 6168 Shadow Lane Citrus Heights, California 95621	916-722-4185 **Ancestor Line:** Daniel Booker Fox, a son of Frederick Fox; Frederick Christman Fox, Frederick Coffman Fox, Winfield Scott Fox	June 7, 1996	0017
Toni Farol Bice 10626 Baker Place Crown Point, Indiana 46307	219-663-4451 **Ancestor Line:** George Fox, a son of Frederick Fox; John L. Fox, Daniel Alexander Fox, William Edward Fox	December 4, 1996	0018
Richard Dale Fox, Jr. P. O. Box 301 Baggs, Wyoming 82321	none **Ancestor Line:** George Fox, a son of Frederick Fox; John L. Fox, Daniel Alexander Fox, William Edward Fox	January 1, 1997	0019
Rachael Lynn Older 618 Tryon Place Gastonia, North Carolina 28054 curtolder@earthlink.net	704-864-3879 **Ancestor Line:** George Fox, a son of Frederick Fox; John L. Fox, Daniel Alexander Fox, Ethel Belle Fox, Mavis Lorene (Gouty) Older	March 20, 1997	0020
Donald A. Smith 7 E. Hill Valley Drive Indianapolis, Indiana 46227	317-865-7761 **Ancestor Line:** George Fox, a son of Frederick Fox; Alexander Fox, Elizabeth Catherine Fox, Walter Alvin Rabold	March 10, 1998	0021
Mr. William Ernest Fox II 8126 West 10 Mile Road Bitely, Michigan 49309	not known **Ancestor Line:** George Fox, a son of Frederick Fox; John L. Fox, Daniel Alexander Fox, Ernest Daniel Fox	January 3, 1999	0022
Alice Takase P. O. Box 6945 Fort Bliss, Texas 79906-0945	not known **Ancestor Line:** George Fox, a son of Frederick Fox; Frederick L. Fox	May 11, 1999	0023
Michael Justin Fox 524 Elm Tree Court Cincinnati, Ohio 45244	513-528-9258 **Ancestor Line:** Daniel Booker Fox, a son of Frederick Fox; Frederick Christman Fox, Frederick Coffman Fox, Winfield Scott Fox, Henry Frederick Fox, Robert Henry Fox	May 17, 1999	0024
Kurt D. Graham 3448 Valley Vista Road Smyrna, Georgia 30080	not known Joined under interest in Battle of South Mountain.	May 20, 1999	0025**H**

Name Address	Phone	Date of Membership	Membership Number
Randy Howald 418 Kelly Court Duncanville, Texas 75137-2511	not known Joined under interest in Battle of South Mountain.	June 8, 1999	0026
George D. Fox 1308 Mound Avenue Miamisburg, Ohio 45342	not known **Ancestor Line:** not known	November 1, 1999	0027
Ann Schulz Trimmer 58 Riverview Terrace Belle Mead, New Jersey 08502 e-mail: ann@trimmer.net	908-359-3876 **Ancestor Line:** Christiana Fox, a daughter of Frederick Fox; George F. Metherd, Benjamin Metherd, Benjamin F. Metherd	November 2, 1999	0028
Robert Eugene Benner 8677 Cook Street Montague, Michigan 49437	231-894-6651 **Ancestor Line:** Mary Magdalena Fox, a daughter of Frederick Fox; Jacob Benner Jr., Valentine Benner, Albert Benner, Robert Ray Benner	December 1, 1999	0029
Terri A. Woods 970 E. College Ave. Westerville, OH 43081-2509	not known **Ancestor Line:** Christiana Fox, a daughter of Frederick Fox; Jacob Metherd, Frederick Metherd, Eliza Ann Metherd	February 18, 2000	0030
Gerald Robert Fox 506 N 300 E Valparaiso, IN 46383	219-531-2852 **Ancestor Line:** George Fox, a son of Frederick Fox; John L. Fox, Daniel Alexander Fox, Ernest Daniel Fox	February 22, 2000	0031
Suella Jane Fenton 17 Sun Cloud Circle Oroville, CA 95965-9268	408-263-8348 **Ancestor Line:** George Fox, a son of Frederick Fox; Frederick L. Fox, Samuel Fox, Orissa J. Fox	February 24, 2000	0032
Peggie Ellen Gallahue 1263 Richmond Drive Wabash, IN 46992	xxx-563-1459 **Ancestor Line:** Christiana Fox, a daughter of Frederick Fox; Jacob Metherd, Frederick Metherd, Eliza Ann Metherd	March 24, 2000	0033
Anne Elizabeth Edgecombe 973 Buchon St. San Luis Obispo, CA 93401	xxx-594-1891 **Ancestor Line:** Elizabeth Fox, a daughter of Frederick Fox; Henry Leiter, John Benton Leiter, Anna Catherine Leiter	April 5, 2000	0034
Homer Carr Hendrickson 876 West Turtlecreek Union Rd Lebanon, Ohio 45036	513-932-6577 **Ancestor Line:** Daniel Booker Fox, a son of Frederick Fox; Christiana Fox, William Perry Hendrickson, Harry Fox Hendrickson	August 30, 2000	0035
Beth Ellen Davis 8355 Camfield Circle Springs, Colorado 80920	719-282-9741 **Ancestor Line:** Mary Magdalena Fox, a daughter of Frederick Fox; Samuel S. Benner, Daniel Benner, Edwin Rabb Benner	October 7, 2000	0036

Name Address	Phone	Date of Membership	Membership Number
Bertha L. Parker 6899 E. So. Barbee Drive Pierceton, Indiana 46562-9152	219-594-5112 **Ancestor Line:** Christiana Fox, a daughter of Frederick Fox; George Metherd, Jacob Metherd, Frederick Metherd, George W. Metherd, Benjamin F. Metherd (went by Frank B. Metherd)	March 18, 2001	0037
Janice Vanderhyde 881 Ursula Street Aurora, Colorado 80011	303-738-0328 **Ancestor Line:** Mary Magdalena Fox, a daughter of Frederick Fox; Jacob Benner Jr., Valentine Benner, Albert Benner, Forrest Benner	January 26, 2001	0038
Roger Lee Benner 881 Ursula Street Aurora, Colorado 80011	303-738-0328 **Ancestor Line:** Mary Magdalena Fox, a daughter of Frederick Fox; Jacob Benner Jr., Valentine Benner, Albert Benner, Forrest Benner	March 19, 2001	0039
Alan K. Sentman 140 Cabrini Blvd., #129 New York, New York 10033-3434	212-740-3532 **Ancestor Line:** Daniel Booker Fox, a son of Frederick Fox; Frederick C. Fox, Caroline Fox, Ida Stansel, James Monroe Sentman, Forrest Eugene Sentman	April 20, 2001	0040
Larry W. Cole 161 Hickory Grove Rd. Leesburg, Georgia 31763-5349 e-mail: lcole@appliedfiber.com	229-432-1068 Joined under interest in Battle of South Mountain.	June 28, 2001	0041
Jon B. Barber 3733 Barmer Drive Jacksonville, Florida 32210-5023	Joined under interest in Battle of South Mountain.	June 28, 2001	0042
Lois Ann Baker 330 East Main Versailles, Ohio 45380	937-526-5493 **Ancestor Line:** Michael Fox, a brother of Frederick Fox; Elizabeth Fox, Elizabeth Beard, George Nischwitz, Charles Nischwitz, Ellen Nischwitz	March 10, 2002	0043

H - denotes Honorary Member

News from Fox's Gap

The Society of the Descendants of Frederick Fox of Fox's Gap in Maryland

Issue 4, Volume 2 **Remember Freedom!** December 1, 2002

Michael Fox, a brother of Frederick, and The Fox - Beard Connection in Ohio

By Lois Ann Baker

This is the second article submitted by Lois Baker on Michael Fox and his descendants. This is the first time this article has been published.

Michael Fox was a brother of Frederick Fox of Fox's Gap in Maryland. Michael and Frederick were sons of John and Christina Fox. Michael preceded Frederick in moving to near Dayton, Ohio, in the early 1800s.

Lois Baker is a descendant of Michael Fox. She has done extensive genealogical research into the descendants of Michael Fox and has graciously submitted the following article.

Lois assisted in marking the grave of Michael Fox as a soldier of the American Revolution. Please also see her article in the June 1, 2002 newsletter.

Lois Anne Baker
330 Main Street
Versailles, Ohio 45380
1-937-526-5493

John Beard, one of the early pioneer settlers of Butler township, Warren County, Ohio, was born in 1778 in Frederick County, Maryland, during the American Revolution. In early manhood, he migrated to Ohio, settling first in Warren County in that section of Franklin Township that later became Clear Creek township. He married Elizabeth (Fox) Robb, a widow, in 1809.

Mrs. John Beard, nee Elizabeth Fox, migrated to Ohio very early in the 1800's. Elizabeth Fox, the daughter of Michael and Susannah Fox, was born April 18, 1778, near Sharpsburg, Maryland. Her grandparents were John and Christina Fox, who settled at Fox's Gap in Maryland, probably before 1760. John and Christina Fox were the parents of Daniel, Frederick, Magdaline, Michael, and Rachael.

In 1790 and 1800, Michael Fox lived in Washington County, Maryland. His brother, Frederick Fox, resided in Frederick County, Maryland, in 1800. After 1800, Michael Fox and family moved to the area now called Cincinnati, Ohio. Frederick Fox and his family moved to Ohio in late 1807 and resided on land located in Warren and Montgomery Counties, Ohio. Michael Fox lived in Warren County in 1830 and died in Franklin, Warren County, Ohio, in 1837.

In 1805, Elizabeth Fox married John Robb. Her son John Robb Junior was born September 20, 1806, in Warren County, Ohio. John Robb Senior died soon after the birth of their son. This information was copied from the application by which Elizabeth applied for a War of 1812 pension after the death of her second husband, John Beard, who died in Butler township, Montgomery County, Ohio, on October 26, 1866.

While living in Warren County, Ohio, John Beard leased 15 acres of timberland from Frederick Fox for a period of six years. This land was located in the northwest quarter of Section 15 in Clear Creek Township.

During the War of 1812, John Beard was drafted for service and was honorably discharged at St. Mary's, Ohio. Family legend says that he served from April 12 until October 26 as a private in the company commanded by Captain Robert Gilchrist. Captain Gilchrist's unit was stationed at Fort Amanda, which is now in Auglaize County, Ohio. Fort Amanda was used as a supply fort to Fort Meigs during the War of 1812.

The pension application of Elizabeth (Fox) Beard was denied because John Beard's name did not appear on Captain Gilchrist's roster list as John Beard. There is a John Beer whose name is found on the roster list but it has never been proven that John Beard and John Beer were the same person. This company was raised in Warren County, Ohio.

John Beard was described in his wife's pension application as six feet tall, auburn hair, hazel eyes, and light skin complexion. The application did not deny that he had served in the War of 1812 but that he got sick and was sent home without completing his 3 months of service.

The John and Elizabeth Beard family lived on a farm near Springboro for about ten years. About 1820, the family moved from Warren County to Montgomery County, settling in Butler township. At one time the Beard family lived on 100 acres of land along the National Road. According to deed record Volume N, page 111, John Beard and Elizabeth, his wife, on December 23, 1829, deeded to Jacob Brandenburg and Jacob Kunkle, directors of the Ninth District in Butler Township, one half acre off the northwest corner of "Beard's Plantation" adjoining the lands of Abraham Hoover, Valentine Nischwitz, and William Erhart, the said piece of ground to be used for a schoolhouse.

The Poplar Hill Cemetery, according to deed records, was once a portion of the old John Beard - Elizabeth Fox farm. John Beard was a landowner in Butler Township, Montgomery County; Allen Township, Darke County; and Cynthiana and Loramie Townships in Shelby County, Ohio.

John Beard lived near the farm of Christian Null where the first camp meeting of the United Brethren Church was held in the state of Ohio in 1812. The Christian Null farm was located a few miles west of Warren County in Montgomery County, Ohio, near Springboro. John Beard attended this camp meeting and immediately joined the Church and thereafter for fifty-four years continued as a faithful and useful member. The first United Church built north of the Ohio River was a log church erected in 1815 near New Hope. The second United Brethren Church built was made of logs and erected on

Clear Creek, about two miles from Springboro, and this is where John Beard attended church until he moved.

The first meeting place of the United Brethren Church in Butler Township was held in the barn and house of the farm of Christian Shupp, located on the Springfield Road and east of the Dayton-Troy Pike. As soon as the barn was closed, Mr. Shupp requested that a meeting be held which resulted in a great revival. This revival was probably the beginning of the Vandalia United Brethren Church.

Until the Church was built, the preaching was regularly held in the homes of Christian Shupp, John Beard, Michael Coover, Benjamin Wilhelm, and others. A brick church was built in Vandalia, the first of its kind north of the Ohio River and the fourth to be built by the United Brethren in the Miami Valley.

John Beard was a trustee of the United Brethren Church of Vandalia for many years. On December 11, 1842, Benjamin Wilhelm and his wife Sarah (Beard) sold to the United Brethren Trustees lot number 24 being 3/4 acre of ground in the south end of Vandalia for a cemetery.

Years later, the old cemetery was sold to Windsor Brussman for an automobile salesroom and after that the land was used for the Butler Township School Administration Building. The old cemetery graves were transferred to Poplar Hill Cemetery.

John Beard and Elizabeth (Fox) Beard raised a family of ten children: Sarah, Mary, Elizabeth, Eve, Samuel, John, Jacob, George, Susan, and Nancy. These children grew to maturity and settled in various areas throughout Ohio.

Jacob Fox, born in 1790 in Washington County, Maryland, and who lived in Clark County, Ohio, is thought to be a brother of Elizabeth Fox Beard. He is buried in Ferncliff Cemetery in Springfield, Ohio.

John and Elizabeth (Fox) Beard lived together as man and wife for a period of 65 years. This union was broken by the death of John Beard in 1866. John Beard, an honored citizen and a member of the United Brethren Church, died at his residence in Vandalia, Ohio. At the time of his death, his widow, two sons, six daughters, fifty-nine grandchildren, and thirty great grandchildren survived him.

After her husband's death and for thirteen years afterwards, Elizabeth Fox Beard lived in and around Vandalia with her children. Mrs. Beard, also a member of the United Brethren Church at Vandalia, died February 13, 1879, aged 100 years, 9 months, and 23 days. At the time of her death, her family consisted of seven children, 54 grandchildren, 79 great grandchildren, and 8 great-great grandchildren.

Both John Beard and his wife Elizabeth Fox Beard are buried in Poplar Hill Cemetery, Vandalia, Ohio, beside many of their descendants.

The following is a brief description of each of the ten children of John Beard and Elizabeth Fox. More detail about each of the ten will appear in the June 1, 2003 newsletter.

1. Sarah, the oldest daughter of John and Elizabeth Fox Beard was born May 10, 1809, in Warren County, Ohio, near Springboro. She married Benjamin Wilhelm on September 12, 1826, in Montgomery County, Ohio. They were the parents of Sarah Naomi, Lucinda, John, Elizabeth, Simon and David.

2. Mary Beard was born July 27, 1810 in Warren County, Ohio. She married Henry Wolaver in Montgomery County on August 15, 1833. This family moved to Shelby County in 1838. They were the parents

of eleven children - John, George, Caroline, Henry, Jacob, Sampson, Sarah, Francis, Mary, Susanna, and James.

3. Elizabeth Beard was born February 10, 1812 in Warren County, Ohio near Springboro. She died January 1, 1900 in Darke County, Versailles, Ohio and was buried in the Reams Cemetery in Newport, Shelby County, Ohio. On April 3, 1836 she was married to Jacob Nischwitz, the son of Valentine Nischwitz and Mary Ockerman. They were the parents of eight children - Susannah, George, Jacob, John, Valentine, Elizabeth, Mary Ann, and David.

4. Eve Beard was born January 15, 1814 in Warren County, Ohio and died June 27, 1901 in Butler Township, Montgomery County, Ohio. She is buried in Poplar Hill Cemetery beside her husband Jacob Coover. Jacob Coover and Eve Beard were married December 12, 1834 in Montgomery County, Ohio. They were the parents of nine children - Henry, Mary E., Michael J., Rosannan, Jacob, Zachariah, Amos J., Anna, and Fidelia.

5. Samuel Beard, the first son of John Beard and Elizabeth Fox, was born January 16, 1816 in Warren County, Ohio near Springboro in Clear Creek Township. He was married in Miami County, Ohio on April 29, 1841 to Anna Matilda Toms, the daughter of Johnston Toms who had migrated from Pennsylvania to Ohio. Samuel and Anna Matilda Beard were the parents of George, Mary Elizabeth, Jonathan Marion, John Oliver, Benjamin, Eleanor, Abner, Jacob, and David Franklin Beard.

6. John Beard Junior, the second son of John Beard and Elizabeth Fox, was born April 5, 1818 in Warren County, Ohio. He married Catharine Warner, the daughter of David Warner and Elizabeth Willet, on November 21, 1842 in Montgomery County, Ohio. They were the parents of three daughters - Susannah, Elizabeth, and Mary.

7. Jacob Beard was born February 7, 1820 in Warren County, Ohio near Springboro. He married Susannah Warner, the daughter of David Warner and Elizabeth Willet, September 23, 1841 in Montgomery County, Ohio. They were the parents of Sarah C., Susanna A., Emmeline Beard, David, and Melinda.

8. George Beard, the son of John Beard and Elizabeth Fox, was born in Butler Township, Montgomery County, Ohio on October 17, 1821. He died on October 6, 1843 at the age of 21 years, 11 month, and 4 days.

9. Susan Beard was born December 5, 1823 in Butler township, Montgomery county, Ohio. She was married June 8, 1851 to John D. Kenney. She died December 7, 1891 and is buried near her parents in Poplar Hill Cemetery in Vandalia, Ohio. John Kenney was buried beside his wife.

10. Nancy Beard, the youngest daughter of John Beard and Elizabeth Fox, was born in Butler Township on March 20, 1826. She was married October 9, 1846 to Amos Maxton. Nancy Maxton died December 21, 1909 aged 84 years and is buried in Forest Hill Cemetery in Piqua, Ohio. Amos Maxton and Nancy Beard were the parents of Catherine, John V., Montgomery, Martha, and Amos Franklin Beard.

Irene Forrer, who assisted Lois Ann Baker in some of the research, is a daughter of Christopher Forrer and Sarah Cotterman. She is a granddaughter of Adam Cotterman and Elizabeth Beard. She is the great granddaughter of John Beard Junior and Catherine Warner. John Beard Senior and Elizabeth Fox were great, great, grandparents of Irene.

John Frederick Fox was a 5th great-grandfather of Lois Ann Baker. The lineage of Lois Ann Baker back to John Fox would be: Lois Ann Baker was a daughter of Ellen Nischwitz and Cleatus Judy. Ellen Nischwitz was the daughter of Charles Nischwitz and Rachel Davidson. Charles Nischwitz was the son of George Nischwitz and Mary Louisa DeFligne. George Nischwitz was the son of Elizabeth Beard and Jacob Nischwitz. Elizabeth Beard was the daughter of Michael Fox and Susannah (last name unknown). Michael Fox was the son of John Frederick Fox and Christena (last name unknown).

John ?Frederick? Fox
of Fox's Gap in Maryland

Some Documentation Presented by Lois Ann Baker

The Fox Genealogy by Daniel Gebhart Fox indicates on page 169, Appendix No. 1 the following:

> The Records of the port of Philadelphia, show that John Frederick Fox landed at the port, which was the principal landing place of the German emigration from 1682 to 1776.
>
> History shows that many of the German emigrants emigrated south, and that from 1748 to 1754, twenty-eight hundred Germans located in Maryland.
>
> Mrs. Christiana (Fox) Allison who was the surviving great-granddaughter of John Frederick Fox, stated to the writer during an interview about two years prior to her death, that "the old man Fox's name was John Frederick."

The third paragraph above, which cites Mrs. Christiana (Fox) Allison, when combined with our knowledge of the port of Philadelphia records, gives us the only evidence we have that the father of Frederick Fox of Fox's Gap in Maryland was named John Frederick Fox. No other records have surfaced that indicate a middle name for the John Fox who settled at Fox's Gap in Maryland.

The following documents, presented by Lois Anne Baker, are published records regarding the John Frederick Fox who landed in Philadelphia on September 27, 1752, on the ship Anderson.

The official lists of persons arriving in the port of Philadelphia are preserved in the archives of the Commonwealth of Pennsylvania. The lists were published for the first time in their entirety in three volumes in 1934. A re-print of this information was made in two volumes in 1975. The second printing did not include the signature page from the first publication.

Page 374 from volume II of the 1975 publication lists a Johann Friederich Fuchs who is found in volume I on pages 461 and 489.

Page 581, Pennsylvania German Pioneers by Strassburger and Hinke in 1934. The tenth signature down in the right column is Johann Friederich Fuchs.

In the State house in Philadelphia Wednesday the 27th September 1752

Present

The Foreigners whose Names are underwritten Imported in the Ship Anderson Captn Hugh Campbell from Rotterdam and last from Portsmouth in England did take and subscribe the usual Qualifications

No 85

Ship Anderson, September 27, 1752,
List 184 C.

In the Statehouse in Philadelphia, Wednesday, the 27th Sept. 1752.
The list on which John Frederick Fox appears begins in the middle of this page.

Johan Gerg Beck	Johann Geörg Haüdt
Andereas Jäckle	Adam Bernhardt
Martin Holtzhäusser	Debalt Grub
Johan Thiel (H) Herman	Johann Wilhelm Stuber
Johanes (H) Herman	Johann Friederich Stuber
Frederik (×) Saamm	Johann Philibpps Stuber
Nicolas Samm	Hans Jerg Eheller [?]
Adam Samm	Daniel Cramer
Theobald Becker	Michael Lauer
Peter (H) Hortt	Johann Wilhellem Stricker
Petter Bien	Balzasor (×) Dikhans
Henrich Müssemer	Georg Peter Eckel
Johannes König	Johannes Küstner
Ludewig (×) Shmit	Georg Seider
Jacob Steinbach	Simon Hermann
Conrad (×) Miller	Caspar (×) Lademan
Henrich Moser	Antonius Walter
Michael ( ) Graff, on board	Nicolaus Walter
Jacob Klar	Hans Jacob Gebhardt
Henrich Bierbauer	Peter Bernhard Henkenius
Andres Petri	Johann Henrich Henkenius
Jost (×) Shoenwalt	Michael (×) Hoffman
Simon Schumacher	

[List 184 C] In the Statehouse in Philadelphia, Wednesday, the 27th September, 1752.

Present: . . .

The Foreigners whose Names are underwritten, Imported in the Ship Anderson, Captn Hugh Campbell, from Rotterdam, and last from Portsmouth in England, took and subscribed the usual Qualifications. No. 85.

Leonhardt Bender	Johannes Weill
Christoph Maurer	Jacob Beittel
Uhlerich (O) Volk	Daniel Reutter
Jerg Riegert	Michael Heim
Peter Miller	Jeremias Ludwig Engelmann
David Hausmann	Johann Schneider
Johann Martin Schweitzer	Philipp Euler
Hans Georg Marquart	Peter (+) Piel
Johannes (+) Strätter	Philipp Graf

**The list from page 488 continues on this page.
The name of Joh Friederich Fuchs appears 20th in the left column.**

Mattheis Beugel
Michael Schmid
Nicklaus Renschler
Peter Dückherdt
Fridrich Steinle
Ulrich Stem [?]
Leonhardt Gnärr
Christian (CH) Rapman
Johannes Waltz
Georg Wetzel
Wilhelm Fridrich Schumann
Carl Friedrich Muckenfus
Simm Zimmerman
Jacob Friedrich Fischer
Johann Georg Breymeyer
Wilhelm Chroph Kestbohrer
Christian Dürr
Nicolaus Schuder
David Wegfaller [?]
Joh Friederich Fuchs
Christof Rothacker
Christoph Österle
Michael Schelling
Martin Betz
Andreas Götz
Andreas Eppler
Johanes Kurtz
Pierre Lageau
Johanes (O) Altig
Adam Weissbahrt
Johannes Weber
Andreas Scheibling
Joh. Caspar Windesch
Andras Weg
Peter (X) Anssel
Joachim Bräuchle
Johan David Horlacher
Johanes (++) Washer
Johann Georg Traub
Johan Jacob Beltz
Georg Michael Beltz
Christoph Gisterer
Johann Jacob Fitzler
Hans Michael (X) Cretel
Georg Ernst Lindenberger
Moritz Baur
J. George (+) Reest
Thomas Knissel
Johann Jerg Schillger
Johann Friderich Läible
Johan Frid König
Mahteus Kühbauch
Johan Fridrich Spur [?]
Wilhelm Garein
Johann Heinrich Von Rahden
Gottlob Hermann
Thomas ( ) Peel, on board
Michel Ritter
Christian (X) Peiffly
Jacob (+) Plessing
M. Jacob Friderich Schertlein *
Jacob Reiser
Balthes Friett
Friderich Masser

[List 185 C] At the Court House in Philadelphia, Wednesday, the 27 September, 1752.

Present: Joshua Maddox, Esquire.

The Foreigners whose names are underwritten, Imported in the Ship President, Captain Dunlop, from Rotterdam and last from . . . in England, did this day take and subscribe the

* A Lutheran Minister. M. = Magister.

President's Message

by Curtis Lynn Older

* We are fortunate to have a second article related to Michael Fox, a brother of Frederick Fox of Fox's Gap in Maryland. Additional material will appear in the June 1, 2003 newsletter that will supplement the current article that begins on page one.

* **Fox related books and documents are now available in Adobe Acrobat Reader Format on my latest CD-Rom disc entitled, *Fox Master CD-Rom Disc.* Everything you wanted to know, well, almost everything, is on this disc. See pages 11 through 15.**

* *Fox's Gap in Maryland Kodak Photo CD-Rom Disc* is another creation of mine. It contains 100 photographs. This disc still is available for $5.00 including shipping. The 100 images also are included in Adobe Acrobat Format on the *Fox Master CD-Rom Disc.*

* **The North Carolina South Mountain Monument will be dedicated in August or September 2003. It will stand near the Reno Monument at Fox's Gap in Maryland. Details in the June 1, 2003 Newsletter. Make plans to be there!**

* Descendants of Daniel Alexander Fox and Elizabeth Jane Ricketts will be interested in the brief article on Jacob Ricketts and Wagner's Division at the Battle of Franklin, Tennessee. Jacob Ricketts was in Wagner's Division and "out in front" at the Battle of Franklin, one of the greatest battles of the Civil War.

Table of Contents for this Newsletter

Frederick Fox Section
by Curtis Lynn Older

"Fox Master CD-Rom Disc"
Now Available!!

Fox Related Books and Documents Available in Adobe Acrobat Reader Format on One CD-Rom Disc

After lots of work, I am proud to announce that I have completed and am ready to distribute the "Fox Master CD-Rom Disc". This disc represents my attempt to put everything you need to know about Frederick Fox and Fox's Gap in Maryland on one CD-Rom disc that I can deliver to you for the price of $5.00, shipping included.

Fox Society members may now obtain copies of *The Fox Genealogy* by Daniel Gebhart Fox and other significant documents related to Fox's Gap in Maryland and The Society of the Descendants of Frederick Fox of Fox's Gap in Maryland in Adobe Acrobat Reader format (.pdf).

The Adobe Acrobat Reader is available FREE to anyone at the Adobe website:

www.adobe.com

The documents were created using Adobe Acrobat version 5.0. Version 5.0 of the Reader must be used to access the documents.

The Acrobat Reader documents that have been created by me will not allow the user to make any changes to the documents. However, copy and paste functions may be used with each document and printing of individual pages or entire documents is allowed. The Acrobat Reader's search and find functions allow a user to quickly locate a key word or phrase within a document. Zoom-in and zoom-out is a key tool in the Reader that allows the user to magnify text and pictures within a document to the desired level.

Another advantage of the Adobe Acrobat program is that it provides another way to archive important photographs. The Adobe Acrobat documents that I created for my Braddock book, my Land Tracts book, and Volume One of the society newsletter have color photographs included within each.

Included on the CD-Rom disc is a scanned version of the original book, *The Fox Genealogy* by Daniel Gebhart Fox. The scanned version has been created as an Adobe Acrobat document. The scanned version allows a user to view the original pages of *The Fox Genealogy*. All documents have been extensively proof-read except the 1000 page Long Version of my Land Tracts book which has not been published.

The CD-Rom disc is now available for a price of $5.00, including shipping and handling. **Please make your check payable to Curtis Older and mail to him at 618 Tryon Place, Gastonia, NC 28054-6066.**

Continued on following page -

Contents of *Fox Master CD-Rom Disc*

1. ***The Fox Genealogy*** by Daniel Gebhart Fox, 172 pages, compiled in 1914 and published in 1924.

(Two versions of this book are available on the cd-rom disc. The first was created in Adobe Acrobat Reader format, version 5.0, from a Microsoft Word document that was typed by Curtis L. Older and Rachael L. Older. A second version was created in Adobe Acrobat Reader format, version 5.0, from scanned images of photocopies made from an original book. Scanned by Curtis L. Older on a Canon Multipass C635 scanner using Scantastic software.)

2. ***The Braddock Expedition and Fox's Gap in Maryland*** by Curtis L. Older, 275 pages, published by Family Line Publications in 1995, now Willow Bend Books.

(Created in Adobe Acrobat Reader format, version 5.0, from Microsoft Word documents that were the same ones used to publish the book. Photographs are from the Kodak Photo CD-Rom disc entitled "Fox's Gap in Maryland" and were edited using Kodak Photo CD Access Plus software.)

3. ***The Land Tracts of the Battlefield of South Mountain*** by Curtis L. Older, 257 pages, published by Willow Bend Books.

(Created in Adobe Acrobat Reader format, version 5.0, from Microsoft Word documents that were the same ones used to publish the book. Most photographs are from the Kodak Photo CD-Rom disc entitled "Fox's Gap in Maryland" and were edited using Kodak Photo CD Access Plus software.)

4. ***The Land Tracts of the Battlefield of South Mountain - Long Version*** - unpublished - by Curtis L. Older, approximately 1000 pages. (Created in Adobe Acrobat Reader format, version 5.0, from Microsoft Word documents of the author.)

5. ***Volume One - News From Fox's Gap,*** the newsletter of The Society of the Descendants of Frederick Fox of Fox's Gap in Maryland, includes the first 10 issues of the newsletter, June 1996 through December 2000, approximately 250 pages, including indexes.

(Created in Adobe Acrobat Reader format, version 5.0, from the Microsoft Word documents that were used to print the copies of the newsletter sent to society members. Includes all maps and photographs as they appeared in the original newsletters.)

6. ***Fox's Gap in Maryland*** - Kodak Photo CD exported to Adobe Acrobat Reader Format - see contents description for "Fox's Gap in Maryland" disc on the following three pages.

7. ***June 1, 2002 Membership Roster of The Society of the Descendants of Frederick Fox of Fox's Gap in Maryland.***

Continued on following page -

Fox's Gap in Maryland Kodak Photo CD

"Fox's Gap in Maryland" is a Kodak Photo CD-Rom disc. The **format** of the images on the disc is **PCD**. The disc includes index pages that describe each of the images on the disc. This disc includes 100 photographic images of the items listed beginning at the bottom of this page and on the two pages following. (The 100 images from the disc also have been converted to Adobe Acrobat Reader format and are included on the "Fox Master CD-Rom Disc" described on the two preceding pages.)

A computer application that is useful to insert Kodak Photo CD images **(PCD format images)** into **Microsoft Word** documents is **Kodak Digital Science**. The "Fox's Gap in Maryland" Kodak Photo CD contains both Macintosh and PC versions of the Kodak Digital Science application on the disc itself. The Macintosh version works with operating systems 7.0, 7.1, and 7.5. The PC version works with operating systems 3.1 and Windows 95. Version Six or higher of **Microsoft Word** is needed to work with either the Mac or PC Kodak Digital Science software that is included on the disc.

The Kodak Photo CD format **(PCD) cannot** be used by **most** photography related computer applications because it is a unique **Kodak** format. One easy solution that enables one to edit, crop, and convert Kodak Photo CD images to a format other than **PCD** is to us **Kodak Photo CD Access Plus** software, available for Macintosh and PC computers.

Kodak Photo CD Access Plus software, version 3.1, is available from Nevada Photo in Las Vegas, Nevada, for about $42.00 including shipping and handling. The disc includes both Macintosh and PC versions of the application. The Macintosh application works with operating systems 7.5 through 9.2.2. The PC application works with Windows 95. You may contact Nevada Photo at:

(702) 735-2211 - phone or (702) 734-2222 - fax

To purchase the "Fox's Gap in Maryland" Kodak Photo CD which includes the Kodak Digital Science software, please make a check payable to Curtis Older in the amount of $5.00 and mail to him at 618 Tryon Place, Gastonia, NC 28054-6066.

Contents of *Fox's Gap in Maryland Kodak Photo CD*

1. Sign about General Braddock.
2. A Rifle of Frederick Fox.
3. Maryland Bicentennial Commission and Maryland Historical Society Marker.
4. Retouched photo of Daniel Booker Fox, a son of Frederick Fox.
5. The Fox Inn, owned by George Fox, son of Frederick Fox, from 1805 to 1807.
6. State Roads Commission Marker.

Continued on following page -

7. The Battle of South Mountain, Md.
8, 9, and 10. Will of John L. Fox.
11, 12, and 13. Will of Frederick Fox.
14. Marriage Register listing George Fox and Elizabeth Ann Link.
15. Part of the Estate Papers of George Fox.
16. Part of Estate Papers of George Fox.
17. Tax receipts in 1848 and 1849 for property of George Fox in Ohio.
18. 17th Michigan Memorial at Fox's Gap.
19. The Reno Monument at Fox's Gap.
20. Map of the Battlefield of South Mountain.
21, 22, 23. Will of Bartholomew Booker.
24. Ft. Frederick, Maryland (probably 1995).
25. Society of Colonial Wars and Maryland Historical Society Marker.
26. 1808 Varle Map.
27. 1808 Varle Map.
28. Will of John Fox. (see #31).
29. Certificate of birth for Johan Jacob Link, October 20, 1682. (English from German version)
30. Certificate of birth for Johan Jacob Link, October 20, 1682. (German from Latin version)
31. Will of John Fox. (see #28.)
32. Photo of Robert William Gouty, Ethel Belle (Fox) Gouty, and Mavis Lorene Gouty (Older).
33. Daniel Alexander Fox and Elizabeth Jane Ricketts on their wedding day, April 1, 1880, taken in Danville, Illinois.
34. The Boulder at Braddock Spring.
35. Fry and Jefferson Map of 1751, 1755, and 1775.
36. Fox's Gap, west side, 1995.
37. 1995 Map of Western Maryland.
38. Fox's Gap, east side, 1995.
39. 1794 Dennis Griffith Map of Maryland.
40. Letter by Jacob Reel of Sharpsburg to Michael and Frederick Fox of Ohio.
41. Birth Certificate for Mavis Lorene Gouty (Older).
42. Grave markers of John L. Fox and his son Daniel Alexander Fox at Hopewell Cemetery west of Covington, Indiana.
43. Grave marker of John L. Fox, son of George Fox, at Hopewell Cemetery, west of Covington, Indiana.
44. Grave marker of Susannah Hiligass, wife of John L. Fox, at Hopewell Cemetery, west of Covington, Indiana.
45. Picture of the Daniel Alexander Fox family, probably around 1900.
46 and 47. National Archives papers for Frederick Fox of the 10th Regiment, Pennsylvania Continental Line.
48 and 49. Will of John Adam Link II.
50 and 51. Receipt for bacon supplied by Adam Link (probably John Adam Link I) May 22, 1778.

Continued on following page -

52. Alexander Ogle, father of Jane Ogle, provided wheat and flour from his mills to the Maryland troops during the American Revolution.
53, 54, 55, and 56. Will of Alexander Ogle.
57, 58, and 59. Part of the Estate Papers of George Fox.
60. Bond of Elizabeth Fox (widow of George Fox) and Adam Fox (son of George Fox).
61. Part of the Estate Papers of George Fox.
62-69. **Index for items 1 through 61 listed above.**
70. John Liter tombstone.
71. Elizabeth (Fox) Liter tombstone.
72. Elizabeth Ann (Link) Fox tombstone.
73. Frederick Fox tombstone.
74. George Mettard tombstone. Jacob Benner and Mary Magdalene (Fox) Benner tombstone. St. John or Gebhart Church in Miamisburg, Ohio.
75. Susannah (Schutt) (Young) Fox tombstone.
76. George Fox tombstone.
77. Daniel Booker Fox tombstone.
78. Susannah (Christman) Fox tombstone.
79. Christiana (Fox) Mettert tombstone.
80. Gebhart Church Cemetery, Miamisburg, Ohio.
81 - 85. Bible Records of Ethel Belle (Fox) Gouty.
86. Ethel Belle, Ruby Dale, William Edward, and Kenneth B. Fox.
87. Curtis Lynn, Linda Sue (Osborn), and Rachael Lynn Older - 1995.
88. Wise Farmhouse at Fox's Gap.
89. 1755 French version of Fry and Jefferson Map; Robert de Vaugondy, Gilles.
90. The Winslow Map of 1736.
91. Land tracts in the area of Boonsboro, Maryland.
92. Fox's Gap land tracts.
93. Land tracts and roads of Fox's and Turner's Gaps.
94. The Fox Inn - land records traced from Daniel Dulany Sr. in 1742 to Helen Rudy, the owner of the Fox Inn, in 1995.
95. The Reno Monument - land records traced from Frederick Fox to the United States Government.
96. Footnotes to the Fox Inn and Reno Monument land tract records.
97. Footnotes to the Fox Inn and Reno Monument land tract records.
98. **Index.**
99. **Index.**
100. **Index.**

News from Fox's Gap

Published June 1 and December 1 of each year by
The Society of the Descendants of Frederick Fox of Fox's Gap in Maryland
Membership dues are $6.00 per year. President of the Society is Curtis L. Older.
Make Society inquiries by the following means:
Curtis L. Older — e-mail: curtolder@earthlink.net
618 Tryon Place — phone: 704-864-3879
Gastonia, NC 28054-6066

Wills Section

Each Newsletter includes one typewritten version of a will that is significant to the preservation efforts of the Society.

Margaret Booker was the wife of Bartholomew Booker and the mother-in-law of Frederick Fox of Fox's Gap in Maryland.

Will of Margaret Book (Booker), Frederick County Md Register of Wills Records GM-3-126, (wife of Bartholomew Booker).

In the Name of God Amen I Margaret Book of Frederick County being very Sick and Weak in body but of Perfect mind and disposing memory, do make this my last Will and Testament in manner & form following . . . I give and bequeath as followeth my Just Debts & funeral charges being first paid Imprimis I give and bequeath every thing or things real or personal that I have in this world to Mary Fox & Elizabeth Fox Daughters of Frederick Fox of Frederick County to be equally Divided between them and their heirs forever and lastly I appoint Frederick Fox my whole & sole Executor of this my last Will & Testament revoking all others heretofore by me made ratifying and confirming this and no other to be my last Will and Testament In Witness whereof I have herunto set my hand & seal this 12th Day of May 1796

Signed Sealed & Delivered in the presence of us and each of us whose names are hereto subscribed

her
Margaret Book
mark

Joseph Chapline (name unclear?)*

her
(name unclear)*, Catherine X Fox
mark

Frederick County August 3rd, 1796 then came Frederick Fox and made Oath on the Holy Evangels of Almighty God that the aforegoing Instrument of writing is the true and whole last will and Testament of Margaret Book late of Frederick County Deceased that hath come to his hands and possession and that he doth not know of any other

George Murdock Reg.

Frederick County August 3rd, 1796 Then came Joseph Chapline and George Medderd two of the Subscribing Witnesses to the aforegoing last will and Testament of Margaret Book . . . and that they did also see Henry Bonsinger and Catharine Fox the other Subscribing Witnesses -- sign their names as Witnesses to said Will in the presence and at the request of the Testator and all in the presence of each other.

Geo Murdoch Regt.

(* **Footnote**: Two names cannot be determined, although the writing is clear. The name to the right of Joseph Chapline can, with a stretch of imagination, be read as George Medderd (Methard). The name to the left of Catharine Fox does not appear to be Henry Bonsinger. Perhaps these two names are written in German.)

Hardbound or Paperback Books

related to Fox genealogy, Fox's Gap in Maryland, the Braddock Expedition, and the Battle of South Mountain

The Braddock Expedition and Fox's Gap in Maryland by Curtis L. Older
available at Will Bend Books, 65 E. Main Street, Westminster, MD 21157-5026, www.willowbendbooks.com, 1-800-876-6102, e-mail: bookorder@willowbend.net

The Land Tracts of the Battlefield of South Mountain by Curtis L. Older
available at Will Bend Books, 65 E. Main Street, Westminster, MD 21157-5026, www.willowbendbooks.com, 1-800-876-6102, e-mail: bookorder@willowbend.net

The Fox Genealogy by Daniel Gebhart Fox
available from Blair's' Book Service, 2503 Springpark Way, Richardson, Texas 75082, reference number XR-2546, e-mail: linda@glbco.com, fax: 972-783-1008
also available on CD-Rom from Curtis L. Older, 618 Tryon Place, Gastonia, NC 28054

Before Antietam, the Battle for South Mountain by John Michael Priest, 206 Weldon Drive, Boonsboro, MD 21713, 301-432-8720; also available in some bookstores

Landscape Turned Red, The Battle of Antietam by Stephen W. Sears; includes a section on The Battle of South Mountain; available in some bookstores

The Pennsylvania Line, Regimental Organization And Operations, 1776-1783, by John B. B. Trussell, Jr., Pennsylvania Historical and Museum Commission

Related Family Lines:

The Link Family by Paxson Link, available from Blair's Book Service, see above

Sir Henry A. Ogle, first published in 1902, *Ogle and Bothal*

The official Ogle Family Library, currently known as "The Ogle Collection," is housed in the Fulton County Museum, 27 E 375 N, Rochester, IN 46975

No new members the past six months!

New addresses:

Alan Sentman
217 Sackett Street, 2R
Brooklyn, NY 11231

Reva Winfred Fox
Jackson Park, 23100 Marine View Drive South
Room 214
Des Moines, Washington 98198

Jacob Ricketts and Wagner's Division at the Battle of Franklin

The following information was received by Curt Older in the Fall of 2001. Anyone who is a descendant of Jacob Ricketts, the father of Elizabeth Jane Ricketts and the father-in-law of Daniel Alexander Fox, should be interested in the Battle of Franklin, Tennessee, where Jacob Ricketts fought. Jacob Ricketts was in the brigade of Col. John Q. Lane, part of Brig. Gen. George D. Wagner's Federal Second Division.

Save the Franklin Battlefield, Inc., of which Curt Older was a member, invited me to the dedication of an historical marker dedicated to the Forward Federal position of Wagner's Division and their actions at the Battle of Franklin on November 30, 1864.

The Wagner maker was unveiled on Saturday, November 3rd, 2001, at 2:00 p.m., one-half mile south of the Carter House on Columbia Pike where Wagner's Division was stationed.

The Wagner marker reads:

Federal Foward Line:
On November 30, 1864, Col. Joseph Conrad's and Col. John Lane's brigades of Brig. Gen. George D. Wagner's Federal Second Division, Fourth Corps, were placed east and west of the road near this position one half mile south of the Federal main line. Acting Federal field commander Maj. Gen. Jacob D. Cox had warned Wagner that if pressed too closely by the enemy to withdraw his two brigades into the main line. Instead of conveying this order to the forward line, Wagner commanded his brigades to stay in position and fight. Lt. Gen. A. P. Stewart's Confederate Corps flanked the Federal line to the east as Brig. Gen. Hiram Granbury's Texas Brigade pierced the center. The Federal line disintegrated into a stampede as the troops raced toward the main line near the Carter House.

Descendants of John Jacob Link

John Jacob Link was an ancestor of Elizabeth Link, the wife of George Fox.
Web site: www.linkreunion.org
Contact person:
Vanda R. White
19618 Stewartown Terrace
Gaithersburg, MD 20886
e-mail: vandaw@erols.com
phone: 301-330-1129

The Link Reunion 50th Anniversary, 1952 - 2002, was held August 24 and 25, 2002, at St. James Lutheran Church, Uvilla, West Virginia.

To reach Uvilla, West Virginia, follow South 230 out of Shepherdstown about two miles to a fork in the road and a stop sign. Proceed left at this intersection, following the sign for Harpers Ferry. Uvilla is about 2.5 miles from the fork. St. James Lutheran church will be on the left.

News from Fox's Gap

The Society of the Descendants of Frederick Fox of Fox's Gap in Maryland

Issue 5, Volume 2 **Remember Freedom!** June 1, 2003

A Photo Heirloom of The Family of Daniel Booker Fox

By Alan Sentman

[We are extremely fortunate to have the following article by Alan Sentman, a member of our Fox Society. In his article, Alan describes the images on a family heirloom related to his Fox ancestors. This family heirloom has to be one of the most significant photographic items related to Frederick Fox and his descendants.

You may contact Alan at:
(e-mail) - alan.sentman@verizon.net
(phone) - 212-740-3532
(mail) - Alan K. Sentman
140 Cabrini Blvd., #129
New York, New York 10033-3434]

As a young boy, learning of Frederick Fox's service as a drummer in the American Revolution not only peaked my curiosity, it summoned the image of one of the drummers in Archibald M. Willard's famous fife and drum painting. This iconographical association allowed for me to place my fifth great grandfather within the broader context of historical events of which he was a part. In a sense this connection created a wonderful backdrop and transition to a photo of Frederick's son, Daniel Booker Fox.

This genealogical jewel is a photo compilation of the family group of Daniel and his ten children. This is one of the earliest Fox families that settled in the Miami Valley area of Ohio in the early eighteen hundreds. They came to Ohio after leaving Frederick Co., Md. This is a photo collection of portraits of Daniel and his children taken at various points in their adult life, which were arranged, printed and affixed onto matte board. It is difficult to say how many prints were made. Although it was generally accepted by my grandfather that the compilation photo was put together around the turn of the century, and may have been distributed at a large Fox family gathering, or handed out individually to the grandchildren of Daniel B. and Susannah (Christman) Fox.

My grandfather recalled attending Fox family reunions in the early nineteen twenties. He told me that the Fox reunions were usually held south of Dayton, Ohio and were attended in great numbers. There was a hill nearby the location where the reunions were held, and many of the attendees at some point during the day, would gather atop the hill where it offered an excellent vantage point of Daniel's old farm.

The photo has passed through many hands, and hints of its origin is found on the reverse side of the photo, which bares the following inscription by my great-great grandmother Caroline (Fox) Stansell, "April 30, 1905 presented Laura Coats by her mother C. Stansell the rest to have a picture off this one if they want." Also, inscribed on the back of the picture, Caroline lists her father, grandfather, aunts and uncle in her handwriting as follows:

(Center) 'Dearest Grandfather' Daniel B. Fox

1. Elizabeth Phillips
2. Theresa 'Tracy' King
3. 'Dearest Father' Fred C. Fox
4. Mahala Reed
5. Susan Mason
6. Catharine Boyd
7. Christiana Ann Hendrickson
8. Malinda Etris
9. Mary Brininger
10. D.C. Fox

The photo's journey began with Caroline (Fox) Stansell outside of the town of Brookville, Ohio. According to the inscription, she gave it to her daughter, Laura E. (Stansell) Robbins-Coats, who lived in Bradford, Ohio. Laura in turn gave the photo to her daughter Ida (Robbins) Royer, who in turn gave it to her daughter, Ruth Royer. Ruth, after having the photo for many years in Bradford, gave it to her cousin James Monroe Sentman.

The Sentman family is related to the Fox family by a marriage in the 1860's between Enoch Van Buren Stansell (1839-1927) and Caroline Fox (1843-1919), daughter of Frederick Christman Fox (1809-1897) and Hannah Coffman-Roberts (1803-1890). Enoch and Caroline had six children, one being my great grandmother Ida Ann Stansell (1872-1948), who in 1903 married Vernon Lewis Sentman (1879-1935). Ida and Vernon had one son named James Monroe Sentman (1915-2003).

It was through my grandfather's genealogical research, photos, family stories, and cemetery visits that I developed a keen interest in genealogical research. I enjoyed for many years pouring over old photos at my grandparents' house and I found the Fox photos to be among my favorite in his collection. This article is respectfully dedicated to him for his dutiful guardianship of so many precious family heirlooms, and, for without his enthusiasm in keeping the family history alive, much would have been lost.

The following is a genealogical report based on compiled information provided in D.G. Fox's book, *The Fox Genealogy*.

Daniel Booker Fox was born June 6, 1781, in Frederick County, Maryland, and died April 30, 1865, in Washington Township, Montgomery County, Ohio. He married Susannah Christman January 15, 1804, in Frederick County, Maryland. She was born January 23, 1782, in Frederick County, Maryland, and died November 5, 1840, in Washington Township, Montgomery County, Ohio. Daniel Booker Fox is buried in the Gephart Cemetery, Miamisburg, Ohio. Susannah (Christman) Fox is buried in the Gephart Cemetery, Miamisbug, Ohio.

Daniel Booker Fox

Children of Daniel Booker Fox & Susannah Christman

1. **Elizabeth Fox** was born December 14, 1804, in Frederick County, Maryland; died December 28, 1867, in Piqua, Miami County, Ohio. Elizabeth Fox married first, John Wesley Samsel who was born in Frederick County, Maryland, and died in Piqua, Miami County, Ohio. Elizabeth Fox married second, William Phillips, in 1826, in Warren County, Ohio. He was born in Frederick County, Maryland. Elizabeth Fox is buried in the Gephart Cemetery in Miamisburg, Ohio.

Elizabeth Fox

2. **Theresa Fox** was born November 20, 1806, in Frederick County, Maryland, and died April 5, 1890, in Washington Township, Montgomery County, Ohio. She married Andrew King on May 2, 1837, in Montgomery County, Ohio. He was born in 1804 in Maryland and died September 1852 in Ohio. Theresa Fox (King) is buried in Ferncliff Cemetery, Springfield, Ohio.

Children of Theresa Fox and Andrew King are:

1. Oliva King, born about 1833
2. David King, born about 1839
3. William King, born about 1840
4. James King, born about 1842
5. Mary King, born about 1843
6. Anna King, born May 1850
7. John King, born 1852

Theresa Fox

3. Frederick Christman Fox was born February 26, 1809, in Miami Township, Montgomery County, Ohio, and died April 30, 1897, in Washington Township, Montgomery County, Ohio. He married Hannah Coffman on August 19, 1829, in Montgomery County, Ohio. She was born September 12, 1803, in Rockingham County, Virginia, and died December 28, 1890, in Washington Township, Montgomery County, Ohio. Frederick Christman Fox and Hannah Coffman are buried in the Hill Grove Cemetery, Miamisburg, Ohio.

Children of Frederick Christman Fox and Hannah Coffman are:

1. Daniel Fox, born August 14, 1830
2. Frederick Coffman Fox, born Feb 25, 1832
3. Susanna Fox, born Dec 16, 1834
4. Hannah Fox, born Aug 21, 1837
5. Catherine Fox, born May 24, 1840
6. Caroline Fox, born Jun 4, 1843
7. Delilah Fox, born Dec 6, 1847

Frederick Christman Fox

5. Susannah Fox was born April 6, 1811 in Miami Township, Montgomery County, Ohio, and died October 1, 1899, in Washington Township, Montgomery County, Ohio. She married Jacob Mason August 19, 1829, in Montgomery County, Ohio. He was born June 6, 1806, in Washington Township, Montgomery County, Ohio, and died July 18, 1891, in Washington Township, Montgomery County, Ohio. Susannah Fox and Jacob Mason are buried in Centerville, Ohio.

Children of Susannah Fox and Jacob Mason are:

1. Lewis V. Mason
2. Martha S. Mason
3. Frances A. Mason
4. Mary E. Mason
5. Mahala J. Mason
6. Catherine M. Mason
7. Sarah A. Mason
8. Daniel C. Mason

Susannah Fox

4. Mahala Fox was born April 24, 1816, in Miami Township, Montgomery County, Ohio, and died June 5, 1897, in Jasper County, Indiana. She married William M. Reed on February 27, 1840, in Montgomery County, Ohio. He was born August 7, 1816, in Maysville, Mason County, Kentucky, and died July 7, 1893, in Jasper County, Indiana. Mahala Fox and William M. Reed are buried in Remington, Indiana.

Children of Mahala Fox and William Reed are:

1. Daniel Webster Reed, born abt. 1841
2. Nathaniel Joshua Reed, born Sep 3, 1843
3. John Reed, born abt. 1846
4. Alonzo Fox Reed, born abt. Dec 1849
5. William Wesley Reed, born aft. 1850

Mahala Fox

-

6. Catharine Fox was born August 13, 1813, in Miami Township, Montgomery County, Ohio. She died March 27, 1884, in Warren County, Ohio. She married James Boyd on August 5, 1846, in Montgomery County, Ohio. He was born September 23, 1817, in Bucks County, Pennsylvania, and died August 1868, in Indianapolis, Indiana. Catherine Fox is buried in Monroe, Butler County, Ohio. James Boyd is buried in Crown Hill Cemetery, Indianapolis, Indiana.

Catharine Fox

-

7. Christiana Ann Fox was born April 26, 1818, in Miami Township, Montgomery County, Ohio, and died March 7, 1900, in Warren County, Ohio. She married William S. Hendrickson on March 17, 1841, in Montgomery County, Ohio. He was born May 22, 1817, in Somerset County, Pennsylvania, and died January 20, 1892, in Warren County, Ohio. Christiana Ann Fox and William S. Hendrickson are buried in Monroe, Butler County, Ohio.

Children of Christiana Fox and William Hendrickson are:

1. W. P. Hendrickson
2. Malinda Hendrickson

Christiana Ann Fox

8. Malinda Fox was born June 15, 1820, in Miami Township, Montgomery County, Ohio, and died April 4, 1903, in Hendricks County, Indiana. She married Pearson Etris on July 31, 1849, in Montgomery County, Ohio. He was born January 18, 1812, in Monmouth County, New Jersey, and died September 11, 1889, in Hendricks County, Indiana. Malinda Fox and Pearson Etris are buried in Green Lawn Cemetery near Brownsville, Indiana.

Children of Malinda Fox and Pearson Etris are:

1. Daniel Pearson Etris, born abt. 1851 in Ohio
2. Hester J. Etris

Malinda Fox

9. Mary Magdalena Fox was born July 6, 1822, in Miami Township, Montgomery County, Ohio, and died June 21, 1893, in the city of Franklin, Warren County, Ohio. She married Daniel Brininger, September 26, 1844, in Warren County, Ohio. He was born July 15, 1818, in Warren County, Ohio, and he died January 25, 1892, in the city of Franklin, Warren County, Ohio. Mary Magdalena Fox and Daniel Brininger are buried in Wood Hill Cemetery, Franklin, Ohio.

Mary Magdalena Fox

10. Daniel Christman Fox was born April 11, 1824, in Miami Township, Montgomery County, Ohio, and died May 18, 1902, in Miami Township, Montgomery County, Ohio. He married Margaret Jane Snyder on May 6, 1847, in Montgomery County, Ohio. She was born April 17, 1829, in Montgomery County, Ohio, and died November 7, 1902, in Miami Township, Montgomery County, Ohio. Daniel Christman Fox and Margaret Jane Snyder are buried in Hill Grove Cemetery, Miamisburg, Ohio.

Children of Daniel Christman Fox and Margaret Snyder are:

1. Martin Fox
2. Mary Fox
3. William Fox
4. Nancy Fox
5. Eveline Fox
6. Mira Fox
7. Erta Fox

Daniel Christman Fox

The Children of John Beard and Elizabeth (Fox) Beard

By Lois Ann Baker

This is the third article submitted by Lois Baker on Michael Fox and his descendants. This is the first time this article has been published.

Michael Fox was a brother of Frederick Fox of Fox's Gap in Maryland. Michael and Frederick were sons of John and Christina Fox. Michael preceded Frederick in moving to near Dayton, Ohio, in the early 1800s.

Lois Baker is a descendant of Michael Fox. She has done extensive genealogical research into the descendants of Michael Fox and has graciously submitted the following article.

Lois assisted in marking the grave of Michael Fox as a soldier of the American Revolution. Please also see her article in the June 1, 2002 newsletter.

Lois Anne Baker
330 Main Street
Versailles, Ohio 45380
1-937-526-5493

Elizabeth Fox was a daughter of Michael Fox and his wife Susannah. Michael Fox was a brother of Frederick Fox of Fox's Gap in Maryland. Elizabeth Fox first married a John Robb in 1805. A son was born to John and Elizabeth (Fox) Robb on September 20, 1806. The son was named John Robb Junior. John Robb Senior died soon after the birth of his son.

Elizabeth Fox (Robb) married second a John Beard. Information on John Beard is included in the article written by Lois Ann Baker in the December 1, 2002, Newsletter.

John Beard and Elizabeth Fox (Robb) (Beard) raised a family of ten children: Sarah, Mary, Elizabeth, Eve, Samuel, John, Jacob, George, Susan, and Nancy. These children grew to maturity and settled in various areas throughout Ohio.

The following descriptions of each of the ten children of John Beard and Elizabeth Fox are more in-depth than those that appeared in the December 1, 2002 Newsletter.

1. Sarah, the oldest daughter of John and Elizabeth (Fox) Beard was born May 10, 1809, in Warren County, Ohio, near Springboro. She married Benjamin Wilhelm on September 12, 1826, in Montgomery County, Ohio. They were the parents of Sarah Naomi, Lucinda, John, Elizabeth, Simon and David.

Benjamin Wilhelm came from Pennsylvania with his father John Wilhelm and family in 1820 to settle in the Miami Valley. Benjamin Wilhelm realized the importance of the National Road as a stopping place for travelers going west and thus the town of Vandalia was laid out in 1838. Mr. Wilhelm laid out 33 lots and constructed several buildings.

The first buildings to be built in the new town were the Wilhelm's home and general store. During the next few years a few more houses were erected. In 1848 the citizens of the village filed incorporation papers. Mr. Wilhelm was elected the first mayor of the village and again re-elected in 1849. Mr. Wilhelm was also the first postmaster.

In 1849 an epidemic of cholera swept the nation. It took its toll in the small town of Vandalia. Fifty of the 200 people who lived there moved for safety's sake. Of the population that remained in Vandalia, fifty died of this dread disease. This disease wiped out entire families. Mr. Wilhelm worked untiringly to help the sick and bury the dead. His wife Sarah Beard Wilhelm and their little daughter Sarah Naomi died during the epidemic. Mother and daughter were buried in the old Vandalia Cemetery.

The obituary of Sarah Beard Wilhelm tells the following story. Mrs. Wilhelm took sick and suffered for two days. On the first morning of her sickness, she told her husband that she was going to die before long. On the morning of the second day, she told her husband that her little baby would follow her in a few days. The little girl took sick the same day and died on the 18th - aged 1 year. Mrs. Wilhelm had died on the 17th. Mrs. Wilhelm was a member of the United Brethren Church for 21 years. She left her husband, Benjamin Wilhelm, and five children as survivors.

On the 29th of January 1850, Benjamin Wilhelm married Mary Jane Linn of Miami County, Ohio. She was the daughter of Daniel and Elizabeth Linn. Benjamin and Mary Jane had a son born in 1851 and named him Orion Oscar Wilhelm. In the year 1855 Benjamin and Mary Jane Wilhelm, along with other family members, moved to Bloomington Township, Muscatine County, Iowa. In the year 1864 Benjamin, Mary Jane, and Orion moved to Tipton, Cedar County, Iowa.

The estate packet for John Beard Senior, who died in 1866, lists his daughter Sarah Beard Wilhelm as deceased and her living children are her heirs. The children of Sarah Beard Wilhelm who were living at that time were Lucinda, John, Elizabeth, Simon P., and David.

Lucinda Wilhelm, born in 1829, married Samuel Taylor. The Taylors lived in Dayton, Ohio, and had a son named Joseph.

John Wilhelm, born in 1831, moved to the state of Illinois and lived in Kendall County.

Elizabeth Wilhelm, born in 1835, married Lewis Brandenburg. The Brandenburgs lived in Vandalia, Ohio, for many years.

Simon P. Wilhelm, born in 1837, moved to the state of Iowa and may have lived in the county of Calhoun.

David Wilhelm, born in 1839, lived in Denver City, County of Arapahoe, Territory of Colorado in 1867.

Benjamin Wilhelm, husband of Sarah Beard, became affiliated with Masonic Cedar Lodge #11 at Tipton, Iowa, on the 25th of April 1866. He was also elected to the office of Constable and Deputy Sheriff and Collector of delinquent taxes between the years of 1864 and 1877. He was elected County Assessor in 1866 and coroner from 1872 to 1875. He was an active member of more than fifty years in the Methodist Episcopal Church.

Mr. Wilhelm was appointed agent to the United Brethren Mutual Aid Society of Pennsylvania in 1872. He remained a Mason until his death on the 19th of May 1888, having lived 83 years, 10 months, and 5 days. He is buried in the Masonic Cemetery at Tipton, Iowa.

2. Mary Beard, daughter of John Beard and Elizabeth (Fox) Beard, was born July 27, 1810 in Warren County, Ohio. She married Henry Wolaver in Montgomery County on August 15, 1833. They were the parents of eleven children - John, George, Caroline, Henry, Jacob, Sampson, Sarah, Francis, Mary, Susanna, and James.

The Wolaver family moved to Shelby County in 1838. Henry Wolaver was elected trustee of Cynthiana Township in Shelby County in 1841 and 1842.

Henry and Mary (Beard) Wolaver are buried in Reams Cemetery, Newport, Ohio, in Shelby County. Mary Beard Wolaver died September 12, 1900, at the age of 90 years, 1 month, and 15 days. She had lived in Cynthiana Township for about sixty-five years.

A son of Henry and Mary (Beard) Wolaver, George M. Wolaver, died in Vandalia, Ohio, on November 26, 1852, aged 17 years, 3 months, and 18 days. He is buried in the old Vandalia Cemetery. There are descendants of the Wolavers living in Shelby County, Ohio, in October 2002.

3. Elizabeth Beard, daughter of John Beard and Elizabeth (Fox) Beard, was born February 10, 1812 in Warren County, Ohio, near Springboro. On April 3, 1836, she was married to Jacob Nischwitz, the son of Valentine Nischwitz and Mary Ockerman. The Valentine Nischwitz family came to Butler Township, Montgomery County, Ohio, from Gettysburg, Adams County, Pennsylvania, about 1820.

After two years of marriage, Jacob Nischwitz and his wife moved to Shelby County, Ohio, in 1838 where they resided for sixty-one years. They were the parents of eight children - Susannah, George, Jacob, John, Valentine, Elizabeth, Mary Ann, and David.

Jacob Nischwitz farmed in Shelby County, Ohio, until his retirement and death on September 26, 1900. Elizabeth (Beard) Nischwitz died January 1, 1900 in Darke County, Versailles, Ohio and was buried in the Reams Cemetery in Newport, Shelby County, Ohio.

4. Eve Beard, daughter of John Beard and Elizabeth (Fox) Beard, was born January 15, 1814 in Warren County, Ohio and died June 27, 1901 in Butler Township, Montgomery County, Ohio. She is buried in Poplar Hill Cemetery beside her husband Jacob Coover.

Jacob Coover and Eve Beard were married December 12, 1834, in Montgomery County, Ohio. Jacob Coover was the son of Michael Coover and Elizabeth Shoup. The Coover family moved to Butler Township from Cumberland County, Pennsylvania.

Jacob Coover and Eve Beard were the parents of nine children - Henry, who married Adaline Johnson; Mary E., who married Darius Hutchins; Michael J., who married Lucy C. Collins; Rosannan, who married Samuel Keplinger; Jacob and Zachariah who never married; Amos J., who married Martha V. Shriver; Anna and Fidelia who never married.

The Coovers were farmers and breeders of horses in Butler Township. Descendants of this family live in the Vandalia area today.

5. Samuel Beard, the first son of John Beard and Elizabeth Fox, was born January 16, 1816, in Warren County, Ohio, near Springboro in Clear Creek Township. He was married in Miami County, Ohio on April 29, 1841, to Anna Matilda Toms, the daughter of Johnston Toms who had migrated from Pennsylvania to Ohio.

Samuel and Anna Matilda (Toms) Beard were the parents of ten children - George, who married Susanna Staudt and resided in Darke County, Ohio; Mary Elizabeth, who married Isaiah Harshman and resided in Tippecanoe County, Indiana; Jonathan Marion, who married Lettie Strimmel and resided in Dayton, Ohio; John Oliver, who married Emma Fudge and worked on the railroad for many years; Benjamin, who died young; Eleanor; Abner, who died young; Jacob, who died young; and David Franklin Beard, who married Laura Fudge and resided in Hagerstown, Indiana.

Samuel Beard lived on 200 acres of land that ran along the present day Dixie Highway to Peter Road. Samuel Beard died July 30, 1867, and was buried in the old Vandalia Cemetery beside his son Abner. They were later interred in Poplar Hill Cemetery in Vandalia.

Anna Matilda (Toms) Beard moved to Darke County, Ohio, to live with George and Susanna (Staudt) Beard. Anna Matilda Beard died February 2, 1892, at Osgood, Ohio, aged 72 years and was buried in Teacup Protestant Cemetery near Delvin, a hamlet that no longer exists. The cemetery is not far from North Star, Darke County, Ohio.

6. John Beard Junior, the second son of John Beard and Elizabeth Fox, was born April 5, 1818 in Warren County, Ohio. He married Catharine Warner, the daughter of David Warner and Elizabeth Willet, on November 21, 1842 in Montgomery County, Ohio. They were the parents of three daughters - Susannah, Elizabeth, and Mary.

Susannah Beard never married but was known as "Aunt Sue" to everyone in Vandalia and the immediate area. Susannah died in 1933 and is buried in Poplar Hill Cemetery.

Elizabeth married Adam Cotterman, the son of Henry Cotterman and Sarah Booher. Elizabeth and Adam Cotterman lived in Butler Township and in Miami County, Ohio.

Mary Beard married Will Tingle and lived in Dayton, Ohio.

John Beard Junior died October 20, 1850, aged 32 years, 6 months, and 16 days. At the time of his death he lived on the SW 1/2 of Section 21 Township 3 Range 6 that contained 160 acres. His father, John Beard Senior, was administrator of his estate. Benjamin Wilhelm was a witness to John Beard Junior's will.

John Beard Junior bought his farmland in 1843, which was Section 21 that lies between what is now Dixie Highway and Peter's Pike on Mulberry Road. John Beard Junior is buried in Poplar Hill Cemetery at the edge of Vandalia. His widow, Catherine Warner Beard, married W. C. Randall. They had several children.

7. Jacob Beard, a son of John Beard and Elizabeth Fox, was born February 7, 1820 in Warren County, Ohio near Springboro. He married Susannah Warner, the daughter of David Warner and Elizabeth Willet, September 23, 1841 in Montgomery County, Ohio. They were the parents of five children.

Sarah C., who never married; Susanna A., who married Jacob Pontius; Emmeline Beard, who never married; David, who lived in Dayton and was a contractor; and Melinda, who married Joseph Stauffer.

Jacob Beard engaged in the distilling business, conducting a distillery for many years near Chambersburg, now Murlin Heights, which is several miles north of Dayton. At the outbreak of the Civil War, he enlisted in Company D 132nd Infantry and was elected Captain of his outfit.

Jacob died at the age of 93 years, 7 months, and 29 days on October 29, 1813. He and his wife are buried at Poplar Hill Cemetery, as are several of their children.

David, a son of Jacob and Susannah Warner Beard, owned a brick factory on Troy Pike, later Route U. S. 25 or now Dixie. He built the original Beardshear Church, which is on Wagner-Ford Road but is now owned by The Church of God.

The Beardshear Cemetery was originally used as a family burial ground in connection with The Beardshear Church. This church was damaged by a storm in 1915, which unroofed the church and caved in one side of the building. During this same storm a horse owned by Clyde Lowry, a relative of the Beards, was killed on a farm where Grafton Kennedy School now stands.

The old Beardshear Church was rebuilt about 1917 and was bought by the Church of God. The new Beardshear Church is located on Stop Eight Road.

David Beard owned a farm at the edge of Vandalia called Poplar Hill on account of a long row of trees that led back to a big brick house which is no longer standing. David Beard died on October 6, 1843, at the age of 21 years, 11 months, and 4 days. He is buried in Poplar Hill Cemetery in Vandalia, Ohio.

8. **George Beard**, a son of John Beard and Elizabeth Fox, was born in Butler Township, Montgomery County, Ohio on October 17, 1821. He died on October 6, 1843 at the age of 21 years, 11 month, and 4 days. He is buried in Poplar Hill Cemetery in Vandalia, Ohio.

9. **Susan Beard**, a daughter of John Beard and Elizabeth Fox, was born December 5, 1823, in Butler township, Montgomery County, Ohio. She was married June 8, 1851, to John D. Kenney. She died December 7, 1891, and is buried near her parents in Poplar Hill Cemetery in Vandalia, Ohio. John Kenney was buried beside his wife.

10. **Nancy Beard**, the youngest daughter of John Beard and Elizabeth Fox, was born in Butler Township on March 20, 1826. She was married October 9, 1846, to Amos Maxton. Before moving to Miami County, the Maxtons lived for many years in Shelby County, Ohio. Nancy (Beard) Maxton died December 21, 1909, aged 84 years and is buried in Forest Hill Cemetery in Piqua, Ohio.

Amos Maxton and Nancy Beard were the parents of Catherine, John V., Montgomery, Martha, and Amos Franklin Maxton.

Relationship of the Author and her assistant to John Fox of Fox's Gap in Maryland

Irene Forrer, who assisted Lois Ann Baker in some of the research that led to this article, is a daughter of Christopher Forrer and Sarah Cotterman. She is a granddaughter of Adam Cotterman and Elizabeth Beard. She is the great granddaughter of John Beard Junior and Catherine Warner. John Beard Senior and Elizabeth Fox were great, great, grandparents of Irene. Elizabeth Fox was a daughter of Michael Fox, who was a brother of Frederick Fox of Fox's Gap in Maryland. Michael Fox, like Frederick Fox, was a son of John Frederick Fox and Christena of Fox's Gap in Maryland.

John Frederick Fox was a 5th great-grandfather of **Lois Ann Baker**. The lineage of Lois Ann Baker back to John Fox would be: Lois Ann Baker was a daughter of Ellen Nischwitz and Cleatus Judy. Ellen Nischwitz was the daughter of Charles Nischwitz and Rachel Davidson. Charles Nischwitz was the son of George Nischwitz and Mary Louisa DeFligne. George Nischwitz was the son of Elizabeth Beard and Jacob Nischwitz. Elizabeth Beard was the daughter of Michael Fox and Susannah (last name unknown). Michael Fox was the son of John Frederick Fox and Christena (last name unknown).

Welcome New Members!

We are pleased to announce the following five new members of our Society who joined after the December 1, 2002, Newsletter:

Name / Address	Phone	Date of Membership	Membership Number
John Lynn Woodard 250 East Center Street Germantown, Ohio 45327 e-mail: jwoodard1@woh.rr.com	937-855-4422 **Ancestor Line:** George Fox, a son of Frederick Fox; George L. Fox, Charles E. Fox, Amos R. Fox, Mildred E. Fox	March 15, 2003	0044

John is a descendant of Frederick Fox of Fox's Gap in Maryland and his oldest son, George Fox, who married Elizabeth Ann Link.

Name / Address	Phone	Date of Membership	Membership Number
Carole Jean Troup 3606 S. W. 5th Street Cape Coral, Florida 33991 e-mail: jtroup@swfla.rr.com	239-283-7219 **Ancestor Line:** Elizabeth Fox, a daughter of Frederick Fox; Frederick Leiter, Elizabeth Leiter, Noah Adam Leis, Ralph Carl Leis	March 22, 2003	0045

Carole is a descendant of Frederick Fox of Fox's Gap in Maryland and one of his daughters, Elizabeth Fox, who married John Leiter.

Name / Address	Phone	Date of Membership	Membership Number
Bonnie Leah Miller 5408 82nd Ave. N. E. Devil's Lake, North Dakota 58301 e-mail: sewgmiller@hotmail.com	701-662-3636 **Ancestor Line:** George Fox, a son of Frederick Fox; John L. Fox, Daniel Alexander Fox, William Edward Fox, Elizabeth Jane Fox	April 5, 2003	0046

Bonnie is a descendant of Frederick Fox of Fox's Gap in Maryland and his oldest son, George Fox, who married Elizabeth Ann Link.

Name / Address	Phone	Date of Membership	Membership Number
Jerry Lee Bucholz 9652 Dolton Court Highland Ranch, Colorado 80126 e-mail: bucholzdj@msn.com	303-791-4761 **Ancestor Line:** George Fox, a son of Frederick Fox; John L. Fox, Daniel Alexander Fox, William Edward Fox, Elizabeth Jane Fox	April 5, 2003	0047

Jerry is a descendant of Frederick Fox of Fox's Gap in Maryland and his oldest son, George Fox, who married Elizabeth Ann Link.

Name / Address	Phone	Date of Membership	Membership Number
Kenneth Eugene Woodard 128 Hummingbird Dr. NW Cleveland, TN 37312 e-mail: kenwoo1@charter.net	423-472-5243 **Ancestor Line:** George Fox, a son of Frederick Fox; George L. Fox, Charles E. Fox, Amos R. Fox, Mildred E. Fox	April 28, 2003	0048

Kenneth is a descendant of Frederick Fox of Fox's Gap in Maryland and his oldest son, George Fox, who married Elizabeth Ann Link.

Fox Society Website is UP!

Enter the following on your Internet Explorer ADDRESS BAR:

http://homepage.mac.com/clo7956/

You can download various Fox Society Related Items in Adobe PDF format. Dial-up Internet may be slow to download. You can print and copy text from these Adobe PDF files. Problems? Send me an e-mail and let me know. You will need Version 5.0 of Adobe Acrobat Reader. Download the Reader for FREE at: www.adobe.com

President's Message
by Curtis Lynn Older

* We have fortunate to have two very significant articles included in this newsletter. Lois Baker provides her third article related to Michael Fox, a brother of Frederick Fox of Fox's Gap in Maryland. Alan Sentman provides photographs and descriptions of Daniel Booker Fox, a son of Frederick Fox, and his children.

* Go to the Fox Society WEBSITE by entering the following in your Internet Explorer ADDRESS BAR: http://homepage.mac.com/clo7956/

You can download various Fox Society Related Items in Adobe PDF format. You will need Version 5.0 of Adobe Acrobat Reader that you may download for FREE at: www.adobe.com

* The North Carolina South Mountain Monument sculpture to be placed at Fox's Gap in Maryland should be ready in September 2003. It will stand near the Reno Monument. No dedication date has been set at this time.

Table of Contents for this Newsletter

News from Fox's Gap

Published June 1 and December 1 of each year by
The Society of the Descendants of Frederick Fox of Fox's Gap in Maryland
Membership dues are $6.00 per year. President of the Society is Curtis L. Older.
Make Society inquiries by the following means:
Curtis L. Older
618 Tryon Place
Gastonia, NC 28054-6066
e-mail: curtolder@earthlink.net
phone: 704-864-3879

"Fox Master CD-Rom Disc" - Now Available!!!!

Contents of the *Fox Master CD-Rom Disc*

1. ***The Fox Genealogy*** by Daniel Gebhart Fox, 172 pages, compiled in 1914 and published in 1924.

(Two versions of this book are available on the cd-rom disc. The first was created in Adobe Acrobat Reader format, version 5.0, from a Microsoft Word document that was typed by Curtis L. Older and Rachael L. Older. A second version was created in Adobe Acrobat Reader format, version 5.0, from scanned images of photocopies made from an original book. Scanned by Curtis L. Older on a Canon Multipass C635 scanner using Scantastic software.)

2. ***The Braddock Expedition and Fox's Gap in Maryland*** by Curtis L. Older, 275 pages, published by Family Line Publications in 1995, now Willow Bend Books.

(Created in Adobe Acrobat Reader format, version 5.0, from Microsoft Word documents that were the same ones used to publish the book. Photographs are from the Kodak Photo CD-Rom disc entitled "Fox's Gap in Maryland" and were edited using Kodak Photo CD Access Plus software.)

3. ***The Land Tracts of the Battlefield of South Mountain*** by Curtis L. Older, 257 pages, published by Willow Bend Books.

(Created in Adobe Acrobat Reader format, version 5.0, from Microsoft Word documents that were the same ones used to publish the book. Most photographs are from the Kodak Photo CD-Rom disc entitled "Fox's Gap in Maryland" and were edited using Kodak Photo CD Access Plus software.)

4. ***The Land Tracts of the Battlefield of South Mountain - Long Version*** - unpublished - by Curtis L. Older, approximately 1000 pages. This book contains the complete text of every land record used by Curtis L. Older in his research of the land tracts of the Battlefield of South Mountain. This book is very valuable to a land tract researcher. (Created in Adobe Acrobat Reader format, version 5.0, from Microsoft Word documents of the author.)

5. ***Volume One - News From Fox's Gap***, the newsletter of The Society of the Descendants of Frederick Fox of Fox's Gap in Maryland, includes the first 10 issues of the newsletter, June 1996 through December 2000, approximately 250 pages, including indexes.

(Created in Adobe Acrobat Reader format, version 5.0, from the Microsoft Word documents that were used to print the copies of the newsletter sent to society members. Includes all maps and photographs as they appeared in the original newsletters.)

6. ***Fox's Gap in Maryland*** - Kodak Photo CD exported to Adobe Acrobat Reader Format, version 5.0. See December 1, 2002, Newsletter for contents of the CD-rom disc.

7. ***June 1, 2002 Membership Roster of The Society of the Descendants of Frederick Fox of Fox's Gap in Maryland.***

The cd-rom is now available for $5.00, including shipping and handling. Please send your check payable to Curtis Older at 618 Tryon Place, Gastonia, NC 28054-6066.

Land Tracts of the Battlefield of South Mountain
by Curtis L. Older

This issue of the newsletter includes a list of all the land records I found for John Fox in Frederick County, Maryland. It is my opinion that several of these records are for a John Fox other than the one of Fox's Gap in Maryland.

Of particular interest is the tract of land named Grim's Fancy. The land record for that tract mentions the house of John Fox and its location along the road through Fox's Gap. The Grim's Fancy tract is about 1/2 mile west of the Reno Monument at Fox's Gap.

John Fox Land Records in Frederick and Washington Counties

Ref No.	Date	From or To	Other party	Name of Tract/Item
J-504	June 2, 1764	From	Daniel Dulaney	Lot #269, Frederick Town*
K-499	May 22, 1766	To	Elias Bruner	Lot #269, Frederick Town*
K-703	Aug. 23, 1766	From	Joseph Chapline	Lot #143, Sharpsburg
K-1231	May 12, 1767	From	Joseph Chapline	Lot #16, Sharpsburg
J-1400	Aug. 18, 1767	From	John Barroughs	Judgment*
K-1278	June 2, 1769	From	Henry Joel	Lot #7, Sharpsburg
K-1279	June 2, 1769	From	Henry Joel	1/2 Lot #6, Sharpsburg

* It is the author's opinion Lot #269 was bought and sold by a John Fox other than the father of Frederick Fox. It is not known which John Fox was the one in the Judgment record. It is the author believes that John Fox, Frederick Fox's father, owned all of the Sharpsburg lots listed.

John Fox's House mentioned in Land Records

(From the Arthur G. Tracey Collection in the Historical Society of Carroll County, Md., 210 East Main Street, Westminster, MD. 21157)

Surname Card:

Fox, John
2-27-1764 Grim's Fancy - 50 A. - CFW: u-40
Near John Fox's House

Land Plat Card:

OFW: u-40 Wash. Co.
GRIMS FANCY
2-27-1764 50 A.
6-12-1769 Alexander Grim
BC & GS 40-114
N.S. Main Road that leads from Fredericktown to Swainingens (Swearingens) Ferry & near to John Fox's house.
On the west side of South Mtn.
On this land is 2 log cabbins 27 x 12 & 14 x 12 & 15 A. cultivated land.
Next to Mt. Atlas.
Wash. Co. near Foxes Gap.
F. C. 1743 Sheet 392

Grims Fancy Land Record in the Maryland Archives

"On the North Side of the Main Road that leads from Frederick Town to Swearingen's Ferry and near to John Foxes House"

Grims Fancy, BC & GS 40, p. 114, Alexander Trim's certificate of survey, examined and passed 5 June 1765, [MdHR 17,451, 1-23-4-5].

Alexander Trim's Cert. 50a Grims Fancy} Frederick County? By virtue of a
Pattd 12th June 1769 Rent ? annum} Special Warrant granted out of his Lordships
2/. ? Chd to the Rent Roll} Land Office of this Province to Alexander Trim of the County aforesaid for fifty acres of land bearing date the 14th of October 1763. I therefore certify as Deputy surveyor under his Excellency Horatio Sharpe Esquire Governor of Maryland that I have carefully surveyed and laid out for and in the name of him the said Alexander Trim all that tract of land called Grims Fancy lying in the County aforesaid beginning at a bounded Black Oak tree standing on the north side of the Main Road that leads from Frederick Town to Swearingen's Ferry and near to John Foxes House on the West side of the South Mountain and running thence

Line No.	North South	Degrees East or West	Length
1	S	West 63	36 perches
2	S	East 18	40 perches
3	S	East 77	58 perches
4	S	East 48	20 perches
5	N	East 60	80 perches
6	N		25 perches

7 then with a straight line to the beginning tree Containing and now laid out for fifty acres of Land to be held of Conegocheigue Manor Surveyed the 27th of February 1764.

John Murdock

June 5th 1765 Examined & Passed}

U. Scott Exr.}

On the back of the aforegoing Certificate was the following Receipt VIZ I have received two pounds one shilling for the within improvement & eleven Shillings & two pence for rents to Mich? 1769 Patent may therefore issue with his Excly approbation June 12th 1769 Danl of St. Thos. Jenifer

Approved Robt. Eden

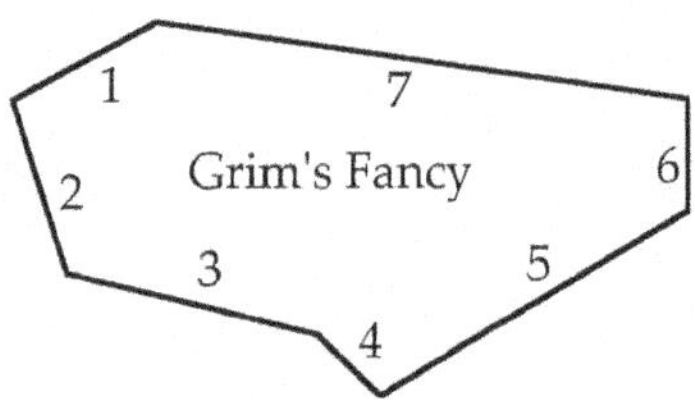

News from Fox's Gap

The Society of the Descendants of Frederick Fox of Fox's Gap in Maryland

Issue 6, Volume 2 **Remember Freedom!** December 1, 2003

The North Carolina South Mountain Monument at Fox's Gap in Maryland

REMEMBERING THE BATTLE OF SOUTH MOUNTAIN

Volunteers begin work on Maryland monument

Sculpture of dying soldier to honor 1,500 from N.C. who fought

---

By Mark Price
Staff Writer
Charlotte Observer

Rex Hovey of Charlotte spent seven years trying to convince Carolinians that they should remember the 1862 Battle of South Mountain, which marked the South's first attack on Northern territory.

He had an idea that someone should erect a grand monument near Boonsboro, Md., honoring the 1,500 North Carolinians who fought there, nearly a third of whom died.

It was an idea the media and politicians largely ignored, but average people listened.

As a result, Hovey and 15 volunteers have been in Boonsboro this week, clearing a spot for a $60,000 monument that was conceived and commissioned with small donations from average people.

"I had to see this thing through or else my reputation in North Carolina would be ruined," says Hovey, 53, who is backed by the Living History Association of Mecklenburg, a Civil War re-enactors group.

"People trusted me: Hundreds who didn't know me from Adam would walk up and give me $20 or $30. Years passed and still there was no monument, but they kept believing I would deliver."

What the believers are getting is a 10-foot-high, 6-foot-long combination of bronze and granite, topped by a life-size sculpture of a dying soldier. It was created by Virginia-based sculptor Gary Casteel, who is also chief designer of the $8 million National Civil War Memorial planned for 2015, the 150th anniversary of the war's end.

The sculpture on the South Mountain monument tells a true story, one involving a flag bearer from the Carolinas who saved his surrounded regiment by jumping on a garden wall and waving his flag. While Union soldiers focused their guns on him, 75 percent of his regiment (most of whom were Carolinians) escaped.

Maryland officials are allowing Hovey to place the monument beside what remains of that garden wall.

"When the viewer looks at the piece, hopefully they'll understand what these soldiers went through," says Casteel. "It was a life-and-death struggle, and they meant to fulfill their obligation."

Ten thousand Confederate troops took on 25,000 Union soldiers at South Mountain on Sept. 14, 1862. an estimated 5,200 soldiers were killed, wounded or turned up missing, including 450 dead from North Carolina.

Want to Donate?

The Living History Association of Mecklenburg County still needs help. To donate, make out a tax-deductible check to The Living History Association of Mecklenburg Inc. and mail to: 9225 Surrey Road, Charlotte, NC 28227.

The battle has been largely overlooked because it occurred within days of Antietam - the bloodiest one-day battle in the Civil War - where the dead, wounded and missing totaled 23,000.

Hovey first visited the area in 1995 and was surprised that locals had trouble giving him directions to the battlefield, claiming they'd never heard of it. When he finally located it on his own, the once open field was thick with brush, poison ivy and diseased pines.

Maryland has since voted to make the South Mountain area its first official state battlefield.

It's a 40-foot-by-40-foot section of the mountain that Hovey and volunteers have been clearing this week, while taking care not to disrupt soil that they saw as hallowed ground.

The work includes cutting a road to bring in the monument's granite base and, in coming weeks, the monument itself. Once it is installed, the road will be removed and a trail will take visitors to the site, 50 yards from the Appalachian Trial.

An estimate $10,000 in donations are still needed, both for installation and to establish a perpetual care fund, Hovey says.

The Living History Association of Mecklenburg plans to have the official unveiling in October. And if doesn't expect the event to become a political issue, since it's a memorial on a battlefield, rather than a courthouse lawn.

"We'd like to get one of the governors there, either from North Carolina or from Maryland," Hovey says, "so we're trying to be flexible on the day."

If neither shows, it won't hold things up.

After seven years, Hovey has learned on whom he can depend.

The North Carolina South Mountain Monument was installed officially on Saturday, October 18, 2003, at Fox's Gap in Maryland. The monument's location is not far from the Reno Monument at Fox's Gap. U. S. Major General Jesse Reno was killed late in the day during the Battle of South Mountain, on Sunday, September 14, 1862. The Reno Monument was erected over one hundred years ago at Fox's Gap. A 17th Michigan marker is across the road from the Reno Monument. Also installed at Fox's Gap a few years ago was a tombstone dedicated to General Samuel Garland, a Confederate General who was killed at Fox's Gap early in the Battle of South Mountain.

The North Carolina South Mountain Monument at Fox's Gap

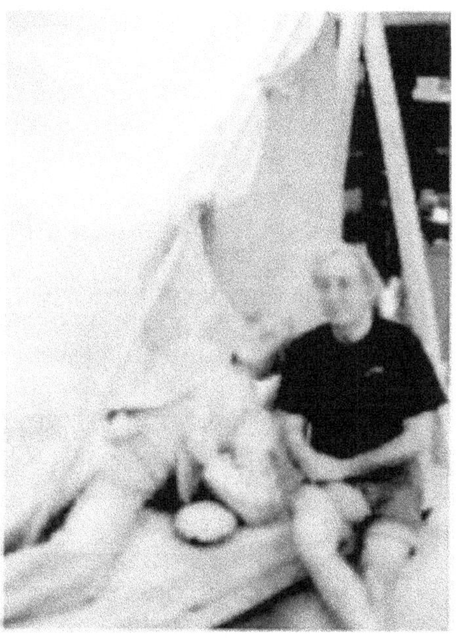

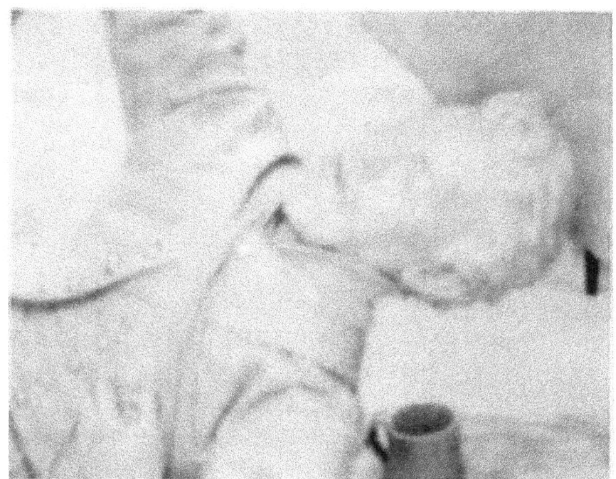

above - close-up of soldier on monument
left - Gary Casteel, sculptor
below - replica of completed monument

Above are photographs of the North Carolina South Mountain Monument under construction and a photograph of a replica of the completed monument.

Documentation

Original Sources related to the Genealogy of Frederick Fox of Fox's Gap in Maryland and his Descendants

By Curtis Lynn Older

The purpose of this article is not only to review the documentary evidence available to prove my own ancestry as it relates to Frederick Fox of Fox's Gap in Maryland, but to review and identify sufficient evidence that is available for others who claim to be a descendant of Frederick Fox. An additional purpose is to identify or clarify to some extent the standards of genealogical proof necessary to satisfy one's self, as well as genealogy-based organizations to which they might apply for membership, that they satisfactorily connected one generation to the next in their chain of ancestors or their family tree.

Genealogy-based organizations, such as the Daughters or Sons of the American Revolution or The Society of Mayflower Descendants, have placed emphasis in recent years on conducting a complete review or reanalysis of the genealogical evidence to support new applications for membership in their organizations. Those individuals who seek membership today in genealogy-based organizations cannot rely solely on listing citations on their application form that were given by others who were successful in the past in gaining admission to an organization.

The focus of many genealogy-based organizations today is upon requiring **Original** material, or **Primary Source** material as some choose to call it, to support the membership application process. Material or sources that were used to gain admission to an organization by successful applicants in the past may not pass muster under today's requirements.

With the above in mind, I thought it would be worthwhile to present Original material as it relates to Frederick Fox and his descendants. I also will present material that will provide the reader with a review some of the most important concepts related to genealogy. I will present and identify for the reader the Original material that I have found to prove my own descent from Frederick Fox. This material should be useful to others who are seeking Original or Primary materials to document or prove to themselves or to others, such as genealogy-based organizations, their descent from Frederick Fox of Fox's Gap in Maryland.

Family genealogy is today one of the most popular avocations on which Americans spend their time. A recent article that I read indicated that perhaps as many as 80 million Americans are working to some degree on developing their family genealogy.

Regardless of our degree of confidence in the evidence we collect along the way to arriving at a genealogical conclusion, we should keep in mind the last point which is made in the following list of Guidelines for Analyzing Evidence. **The case is never closed on a genealogical conclusion.**

[The following material was taken from, ***Evidence! Creation & Analysis for the Family Historian,*** Elizabeth Shown Mills, Genealogical Publishing Co., Inc., Baltimore, MD, 1997.]

Original material, as defined by the purist, is based on firsthand knowledge--be it oral or written. It is the testimony of a person relating events that he or she personally experienced or witnessed. It is an original document created by a party with firsthand knowledge of the information being recorded.

Derivative material is all else. Its weight can span the entire spectrum of reliability--depending upon the form that it takes, the circumstances of its creation, and the skill and reliability of its creator. A debatable hierarchy for appraising derivative material might be: 1) duplicates, 2) transcripts, 3) edited transcripts, 4) abstracts, 5) extracts, 6) compendiums, 7) histories, genealogies, and expository essays, and 8) traditions.

Guidelines for Analyzing Evidence

1) Direct evidence is easier to understand, but indirect evidence can carry equal weight.
2) Reliable genealogical conclusions are based on the weight--not quantity--of evidence found.
3) Evidence should be drawn from a variety of independently created sources.
4) Original source material generally is more reliable than derivative material.
5) The reliability of a derivative work is influenced by the degree of processing it has undergone.
6) The purpose of a record and the motivation of its creators frequently affect its truthfulness.
7) The most reliable informants have firsthand knowledge of the events to which they testify.
8) The veracity and skill of a record's creator will have shaped its content.
9) Timeliness generally adds to a document's credibility.
10) Penmanship can establish identity, date, and authenticity.
11) A record's custodial history affects its trustworthiness.
12) All known records should be used and a thorough effort made to identify unknown materials.
13) **The case is never closed on a genealogical conclusion.**

The remainder of this article will present Original material that I collected over a number of years which I use as evidence to document my ancestors back to John Fox of Fox's Gap in Maryland. Also provided for each ancestor in my Fox line is a list of all the material, both Original and Derivative, that I collected over the years of which I am aware that I used to evaluate my family tree related to my Fox ancestors and that I may have used to gain admission to a genealogy-based organization. Perhaps you will agree or disagree with the category under which I place an item, as either Original or Derivative. Please send me any comments you might have in the form of letters or e-mails, as I would be happy to discuss them with you.

Documentation for John Fox of Fox's Gap in Maryland

will of John Fox

Book A Liber 102, will of John Fox, January 17, 1784
Washington County, Maryland (probated December 4, 1784)

In the name of God Amen I John Fox of Sharpsburg Washington County and State of Maryland being very sick and weak in body but of perfect mind and memory thanks be given to God calling to mind the mortality of my body and knowing that it is appointed for all men once to die do make and ordain this my last Will and Testament, that is to say principally & first of all I give and Recommend my Soul unto the Earth to be buried in decent Christian burial at the discretion of my Executors nothing doubting but at the General Resurrection I shall receive the same again by the Almighty power of God. And as touching such worldly Estate as it has pleased God to bless me with in this life. I give devise and dispose of the same in the following manner and form.

First I give and bequeath unto my beloved Wife Christina all that I do possess of during her Natural life

and at her Death it is well that my Son Frederick shall have the Clock and one half of the skin-dressing tools used.

My son Michael is to have the Young Mare with the Other half of the Aforesaid tools and also my Wearing Apparel Except my fine fur hat which I leave to Frederick,

and the remaining and Residue of my Estate I leave and bequeath unto my Children and Grand Children viz. as follows,

Frederick, Magdelin & Michael is to have three fourth of it divided Equally amongst them

and the remaining fourth part I give and Bequeath unto my live Grand Children, Elizabeth & Catherine Furtnay (?Fortney?),

and also I leave and bequeath unto my Oldest Son Daniel and my Daughter Rachel five shillings each to be paid when demanded

And also I Constitute and appoint my Wife Christina and my Son Frederick to be the Executors of this my last Will and Testament

and I do hereby utterly disallow revoke and dis(?) all and every Other Testaments Wills Legacies bequests and Executors by me in any wise before named Willed and bequeathed Ratifying and Confirming this and no other to be my last Will and Testament

In Witness whereof I have hereunto set my hand and seal this 17 day of January in the Year of our Lord Seventeen Hundred & Eighty Four.

Signed Sealed published & delivered before the Said John Fox as his last Will and Testament in the presence of us who in his presence and in the presence of each other have hereto subscribed our names

John X Fox (seal)
his mark

Peter Dick Mathias Coons Christopher Cruse

The following is a list of Original and Derivative material related to John Fox of Fox's Gap in Maryland collected by me. You may agree or disagree with the classification under which I list each item. I hope the reader will review the list and evaluate the genealogical evidence presented to connect one generation to the next, from John Fox to Frederick Fox to George Fox to John L. Fox.

Original Material Related to John Fox of Fox's Gap in Maryland

1. Will of John Fox, Book A Liber 102, Washington County, Maryland. Jan. 17, 1784.

This document lists his wife: Christina; his children: Frederick, Magdelin, Michael, Daniel, and Rachel; his grandchildren: Elizabeth and Catherine Furtnay (?Fortney?); and names his wife Christina and his son Frederick as the Executors. Frederick, Magdelin, and Michael were to receive three-fourths of the residue of the estate and two grandchildren, Elizabeth and Catherine Furtnay (?Fortney?), were to receive one-four of the residue of the estate. His oldest son Daniel and daughter Rachel were to receive five shillings each.

2. Frederick County, Maryland, The Account of Joseph and Jennett Chapline Executors of Moses Chapline late of Frederick County Deceased, bearing a date of June 19, 1766. This court record lists John Fox as among those owed money by the estate of Moses Chapline.

3. John Fox's house is identified in Maryland land records. The following record places John Fox's house at or very near to Fox's Gap in Maryland. Maryland Archives - Grim's Fancy, BC & GS 40, p. 114, Alexander Trim's (Grim's) certificate of survey, examined and passed 5 June 1765, [MdHR 17, 451, 1-23-4-5]. This land record states in part, "on the North Side of the Main Road that leads from Frederick Town to Swearingen's Ferry and near to John Foxes House."

4. Washington County Land Records, K-703, K-1231, J-1400, K-1278, and K-1279 in the years 1766 to 1769.

5. I. Daniel Rupp, *Thirty-Thousand Names of Immigrants* (Baltimore: Genealogical Publishing Co., 1971), 280-1. Johan Frederich Fuchs and his wife Christiana arrived at the port of Philadelphia on the ship Anderson, Captain Hugh Campbell, September 27, 1752.

6. R. B. Strassburger and W. J. Hinke, *Pennsylvania German Pioneers, Lists of Arrivals* (Norristown, Pa.: Pennsylvania German Society, 1934), 488-9. John Fox appeared in the state house in Philadelphia the day of his arrival and "took and subscribed the usual Qualifications."

John Fox Land Records in Frederick County, Maryland

Ref No.	Date	From or To	Other party	Name of Tract/Item
J-504	June 2, 1764	From	Daniel Dulany	Lot #269, Frederick Town*
K-499	May 22, 1766	To	Elias Bruner	Lot #269, Frederick Town*
K-703	Aug. 23, 1766	From	Joseph Chapline	Lot #143, Sharpsburg
K-1231	May 12, 1767	From	Joseph Chapline	Lot #16, Sharpsburg
J-1400	Aug. 18, 1767	From	John Burroughs	Judgment*
K-1278	June 2, 1769	From	Henry Joel	Lot #7, Sharpsburg
K-1279	June 2, 1769	From	Henry Joel	1/2 Lot #6, Sharpsburg

* It is the author's opinion Lot #269 was bought and sold by a John Fox other than the father of Frederick Fox. It is not known which John Fox was the one in the Judgment record. In the author's opinion John Fox, the father of Frederick Fox, owned all of the Sharpsburg lots listed above.

Derivative Material Related to John Fox of Fox's Gap in Maryland

1. Daniel Gebhart Fox, *The Fox Genealogy including the Met herd, Benner and Loiter Descendants.* (n.p., 1914).

2. Older, Curtis L., *The Braddock Expedition and Fox's Gap in Maryland.* Westminster, Md: Family Line Publications, 1995.

3. Older, Curtis L., *The Land Tracts of the Battlefield of South Mountain*, Westminster, Md: Willow Bend Books, 1999.

4. Letter from Jacob Reel to Michael and Frederick Fox, dated at Sharpsburg, Aug. 9, 1812, from a copy obtained from Robert H. Fox of Cincinnati, Ohio. "The following letter received and forwarded from Lebanon, Warren County, Ohio, Sept. 8, 1812, addressed to Msrs. Fredric(k) & Michael Fox, Franklin Township, Warren Co. Ohio".

Documentation for Frederick Fox of Fox's Gap in Maryland

will of Frederick Fox

Montgomery County, Ohio, Will Book C, case #1444

In the name of God, Amen, I Frederick Fox of the County of Montgomery and State of Ohio, being far advanced in years but of sound mind and memory considering the certainty of death and the uncertainty of this mortal life, and as it hath pleased God to bless me with some worldly estate, and to be better prepared to leave this world, whenever it may please God to call me hence, do make and publish this to be my last will and testament, in manner following that is to say:

First, I give and devise unto my son Joseph Fox the use and occupancy of the south west quarter of Section No. twenty two, of Township two in Range five, of the land between the Miami rivers, to my said son Joseph Fox, to have and to hold the aforesaid quarter section, except twenty five acres including a certain lease given to Mathias Wolff for payment of the said twenty five acres, to my said son Joseph to have and to hold the aforesaid quarter section except as aforesaid excepted to him and his wife Elizabeth now living during the life of my said son Joseph and his said wife Elizabeth provided that my said son is not to commit any waste by selling or destroying any timber on the aforesaid premises more than for the use & benefit of said premises on forfeiture of the aforesaid devise.

2nd I give and devise unto my grand son Frederick Fox and son of the aforesaid Joseph Fox twenty five acres of land, to be laid off by said Executors herein after named to my (?) in said twenty five acres the lease given Mathias Wolff in the greater section aforesaid to him my said grand son Frederick Fox and heirs and assigns to have and to hold the aforesaid 25 acres for ever

3rd After the death of my said son Joseph Fox and his wife Elizabeth, I give and devise the aforesaid quarter section except as above excepted to my grand children one son and seven daughters share and share equal alike all children of my son Joseph Fox.

4. It is my will and wish that after my death that my executor herein after named will make sale of the north west quarter of section fifteen of Township Two in Range five of the lands between the Miami Rivers, wherein I formerly lived and also to make sale of my house and lot in the town of Franklin in Warren County to the best advantage and the monies arising from the sale of the said premises to be equally divided between my lawful heirs share and share alike that is to say my son George and Daniel B. Fox and my four daughters to wit: Christena Metherd, Meahany Benner, Rosannah Hogee living in Virginia near Shanodore River, and my daughter Elizabeth Lighterd and to my son Joseph Fox an equal share with all the rest of my aforesaid children to be paid to my son Joseph by my Executor herein named as he thinks the said Joseph stands in need of money at any time or times-

5. I give and bequeath to my daughter Rosannah Hoge's four children that she had by her first husband that is to say one son and three daughters receive of my estate to the amount of the balance of my daughter Rosannah legacy ??? the amount of my daughter Rosannah shall be equal with all ??? ?? ?? as aforesaid-

And lastly I do hereby nominate & appoint my son Daniel B. Fox to this my last will and testament ??? Sole and Sole Executor revoking and ?? Annulling all former wills by me heretofore made allowing this and none other to be my last will and testament. In Witness whereof I the said Frederick Fox have hereunto set my hand and seal this tenth day of December in the year of our Lord One thousand eight hundred and thirty three

Frederick Fox (Seal)

Signed, sealed and declared by the testator Frederick Fox to this will to be his last will and testament who called on us who have subscribed our names to witness the same,

John Liter
Frederick Liter
James Russell

will of Frederick Fox continued -

The State of Ohio
Montgomery County (?) Court of Common pleas, March Term 1837.

Personally appeared in open Court John Liter, and Frederick Liter, who being duly sworn depose and say that the paper now before them purporting to be the last will and testament of Frederick Fox now deceased, was by the said Frederick Fox acknowledged, published and declared by him to be his last will and testament in the presence of these deponents, that the said deceased was of lawful age, that he was of sound and disposing mind and memory, and under no restraint as they verily believe that they subscribed the same as witnesses in the presence and at the request of the testator and in the presence of each other,
John Liter
Frederick Liter
Sworn and subscribed this 20 day of March 1837 in Open Circuit
Edward (?) Daniel Clerk
The State of Ohio Montgomery Circuit Ct.

Original Material Related to Frederick Fox of Fox's Gap in Maryland

1. Will of Frederick Fox - Will Book C, case #1444, Montgomery County, Ohio, December 10, 1833.

2. Catharine, the wife of Frederick Fox, was buried November 4, 1800. Frederick S. Weiser, ed., *Maryland German Church Records* Vol. 2, Zion Lutheran Church 1781-1826 (Manchester, Md.: Noodle-Doosey Press, 1987), 77. The Death Register of Zion Lutheran Church indicates "Catarin, wife of Friedrich Fuchs, bur. 4 Nov. 1800. Heb. 4:9."

3. 1790 Maryland federal census, Frederick County, Unknown Township, Page 66, Roll M637_3, Image 0491. Frederick Fox appears in the first census of the United States in 1790.

4. 1800 Maryland federal census, Frederick County, District No. 3, Page 123, Roll M32_10, Image 124. Frederick Fox is in the Maryland census for the last time.

5. 1809 Ohio state census, Warren County, Franklin Township, page 13.

6. 1810 Ohio federal census, Warren County, Franklin Township, page 28.

7. 1830 Ohio federal census, Warren County, Clear Creek township, Page 173, Roll M19_142, Image 340.

8. Tombstone of Frederick Fox at the Gebhart or St. John Cemetery, Miamisburg, Ohio.

9. Frederick Fox was an Elder in the Zion Lutheran Church, Middletown, Maryland. Weiser, Frederick S., *Zion Lutheran Church 1781-1826*, Maryland German Church Records 2:4.

10. Frederick Fox and Margaret Booker were the executors of the estate of Bartholomew Booker. See the will of Bartholomew Booker, Frederick County, Maryland, Register of Wills Records, GM-2-431, October 21, 1791.

12. Frederick Fox was a farmer. See Frederick County Land Records, WR-19-206, mortgage from Christian Benner to Frederick Fox, recorded April 11, 1799, Shaff's Purchase and Mount Sinai.

12. Frederick Fox signed the Patriot's Oath of Fidelity and support. See NGSQ Volume 6, #1, April 1917, Unpublished Revolutionary Records of Maryland, page 13, Patriot's Oaths of Fidelity and Support, 1778, Sharpsburgh Hundred. Washington County, MD, Patriot's Oath, March Court, 1778, Sharpsburgh Hundred, March 2, 1778, Christopher Cruss's Returns.

13. Frederick Fox served for a period in the Maryland Militia. See S. Eugene Clements and F. Edward Wright, The Maryland Militia in the Revolutionary War (Silver Spring, Md.: Family Line Publications, 1987), 241. Maryland Historical Society Records for Washington County, Militia Lists of Daughters of Founders and Patriots.

14. Daughters Mary and Elizabeth Fox are mentioned in the will of Margaret Booker. See Frederick County, MD, Register of Wills Records, GM-3-126, will of Margaret Book (Booker).

15. Frederick Fox served as a drummer in the Lieutenant Colonel's Company of the 10th Regiment, Pennsylvania Continental Line, American Revolution, from April 22, 1777, until January 1, 1781. National Archives, card numbers 37404176, 4837, 37188278, and 39144421; National Society of the Daughters of the American Revolution. 17th Report, Pierce's Register, #67913. Also see Pennsylvania Archives, Series 5, 3:487, 529, 533, and 572.

16. Maryland newspaper items related to Frederick Fox in Maryland. See Edward Wright, Western Maryland Newspaper Abstracts 1786-1798 (Silver Spring, Md.: Family Line Publications, 1985), 1:14.

Item101.FTMAug28 1792/MargareBookerFrederickFox,exec,to sellfarm,late the prop of Bartholomew Booker, decd, 304 a., on road from Fred Town to Williams Port, and Hager's Town, about 3 miles above Middletown/

Item 466. EAM Aug 31 1797/Frederick Fox to petition the Assembly to confirm his title to 2 lots in Village of Boonsberry, formerly deeded by William and George Boone to Michael Booch.

Item 485. EAM Jan 11 1798/Letters remaining at P.O. Hagerstown: Frederick Fox

17. *Ohio Wills and Estates to 1850: An Index,* by Carol Willsey Bell, published by Carol Willsey Bell, C.G., 4801 Mockingbird Court, South, Columbus, Ohio 43229.
Fox, Frederick - W-1837 MT wbC p46; c1444 (MT = Montgomery)
Fox, Frederick - W-1849 WR wbB p301 (WR = Warren)

18. Book B, page 38. Deed dated 1811. Jacob Long to Frederick Fox. Sec 18, T 2, R 5S. Signed Jacob Long. Witness: W. C. Schenck, #2 ? (german script) rec 1812. p 465.

19. Common Pleas (Probate) Docket Book C-1, Term of August 1816. Case 239. Will of Benjamin Richards. Exec: Massy Richards & Benjamin Richards. Witness: Charles Hardy, Frederick Fox. Appr: Nicholas Horner, James Petticrew, William Brown, p. 98.

20. An Index of Wills and Administrations In Montgomery County, Ohio, Book I, 1803-1893, Transcribed by Lindsay M. Brien from the Probate Records of Montgomery County, Volume I, Chronological Index, Miami Valley Records, Vol. 2, Pt. 1, Typed by W. P. A. Workers, Dayton, O., Dayton Public Library, 1940 [0 00 60 3716119 4].

Doc AI Page 7 Fox Frederick Will Book Cl Page 46, Jan. 10, 1837 to Sept. 10, 1851.

21. Marriage Record - See Ohio D.A.R. Soldiers Rosters, 2 vol., 1:146.

22. *Early Settlers of Montgomery County, Ohio, Genealogical Abstracts from Land Records, Tax Lists, and Biographical Sketches,* Compiled and Edited by Shirley Keller Mikesell, Heritage Books, Inc.

23. Common Pleas (Probate) Docket Book C-1. Term of August 1816. Case 239. Will of Benjamin Richards. Exec: Massy Richards & Benjamin Richards. Witness: Charles Hardy, Frederick Fox. Appr: Nicholas Horner, James Petticrew, William Brown. p. 98.

Frederick Fox Land Records in Frederick County, Maryland

Reference No.	Date	From or To	Other Party	Name of Tract
WR-7-213	Apr 4, 1787	From	Bartholomew Booker	I Hope It's Well Done
WR-10-643	May 2, 1792	From	Christian Kiser	Pick All
WR-12-367	Apr 23, 1794	To	Peter Hutzele	Fredericksburg
WR-13-488	Aug 21, 1795	From	William Widmeyer	I Hope It's Well Done
WR-17-158	Jul 24, 1798	To	George Methard	Fredericksburg
WR-18-206	Apr 11, 1799	From	Christian Benner	Shaaf's Purchase, Mt. Sinai
WR-22-477	Apr 17, 1802	To	Christian Benner	Shaaf's Purchase, Mt. Sinai
WR-23-286	Aug 9, 1802	From	Joseph Chapline	Exchange
WR-25-556	May 5, 1804	To	Conrad Miller	I Hope It's Well Done
WR-31-319	Aug 1, 1807	From	George Fox	Mt. Pleasant
WR-32-26	Oct 7, 1807	To	Joseph Sweringen	Fredericksburg
WR-32-28	Oct 7, 1807	To	John Ringer	I Hope It's Well Done, Pegging Awl, Turkey Foot, Mt. Pleasant

Reference No.	Date	From or To	Other Party	Name of Tract
WR-32-63	Oct 14, 1807	To	Henry Ascherman	I Hope It's Well Done, Shettle, Exchange, Pegging Awl, Turkey Foot, Peter's Neglect, Mt. Pleasant
Slave:				
WR-25-424	Mar 3, 1804	From	Abraham Boyer	Negro Woman Eleana

Frederick Fox Land Records in the Tracey Collection, Westminster, Maryland

Acreage	Date	Name of Tract
231 1/2 Ac	June 8, 1795	Friendship (unpatented certificate #228)
202 Acres	May 9, 1797	Addition to Friendship

Frederick Fox Land Records in Washington County, Maryland

Reference No.	Date	From or To	Other Party	Name of Tract
A-368-370	Nov 27, 1778	From	Jacob Soufrank	1/2 Lot #4, Sharpsburg
A-536-537	Apr 29, 1779	To	Philip Waggoner	Lot #55, Sharpsburg
C-510	1783	To	Adam Deats	1/2 Lot #4, Sharpsburg
D-579	1783	From	Jacob Nafe	Lot #5, Sharpsburg
G-441	1791	To	Jacob House	Lot #15, Sharpsburg
G-442	1791	To	Jacob House	Lot #6, Sharpsburg
G-443	1791	To	Jacob House	Lot #17, Sharpsburg
G-444	1791	To	Jacob House	Lot #123, Sharpsburg
G-445	1791	To	Jacob House	Lot #5, Sharpsburg
H-601	1794	From	Peter Conn	Lot #175, Sharpsburg
I-330	1795	From	William Widmyer	Bill of Sale
L-128	1798	To	Henry Shrader	Lot #177, JerusalemTown
W-285	1810	To	Peter Ham	(Out?) Lot #1, Sharpsburg

Frederick County, Maryland, Survey Records

Tract Name	Acreage	Ref. No.	Date	Survey Done For
Fredericksburg	75 Acres	HGO-1-564	Jul 6, 1792	Frederick Fox
Mt. Pleasant	23 Acres	HGO-1-534	Jan 10, 1791	Thomas Van Swearing
Peter's Neglect	37 Acres	THO-1-75	May 1, 1796	Adam Rowsann
Turkey Foot	6 Acres	HGO-1-267	Mar 13, 1788	Henry Cullman

Derivative Material Related to Frederick Fox of Fox's Gap in Maryland

1. *Early Settlers of Montgomery County, Ohio, Genealogical Abstracts from Land Records, Tax Lists, and Biographical Sketches*, Compiled and Edited by Shirley Keller Mikesell, Heritage Books, Inc.

2. Daniel Gebhart Fox, *The Fox Genealogy including the Metherd, Benner and Leiter Descendants.* (n.p., 1914).

3. Older, Curtis L., *The Braddock Expedition and Fox's Gap in Maryland.* Westminster, Md: Family Line Publications, 1995.

4. Older, Curtis L., *The Land Tracts of the Battlefield of South Mountain*, Westminster, Md: Willow Bend Books, 1999.

5. Fredrick Fox was born on the ocean while his parents were immigrating to America. *History of Vermillion County, Indiana*, Biographical Sketches: page 491 indicates, under the biography of John L. Fox, a grandson of Frederick Fox, "The father of our subject was a native of Maryland, and a son of Frederick Fox, who was born on the ocean while his parents were immigrating to America." This statement supports the record of John Frederick Fox who came to the Port of Philadelphia in 1751 as being the John Fox who was the father of Frederick Fox.

Documentation for George Fox, a son of Frederick Fox

The Estate Papers of George Fox - (in part)

Obtained through the Warren County Genealogical Society, 300 East Silver Street, Lebanon, Ohio 45036.

Elisabeth Fox and Adam Fox Adm of George Fox Decd In acpt with the widow and Heirs of said Estate.
Debtor
%? Amounts found remaining in the hands of said Admrs are final settlement at the October Term 1850
$ 2591.54 1/2

	Credits
Vouchers No. 1 to 7 inclusive Elisabeth Fox widow of said Decd	930.51
Vouchers No. 8 to 12 inclusive Adam Fox	184.63
Vouchers No. 13 to 17 inclusive Frederick L. Fox	184.63
Vouchers Nos. 18 to 22 inclusive Daniel L. Fox	184.63
Vouchers Nos. 23 to 28 inclusive George L. Fox	184.63
Vouchers Nos. 29 to 33 inclusive John L. Fox	184.63
Vouchers Nos. 34 to 38 inclusive Alexander Fox	184.63
Vouchers Nos. 39 to 42 inclusive Elisabeth L. Fox	184.63
Vouchers Nos. 43 to 46 inclusive Mary L. Fox (now deceased)	184.00
Vouchers No. 47 John Fox guardian of Elisabeth Ann & David M. Fox	184.63

State of Ohio Warren County

Personally appeared in open court Adam Fox one of the administrators of George Fox Decd and was duly sworn according to law deposeth and saith that the foregoing accounts & vouchers therein referred to is last & correct to best of his knowledge & belief and he further saith that after they had paid out to each of the heirs at law (except the two minors entitled to one share) that Mary L. Fox died intestate and without issue and then the small balance remaining in the hands of the Adms was divided among the remaining heirs & saith he saith not
Sworn to & subscribed in
open court this 23rd Nov 1850} Adam Fox
A W Stokes Clk

Received of Elisabeth Fox and Adam Fox administrators of the Estate of George Fox decd the sum of fifty dollars, part of the above - named Estate
January 4th 1848 Susannah Fox for John L Fox (signed)

June 23rd 1849.

Received of Adam Fox one of the administrators of the Estate of George Fox Decd, the sum of fifty dollars part of the above named Estate due the widow.
Elisabeth Fox (signed)

Received of Elisabeth Fox and Adam Fox administrators of the Estate of George Fox Decd the sum of one hundred and eighty four dollars & sixty-three cents it being paid as the distributive share of Elisabeth Ann, & David, M. Fox minor heirs of Catharine L. Fox Decd and heirs at Law of said George Fox Decd. Also nine dollars and fifteen cents interest received thereon.
Nov 11th 1850

John Fox (signed)
Guardian of Elisabeth
Ann & David M. Fox

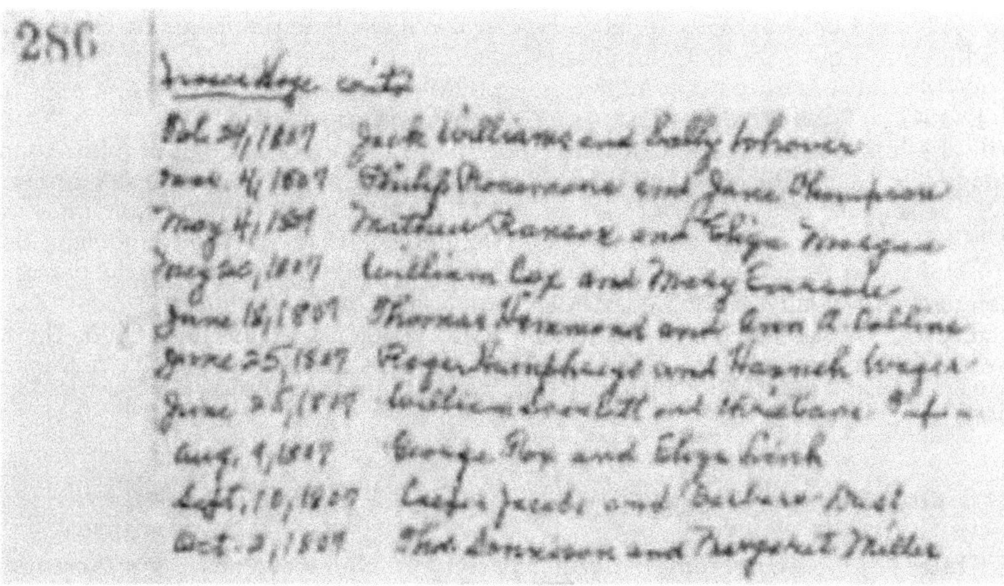
286

Marriage Record for George Fox and Elizabeth Link

Original Material Related to George Fox of Maryland and Ohio

1. Marriage record for George Fox and Elizabeth Ann Link. Jefferson County, West Virginia, Marriage Records, 1807, page 286.

2. Ohio state census, 1809, Warren County, Franklin Township, page 13.

3. Ohio federal census, 1810, Warren County, Franklin Township, page 28.

4. 1830 Ohio federal census,

5. 1840 Ohio federal census,

6. 1847 and 1848 tax bills of George Fox.

7. Newspaper notice concerning the estate of George Fox published in the *Sober Second Thought*, a newspaper of general circulation in Warren County, Ohio, by Adam Fox, one of the administrators for George Fox deceased. The notice was published for three consecutive weeks beginning on August 27, 1847.

8. Estate Papers of George Fox, Warren County Genealogical Society, Lebanon, Ohio.

The estate papers of George Fox mention the following individuals:

a. Elizabeth Fox, widow of the deceased
b. Adam Fox
c. Frederick L. Fox
d. Daniel L. Fox
e. George L. Fox
f. John L. Fox
g. Alexander Fox
h. Elizabeth L. Fox
i. Mary L. Fox
j. John Fox, guardian of Elizabeth Ann & David M. Fox
k. Susannah Fox for John L. Fox
l. Elizabeth Ann & David M. Fox, minor heirs of Catharine L. Fox
m. John Fox
n. Mary L. Fox

9. *Ohio Wills and Estates to 1850: An Index,* by Carol Willsey Bell, published by Carol Willsey Bell, C.G., 4801 Mockingbird Court, South, Columbus, Ohio 43229.
Fox, George - W-1845 HM wb1 p393; cA2535 (HM = Hamilton)
Fox, George - E -1847 WR wbB p80; bx31 (WR = Warren)

10. Will of John Adam Link II includes his daughter, Elizabeth Fox. Will of John Adam Link II. Will Book 8, pages 88, 89, and 90, Jefferson County Court House, Charles Town, West Virginia

11. Frederick S. Weiser, ed., *Zion Lutheran Church 1781-1826,* Maryland German Church Records Vol. 2, (Manchester, Md.: Noodle-Doosey Press, 1987), 25. "Samuel, son of Jacob and Magdelena Benner was born April 14, 1801. Baptized June 21, 1801. Sponsored by George Fox, a single person." (Mary) Magdelena Benner was the daughter of Frederick Fox and a sister of George Fox.

12. Tombstone for George Fox. Gebhart or St. John Cemetery, Miamisburg, Ohio. The tombstone of George Fox states, "Born March 10, 1781: In the State of Md. Died June 14, 1847". A tombstone next to the George Fox tombstone indicates, "Elizabeth wife of George Fox died March 9, 1872 aged 88 Yrs. 1 Mo. & 11 Ds".

George Fox Land Records in Frederick County, Maryland*

Ref. No.	Date	To or From	Other Party	Name of Tract	Acreage
WR-31-319	Aug 1, 1807	To	Frederick Fox	Mt. Pleasant	13
WR-32-30	Oct 7, 1807	To	John Ringer	Exchange, Bubble, Deefer Snay	100

*There are numerous George Fox Land Records in Frederick County, MD. Only those in the opinion of the author that were related to George Fox, a son of Frederick Fox, are included.

Derivative Material Related to George Fox of Maryland and Ohio

1. Daniel Gebhart Fox, *The Fox Genealogy including the Metherd, Benner and Leiter Descendants.* (n.p., 1914).
2. Older, Curtis L., *The Braddock Expedition and Fox's Gap in Maryland,* Westminster, Md: Family Line Publications, 1995.
3. Older, Curtis L., *The Land Tracts of the Battlefield of South Mountain,* Westminster, Md: Willow Bend Books, 1999.

The Fox Society Website is UP!

Enter the following on your Internet Explorer address bar:

http://homepage.mac.com/clo7956/

You can download various Fox Society Related Items in Adobe Acrobat Reader PDF format. Dial-up Internet may be slow to download. You can select and copy text from these Adobe Acrobat Reader PDF files or print entire documents. Problems? Send an e-mail to: curtolder@earthlink.net

You will need Version 5.0 of Adobe Acrobat Reader.
You may download the Reader for FREE at: www.adobe.com

Documentation for John L. Fox, a son of George Fox

will of John L. Fox

Will Record of John L. Fox, at Vermillion County, Indiana, Court House, Newport, page 520

John L. Fox
Vermillion County, Indiana
Court House, Newport

520 John L. Fox

WILL RECORD

In the name of God, Amen:
I John L. Fox of the County of Vermillion and State of Indiana being weak in body and of sound mind, memory and understanding but considering the uncertainly of this transitory life, do make and publish this my last Will and Testament in manner and form following, to wit:
First, - It is my Will and I do order that all my just debts and Funeral expenses be duly paid and satisfied as soon as conveniently can be after my decease,
Second, -
Item, - I give unto my Daughter Margaret Ricketts ($5.00) Dollars.
Item, - I give unto my son John A. Fox Five ($5.00) Dollars.
Item, - The balance of my Estate shall be equally divided between my Daughters Anna E. Goff, Mary Burnett and Daniel A. Fox.
The said Margaret Ricketts and John A. Fox have already received more of my estate than their shares.
And, lastly, I nominate, constitute and appoint W. H. Goff of Gessie, Ind. To be the Executor of this, my Will, hereby revoking all other Wills, legacies and bequests by me heretofore made, and declaring this, and no other, to be my last will and testament.
In Witness Whereof I have hereunto set my hand and seal this 8th day April, in the year 1898.

John L. Fox (seal)
Signed, sealed, published, and declared by the said John L. Fox as and for his last Will and Testament, in the presence of us who at his request and in his presence and in the presence of each other, have subscribed our names as witnesses thereto.

Alexander Swisher (seal)
Jacob B. Swisher (seal)

State of Indiana, Vermillion County, SS:

Before me, John T. Lowe Clerk of the Vermillion Circuit Court, personally came Jacob B. Swisher one of the subscribing witnesses to the foregoing last Will and Testament of John L. Fox late of Vermillion County, Indiana, deceased, and being duly sworn on oath says that he was present at the execution of said last will: that the same was duly executed: that said testator requested said Jacob B. Swisher and Alexander Swisher to sign said will as Witnesses thereto, which they accordingly did in the presence of said testator, and in the presence of each other as subscribing witnesses thereto.

Jacob B. Swisher
Subscribed and sworn to before me this 28th day of January 1899,

John T. Lowe clerk

521

State of Indiana} SS:
Vermillion County}

I John T. Lowe Clerk of the Vermillion Circuit Court do hereby certify that the above and foregoing last will and testament of John L Fox late of Vermillion County State of Indiana deceased was this day duly admitted to probate and record and the proof thereof duly made by Jacob B. Swisher one of subscribing witnesses thereto which said Will together with such proof have been duly recorded in Record of Will Lo 3 Page 520 in this office

Witness my name and the seal of said Court this 28th day of Jany 1899
John T. Lowe Clerk

Original Material related to John L. Fox of Ohio and Indiana

1. Will record of John L. Fox, at Vermillion County, Indiana, Court House, Newport, page 520.
2. Vermillion County, Indiana, Highland Township, land record for John L. Fox.

Joseph Howard & wife to John L. Fox Warranty Deed By this deed Joseph Howard and his ___ Susan Howard of Vermillion County in the State of Indiana Convey & warrant to John L. Fox of Vermillion County in the State of Indiana for the sum of six thousand five hundred and sixty dollars the receipt whereof is hereby acknowledged the following real estate in Vermillion County in the State of Indiana to wit: The North west fractional quarter of section eighteen in Township Nineteen north of Range nine west, containing one hundred and fifty nine and 60/100 acres more or less - also the west fraction of the south west fractional quarter of section seven, in Township nineteen, north of Range nine west, containing eighty and 12/100 acres more or less _ _ also one acre being two rods wide off the south end of the east half of the northwest quarter of section seven in Township nineteen north of range nine west, _ Also the west half of the north east quarter of section seven in township nineteen north of range nine west, except two acres in the south east corner thereof on which the widow Brown resides being sixteen rods wide from south to north and twenty rods from east to west leaving seventy seven acres more or less also ten acres off the south end of the west half of the south east quarter of section six in Township nineteen north of range nine west, in a three hundred and twenty eight and 32/100 acres more or less, actual possession of said premises being hereby given to the said John L. Fox March 10, 18?? In witness whereof the said Joseph Howard and Susan Howard, have hereunto set their hands and seals this seventh day of April 1858
Joseph Howard (seal)
Susan Howard (seal)
State of Indiana
Vermillion County
Before me George H McNeil a notary public in and for said county came Joseph Howard and Susan Howard to me personally known and acknowledged the execution of the foregoing deed. Witness my hand and notarial seal this seventh day of April AD 1858 George H. McNeil Notary Public Recorded July 5th 1858 W B Florer Recorder

2. 1860 Indiana Federal Census, Vermillion County, Highland Township:
Family #0076, Dwelling #0076 census line 09a, page 0064

John L. Fox, age 41, white, born in Ohio, farmer, real property = $6,560, personal property = $1,500, head of household = y; literate = y
Susannah Fox, age 40, white, born in Ohio, literate = y
Mary S. Fox, age 10, female, white, born in Ohio, literate = y;
Ann E. Fox, age 12, female, white, born in Ohio, literate = y
Catharine F. Fox, female, age 8, white, born in Ohio, literate = y
Margaret P. Fox, female, age 6, white, born in Ohio, literate = y
John A. Fox, male, 3, white, born in Ohio, literate = y
Daniel A. Fox, male, age 5 months, white, born in Indiana, literate = y

Original Material **related to John L. Fox continued -**

3. Tombstones of John L. Fox and his wife, Susannah Hilligass, at Hopewell Cemetery, Vermillion County, Indiana. Photographs of these tombstones appear on the Fox's Gap in Maryland Kodak Photo CD-rom disc at the Fredrick County Historical Society and the Maryland Historical Society.

Derivative Material Related to John L. Fox of Ohio and Indiana

1. Daniel Gebhart Fox, *The Fox Genealogy including the Metherd, Benner and Leiter Descendants.* (n.p., 1914).

Documentation for Daniel Alexander Fox, a son of John L. Fox

will of Daniel Alexander Fox

will record at Vermillion County, Indiana, Newport Court House, Record number 6, page 218

218

WILL OF

Daniel A Fox

I, Daniel A. Fox of Highland Township, in Vermillion County, State of Indiana, being of sound and disposing mind and memory, do hereby make ordain and publish this my last will and testament hereby revoking any and all other wills heretofore made by me.

Item I It is my will that all my just debts including funeral expenses and expenses of last sickness, or m? a first charge upon my estate, and be paid by my ? Executor out of the first-moneys coming into his hands.

Item II It is my will that all my real and personal property, shall as soon after my death as is practical be sold either at public or private sale as my executor shall deem most advisable and in the manner he believe in it will sell for the most money, and after the payments of my debts and funeral expenses as set out in Item I of this will the residue of the moneys left in the hands of my executor shall be divided share and share alike between my following named children, to-wit Ruby Hines, Ethel Gouty, Kenneth B. Fox and William E. Fox. In event that any or either of my above named children should die before the time they or either of them would inherit hereunder, then the share which would have gone to such child living shall go to his or her children in equal shares.

Item III I make no provision in this will for my son Ernest E. Fox, as I have heretofore paid out for him, as much or more than what I would deem to be his interest in my Estate and for that (?) I am giving him nothing by this will.

Item IV I do hereby nominate and appoint my ??? John W. Carithers?, Executor of this Will.

In testimony? ????, I Daniel A. Fox, have here unto set my hand and seal at Newport, Vermillion County Indiana, this 6th day of May 1927

Daniel A Fox

The above and foregoing instrument was signed by the said Daniel A Fox in our presence and declared by ?? to be his last will and testament and at his request and in his presence and in the presence of each other we now subscribed our names hereto as witnesses this 6th day of May - 1927

Edgar Prather

witnesses Geo D. Sunkel

will of Daniel Alexander Fox continued -

Proof of Will
State of Indiana
County of Vermillion

Edgar Prather personally appeared before the Clerk of Vermillion Circuit Court, and being duly sworn says that Daniel A Fox signed his name to the above writing of date of May 6 - 1927 as and for his last will and that the same was attested and subscribed by said offiant(?) and Geo D Sunkel as witnesses hereunto in the presence of said Testator and by his request and in the presence of each other that said Testator declared to same to be his last Will and that said Testator was not at the time of executing said will an infant or of unsound mind, or under coercion

Edgar Prather

Certificate of Probate
State of Indiana
County of Vermillion
Court I J N Jones, Clerk of the Vermillion Circuit Court Certified the within last Will of Daniel A Fox late of said County, deceased has been duly admitted to probate: that its due execution was this day proofed by Edgar Prather whose proofs together with such Will, have been duly recorded on page 218 of Record No 6 of Wills in my office

In witness whereof I have hereunto set my hand and affixed the seal of said Court this 1st Day of August 1932

J N Jones clerk (seal)

Original Material related to Daniel Alexander Fox of Indiana

1. Will record of Daniel Alexander Fox, at Vermillion County, Indiana, Court House, Newport, Record number 6, page 218.

2. The marriage license of Daniel Alexander Fox and Elizabeth Jane Ricketts is at the Fountain County Court House, Covington, Indiana, Book 8, #350. The marriage license gives a date of April 1, 1881.

3. A picture of Daniel Alexander Fox and Elizabeth Jane Ricketts on their wedding day in Danville, Illinois. The original photo is in the possession of Curtis Lynn Older. A copy of photograph is on Fox's Gap in Maryland Kodak Photo CD-rom disc at the Frederick County Historical Society and the Maryland Historical Society.

4. Census record: 1920 Indiana Federal Census, Highland Township.

5. Article entitled, *Daniel Alexander Fox and Elizabeth Jane Ricketts Fox* by Carmen Hines Abernathy, daughter of Ruby Dale Fox Hines. Ruby Dale Fox was a daughter of Daniel Alexander Fox. Carmen was a daughter of Everett and Ruby Dale Fox Hines and a granddaughter of Daniel Alexander Fox. The article appears in the December 1, 1996, News from Fox's Gap newsletter of The Society of the Descendants of Frederick Fox of Fox's Gap in Maryland.

Derivative Material Related to Daniel Alexander Fox of Indiana

1. Daniel Gebhart Fox, *The Fox Genealogy including the Metherd, Benner and Leiter Descendants.* (n.p., 1914).

Welcome New Members!

We are pleased to announce the following new members of our Society who joined after the June 1, 2003 newsletter was completed:

Name Address	Phone	Date of Membership	Membership Number
Larry Leo Bucholz	386-917-0401	May 15, 2003	0049

121 Bradwick Circle
DeBary,FL 32713
lbucholz@cfl.rr.com

Ancestor Line: George Fox, a son of Frederick Fox; John L. Fox, Daniel Alexander Fox, William Edward Fox, Elizabeth Jane Fox

Larry is a descendant of Frederick Fox of Fox's Gap in Maryland and his oldest son, George Fox, who married Elizabeth Ann Link.

William Ross Hendrickson	513-539-8084	July 15, 2003	0050

Box 360
Monroe,OH 45050
Glohen1@juno.com

Ancestor Line: Daniel Booker Fox, a son of Frederick Fox; Christiana Ann Fox, William P. Hendrickson, Huber E. Hendrickson

William is a descendant of Frederick Fox of Fox's Gap in Maryland and one of his sons, Daniel Booker Fox, who married Susannah Christman.

Mary Louise Githens	937-855-2304	September 22, 2003	0051

44 Moler Ave.
Germantown, OH 45327

Ancestor Line: Daniel Booker Fox, a son of Frederick Fox; Daniel C. Fox, Martin F. Fox, Howard Fox

Mary is a descendant of Frederick Fox of Fox's Gap in Maryland and one of his sons, Daniel Booker Fox, who married Susannah Christman.

The Fox Society Website is UP!

Enter the following on your Internet Explorer address bar:

http://homepage.mac.com/clo7956/

You can download various Fox Society Related Items in Adobe Acrobat Reader PDF format. Dial-up Internet may be slow to download. You can select and copy text from these Adobe Acrobat Reader PDF files or print entire documents. Problems? Send an e-mail to: curtolder@earthlink.net

You will need Version 5.0 of Adobe Acrobat Reader.
You may download the Reader for FREE at: www.adobe.com

President's Message
by Curtis Lynn Older

*
Please consider writing an article about your Fox family relatives for the newsletter. Publishing an article in the Fox newsletter is a good way to archive your family information.

*
Access the Fox Society website by entering the following in your Internet Explorer Address Bar: **http://homepage.mac.com/clo7956/**

You can download various Fox Society Related Items in Adobe Acrobat PDF format. You will need Version 5.0 of the Adobe Acrobat Reader that you may download for FREE at:

www.adobe.com

*
We now are over the 50-member milestone. A current membership roster in Adobe Acrobat 5.0 PDF format is posted on the Fox Society website. Please download the file from the website so that you can review the list of all those who have joined during the Fox Society's first eight years.

Table of Contents for this Newsletter

Page

News from Fox's Gap
Published June 1 and December 1 of each year by
The Society of the Descendants of Frederick Fox of Fox's Gap in Maryland
Membership dues are $6.00 per year. President of the Society is Curtis L. Older.
Make Society inquiries by the following means:

Curtis L. Older
618 Tryon Place
Gastonia, NC 28054-6066
e-mail: curtolder@earthlink.net
phone: 704-864-3879

News from Fox's Gap

The Society of the Descendants of Frederick Fox of Fox's Gap in Maryland

Issue 7, Volume 2 **Remember Freedom!** June 1, 2004

The Mysterious Confederate Color Bearer of Fox's Gap

by Steven R. Stotelmyer

(Steve Stotelmyer is the author of *The Bivouacs of the Dead, the story of those who died at Antietam and South Mountain.* Steve has done extensive research on Fox's Gap in Maryland. He helped form the Central Maryland Heritage League in 1989 and has been an active volunteer at the Antietam Battlefield.)

The purpose of this narrative is to set the record straight on an event related to the Battle of South Mountain. There exists a popular story concerning the color bearer of the Thirteenth North Carolina Infantry and his death at South Mountain during the late morning action at Fox's Gap. The Thirteenth North Carolina was one of the five regiments of General Samuel Garland's Brigade and it was involved in combat with the Kanawha Division of Ohio troops at Fox's Gap. As stated before, this combat climaxed in the late morning, near noon, in the vicinity of Wise's cabin at Fox's Gap.

It is also important to note that this was not the only combat in the vicinity of Wise's cabin that day. There was intense fighting in the afternoon in the area of Wise's cabin as well. This combat included the Confederate troops of General Thomas Drayton's Brigade and General Reno's IX Corps, which included the Kanawha Division. Both of these actions were part of the Battle of South Mountain on Sunday, September 14, 1862.

So popular, and accepted as fact, is the story of the color bearer of the Thirteenth North Carolina Infantry that a monument to North Carolina soldiers, installed at Fox's Gap in October 2003, bears the following inscription: "Driven back from the front, the enemy falling back through Wise's garden, were met by our line coming up from the rear in the flank, and a terrific fight ensued. The color bearer of a Confederate Regiment jumped up on the rear wall of the garden, and defiantly waving his flag refused the many calls to surrender which he received, was shot and fell inside the garden wall. Private Hoagland of my company jumped over the fence and secured the flag. Lt. Col. Coleman of the 11th, who was present and had called upon the man to surrender, ordered Hoagland to deliver the flag to him, and afterwards claimed credit for its capture. R. B. Wilson, 12th Ohio, Letter to Gen. E. A. Carmen, Antietam Board, July 22, 1899." On the surface this quote seems very reliable, an eyewitness account from a veteran of the battle. However, closer scrutiny will reveal some serious flaws with this text's inference that the color bearer was one of Samuel Garland's North Carolinians.**(1)**

Did the incident really happen as described on the monument, and if so, what historical evidence exists to support the story of a Confederate color bearer being killed at Fox's Gap? The answer seems to be yes, there was a Confederate color bearer killed at Fox's Gap. However, most of the source material for this incident comes from Union sources and none of them identify the Confederate regiment to which the unfortunate color bearer belonged.

The only Confederate source, to date, that mentions the loss of a color bearer during the morning combat is Colonel Duncan McRae's after action report, which references the loss of the Fifth North Carolina Infantry's Flag on the other end of the battlefield, more than 1,000 yards south of Fox's Gap. In his report, dated October 18, 1862, Colonel McRae writes, "Captain Garrett ordered his flag to be placed upon the Ridge Road, and was endeavoring to make a rally there, when his color bearer was shot down, and he was compelled to fall back farther down the hill." The Fifth North Carolina Infantry was located two thirds of a mile south of Fox's Gap during the battle of South Mountain. Clearly then McRae's report offers us no help in identifying our mysterious color bearer back at Fox's Gap.**(2)**

As stated before, it has been asserted in the popular account of the incident that the color bearer belonged to the Thirteenth North Carolina Infantry. And it is true that the Thirteenth North Carolina was in the area of Wise's cabin during the late morning combat. However, (as of this writing) I cannot substantiate the popular claim that the color bearer belonged the Thirteenth North Carolina Infantry. Colonel Thomas Ruffin, commander of the Thirteenth North Carolina, makes no mention of the incident in his after action report, in his postwar correspondence to General D. H. Hill, or in a letter to his father written shortly after the battle. As a matter of fact, it could just have easily been the color bearer of the Twelfth North Carolina Infantry, Second North Carolina Infantry, or the Fourth North Carolina Infantry, as these regiments were also involved in the late morning combat in the vicinity of the Wise cabin. None of the current source material regarding these regiments mentions the death of a color bearer.**(3)**

A close scrutiny of the source material available at this time will reveal quite a different story from the popular account.

The earliest telling of the incident is from Major Lyman J. Jackson's after action report for the Eleventh Ohio Regiment. At South Mountain Lieutenant Colonel Augustus H. Coleman commanded the Eleventh Ohio. However, Coleman was killed three days later at Antietam and consequently did not survive to write the after action report for the regiment. That duty fell to Major Jackson. From Jackson's report, dated September 20, 1862, we find, "The first Brigade made the advance up the hill. After our ascent to the open field on the left... we were ordered to skirmish the woods beyond the field. The right wing, under Lieutenant-Colonel Coleman, deployed and advanced... We then fell back to the hillside in the open fields, where we were out of reach of their guns, and remained here with the rest of our brigade until an advance was made against the enemy by the Pennsylvania and Rhode Island troops on our right. We then, in conjunction with them and the other troops of our division, made a bayonet charge through the woods on the battery and over the stone fences held by the enemy, driving them from it with fearful slaughter. Lieutenant Colonel Coleman took down the enemy's colors with his own hands."**(4)**

Here we have an eyewitness account from a participant written only six days after the battle. It is important to note Jackson's chronology of events. The Eleventh Ohio participated in the morning action on the far left (south) of the battlefield. They were not in the vicinity of Fox's Gap in the morning. After the morning action they fell back and rested until the afternoon's combat. Jackson's statement regarding the Pennsylvania and Rhode Island troops is a direct reference to other troops of General Reno's IX Corps that were on the field during the afternoon attack. The Eleventh Ohio, along with the rest of the Kanawha Division, also participated in that attack.**(5)**

There are two important facts to be gleaned from Major Jackson's report: 1. The report definitely links Colonel Coleman with the Confederate colors, and by inference the Confederate color bearer (The linkage of Colonel Coleman and the Confederate colors will become a recurrent theme in the postwar accounts of the incident). 2. The incident involving Colonel Coleman and Confederate colors occurred in the afternoon, not in the morning!

The earliest postwar account, and perhaps, because of language and romantic sentiment, the most amusing, comes in 1864. It is found in a regimental history of the 12th Ohio Infantry by James E. D. Ward. The 12th Ohio was another regiment of the Kanawha Division, and Ward was a private in that regiment during the battle. "A rebel color sergeant being surrounded tore off the flag he was carrying and wrapped it around his body. Commanded to surrender, he replied, 'Gentleman, I am a color sergeant and cannot surrender.' At the same time he jerked out a revolver and began firing. In an instant a dozen balls pierced his body and he fell dead. It was as instance of rash heroism which was admired by all who witnessed it, and those who shot him did it with tears in their eyes."**(6)**

The Twelfth Ohio, unlike the Eleventh, was involved in the late morning's action in the vicinity of Wise's Cabin at Fox's Gap. Others have used this account in an attempt to link the color bearer incident with the morning's action. However, it should be noted that Ward makes no statement as to the time of day or the identity of the Confederate color bearer. It should be pointed out that any footnote in any account that uses this anecdote to link the color bearer incident with the 13th North Carolina Regiment, is an inference drawn by the particular author using Ward's anecdote.**(7)**

The next account of the incident appears in 1866. It occurs in a regimental history of the Eleventh Ohio Infantry. Two veterans of Company F of the regiment, Second Lieutenant J. H. Horton and Second Lieutenant Solomon Teverbaugh, wrote it. In a passage titled "At South Mountain" we find the following regarding Colonel Coleman: "The Eleventh, with other regiments, had reached the rear of the enemy, after very severe fighting, and the rebels were retreating in disorder. At this time a rebel color sergeant and color guard emerged from the chestnut undergrowth, and marched directly toward the place where Colonel Coleman, with a squad of men, happened then to be. When about forty paces away, a shot was fired and one of the guard fell, but the color bearer kept steadily on his course until halted by Colonel Coleman, who ordered him, in the usual terms adopted on such occasions, to surrender. When the rebel stopped, a stone fence, behind which our boys were lying, was all that separated them. After pausing a moment the rebel hastily raised a pistol and fired directly at Colonel Coleman, strangely missing him. The rebel (who was certainly a brave fellow) immediately turned to run, but a shot in the shoulder and another in the head felled him to the earth. Several other shots were fired at him just as he was falling, and upon examination it was found that seven or eight bullets had entered his body."**(8)**

As with the Ward anecdote, there is no direct reference as to the time of day or the identity of the regiment to which the Confederate color bearer belonged. What we do have once again is a definite linkage between Colonel Coleman and the color bearer. We also, for the first time, have a reference to a Confederate color "guard." Some Civil War infantry regiments had a small group who were responsible for displaying and guarding the regimental flags. This group was known as a color guard. It usually consisted of a color sergeant and a couple of corporals. This reference will later prove to be crucial in identifying the regiment to which the color bearer belonged.**(9)**

And now we come to what is perhaps the most misinterpreted account of the incident. It is a letter, written in 1899, by Robert E. Wilson. Wilson, a veteran of the 12th Ohio Infantry, was writing to Ezra A. Carman regarding the part taken by the 12th

Ohio in the Battle of South Mountain. At one particular juncture of Wilson's letter he enters into a discourse about the position of the 11th Ohio Infantry: "If the 11th Ohio was sent to the left of the 23rd I think it must have been at the time of the reformation of our Brigade after the first charge. I feel sure it was not there at the time of the first charge. I was not aware before receiving your letter that the 11th had been so separated from its brigade, and my impression that the 11th was immediately on the right of the 12th grew out of the fact, that in the 2nd charge to the rear of the cabin and garden, the men of the 11th and 12th were mixed together." Much of the mystery regarding the Confederate color bearer of Fox's Gap will turn on the phrase "in the 2nd charge to the rear of the cabin."

Wilson continued with a new paragraph, "One incident will show how closely: Driven back from the front, the enemy falling back through the garden were met by our line coming up from the rear and in the flank, and a terrific fight ensued. The color bearer of a Confederate regiment jumped up on the rear wall of the garden, and defiantly waving his flag, refused the many calls to surrender which he received, was shot and fell inside the garden wall. Private Hoagland of my company jumped over the fence and secured the flag. Lt. Col. Coleman of the 11th, who was present, and had called upon the man to surrender, ordered Hoagland to deliver the flag to him, and afterwards claimed the credit of its capture."**(10)**

Wilson's account has been used by others to place the 11th Ohio Regiment in the late morning's action in the vicinity of Wise's cabin. And why should they not? It is a primary source and on the surface it seems a trustworthy account. As stated previously, the key to understanding Wilson's explanation hinges on how one interprets the phrase "in the 2nd charge to the rear of the cabin." In order to understand Wilson's statement a brief synopsis of the morning's battle is required.

The morning's combat at South Mountain mostly involved the Union troops of the Kanawha Division, commanded by Brigadier General Jacob D. Cox, and the Confederates of Brigadier General Samuel Garland. Late in the morning two regiments of Brigadier George B. Anderson's Brigade arrived to reinforce Garland. The Kanawha Division consisted of two brigades of three regiments each. The First Brigade, commanded by Colonel Eliakim Scammon, opened the attack about 9:00 AM that morning. Scammon had three regiments, the Twenty-third Ohio, posted on the far left, the Twelfth Ohio, in the middle, and the Thirtieth Ohio, on the far right. The attack of Scammon's Brigade represents the first Union charge.

Garland's men proved to be up to the task and managed to beat back the first Union assault, but it cost Garland his life. Cox then repositioned his line somewhat and called for reinforcements from his Second Brigade, commanded by Colonel George Crook. The Eleventh Ohio, of Crook's Brigade, was sent to the left of the Twenty-third Ohio on the far left of the field. The Twenty-third was moved a little to the right to make contact with the Twelfth Ohio, and the Thirty-sixth Ohio, of Crook's Brigade, was moved to the right of the Twelfth Ohio to fill the void between the Twelfth and the Thirtieth Ohio. The Twenty-eighth Ohio Regiment was held in reserve. This arrangement provide Cox with a strong center, the Twenty-third, Twelfth, and Thirty-sixth Ohio Infantry Regiments with which to attack Garland (**see Situation Map, Second Union Attack**).

Sometime between 10:00 and 10:30 AM the Union line sprang forward once again. This was the second charge of the morning. Garland's successor, Colonel Duncan McRae, was not up to the task and, after a brief period of intense and savage combat, the Union troops won the crest at South Mountain south of Fox's Gap. Most of the Confederates fled down the West Side of the crest. Only Colonel Ruffin and the Thirteenth North Carolina Infantry remained in the area of Wise's cabin at Fox's Gap. It was about this time, 11:00 AM that the Second and Fourth

North Carolina Regiments, commanded by Colonel Charles C. Tew, arrived to reinforce Ruffin. The Twelfth and Thirty-sixth Ohio reformed and moved northwards towards Fox's Gap to join up with the Thirtieth Ohio. Together these three Union regiments attack the three Confederate Regiments of Ruffin and Tew. The Eleventh and Twenty-third Ohio regiments remained to the left on the southern part of the field. They did not participate in the late morning attack in the area of Wise's cabin (**see Situation Map, Cox's Attack Culminates**).**(11)**

But what should we make of the account of Wilson? According to Captain Wilson, the troops of the Eleventh and Twelfth Ohio were mixed together "in the 2nd charge to the rear of the cabin." Was Wilson lying? The answer is no, Wilson was correct. The truth lies in the fact that the Twelfth Ohio made two charges to the area of Wise's cabin, one in the morning, and another in the late afternoon. It was in the second charge to the cabin, in the late afternoon, that the troops of the Eleventh and Twelfth Ohio were mixed together. Therein lies the confusion, others have interpreted the phrase "2nd charge to the rear of the cabin" to mean the morning's second charge.

It has already been established from the after action reports of General Cox and Major Jackson that the Eleventh Ohio Infantry did not participate in the late morning action at the Wise cabin area of Fox's Gap. There is ample primary source material, which shows that the Twelfth Ohio Infantry did participate in that action near the Wise cabin. From the diary of First Sergeant Harrison G. Otis, Twelfth Ohio Infantry, we find, "The 12th, 23rd, and 36th charged the Rebel position in the forenoon." As stated before, the Twelfth Ohio, Twenty-third Ohio, and the Thirty-sixth Ohio, represented the "center" of Cox's line and did charge in the morning, or forenoon as Sergeant Otis described it. According to General Cox after charging and winning the crest of the mountain, "The Thirtieth and Thirty-sixth... attacked the remnant of Garland's Brigade... Meanwhile the Twelfth Ohio, also changing front, had threaded its way in the same direction... attacking suddenly the force at Wise's as the other two regiments charged." It is important to note that this was the second Union charge of the morning, but it was the first charge of the Twelfth Ohio "to the rear of the cabin."**(12)**

After winning the crest Cox withdrew from the area around Wise's cabin and consolidated his position and waited fro reinforcements from Reno's IX Corps to arrive. By late afternoon, the other divisions of the corps had arrived and a general advance was made against the Confederates at Fox's Gap. By this time the Confederates of Brigadier General Thomas F. Drayton's Brigade defended the area in and around the Wise cabin. As Sergeant Otis recorded in his diary, "Later in the day the battle raged even more furiously. Our division again charged." In the ranks of the men of the Kanawha Division an anonymous newspaper correspondent for the Youngstown Mahoning Register reported, "About four o'clock we were again ordered into line... the line being formed as follows: the 12th in advance and center, the 36th in the rear, the 23rd and 11th on the left flank, and the 28th and 30th on the right flank." No doubt, it was this late afternoon action that Robert Wilson was attempting to clarify for Ezra Carman. This was the only time that day that the troops of the Eleventh Ohio and Twelfth Ohio Infantry could have been mixed together. This was the "2nd charge to the rear of the cabin" for the men of the Twelfth Ohio Infantry Regiment.**(13)**

This then begs the question, if the combat involving the Confederate color bearer of Fox's Gap did not happen in the morning, is there a Confederate source that mentions the death of a color bearer in the afternoon? The answer is a resounding, "Yes, there is." There was a South Carolina color bearer of Drayton's Brigade killed in the afternoon's actions near Wise's cabin.

The area around Wise's cabin became a "no man's land" during the early afternoon of September 14, 1862, with both sides trading occasional small arms fire. Union reinforcements from Reno's IX Corps began to arrive in the area of Fox's Gap before Confederate reinforcements. Around 3:30 PM Confederate reinforcements began arriving. Although the Confederate commander, Major General D. H. Hill, had planned to counterattack with four Confederate brigades, things immediately began to go wrong. Due to the action of Brigadier General Roswell S. Ripley, three of those brigades spent the afternoon marching about ineffectually on the western slope of the mountain. Consequently, the full responsibility for the success or failure of the counterattack fell to the line brigade of Thomas F. Drayton.

Drayton initially deployed his brigade in an inverted "L" shaped formation that bordered the southern and eastern extents of the large field north of the Old Sharpsburg Road. Drayton determined to carry out his orders to sweep the woods and clear them of enemy troops, launched an attack that would prove to be disastrous to his command. That attack, led by the Fifteenth South Carolina Regiment, the Third South Carolina Battalion, and the Phillips Georgia Legion, initiated with a furious charge straight south through Wise's field. As the charge went into full swing, Drayton shifted the remaining Georgia troops, The Fiftieth and Fifty-first Infantry Regiments, into the Old Sharpsburg Road. As this attack was transpiring, Drayton's position was assailed by the full weight of Reno's IX Corps and the 50th and 51st Georgia retreated from their position in the Old Sharpsburg Road. Parts of the original force, which had charged south, were forced to seek shelter behind the double stone walls lining the Ridge Road east of the Wise cabin. These stone walls became a "fall back" position as they sought shelter against an overwhelming assault. Eventually the Union troops ravaged Drayton's men simultaneously from the front and both flanks (**see Situation Map, Drayton's Last Stand**).**(14)**

It is at this point that our attention is drawn to the color bearer of the Third South Carolina Battalion, commanded by Colonel George S. James. In the ranks of this regiment, sometimes referred to simply as "James Battalion," was a young private by the name of Sam Puckett. In an account first published in 1903, Puckett attempted to describe some of the carnage of that action, "Col. James, seeing the enemy to be too strong, wheeled the battalion to the right between two rock fences, where we attempted to check them... Col. James was killed, and Major Rice severely wounded... Simpson, the color bearer, and one of the color guards was shot down, then the other color guard, R. C. Puckett, was also shot down. The flag was shot to pieces and the staff was broken."**(15)**

And there it is: not only does this incredible anecdote mention the loss of a color bearer, but it cross references Horton and Teverbaugh's account that also mentions the death of the color "guard" as well! Rarely does one get such agreement between Union and Confederate source material. It all seems to come together, the mysterious color bearer of Fox's Gap, which the sources of the Eleventh Ohio and Captain Wilson reference, probably belonged to the Third South Carolina Battalion.

Does this then mean that no North Carolina color bearer died at South Mountain? It absolutely does not. We have documentation for the death of the color bearer of the Fifth North Carolina Infantry. One cannot discount the possibility that another North Carolina color bearer was also killed at Fox's Gap, and that someday a document may surface supporting such a claim, but as of this writing no documentation exists to support that occurrence. What does exist is inference and speculation. Ward's anecdote, which does not link Colonel Coleman to the color bearer nor include a reference to the time of day, could be loosely used to support a claim for capture of a North Carolina Flag in the morning action. However, it is important to note that Sergeant Giles Jones, the color bearer of the Thirteenth North Carolina, survived the Battle of South Mountain.

What is known conclusively is that the other Union sources linking Colonel Coleman and the hapless Confederate color bearer clearly reference the afternoon's combat, and this definitely makes a strong case for the identity of our confederate color bearer's regiment as being the Third South Carolina Battalion.

End Notes

Stephen R. Stotelmyer article

The Mysterious Confederate Color Bearer of Fox's Gap

(1) N.C. South Mountain News, Fall, 1999. The authors of the Newsletter provide this footnote regarding the inscription on the back of the monument: "Footnote: LHAM has a copy of the entire above letter from the Library of Congress describing the entire battle from Capt. Wilson's perspective. The referral to the flag being the 13th's is documented in a book by Scott Hartwig, *Civil War Regiments, Antietam: The Maryland Campaign*. Hartwig, with the Gettysburg National Military Park, spoke with us concerning the color bearer and his conclusion that it was the 13th's. He has done a thorough examination of the battle and claims the 13th was the only unit in the area during this fighting."

Scott Hartwig did not write a book by the title named in the footnote. "Civil War Regiments" is a periodical published quarterly by Savas Publishing Company. Hartwig did write an article for the Volume Five, No. #3 edition (This edition was subtitled "Antietam, The Maryland Campaign of 1862"). Hartwig's article was titled "My God Be Careful!" Morning Battle at Fox's Gap, September 14, 1862." I seriously doubt that Scott Hartwig would make the claim that "the 13th was the only unit in this area during the fight." For more on Hartwig's inference that the color bearer was that of the Thirteenth North Carolina Infantry see footnote #12.

(2) McRae, Duncan, Official Records, Vol. 19 Part I, p. 1042. We know the 5th North Carolina's position from McRae's report, "The Fifth, on the extreme right, was nearest to the intersecting road, which was threatened." The road that McRae speaks of is the Loop Road approximately 2/3 mile south of Fox's Gap. Clearly then it was not the color bearer of the 5th North Carolina Infantry who was killed at Fox's Gap.

(3) Ruffin, Thomas, Official Records, Vol. 19 Part I, p. 1047, "I feel it to be just that I should acknowledge the fact that we were joined by a small party of the Twelfth North Carolina Regiment early in the morning." And also concerning the Twelfth, from Montgomery, Walter, Histories of the Several Regiments and Battalions from North Carolina. Voume II, p. 627, "The greater part of the regiment, with the flag, was in its place the whole day." Clearly then the color bearer of the Twelfth North Carolina Regiment was also with the Thirteenth North Carolina Regiment. It is also documented fact that two regiments of Brigadier General George B. Anderson's Brigade were sent to Fox's Gap by General Hill during the late morningg action. The Second North Carolina and the Fourth North Carolina Regiments, commanded by Colonel Charles C. Tew, also participated in the late morning action and also, it is assumed, had their colors and color bearers with them as well.

(4) Jackson, Lyman, Official Records, Vol. 19 Part I, pp. 472-473.

(5) Cox, Jacob D., Official Records, Vol. 19, Part I, p. 459, "The Eleventh Ohio, of the Second Brigade, Lieut. A. H. Coleman commanding, was now sent to support the left, and formed on the left of the Twenty-third." And on p. 460, concerning the afternoon action, Cox wrote, "About 4 o'clock p. m., most of the reinforcements being in position, the order was received to advance the whole line."

(6) Ward, James E. D., Twelfth Ohio Volunteer Infantry, p. 59.

(7) See Hartwig, Scott, Civil War Regiments, Volume Five, No. 3, pp. 52-53, for his account involving the color bearer. Hartwig definitely names the color bearer as belonging to the Thirteenth North Carolina and his footnote (#51) includes the reference to Ward. See also Priest, John M., Before Antietam, The Battle for South Mountain, pp. 167-168. Priest uses McRae's after action report (although he doesn't reference it) to identify the color bearer as belonging to the Fifth North Carolina Regiment. These two references are provided so that the reader may see how two authors can use much of the same material and yet come up with two different accounts.

(8) Horton and Teverbaugh, A History of the Eleventh Regiment, pp. 269-270.

(9) Once again see Hartwig and Priest, both authors reference the Horton and Teverbaugh anecdote.

(10) Wilson, Robert E., Letter to Ezra A. Carman dated July 22, 1899. To fully understand the importance of this letter, one has to understand why it was written. General Ezra A. Carman, veteran of the Battle of Antietam, became a member of the Antietam Battlefield Board in October 1894. The Board was charged with the task of marking the positions of the various units on the battlefield. Their labors eventually culminated with the placement of the descriptive cast iron tablets and the creation of what was to become the Antietam National Battlefield Park. General Carman corresponded with many of the veterans of the Maryland Campaign as to the actual locations of the units. Carman and the veterans visited the sites repeatedly in their attempts to accurately document the campaign. In addition to the Battle of Antietam, Gen. Carman also queried the veterans about the Battle of South Mountain. Much of this correspondence still survives today. It should be noted that a large portion of General Carman's work was based on the actual recollections of the veterans. Robert Wilson's letter was one of those first-hand accounts. Once again, both Hartwig and Priest reference Wilson's letter.

(11) McRae *Op. Cit.*, and Cox, *Op. Cit.* In addition I would also recommend Cox, Jacob D., Reminiscences of the Civil War, pp. 280-285. The times of day are my inferences based upon my research.

(12) Otis, Harrison G., Diary Entry September 15, 1862, and Cox, *Reminiscences*, p. 284. In defense of Scott Hartwig, who I consider an excellent historian, I have to say that I made the same mistake as he. I also interpreted Wilson's statement "2nd charge to the rear of the cabin" to mean the second charge of the morning. I did not like it, but I accepted it. I did not like it for two reasons: 1. I felt that it was too much ground for the Eleventh Ohio to cover. It is over 1,000 yards from the Loop Road/Ridge Road intersection to Fox's Gap. That seemed to me too much distance too soon for the Eleventh to cover. 2. I could not find a reliable cross-reference that placed the Eleventh Ohio at the Wise cabin in the late morning's combat. The source material was strangely quiet on this topic. Indeed, the most reliable source, Major Jackson's after action report, contradicted Wilson's letter. I was even ready to explain away Jackson's report as his telescoping events out of chronological sequence. So convincing is Wilson's letter and his use of the phrase "2nd charge to the rear of the cabin," that it took a fresh pair of eyes, those of my daughter, to point out that Wilson was not talking about the second charge of the morning. He was making reference to the second charge of the Twelfth Regiment that day to the rear of the cabin.

(13) Otis, *Op. Cit.*, and "Army Correspondence," Youngstown Mahoning Register, October 9, 1862.

(14) Graham, Kurt, "Death of a Brigade," Newsletter, The Society of the Descendants of Frederick Fox, Issue 9, Volume I, June 1, 2000. This is to date, in my opinion, the best research regarding the afternoon's action at Fox's Gap.

(15) Calhoun, C. M., Liberty Dethroned, p. 228.

Situation Map, Second Union Attack

The above named map will be added to the Adobe Acrobat version of the June 1, 2004, *News from Fox's Gap* newsletter as soon as the software driver for the Microtek 4800 scanner used to scan images to my computer becomes available from Microtek for Macintosh OS 10.3.

Situation Map, Cox's Attack Culminates

The above named map will be added to the Adobe Acrobat version of the June 1, 2004, *News from Fox's Gap* newsletter as soon as the software driver for the Microtek 4800 scanner used to scan images to my computer becomes available from Microtek for Macintosh OS 10.3.

Situation Map, Drayton's Last Stand

The above named map will be added to the Adobe Acrobat version of the June 1, 2004, *News from Fox's Gap* newsletter as soon as the software driver for the Microtek 4800 scanner used to scan images to my computer becomes available from Microtek for Macintosh OS 10.3.

President's Message

by Curtis Lynn Older

* No new members have joined the Society since the December 1, 2003 newsletter was finalized.

* Get on the Fox Society website by entering the following in your Internet Explorer search:

http://homepage.mac.com/clo7956/

* You can download various Fox Society Related Items in Adobe PDF format from the Fox Society website. You will need Version 5.0 of Adobe Acrobat that you may download for FREE at:

www.adobe.com

News from Fox's Gap
Published June 1 and December 1 of each year by
The Society of the Descendants of Frederick Fox of Fox's Gap in Maryland
Membership dues are $6.00 per year. President of the Society is Curtis L. Older.
Make Society inquiries by the following means:

Curtis L. Older
618 Tryon Place
Gastonia, NC 28054-6066

e-mail: curtolder@earthlink.net
phone: 704-864-3879

News from Fox's Gap

The Society of the Descendants of Frederick Fox of Fox's Gap in Maryland

Issue 8, Volume 2 **Remember Freedom!** December 1, 2004

The Truth About Wise's Well

Setting the Record Straight on South Mountain

By Steven R. Stotelmyer

The following article is reprinted from the *Blue and Gray Magazine* of October 1990.

[Steven R. Stotelmyer is a native of Hagerstown, Maryland. As a child he and his sister played among the monuments at Antietam National Battlefield during the many family picnics to the Philadelphia Brigade Park. When he graduated from high school in 1968, Mr. Stotelmyer enlisted in the United States Navy and served as a radar man on a destroyer. Returning to civilian life, he earned a Bachelor of Science degree from Frostburg State College and a Masters of Arts from Hood College.

Always interested in local history, especially South Mountain and Antietam, Mr. Stotelmyer helped form the Central Maryland Heritage League in 1989. The League has been successful in acquiring land of the South Mountain Battlefield--an area often overshadowed by Antietam. He has also written magazine articles on the Civil War in Western Maryland and is an active volunteer at the Antietam Battlefield. His favorite "duty station" is the National Cemetery.]

They were thrown into a well instead of receiving a proper burial. They were dead Confederate soldiers, and as the legend goes, they were thrown down an abandoned well by an old farmer named Daniel Wise on September 15, 1862, after the battle of Fox's Gap in Maryland.

The veterans of the fighting at Fox's Gap would remember the combat as being "as hot as any action of the entire war." Fox's Gap was one of the areas where the battle of South Mountain occurred on Sunday, September 14, 1862. There had been fighting all day between Union Gen. Jesse Lee Reno's IX Corps and Confederate Gen. D. H. Hill's division, with the action beginning around 9:00 a.m. At times thousands of men were involved, at other times just a few skirmishers. At its worst, the fighting was fierce hand-to-hand combat with clubbed rifles and bayonets.

The Confederates withdrew that Sunday night. They left their dead and wounded on the battlefield. It was a cold night, and either as a gesture of compassion toward a gallant enemy, or simply because the dead were too gruesome to view throughout the night, Union boys unrolled

Wall with Confederate dead at Fox's Gap after the Battle of South Mountain

blankets and spread them over Confederate corpses. And, as David L. Thompson of the 9th New York Volunteers remembered, "we went to sleep, lying upon our arms in line as we had stood, living Yankee and dead Confederate side by side, and indistinguishable." As dawn broke on September 15, and the difference between the dead and living once again became apparent, the living were faced with the problem of burying the dead. There were a lot of dead.

All this had been the result of Gen. Robert E. Lee's Maryland Campaign, which culminated in the battle of Antietam (or Sharpsburg) on September 17, 1862. As with many events of the Maryland Campaign there are actually two stories: the legend and the fact. And with the story of Wise's well there is some truth to the old adage, "When the legend becomes fact, print the legend."

The legend of farmer Wise has its origin in the regimental history of the 21st Massachusetts. Published 20 years after the battle, it was written by Charles F. Walcott, a member of the 21st, who was at Fox's Gap on the 14th and15th of September 1862. It is from the following account that most historians have based their narratives concerning farmer Wise:

The burial of a portion of the rebel dead was peculiar enough to call for special mention. Some Ohio troops had been detailed to bury them, but not relishing the task, and finding the ground hard to dig, soon removed the covering of a deep well connected with Wise's house on the summit, and lightened their toil by throwing a few bodies into the well. Mr. Wise soon discovered what they were about, and had it stopped: and then the Ohioans went away, leaving their work unfinished. Poor Mr. Wise, anxious to get rid of the bodies, finally made an agreement with General Burnside to bury them for a dollar apiece. As long as his well had been already spoiled, he concluded to realize on the rest of its capacity, and put in fifty-eight more rebel bodies, which filled it to the surface of the ground.

Others elements of the legend would be added as time passed. A local source that propagated the legend was *The Valley Register*, a weekly newspaper of Middletown, Maryland, in circulation since 1844. Both Union and Confederate troops had passed through Middletown on their way to the battle. The town was strongly pro-Union in sentiment. Adam C. Koogle of Middletown had enlisted in the 1st Maryland (Union) Artillery. War touched Koogle's family when his father's barn was burned as the Confederates torched the wooden bridge over Catoctin Creek when they withdrew from Middletown on their way toward Boonsboro. Koogle fought at Crampton's

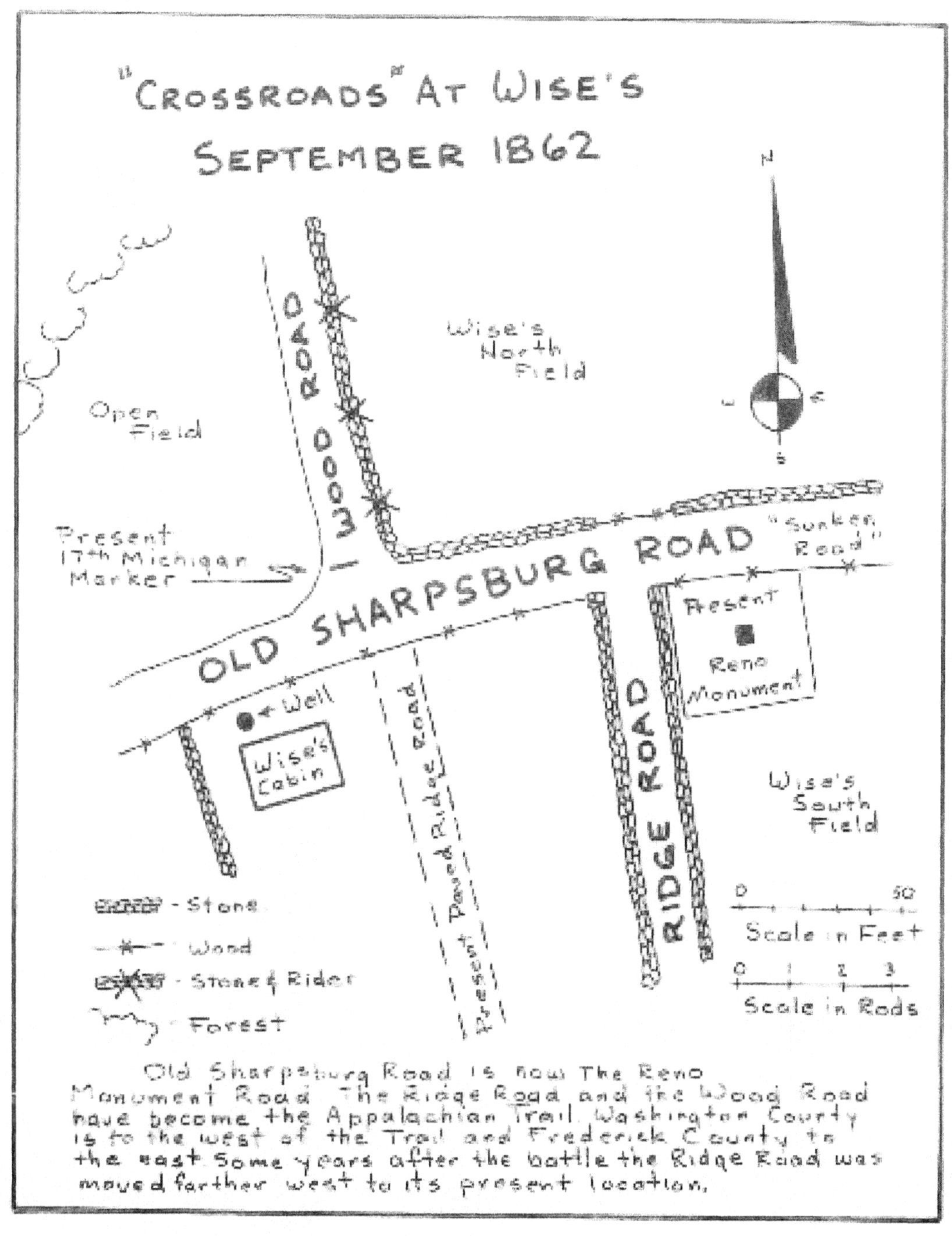

Gap (about six miles south of Fox's Gap), and at Antietam he was wounded. He made his way to an aunt's house to escape the surgeon's saw. He recovered from his wounds, rejoined his unit, and survived 50 more years to write about the battle of South Mountain, and about farmer Wise.

In 1912 the *Register* published a special 50th anniversary issue on the battle. Mr. Koogle wrote an article that took up an entire page. Although he had fought at another gap, Mr. Koogle had the opportunity to say something about farmer Wise:

During the night of the 14th, the Confederates withdrew from the mountain, going in the direction of Sharpsburg, leaving their dead and wounded for the Union Army to care for. The Confederates left many of their wounded in

Boonsboro, where they were well cared for. Burial details were soon at work burying the dead. Mr. Wise, who lived just at the top of the mountain, on the Old Sharpsburg Road, was given $1.00 each to bury a lot of dead Confederates that lay all around his yard and in the road. He threw 58 of the dead in an old abandoned well, which at the time seemed quite revolting, but when we consider the condition the bodies were in, and the hard time of digging trenches in that locality, we cannot so much blame him. This well never had any water in it. The remains of all were finally removed and taken to Hagerstown, Md. as well as the remains of all others that could be located.

Fifty years after the battle the well was reported as "abandoned" by Wise. It never had any water, so no harm had been done by tossing bodies into it. How could it have been ruined if it was abandoned? Koogle's text is a sort of exoneration of Wise: the farmer did everyone a favor, because the ground was too hard to dig and the condition of the bodies warranted a quick burial. Most of what Koogle wrote is incorrect.

* * * * *

This photo of the Wise cabin appeared in the June 4, 1909 edition of Middletown's Valley Register. A chimney has been added and a new window, but the old fence is the same from Civil War days. The "X" on the fence at far right marks the location of Wise's well, according to the newspaper's caption.

(The picture above was cropped slightly from the original photo that appeared in the article.)

This article will be continued in the June 1, 2005, issue of *News from Fox's Gap*!

Genealogy Documentation Section

by Curtis L. Older

A new feature of each Fox Society Newsletter will be the inclusion of an article that will document a descendant or spouse of a descendant of John Fox of Fox's Gap in Maryland. The article will present a written description about the individual and his or her family as well as a listing of the related genealogical source records that support the written description. The first individual to be presented is Frederick Fox of Fox's Gap in Maryland. Frederick was a son of John Fox, the man for whom Fox's Gap in Maryland is named.

Documentation for Frederick Fox, father of George Fox

Frederick Fox was born May 10, 1751, in Hesse-Cassel, Germany.(**1**) He was the son of John Frederick Fox and Christina.(**2**) The brothers and sisters of Frederick Fox were: Daniel, Magdelin, Michael, and Rachael.(**3**) John Fox was a skin-dresser by trade.(**4**) John Fox died between January 17, 1784, when he wrote his will, and December 4, 1784, when his will was probated.(**5**) Christiana Fox died Aug. 6, 1812, probably in Sharpsburg, Maryland.(**6**)

Frederick Fox and his parents probably lived at or near Fox's Gap, Maryland, during the 1760s. The gap received its name from Frederick's father, John Fox, because he was the earliest settler in the immediate vicinity of the gap.(**7**) Fox's Gap in Maryland is where the Old Sharpsburg Road from Frederick, Maryland, to Sharpsburg, Maryland, crosses the South Mountain.(**8**) The Old Sharpsburg Road was part of the Great Wagon Road to Philadelphia, which also was known as the German Monocacy Road.(**9**)

Fox's Gap was the scene for a major portion of the battle between forces under Confederate General Robert E. Lee and Union General George B. McClellan on September 14, 1862.(**10**) The Reno Monument, dedicated to U. S. Major Jesse Lee Reno who was killed in the Battle of South Mountain, stands at Fox's Gap.(**11**) A little more than one hundred years prior to the Battle of South Mountain, on May 2, 1755, the road through Fox's Gap was used by General Braddock, George Washington, and Maryland's Governor Sharpe to travel from Frederick Town to Swearingen's Ferry on the Potomac River, while on their way to Fort Cumberland during the Braddock Expedition.(**12**)

Frederick Fox was a farmer and perhaps a tavern keeper.(**13**) He married Catherine Booker on March 1, 1773, probably at or near Middletown, Maryland.(**14**) Catherine was a daughter of Bartholomew Booker and Margaret.(**15**) She was born May 1, 1748.(**16**)

The Fox Genealogy by Daniel Gebhart Fox indicates that The Fox Inn, which still is standing and is occupied by renters in the year 2004, was built on land owned by Frederick Fox.(**17**) However, Curtis L. Older found no land records that support Frederick Fox as the owner of the land upon which the Fox Inn stands. Curtis did find that George Fox, at age 24, the oldest son of Frederick and Catherine Fox, acquired the Fox Inn along the Old Sharpsburg Road in 1805.(**18**) The inn stands about two miles east of Fox's Gap and about two miles west of Middletown, Maryland, along the Old Sharpsburg Road from Frederick to Sharpsburg.

Frederick Fox served in Joseph Chapline Junior's Company of Militia, Sharpsburg, Maryland, probably between 1775 and 1777.(**19**) He signed the Patriot's Oath of Fidelity and Support in 1778.(**20**)

Frederick served as a drummer in the Lieutenant Colonel's Company of the 10th Regiment, Pennsylvania Continental Line from April 22, 1777, to January 1, 1781.(**21**) He probably fought in the battles of Brandywine, Paoli "Massacre", Germantown, and Monmouth and he was at the Valley Forge Encampment.(**22**)

Frederick was short and of rather stout build and wore his hair in the olden time cue style.(**23**) He was an elder in the Zion Lutheran Church of Middletown, Maryland, from 1787 until 1790.(**24**)

Frederick Fox and Catherine Booker Fox were the parents of seven children: Christiana, Rose, George, Daniel Booker, Elizabeth, Mary Magdalena, and Joseph.(**25**) Catherine Booker Fox died November 1, 1800, and was buried in the Middletown, Maryland, area.(**26**)

Sometime between 1800 and 1807 Frederick Fox married a widow, Susannah (Schutt) Young. She was born April 19, 1754 and died November 13, 1831.(**27**) "Frederick Fox and thirty-two other persons, thirty-one of whom are known, emigrated to Ohio in the early day canvas covered wagons, coming by the way of Wheeling, West Virginia, and arriving in Franklin, Warren county, in the fall of 1807."(**28**) Frederick Fox died February 27, 1837, in Miamisburg, Ohio, and was buried in the Gebhart or St. John Cemetery in Miamisburg.(**29**)

Frederick Fox appears as a head of household in the 1790 Maryland Federal census for Frederick County.(**30**) The household contained 3 free white males of 16 and upwards, including heads of families, 3 free white males under 16 years, 5 free white females including heads of families, 0 all other free persons, 0 slaves.

The 1800 Maryland Federal census list Frederick Fox as a head of household in Frederick County.(**31**) The Frederick Fox household reported: free white males - none under age 10, one male age 10 to 15, 2 males age 15 thru 25, no males age 26 thru 44, one male age 45 and over. Free white females included: none age under 10, one age 10 to 15, 3 age 15 thru 25, one age 26 thru 44, and none age 45 and over.

The 1809 Ohio state census for Warren County, Franklin Township, lists Frederick Fox.(**32**) The 1810 Ohio Federal census for Warren County, Franklin Township shows the Frederick Fox household.(**33**)

The 1830 Ohio Federal Census lists the Frederick Fox household of Warren County, Clear Creek Township, as containing: one male at least 70 and under 80, one female at least 40 and under 50, and one female at least 70 and under 80.(**34**)

Children (**Fox**) born in Frederick County, Maryland:(**35**)

i. **Christiana**, born January 20, 1774
ii. **Rose**, born September 9, 1775
iii. **Mary Magdelena**, born December 17, 1778
iv. **George**, born March 10, 1781
v. **Daniel Booker**, born June 6, 1783
vi. **Joseph**, born April 12, 1785
vii. **Elizabeth**, born September 27, 1788

REFERENCES

1. Tombstone of Frederick Fox, Gebhart or St. John Cemetery, Miamisburg, Ohio; *The Fox Genealogy including the Metherd, Benner, and Leiter descendants, giving biographies of the first and second generations, with sketches of the third generation*, compiled by D. G. Fox, 1914. (n.p) 1924. 1 p. 1., (5)-172 p. 20 com. 37-9439 CS71.F79 1924 Library of Congress, 82. **2.** Will of John Fox, Book A Liber 102, Washington County, Maryland, January 17, 1784; *Fox Genealogy*, p. 12. **3.** Will of John Fox; Michael Fox, Frederick's brother, was a member of Joseph Chapline's Company of Militia. See S. Eugene Clements and F. Edward Wright, *The Maryland Militia in the Revolutionary War* (Silver Spring, Md.: Family Line Publications, 1987), 241; Maryland Historical Society Records for Washington County. Militia Lists of Daughters of Founders and Patriots. **4.** *Fox Genealogy*, pp. 12 and 13; The *Bierly Tannery Report*, held by the Frederick, Maryland, library, is a report on the tannery business in and about Frederick, Maryland, in the mid 1700s. **5.** Will of John Fox. **6.** *Fox Genealogy*, p. 12; Letter from Jacob Reel to Michael and Frederick Fox, dated at Sharpsburg, Aug. 9, 1812, from a copy obtained from Robert H. Fox of Cincinnati, Ohio. "The following letter received and forwarded from Lebanon, Warren County, Ohio, Sept. 8, 1812, addressed to Msrs. Fredric(k) & Michael Fox, Franklin Township, Warren Co. Ohio". **7.** Curtis L. Older, *The Braddock Expedition and Fox's Gap in Maryland* (Westminster, Md.: Family Line Publications, 1995), p. 77-79. **8.** *Braddock Expedition and Fox's Gap in Maryland*, Chapter Three, pp. 69-116. **9.** *Braddock Expedition and Fox's Gap in Maryland*, p. 87. **10.** *Braddock Expedition and Fox's Gap in Maryland*, Afterword, pp. 177-182. **11.** Curtis L. Older, *The Land Tracts of the Battlefield of South Mountain* (Westminster, Md.: Willow Bend Books, 1999), 206; *Braddock Expedition and Fox's Gap in Maryland*, p. 99. **12.** *Braddock Expedition and Fox's Gap in Maryland*, p. 70. **13.** FCLR, WR-19-206, Mortgage from Christian Benner to Frederick Fox, recorded April 11, 1799, Shaaffs Purchase and Mount Sinai. "Between Christian Benner Sen. of Frederick County farmer of the one part; and Frederick Fox of the same county farmer of the other part."; Lemoine Cree, *A Brief History of the South Mountain House* (Boonsboro, Md.: Dodson, 1963); Ohio D.A.R. Soldiers Rosters, 2 Vols., 1:146; *Fox Genealogy*, pp. 13-14. **14.** *Ohio D.A.R. Soldiers Rosters*, 2 vols., 1:146; *Fox Genealogy*, p. 12. **15.** *Fox Genealogy*, p. 12; will of Bartholomew Booker, Frederick County, Maryland, Register of Wills Records, GM-2-431; will of Margaret Book (Booker) Frederick County, Maryland, Register of Wills Records GM-3-126. **16.** *Fox Genealogy*, p. 12. **17.** *Fox Genealogy*, p. 13. **18.** *Braddock Expedition and Fox's Gap in Maryland*, p. 98; *Land Tracts of the Battlefield of South Mountain*, p. 211. **19.** *Maryland Militia in the Revolutionary War* (Silver Spring, Md.: Family Line Publications, 1987), 241; Maryland Historical Society Records for Washington County, Militia Lists of Daughters of Founders and Patriots. **20.** Washington County, Maryland, Patriot's Oath, March Court, 1778. Sharpsburgh Hundred, March 2, 1778, Christopher Cruss's Returns. **21.** National Archives, card numbers 37404176, 4837, 37188278, and 39144421; National Society of the Daughters of the American Revolution. 17th Report, *Pierce's Register*, #67913. Also see Pennsylvania Archives, Series 5, 3:487, 529, 533, and 572. **22.** Ibid; *Braddock Expedition and Fox's Gap in Maryland*, p. 212. **23.** *Fox Genealogy*, p. 18. **24.** Frederick S. Weiser, ed., *Zion Lutheran Church 1781-1826*, Maryland German Church Records, Vol. 2, (Manchester, Md.: Noodle-Doosey Press, 1987), 4. **25.** Will of Frederick Fox, Will Book C, case #1444, Montgomery County, Ohio; *Fox Genealogy*, p. 18. **26.** Frederick S. Weiser, ed., Maryland German Church Records Vol. 2, *Zion Lutheran Church 1781-1826* (Manchester, Md.: Noodle-Doosey Press, 1987), 77. The Death Register of Zion Lutheran Church indicates "Catarin, wife of Friedrich Fuchs, bur. 4 Nov. 1800. Heb. 4:9."; *Fox Genealogy*, p. 12. **27.** *Fox Genealogy*, p. 15; tombstone of Susannah Fox, Gebhart Cemetery, Miamisburg, Ohio. **28.** *Fox Genealogy*, pp. 15-16. **29.** Tombstone of Frederick Fox, Gebhart or St. John Cemetery, Miamisburg, Ohio; *Fox Genealogy*, pp. 17-18. **30.** 1790 Maryland Federal census, Fredrick County, unknown township, image 0491, roll M637_3, page 66. **31.** 1800 Maryland Federal census, Frederick County, township District No. 3, image 124, roll M32_10, page 123. **32.** 1809 Ohio state census, Warren County, Franklin township, page 13. **33.** 1810 Ohio Federal census, Warren County, Franklin township, page 28. **34.** 1830 Ohio Federal census., Warren County, Clear Creek township, image 340, roll M19_142, page 173. **35.** *Fox Genealogy*, various pages; will of Frederick Fox, Will Book C, case #1444, Montgomery County, Ohio.

President's Message

by Curtis Lynn Older

* The Civil War Preservation Trust Memorandum dated October 8, 2004, entitled Battlefield Preservation Status Report indicates the following regarding preservation efforts for the Battlefield of South Mountain: "**Maryland - South Mountain** (Fox's Gap, near McClellan's headquarters) - 36.5 acres. Thanks to CWPT members, we raised the $10,000 we needed. The deal has closed and the Maryland Environmental Trust now holds the easement. More land saved forever!" This certainly is great news regarding the preservation efforts near Fox's Gap.

* No new members have joined the Society since the June 1, 2004 newsletter was finalized.

* You can download various Fox Society Related Items in Adobe PDF format from the Fox Society website. You will need Version 5.0 of Adobe Acrobat that you may download for FREE at:

www.adobe.com

* Get on the Fox Society website by entering the following in your Internet Explorer search:

http://homepage.mac.com/clo7956/

* Membership Dues have been reduced to $5.00 per year as the result of a decision to make the Fox Society Newsletter an average of 10 to 12 pages instead of the previous 18 to 22 pages.

News from Fox's Gap

Published June 1 and December 1 of each year by
The Society of the Descendants of Frederick Fox of Fox's Gap in Maryland

Membership dues are $5.00 per year. President of the Society is Curtis L. Older.
Make Society inquiries by the following means:

Curtis L. Older
618 Tryon Place
Gastonia, NC 28054-6066

e-mail: curtolder@earthlink.net
phone: 704-864-3879

Land Tracts of the Battlefield of South Mountain
by Curtis L. Older

Most Fox Society Newsletters include a survey, patent, or deed related to the land tracts in the vicinity of Crampton's, Fox's, and Turner's Gaps. These three gaps in South Mountain represent the main area contested by the Union and Confederate Armies in the Battle of South Mountain on September 14, 1862.

Previous issues of the Society Newsletter contained descriptions of the following tracts:

June 1, 1997	Addition to Friendship of Frederick Fox
December 1, 1997	Fredericksburgh of Frederick Fox
June 1, 1998	Pick All of Bartholomew Booker
December 1, 1998	Bowser's Addition of David Bowser
June 1, 1999	Partnership of John Mansberger
December 1, 1999	Mountain of John Baley
December 1, 2000	Flonham of Philip Jacob Shafer
June 1, 2001	The Exchange of Daniel Dulaney
December 1, 2001	Betty's Good Will of Robert Evans

The Resurvey on Exchange is a resurvey on The Exchange, surveyed October 5, 1742, for Daniel Dulaney. The Fox Inn stands on the northern portion of this tract of land.

(Maryland Hall of Records, Annapolis, Maryland) MdHR 17,405-2, 1-23-2-43, BY & GS 4, 586-586, Casper Shaff, resurveyed 1 Sep 1751, 275 acres. (Resurvey on Exchange)

Casper Shaff's Patent 275 Acres the Resurvey on Exchange} Frederick ? Know ye that whereas Joseph Chapline of Frederick County by his humble petition to our agents for management of land affairs within this province did set forth that he was seized in fee of and in ascertain tract or parcel of land called Exchange lying and being in the county aforesaid originally on the twenty ninth day of September Anno Domini Seventeen hundred and forty nine granted unto the petitioner for one hundred acres under new rent contiguous to which the petitioner had lately discovered some vacant land and being desirous to add the same humbly prayed a special warrant to resurvey the aforesaid tract for that intent and purposes and that on return of a certificate of such resurvey he making good rights to the vacancy added and complying with all other requisites usual in such cases might have our grant of confirmation issue unto him thereon which was granted him and accordingly a warrant on the twenty second day of March seventeen hundred and fifty unto him for that purposes did issue In pursuance whereof it is certified into our land office that the aforesaid tract or parcel of land is resurveyed by which it appears the same contains only the quantity of seventy five acres and that there is the quantity of two hundred acres of vacant land added so that there appears to be a deficiency in the original tract of twenty five acres to make good which is applied so much part of the vacancy aforesaid and for the remaining and hundred and seventy five acres he has paid and satisfied unto Benjamin Tasker Esq our present agent and receiver general for our use as well the sum of eight pounds fifteen shillings sterling caution for the same as the sum of ten shillings for the improvements mentioned to be more thereon according to charter lord Baron of Baltimore our great grand Father of Noble memory his instruction to Charles Carroll Esq his then agent bearing date at London the twelfth day of September seventeen hundred and twelve and registered in our secretary's office of our said province Together with a paragraph of our instructions bearing date at London the fifteenth day of December seventeen hundred and thirty eight and registered in our land office ? before the said Joseph Chaplin ? out our grant thereon he did on the ninth day of May seventeen hundred and fifty four assign over all his right title interest claim and domain whatsoever of in and unto the certificate of resurvey aforesaid and the land and premises therein mentioned unto a certain Casper Shaff who hath since supplicated us that our grant might issue in his name for the same which we have thought fit to condescend unto We do therefore hereby grant and confirm unto him that said Casper Shaff all that the aforesaid tract or parcel of land now resurveyed with the vacancy added reduced into one entire tract and called the Resurvey on Exchange beginning at the original beginning tree running thence

Line No.	North South	Degrees East or West	Length
1	N	68 west	140 perches
2	N	35 west	69 perches
3	N	71 east	69 perches
4	S	56 east	88 perches
5	N	43 east	30 perches
6	S	52 east	64 perches
7	S	5 east	61 perches
8	S	37 east	74 perches
9	S	14 east	138 perches
10	N	74 west	118 perches
11	N	45 west	36 perches
12	S	59 west	40 perches
13	S	22 west	36 perches
14	N	66 west	23 perches
15	N	40 west	34 perches
16	N		57 perches
17	N	34 east	94 perches
18	N	80 east	12 perches

19 then by a straight line to the beginning tree containing and now laid our for two hundred and seventy five acres of land more or less according to the certificate of Resurvey thereof taken and returned into our land office bearing date the first day of September seventeen hundred and fifty one and there remaining together with all rights profits benefits and privileges thereunto belonging . . . . . given under our great seal of our said province of Maryland this ninth day of may Anno Domini seventeen hundred and fifty four witness our trusty and well beloved Horatio Sharpe esq lieutenant general and chief governor of our said province of Maryland chancellor & keeper of the great seal thereof

Horo (the great seal) Sharpe

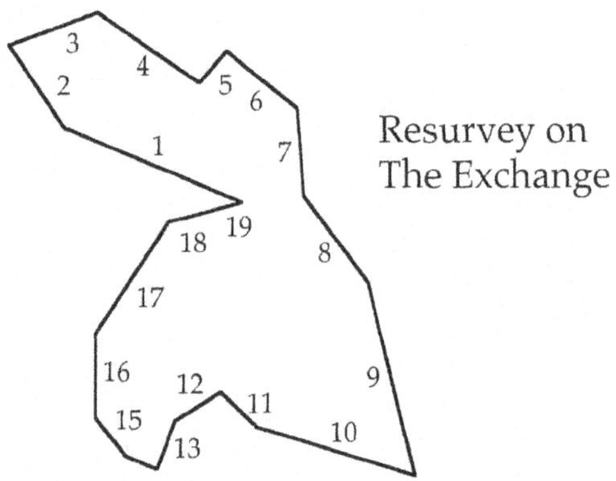

News from Fox's Gap

The Society of the Descendants of Frederick Fox of Fox's Gap in Maryland

Issue 9, Volume 2 **Remember Freedom!** June 1, 2005

The Truth About Wise's Well

Setting the Record Straight on South Mountain

By Steven R. Stotelmyer

The following article is reprinted from the *Blue and Gray Magazine* of October 1990.

[Steven R. Stotelmyer is a native of Hagerstown, Maryland. As a child he and his sister played among the monuments at Antietam National Battlefield during the many family picnics to the Philadelphia Brigade Park. When he graduated from high school in 1968, Mr. Stotelmyer enlisted in the United States Navy and served as a radar man on a destroyer. Returning to civilian life, he earned a Bachelor of Science degree from Frostburg State College and a Masters of Arts from Hood College.

Always interested in local history, especially South Mountain and Antietam, Mr. Stotelmyer helped form the Central Maryland Heritage League in 1989. The League has been successful in acquiring land of the South Mountain Battlefield--an area often overshadowed by Antietam. He has also written magazine articles on the Civil War in Western Maryland and is an active volunteer at the Antietam Battlefield. His favorite "duty station" is the National Cemetery.]

Continued from the December 1, 2004, *News from Fox's Gap* Newsletter

As the years wore on and the legend grew, so did the number of bodies, and the Ohio troops faded from the scene altogether. In the closing months of 1919 the Wise cabin was demolished and there was an article in the *Register* to protest the loss of the historic landmark. The staff writer noted: *The old Wise house was made famous by an act of its owner, the day following the battle. Wise was paid $1 per head to bury the dead soldiers. Instead of giving them a decent burial, he gathered up about 75 bodies and threw them into an old well in the yard, at the west side of the house. Later, when the government officials heard of Wise's act, he was compelled to remove every one of the bodies, and they were taken away and properly buried, later being removed to Antietam National Cemetery.*

By 1919 farmer Wise was suddenly responsible for taking the bodies *out* as well as putting them in. It is interesting to note also that the *Register* article said that farmer Wise somehow managed to get the

Confederates buried at Antietam National Cemetery. That never happened.

As recently as October 1989 a Hagerstown paper ran a story about farmer Wise and his legendary well. In a Halloween article about the ghosts of South Mountain appeared the following:

When the smoke cleared from the Battle of South Mountain in 1862, farmer Daniel Wise was offered a dollar for every Confederate body he buried. Wise had a well that wasn't working, so he dumped 58 bodies there. . . That night, wise was sitting on his porch, enjoying the tobacco he bought with his $58.

A clue in the search for what really happened will once again be furnished by Mr. Walcott of the 21st Massachusetts. At the end of his account of the "peculiar" burial of the Confederate dead, he provides the following footnote:

This account of the burial of the rebels was given by Mr. Wise himself, a few weeks after the act to a gentleman connected with the Sanitary Commission, who noticed that the well had been filled up, and asked him how a man's hand came to be projecting through the sunken earth, with which it had been covered.

It would seem, then, that Mr. Wise was responsible for starting his own legend.

A review of the legend of farmer Wise would go something like this: On the day after the fighting at Fox's Gap, some Ohio troops, assigned a task they didn't particularly like, sought a short-cut by dumping some of the bodies down a well. The old man who lived in the cabin, being a shrewd old codger, made the most of a bad situation by contracting with Gen. Burnside to continue the process for a dollar a body. He then threw in 58 bodies (or more), sealed the well and earned himself a tidy sum. Farmer Wise was caught and made to put things right by removing the dead Rebels himself. The storytellers all agree that Wise was paid for his troubles.

Did farmer Daniel Wise throw the bodies of 58 dead Confederate soldiers down his will? To address this question we will have to take a look at the gruesome scene the day after the battle. There were many Union regiments of the IX Corps involved at Fox's Gap. Many of the survivors had a chance to view the battlefield the next day and record their impressions.

At the time of the battle the cabin at Fox's Gap was occupied by the Wise family, which consisted of Daniel Wise, age 62, his son John, age 24, and a spinster daughter, Matilda, age 29. It was actually John and Matilda who had purchased the land in 1858. In addition to farming, Daniel Wise earned a living as a "root doctor"--not as a physician, but rather as a local expert in folk medicine. On the morning of the battle the family had fled their cabin to seek safety elsewhere.

Gen. Orlando B. Willcox had led the First Division of the IX Corps at Fox's Gap. On September 14, 1889, he was a speaker at the dedication of the Reno Monument at the site where Gen. Reno fell in the battle. Willcox was one of the three original trustees for the monument, and as a veteran of the battle he was reporting first-hand when he said, "such a picture of the killed and wounded as the view presented next day was rarely seen during the whole war."

That part of the Old Sharpsburg Road that passed over the ridge of South Mountain at Fox's Gap would after the battle come to be known to the veterans as the Sunken Road. The 35th Massachusetts was one of the last units to occupy the Sunken Road. Years later the regimental historian wrote:

. . . the sunken road. . . we found encumbered with dead and wounded confederates. . . . Some of the poor fellows in the road had strength enough to speak, and beg for water or a change of position, which was willingly rendered them. When the contest had ceased General Sturgis send up a section of artillery; and, to let the guns pass, our men moved the wounded and dead from the road upon the bank, sometimes in the darkness placing several bodies together, which led observers in the morning to report to the newspapers that "the rebels were piled in heaps as high as the wall."

William Todd of the 79th New York remembered:

All about us lay the dead and dying, while the groans and cries of the wounded sounded in our ears throughout the long hours of that weary night. . . . Morning of the 15th dawned at last, and on such a sight as none of us ever wish to look upon again. Behind and in front of us, but especially in the angles of the stone walls, the dead bodies of the enemy lay thick; near the gaps in the fences they were piled on top of each other like cord-wood dumped from a cart. . . . About noon we moved off the field, and on our way saw many more evidences of the battle. At one angle of the stone walls fourteen bodies of the enemy were counted lying in a heap, just as they had fallen, apparently, [and] *we referred to that spot as "Dead Man's Corner." A curious sight presented itself in the body of a rebel straddling a stone wall; he must have been killed while in the act of climbing over, for with a leg on either side, the body was thrown slightly forward stiff in death. We were glad to leave these scenes behind us.*

The Confederates had used the stone walls as breastworks. Dr. Thomas T. Ellis, a Union surgeon, noted that . . .

. . . from their [the Rebels] position behind the stone walls, when struck it was mortal, being chiefly in the head or chest. The appearance of the field the morning after the fight was a terrible sight. In some places the dead were lying two or three deep. On the road or pass along which ran the stone walls, the dead lay thickly strewn. The death of many was so instantaneous that their arms were in position of firing their pieces, while others still retained the bitten cartridge in their hands. They appeared to be mostly young men, many of them mere boys.

Walcott of the 21st Massachusetts found the scene on the 15th "interestingly horrible." He wrote:

. . . the rebel dead were lying more thickly, though

By referring to the author's "Crossroads" map (12-1-04 newsletter), this view of Wise's cabin as it appeared in the 1880s was taken from near where the 17th Michigan maker now stands. The road in the left foreground is Wood Road, the one passing across the view left to right is the Old Sharpsburg road (now Reno Monument Road), and the buggy is sitting in the relocated Ridge Road. Unfortunately the well site didn't make it into the photo, and is just out of view at the right edge. (MOLLUS Coll., USAMHI)

(1)

HISTORICAL TIME-LAPSE PHOTOGRAPHY--Three views of the Wise farm. **(1)**The above composite sketch appeared in *Battles and Leaders*, accompanying an article by Confederate Gen. D. H. Hill, defender of South Mountain. The left half is entitled "Fox's Gap--the Approach to Wise's Field," the right, "Fox's Gap--Wise's Field As Seen from the Pasture North of the road" (that's Wise's cabin in the far right). Take notice of the large tree to the left of the cabin, and a smaller sapling to the left of the big tree. **(2)**The same two trees appear in the 1924 photograph by Fred Cross. The Wise cabin is gone. At left is the Reno Monument. **(3)**This is the same view in November 1988. The three views show how much the character of the terrain has changed over a century and a quarter. They also help the modern battlefield tramper identify where the Wise house stood, which in turn helps pinpoint the site of Wise's legendary well.

(2)

(3)

This photo was taken in 1895 and appeared in a book entitled *Echoes of Battle* by Bushrod Washington James. The caption reads: "The Old Stone Fence, Hagerstown Road, Antietam." That's wrong. Observe the building closely. It is Wise's cabin at Fox's Gap, viewed from the northeast.

in narrow spaces, than we had ever seen before, and the woods were full of their wounded. In an outbuilding of a little house belonging to a man named Wise . . . was a savage spectacle, in the bodies of two men, a Union and rebel soldier, who seemed to have killed each other in a hand-to-hand fight.

Some time around noon on the 15th, Walcott and his unit headed down the mountain toward Sharpsburg. Pursue the enemy, take care of the wounded, and bury the dead. These constitute the common routine of an army at war. All day long on the 15th troops were on the move, regrouping and passing by the Wise cabin on their way down the mountain. Field hospitals were established and the burial details were starting their task.

Capt. James Wren was a member of the 48th Pennsylvania. Later in his life he became one of the trustees for the Reno Monument. On September 15, 1862, he had some time to view the battlefield before his regiment headed for Sharpsburgh. The following is from his personal diary. The spelling is his, but some punctuation has been added to assist the reader.

Just to the right of my skirmish line of yesterday war two Cross roads in the shape of an X. On our frut thear was a stone fence & behind that fence & in this ex road the enemy lay verey thick. One rebil in crossing the fence was Killed in the act & his clothing caught & he was haning on the fence . . . this place being the top of South Mountain. The Hospittle was an aufil sight, being a little house by its self. In the yard thear was 3 or 4 large Tables in it. As the soldiers was put on it that was wounded the sergical Core Came along. The head of the Core had in his hand a peic of white Chalk. He marked the place whear the Linb was to be Cut of. Right behind him was the line of sergons with thear instruments & procedid to amputate.

In looking around in the yard I saw a Beautiful plump arm Laing which drew my attention. In looking a Little . . . and seeing another of the same Kind . . . I picked them up & Laid them together & found that thay a right & one a Left Arm which Convinced me that thay war of the one man. You Could see meney legs Laing in the yard with the shoes & stocking on.

During the Civil War, responsibility for the burial of the dead usually fell upon the side that found itself in possession of the field after the battle. Sometimes civilians would be contracted, usually at the rate of a dollar a body, but most of the time the duty fell to the common soldier. burial details were usually a "pick-up" affair, with a few men from each regiment assigned the duty. And it wasn't always the straggler or shirker who got the duty. The good soldier could simply be in the wrong place at the wrong time and find himself on burial detail. There was no standardized system for identification of the dead, and this was usually accomplished by friends and comrades who had survived. When possible, a head-board of scrap wood was marked with the soldier's name and regiment and placed at the head of the grave. Photographs of loved ones, notes and letters, and other personal memorabilia were often buried with the soldier. there were no "dog tags." Indeed, the dead soldier's next of kin often had to consult the newspapers of the day for casualty lists.

The men assigned burial detail had their "tricks of the trade." A bayonet picked up on the battlefield could be heated and bent into the shape of a hook for dragging the corpses to a centralized spot. Trench burial was the norm. A shallow hole was dug and a body rolled in, while another hole dug beside it provided the earth for covering the first body. The next body was placed in the new hole and the procedure was repeated as needed. At South Mountain, where the Union held the field, attention was naturally given to the Yankee dead first.

The above article will be continued in the December 1, 2005, issue of *News from Fox's Gap*!

Welcome New Members!

****

We are pleased to announce the following new member of our Society who joined after the June 1, 2004 newsletter was completed:

Name Address	Phone	Date of Membership	Membership Number
Michael Todd Beachley	717-540-5772	June 1, 2004	0052

885 Sunny Hill Lane — **Ancestor Line:** Joined under interest in Battle of South Mountain.
Harrisburg, PA 17111

Michael had ancestors living in the vicinity of Fox's Gap. He joined the Fox Society under Interest in the Battle of South Mountain. A study of the Civil War period map of The Battlefield of South Mountain reveals many Beachley families living in the Fox's Gap area.

Continued on the following page

Continued from the preceding page

Welcome New Members!

****

We are pleased to announce the following new members of our Society who joined after the December 1, 2004 newsletter was completed.

All of the following new members are descendants of Frederick Fox of Fox's Gap in Maryland and his oldest son, George Fox, who married Elizabeth Ann Link.

Name / Address	Phone	Date of Membership	Membership Number
Timothy Fox Woodard Sr. 4 Kimberly Court Germantown, Ohio 45327		December 10, 2004	0053
Timothy Fox Woodard Jr. 1027 Heatherwood Drive Englewood, OH 45322		December 10, 2004	0054
Kimberly Shay Hayslett 718 Jamestown Drive Miamisburg, OH 45342		December 10, 2004	0055
Elizabeth Bissel 193 East Main Street Norwalk, OH 44857		December 10, 2004	0056
Andrew J. Woodard 250 East Center Street Germantown, OH 45327		December 10, 2004	0057
John Paul Woodard 250 East Center Street Germantown, OH 45327		December 10, 2004	0058

Ancestor Line (each member above): George Fox, a son of Frederick Fox; George L. Fox, Charles E. Fox, Amos R. Fox, Mildred Elizabeth Fox

Genealogy Documentation Section
by Curtis L. Older

A new feature of each Fox Society Newsletter that was begun with the December 1, 2004 , newsletter is the inclusion of an article that documents a descendant or spouse of a descendant of John Fox of Fox's Gap in Maryland. The article will present a written description about the individual and his or her family as well as a listing of the related genealogical source records that support the written description.

The second individual to be presented in this new feature of the newsletter is George Fox of Fox's Gap in Maryland. George was a son of Frederick Fox, the man for whom The Society of the Descendants of Frederick Fox of Fox's Gap in Maryland is named.

Previous issues of the Fox Society Newsletter contained documentation for the following individuals:

December 1, 2004 - Frederick Fox

Documentation for George Fox, father of John L. Fox

George Fox was born March 10, 1781, in Frederick County, Maryland.(**1**) He was the son of Frederick Fox and Catherine Booker.(**2**) George may have been born at or near Fox's Gap in Maryland. The gap received its name from George's grandfather, John Fox, who was the earliest settler in the immediate vicinity of the gap.(**3**) Fox's Gap is where the Old Sharpsburg Road from Frederick, Maryland, to Sharpsburg, Maryland, crosses the South Mountain.(**4**) The Old Sharpsburg Road was part of the Great Wagon Road to Philadelphia, which also was known as the German Monocacy Road.(**5**)

Fox's Gap was the scene for a major portion of the Battle of South Mountain between forces under Confederate General Robert E. Lee and Union General George B. McClellan on September 14, 1862.(**6**) The Reno Monument, dedicated to U. S. Major Jesse Lee Reno who was killed in the Battle of South Mountain, stands at Fox's Gap.(**7**) A little more than one hundred years prior to the Battle of South Mountain, on May 2, 1755, the road through Fox's Gap was used by General Braddock, George Washington, and Maryland's Governor Sharpe to travel from Frederick Town to Swearingen's Ferry on the Potomac River, while on their way to Fort Cumberland during the Braddock Expedition.(**8**)

George Fox was a member of the Zion Lutheran Church of Middletown, Maryland.(**9**) In 1805, at age 24, George acquired the Fox Inn along the Old Sharpsburg Road, about 2 miles east of Fox's Gap.(**10**) *The Fox Genealogy* by Daniel Gebhart Fox indicates that the Fox Inn, which still is standing and is occupied by renters in the year 2004, was built on land owned by Frederick Fox, George's father.(**11**) However, Curtis L. Older found no land records that support Frederick Fox as the owner of the land upon which the Fox Inn stands.(**12**)

George married Elizabeth Ann Link on August 9, 1807, at Shepherdstown, Virginia, now West Virginia.(**13**) Elizabeth was the daughter of John Adam Link II and Jane Ogle.(**14**) Elizabeth's father was a grandson of John Jacob Link, who was an ancestor of Dwight D. Eisenhower.(**15**) Jane Ogle, a daughter of Alexander Ogle of Frederick, Maryland, was a descendant of John Ogle of Delaware.(**16**)

Elizabeth Ann Link was born on January 28, 1784, near Frederick in Frederick County, Maryland.(**17**) She was baptized in the Frederick Lutheran Church.(**18**) George and Elizabeth Fox moved west to near Miamisburg, Ohio, in late 1807 along with a number of other families with ties to George's parents, Frederick and Catherine Fox.(**19**)

George and Elizabeth Fox were the parents of ten children: Adam, Frederick L., Daniel L., Catharine (Mrs. John Fox), George L., Alexander, Susanna Jane, Elizabeth, John L., and Mary L. Fox.(**20**) George Fox died June 14, 1847, in Miamisburg, Ohio, and was buried in the Gebhart or St. John Cemetery in Miamisburg.(**21**) Elizabeth Ann (Link) Fox died March 9, 1872, in Miamisburg, Ohio, and is buried next to her husband in the Gebhart or St. John Cemetery.(**22**)

George Fox is listed in the 1809 Ohio state census for Franklin Township in Warren County.(**23**) The 1810 Ohio Federal census for Warren county, Franklin township, lists the George Fox household.(**24**)

The 1830 Ohio Federal census for Warren county, Clear Creek township, lists the George Fox household as consisting of 7 males and 2 females: one male was 5 and under 10, two males were 10 and under 15, two males were 15 and under 20, one male was twenty and under thirty, one male was 40 and under 50; one female was 5 and under 10 and one female was 15 and under 20.(**25**)

The 1840 Ohio Federal census for Warren county, Clear Creek township, lists the George Fox household as consisting of 5 males and 4 females: one male was age 15 and under 20, two males were 20 and under 30, one male was 30 and under 40, and one male was 50 and under 60; two females were age 5 and under 10, 1 was age 15 and under 20, and one was age 50 and under 60.(**26**)

Children (**Fox**) born in Warren County, Ohio:(**27**)

- i. **Adam**, born October 1, 1808
- ii. **Frederick L.**, born February 28, 1810
- iii. **Daniel L.**, born August 17, 1811
- iv. **Catharine**, born May 6, 1813
- v. **George L.**, born September 12, 1816
- vi. **John L.**, October 18, 1818
- vii. **Alexander**, born September 21, 1820
- viii. **Susanna Jane**, born November 17, 1824
- ix. **Elizabeth** L., born October 1, 1830
- x. **Mary L.**, born October 1, 1830

REFERENCES

1. Tombstone of George Fox, Gebhart or St. John Cemetery, Miamisburg, Ohio; *The Fox Genealogy including the Metherd, Benner, and Leiter descendants, giving biographies of the first and second generations, with sketches of the third generation*, compiled by D. G. Fox, 1914. (n.p) 1924. 1 p. 1., (5)-172 p. 20 com. 37-9439 CS71.F79 1924 Library of Congress, 82. **2.** *Ohio D.A.R. Soldiers Rosters*, 2 vols., 1:146; will of Frederick Fox, Will Book C, case #1444, Montgomery County, Ohio. **3.** Curtis L. Older, *The Braddock Expedition and Fox's Gap in Maryland* (Westminster, Md.: Family Line Publications, 1995), 77-79. **4.** *Braddock Expedition and Fox's Gap in Maryland*, Chapter Three, pp. 69-116. **5.** Curtis L. Older, *The Land Tracts of the Battlefield of South Mountain* (Westminster, Md.: Willow Bend Books, 1999), 42; *Braddock Expedition and Fox's Gap in Maryland*, p. 87. **6.** *Braddock Expedition and Fox's Gap in Maryland*, Afterword, pp. 177-182. **7.** *Land Tracts of the Battlefield of South Mountain*, p. 99. **8.** *Braddock Expedition and Fox's Gap in Maryland*, p. 70. **9.** Frederick S. Weiser, ed., *Zion Lutheran Church 1781-1826*, Maryland German Church Records, Vol. 2, (Manchester, Md.: Noodle-Doosey Press, 1987), 77. **10.** *Braddock Expedition and Fox's Gap in Maryland*, p. 98; *Land Tracts of the Battlefield of South Mountain*, p. 211. **11.** *Fox Genealogy*, p. 13. **12.** *Braddock Expedition and Fox's Gap in Maryland*, p. 98; *Land Tracts of the Battlefield of South Mountain*, p. 211. **13.** Jefferson County, West Virginia, Marriage Records, 1807, page 286; Paxson Link, *The Link Family* (Paris, Illinois: [s.l.], 1951). **14.** *Index to Marriage Licenses, Frederick County, 1778-1810*, married April 14, 1783. **15.** Paxson Link, *The Link Family* (Paris, Illinois: [s.l.], 1951).

Adam Link, the grandfather of Elizabeth Ann Link, supplied bacon during the American Revolution. See Maryland State Papers, Series A, MdHR 4586-15 1/6/4/18. Adam Link, the father of Elizabeth Ann Link (Fox), was an officer during the American Revolution. See *The Link Family* by Paxson Link. **16.** *Land Tracts of the Battlefield of South Mountain*, 236; *Braddock Expedition*, 98; Francis Hamilton Hibbard, assisted by Stephen Parks, The English origin of John Ogle, first of the name in Delaware (Pittsburgh: n.p., 1967); Sir Henry Asgill Ogle, Ogle and Bothal (Newcastle-upon-Tyne: Andrew Reid & Company, 1902). Alexander Ogle, the father of Jane Ogle, provided wheat and flour from his mills to the Maryland troops during the American Revolution. See Maryland State Papers, Series A, MdHR 6636-23-29/7 1/7/5 and related papers. **17.** Tombstone of Elizabeth Ann (Link) Fox, Gebhart or St. John Cemetery, Miamisburg, Ohio; *Fox Genealogy*, 82. **18.** *Link Family*, p. 81. **19.** *Fox Genealogy*, pp. 15-16. **20.** Warren County Genealogical Society, Lebanon, Ohio, estate papers of George Fox; Fox Genealogy, p. 83. **21.** Tombstone of George Fox, Gebhart or St. John Cemetery, Miamisburg, Ohio; *Fox Genealogy*, 82. **22.** Tombstone of Elizabeth Ann (Link) Fox, Gebhart or St. John Cemetery, Miamisburg, Ohio; *Fox Genealogy*, 82. **23.** *Ohio Early Census Index*, 1809 Tax List, Warren County, Franklin Township, page 013, George Fox. **24.** 1810 Ohio Federal Census, Franklin township, Warren County, page 28. **25.** 1830 Ohio Federal Census, Clear Creek township, Warren County, roll M19_142, page 173, image 340. **26.** 1840 Ohio Federal Census, Clear Creek township, Warren County, roll M704_431, page 178, image 356. **27.** Warren County Genealogical Society, Lebanon, Ohio, estate papers of George Fox; *Fox Genealogy*, pp. 82-100.

President's Message

by Curtis Lynn Older

* The end of 2005 will mark the end of our tenth year as an organization. I wish to thank everyone who helped make this adventure a success. We had 58 individuals join the Society during the past nine and one half years. Let all of us increase our pursuit of new members during the next ten years and may we continue to strive to preserve the history of Fox's Gap in Maryland and the genealogy of the Fox family that lived there many years ago.

* Braddock Heights, Maryland, celebrated May 1st as the 250th Anniversary of the Braddock Expedition during a two-hour event that included living historians, music, and wagons. It was 250 years ago on May 2, 1755, when General Braddock, George Washington, and Maryland Governor Sharpe departed Frederick, Maryland, and passed through Fox's Gap on their way to Ft. Cumberland in their attempt to capture Ft. DuQuesne from the French and Indians.

News from Fox's Gap

Published June 1 and December 1 of each year by
The Society of the Descendants of Frederick Fox of Fox's Gap in Maryland
Membership dues are $6.00 per year. President of the Society is Curtis L. Older.
Make Society inquiries by the following means:

Curtis L. Older
618 Tryon Place
Gastonia, NC 28054-6066

e-mail: curtolder@earthlink.net
phone: 704-864-3879

Land Tracts of the Battlefield of South Mountain
by Curtis L. Older

Most Fox Society Newsletters include a survey, patent, or deed related to the land tracts in the vicinity of Crampton's, Fox's, and Turner's Gaps on the Battlefield of South Mountain.

Previous issues of the Society Newsletter contained descriptions of the following tracts:

June 1, 1997	Addition to Friendship of Frederick Fox
December 1, 1997	Fredericksburgh of Frederick Fox
June 1, 1998	Pick All of Bartholomew Booker
December 1, 1998	Bowser's Addition of David Bowser
June 1, 1999	Partnership of John Mansberger
December 1, 1999	Mountain of John Baley
December 1, 2000	Flonham of Philip Jacob Shafer
June 1, 2001	The Exchange of Daniel Dulaney
December 1, 2001	Betty's Good Will of Robert Evans
December 1, 2004	Resurvey on Exchange

Two land records from the Maryland Archives (Maryland Hall of Records) are included below. Each tract is on the east side of the South Mountain, not far from Fox's Gap.

MdHR 17, 435, 1-23-3-35, BC & GS 24, p. 270, Joseph Chapline, The Gap, surveyed 29 Mar 1761, 50 acres.

Frederick County By virtue of a Warrant granted out of his lordships land office of this province to Joseph Chapline of the aforesaid county for one hundred acres of land bearing date 21 Feby 1761. I therefore certify as Deputy surveyor under his Excellency Horatio Sharpe Esq. Governor of Maryland that I have carefully laid out for and in the name of him the said Joseph Chaplin all that tract of land called The Gap lying in the aforesaid county beginning at the end of the third line of Wardrop's Land called Curry's Old Place running thence

Line No.	**North South**	**Degrees East or West**	**Length**
1	S	west 58	88 perches
2	N	west 37	106 perches
3	N	east 35	50 perches

4 then by a straight line to the beginning containing and now laid out for fifty acres of land to be held of Conogocheige Manor Surveyed 29th March 1761

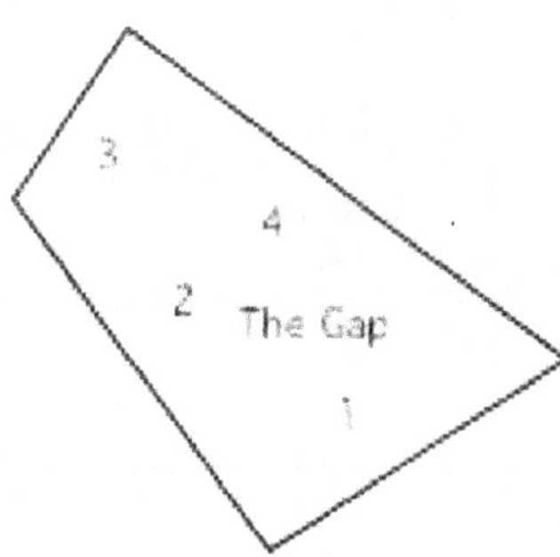

(**Note:** Line 1 of the above tract is the same as line 4 of the John's Delight tract.)

MdHR 17, 406, 1-23-2-44, BY & GS 5, p. 59, James Wardrop, John's Delight, surveyed 17 May 1750, 104 acres.

James Wardrop's Cert 104 a John's Delight Pattd 17th May 1750 Frederick County By virtue of a warrant granted out of his lordships land office of this province to Ms? James Wardrop for fifty acres of land bearing date April 30th 1750 I Therefore Certifie as deputy surveyor and in his excy Samuel Ogle Esqr governor of Maryland I have Carefully laid out for and in the name of him the said Wardrop all that Tract of land called Johns Delight Beginning at a bounded white oak standing about thirty feet from a small run called Carry's Branch nigh the foot of Shanondore Mountain near Curry's Gap Running thence

Line No.	North South	Degrees East or West	Length
1	N	15 east	40 perches
2	N	14 west	80 perches
3	N	73 west	140 perches
4	S	58 west	88 perches

5 then by a straight line to the beginning tree containing and now laid out for one hundred and four acres of land to be held of Conogocheige Manor Surveyed 17 th May 1750

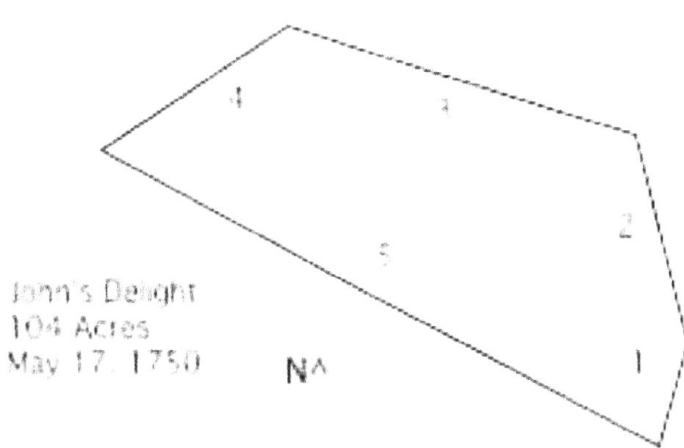

in the name of him the said Wardrop all that tract of land called Johns Delight Beginning at a bounded white oak standing about 30 feet from a small run called Carry's Branch nigh the foot of Shanondore Mountain near Curry's Gap

(**Note:** Line 4 of the above deed is the same as line 1 of The Gap.)

News from Fox's Gap

The Society of the Descendants of Frederick Fox of Fox's Gap in Maryland

Issue 10, Volume 2 **Remember Freedom!** December 1, 2005

The Truth About Wise's Well

Setting the Record Straight on South Mountain

By Steven R. Stotelmyer

The following article is reprinted from the *Blue and Gray Magazine* of October 1990.

[Steven R. Stotelmyer is a native of Hagerstown, Maryland. As a child he and his sister played among the monuments at Antietam National Battlefield during the many family picnics to the Philadelphia Brigade Park. When he graduated from high school in 1968, Mr. Stotelmyer enlisted in the United States Navy and served as a radar man on a destroyer. Returning to civilian life, he earned a Bachelor of Science degree from Frostburg State College and a Masters of Arts from Hood College.

Always interested in local history, especially South Mountain and Antietam, Mr. Stotelmyer helped form the Central Maryland Heritage League in 1989. The League has been successful in acquiring land of the South Mountain Battlefield--an area often overshadowed by Antietam. He has also written magazine articles on the Civil War in Western Maryland and is an active volunteer at the Antietam Battlefield. His favorite "duty station" is the National Cemetery.]

Continued from the June 1, 2005, *News from Fox's Gap* Newsletter

As Capt. Wren observed:

. . . in a field to the left of this house [Wise's] *was a long line of dead Soldiers Laing sid by sid with a Little inscription on thear brest giving thear Names & thear Compy & Reigmt & the state thay ware from. The pionear or ambulenc Cor engaged diging a long trench 7 feet wid to bury them in which makes the troops feal desperate towards the rebels. Meney of them had brave Comrads whou stod in Line with them was now taking thear posision in ther Last Line.*

The field to the left of the cabin was known as Wise's south field, and at the time of the battle it was cultivated.

One of the main themes of the legend of farmer Wise, and the most often cited excuse for putting the Rebels in the well, is the belief that the ground was too hard for digging graves- even though most of the ground around the cabin was being farmed. Perhaps the following account from an observer in the 9th New Hampshire provides a clue: *The work of removing and burying the dead went forward with all possible speed, though the rapid digging of so many graves was made extremely difficult by the stony character of the ground. In long windrows they lay, like wheat from the sickle, in fence corners, on the banks, along the sunken road, and beside the stone wall.*

Perhaps it is not so much that the ground was too hard for digging, but rather that those involved in the task were simply overwhelmed by the number of dead. There were 325 Union soldiers of the IX Corps killed at Fox's Gap (including Maj. Gen. Reno). And, although some of the Union dead were transported home for burial, the majority of them were buried at the gap. A descriptive list of Confederate burial places, published by authority of Maryland Governor Oden Bowie in 1869 (two years after the Union soldiers had been reintered at Antietam), shows a total of 130 Confederates buried in the fields near Wise's cabin (including the 58 in the well). The same list shows 66 confederates in the area east of Fox's Gap. Assuming then that some of the Union dead were buried at home, the burial details at Fox's Gap probably had to deal with some 400 bodies.

What about the Wise family? Were they present on the 15th of September? There were civilians on the battlefield. David Thompson remembered that, "Before we left the spot, some of the country people living thereabout, who had been scared away by the firing, ventured back, making big eyes at all they saw, and asking most ridiculous questions."

Dr. Ellis related that, "A number of farmers came on the field to witness the sight, of which they had so often heard but never seen. They collected as relics everything portable: cartridge-boxes, bayonet scabbards, old muskets, and even cannon-balls were carried away by them." It is quite possible that Daniel Wise and his family were on the scene along with many others who were souvenir hunting and sightseeing. One of the events they would have witnessed was the passage of Gen. Burnside. As Dr. Ellis wrote, "Gen. Burnside rode by this morning, and is again to take command of the Corps in person. He was welcomed by the men with shouts of delight."

This photo of Fox's Gap in 1912 appeared in the regimental history of the 45th Pennsylvania. The view is looking west along the Old Sharpsburg Road toward the Wise cabin, which is barely visible at far left, from the wall of the Reno Monument, a corner of which can be seen in the bottom left of the photo. Note the stone wall in the right distance; it borders Wood Road. It was this wall that had the dead "Johnnie" straddling it. We'll never know if he became one of the occupants of Wise's well . . .

All day long on September 15, 1862, elements of the Union Army of the Potomac passed through Fox's Gap on their way toward Sharpsburg. There were many unusual sights to behold and one of them was that dead Confederate hung up on the fence along Wood Road. (The fence was a type known as "stone and rider," a combination of stone wall and wooden railing.) The historian for the 9th New Hampshire remembered him thus: *Clearly, too, does one remember the strangely lifelike position of that dead Confederate soldier sitting astride the stone wall near Wise's house, his body bent slightly forward, killed just in the act of climbing over. . . . Yet, with the quickly aquired tendency of the soldier to turn anything into a jest, entirely regardless of his own feelings, a Company E boy, noting the well shod feet of the dead man, exclaimed, "That's the first rebel I've seen with a decent pair of boots on, and by thunder, if he ha'nt got up there to show 'em."*

Pvt. Samuel Compton of the 12th Ohio remembered the dead man too: *As we passed the corner of the little field, astride of the wall was a husky Reb. Stone dead, bolt upright, his haversack had fallin in front, both arms extended palms up and mouth open. Under any circumstances men will joke. Some "smart alec" of a yank had placed a yeast biscut from his haversack, one in his mouth and one in each hand. The following was hurled at him. "Say Johnnie your a hog! You need ice, not ratios where you are going! Was that gal good lookin that baked them biscuts?" Many more equally cantankerous jibes were hurled at Johnnie.*

Capt. Lyman Jackman of the 6th New Hampshire remembered that as his regiment was passing through Fox's Gap. . . *it came upon a heap of the enemy's dead. Just beyond was a stone wall, and astride it sat a "Johnnie." Sergent French of Company B thought he would go up and speak to him. Going near, he asked him what he wanted. Getting no reply, French mover up nearer. . . . French had got near enough to see that his man was dead. He had been killed while getting over the wall, and a stake by his side held him up in the position in which he was found. The boys used to joke French somewhat about his trying to make a dead rebel talk.*

In perhaps the most gruesome account of that day, Capt. Jackman continued: *Just over this wall was a lane that led down the mountain. Our men will remember how thick the ground there was covered with the enemy's dead. The bodies were lying in all positions imaginable. . . . A few minutes after we came up, a battery tore along the road and down this lane, to take position in front. Orders were urgent, and there was no stopping for dead rebels, so the battery was driven over them. It was a sickening sight after the last caisson had passed along.*

By the end of the day most of the Union army was off the mountain. As far as the burial details were concerned, the day of September 15 had been spent digging graves for Union dead. There had been some civilians and some Confederate prisoners put to work burying Confederate dead that day, but the bulk of the dead Southerners still awaited burial. The area around the Wise cabin presented a bizarre scene of war. In addition to the constant noise and confusion of the passage of thousands of troops by the cabin, there were the headshot Rebels piled behind the stone walls. . . the field hospital in and around the cabin with the screams of the wounded as their limbs were amputated and dumped in the yard. . . the macabre comedy of the dead "Johnnie" on the fence. . . and those mutilated corpses that had been ground under the wheels and hooves of the artillery.

The Wise farm had been a crowded place at times during the day. Many of the survivors of the fight at Fox's Gap took the opportunity to tour the field, and many of the local citizenry came by to sight-see and collect curios. It is not unreasonable, then, to assume that had a 62-year old man been dumping dead Confederates down his well there would have been someone around to take notice. The truth is, there were no bodies thrown down the well on September 15, 1862. They were put in the well on September 16th. Pvt. Compton of the 12th Ohio was there to observe the following: *On the morning of the 16th I strolled out to see them bury the Confederate dead. I saw but I never want to another sight.*

The squad I saw were armed with a pick & a canteen full of whiskey. The whiskey the most necessary of the two. The bodies had become so offensive that men could only endure it by being staggering drunk. To see men stagger up to corpses and strike four or five times before they could get a hold, a right hold being one above the belt. Then staggering, as very drunk will, they dragged the corpses to a 60 foot well and (were) tumbling them in. What a sepulcher and what a burial! You don't wonder I had no appetite for supper.

You must remember that Charles Walcott of the 21st Massachusetts, whose account of the incident became the basis for the Wise's well legend, footnoted his account by saying that the story as he reported it was told originally to a member of the Sanitary Commission by Wise. Walcott was not there when the incident happened, because he was off the mountain on the 15th. Walcott received his information second-hand. But his account has been accepted over others, who observed firsthand what transpired at Wise's farm. As we have seen, there were civilians on the battlefield on the 15th, and it is reasonable to assume that at least one member of the Wise family was there in the days following the battle.

PHOTOGRAPHIC ELOQUENCE—All of you hardcore battlefield trampers should copy this article—this page at the very least—and tuck it into the pages of your dog-eared copy of B&G's South Mountain issue of a few years back. Then, the next time you venture to South Mountain, you can add to your Tour the "exact" site of Daniel Wise's well (plus or minus 10 feet, according to the author, a professional surveyor). The top photo shows the author's daughter, Amber, standing alongside modern-day Reno Monument Road—the road, also known as the Old Sharpsburg Road, and simply as the Sunken Road by veterans of the battle, was widened considerably in the 1950s. She is marking the site of Wise's well. In the bottom photo, Amber hasn't moved (see her in the bottom right-hand corner?), but her daddy has. He's moved to the position of a photographer who made the image of Wise's cabin in the 1880s (see Pg. 30). Superimposed on the author's modern-day photo is that 1880s picture. From this angle you can't see Reno Monument Road passing in front of Amber. But to the far left, among the trees, is a faint image of the Reno Monument. The slight depression in left-center is the trace of Wood Road, now part of the Appalachian Trail. Just behind the trees in the center, largely obliterated by them, is the marker for the 17th Michigan. (Please bear in mind that most of this area is private property, so don't get too involved in exploring around without first obtaining permission from property owners. B&G's South Mountain issue made us a host of enemies in the area, some of whom, we're told, don't mind sending a load of buckshot in the direction of intruders.)

But, since Gen. Burnside passed through Fox's Gap on the 15th and the bodies were put in the well on the 16th, it follows that Daniel Wise could not have stopped the "Ohio troops" in their task, and then contracted with Burnside to finish the job himself. Assuming that at least one member of the Wise family was there, they probably just looked on helplessly as the men dragged rotting bodies to the well.

It is also reasonable to assume that staggering drunk men would not be able to drag two-day old bodies very far. Most of the dead Confederates in the well probably came from the are between the stone walls along the Ridge Road, the Sunken Road, and the Wood Road. An analysis of the battle indicates that these positions were defended at various times during the day by troops from North Carolina, South Carolina, Georgia and Virginia. And that is almost all that we will ever know about the fellows tossed down the well.

And, given the condition of the bodies as already described, plus the two days of already described, plus the two days of exposure to the warm September sunshine, it is understandable that the men on the burial detail would want a drink. Under the best of circumstances it was not pleasant duty. One wonders if perhaps it started out as a lark or a joke. Certainly the dead Rebel on the fence had already provided a sort of carnival atmosphere that would only have been amplified by alcohol: "Say, we already have a hole here, let's fill it up!" Or perhaps it started by someone dumping amputated limbs into the well, and then naturally continuing with whole bodies. Whatever the spark of origin, 58 bodies ended up in Wise's well.

It must have been a very frustrating couple of days for the Wise family. Not only were they unable to get back into their home because it was being used as a field hospital, but then they had to suffer the contamination of their well. It is not unreasonable to assume that at least one member of the family noted the number of bodies put in the well. And some weeks later, when the gentleman from the Sanitary Commission noticed the hand protruding from the dirt and made his inquiries, Daniel Wise, in an attempt to get some sort of recompense for his ruined well, might have answered: "The Ohio boys started it, but I stopped them. And Gen. Burnside said he'd give me a dollar for every body if I agreed to finish it. A dollar a body, that's the going rate. . ." Of course, this is speculation, and we may never know what Daniel Wise said. But we do know that Daniel Wise did not put those bodies in his well - not on September 15 or 16 or any other day - and there is no record to indicate that any member of the Wise family was ever paid a cent by the Federal government for their ruined well. Like many other civilians of the area, the Wise family were also victims of the battle of South Mountain, and around them has grown a legend too long accepted as fact.

John Wise sold the farm in 1878 after his father's death. There was never any contemporary local story about Daniel Wise putting bodies down his well. The only local reference of the well before 1882 was by the Hagerstown press. In 1874, when the South Mountain dead were being exhumed, the *Hagerstown Mail* reported, "Some of these bodies we have heretofore noticed as having been taken from the historical well on South Mountain battle-field, where they were thrown by Gen. Reno's command . . ." Daniel Wise never knew of the legend that grew from Walcott's regimental history, published in 1882.

As for the 58 unknown Confederates who were dumped into Wise's well by burial details, they would stay in the well for 12 years. By that time, the men who did the exhumations were removing nothing but bones. Any trace of the soldiers' identities had long since vanished. Mr. Henry C. Mumma of Sharpsburg was contracted by the trustees of the Washington Confederate Cemetery at Rose Hill in Hagerstown to exhume the Rebel dead on South Mountain. He was paid $1.65 per head. It is reasonable to assume that if he had to excavate a 60-foot well, he made sure he got them all.

Because the cemetery trustees in Hagerstown were operating under a strict budget with limited funds - these funds being provided by the states of Maryland, Virginia and West Virginia, and not by the Federal government - when unknown soldiers were encountered, the remains of two of them were placed together in a small wooden casket three feet long and a foot in depth. On the metal plaque that serves as the marker for almost 2500 bodies in Hagerstown's Confederate Cemetery, there is an inscription that reads: "29 boxes, 58 bodies unknown." It is the only place where the number 58 appears on the plaque, and that agrees with the only place in Governor Bowie's descriptive list where the same number appears: "58 Unknown, In Wise's well on South Mountain."

Setting the historical record straight is often condemned as "revisionism." The story of Daniel Wise's well has become cemented as fact in the history of the Maryland Campaign and, unfortunately, much of it is legend. The campaign has more than ample drama and human interest - documented - without having to include incidents that can be proven false or are riddled with errors. To "revise," by definition, implies correction and improvement. The foregoing essay corrects the Wise's well story, it doesn't demolish it. Without doubt the well became a mass grave for 58 Confederates. What I have done is merely corrected the history behind how they got there. They weren't put there on September 15, but rather the next day. Daniel Wise didn't put them there, burial details did. And there is no evidence that Wise or his family got a dollar per body or even one red cent for having their well contaminated. I rest my case.

SOURCES: Books - *A Descriptive List of the Burial Places and Remains of Confederate Soldiers,* published under the direction of Governor Oden Bowie; *History of the Thirty-fifth Regiment Massachusetts Volunteers,* published by a committee of the Regimental Association; Ellis, Thomas T., M.D., *Leaves From the Diary of an Army Surgeon*; Jackman, Lyman, *History of the Sixth New Hampshire Regiment*; Lord, Edward O. ed., *History of the Ninth Regiment New Hampshire Volunteers*; Todd, William, *The Seventy-ninth Highlanders New York Volunteers*; and Walcott, Charles F., *History of the Twenty-first Regiment Massachusetts Volunteers.* **Articles** - "In the Ranks to the Antietam," by David L. Thompson, in *Battles and Leaders of the Civil War,* **Manuscripts** - Letter of Capt. Gabriel Campbell, 17th Michigan, in the Antietam battlefield library; "The Maryland Campaign of 1862," by Ezra Carmen, in the Western Maryland Room of Washington County Library, Hagerstown, MD; Samuel Compton's "Memoirs," in the Manuscript Department of Duke Univ.; and Capt. James Wren's "Diary," in the possession of the Antietam battlefield library. **Newspapers** - *Hagerstown Mail,* June 26, 1874; *The Morning Herald* (Hagerstown), October 31, 1989; and *The Valley Register* (Middletown), September 20, 1889, September 13, 1912, and December 26, 1919. **Miscellaneous** - U. S. Census for 1850, 1860 and 1870; and "Report of the Trustees of Washington Cemetery," December 9, 1873, in the Western Maryland Room of Washington County Library, Hagerstown, MD.

Fox Society website

http://homepage.mac.com/clo7956

Genealogy Documentation Section

by Curtis L. Older

A new feature of each Fox Society Newsletter that was begun with the December 1, 2004, newsletter is the inclusion of an article that documents a descendant or spouse of a descendant of John Fox of Fox's Gap in Maryland. The article will present a written description about the individual and his or her family as well as a listing of the related genealogical source records that support the written description.

The third individual to be presented in this new feature of the newsletter is John L. Fox. John L. Fox was a son of George Fox.

Previous issues of the Fox Society Newsletter contained documentation for the following individuals:

December 1, 2004 - Frederick Fox June 1, 2005 - George Fox

Documentation for John L. Fox, father of Daniel Alexander Fox

John L. Fox was born October 18, 1818, near Miamisburg, Ohio.(**1**) He was the son of George Fox and Elizabeth Ann Link.(**2**)

John L. Fox married Susannah Hiligass on November 11, 1845, in Miami Township, Montgomery County, Ohio, by the Reverend George Long.(**3**) Susannah Hiligass was the daughter of Michael Hiligass and Anna Yeakel(Weikel). She was born November 30, 1819, in Montgomery County, Ohio .(**4**)

John L. Fox and Susannah Hiligass were the parents of seven children: Anna Elizabeth, Mary Susannah, Catherine Florence, Martha Jane, Margaret Persilla, John Adam, and Daniel Alexander Fox. All of the children were born in Ohio except Daniel, who was born in Vermillion County, Indiana.(**5**)

Susannah Hiligass Fox died August 11, 1894, in Gessie, Highland Township, Vermillion County, Indiana.(**6**) John L. Fox died January 6, 1899, probably in Highland Township, Vermillion County, Indiana.(**7**) Both Susannah (Hiligass) Fox and John L. Fox are buried in Hopewell Cemetery west of Covington, Indiana.(**8**) The will of John L. Fox lists the following children: Margaret Ricketts, John A. Fox, Anna E. Goff, Mary Burnett, and Daniel A. Fox.(**9**)

John L. Fox is listed under the U. S. Census of Ohio, 1850, Miami Township, Montgomery County, as age 32 value of real estate = $2,500. Also listed with him are Susannah age 30, Ann age 2, and Mary Fox age 8 months. All are listed as born in Ohio.**(10)** John L. Fox and family moved to Vermillion County, Indiana about 1857.

John L. Fox appears in the U. S. Census of Indiana, 1860, Highland Township, Vermillion County, Indiana. His real estate was valued at $6,560 and his personal property was valued at $1,500. Also listed in the household is: Susannah Fox, age 40, born in Ohio; Ann E. Fox, age 12, born in Ohio; Mary S. Fox, age 10, born in Ohio; Catherine F. Fox, age 8, born in Ohio; Margaret P. Fox, age 6, born in Ohio; John A. Fox, age 3, born in Ohio; Daniel A. Fox, age 5/12, born in Indiana; and Allen Rager, age 45, a laborer, who was born in Indiana.(**11**)

John L. Fox is listed under the U. S. Census of Indiana, 1870, Highland Township, Vermillion County, Post Office - Perrysville, enumerated June 21, 1870, by A. J. Adams, pages 14 and 15, dwelling number 94, family number 94. John L. Fox is listed as age 53, real estate value = $6,780 and personal estate value = $1,400. Susannah is listed as age 50.**(12)**

John L. Fox is listed in the U. S. Census of Indiana, 1880, Highland Township, Vermillion County, dwelling 16, family 16, age 60, a farmer, living with Susannah Fox and Daniel Fox.(**13**).

For a Biographical Sketch of John L. Fox, see *History of Vermillion County, Indiana,* Biographical Sketches: page 491. The article indicates John L. Fox owned 331 acres of choice land at one time in Highland Township. He was farming 186 acres at the time the book was published.**(14)** Also see *The Peoples' Guide, a business political and religious directory of Vermillion County, Indiana,* by Cline and McHaffie, 1874. A listing includes John L. Fox, farmer, 1 1/4 miles north east of Gessie, born in OH, 1818, settled in Vermillion Co., IN, 1858.**(15)**

Children (**Fox**):

i. **Anna Elizabeth**, born February 25, 1848, in Miamisburg, Montgomery County, Ohio

ii. **Mary Susannah**, born January 1850 in Ohio

iii. **Catherine Florence**, born in 1852 in Ohio

iv. **Martha Jane** born in Ohio

v. **Margaret Persilla**, born in 1854 in Warren County, Ohio

vi. **John Adam**, born in July 1857 in Warren County, Ohio

vii. **Daniel Alexander**, born January 13, 1860, in Highland Township, Vermillion County, Indiana

REFERENCES

1. *The Fox Genealogy including the Metherd, Benner, and Leiter descendants, giving biographies of the first and second generations, with sketches of the third generation,* compiled by Daniel Gebhart Fox, 1914. (n.p) 1924. 1 p. 1., (5)-172 p. 20 com. 37-9439 CS71.F79 1924 Library of Congress, page 94; Tombstone of John L. Fox, Hopewell Cemetery west of Covington, Indiana. Date of death is given as January 6, 1899. The tombstone indicates he was 80 years, 2 months, 28 days old. Tombstone photograph by Curtis L. Older. **2.** Estate Papers of George Fox, Warren County Genealogical Society, 300 East Silver Street, Lebanon, Ohio 45036, includes a receipt in the amount of $50 signed by Susannah Fox for John L. Fox; *The Fox Genealogy* by D. G. Fox, p. 94. **3.** *The Fox Genealogy* by D. G. Fox, p. 94; John L. Fox and Susannah Hiligass, married November 11, 1845, in Miami Township, Montgomery County, Ohio, by Reverend George Long; Susannah Hiligass and John L. Fox marriage record, source #492.000, Yates Publications. **4.** *The Fox Genealogy* by D. G. Fox, p. 94; tombstone of Susannah Hiligass, Hopewell Cemetery west of Covington Indiana. The tombstone states, "Susannah Hiligass, wife of John L. Fox, died August 11, 1894, 74 years, 2 months, 11 days." **5.** *The Fox Genealogy* by D. G. Fox, p. 94; U. S. Census for Ohio, 1850, Montgomery County, Miami Township, enumerated by J. Hokidry on August 4, 1850, dwelling number 473, family number 473; U. S. Census for Indiana, 1860, Vermillion County, Highland Township, Post Office - Perrysville, enumerated by A. J. Adams on June 30, 1860, dwelling number 76, family number 76; U. S. Census for Indiana, 1870, Vermillion County, Highland Township, Post Office - Perrysville, enumerated by A. J. Adams on June 21, 1870, dwelling number 94, family number 94, pages 14 and 15; U. S. Census for Indiana, 1880, Vermillion County, Highland Township, enumerated June 8, by Joshua Lewis, dwelling number 16, family number 16; will of John L. Fox, Court House, Newport, Vermillion County, Indiana, pages 520 and 521. **6.** Tombstone of Susannah Hiligass, Hopewell Cemetery west of Covington Indiana. The tombstone states, "Susannah Hiligass, wife of John L. Fox, died August 11, 1894, 74 years, 2 months, 11 days." 7. Tombstone of John L. Fox, Hopewell Cemetery west of Covington, Indiana. Date of death is given as January 6, 1899. The tombstone indicates he was "80 years, 2 months, 28 days old". **8.** Tombstones of John L. Fox and Susannah Hiligass at Hopewell Cemetery west of Covington, Indiana. **9.** Will of John L. Fox, Court House, Newport, Vermillion County, Indiana, pages 520 and 521.

10. U. S. Census for Ohio, 1850, Miami Township, Montgomery County, enumerated August 4, 1850, by J. Hokidry, Dwelling 473, Family 473, John L. Fox, age 41, John Fox, age 32, farmer, real estate value = $2,500, born in Ohio; Susannah Fox, age 30, female, born in Ohio, Ann Fox, age 2, female, born in Ohio, Mary Fox, age 8 months, born in Ohio. **11.** U. S. Census for Indiana, 1860, Highland Township, Vermillion County, enumerated by A. J. Adams on June 30, 1860, Dwelling 76, Family 76, John L. Fox, age 41, farmer, real estate value = $6,560, personal property value = $1,500, born in Ohio; Susannah Fox, age 40, born in Ohio; Ann E. Fox, age 12, born in Ohio; Mary S. Fox, age 10, born in Ohio; Catherine F. Fox, age 8, born in Ohio; Margaret P. Fox, age 6, born in Ohio; John A. Fox, age 3, born in Ohio; Daniel A. Fox, age 5/12, born in Indiana. **12.** U. S. Census for Indiana, 1870, Vermillion County, Highland Township, Post Office - Perrysville, enumerated June 21, 1870, by A. J. Adams, pages 14 and 15, Dwelling number 94, Family number 94, John L. Fox, age 53, male, white, farmer, real estate value = $6,780, personal estate vale = $1,400, born in Ohio, citizen of the U. S.; Susannah Fox, age 50, female, white, at home, born in Ohio; Anna Fox, age 22, female, white, at home, born in Ohio; Mary Fox, age 20, female, white, at home, born in Ohio; Catherine Fox, age 18, female, white, at home, born in Ohio, attended school within the year; Margaret Fox, age 14, female, white, at home, born in Ohio, attended school within the year; John Fox, age 13, male, white, at home, born in Ohio, attended school within the year; Daniel Fox, age 10, male, white, at home, born in Indiana, attended school within the year. **13.** U. S. Census for Indiana, 1880, Highland Township, Vermillion County, enumerated June 8, 1880, by Joshua Lewis, Dwelling number 16, Family number 16, John L. Fox, age 60; Susannah Fox, age 59; Daniel Fox, age 20. **14.** *History of Vermillion County, Indiana,* under Biographical Sketches, page 491, there appears a sketch of John L. Fox. The biographical sketch indicates he owned 331 acres of choice land at one time in Highland Township. He was farming 186 acres at the time the book was published. **15.** *The Peoples' Guide, a business political and religious directory of Vermillion County, Indiana,* by Cline and McHaffie, Indianapolis, Indianapolis Printing and Publishing House 1874: John L. Fox, farmer, 1 1/4 miles north east of Gessie, born in OH, 1818, settled in Vermillion Co., IN, 1858.

Brothers and Sisters of John L. Fox

Adam Fox was born Oct. 1, 1808, and died May 1, 1881, in Ohio. He married Elizabeth F. Heiss.

Frederick L. Fox was born Feb. 28, 1810, in Montgomery Co., Ohio, and died Nov. 20, 1851. He is buried at the St. John or Gebhart Church Cemetery in Miamisburg, Warren Co., Ohio. He married Anna Maria Zehring on Mar. 28, 1833.

Daniel L. Fox was born Aug. 17, 1811 and died Sep. 8, 1889. He married Rosannah Christman on Sep. 12, 1833.

Catharine Fox (Mrs. John Fox) was born May 6, 1813 and died Sep. 19, 1841. She married John Fox on Sep. 20, 1832.

George L. Fox was born Sep. 12, 1816 and died Apr. 17, 1893. He married Susannah Manning on Dec. 27, 1842.

Alexander Fox was born Sep. 21, 1820 and died Sep. 15, 1900. He married Anna Eagle on Apr. 9, 1845.

Susanna Jane Fox was born Nov. 17, 1824 and died Nov. 17, 1824.

Elizabeth Fox was born Oct. 1, 1830 and died Oct. 23, 1868. She married Peter Eagle on Nov. 11, 1854.

Mary L. Fox was born Oct. 1, 1830 and died Oct. 5, 1850.

President's Message
by Curtis Lynn Older

* The end of 2005 will mark the end of our tenth year as an organization. I wish to thank everyone who helped make this venture a success. We had 58 individuals join the Society during the past nine and one half years. Let all of us increase our pursuit of new members during the next ten years and may we continue to strive to preserve the history of Fox's Gap in Maryland and the genealogy of the Fox family that lived there many years ago.

* The next two issues of *News from Fox's Gap* will contain an article published in the Spring/Summer edition of *Catoctin History. Catoctin History* is the magazine of the Catoctin Center for Region Studies, a program of Frederick Community College, Frederick, Maryland, and co-sponsored by the National Park Service.

The article is entitled, "Catoctin History Tour #5, The French and Indian War in Mid-Maryland." It discusses a new history tour that has been established in Western Maryland, principally in Washington and Frederick Counties. The tour traces the routes of General Braddock and his forces during the Braddock Expedition of 1755. The article was written by Angela R. Commito, Research Assistant, The Catoctin Center for Regional Studies. Angela uses a book written by Curtis L. Older, *The Braddock Expedition and Fox's Gap in Maryland,* to substantiate most of the statements made in the article.

Catoctin History was a Winner of the 2004 Certificate of Commendation from the American Association for State and Local History! Winner of a 2004 Educational Excellence Award from the Maryland Historical Trust! Winner of a 2004 Award of Excellence from the Printing and Imaging Industries of Maryland!

* Please visit the Indiana University of Pennsylvania website on Fox's Gap in Maryland at:

http://www.iuparchaeology.iup.edu/FoxGap/

News from Fox's Gap

Published June 1 and December 1 of each year by
The Society of the Descendants of Frederick Fox of Fox's Gap in Maryland
Membership dues are $5.00 per year. President of the Society is Curtis L. Older.
Make Society inquiries by the following means:

Curtis L. Older
618 Tryon Place
Gastonia, NC 28054-6066

e-mail: curtolder@earthlink.net
phone: 704-864-3879

Land Tracts of the Battlefield of South Mountain

by Curtis L. Older

Many Fox Society Newsletters include a survey, patent, or deed related to the land tracts in the vicinity of Crampton's, Fox's, and Turner's Gaps on the Battlefield of South Mountain.

Previous issues of the Society Newsletter contained descriptions of the following tracts:

June 1, 1997	Addition to Friendship of Frederick Fox
December 1, 1997	Fredericksburgh of Frederick Fox
June 1, 1998	Pick All of Bartholomew Booker
December 1, 1998	Bowser's Addition of David Bowser
June 1, 1999	Partnership of John Mansberger
December 1, 1999	Mountain of John Baley
December 1, 2000	Flonham of Philip Jacob Shafer
June 1, 2001	The Exchange of Daniel Dulaney
December 1, 2001	Betty's Good Will of Robert Evans
December 1, 2004	Resurvey on Exchange
June 1, 2005	The Gap and John's Delight

A land record for the Resurvey on Well Done from the Maryland Archives (Maryland Hall of Records) is included below. This tract was on the west side of Fox's Gap and began at the beginning tree of Grims Fancy. The Grims Fancy tract description mentions John Fox's house and the Road from Frederick Town to Swearingen's Ferry.

MdHR 17,458, 1-23-4-12, BC & GS 47, pp. 39-40, Philip Booker, Resurvey on Well Done, resurveyed 10 May 1771, 332 acres. completed 10-1-95.

Philip Booker his cert 332 acres The Resurvey on Well Done Pattd 10th Nov 1772 Ren ? ? ?/3/2/ Stg Charged to the rent Roll} Frederick County ? by virtue of a warrant granted out of his lordships land office unto Philip Booker of said county to resurvey a tract or parcel of land called well done lying and being in the county afsd originally on the 4th day of Sept Anno Domini 1761 granted unto Moses Chaplaine for 100 acres under new rent to correct and amend all errors in the original survey and to add any vacant land thereto contiguous not exceeding two hundred and fifty acres bearing date by renewment the 2d April 1771 I certifie as deputy surveyor of Frederick county under George? Lee? Esqr. surveyor general of the western shore of Maryland that I have carefully resurveyed for and in the name of him the said Philip Booker his tract of land afsd according to the ancient meets and bounds and find it contains ninety seven acres and three quarters of an acre being two acres and one quarter of an acres less that it was granted for that I have added one parcel of vacancy containing two hundred and thirty four acres and one quarter of an acre and reduced the whole into one entire tract beginning for the out lines thereof at the beginning tree of a tract of land called Grims Fancy and running thence

Line No.	North South	Degrees East or West	Length
1	S	82 east	121 perches
2	S		25 perches
3	S	60 west	26 perches
4	S	30 east	24 perches

Line No.	North South	Degrees East or West	Length
5	N	east 71	60 perches
6	N		141 perches
7	S	88 1/4 west	266 perches to the beginning tree of Well Done
8	S	82 1/2 west	167 perches to the end of the 6?th line of original
9	S		126 perches to the end of the 5th line of the original
10	N	63 east	48 perches
11	N	78 east	40 perches
12	N	50 east	26 perches to the end of the 2nd line of original
13	S		30 perches
14	S	79 east	194 perches
15	N	21 1/2 east	8 perches
16	N	42 west	36 perches
17	N	77 west	25 perches
18	N	18 west	40 perches then with

19 a straight line to the beginning containing three hundred and thirty two acres to be held of his lordships manor of Monocacy by the name of the Resurvey on Well Done resurveyed the 10th May 1771 John Hanson ?
April 2d 1772 examd & passed U. Scott Exr.

On the back of the foregoing certificate was the following receipt vizt,

I have received eleven pound twelve shillings for the within vacancy and twelve shilings and six pence rent to Michemas 1772 patent may therefore issue with his excellencys approbation

3d April 1772 approved Robt Eden Danl of St. Thos Jenifer

Resurvey on Well Done
Phillip Booker
BC & GS 47, 39-40
resurveyed 10 May 1771
332 acres

Beginning for the out lines thereof at the beginning tree of a tract of land called Grim's Fancy.

(**Author's Note:** The original tract named Well Done is in the westernmost portion of this tract.)

News from Fox's Gap

The Society of the Descendants of Frederick Fox of Fox's Gap in Maryland

Issue 1, Volume 3 **Remember Freedom!** June 1, 2006

The French and Indian War in Mid-Maryland

By Angela R. Commito

The following article appeared beginning on page 42 of *Catoctin History* Spring/Summer 2005.

Angela Commito is a Research Assistant at the Catoctin Center for Regional Studies.

Catoctin History is the magazine of the **Catoctin Center for Regional Studies**, a program of **Frederick Community College, Frederick, Maryland**, and co-sponsored by the **National Park Service**.

Catoctin History is a non-profit educational magazine that serves as a forum for information about the history and culture of mid-Maryland and the surrounding region. For additional information about the Catoctin Center for Regional Studies, please see the Center's website at:

http://catoctincenter.frederick.edu

The first half of this article is presented in this issue of *News from Fox's Gap*. The second half of this article will be presented in the December 1, 2006, issue of *News from Fox's Gap*.

In the spring of 1755 the settlers of mid-Maryland became enmeshed in international politics. Since the end of the seventeenth century, French and British colonists in North America had been embroiled in conflict over rights to settlement in the Ohio Valley. These conflicts were part of a worldwide struggle for power between Great Britain and France that saw fighting in North America, Europe, India, and elsewhere. The North American front of the last of these conflicts is called the French and Indian War (1754-1763) and corresponds with the Seven Years' War (1756-1763) in Europe. On a local level, mid-Maryland played a role in the beginning of this struggle, and this tour highlights several sites related to the war.

Beginning in the 1740's, French colonists in North America began to lay claim to the rich Ohio Territory by building a chain of forts from Lake Erie to southern Pennsylvania. A group of Virginia businessmen, organized as the Ohio Company, began exploring the same territory with plans to expand into it from the east. Rising hostilities between the British-endorsed Ohio Company and the French over control of these lands erupted when

General Braddock and the two regiments of his army traveled through Virginia and Maryland on their way to Fort Duquesne in the spring of 1755. This map shows the routes that Braddock's party, Dunbar's 48th Regiment, and Halkett's 44th Regiment used to reach Fort Cumberland by May before continuing to Fort Duquesne. The routes have been drawn on modern state and county borders. [Walter S. Hough, *Braddock's Road Through the Virginia Colony, Volume VII: Winchester-Frederick County Historical Society* (Winchester, VA: Winchester-Frederick County Historical Society, 1970), 2, 4; Curtis L. Older, *The Braddock Expedition and Fox's Gap in Maryland* (Westminster, MD: Willow Bend Books, 2000), 46, 173.]

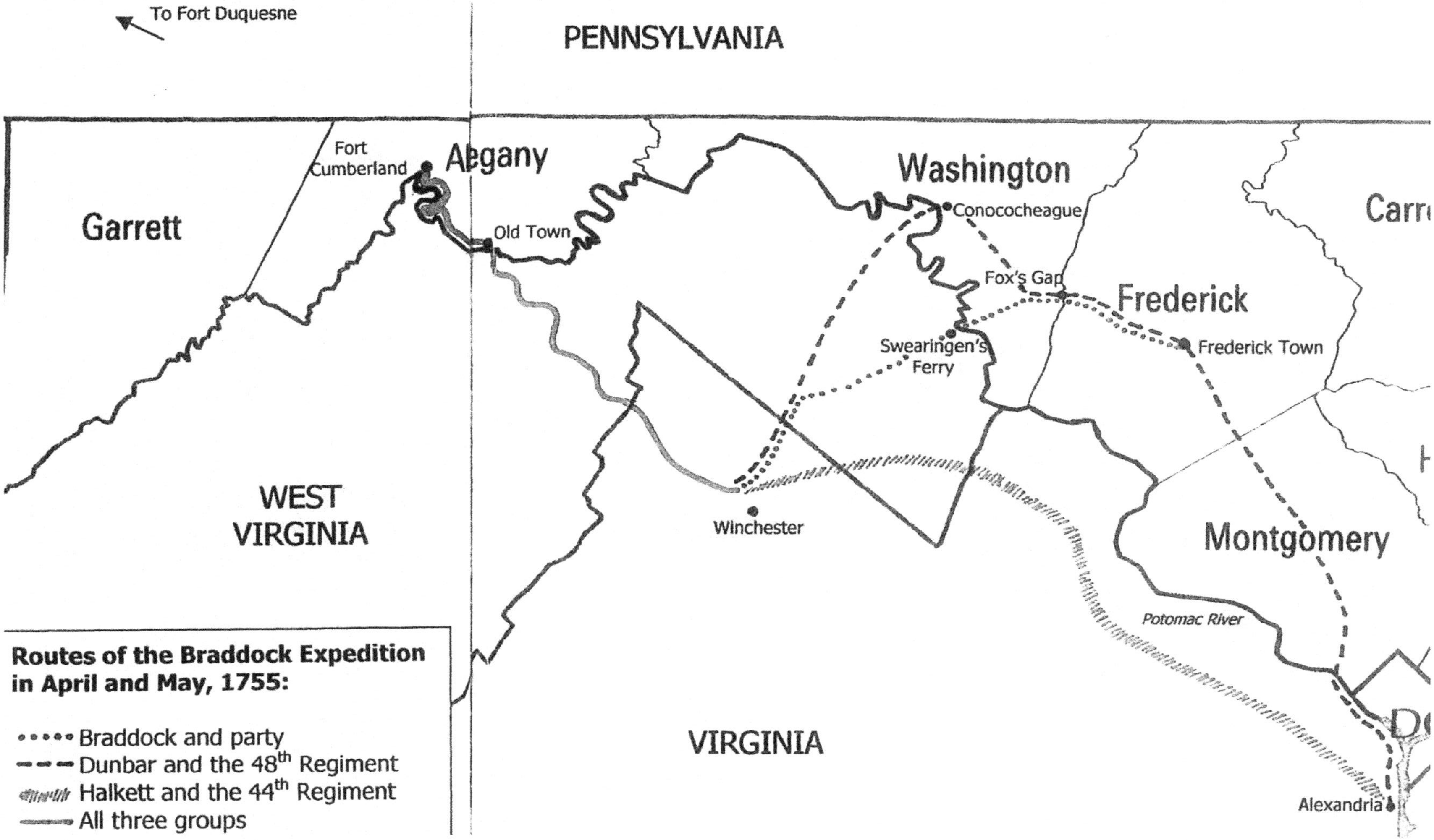

To Fort Duquesne
PENNSYLVANIA
Fort Cumberland
Alegany
Garrett
Old Town
Washington
Conococheague
Fox's Gap
Frederick
Swearingen's Ferry
Frederick Town
Carr
WEST VIRGINIA
Winchester
Montgomery
Potomac River
VIRGINIA
Alexandria

Routes of the Braddock Expedition in April and May, 1755:

Braddock and party
Dunbar and the 48th Regiment
Halkett and the 44th Regiment
All three groups

French forces took possession of the site where the Monongahela and Allegheny Rivers meet the Ohio River (the location of modern Pittsburg) and built Fort Duquesne in 1754.

Virginia Governor Robert Dinwiddie sent George Washington and his Virginia troops to take the fort later that year. Washington built Fort Necessity near Fort Duquesne as headquarters for his campaign but was soon defeated and forced to retreat from the site. In reaction to this defeat, Great Britain sent General Edward Braddock and two regiments of infantry to the colonies. The goal of the British was to capture Fort Duquesne and, having accomplished that, to continue seizing all French holdings from Pennsylvania to Canada. Braddock's campaign would turn out to be more costly and embarrassing than the British could ever have imagined.

Getting Started

General Braddock arrived in advance of his army at Hampton, Virginia, on February 20, 1755. The first problem the general faced was determining the best route for transporting all the troops, artillery, and supplies of his army from the coast of Virginia to Fort Duquesne. The strategic link connecting Fort Duquesne with the towns to the east was Fort Cumberland at Will's Creek in western Maryland, built in 1754 at the site of modern Cumberland. Braddock decided to use Fort Cumberland as a staging point where he would reassemble the two legs of his army after their separate journeys through Virginia and Maryland. The army was forced to split because Virginia was unable to supply an adequate number of wagons and horses for the campaign, and Marylanders would only allow use of their wagons north of the Potomac River.**(1)** Another enticement for travel through Maryland was a new road initiated by Governor Sharpe in 1754 that was to stretch from Rock Creek to Fort Cumberland.**(2)** Braddock may have been led to believe that this road would be ready by the time he and his troops arrived. The British troops that marched through Maryland may have used this road on the first part of their journey. It seems, however, that the road had not been completed to Fort Cumberland by spring 1755, because the troops actually crossed back into Virginia from Maryland on their way to Fort Cumberland.

Braddock spent two months deliberating with the governors of the surrounding colonies about the availability of supplies and reconnaissance of the roads that were to be used by his army. He then met his troops in Alexandria, where they had disembarked at the end of March, and from there ordered the two main legs of his army to proceed to Fort Cumberland.**(3)** Sir Peter Halkett and the 44th Regiment left Alexandria in stages throughout April to march to the fort through Virginia.**(4)** Colonel Thomas Dunbar and the 48th Regiment set out on their longer journey through Maryland on April 12.**(5)**

Two journals kept by men traveling with Dunbar's group record the daily activities of the regiment as it marched from Alexandria up to Conococheague, now Williamsport.**(6)** Dunbar's regiment included 700 regulars, 350 Rangers from Virginia and the Carolinas, 50 carpenters, and a group of British sailors to supervise ferrying the soldiers over the Potomac and the block and tackle work needed to help transport heavy artillery across the mountains. On the morning of April 12, Dunbar and his men left Alexandria and marched to Rock Creek. Here they crossed the Potomac River in flat boats provided by the British Navy. The regiment continued to Lawrence Owen's Ordinary, fifteen miles from Rock Creek, perhaps near today's Rockville, and then marched another fifteen miles to Michael Dowden's residence.**(7)**

Eleven miles later they reached the Monocacy River. By 1751 the main road between Frederick and Georgetown crossed the Monocacy at a point called the Middle Ford.**(8)** Dunbar's regiment probably crossed the Monocacy at the Middle Ford using the ferry that had been established there in 1748 by Henry Ballenger. One soldier described this portion of the trip as follows: "4 miles this side of Frederick we crossed the River Menurcus (Monocacy), it being a hundred yards over and only one flat made the Baggage so late before it got over that we was oblig'd to lay in quarters that night... in a pleasant fine Country."**(9)** Textual evidence of a tavern by the Middle Ford was confirmed in 2004 with the identification of a mid-eighteenth-century domestic site by archeologists from the National Park Service. Excavation of a portion of a cellar hole at the site revealed artifacts dating to the mid- and late eighteenth century. The tavern was in use from the 1740's until about 1830 and may have hosted those members of the 48th Regiment delayed by the slow process of ferrying supplies across the river. By April 18 the entire regiment was encamped on the north side of Frederick.**(10)**

Braddock and Dunbar's 48th Regiment in Frederick

According to one of the diarists with Dunbar's group, the young town of Frederick had at that time "200 Houses & 2 Churches- 1 Dutch (German), 1 English; the inhabitants chiefly Dutch, Industrious, but imposing People; Provisions & Forrage in Plenty."**(11)** During the twelve days they camped in Frederick, the soldiers and sailors foraged for provisions, tried to enlist locals into the army, and were repeatedly punished for drunkenness.**(12)**

Braddock arrived in Frederick from Alexandria on April 21 and during his short stay in the town managed to meet over the course of several days with Benjamin Franklin, Governor Horatio Sharpe, and the young George Washington.**(13)** Frustrated by the lack of wagons and provisions made available to his army by Maryland and Virginia, Braddock was placated by Franklin's offer to advertise for and send supplies from Pennsylvania. The Assembly in Pennsylvania, worried that Braddock held it in contempt for its apparent unwillingness to cooperate with the British forces, had sent Franklin under the guise of postmaster-general to assess the general's opinion of the Assembly and alleviate his dissatisfaction over the scarcity of supplies. Franklin's summation of Braddock was written with the clarity of hindsight: "This general was, I think, a brave man, and might probably have made a figure as a good officer in some European war. But he had too much self-confidence, too high an opinion of the validity of regular troops, and too mean a one of both Americans and Indians."**(14)** Franklin did succeed in raising 150 wagons and 259 carrying horses, for which Braddock gave him £800, an insufficient sum Franklin had to augment with his own money.**(15)** At Dunbar's request, Franklin also sent along twenty parcels of choice provisions, including sugar, tea, coffee, chocolate, Gloucester cheese, Madeira wine, Jamaica spirits, cured ham, dried tongues, and raisins.**(16)**

Governor Sharpe met with Braddock in Frederick on April 23, and Washington arrived eight days later.**(17)** Braddock had asked Washington to join the expedition, and the young Virginian was eager to prove himself after his defeat at Fort Necessity a year before. Dunbar and his troops left Frederick on April 29 to begin their journey over South Mountain and on to Conococheague, where they were to cross the Potomac and travel on to Fort Cumberland through Virginia. Three days later on May 2, Braddock, Washington, Governor Sharpe, and Braddock's aides-de-camp Orme and Morris and secretary Shirley also left Frederick for Fort Cumberland. The two groups, separated by three days, followed the same route over South Mountain, but at a point south of today's Keedysville their paths diverged.

What Route did They Take?

In the spring of 1755, the only viable road to Fort Cumberland started near Winchester, Virginia.**(18)** In order to get to Winchester from Maryland, the troops could use one of two roads. One ran through Conococheague, and the other passed through Swearingen's Ferry, by Shepherdstown, West Virginia. Dunbar's regiment took the road that passed through Conococheague, which was also used as a supply station for the wagons and provisions needed by the army. Braddock himself took the road that passed through Swearingen's Ferry.

A clue to the route Braddock's party traveled over South Mountain is divulged in a letter written by Governor Sharpe to Governor Dinwiddie of Virginia:

May 9th 1755.

D[r] Sir

I take this Opportunity of acquainting you that I left the General Capt. Orme & Morris Col. Washington & Mr Shirley this Day Sen'net at Swerengen's Ferry on their way to Winchester I suppose they will reach Wills-Creek (Fort Cumberland) to morrow. Col. Dunbar's Regiment marched from Frederickton the 29th of April, Col. Halketts & the Virg[a] Companies had I hear left Winchester some Days before...**(19)**

On May 2, seven days before Governor Sharpe wrote this letter, Braddock and his party traveled from Frederick to Swearingen's Ferry, where the governor left the group to its expedition. The main road from Frederick to Swearingen's Ferry in 1755 was part of the Great Philadelphia Wagon Road, which stretched from Philadelphia to Winchester, running through Maryland via Taney Town and a pass in the South Mountains known as Fox's Gap. Another road cut through the mountains at Crampton's Gap, south of Fox's Gap, but this seems to have been only a horse trail at this time, and so would have been an improbable route for the coach and six horses (purchased from Governor Sharpe) that carried Braddock in addition to his party.**(20)** The stretch of road from Frederick to Swearingen's Ferry passed through Sharpsburg on its way to the Potomac River and is labeled the Old Sharpsburg Road in the 1891-1895 *Atlas to Accompany the Official Records of the Union and Confederate Armies.***(21)**

There is less definite evidence for the route Dunbar's group took over South Mountain, but several facts suggest that he and his men also passed through Fox's Gap on their way to Conococheague. A land tract by Keedysville surveyed in 1739 describes a "Conegochieg Road" that crosses Antietam Creek.**(22)**

The Braddock-Washington Monument (**above**) stands beside Alternate Route 40 on the east side of Braddock Heights, Maryland. The monument's plaque (**below**) depicts Braddock, Washington, and a third man drinking at nearby Braddock Springs on their way to Fort Duquesne in 1755.

Braddock had ordered a bridge to be constructed over Antietam Creek for the transportation of supply wagons sent in advance to Conococheague and for Dunbar and his men. It was probably built in the vicinity of today's Hicks Bridge west of Keedysville and may have been located on the "Conegochieg Road" mentioned in the land tract.**(23)** Hicks Bridge is located on the present route from Keedysville through Bakersville to Williamsport, which may be the same route that Dunbar used in 1755.**(24)**

The only detail diarists with Dunbar's group give of the route is their stopping place outside Frederick called Chapman's Ordinary, which seems to refer to the property of Moses Chapline, Sr., located approximately two miles west of Fox's Gap.**(25)** The proximity of the stopping place to Fox's Gap suggests that the regiment did indeed use this pass to cross South Mountain. In addition, wagons laden with supplies had been sent from Frederick to off-load in Conococheague, where provisions were stored before being sent on to Fort Cumberland. These wagons could travel one of only two roads from Frederick to Conococheague wide enough to accommodate them. One of these passed through Fox's Gap, and the other ran through Orr's Gap.**(26)** Days earlier Braddock and Washington had used the road through Fox's Gap because it was wide enough to accommodate the coach in which Braddock traveled and because it was the main road from Frederick to Swearingen's Ferry. It is likely that all three groups- the advance supply wagons, Dunbar's regiment, and Braddock's party- used the same route over South Mountain.

Driving Tour

The route that Braddock's party took to Swearingen's Ferry, part of which Dunbar's 48th Regiment also traveled, can be easily followed today and passes through both attractive countryside and smatterings of new housing developments. It begins in Frederick, and ends at the Potomac River by Shepherdstown.

Start the tour at the intersection of Patrick and Market Streets in downtown Frederick. Drive west on Patrick Street, which becomes Route 40, past the Route 15 overpass and rows of shopping centers until the Old National Pike (Alternate Route 40 West) branches off to the left from Route 40 directly after you cross Waverley Drive (2.8 miles). Take this left (by doing so you cross the traffic lanes of Route 40 East) and continue west towards Braddock Heights, named in honor of the general. A little more than 4 miles from the Interstate 70 overpass, a monument stands on the left side of the road. **(The monument is unfortunately located behind the guardrail at such a dangerous point in the road that we do not recommend that you park your car and walk to view it. Instead, look to your left as you drive by a house on the right with the mailbox number 4930.)**

The Braddock-Washington Monument is a large boulder decorated with a bronze plaque, designed by sculptor Edward Berge, that depicts Braddock, Washington, and a third man stopping to drink at nearby Braddock Springs on their way to Fort Duquesne. The dedication reads: "This boulder marks the National Trail over which traveled Gen. Edward Braddock and Lieutenant Colonel George Washington 1755. Erected by the Frederick Chapter, Daughters of the American Revolution 1924."

The monument, draped with the flags of America, Great Britain, and Maryland, was unveiled at its nearby original location at Braddock Springs on July 10, 1924, during a patriotic ceremony that included musical performances and speeches by members of the Daughters of the American Revolution.**(27)** There is no evidence that Braddock and Washington actually drank from the springs that now bear the general's name. However, the site is located in the general are of the path that the men took to cross the mountains. The monument was moved to its current inaccessible location by the Maryland State Roads Commission when Alternate Route 40 was widened and elevated in the 1950s.**(28)** **(Continued in next issue!)**

Genealogy Documentation Section
by Curtis L. Older

A feature of each Fox Society Newsletter that was begun with the December 1, 2004, newsletter is the inclusion of an article that documents a descendant or spouse of a descendant of John Fox of Fox's Gap in Maryland. The article will present a written description about the individual and his or her family as well as a listing of the related genealogical source records that support the written description.

The fourth individual to be presented in this feature of the newsletter is Daniel Alexander Fox. Daniel Alexander Fox was a son of John L. Fox.

Previous issues of the Fox Society Newsletter contained documentation for the following individuals:

December 1, 2004 - Frederick Fox
June 1, 2005 - George Fox
December 1, 2005 - John L. Fox

Documentation for Daniel Alexander Fox, father of Ethel Belle Fox

Daniel Alexander Fox was born January 13, 1860, in Highland Township, Vermillion County, Indiana.(**1**) He was the son of John L. Fox and Susannah Hiligass.(**2**) Daniel married Elizabeth Jane Ricketts on April 1, 1881.(**3**) Elizabeth was the daughter of Jacob Ricketts and Melissa Barnard. Elizabeth was born on October 18, 1861, in Vermillion County, Indiana.(**4**)

Daniel and Elizabeth Fox were the parents of five children. Kenneth Benjamin Fox was born November 17, 1882, in Gessie, Highland Township, Vermillion County, Indiana. He died September 30, 1971, in Richmond, Indiana. He married Virga Butche in 1900. Virga was born August 4, 1885, and died November 2, 1983, in Salt Lake City, Utah. (**5**)

Ernest Daniel Fox was born December 1, 1885 near Gessie, Vermillion County, Indiana. He married Lola Frances Jackson on January 8, 1908, in Vermilion County, Illinois. She was born January 1, 1890, and died June 28, 1943. Ernest died October 3, 1940, at Lakeview Hospital in Danville, Illinois. He is buried at Niccum Cemetery in Vermilion County, Illinois. (**6**)

William Edward Fox was born Jan 5, 1888, and died Apr 16, 1974. He married Marguerite Clem on Feb 10, 1909, in Danville, IL. She was born Mar 9, 1894, in Mound Township, Warren County, IN. She died Jan 27, 1970, at Danville, IL. Her parents were Augustus Elmer Clem and Malinda Lloyd Cunningham. William and Marguerite are both buried at the Lower Mound Cemetery west of Covington, Indiana. (**7**)

Ethel Belle Fox was born on October 6, 1892. On February 3, 1917, Ethel Belle Fox married Robert William Gouty. He was the son of Joseph P. Gouty and Luella Marie Hartman. Robert was born August 26, 1889, in Gessie, Vermilion County, Indiana. (**8**)

Ruby Dale Fox was born December 13, 1896. She died November 12, 1990, in Grand Rapids, Michigan. She married Everett Hines on April 10, 1920, in Covington, Indiana. Everett was born July 30, 1894, and died April 5, 1963. Both Everett and Ruby are buried in the Lower Mound Cemetery west of Covington, Indiana. (**9**)

Elizabeth Jane (Ricketts) Fox was burned to death on Tuesday, February 28, 1922, when her clothes caught fire from the kitchen stove and she ran onto the back porch and fell upon a bottle of gasoline.(**10**) Daniel Alexander Fox died July 29, 1932, in Covington, Indiana.(**11**) Both Daniel and

Elizabeth Fox are buried in Hopewell Cemetery west of Covington, Indiana. The will of Daniel Alexander Fox lists the names of all of his children and is recorded in the Vermillion County, Indiana Court House.(**12**)

Daniel A. Fox is listed in the 1880 Indiana Federal census as age 20, living at home with his parents, John L. Fox and Susannah Fox, in Highland Township, Vermillion County.(**13**). Daniel A. Fox is listed in the 1920 Indiana Federal census as age 60, living with his wife, Lizzie J. Fox, and Ruby D. Fox, a daughter.(**14**) Daniel also is listed in the 1930 Indiana federal census, Vermillion County, Highland, Dist. 18, p. 220, sheet 1A: household of son-in-law Everett Hines. Daniel was listed as age 70, widowed.**(15)**

Children (**Fox**) born in Highland Township, Vermillion County, Indiana:

i. **Kenneth Benjamin**, born November 17, 1882
ii. **Ernest Daniel Fox,** born December 1, 1885
iii. **William Edward**, born January 5, 1888
iv. **Ethel Belle**, born October 6, 1892
v. **Ruby Dale**, born December 13, 1896

REFERENCES

1. Ethel Belle (Fox) Gouty Family Bible in the possession of Curtis Lynn Older. Copies of pages from the Ethel Belle Fox Family Bible are in a CD-rom disc entitled Fox's Gap in Maryland, which is at the Frederick County Historical Society, Frederick, Maryland. **2.** Ibid; *The Fox Genealogy including the Metherd, Benner, and Leiter descendants, giving biographies of the first and second generations, with sketches of the third generation,* compiled by D. G. Fox, 1914. (n.p) 1924. 1 p. 1., (5)-172 p. 20 com. 37-9439 CS71.F79 1924 Library of Congress. **3.** Ibid; Marriage records, Fountain County Court House, Covington, Indiana, Book 8, #350, April 1, 1881, Daniel Alexander Fox and Elizabeth Jane Ricketts. Fountain County, Indiana, Index to Marriage Record 1848 - 1920 Inclusive Volume I Letters A - G Inclusive, W. P. A. Original Record Located: County Clerks Office Covington Compiled by Indiana Works Projects Administration 1941, County: Fountain, Name: Daniel A Fox, Spouse: Lizzie J Ricketts, Marriage Date: 01 Apr 1881, Book: 8, Original Source Page: 350. **4.** Ibid. **5.** *The Fox Genealogy* by Daniel Gebhart Fox; Issue 9, Volume 1, *News from Fox's Gap,* published by The Society of the Descendants of Frederick Fox of Fox's Gap in Maryland, page 19, "The Children of Daniel Alexander Fox and Elizabeth Jane Ricketts", by Curtis Lynn Older, information provided by Mildred Fox Metcalf, daughter of Kenneth Fox. **6.** Ibid. **7.** Ibid; Issue 1, Volume 1, *News from Fox's Gap,* page 6, "Descendants of William Edward Fox" by Dellie Jean Fox Craig. **8.** *The Fox Genealogy* by Daniel Gebhart Fox; Issue 9, Volume 1, *News from Fox's Gap,* published by The Society of the Descendants of Frederick Fox of Fox's Gap in Maryland, page 19, "The Children of Daniel Alexander Fox and Elizabeth Jane Ricketts", by Curtis Lynn Older. **9.** Ibid. **10.** Covington (Indiana) Republican Newspaper, obituary notice, front page, column one, probably about March 1, 1922; The Ethel Belle Fox Gouty Family Bible. **11.** Ethel Belle (Fox) Gouty Family Bible; Daniel A. Fox obituary, Reel #182072, Covington (Indiana) Republican, January 1931 - December 1932, August 5, 1932. **12.** Will of Daniel Alexander Fox, Newport, Vermillion County, Indiana, Court House, page 218, record number 6, August 1, 1932. **13.** 1880 Indiana Federal census, Highland Township, Vermillion County, enumerated June 8, 1880, by Joshua Lewis. **14.** 1920 Indiana Federal census, Highland Township, Vermillion County, enumerated February 13, 1920, by Dale E. Hughes. **15.** 1930 Indiana Federal census, Highland Township, Vermillion County, District 18, page 220, sheet 1A, household of Everett Hines.

President's Message

by Curtis Lynn Older

* The numbering system for *News from Fox's Gap* considers a Volume to consist of 10 issues of the newsletter over a period of five years. Thus, with the current issue of *News from Fox's Gap* we begin our third period of five years of publication. The current Volume is thus number 3 and the Issue starts over at number 1. The December 1, 2005, printing of the newsletter was the 20th newsletter that had been published prior to this current issue.

* The next issue of *News from Fox's Gap* will contain the second half of an article published in the Spring/Summer edition of *Catoctin History.* Angela Commito, the author of the article, uses a book written by Curtis L. Older, *The Braddock Expedition and Fox's Gap in Maryland,* to substantiate most of the statements made in her article.

Catoctin History was a Winner of the 2004 Certificate of Commendation from the American Association for State and Local History! Winner of a 2004 Educational Excellence Award from the Maryland Historical Trust! Winner of a 2004 Award of Excellence from the Printing and Imaging Industries of Maryland!

* If you have not already done so, please visit the Indiana University of Pennsylvania website on Fox's Gap in Maryland at:

http://www.iuparchaeology.iup.edu/FoxGap/

News from Fox's Gap

Published June 1 and December 1 of each year by
The Society of the Descendants of Frederick Fox of Fox's Gap in Maryland
Membership dues are $5.00 per year. President of the Society is Curtis L. Older.
Make Society inquiries by the following means:

Curtis L. Older
618 Tryon Place
Gastonia, NC 28054-6066

e-mail: curtolder@earthlink.net
phone: 704-864-3879

Land Tracts of the Battlefield of South Mountain

by Curtis L. Older

Many Fox Society Newsletters include a survey, patent, or deed related to the land tracts in the vicinity of Crampton's, Fox's, and Turner's Gaps on the Battlefield of South Mountain.

Previous issues of the Society Newsletter contained descriptions of the following tracts:

June 1, 1997	Addition to Friendship of Frederick Fox
December 1, 1997	Fredericksburgh of Frederick Fox
June 1, 1998	Pick All of Bartholomew Booker
December 1, 1998	Bowser's Addition of David Bowser
June 1, 1999	Partnership of John Mansberger
December 1, 1999	Mountain of John Baley
December 1, 2000	Flonham of Philip Jacob Shafer
June 1, 2001	The Exchange of Daniel Dulaney
December 1, 2001	Betty's Good Will of Robert Evans
December 1, 2004	Resurvey on Exchange
June 1, 2005	The Gap and John's Delight
December 1, 2005	Resurvey on Well Done

The tract presented in this issue of *News from Fox's Gap* is named Foxes Last Shift. There has been considerable debate over the significance, if any, of the name given to this tract and the tract's location just north of Fox's Gap and on the road from Frederick to Fort Frederick. Did the name imply that the "new" route from Frederick to Fort Frederick eliminated the need for someone to pass through Fox's Gap in order to go from Frederick (Town) to Fort Frederick? Fort Frederick was built almost immediately after the Braddock Expedition of 1755 and a shorter route was created through Turner's Gap in order to reach the fort from Frederick Town in Maryland. The fort was located a little west of Williamsport, Maryland, previously known as Conococheague.

(Note: a perch is 16 and 1/2 feet in length)

MdHR 17,438, 1-23-3-38, BC & GS 27, p. 331, Robert Smith, Foxes Last Shift, examined and passed 5 Oct 1764, 72 acres.

Robert Smith, his cert 72 acres Foxes Last Shift Patt 27th Feb? ? retn ? ? ?
Frederick County - By virtue of a warrant granted out of his lordships land office of this province to George William Laurpuco? of the county aforesaid for seventy two acres of land bearing date by renewment the 20th of January 1761? and which said warrant is assigned to Robert Smith of the same county - I Therefore certify as deputy surveyor under his excellency Horatio Sharpe Esq. Governor of Maryland that I have carefully surveyed and laid out for and in the name of him the said Robert Smith all that tract of land called Foxes Last Shift lying in the county afsd beginning at a bounded white oak tree standing on the north side of the main country road that leads from Frederick Town to Fort Frederick in the South Mountain and running thence

Line No.	North South	Degrees East or West	Length
1	N	52 west	32 perches

Line No.	North South	Degrees East or West	Length
2	S	52 west	20 perches
3	S	15 west	107 perches
4	S	60 west	38 perches
5	N	6 west	16 perches
6	S	75 west	40 perches
7	S	23 west	85 perches
8	S	89 east	103 perches
9	N	19 east	158 perches (168?)
10	N	59 west	17 perches
11	N	12 perches	

12 then with a straight line to the beginning tree containing and now laid out for seventy two acres of land to be held of Conococheigue Manor October 5th 1764 Examined & Passed U Scott Exc.

Enclosed in the foregoing certificate was the following assignment viz. - I do hereby assign transfer and make over unto Robert Smith of the County of Frederick and Province of Maryland all my right title interest claim and demand of in and unto seventy two acres of land warrant granted unto me out of his lordships land office for that quantity of land which land warrant is now laying in the hand of Mr. John Murdock Surveyor of Frederick County; hereby desiring that upon return of a certificate in the name of him the said Robert Smith by virtue of the said Warrant for the quantity of land thereby granted unto me that his lordships right of confirmation may in no unto ? heirs and assigns forever for the same as witnessing? hand this 25th day of February 1764.

Test Jas Smith George William A Laurence his mark

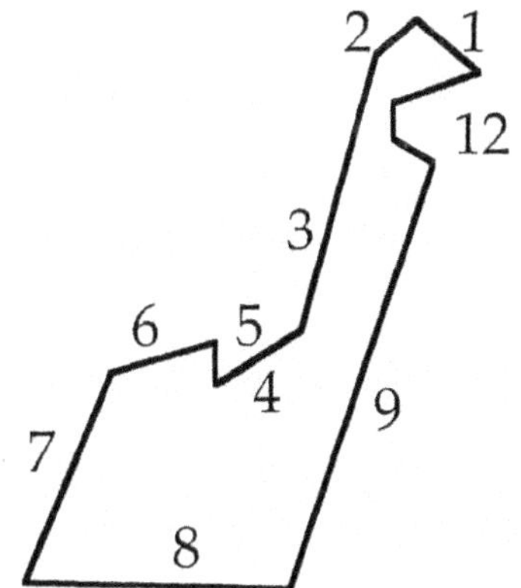

N ^

Foxes Last Shift

72 acres

Beginning at a bounded white oak tree standing on the north side of the main country road that leads from Frederick Town to Fort Frederick in the South Mountain

Membership Correspondence Section

Items of Interest from the Membership

Michael J. Fox, a son of Robert H. Fox (deceased) of Cincinnati, Ohio, writes the following:

"I was reading the information about John L. Fox in the newsletter. I saw that Elizabeth Fox, 10/01/1830 - 10/23/1868, was married to Peter Eagle on 11/11/1854. Peter Eagle fought in the Civil War. I did a little research and found the following:

Fourth Regiment Ohio Volunteer Cavalry, Company D
Rank Sergeant
Entered 11/22/1861 Period of Service 3 Years
Appointed, captured, and paroled 10/18/1862 at The Battle of Lexington, KY
Discharged 3/21/1863 by order of the War Department

I may have some of the details wrong by my Dad Robert H. Fox used to tell a story about Fredric Coffman Fox, 2/25/1832 - 6/25/1882. He was a political figure in Miamisburg, OH, during the Civil War. Because Peter Eagle was captured he went to Washington, D.C. to see President Abraham Lincoln. Lincoln gave him a pass to get through the lines and travel to Andersonville, Georgia. Fredric Coffman Fox bribed the prison commandant and gained the release of Peter Eagle.

I do not know if this is true or not, however, it always fascinated me and I thought you might be interested in hearing it."

News from Fox's Gap

The Society of the Descendants of Frederick Fox of Fox's Gap in Maryland

Issue 2, Volume 3 **Remember Freedom!** December 1, 2006

The French and Indian War in Mid-Maryland

By Angela R. Commito

The following article appeared beginning on page 42 of *Catoctin History* Spring/Summer 2005.

Angela Commito is a Research Assistant at the Catoctin Center for Regional Studies.

Catoctin History is the magazine of the **Catoctin Center for Regional Studies**, a program of **Frederick Community College, Frederick, Maryland**, and co-sponsored by the **National Park Service.**

Catoctin History is a non-profit educational magazine that serves as a forum for information about the history and culture of mid-Maryland and the surrounding region. For additional information about the Catoctin Center for Regional Studies, please see the Center's website at:

http://catoctincenter.frederick.edu

Continued from the June 1, 2006, newsletter-

Continue through Middletown and take a left onto Marker Road as soon as you cross the bridge that spans Catoctin Creek (8.9 miles; the turn is easily spotted by a farm with a large red barn). Turn right onto Bolivar Road (10.7 miles) and then left onto Reno Monument Road (11.5 miles). Continue up the mountain until you reach Fox's Gap, where there is a small parking area, several Civil War monuments and explanatory markers, and access to the Appalachian Trail (12.6 miles).

The Reno Monument commemorates Union General Jesse Lee Reno, who commanded the divisions of the Union IX Corps that fought at Fox's Gap during the Battle of South Mountain on September 14, 1862, and died that same day. Here, where the Old Sharpsburg Road passed over South Mountain, you can walk along the Appalachian Trail and wander south through the ten acres of land owned by the Central Maryland Heritage League.**(29)** More than a century before Union and Confederate soldiers fought for control of the mountain pass, Braddock, Washington, and Dunbar's regiment traveled through Fox's Gap on their way to Fort Cumberland.

Continuing on Reno Monument Road, you will cross Route 67 and continue straight onto Mount Carmel Church Road (14.7 miles). Soon after passing Mount Carmel Church on your left, take a right onto Dogstreet Road and continue until you reach Felfoot Bridge, which spans Little Antietam Creek (16.5 miles). The sign by the bridge explains that the structure was built by George Burgan in 1854 on land that was once patented in 1737 to Thomas Swearingen, who owned the ferry that Braddock and his group used to cross the Potomac River by Shepherdstown.

The Routes Diverge

After Felfoot Bridge, Dogstreet Road makes a sharp right (17.1 miles) and continues into Keedysville. At this point the routes of Braddock and Dunbar split. On April 29 Dunbar and the 48th Regiment turned right and traveled north to Conococheague. Three days later on May 2, Braddock, Washington, Governor Sharpe, and the others arrived at this point and turned left, continuing south into Virginia.

To follow Braddock's route, take this left onto Red Hill Road and an almost immediate right onto Geeting Road. A mile later turn right onto Porterstown Road and continue until you reach Route 34 (18.7 miles). Turn left (west) onto Route 34 and drive into downtown Sharpsburg. At the center of downtown Sharpsburg, in front of the library on the left, there is a marker commemorating General Braddock's stay in Frederick and his journey from Frederick to Virginia (20.3 miles).

Continue on Route 34 until you reach a turnoff to the left before the bridge across the Potomac River where several markers are located (23.3 miles). One of these markers describes Swearingen's Ferry, which was located near the site of the current bridge that crosses the river into Shepherdstown. Thomas Swearingen, the same man to whom the land around Felfoot Bridge was patented, began operating the ferry in 1755.**(30)** Since Governor Sharpe used the name Swearingen's Ferry in the letter quoted above, the ferry must have been active when Braddock and his group crossed into Virginia. At this point in the journey, Governor Sharpe left Braddock, Washington, and the other men to continue on their way to Fort Cumberland and finally to Fort Duquesne.

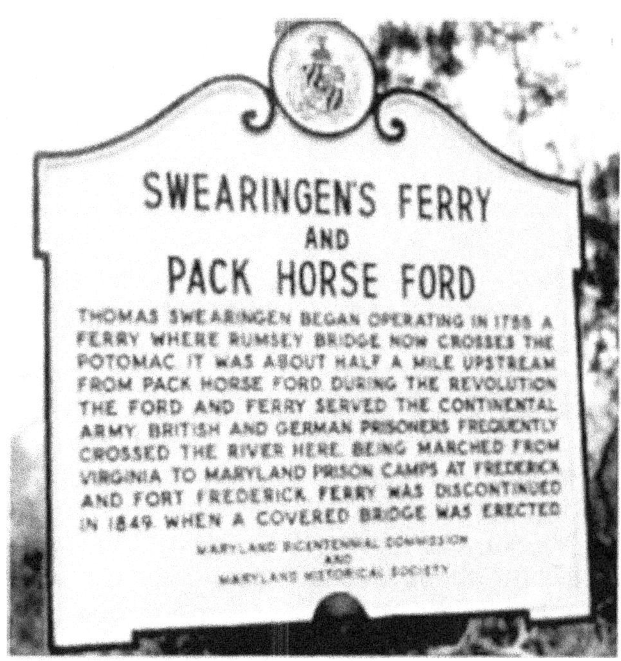

A marker (**above**) on the Maryland side of the Potomac River near Shepherdstown, West Virginia, commemorates Swearingen's Ferry, which began operation in 1755 and was used by Braddock, Washington, and Governor Sharpe on May 2 of that same year.

While Braddock and Washington were traveling through Sharpsburg and Shepherdstown, Dunbar and his long train of men had already marched to Conococheague, crossed the Potomac River into Virginia, and were enjoying a day of rest twenty miles northeast of Winchester.**(31)** The route Dunbar traveled from Frederick to Conococheague is not known conclusively, though there is evidence that the regiment, after passing through Fox's Gap, continued north through Keedysville, crossed Antietam Creek at the Upper Bridge (Hicks Bridge), and traveled northwest through Bakersville and into Williamsport, following today's Keedysville Road, Bakersville Road, and Route 63.**(32)**

Springfield Farm in Williamsport is an interesting site that contains buildings that were probably standing during the French and Indian War and are connected to Braddock's campaign. Unfortunately, the structures of Springfield Farm have been altered and are currently managed by several different owners, so visiting the site is not recommended. A man named George Ross of Conococheague is mentioned in 1755 as Commissary for Braddock at the mouth of the Conococheague River.**(33)** During the early 1760s, Ross leased land called Ezekiel's Inheritance, which included Springfield Farm, from the Lord Proprietary. In 1750 Ezekiel's Inheritance corresponded to a tract called Store House land.**(34)** The store house (or stillhouse) to which the name Store House land refers, along with an adjacent springhouse and main house, were all part of Ezekiel's Inheritance and are collectively referred to as Springfield Farm. The store house of 1750 was later used by George Ross in his capacity as Commissary at Conococheague, and the main house was probably Ross's residence in the 1760s.**(35)**

The store house and springhouse at Springfield Farm in Williamsport, Maryland, c. 1941.

Local tradition purports that the stone springhouse was used for trade operations by Thomas Cresap, who was a member of the Ohio Company and in 1755 was enlisted to gather and store supplies for Braddock's army.**(36)** Legend also claims that Braddock and Washington drank from the spring, though there is little evidence that Braddock ever visited the area.**(37)**

"Who Would Have Thought It?"

By the end of May, General Braddock, Halkett's 44th Regiment, Dunbar's 48th Regiment, and several companies from the colonies had assembled at Fort Cumberland and were making preparations to march to Fort Duquesne.**(38)** Halkett and the 44th Regiment had traveled to Fort Cumberland through Virginia, and sections of the regiment had arrived before Dunbar's group. The army began its slow journey to Fort Duquesne through the forests of Maryland and Pennsylvania, cutting trees and clearing the path that later became the National Road. Seeing that the long train of supply wagons and artillery was slowing the army's progress tremendously, Braddock decided to advance with a group of select men, artillery, and stores and left the cumbersome baggage, wagons, and sick men with Dunbar to proceed at a slower pace.

On July 9 the advance party and the remainder of the army except Dunbar's slower group crossed the Monongahela River approximately nine miles south of Fort Duquesne. The advance party was routed by the French and Indian forces in a surprise attack and fell back into the main body of the British army that had been traveling behind it. The British troops were unprepared for the attack and unaccustomed to fighting to fighting on uneven, forested ground. The confusion was so complete that the British army, though the larger force, could not overtake the French and their allies. Braddock was wounded, and many of his officers were injured or killed. The army retreated back to the river, where the French and Indian forces stopped their pursuit, and continued on to Dunbar's camp about fifty miles back down the road. Braddock died not long after and was buried under the road by Washington in mid-July. According to Captain Orme, the day before he died Braddock wondered aloud, "Who would have thought it?" Before dying the next day, the general responded optimistically, "We shall better know how to deal with them another time."**(39)**

Retreat through Maryland

After assuming control of the debilitated army, Dunbar made no plans for a second attack. Instead, he decided to destroy the artillery and most of the supplies and leave for Philadelphia. The defeated troops marched back to Fort Cumberland at the end of July and left for Winchester at the beginning of August.**(40)** From Winchester the troops traveled back up to Maryland, probably crossing the Potomac River at Conococheague, and continued through Pennsylvania to Philadelphia.**(41)**

Jonathan Hager emigrated from Germany to Maryland in the 1730s and built this fortified home in Hagerstown in 1739.

The sick and wounded soldiers and a group of army followers retreated from Fort Cumberland at a slower pace and stopped in Frederick, where there was an army hospital, on their way to Philadelphia.**(42)** A woman within this group named Mrs. Charlotte Browne had traveled from England with her brother, a commissary officer to the expedition, to act as a nurse, and recorded the journey to Frederick and her activities while staying in the city.**(43)** Weary with sickness and fatigue, Mrs. Browne did not write in her journal during the march to Frederick, and so the route she took remains unknown. She either retraced Dunbar's steps through Conococheague or Braddock's route through Swearingen's Ferry.

Mrs. Browne's party left Fort Cumberland on August 20 and arrived in Frederick ten days later. She remained in Frederick through September while awaiting the arrival of the sick and wounded soldiers from Fort Cumberland.**(44)** These soldiers arrived on October 5, followed two days later by news that Indians had scalped five families around the fort, which was now defended only by the companies from Virginia, North Carolina, and Maryland.**(45)** The remains of the British army and its followers packed their bags and left Frederick for Philadelphia soon after.

The beginning of the North American campaign had not begun well for the British. Despite their unsuccessful start, British forces did eventually capture French holdings through the Ohio Territory and in Canada. The French and Indian War ended in 1763 with the signing of the Treaty of Paris, under which Britain received control of all French territories in North America with the exception of the Caribbean island Guadeloupe. General Braddock and his army constituted the first considerable British force sent to America to fight the French. Mid-Maryland played an important role as a staging ground for a war that resonated worldwide.

Other Sites to Visit

Thought not related to the Braddock Expedition, two other sites in central Maryland are relevant to the French and Indian War and are worthy of note. The Jonathan Hager House and Museum, located in Hagerstown City Park, was built in 1739 in the wilds of Maryland's western frontier as a fortified house, complete with twenty-two-inch thick stone walls and a protected water supply. Recognized as the founder of Hagerstown, Jonathan Hager emigrated from Germany to Maryland in the 1730s and served during the French and Indian War. The site is open Tuesday through Saturday from 10 a.m. to 4 p.m. and on Sunday from 2 to 5 p.m. but remains closed during the winter. There is also a museum exhibiting artifacts found during restoration of the house. For more information, call 301-739-8393 or visit the website at www.hagerhouse.org.

The reconstructed barracks inside Fort Frederick, which was built in 1756 to protect eastern Maryland from attacks by the French and their allies.

After Braddock's failure to capture Fort Duquesne made the western Maryland frontier vulnerable to French and Indian attacks, the Assembly of Maryland, urged by Governor Sharpe, decided in 1756 to build a new fort sixty miles to the east of Fort Cumberland "to provide for the Defence & Security of the Frontiers of the Province on which some parties of Indians have begun to make Incursions."**(46)** Fort Frederick played important roles during the French and Indian, Revolutionary, and Civil Wars but was never actually attacked. For detailed information on the fort and its history, please read Stephen Robertson's article on Fort Frederick in this issue of *Catoctin History*. Fort Frederick State Park, located near Big Pool, Maryland, is open from 8 a.m. to sunset, but the Visitor's Center is open on weekends only from 9 a.m. to 5 p.m. Evening hours are subject to change, so call in advance 301-842-2155 or visit the website at www.dnr.state.md.us/publiclands/western/fortfrederick.html for up-to-date times and directions.

Angela R. Commito is a Research Assistant at the Catoctin Center for Regional Studies.

Notes

1. Curtis L. Older, *The Braddock Expedition and Fox's Gap in Maryland* (Westminster, MD: Willow Bend Books, 2000), 49.

2. Letter from Governor Dinwiddie to Governor Sharpe, July 31, 1754, *Correspondence of Governor Horatio Sharpe, Volume 1*, 1753-1757, Archives of Maryland Online, vol. 6, 77, http://www.mdarchives.state.md.us; letter from Governor Dinwiddie to Governor Sharpe, September 5, 1754, *Correspondence of Governor Horatio Sharpe, Volume 1, 1753-1757*, Archives of Maryland Online, vol. 6, 97, http://www.mdarchives.state.md.us.

3. T. J. C. Williams and Folger McKinsey, "Braddock's Orderly Books," in *History of Frederick County*, vol. 1 (1910; reprint, Baltimore: Regional Publishing Company, 1979), 54-59; Older, *Braddock Expedition*, 27.

4. Walter S. Hough, *Braddock's Road Through the Virginia Colony, Volume VII: Winchester-Frederick County Historical Society* (Winchester, VA: Winchester-Frederick County Historical Society, 1970), 2.

5. Charles Hamilton, ed., "The Journal of Captain Robert Cholmley's Batman," in

Braddock's Defeat (Norman: University of Oklahoma Press, 1959), 10.

6. Ibid.; Archer Butler Hulbert, "A Seaman's Journal," in *Braddock's Road and Three Relative Papers*, Historic Highways of America, vol. 4 (Cleveland: Arthur H. Clark Company, 1903), 84; Allan Powell, *Maryland and the French and Indian War* (Baltimore: Gateway Press, 1998), 53. Information on the journey of Dunbar and the 48th Regiment is from Hamilton, "Batman," and Hulbert, "Seaman."

7. Older, *Braddock Expedition*, 13-14; Hamilton, "Batman," 10; Hulbert, "Seaman," 85; Andrew J. Wahll, *Braddock Road Chronicles*, 1755 (Bowie, MD: Heritage Books, 1999), 134.

8. Information on the Middle Ford ferry and tavern is from personal correspondence with Joy Beasley, Archeologist, Cultural Resources Program Manager, Monocacy National Battlefield, May 25, 2005.

9. Hamilton, "Batman," 10-11.

10. Ibid., 11; Hulbert, "Seaman," 85-86.

11. Hulbert, "Seaman," 85-86.

12. Ibid., 86; Hamilton, "Batman," 11-12.

13. Hulbert, "Seaman," 86; Hamilton, "Batman," 11.

14. Benjamin Franklin, *The Autobiography of Benjamin Franklin* (McLean, VA: IndyPublish.com, 2001), 102, 106.

15. Ibid., 105.

16. Ibid., 106.

17. Hulbert, "Seaman," 86-87; Hamilton, "Batman," 12; Older, *Braddock Expedition*, 75.

18. Older, *Braddock Expedition*, 5-6.

19. Letter from Governor Sharpe to Governor Dinwiddie, May 9, 1755, *Correspondence of Governor Horatio Sharpe, Volume 1, 1753-1757*, Archives of Maryland Online, vol. 6, 205, http://www.mdarchives.state.md.us.

20. Older, *Braddock Expedition*, 14-15, 109-110. The Great Philadelphia Wagon Road was also known as the road from Conestoga to Opequon and is not to be confused with the Great Wagon Road to Philadelphia, which also ran from Philadelphia to Winchester but north through Conococheague, not Frederick. Documentation of Braddock's use of a coach purchased from Governor Sharpe includes a letter from Braddock to the Governor.

21. Ibid., 46, 77; U. S. War Department, *Atlas to Accompany the Official Records of the Union and Confederate Armies* (Washington, DC: Government Printing Office, 1891-1895), Plate 27, No. 3, Battle of South Mountain.

22. Older, *Braddock Expedition*, 167.

23. Ibid., 122-123.

24. Ibid., 172-173.

25. Ibid., 173; Hamilton, "Batman," 12.

26. Older, *Braddock Expedition*, 173.

27. "Unveil Marker Braddock Spring," *The Frederick Post*, July 11, 1924.

28. Anne B. Hooper, *Braddock Heights: A Glance Backward* (Braddock Heights, MD: R. and A. Hooper, 1974), 65; "Braddock Monument," Maryland Military Monuments Commission Guided Tour, http://www.sos.state.md.us/mmmc/vt1-braddock.html.

29. For more information, visit the website of the Central Maryland Heritage League Land Trust at http://www.cmhl.org or call 301-371-7090.

30. Older, *Braddock Expedition*, 85.

31. Hulbert, "Seaman," 87; Hamilton, "Batman," 12-13.

32. Older, *Braddock Expedition*, 172-173.

33. Mary Vernon Mish, "Springfield Farm of Conococheague," *Maryland Historical Magazine* 47 (1952): 314-335, citing the Colonial Records of Pennsylvania, VI, 379.

34. Ibid., 319, citing Survey, Book No. 2, pg. 79, Surveyor's Office, Washington County Court House.

35. Ibid., 319.

36. Ibid., Hough, *Braddock's Road*, 49; Older, *Braddock Expedition*, 43.

37. Mary H. Rubin, *Images of America: Washington County* (Charleston, SC: Arcadia, 2001), 85.

38. Older, *Braddock Expedtion*, 54-61.

39. Franklin, *Autobiography*, 108.

40. Hough, *Braddock's Road*, 6.

41. Older, *Braddock Expedition*, 63, citing a letter from Robert Dinwiddie to William Shirley, Sept. 7, 1755, and a letter from Robert Hunter Morris to William Shirley, Sept. 5, 1755, Pennsylvania Archives, 2:400.

42. Letter from Governor Sharpe to Governor Dinwiddie, Augustu 23, 1755, *Correspondence of Governor Horatio Sharpe, Volume 1, 1753-1757*, Archives of Maryland Online, vol. 6, 271, http://www.mdarchives.state.md.us.

43. Fairfax Harrison, ed., "Mrs. Browne's Diary," Virginia Magazine of History and Biography, vol. 32, no. 4 (October 1924): 305-20, quoted in Older, *Braddock Expedition*, 65, and Wahll, *Braddock Road Chronicles*.

44. Harrison, "Mrs. Browne's Diary," quoted in Older, *Braddock Expedition*, 65.

45. Letter from Governor Sharpe to Thomas Robinson, August 11, 1755, *Correspondence of Governor Horatio Sharpe, Volume 1, 1753-1757*, Archives of Maryland Online, vol. 6, 265, http://www.mdarchives.state.md.us.

46. Letter from Governor Sharpe to Secretary of State Fox, May 3, 1756, *Correspondence of Governor Horatio Sharpe, Volume 1, 1753-1757*, Archives of Maryland Online, vol. 6, 404, http://www.mdarchives.state.md.us.

News from Fox's Gap

Published June 1 and December 1 of each year by
The Society of the Descendants of Frederick Fox of Fox's Gap in Maryland

Membership dues are $5.00 per year. President of the Society is Curtis L. Older.
Make Society inquiries by the following means:

Curtis L. Older
618 Tryon Place
Gastonia, NC 28054-6066

e-mail: curtolder@earthlink.net
phone: 704-864-3879

Genealogy Documentation Section
by Curtis L. Older

A new feature of each Fox Society Newsletter that was begun with the December 1, 2004, newsletter is the inclusion of an article that documents a descendant or spouse of a descendant of John Fox of Fox's Gap in Maryland. The article will present a written description about the individual and his or her family as well as a listing of the related genealogical source records that support the written description.

The third individual to be presented in this new feature of the newsletter is John L. Fox. John L. Fox was a son of George Fox.

Previous issues of the Fox Society Newsletter contained documentation for the following individuals:

December 1, 2004 - **Frederick Fox**
June 1, 2005 - **George Fox**
December 1, 2005 - **John L. Fox**
June 1, 2006 - **Daniel Alexander Fox**

Documentation for Elizabeth Jane Ricketts, mother of Ethel Belle Fox

Elizabeth Jane Ricketts was born October 18, 1861, Vermillion County, Indiana.(**1**) She was the daughter of Jacob Ricketts and Melissa Barnard.(**2**) Elizabeth Jane Ricketts married Daniel Alexander Fox on April 1, 1881.(**3**) Daniel Alexander Fox was the son of John L. Fox and Susannah Hiligass.(**4**)

Daniel and Elizabeth Fox were the parents of five children. Kenneth Benjamin Fox was born November 17, 1882, in Gessie, Highland Township, Vermillion County, Indiana. He died September 30, 1971, in Richmond, Indiana. He married Virga Butche in 1900. Virga was born August 4, 1885, and died November 2, 1983, in Salt Lake City, Utah. (**5**)

Ernest Daniel Fox was born December 1, 1885 near Gessie, Vermillion County, Indiana. He married Lola Frances Jackson on January 8, 1908, in Vermilion County, Illinois. She was born January 1, 1890, and died June 28, 1943. Ernest died October 3, 1940, at Lakeview Hospital in Danville, Illinois. He is buried at Niccum Cemetery in Vermilion County, Illinois. (**6**)

William Edward Fox was born Jan 5, 1888, and died Apr 16, 1974. He married Marguerite Clem on Feb 10, 1909, in Danville, IL. She was born Mar 9, 1894, in Mound Township, Warren County, IN. She died Jan 27, 1970, at Danville, IL. Her parents were Augustus Elmer Clem and Malinda Lloyd Cunningham. William and Marguerite are both buried at the Lower Mound Cemetery west of Covington, Indiana. (**7**)

Ethel Belle Fox was born on October 6, 1892. On February 3, 1917, Ethel Belle Fox married Robert William Gouty. He was the son of Joseph P. Gouty and Luella Marie Hartman. Robert was born August 26, 1889, in Gessie, Vermilion County, Indiana. (**8**)

Ruby Dale Fox was born December 13, 1896. She died November 12, 1990, in Grand Rapids, Michigan. She married Everett Hines on April 10, 1920, in Covington, Indiana. Everett was born July 30, 1894, and died April 5, 1963. Both Everett and Ruby are buried in the Lower Mound Cemetery west of Covington, Indiana. (**9**)

Elizabeth Jane (Ricketts) Fox burned to death on Tuesday, February 28, 1922, when her clothes caught fire from the kitchen stove and she ran onto the back porch and fell upon a bottle of gasoline.(**10**) Daniel Alexander Fox died July 29, 1932, in Covington, Indiana.(**11**) Both Daniel and Elizabeth Fox are buried in Hopewell Cemetery west of Covington,

Indiana. Their tombstone is near that of John L. Fox and his wife Susannah Hillegas. The will of Daniel Alexander Fox lists the names of all of his children and is recorded in the Vermillion County, Indiana Court House, Newport, Indiana.(**12**)

Elizabeth Jane Ricketts, age 8, is listed in the 1870 U. S. Federal Census for Indiana, Highland Township, Vermillion County, living with her parents, Jacob and Melissa (Barnard) Ricketts, (**13**). The 1870 census record indicates that Elizabeth Jane was a twin sister to Abraham Lincoln Ricketts. Elizabeth Jane Ricketts is listed in the 1880 U. S. Federal Census for Indiana, Mound Township, Warren County, enumerated June 11, 1880, by George W. Main. Her age is listed as 19 and she was living with her parents, Jacob and Melissa (Barnard) Ricketts, (**14**).

The 1900 U. S. Census for Indiana, Vermillion County, Highland Township, East part, enumerated June 11 & 12, 1900, John L. Webster, shows Elizabeth J. Fox, age 38, born in October 1861, mother of five children, all five living in 1900.**(15)** The 1910 U. S. Census for Indiana, Vermillion County, Highland Township, enumerated April 20 and 21, 1910 by Jno. L. Webster, shows Elizabeth J. Fox, wife, female, white, age 48, mother of 5 children, 5 living, born in Indiana, father born in Indiana, mother born in Indiana.**(16)** Lizzie J. Fox (Elizabeth Jane Fox) is listed in the 1920 U. S. Federal Census for Indiana, Vermillion County, Highland Township, age 60, living with her husband, Daniel A. Fox, and Ruby D. Fox, a daughter.(**17**) Daniel Alexander Fox should be listed in the 1930 U. S. Federal Census for Indiana.

Children (**Fox**) born in Highland Township, Vermillion County, Indiana:

i. **Kenneth Benjamin**, born November 17, 1882

ii. **Ernest Daniel Fox,** born December 1, 1885

iii. **William Edward**, born January 5, 1888

iv. **Ethel Belle**, born October 6, 1892

v. **Ruby Dale**, born December 13, 1896

REFERENCES

1. Ethel Belle (Fox) Gouty Family Bible in the possession of Curtis Lynn Older. Copies of pages from the Ethel Belle Fox Family Bible are in a CD-rom disc entitled Fox's Gap in Maryland, which is at the Frederick County Historical Society, Frederick, Maryland. **2.** 1870 U. S. Federal Census for Indiana, Highland Township, Vermillion County, Post Office - Perrysville, enumerated June 24, 1870; 1880 U. S. Federal Census for Indiana, Warren County, Mound Township, enumerated June 11, 1880 by George W. Main. **3.** Marriage records, Fountain County Court House, Covington, Indiana, Book 8, #350, April 1, 1881, Daniel Alexander Fox and Elizabeth Jane Ricketts. Fountain County, Indiana, Index to Marriage Record 1848 - 1920 Inclusive Volume I Letters A - G Inclusive, W. P. A. Original Record Located: County Clerks Office Covington Compiled by Indiana Works Projects Administration 1941, County: Fountain, Name: Daniel A Fox, Spouse: Lizzie J Ricketts, Marriage Date: 01 Apr 1881, Book: 8, Original Source Page: 350; *The Fox Genealogy including the Metherd, Benner, and Leiter descendants, giving biographies of the first and second generations, with sketches of the third generation*, compiled by D. G. Fox, 1914. (n.p) 1924. 1 p. 1., (5)-172 p. 20 com. 37-9439 CS71.F79 1924 Library of Congress. **4**. *The Fox Genealogy*, page 96. **5**. *The Fox Genealogy*, page 96; Issue 9, Volume 1, *News from Fox's Gap,* published by The Society of the Descendants of Frederick Fox of Fox's Gap in Maryland, page 19, "The Children of Daniel Alexander Fox and Elizabeth Jane Ricketts", by Curtis Lynn Older. **6.** Ibid. **7**. Ibid; Issue 1, Volume 1, *News from Fox's Gap*, page 6, "Descendants of William Edward Fox" by Dellie Jean Fox Craig. **8.** Issue 9, Volume 1, *News from Fox's Gap*, published by The Society of the Descendants of Frederick Fox of Fox's Gap in Maryland, page 19, The Children of Daniel Alexander Fox and Elizabeth Jane Ricketts, by Curtis Lynn Older. **9.** Ibid. **10.** Covington (Indiana) Republican Newspaper, obituary notice, front page, column one, probably about March 1, 1922; The Ethel Belle Fox Gouty Family Bible; Issue 2, Volume 1,

News from Fox's Gap, published by The Society of the Descendants of Frederick Fox of Fox's Gap in Maryland, page 5. **11.** Ethel Belle (Fox) Gouty Family Bible; Daniel A. Fox obituary, Reel #182072, Covington (Indiana) Republican, January 1931 - December 1932, August 5, 1932. **12.** Will of Daniel Alexander Fox, Newport, Vermillion County, Indiana, Court House, page 218, record number 6, August 1, 1932. **13.** 1870 U. S. Federal Census for Indiana, Highland Township, Vermillion County, Post Office - Perrysville, enumerated June 24, 1870. **14.** 1880 U. S. Federal Census for Indiana, Warren County, Mound Township, enumerated June 11, 1880 by George W. Main. **15.** 1900 U. S. Census for Indiana, Vermillion County, Highland Township, East part, enumerated June 11 & 12, 1900, John L. Webster. **16.** 1910 U. S. Census for Indiana, Vermillion County, Highland Township, enumerated April 20 and 21, 1910 by Jno. L. Webster. **17.** 1920 Indiana Federal census, Highland Township, Vermillion County, enumerated February 13, 1920, by Dale E.

New Member Section

We are pleased to announce the following new member of our Society:

Name / **Address**	**Phone**	**Date of Membership**	**Membership Number**
Bruce L. Barnheiser 1777 Lariat Trail Edmond, OK 73003 BBarnheise@aol.com	**Ancestor Line:** Leiter	August 1, 2006	0059

President's Message

by Curtis Lynn Older

* ***News from Fox's Gap* is seeking articles by Fox Society members about their family genealogy, primarily as it relates to their descent from Frederick Fox. We hope to publish a number of articles in the future that were contributed by Society members.**

* Please visit the Indiana University of Pennsylvania website of Fox's Gap in Maryland at:

http://www.iuparchaeology.iup.edu/FoxGap/

Land Tracts of the Battlefield of South Mountain

by Curtis L. Older.

Many Fox Society Newsletters include a survey, patent, or deed related to the land tracts in the vicinity of Crampton's, Fox's, and Turner's Gaps on the Battlefield of South Mountain. Previous issues of the Society Newsletter contained descriptions of the following tracts:

June 1 1997	Addition to Friendship of Frederick Fox
December 1, 1997	Fredericksburgh of Frederick Fox
June 1, 1998	Pick All of Bartholomew Booker
December 1, 1998	Bowser's Addition of David Bowser
June 1, 1999	Partnership of John Mansberger
December 1, 1999	Mountain of John Baley
December 1, 2000	Flonham of Philip Jacob Shafer
June 1, 2001	The Exchange of Daniel Dulaney
December 1, 2001	Betty's Good Will of Robert Evans
December 1, 2004	Resurvey on Exchange
June 1, 2005	The Gap and John's Delight
December 1, 2005	Resurvey on Well Done
June 1, 2006	Foxes Last Shift

Additional information related to land records in the vicinity of Fox's Gap is available in *The Land Tracts of the Battlefield of South Mountain* by Curtis L. Older, published by Willow Bend Books, Westminster, Maryland, ISBN: 1-58549-066-0. The book contains over six years of research by the author involving over 300 land records of Frederick County, Washington County, and the Maryland Archives.

Land records are traced from the earliest landowner to the owner of the property in 1995 for the following historic sites:

The Fox Inn
The Mountain House
The Reno Monument
The War Correspondents Memorial Arch
and others

Land records which help identify the route of the following roads also are included in the book:

The Road through Fox's Gap
The Road through Turner's Gap

Anyone interested in researching or learning about the historic area surrounding Fox's Gap in Maryland can save themselves a lot of work by starting with a copy of *The Land Tracts of the Battlefield of South Mountain* by Curtis L. Older.

A land record from the Maryland Archives (Maryland Hall of Records) is included below. The tract is on the west side of the South Mountain and is a key tract in helping document where Robert Turner lived. Robert Turner owned a tract of land named Nelson's Folly at the present site of Boonsboro, Maryland. Charlemount Pleasant was located "about half a mile to the southward of Robert Turners". Robert Turner did not live at the "Mountain House" at Turner's Gap as many people incorrectly assume.

The land record in the Maryland Archives for Charlemount Pleasant appears on the following page:

MdHR 17,420, 1-23-3-14, BC & GS 9, pp. 405-406, Samuel Ogle Esqr., Charlemount Pleasant, surveyed 1 Jan 1745, 100 acres.

Samuel Ogle Esqr Cert. Charlemount Pleasant 100 acres Patd ??} Prince Georges County by virtue of a warrant granted out of his lordships land office of this province unto Samuel Ogle Esqr for five hundred and sixteen acres of land bearing date the twenty fifth day of September Anno Domini 1745 I therefore certify as deputy surveyor of Prince Georges County under his excellency Thomas Bladen Esqr Governor of Maryland I have carefully laid out for and in the name of him the said Samuel Ogle Esqr all that tract of land lying in the said county called Charlemount Pleasant Beginning at a bounded Black Oak standing on a small hill to the eastward of a spring that falls in Little Antieatom about half a mile to the southward of Robert Turners and running thence

Line No.	North South	Degrees East or West	Length
1	N	5 east	40 perches
2	S	87 west	48 perches
3	S	26 west	207 perches
4	S	77 east	110 perches

5 then by a straight line to the beginning tree containing and now laid out for 100 acres of land to be held of Calverton or Conegochieg Mannor Surveyed this 1st day of January Anno Domini 1745.

? Thos Cresap D S of Prince Georges County

Nov ? 1746 Examd & Passed } On the back of the forgoing certificate
R of Exam? } was this following assignment receipt Know all men by these presents that we the subscribers executers of Samuel Ogle Esqr Deceased do for a valuable consideration assign over all our right title Interest of in ? unto the within certificate unto John Darnall of Frederick County Esqr In Witness whereof we have hereunto set our hands this ?th day of Sept? 1758. Benja Tasker

Benja Tasker Junr

I have received the sum of two pounds fourteen shillings for thirteen years and a half years rent of the within land to ? 1758. Patent may therefore issue with his excellencys approbation. September 1758 approved H Sharpe Edwd Lloyd

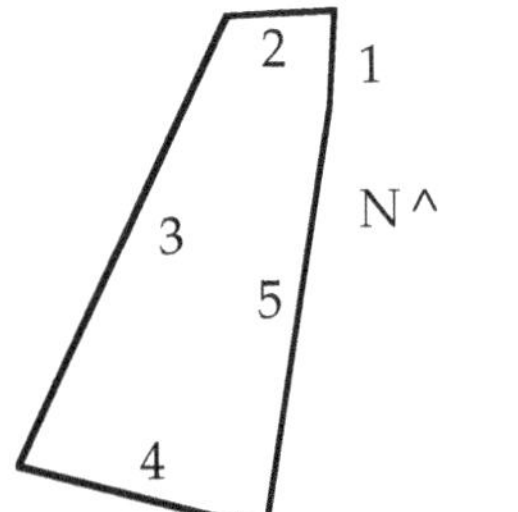

Charlemount Pleasant

100 acres

Beginning at a bounded Black Oak standing on a small hill to the eastward of a spring that falls in Little Antieatom about half a mile to the southward of Robert Turners

News from Fox's Gap

The Society of the Descendants of Frederick Fox of Fox's Gap in Maryland

Issue 3, Volume 3 **Remember Freedom!** December 1, 2007

The Family of Charles E. Fox, a son of George L. Fox

Charles (4) and Ella Shinn Fox Family
Front: Amos(5), Charles Fox, Ella Shinn Fox, Herbert(5)
Back: Emma Fox(5) Robinson, Lizzie Fox(5) Heffner, Maggie Fox(5) Anke

Lynn Woodard provided the above picture of the Charles E. Fox family. Charles was a son of George L. Fox who was a son of George and Elizabeth Ann (Link) Fox and a grandson of Frederick Fox. Charles married Ella Chinn. The children of Charles E. and Ella Fox were Amos, his brother Herbert, and sisters Emma, Lizzie M., and Maggie M. Fox. Lynn estimates the date of this family portrait as circa 1900. See pages 92 and 93 of ***The Fox Genealogy*** by Daniel Gebhart Fox for the descendants of George L. Fox.

Genealogy Documentation Section

by Curtis L. Older

A feature of each Fox Society Newsletter that began with the December 1, 2004, newsletter is the inclusion of an article that documents or genealogically proves a descendant or spouse of a descendant of John Fox of Fox's Gap in Maryland. The article will present a written description about the individual and his or her family as well as a listing of the related genealogical source records that support the written description. This newsletter contains documentation for two individuals.

The sixth and seventh individuals to be presented in this section of the newsletter are Elizabeth Ann Link, the wife of George Fox and Susannah Hilligass, the wife of John L. Fox.

Previous issues of the Fox Society Newsletter contained documentation for the following individuals:

December 1, 2004 - **Frederick Fox**
December 1, 2005 - **John L. Fox**
December 1, 2006 - **Elizabeth Jane Ricketts**
June 1, 2005 - **George Fox**
June 1, 2006 - **Daniel Alexander Fox**

Documentation for Elizabeth Ann Link, the mother of George L. Fox and the wife of George Fox

Elizabeth Ann Link was born on January 28, 1784, near Frederick in Frederick County, Maryland.**(1)** She was baptized in the Frederick Lutheran Church.**(2)** She was the first child of John Adam Link II and Jane Ogle.**(3)** Elizabeth's father was a grandson of John Jacob Link, an ancestor of Dwight D. Eisenhower.**(4)** Jane Ogle, a daughter of Alexander Ogle of Frederick, Maryland, was a descendant of John Ogle of Delaware.**(5)** Elizabeth's parents moved the family to near Shepherdstown, Virginia, in early 1784.**(6)**

Elizabeth Ann Link married George Fox on August 9, 1807, at Shepherdstown, Virginia, now West Virginia.**(7)** George Fox was born March 10, 1781, in Frederick County, Maryland.**(8)** George was the oldest son of Frederick Fox and Catharine Booker.**(9)**

George Fox was a member of the Zion Lutheran Church of Middletown, Maryland.**(10)** In 1805, at age 24, George Fox acquired the Fox Inn along the Old Sharpsburg Road, about 2 miles east of Fox's Gap.**(11)** Fox's Gap is where the Old Sharpsburg Road from Frederick, Maryland, to Sharpsburg, Maryland, crosses the South Mountain.**(12)** The Old Sharpsburg Road was part of the Great Wagon Road to Philadelphia, which also was known as the German Monocacy Road.**(13)**

Fox's Gap was named for John Fox, the grandfather of George and the father of Frederick Fox. John Fox settled at the gap by the early 1760s. Fox's Gap was the scene for a major portion of the Battle of South Mountain between forces under Confederate General Robert E. Lee and Union General George B. McClellan on September 14, 1862.**(14)** A little more than one hundred years prior to the Battle of South Mountain, on May 2, 1755, the road through Fox's Gap was used by General Braddock, George Washington, and Maryland's Governor Sharpe to travel from Frederick Town to Swearingen's Ferry on the Potomac River, while on their way to Fort Cumberland during the Braddock Expedition.**(15)** Swearingen's Ferry was near the sight of present day Shepherdstown, West Virginia, formerly Virginia.

George and Elizabeth Fox moved west to near Miamisburg, Ohio, in late 1807 along with a number of other families with ties to George's parents, Frederick and Catherine Fox.**(16)** George and Elizabeth Fox were the parents of ten children:**(17)**

Adam Fox was born Oct 1, 1808, and died May 1, 1881, in OH. Late in his life he married Elizabeth F. Heiss.

Frederick L. Fox was born Feb 28, 1810, in Montgomery Co., OH, and died Nov 20, 1851. He is buried at the St. John or Gebhart Church Cemetery in Miamisburg, Warren Co., OH. He married Anna Maria Zehring on Mar 28, 1833. She was a daughter of Johann Zehring and Frances Garst. The seven children of Frederick L. and Anna (Zehring) Fox are: Samuel Fox, George Fox, Lavinia Fox, John P. Fox, Frances A. Fox, Elizabeth Fox, and Jacob Henry Fox. (See Family Tree Maker CD, U.S. and International Marriage Records, 1340-1980)

Daniel L. Fox was born Aug 17, 1811 and died Sep 8, 1889. He married Rosannah Christman on Sep 12, 1833.

Catharine Fox (Mrs. John Fox) was born May 6, 1813 and died Sep 19, 1841. She married John Fox on Sep 20, 1832.

George L. Fox was born Sep 12, 1816 and died Apr 17, 1893. He married Susannah Manning on Dec 27, 1842.

John L. Fox was born October 18, 1818 and died January 6, 1899. He married Susannah Hilligass on November 11, 1845.

Alexander Fox was born Sep 21, 1820 and died Sep 15, 1900. He married Anna Eagle on Apr 9, 1845.

Susanna Jane Fox was born Nov 17, 1824, and died September 9,1841.

Elizabeth Fox was born Oct 1, 1830 and died Oct 23, 1868. She married Peter Eagle on Nov 11, 1854.

Mary L. Fox was born Oct 1, 1830 and died Oct 5, 1850.

George Fox died June 14, 1847, in Miamisburg, Ohio, and was buried in the Gebhart or St. John Cemetery in Miamisburg.**(18)** Elizabeth Ann (Link) Fox died March 9, 1872, in Miamisburg, Ohio, and is buried next to her husband in the Gebhart or St. John Cemetery.**(19)**

George Fox is listed in the 1809 Ohio state census for Franklin Township in Warren County.**(20)** The 1810 Ohio Federal census for Warren county, Franklin township, lists the George Fox household.**(21)**

The 1830 Ohio Federal census for Warren county, Clear Creek township, lists the George Fox household as consisting of 7 males and 2 females: one male was 5 and under 10, two males were 10 and under 15, two males were 15 and under 20, one male was twenty and under thirty, one male was 40 and under 50; one female was 5 and under 10 and one female was 15 and under 20.**(22)**

The 1840 Ohio Federal census for Warren county, Clear Creek township, lists the George Fox household as consisting of 5 males and 4 females: one male was age 15 and under 20, two males were 20 and under 30, one male was 30 and under 40, and one male was 50 and under 60; two females were age 5 and under 10, 1 was age 15 and under 20, and one was age 50 and under 60.**(23)**

The 1850 U. S. Census for Ohio, Warren County, Clear Creek Township, dwelling number 439 and family number 439 lists the Elizabeth Fox household. Elizabeth is listed as age 66 and born in Maryland. Also living in the household are Adam Fox age 42, a farmer born in Ohio; Elizabeth Fox, age 19 and born in Ohio; and Mary Fox, age 19 and born in Ohio. Also listed on the same census page are the households of George L. Fox and Frederick L. Fox.**(24)**

The 1860 U. S. Census for Ohio, Warren County, Clear Creek Township, dwelling number 287 and family 287 lists the Elizabeth Fox household. Elizabeth Fox is listed as age 76 and born in Maryland. Her real estate value is given as $3,862 and her personal estate value is given as $2,110. Also living in the household are Adam Fox, age 51, farmer, born in Ohio and Elizabeth A. fox, age 25, born in Ohio.**(25)**

The 1870 U. S. Census for Ohio, Warren County, Clear Creek Township, lists the Adam Fox household. Adam Fox is listed as age 61, a farm laborer who was born in Ohio. Also listed are Elizabeth Fox, age 36, who keeps house for her brother and Elizabeth Fox age 86, born in Maryland, who lives with her son.**(26)**

Children (**Fox**) born in Warren County, Ohio:

i. **Adam**, born October 1, 1808
ii. **Frederick L.**, born February 28, 1810
iii. **Daniel L.**, born August 17, 1811
iv. **Catharine**, born May 6, 1813
v. **George L.**, born September 12, 1816
vi. **John L.**, born October 18, 1818
vii. **Alexander**, born September 21, 1820
viii. **Susanna Jane**, born Nov. 17, 1824
ix. **Elizabeth** L., born October 1, 1830
x. **Mary L.**, born October 1, 1830

REFERENCES

1. Tombstone of Elizabeth Ann Link, Gebhart or St. John Cemetery, Miamisburg, Ohio, "Elizabeth wife of George Fox died March 9, 1872, aged 88 Yrs. 1 Mo. & 11 Ds." photograph by Curtis L. Older; *The Fox Genealogy including the Metherd, Benner, and Leiter descendants, giving biographies of the first and second generations, with sketches of the third generation*, compiled by D. G. Fox, 1914. (n.p) 1924. 1 p. 1., (5)-172 p. 20 com. 37-9439 CS71.F79 1924 Library of Congress, p. 82; see Paxson Link, *The Link Family* (Paris, Illinois: [s.l.], 1951), 81, " John Adam II and Jane spent the first year of their married life in Maryland, where their first child, Elizabeth Ann, was born January 29, 1784, and baptized in the Frederick Lutheran Church. She married George Fox, August 9, 1807, and has not been contacted in our research work." **2.** *The Link Family*, p. 81. **3.** *Index to Marriage Licenses, Frederick County, 1778-1810*, John Adam Link II and Jane Ogle, married April 14, 1783; *The Link Family*, p. 81, "on April 15, 1783, John Adam and Jane, accompanied by her brother and sister and his father and brother, Jacob, were married in the Frederick Lutheran Church." **4.** *The Link Family*, chapter on Dwight D. Eisenhower; letter from Dwight D. Eisenhower to Paxson Link dated October 10, 1950, copy in the possession of Curtis L. Older; Adam Link I, the grandfather of Elizabeth Ann Link , supplied bacon during the American Revolution, see Maryland State Papers, Series A, MdHR 4586-15 1/6/4/18; John Adam Link II, the father of Elizabeth Ann Link, was an officer during the American Revolution, see Paxson Link, *The Link Family*, 78. **5.** Francis Hamilton Hibbard, assisted by Stephen Parks, *The English origin of John Ogle, first of the name in Delaware* (Pittsburgh: n.p., 1967); Sir Henry Asgill Ogle, *Ogle and Bothal* (Newcastle-upon-Tyne: Andrew Reid & Company, 1902). Alexander Ogle, father of Jane Ogle, provided wheat and flour from his mills to the Maryland troops during the American Revolution. See Maryland State Papers, Series A, MdHR 6636-23-29/7 1/7/5 and related papers. **6.** *The Link Family*, p. 81, "During the first part of 1784 John Adam II and Jane moved across the Potomac River to take possession of Jane's inheritance and make for themselves a homestead." **7.** Jefferson County, West Virginia, Marriage Records, 1807, page 286; *The Link Family*, p. 81. **8.** Tombstone of George Fox, Gebhart or St. John Cemetery, Miamisburg, Ohio; *Fox Genealogy*, 82. **9.** Curtis L. Older, *The Braddock Expedition and Fox's Gap in Maryland* (Westminster, Md.: Family Line Publications, 1995), p. 98; *Ohio D.A.R. Soldiers Rosters*, 2 vols., 1:146; will of Frederick Fox, Will Book C, case #1444, Montgomery County, Ohio; *Fox Genealogy*, p. 82. **10.** Frederick S.Weiser, ed., *Zion Lutheran Church 1781-1826*, Maryland German Church Records, Vol. 2, (Manchester, Md.: Noodle-Doosey Press, 1987), 25. "Samuel, son of Jacob and Magdelena Benner was born April 14, 1801. Baptised June 21, 1801. Sponsored by George Fox, a single person." (Mary) Magdelena Benner was the daughter of Frederick Fox and sister of George. **11.** *Braddock Expedition and Fox's Gap in Maryland*, pp. 97-99 and Appendix D; Curtis L. Older, *The Land Tracts of the Battlefield of South Mountain* (Westminster, Md.: Willow Bend Books, 1999), pp. 211-13, 227. **12.** *Braddock Expedition and Fox's Gap in Maryland*, pp. 99-104; *Land Tracts of the Battlefield of South Mountain*, pp. 40-41. **13.** *Land Tracts of the Battlefield of South Mountain*, p. 42; *Braddock*

Expedition and Fox's Gap in Maryland, p. 87. **14.** *Braddock Expedition and Fox's Gap in Maryland*, Afterword, pp. 177-182. **15.** *Braddock Expedition and Fox's Gap in Maryland*, p. 70. **16.** Sale of the Fox Inn property, Frederick County, Maryland, Land Records, WR-32-30, George Fox to John Ringer, 1807, 100 acres; Fox, *Fox Genealogy*, 15-6. **17.** Warren County Genealogical Society, Lebanon, Ohio, estate papers of George Fox; *Fox Genealogy*, pp. 82-100. **18.** Tombstone of George Fox, Gebhart or St. John Cemetery, Miamisburg, Ohio, "died June 14, 1847, aged 66 yrs, 3 mos, and 4 ds", photograph by Curtis L. Older; *Fox Genealogy*, 82. **19.** Tombstone of Elizabeth Ann Link, Gebhart or St. John Cemetery, Miamisburg, Ohio, "Elizabeth wife of George Fox died March 9, 1872, aged 88 Yrs. 1 Mo. & 11 Ds." photograph by Curtis L. Older; *Fox Genealogy*, 82. **20.** *Ohio Early Census Index*, 1809 Tax List, Warren County, Franklin Township, page 013, George Fox. **21.** 1810 Ohio Federal Census, Warren County, Franklin Township, page 28. **22.** 1830 Ohio Federal Census, Warren County, Clear Creek Township, roll M19_142, page 173, image 340. **23.** 1840 Ohio Federal Census, Warren County, Clear Creek Township, roll M704_431, page 178, image 356. **24.** 1850 Ohio Federal Census, Warren County, Clear Creek Township, page 446, roll M432_737, dwelling 439 and family 439, Elizabeth Fox household. **25.** 1860 Ohio Federal Census, Warren County, Clear Creek Township, page 314, roll M653_1047, enumerated August 3, 1860, Elizabeth Fox household, dwelling 287 and family 287. **26.** 1870 Ohio Federal Census, Warren County, Clear Creek Township, Post Office - Lebanon, enumerated August 1, 1870, page 225, roll M593_1277, image 54, Adam Fox household.

Please visit the Indiana University of Pennsylvania website for Fox's Gap in Maryland at:

http://www.iuparchaeology.iup.edu/FoxGap/

News from Fox's Gap

Published December 1 of each year by:

The Society of the Descendants of Frederick Fox of Fox's Gap in Maryland

Membership dues are $3.00 per year. President of the Society is Curtis L. Older.

Make Society inquiries by the following means:

Curtis L. Older
2417 Kinmere Road
Gastonia, NC 28056-7818

e-mail: curtolder@earthlink.net

phone: 704-864-3879

Documentation for Susannah Hilligass, the mother of Daniel Alexander Fox and the wife of John L. Fox

Susannah Hilligass was born November 30, 1819, in Montgomery County, Ohio.**(1)** Susannah Hilligass was the daughter of Michael Hilligass and Anna Yeakel(Weikel).**(2)** Susannah Hilligass married John L. Fox on November 11, 1845, in Miami Township, Montgomery County, Ohio, by the Reverend George Long.(**3**) John L. Fox was born October 18, 1818, near Miamisburg, Ohio.**(4)** He was the son of George Fox and Elizabeth Ann Link.**(5)**

John L. Fox and Susannah Hilligass were the parents of seven children: Anna Elizabeth, Mary Susannah, Catherine Florence, Martha Jane, Margaret Persilla, John Adam, and Daniel Alexander Fox. All of the children were born in Ohio except Daniel, who was born in Vermillion County, Indiana.**(6)**

Susannah Hilligass Fox died August 11, 1894, in Gessie, Highland Township, Vermillion County, Indiana.**(7)** John L. Fox died January 6, 1899, probably in Highland Township, Vermillion County, Indiana.**(8)** Both Susannah (Hilligass) Fox and John L. Fox are buried in Hopewell Cemetery west of Covington, Indiana.**(9)** The will of John L. Fox lists the following children: Margaret Ricketts, John A. Fox, Anna E. Goff, Mary Burnett, and Daniel A. Fox.**(10)**

John L. Fox is listed under the U. S. Census of Ohio, 1850, Miami Township, Montgomery County, as age 32 value of real estate = $2,500. Also listed with him are Susannah age 30, Ann age 2, and Mary Fox age 8 months. All are listed as born in Ohio.**(11)** John L. Fox and family moved to Vermillion County, Indiana about 1857.**(12)**

John L. Fox appears in the U. S. Census of Indiana, 1860, Highland Township, Vermillion County, Indiana. His real estate was valued at $6,560 and his personal property was valued at $1,500. Also listed in the household is: Susannah Fox, age 40, born in Ohio; Ann E. Fox, age 12, born in Ohio; Mary S. Fox, age 10, born in Ohio; Catherine F. Fox, age 8, born in Ohio; Margaret P. Fox, age 6, born in Ohio; John A. Fox, age 3, born in Ohio; Daniel A. Fox, age 5/12, born in Indiana; and Allen Rager, age 45, a laborer, who was born in Indiana.**(13)**

John L. Fox is listed under the U. S. Census of Indiana, 1870, Highland Township, Vermillion County, Post Office - Perrysville, enumerated June 21, 1870, by A. J. Adams, pages 14 and 15, dwelling number 94, family number 94. John L. Fox is listed as age 53, real estate value = $6,780 and personal estate value = $1,400. Susannah Fox is listed as age 50.**(14)**

John L. Fox is listed in the U. S. Census of Indiana, 1880, Highland Township, Vermillion County, dwelling 16, family 16, age 60, a farmer, living with Susannah Fox and Daniel Fox.**(15)**.

For a Biographical Sketch of John L. Fox, see *History of Vermillion County, Indiana,* Biographical Sketches: page 491. The article indicates John L. Fox owned 331 acres of choice land at one time in Highland Township. He was farming 186 acres at the time the book was published.**(16)** Also see *The Peoples' Guide, a business political and religious directory of Vermillion County, Indiana,* by Cline and McHaffie, 1874. A listing includes John L. Fox, farmer, 1 1/4 miles north east of Gessie, born in OH, 1818, settled in Vermillion Co., IN, 1858.**(17)**

Children (**Fox**):

i. **Anna Elizabeth**, born February 25, 1848, in Miamisburg, Montgomery County, Ohio

ii. **Mary Susannah,** born January 1850 in Ohio

iii. **Catherine Florence**, born in 1852 in Ohio

iv. **Martha Jane** born in Ohio

v. **Margaret Persilla**, born in 1854 in Warren County, Ohio

vi. **John Adam**, born in July 1857 in Warren County, Ohio

vii. **Daniel Alexander**, born January 13, 1860, in Highland Township, Vermillion County, Indiana

REFERENCES

1. Tombstone of "Susannah Hilligass wife of John L. Fox", Hopewell Cemetery west of Covington, Indiana. Date of death is given as August 11, 1894. The tombstone indicates she was 74 years, 8 months, 11 days old. Tombstone photograph taken by Curtis L. Older. **2.** *The Fox Genealogy including the Metherd, Benner, and Leiter descendants, giving biographies of the first and second generations, with sketches of the third generation,* compiled by Daniel Gebhart Fox, 1914. (n.p) 1924. 1 p. 1., (5)-172 p. 20 com. 37-9439 CS71.F79 1924 Library of Congress, page 94; Tombstones for Michael Hilligass and Anna, wife of Michael Hilligass are at the St. John, or Gebhart Cemetery, Miamisburg, Ohio. **3.** *The Fox Genealogy* by D. G. Fox, p. 94; John L. Fox and Susannah Hilligass, married November 11, 1845, in Miami Township, Montgomery County, Ohio, by Reverend George Long; Susannah Hilligass and John L. Fox marriage record, source #492.000, Yates Publications. **4.** *The Fox Genealogy* by D. G. Fox, p. 94; tombstone for John L. Fox, Hopewell Cemetery west of Covington Indiana. The tombstone states, "John L. Fox, died January 6, 1899, aged 80 years, 2 months, 28 days." **5.** *The Fox Genealogy* by D. G. Fox, p. 94; Estate Papers of George Fox, Warren County Genealogical Society, 300 East Silver Street, Lebanon, Ohio 45036, includes a receipt in the amount of $50 signed by Susannah Fox for John L. Fox. 6. *The Fox Genealogy* by D. G. Fox, p. 94-96; will of John L. Fox, Court House, Newport, Vermillion County, Indiana, pages 520 and 521; U. S. Census for Indiana, 1860, Highland Township, Vermillion County, enumerated by A. J. Adams on June 30, 1860, Dwelling 76, Family 76, John L. Fox, age 41, farmer, real estate value = $6,560, personal property value = $1,500, born in Ohio; Susannah Fox, age 40, born in Ohio; Ann E. Fox, age 12, born in Ohio; Mary S. Fox, age 10, born in Ohio; Catherine F. Fox, age 8, born in Ohio; Margaret P. Fox, age 6, born in Ohio; John A. Fox, age 3, born in Ohio; Daniel A. Fox, age 5/12, born in Indiana. **7.** Tombstone Susannah Hilligass. **8.** Tombstones of John L. Fox. **9.** Tombstones of John L. Fox and Susannah Hilligass at Hopewell Cemetery west of Covington, Indiana. **10.** Will of John L. Fox, Court House, Newport, Vermillion County, Indiana, pages 520 and 521. **11.** U. S. Census for Ohio, 1850, Miami Township, Montgomery County, enumerated August 4, 1850, by J. Hokidry, Dwelling 473, Family 473, John L. Fox, age 41, John Fox, age 32, farmer, real estate value = $2,500, born in Ohio; Susannah Fox, age 30, female, born in Ohio, Ann Fox, age 2, female, born in Ohio, Mary Fox, age 8 months, born in Ohio. **12.** *The Fox Genealogy* by D. G. Fox, p. 94. **13.** U. S. Census for Indiana, 1860, Highland Township, Vermillion County, enumerated by A. J. Adams on June 30, 1860, Dwelling 76, Family 76, John L. Fox, age 41, farmer, real estate value = $6,560, personal property value = $1,500, born in Ohio; Susannah Fox, age 40, born in Ohio; Ann E. Fox, age 12, born in Ohio; Mary S. Fox, age 10, born in Ohio; Catherine F. Fox, age 8, born in Ohio; Margaret P. Fox, age 6, born in Ohio; John A. Fox, age 3, born in Ohio; Daniel A. Fox, age 5/12, born in Indiana. **14.** U. S. Census for Indiana, 1870, Vermillion County, Highland Township, Post Office - Perrysville, enumerated June 21, 1870, by A. J. Adams, pages 14 and 15, Dwelling number 94, Family number 94, John L. Fox, age 53, male, white, farmer, real estate value = $6,780, personal estate vale = $1,400, born in Ohio, citizen of the U. S.; Susannah Fox, age 50, female, white, at home, born in Ohio; Anna Fox, age 22, female, white, at home, born in Ohio; Mary Fox, age 20, female, white, at home, born in Ohio; Catherine Fox, age 18, female, white, at home, born in Ohio, attended school within the year; Margaret Fox, age 14, female, white, at home, born in Ohio, attended school within the year; John Fox, age 13, male, white, at home, born in Ohio, attended school within the year; Daniel Fox, age 10, male, white, at home, born in Indiana, attended school within the year. **15.** U. S. Census for Indiana, 1880, Highland Township, Vermillion County, enumerated June 8, 1880, by Joshua Lewis, Dwelling number 16, Family number 16, John L. Fox, age 60; Susannah Fox, age 59; Daniel Fox, age 20. **16.** *History of Vermillion County, Indiana,* under Biographical Sketches, page 491, there appears a sketch of John L. Fox. The biographical sketch indicates he owned 331 acres of choice land at one time in Highland Township. He was farming 186 acres at the time the book was published. **17.** *The Peoples' Guide, a business political and religious directory of Vermillion County, Indiana,* by Cline and McHaffie, Indianapolis, Indianapolis Printing and Publishing House 1874: John L. Fox, farmer, 1 1/4 miles north east of Gessie, born in OH, 1818, settled in Vermillion Co., IN, 1858.

President's Message

by Curtis Lynn Older

* **Membership in the Society will be $3.00 per year beginning January 1, 2008.**

* **News from Fox's Gap will be published only once per year, on each December 1st , beginning with this issue.**

* ***News from Fox's Gap* is seeking articles by Fox Society members about their family genealogy, primarily as it relates to their descent from Frederick Fox. I hope to publish a number of articles in the future that were contributed by Society members.**

* **There were no new Society members for the calendar year 2007.**

* **Please note a new home address for me. My family and I moved about four miles to a new home during June of this year.**

Land Tracts of the Battlefield of South Mountain

by Curtis L. Older.

Many Fox Society Newsletters include a survey, patent, or deed related to the land tracts in the vicinity of Crampton's, Fox's, and Turner's Gaps on the Battlefield of South Mountain. Previous issues of the Society Newsletter contained descriptions of the following tracts:

June 1 1997	Addition to Friendship of Frederick Fox
December 1, 1997	Fredericksburgh of Frederick Fox
June 1, 1998	Pick All of Bartholomew Booker
December 1, 1998	Bowser's Addition of David Bowser
June 1, 1999	Partnership of John Mansberger
December 1, 1999	Mountain of John Baley
December 1, 2000	Flonham of Philip Jacob Shafer
June 1, 2001	The Exchange of Daniel Dulaney
December 1, 2001	Betty's Good Will of Robert Evans
December 1, 2004	Resurvey on Exchange
June 1, 2005	The Gap and John's Delight
December 1, 2005	Resurvey on Well Done
June 1, 2006	Foxes Last Shift
December 1, 2006	Charlemount Pleasant

Additional information related to land records in the vicinity of Fox's Gap is available in *The Land Tracts of the Battlefield of South Mountain* by Curtis L. Older, published by Willow Bend Books, Westminster, Maryland, ISBN: 1-58549-066-0. The book contains over six years of research by the author involving over 300 land records of Frederick County, Washington County, and the Maryland Archives.

Land records are traced from the earliest landowner to the owner of the property in 1995 for the following historic sites:

The Fox Inn
The Mountain House
The Reno Monument
The War Correspondents Memorial Arch
and others

Land records which help identify the route of the following roads also are included in the book:

The Road through Fox's Gap
The Road through Turner's Gap

Anyone interested in researching or learning about the historic area surrounding Fox's Gap in Maryland can save themselves a lot of work by starting with a copy of *The Land Tracts of the Battlefield of South Mountain* by Curtis L. Older.

The land record in the Maryland Archives for The Forrest appears on the following page:

MdHR 17,386, 1-23-2-18, AM 1, pp. 365-366, John Magrudar, Forrest, examined and allowed 2 Oct 1733, 300 acres.

Note: The road mentioned in the land record, i.e., "from Conestoga to Opeckin", was another name for the road that went through what was to become Fox's Gap.

Maryland Prince Georges County ? April the 9th 1734
Jn Magruder platd ? cert ? 300a Forrest By virtue of a warrant granted out of his Lordships Land Office the 23d day of December last ? renewment unto John Magruder of the afd county for six hundred and fifty acres of land I have surveyed for the said John Magrudar all that tract or parcel of land called **The Forrest** lying in the said county and beginning at a bounded hickory standing **about half mile above the wagon road that goes from Conestoga to Opeckin Crosses a creek called Katankin Creek** which falls into Potomack River about six miles above Monocacy and running thence

Line No.	North South	Degrees East or West	Length
1	S	25 east	120 perches
2	N	70 east	80 ps.
3	S	30 east	72 ps.
4	S	10 west	146 ps.
5	S	15 east	202 ps.
6	N	East	80 ps.
7	N	15 west	202 ps.
8	N	10 east	146 ps.
9	N	30 west	226 ps.

10 then with a straight line to the first trace and now laid out for **three hundred acres of land** more or less to be held of Calverton Mannor

October 1733 Examined and allowed R Francis Examiner George Nbole ???
On the back of the aforegoing cert was written the following assignment viz--
Know all men by these presents that I John Magruder of Prince Georges County for a valuable consideration assign sell transfer and make over unto Samuel Magrudar ? of the same county all any right title and interest of in and to the ? in ? and the land therein mentioned To have and to hold the same unto him the said Samuel his heirs and assigns for ever as witness my hand and seal this tenth day of June Anno Domi 1734
Jon Magruder
Witnesseth?
William Scott
James Magrudar

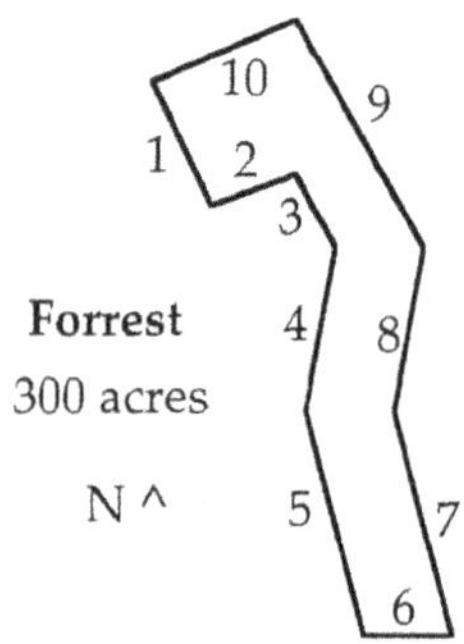

Beginning at a bounded hickory standing about half mile above the wagon road that goes from Conestoga to Opeckin Crosses a creek called Katankin Creek which falls into Potomack River about six miles above Monocacy

Note: Catoctin Creek cuts across this property, probably parallel and close to line 2 of this tract
. This tract apparently is adjacent to the south side of a tract named Wooden Platter. The beginning point is 1/2 mile above Catoctin Creek.

News from Fox's Gap

The Society of the Descendants of Frederick Fox of Fox's Gap in Maryland

Issue 4, Volume 3 **Remember Freedom!** December 1, 2008

The Pioneer Spirit of Elizabeth Booker Fox Leiter, Daughter of Frederick Fox and Catherine Booker

By Carole Leis Troup

Elizabeth Booker Fox Leiter was born in Frederick County, Maryland 27 September 1788; (3, 5, 10, 11, 21) she died 14 March 1854 (3, 5, 12, 16, 21) aged 65 years, married John Leiter 7 December 1805 at Frederick County, Maryland (6). John was born 1779 in Frederick County, Maryland; he died 16 September 1825, aged 46 years, buried in the St. John (Gebhart) Church Yard, (3, 5, 10, 11, 16) Miamisburg, Montgomery County, Ohio. He was the child of Henry Leiter and Catherine Stahley who were early settlers of the Middletown Valley in Maryland (12, 13, 14). He was one of nine children (13). John's parents did not immigrate to Ohio. They both died in Maryland and are buried in the German Reformed Cemetery in Middletown, Maryland (12, 13). (U.S. Census 1790 A.) US Census 1800 (B.) US Census 1810 (C.) (Frederick Co., MD) (21). US 1820 Census, John Leighter, Washington Twp., Montgomery Co., Ohio (E.) Roll 94, Book 1, page 164; US 1830 Census Miami Twp., (F.) Montgomery Co., OH. (Widow Lighter, page 216, Roll 136, Book 1). US 1840 Census, Miami Twp., Montgomery Co., OH (G.): Roll 414, Book 1: Henry Liter, John Liter, Elizabeth Liter Daniel Fox, all living next door to each other with their families; US 1850 Census, Roll 713, Book 1 Miami Twp., Montgomery Co., Ohio (H.): Elizabeth Liter, 62, f, w, head, $3500, PA, Catherine Eagle, 32, her widowed daughter and grandson William Eagle, 10).

Elizabeth's parents were Frederick Fox and Catherine Booker (12, 21). Frederick Fox was born 10 May 1751 in Hesse-Cassel, Germany; he died 27 February 1837at the age of 85 years 9 months 17days. (5, 7, 8, 10, 16, 17, 18, 13, 21) (Census Records 1790 (A.) 1800 (B.) Frederick Co., MD) (State of Ohio Census 1809, 1810) (US 1820, 1830 Franklin Twp., (BB.) Warren Co., Ohio; Miami Twp.(F.) Montgomery Co., Ohio.

He was the son of John Frederick and Christiana Fox (10, 11, 12, 13, 14, having come aboard the ship Anderson from Rotterdam Holland which landed at Philadelphia 27 September 1752 (12, 13). His parents were born in Germany (12, 13). He married Catherine Booker who was born 1 May 1748 and died 1 Nov. 1800 (12, 13). She was the daughter of Bartholomew Booker and Margaret Comes (10, 11, 12, 13, 15, 23, 25. She was one of fourteen children (10, 11). Frederick Fox served in the Revolutionary War as a Drummer. He served in the Pennsylvania Militia even though he lived in Maryland (18, 24, 25, 26).

John and Elizabeth Leiter joined the seven families with ties to his family--there being thirty-two pioneers emigrating from Washington County, Sharpsburg, MD to Ohio in covered wagons nearby Miamisburg, Ohio in late 1807 (10, 11, 12, 13, 16, 21). John and Elizabeth were the parents of nine children.

(13) Three of their children married Gebharts. Their children were: (13)

1. **Henry Leiter.** He was born 14 November 1806 Frederick County, Maryland (3, 10, 14, 21). He was baptized at the Reformed Church in Middletown, MD (14). He married Anna LaRose Gebhart on 22 December 1831 in Miamisburg (1 pg. 191 & 114) Montgomery Co., OH. He died on 29 September 1859 in Miamisburg, (3, 10, 31). He is buried at Gebhart (St. John's) Church Yard (3, 10, 14, 16) 29 September 1859 aged 52y 10m 15 d. US 1850 Census, Miami Twp., Montgomery CO., OH (H.). After Henry Leiter died, Anna LaRose Gebhart Leiter US 1860 Census Miami Twp., Montgomery Co., (K.) OH, 48, f, w, Widow, living with children Emanuel G., William A., Lewis, Elizabeth, Albert, Noah and son John, married, 25, living next door. Originally, Henry and Anna located on a tract of land adjoining the Gebhart (St. John's) Church on the South (14, 21). He was listed in the Miami Twp. Census with his wife's parents living in the same house with them (14, 21). After Henry Leiter's death his wife, Anna Leiter moved to Sedalia, Missouri in January 1869. She bought a farm 5 _ miles southeast of town where she and her children resided. Anna Leiter lived near her sister Mary LaRose Gebhart Leiter Houk. US 1870 Census, Flat Creek Twp., Pettis Co., Missouri (DD.) Anna, 57, f, w, living with Children: William, 25, Lewis, 22, Elizabeth, 20, Albert, 17, Noah, 12. (See 1870 Census, Butler Twp., Faberville, St. Clair Co., Missouri .GG.) William Houk--Mary LaRose Gebhart Leiter Houk). US 1880 Census, Flat Creek Twp., Pettis Co., Missouri (EE.) Leiter: Albert, 27, farmer, head, Isabel, w, f, 22, wife housekeeper, Anna F., f, 7/12 daughter, Anna, w, f, 68, Mother, lives with son, Noah, w, m, 23, brother, farmer. Anna Leiter died 2 December 1896 (28). Anna is buried in Pleasant Hill Methodist Cemetery, Flat Creek Twp., Missouri (28). Anna lived with her son Noah K. until her death (28c, 29). They are together on all Censuses from 1850 forward.

2. **John Benton Leiter.** He was born on 4 October 1809 (11, 13, 18 pg.143) and died 1 February 1872 (2, 13, 14, 18) in Miami Township, Montgomery County, Ohio. He married Susan Crider (1) who was born 31 August 1816 and died 23 Jun 1886. (2, 10, 13, 18). They were married on 12 February 1834, (Montgomery County Court Document, Ohio. (1 pg. 85, 2 pg. 140 Vol. B Montgomery Co. Court). Both are buried in the Gebhart (St. John's) Church Yard (10, 13, 14, 18 pg. 194).

3. **Frederick Leiter.** He was born 22 March 1813 (3, 5, 11) in Miamisburg, Miami Township, Montgomery County, Ohio (4, 10, 13, 14, 21). He married Mary LaRose Gebhart (1 pg. 114, 33, 5) on 11 February 1836 in Miami Township, Montgomery County, Ohio. He died 14 October 1838 (3, 5,) in Miami Township, Montgomery County, Ohio (12, 18).

Frederick Lighter's tombstone inscription at the Gebhart Church Yard reads (3, 13, 18, 33, 34):

"In Memory of
Frederick Lighter
Who was born March the 23
1813 and died October 11, 1838,
Aged 25 years 6 months and 22 days
Why do we mourn departing friends
Or them? At Death's alarmes
Tis but a voice that Jesus sends
To all of them? His arms...."

Two children were born to Frederick Leiter and Mary LaRose Gebhart. They were: (4, 10, 11, 21,13).

- **Emanuel L. Leiter** was born 1837 in Miami Township, Montgomery County, Ohio. (13). Emanuel, age 12, was listed on US 1850 Census, Miami Twp., Montgomery Co., Ohio (H.) living with his mother, Mary and step-father William S. Houk. His sister, Elizabeth Leiter, age 11 was listed. He married Malissa A. More on 4 December 1859 in Parke County (11, 21), Indiana. US 1860 Census, Parke Co., Indiana (J) Emanuel and Malissa were living with his cousin, Lewis Gebhart and family. US 1880 Census, Penn Twp., Parke Co., Indiana, page 452a Roll 303 8th June (FF.) Emanuel Lighter, w, m, 43 married farmer OH MD OH living with Melissa A., w, f, 40 wife keep house IN PA OH, George, 15, MO OH Indiana. Leroy, 10

Sallie, 5. (Note: This lineage will continue in December 2009 newsletter.)

• **Elizabeth Leiter** was born on 5 February 1839 in Miamisburg, Montgomery Co., Ohio (5, 7). She is listed on the US 1850 Census, Miami Twp., Montgomery Co., Ohio (H) age 11, living with her mother, Mary and step-father, William S. Houk and brother, Emanuel, 12 (H). She married John Adam Leis (9) who was born 11 October 1836 and died in May 1924 (7). They were married on 4 July 1861 (7) in Montgomery Co., Ohio. She died on 19 July 1917 in Miamisburg, Montgomery Co., Ohio (3 pg.183, 31, 35). Both are buried in Hillgrove Cemetery, Miamisburg, Ohio. (31, 34, 35 18 pg. 183). (Note: This lineage will continue in December 2009 newsletter.)

4. **Elizabeth Leiter.** She was born 9 April 1815 in Miamisburg, Miami Township, Montgomery Co., Ohio and died on 19 March 1885 (11). She married Emanuel B. Gebhart 3 April 1836 by Reverend H. Heincke (1 pg. 115 and 1 pg 140 Vol. B. Montgomery County Court Record, 11). He was born in Lebanon Co., PA 25 March 1814; died 24 July 1895, aged 81 y 3m 29d. They had located on a tract of land in Miami Twp., Montgomery Co., Ohio, residing there until 1883 when they sold it and moved to Salina, KS (11). Both are buried in Salina, KS (11).

U S 1860 Census (K) Miami Twp., Montgomery Co., Ohio: E.B. Gebhart, 46, m, w, farmer $13,500, 1400 PA, Elizabeth, 44, Jacob, 22, John, 21, Mary, 18, Elizabeth, 16, Perry, 12, Lucinda, 10, Elmira, 8, James, 4, Barbara Gebhart, 77, f, Widow.

5. **Catherine Leiter.** She was born on 5 October 1817 in Miami Township, Montgomery County, Ohio. She married (1st John Eagle 21 March 1839 (2 pg. 87) (2nd 11 pg 152 Johannes Leis 16 October 1851. He was born in Berks Co., PA 25 Jan 1810; died 19 May 1897 aged 87 y 3 m 21 d 11, pg. 152. She died 23 February 1854 in Montgomery County, Ohio 11, pg. 152). Burial in Slifer's Church Yard, Jackson Township, Montgomery Co., Ohio (11, pg. 152.) Catherine Eagle, age 32, is listed on the US 1850 Census Miami Twp., Montgomery Co., Ohio (H.) living with her widowed mother, Elizabeth Leiter, 62, her son, William Eagle, age 10.

6. **Christiana Leiter.** She was born on 26 June 1819 in Miami Township, Montgomery County, Ohio. She married John M. Lesher on 17 September 1845. (2 pg. 193). She died on27 February 1897 age 77y 8m 2d 1st Reformed Church Zion Cemetery Section II Row 9 (16 pg. 337). John M Lesher was born December 1814 and died 1 January 1858 age 44y 7d (16 pg. 337 Row 9ss). Burial in Zion Church Yard, Miami Township, Montgomery Co., Ohio.

7. **Mary Ann (13) Leiter** was born on 4 December 1821 in Miami Township, Montgomery Co., Ohio. She married Samuel Eckhart (11, pg. 55, 13, 2 pg. 47 24 October 1844, filed same day, her brother John present, Reverend Long's records). She died on 9 July 1908 in Miamisburg, Ohio, Montgomery Co., Ohio. She is buried in Woodland Cemetery, Dayton, Montgomery Co., Ohio. Samuel was a blacksmith by trade. He served in the Civil War, Company C, 66th Ohio, V.I. (11, pg 155). He was born in Pennsylvania 1 June 1819; died 8 April 1904 aged 84 y 10 m 7 d buried at the National Military Home, Montgomery Co., Ohio (11 pg. 155).

Samuel and Mary Ann lived in Johnsville, Montgomery Co., Ohio. They are listed on the US 1850, 1860 and 1870 Census Records (I., L., N.)

8. **Daniel Leiter.** He was born 19 May 1824 in Miami Township, Montgomery Co., Ohio (31 pg. 122) He married Lucinda Clevenger born 1824 died 1906 (2 pg. 18, 47 & 188). They were married on 15 January 1844 in Montgomery Co., Ohio at the First Reformed Church, Miamisburg, Ohio. (2, pg. 47 1, pg. 56. Her brother/father Jona Clevinger, sworn, cousin of artist-Rev. Long's records). He died 23 June 1863 (2 pg. 122 42y 1m 4d). They are buried in Hillgrove Cemetery (2 pg. 122, 31, pg. 80 Lot 482 & 482 - 2) in Miamisburg, Montgomery Co., Ohio.

9. **George Leiter.** He was born on 27 May 1826 (2, 3, 10) in Miami Township, Montgomery Co., Ohio and died on 23 March 1855 (2, 10) in Miami Township, Montgomery

Co., Ohio (28y 9m 26d) (2, 3, 10). He married Mary Ann Snyder on 4 January 1849. Burial was at Gebhart Church Yard, Miamisburg, Ohio (2 pg. 115, 3, 10). George Leiter St. John's Church (funeral 25th St. John's Church and Cemetery-Typhoid fever). Lindsay Brien (37 1930 reading of cemetery pg. 203 Records of 1st Reformed Church, Miamisburg, Ohio). US 1850 Census, Miami Twp., Montgomery Co., Ohio, Roll 713, Book 1, 4th August 1850 (H.) lists George Liter, 24, m, w, farmer $4,000 Ohio, Mary, 18, f, w, Ohio, John 4/12 m, w, Ohio. Several of George's family living next door.

REFERENCES

1. A Register of Marriage Certificates Recorded in Montgomery Co., Ohio July 26, 1803 to July 20, 1851 Transcribed by Lindsay M. Brien from Montgomery Common Pleas Record of Marriage Certificates Book A, B, A2 and B2. Other Montgomery County Court Marriage Documents. Copied these records from book from Inter-loan Libraries.
2. Montgomery Co., Ohio German Church Records Volume II Transcripts of the Records of First Reformed German Church Book of Miamisburg, Ohio including: Membership, Marriages, Baptisms, and Deaths and Funerals Extracted Edited and Indexed by Anne and Bob Johnson Published by Montgomery Co. Chapter Genealogical Society 1999.
3. Tombstone pictures of Henry, John and Frederick Leiter, Elizabeth Booker Fox, Leiter, Frederick Fox and other family members – Gebhart (St. John's) Church Yard, Miamisburg, Ohio
4. Estate Records of Frederick and John Leiter – Montgomery County Court
5. Archivist Nita Petticrew Gebhart (St. John) Lutheran Church & Historian Miamisburg Historical Society, Miamisburg, Ohio. Sent me on the church letterhead her records of Leis/Leiter/Fox/Gebhart, LaRose and related families in 2003.
6. Marriage Documentation of John Leiter and Elizabeth Booker Fox, Marriage Licenses (2nd Edition 1778-1810) pages 90 and 91. Received from Washington County Marriage License by Margaret E. Myers, Frederick County, Maryland.
7. Marriage License, Death Certificates Elizabeth Leiter and John Adam Leis – Montgomery County Court, Ohio.
8. Death Record of Catherine Booker Fox (wife of Frederick Fox) Maryland Lutheran Church, Frederick Co., MD
9. Slifer's Church, Farmersville, Montgomery County, Ohio – Baptismal record Noah Adam Leis
10. Notes and documentation from Suella Leis-Fenton – Leis, Leiter, Fox, Gebhart and related families readings taken of Gebhart (St. John's) Church Yard. Suella Leis-Fenton has been researching and documenting the family data for many years. We have worked together since 1999 when I began my Genealogical Research.
11. The Fox Genealogy Book by D.G. Fox, Compiled 1914 Published 1924 Including the Metherd, Benner and Leiter Descendants giving Biographies of the First and Second Generations with Sketches of the Third Generation. Note: "All dates quoted as transpiring in Miami Twp., Montgomery Co. prior to 1830 occurred in Washington Twp., as the portion of Miami Twp., lying east of the river was deducted from Washington Twp. All dates quoted as transpiring in Clear Creek Twp., Warren Co., Ohio, prior to October 17, 1815, occurred in Franklin Twp., as that portion of Clear Creek Twp., was deducted from Franklin Twp., at the organizing of Clear Creek Twp., /s/ D.G. Fox, 5th."
12. Notes and documentation from Charles Leis, descendant of Mary LaRose Gebhart Leiter Houk. He sent me a notebook on Leis/Leiter/Gebhart/Fox/LaRose and related families. Received in 2002.

13. Notes and documentation from Bruce Barnheiser +"Descendants of Melchior Leiter and Related Families, descendant of Anna LaRose Gebhart Leiter. Copywrite 2004 by Bruce L. Barnheiser. All rights reserved. Bruce allows anyone researching these families to copy for family research but not use for any monetary cause. BBarnheise@aol.com.
14. Notes and documentation from Anne Edgecombe including Genealogy and History of Leiter family by Roger Merrill Leiter. She sent to me in 2003, 2005.
15. Wills and documentation from Curtis Older (wills of Frederick Fox and Bartholomew Booker). Received from Curt via email in 2005.
16. Montgomery Co., Ohio Cemetery Inscriptions VI Miami Twp., Book A—All Except Hillgrove Cemetery Published by Montgomery Co. Chapter OGS Compiled and Edited by Anne & Robert Johnson 2000 – Cemetery Inscriptions and Records, Miamisburg, Ohio – Published by Miamisburg Historical Society. Cemeteries: Ungerer (Benner) Butt (Munger) Evergreen (West Carrollton) Gebhart (St. John) Highland, Schoolhouse (Canal) Library (Old Miamisburg) Cedar Grove (Kirchner) Our Lady of Good Hope, Moyer, Stettler, Troxel, Zion (Hetzell) Root (Zeller).
17. Microfiche of St. Jacob's Lutheran Church from 1821 forward showing marriages, births, deaths, funerals of multiple family members into the 1980's. St. Jacob's was formerly First Lutheran Church in Miamisburg. Colonel Emanuel Gebhart was a founder of this church, an officer and President of the Council at the time of his death in 1868. Emanuel fought in War of 1812. His family was one of the founders of the village of Miamisburg, Oh. His wife was Elizabeth LaRose whose famous father was the Reverend John Jacob LaRose, another founder of Miamisburg and the first circuit rider in the county. Emanuel and Elizabeth Gebhart were the parents of my 2nd great grandmother, Mary LaRose Gebhart. Both Emanuel's father, John Nicholas Gebhart and Elizabeth's father, Reverend LaRose fought in the Revolutionary War and are buried with Emanuel and Elizabeth atop the Hillgrove Cemetery. They are listed in the inscriptions of Hillgrove Cemetery Book published by the Miamisburg Historical Society. Montgomery Co., Ohio Cemetery Inscriptions VI Jefferson Twp., Book B All Except Dayton National Cemetery Published by Montgomery Co. Chapter of the OGS Compiled and Edited by Bob & Anne Johnson, 2002.
18. Montgomery Co., Ohio German Church Records VI including: Emmanuel's Evangelical Lutheran Church (Germantown, OH, Salem's Evangelical Lutheran Church (Ellerton, OH) and Slifer's Reformed Church in Jackson Twp., OH. Extracted, Edited and Indexed by Anne W. and Robert E. Johnson published by Montgomery Co., Chapter OGS 1998.
19. David Cemetery Letter Documentation of Family Burials: David's Cemetery Association of Kettering, Ohio, City of Kettering, Co. of Montgomery and State of Ohio and being Lot 319, Section2 - South Graves – west half – located at the Church on David Road and Mad River Road. Certificates in my files. Original purchase 1937 by my grandparents.
20. Missouri Records "Compliments of Osage Chapter DAR, Sedalia, Missouri, 1962" Missouri Records "Genealogy & History of the Leiter and Connected Families; Gebhart, Fox and LaRose" – Author, Fay Cole Leiter – State Regent: Mrs. Walter e. Diggs – Chapter Regent: Mrs. Ira A. Leiter – Compilation by Mrs. Ira Leiter, Regent Osage Chapter (Leiter B.F. DARR) Mrs. Joseph Jannuzzo State Chairman of Genealogical Records MISSOURI: 1963 C004959 Call #929.2 Publisher: Sedalia, MO DAR, OSAGE CHAPTER, 1962 DBCN: ABB-4713 Interlibrary Loan 20 April 2005 from St. Louis Public Library Catalogue
21. Pennsylvania Archives Fifth Series VOLUME III Edited by Thomas Lynch Montgomery Secretary of the Commonwealth Harrisburg, PA Continental Line Pennsylvania Archives Fifth Series VOLUME III Edited by Thomas Lynch Montgomery Secretary of the Commonwealth Harrisburg, PA Continental Line Depreciation Pay – Revolutionary War – Tenth Pennsylvania

Maryland Militia in the Revolutionary War – by Eugene Clements and F. Edward Wright – Military papers of Frederick Fox – Drummer Boy – Frederick Fox, Pennsylvania Archives Fifth Series VOLUME III Edited by Thomas Lynch Montgomery Secretary of the Commonwealth Harrisburg PA Continental Line

22. Western Maryland Newspaper Abstracts 1786-1798 Compilation of items taken from the available newspapers of Hagerstown and Frederick, MD:
    101.FTM Aug. 28 1792/Margaret Booker, Frederick Fox, exec. To sell farm, late the prop of Bartholomew Booker, decd. 304 a., on road from Fred Town to Williams Port p.14 – 485. EAM Jan. 11 1798/Sale of 328 a. Letters remaining at P.O. Hagerstown: Letters remaining at P.O. Hagerstown: Frederick Fox.
23. "Inhabitants of Frederick Co., MD Volume I 1750-1790 "includes a note on a Frederick Fox. Similarly volume 2 contains a couple of notes on persons named Frederick Fox.
24. 1786-1789 Volume of Western Maryland Newspaper Abstracts contains a note on the family providing location of the Booker farmstead, Frederick Fox executor of the estate of his mother-in-law Margaret Booker wife of Bartholomew Booker and mother of Frederick's wife Catherine Booker.
25. Copy of Deed for Washington County resident named Frederick FOX received from Washington County Historical Society.
26. Leis Family Bible Statistics
27. Pleasant Hill Cemetery Readings of Flat Creek Twp., Section 36, Southern Methodist Cemetery 6 miles southeast of Sedalia on M to Pleasant Hill Rd. West on Pleasant Hill Rd. 1.6 miles to the Methodist Church on right. Cemetery is behind the church and surrounded by a chain link fence. Well-attended and currently accepting burials. Pettis Co., MO. Updated and photographed 8 June 2003 by George C. Willick. All rights reserved. 10 pages printed out 1 Nov. 2008:
    a. Leiter, Albert J., 1852-1928
    b. Leiter, Isabelle; 1858-1925 wife of Noah
    c. Leiter, Anna; May 1, 1812 – Dec 2, 1896
    d. Leiter, Infants of Noah K. & Mattie
    e. Leiter, Mattie A. wife of Noah, died Jan. 30, 1890 – aged 32y (1)
    f. Leiter, Noah K.; 1857-1931
    g. Leiter, Christena; 1858-1933
    h. Leiter, Raymond G.; Mar. 7, 1896-Apr. 25, 1918
    i. Leiter, William A. Jan. 1, 1845 – Feb. 18, 1911
28. Picture of Tombstone Anna Leiter – Wife of Henry – Inscription) Pleasant Hill Cemetery, Flat Creek Twp., Pettis Co., MO – Picture of Henry – Gebhart (St. John's Cemetery – Miamisburg, Ohio
29. State of Missouri Death Certificate #152161931 Noah K. Leiter 1931
30. Hillgrove Cemetery Inscriptions & Records Miamisburg, Ohio Published by Miamisburg Historical Society Resources and Research Committee 2005.
31. Picture of John Adam and Elizabeth Leiter Leis Tombstone at Hillgrove Cemetery, Miamisburg, Ohio Lots 1177 nh – and 1177sh
32. Marriage Record of Frederick Leiter and Mary LaRose Gebhart Montgomery County Court Document #131, Ohio
33. Frederick Leiter's tombstone (Gebhart (St. John's Cemetery) Miamisburg, Ohio
34. Photo of John Adam Leis and Elizabeth Leiter Gebhart (St. John's Cemetery) Miamisburg, Ohio
35. Slifer Reading of Slifer Cemetery, Farmersville, Montgomery Co., OH
    Lindsey Brien's 1930 Reading of Gebhart (St. John's) Cemetery, Additional Burial Records 1st Reformed Church, Page 203 (2)

US Census Records Citations for Above Article

A. US 1790 Census, Frederick Co., MD
B. US 1800 Census, Frederick Co., MD
C. US 1810 Census, Frederick Co., MD
D. US 1820 Census, Miami Twp., Montgomery Co., OH
E. US 1820 Census, Washington Twp., Montgomery Co., OH
F. US 1830 Census, Miami Twp., Montgomery Co., OH
G. US 1840 Census, Miami Twp., Montgomery Co., OH
H. US 1850 Census, Miami Twp., Montgomery Co., OH
I. US 1850 Census, Johnsville, Montgomery Co., OH
J. US 1860 Census, Parke Co., IN
K. US 1860 Census, Miami Twp., Montgomery Co., OH
L. US 1860 Census, Johnsville, Montgomery Co., OH
M. US 1870 Census, Miami Twp., Montgomery Co., OH
N. US 1870 Census, Johnsville, Montgomery Co., OH
O. US 1880 Census, Miami Twp., Montgomery Co., OH
P. US 1900 Census, Miami Twp., Montgomery Co., OH
Q. US 1910 Census Miami, Twp., Montgomery Co., OH
R. US 1920 Census, Miami Twp., Montgomery Co., OH
S. US 1930 Census, Miami Twp., Montgomery Co., OH
T. US 1860 Census, Indiana
U. US 1870 Census, St. Clair Twp., Grundy Co., IA –
V. US 1880 Census, Henry Co., MO
W. US 1900 Census, Bruceport Twp., Grundy Co., IA
X. US 1900 Census, Portland, OR
Y. US 1900 Census, Williapa, Everette Co., WA
Z. US 1910 Census, Washington Twp., Montgomery Co., OH
AA. US 1920 Census, Beavercreek Twp., Montgomery Co.
BB. US 1820 Census, Franklin Twp., Warren Co., OH
CC. US 1830 Census, Franklin Twp., Warren Co., OH
DD. US 1870 Census Flat Creek Twp., Pettis Co., MO
EE. US 1880 Census, Flat Creek Twp., Pettis Co., MO
FF. US 1880 Census, Penn Twp., Parke Co., IN
GG. US 1870 Census, Butler Twp., Faberville, St. Clair Co., MO, pg. 13
HH. US 1880 Census, Jackson Twp., Montgomery Co., OH
ii. US 1860 White River Twp., Randolph Co., IN pg. 144 27th July 1860

Next Issue, December 1, 2009, of *News from Fox's Gap*
Mary LaRose Gebhart's marriage to William Shepherd Houk

Genealogy Documentation Section
By Curtis L. Older

A feature of each Fox Society Newsletter that began with the December 1, 2004, newsletter is the inclusion of an article that documents or genealogically proves a descendant or spouse of a descendant of John Fox of Fox's Gap in Maryland. The article will present a written description about the individual and his or her family as well as a listing of the related genealogical source records that support the written description. This newsletter contains documentation for two individuals.

The eighth and ninth individuals to be presented in this section of the newsletter are John Adam Link II and Jane Ogle, the parents of Elizabeth Ann Link (Mrs. George Fox).

Previous issues of the Fox Society Newsletter contained documentation for the following individuals:

December 1, 2004 - **Frederick Fox**
December 1, 2005 - **John L. Fox**
December 1, 2006 - **Elizabeth Jane Ricketts**
December 1, 2007 - **Susannah Hiligass**
June 1, 2005 - **George Fox**
June 1, 2006 - **Daniel Alexander Fox**
December 1, 2007 - **Elizabeth Ann Link**

Documentation for John Adam Link II, Father of Elizabeth Ann Link and husband of Jane Ogle

John Adam Link II was born December 31, 1756, in Oley Hill, Pennsylvania.**(1)** He was the fifth child of John Adam Link I and Elizabeth Miller and he was born in their Oley Hill home.**(2)** He was a grandson of John Jacob Link, an ancestor of Dwight D. Eisenhower.**(3)**

John Adam Link II was baptized in St. Joseph's Church, January 16, 1757, near Oley Hill, Pennsylvania.**(4)** John Adam Link II was sponsored at his baptism by Catherine, daughter of Stephan Houck, and Philip, son of Jacob Matthias.**(5)**

John Adam Link II grew up at his parent's home on Israel's Creek in Frederick County, Maryland.**(5A)** John Adam Link II was confirmed in the Lutheran Church of Frederick, Maryland, on May 25, 1775.**(6)** He was commissioned on June 29, 1782, as an Ensign in Captain Peter Barrick's Company, the Catoctin Battalion, Militia of Frederick County, Maryland.**(7)**

John Adam Link II married Jane Ogle.**(8)** Jane, a daughter of Alexander Ogle and Martha of Frederick, Maryland, was a descendant of John Ogle of Delaware.**(9)** John Adam II and Jane, accompanied by her brother and sister and by his father and brother, Jacob, were married in the Frederick Lutheran Church on April 15, 1783. **(10)**

Jane Ogle and her twin sister, Martha, were born September 23, 1761.**(11)** Jane lived on the west bank of the Monocacy near the Devilbiss Bridge, some four miles from where John Adam Link II lived on Israel's Creek.**(12)**

Elizabeth Ann Link, the first child of John Adam Link II and Jane Ogle, was born January 24, 1784, near Frederick in Frederick County, Maryland.**(13)** She was baptized in the Frederick Lutheran Church.**(14)**

John Adam Link II, his wife Jane Ogle, and their first child, Elizabeth Ann Link, moved across the Potomac River in 1784 to take possession of Jane's inheritance. **(15)** "Alexander Ogle purchased of Andrew Lucas, son of Edward Lucas, May 19, 1778, 208 acres in Berkeley, now Jefferson County, West Virginia, part of a 417-acre grant to Edward

Lucas by Lord Fairfax, for 552 pounds current and lawful money of Virginia. These 208 acres were willed to Jane."**(16)** John Adam Link II, with assistance from his brother Jacob Link and perhaps from his brother John George Link, built a stone dwelling for a home on the 208 acres.**(17)**

"On June 9, 1811, Henry Buckles and Mary, his wife, of Jefferson County, Commonwealth of Virginia, deeded to John Adam Link II, in consideration of the sum of $2,943.50 lawful money of the United States, what is known as the Buckles farm in John Adam Link II's estate, containing 73 acres, 2 roods, and 14 poles. This is a parcel of land of a greater tract granted Robert Buckles by Lord Fairfax, June 14, 1751, and bequeathed to his son, Robert Buckles, Junior, by will dated June 7, 1787."**(18)**

"On October 13, 1819, John B. Henry and Ann, his wife, of Jefferson County, Virginia, conveyed by deed to John Adam Link II for $6,500, lawful money of the United States, two parcels of land, one of 100 acres and one of 10 acres, lying on Elk Branch in Jefferson County, Virginia. Said tracts were purchased from the heirs of James Young by said John B. Henry. Said tracts were conveyed to James Young by Robert Lowry and Agnes, his wife, by deed, February 21, 1793."**(19)**

"On November 22, 1822, William Burr and Margaret Young, his wife, of Logan County, Kentucky, conveyed by deed to John Adam Link II, two parcels of land, one of 100 acres and one of 10 acres, formerly belonging to the James Young estate and transferred by legacy to Margaret for $1,830.00."**(20)**

John Adam Link II was a member of St. Peter's Lutheran Church in Shepherdstown, Virginia (now West Virginia).**(21)** John Adam Link II and Jane Ogle were the parents of seven children:**(22)**

Elizabeth Ann Link, born January 29, 1784, married George Fox on August 9, 1807, at Shepherdstown, Virginia, now West Virginia. George was the oldest son of Frederick Fox and Catharine Booker. They were the parents of ten children. The family moved west to near Miamisburg, Ohio, in late 1807 along with a number of other families with ties to George's parents. George Fox died June 14, 1847, in Miamisburg, Ohio. Elizabeth Ann (Link) Fox died March 9, 1872, in Miamisburg, Ohio. Both George and Elizabeth Fox are buried in the Gebhart or St. John Cemetery in Miamisburg.

Maria Catherine Link, born December 18, 1785, and died September 8, 1866. She married Henry Remsberg, June 4, 1805. He was born August 10, 1781, and died February 16, 1852. Both are buried in the Old Lutheran Cemetery in Middletown, Maryland.

Martha Link, born October 23, 1787. She married her uncle, John George Link on January 3, 1809, in Washington County, Maryland. They moved from Jefferson County, Virginia, to Bourbon County, and thence to Fayette County, Kentucky.

John Alexander Link, born March 7, 1790, and named for his grandfather Ogle. He married Nancy Dust on June 6, 1816. John Alexander Link died on March 7, 1864. Nancy (Dust) Link died June 17, 1876. They are buried in St. James Cemetery, Uvilla, West Virginia.

Mary Link, born December 11, 1792, and married Samuel Crowell on June 16, 1814. They moved to a farm near Sandusky, Ohio. See *The Link Family* by Paxson Link for additional information on this family.

Rebecca Link, born February 11, 1795, married Elias Crowell on September 8, 1820. Elias died after a few years of the marriage and Rebecca next married William Demory. Rebecca died April 7, 1877. Both William and Rebecca Demory are buried at the Old Ebenezer Cemetery near Huntsville, Ohio.

John Adam Link III, born September 14, 1797, and died January 4, 1873. He was married four times. See *The Link Family*, page 84, for details of the marriages of John Adam Link III.

John Adam Link II died September 28, 1835, in Shepherdstown, Virginia (now West Virginia).**(23)** He was buried near the brick wall of the old St. Peter's Lutheran Church in Shepherdstown, West Virginia.**(24)** Jane (Ogle) Link died October 7, 1836, in Shepherdstown, Virginia (now West

Virginia). She also was buried near the brick wall of the old St. Peter's Lutheran Church in Shepherdstown, West Virginia.**(25)**

The 1810 U. S. Census for Virginia, Jefferson County, lists the Adam Link household.**(26)** The census lists one male under age 10, one male age 16 through 25, and one male age 45 or over. Females included one age 10 through 15, one female age 16 through 25, and one female age 45 or over.

The 1820 U. S. Census for Virginia, Jefferson County, Lee Township, lists the Adam Link household. **(27)** Adam Link was listed as a farmer. Household members included one male of age 16 and under 26; one male of age 45 and upwards; one female of age 16 and under 26; and one female of age 45 and upwards. The household included 6 male slaves and 4 female slaves.

The 1830 U. S. Census for Virginia, Jefferson County, Adam Link household, lists one male of age 70 and under 80 and one female of age 60 and under 70. These ages would fit with the birthdates of John Adam Link II and Jane (Ogle) Link.**(28)**

Children (**Link**):

i. **Elizabeth Ann**, born January 29, 1784

ii. **Maria Catherine**, born December 18, 1785

iii. **Martha**, born October 23, 1787

iv. **John Alexander**, born March 7, 1790

v. **Mary**, born December 11, 1792

vi. **Rebecca**, born February 11, 1795

vii. **John Adam III**, born September 14, 1797

REFERENCES

1. Paxson Link, *The Link Family* (Paris, Illinois: [s.l.], 1951),p. 78. **2.** *The Link Family*, p. 78; Adam Link I, father of John Adam Link II, supplied bacon during the American Revolution, see Maryland State Papers, Series A, MdHR 4586-15 1/6/4/18. **3.** *The Link Family*, various pages including 26, 72, 284, 192, 374, 543, chapter on Dwight D. Eisenhower; letter from Dwight D. Eisenhower to Paxson Link dated October 10, 1950, copy in the possession of Curtis L. Older. **4.** *The Link Family*, p. 78. **5.** Ibid. **6.** Ibid, p. 78-9. **7.** Ibid, p. 79. **8.** *Index to Marriage Licenses, Frederick County, 1778-1810*, John Adam Link II and Jane Ogle, married April 14, 1783. **9.** *The Link Family*, p. 79; Francis Hamilton Hibbard, assisted by Stephen Parks, *The English origin of John Ogle, first of the name in Delaware* (Pittsburgh: n.p., 1967); Sir Henry Asgill Ogle, *Ogle and Bothal* (Newcastle-upon-Tyne: Andrew Reid & Company, 1902). Alexander Ogle, father of Jane Ogle, provided wheat and flour from his mills to the Maryland troops during the American Revolution. See Maryland State Papers, Series A, MdHR 6636-23-29/7 1/7/5 and related papers. **10.** Ibid. A wedding date of April 15, 1783 is given in *The Link Family*. **11.** *The Link Family*, p. 80. **12.** Ibid, p. 79. **13.** Ibid, p. 81. **14.** Ibid, p. 81. **15.** *The Link Family*, p. 81, "During the first part of 1784 John Adam II and Jane moved across the Potomac River to take possession of Jane's inheritance and make for themselves a homestead." **16.** Ibid, pp. 81-2. **17.** Ibid, p. 82. **18.** Ibid, p. 85. **19.** Ibid. **20.** Ibid. **21.** Ibid, p. 84. **22.** Ibid, pp. 81-4. **23.** Ibid, p. 85. **24.** Ibid. **25.** Ibid. **26.** 1810 U. S. Census for Virginia, Jefferson County, Township Not Stated, Roll M252_69, page 85, Adam Link household. **27.** 1820 U. S. Census for Virginia, Jefferson County, Lee Township, Roll M33_34, page 101, Image Number 102, Adam Link household. **28.** 1830 U. S. Census for Virginia, Jefferson County, Township Not Stated, Roll 191, page 129, Adam Link household.

The following books discuss Link and Ogle genealogies:

10569 LINK. The Link Family; antecedents and descendants of John Jacob Link, 1417-1951, with much history about the Stoner, Crowell, Demory, Remsburg, Thraves, Ropp, Boyer, Fuchs (Fox), Beard (Bart), Miller, Filler, Hanger, Wayland, Osbourn, Hendricks, Reinhart, Stone, Burrier, Root, Houff, Stover, Turner, LaGrange, Smith, Kneiple, Shank, Grove, Cale, Palmer, Lewis, Woodward, Burnett, McChesney, Baylor, Freer, Garrett, Girdner, Creager, Burckhardt, and Eisenhower families. (Paris, Ill.) 1951. xiv. 872

p. illus., ports., maps. 24 cm. 53-22402. CS71.L7563 1951

S1844 OGLE. The English origin of John Ogle, first of the name in Delaware, by Francis Hamilton Hibbard, assisted by Stephen Parks. (Pittsburgh) 1967. 30 p. general. table. 22 cm. Bibliography: p. 29 - 30. 73-156908 MARC. CS71.O36 1967

12739 OGLE. Ogle and Bothal: or, A history of the baronies of Ogle, Bothal, and Hepple, and of the families of Ogle and Bertram . . . To which is added, accounts of several branches of families bearing the name of Ogle settled in other counties and countries; with appendices and illustrations compiled from ancient records and other sources, by Sir Henry A. Ogle, baronet. (Printed privately) Newcastle-upon-Tyne, A. Reid & company, limited, 1902. 1 p. 1., 426, lxx p. 14 pl. incl. front. (parts coats of arms) general. tables (part fold.) 29 cm. Works consulted: p. ii-iii. 15-19676. CS439.O5

12740 OGLE. . . . A short history of the Ogle family, compiled by Anna Ogle Kirkpatrick. Morrison, Ill., The Shawver publishing co., 1927. (21)p. 17 1/2 cm. (American families series) A 32-2439. CS71.O36 1927

Abstract of Graves of Revolutionary Patriots Record about Adam LINK
Name: **Adam LINK**
Cemetery: Luth Cem
Location: Shepherdstown, Jefferson Co WV
42
Reference: *Abstract of Graves of Revolutionary Patriots, Vol.3, p. Serial: 10675; Volume: 7*

News from Fox's Gap

Published December 1 of each year by:

The Society of the Descendants of Frederick Fox of Fox's Gap in Maryland

Membership dues are $3.00 per year. President of the Society is Curtis L. Older.

Make Society inquiries by the following means:

Curtis L. Older
2417 Kinmere Road
Gastonia, NC 28056-7818

e-mail: curtolder@earthlink.net
cell: 704-685-2760
phone: 704-864-3879

Please visit the Indiana University of Pennsylvania website for Fox's Gap in Maryland at:

http://www.iuparchaeology.iup.edu/FoxGap/

President's Message

By Curtis Lynn Older

* The biggest news item of 2008 was the attempt by Dominion Transmission, Inc. to build a natural gas booster station on land adjacent to the Fox Inn near the intersection of Marker and Bolivar roads at Middletown, Maryland. The residents of the surrounding area gave considerable opposition to the project and at the present time, it appears the natural gas booster station will be built elsewhere. However, the issue is far from being resolved.

To stay abreast of the Dominion Transmission, Inc. natural gas booster station issue, please monitor the following website:

www.cpmv.org

* Membership in the Society will be $3.00 for the 2009 calendar year.

* News from Fox's Gap is published only once per year, on each December 1st.

* There were no new Society members for the calendar year 2008.

* Wilma "Billie" Fox Gose of Griffith, Indiana, died Friday, November 7, 2008.

News from Fox's Gap

The Society of the Descendants of Frederick Fox of Fox's Gap in Maryland

Issue 5, Volume 3 **Remember Freedom!** December 1, 2009

Descendants of Frederick Leiter (22 Mar 1813 to 14 Oct 1838) and Mary LaRose Gebhart (7 Oct 1815 to 5 Jan 1877)

by Carole Leis Troup

[Note: Numbers in parentheses are **REFERENCE** numbers. The **REFERENCE** number section is at end of this article. Each reference number refers to an original source document or other record that helps substantiate the statement presented in the article.]

Mary LaRose Gebhart was born on 7 October 1815 in Miamisburg, Miami Township, Montgomery County, Ohio. She died 5 January 1877 in Beulah, Gerard Township, Crawford County, Kansas.**(1)** The marriage of **Mary LaRose Gebhart** to **Frederick Leiter**, a descendant of Frederick Fox, took place 11 February 1836, in Miami Township, Montgomery County, Ohio.**(2)** The Reverend Henry Heineke, M.G. presided over the ceremony.**(3)** The Reverend Henry Heineke led a rigourous and interesting life. He served the Miamisburg congregation for 33 years until his death in July 1859.**(4)**

Frederick Leiter was born 22 March 1813 in Miami Township, Montgomery County, Ohio.**(5)** He died 14 October 1838 in Miami Township, Montgomery County, Ohio.**(6)** Frederick was the son of John Leiter and Elizabeth Fox. **(7)** Family sources described Mary as being a nurse.**(8)** After her husband, Frederick Leiter, died in 1838, Mary returned to her parents' home with her two young children, Emanuel, and Elizabeth, in Miami Township, where she lived with them until she married her second husband, William Shepherd Houk in 1845.**(9)**

Two children, Emanuel and Elizabeth, were born to Mary LaRose Gebhart and Frederick Leiter:

1. **Emanuel Leiter** born 1837 in Miami Township, Montgomery County, Ohio.**(9A)** Emanuel married Malissa A. More. They

were married on 4 December 1859 in Parke County, Indiana.**(10)** Emanuel L. Leiter and Malissa A. More had 4 children:

I - Lewis Leiter. He was born between 1865-1870.

II - George Leiter. He was born 1865 in Missouri.

III - Leroy Leiter. He was born 1870 in Missiouri.

IV - Sadie Leiter. She was born 1875 in Indiana.

2. **Elizabeth Leiter** was born 5 February 1839 in Miamisburg, Montgomery County, Ohio and died 21 July 1917 in Miami Township, Montgomery County, Ohio.**(11)** **Elizabeth Leiter** married **John Adam Leis** on 4 July 1861 in Montgomery County, Ohio.**(12)** John Adam Leis was born 11 October 1836 and died 16 Mary 1925, also in Miami Township, Montgomery County, Ohio.**(13)** **John Adam Leis** was the son of **George Leiss** and **Salome Leiss**, both born in Berks County, Pennsylvania. They came to Miamisburg, Ohio, in 1836 shortly after their marriage.**(14)** George and Salome Leiss are buried at Gebhart Church Cemetery (St. John's Lutheran Church), Miamisburg, Ohio.**(15)**

According to my father, Ralph Leis, John Adam Leis lost his left eye when he was a small child growing up in Miami Township, Ohio, when he fell by accident on a stick. My father indicated that John Adam Leis never seemed to have felt that the loss of his eye was of great consequence.

The following is a family story as told to me by my father, Ralph Leis, in 1999:

John Adam Leis and Elizabeth Leiter Leis decided to move from Ohio to Missouri in the spring of 1970 in order to be near Elizabeth Leiter Leis's mother, Mary LaRose Leiter Houk. The railroads were offering free passage to the western frontier at this time so the women and children rode on the train, the men and boys old enough to do so traveled by river on flatboats. The men carried supplies, produce and farm animals on the flatboats. They left Miamisburg in wagons to travel the approximately 50 miles south to Cincinnati, Ohio, to board the train and river flatboats. Exactly the length of time traveled is not known. There were about ten families who made this journey. The times were bad in Missouri when the families arrived. They had a difficult time farming and at times did not have enough food to eat. My Leis Family stayed approximately six years. For many generations the three families - John Adam, Noah Adam, all the children and grandchildren lived in the same household, consequently my dad heard many stories about the trip to Sedalia, Missouri, and the return to Jackson and Miami Township, Ohio, where the family remained their entire lives. These stories were legend in our family, repeated through the years

John Adam Leis and Elizabeth Leiter Leis were the parents of eleven children:**(16)**

1. **Irvin George William Leis** was born November 1862 in Montgomery County, Ohio, and died 23 April 1853 in Ohio.**(17)** He married (1) **Phoebe Slaughman**. He married (2) **Sarah Bell Breen** 7 June 1898, at First Reformed Church Pasonage.**(18)**

2. **Clement Emanuel Leis** was born 11 February 1865 in Montgomery County, Ohio. He was baptized 12 February 1867 and died 17 October 1867 in Montgomery County, Ohio. Tombstone reads "Lyce".**(19)**

3. **Peter Frederick Leis** was born on 14 October 1866, He was baptized 16 February 1867.**(20)** He married **Rosa Berger-Hannah** on 17 April 1892.**(21)** He died 1945 in Dayton, Montgomery County, Ohio. They were buried in Memorial Park Cemetery, Montgomery County, Ohio.**(22)**

4. **Eva Anna Leis** was born on 1 March 1869 in Montgomery County, Ohio. She died in November 1869 in Montgomery County, Ohio. Her tombstone at St. John's Church reads, "8m 24d".**(23)**

5. **Amelia Ella Leis** was born 8 December 1869 and was baptized 6 February 1870.**(24)** She married **Abraham George** in

1888 in Preble County, Ohio.**(25)** She died 26 September 1954 in Darke County, Ohio. They are both buried at Lower Miami Cemetery, Jefferson Township, Montgomery County, Ohio.**(26)**

6. **Cora Belle Leis** was born on 8 January 1872 in Sedalia, Pettis County, Missouri, and was baptized 3 January 1875.**(27)** She married Charles E. Myers. They were married on 14 January 1897 in Preble County, Ohio, She died in 1957.**(28)** She and her sister, Clara, married Myers brothers.**(29)**

7. **Elva Alzonia Leis** was born on 21 October 1873 in Sedalia, Pettis County, Missouri.**(30)** She married Charles Carey in February 1899.**(31)** He was born in 1872 and he died 3 September 1940 in Ohio.**(32)** Elva died 13 November 1955 in Dayton, Ohio. Elva and Charles are buried at Hillgrove Cemetery.**(33)**

8. **Clara Elizabeth Leis** was born on 1 July 1876 in Ohio. She was baptized on 2 February 1877. She married Ambert M. Myers. They were married in 1895. Ambert Myers was Treasurer-Elect of Montgomery County when he died at the age of 58. Clara died in 1973 in Ohio. Clara and Ambert are buried in Memorial Park Cemetery, Dayton, Ohio.**(34)**

9. **Early John Henry Leis** was born on 7 March 1878 in Ohio.**(35)** He married Maud Elizabeth Smith on 30 December 1900 at First Reformed Church Parsonage.**(36)** He died 22 January 1951 in Montgomery County, Ohio. They are buried in Hillgrove Cemetery.**(37)**

10. Noah Adam Leis was born 10 April 1880 in Miami Township, Montgomery County, Ohio. and he was baptized 14 August 1881 at Slifer's Church in Farmersville by Reverend Milton Frank.**(38)** Noah Adam Leis married **Edith Mary Beck** on 18 January 1904.**(39)** Edith was 17 at the time of marriage. Her father, **Samuel Beck**, signed the marriage license with permission for her to marry Noah Adam Leis. Edith's mother was **Martha Houser.(40)** Noah and Edith were married by Reverend H. M. Herman, Minister, First Reformed Church, Miamisburg, Ohio.**(41)**

After Edith died in 1947, Noah married Louise Stamm, a widow, in 1951. They moved to Lee County, Florida, and lived there until he died 16 October 1966.**(42)** Noah was buried beside his first wife at Ellerton Cemetery.**(43)** His last will and testament appointed his son, Ralph Leis, executor of his estate. Noah Adam Leis, the youngest son of John Adam Leis and Elizabeth Leiter, was the grandfather of Carole Leis Troup. **Ralph Leis**, the father of Carole Leis Troup, was the son of Noah Leis.**(44)**

11. Bessie Catherine Leis was born on 26 December 1882 in Montgomery County, Ohio.**(45)** She married Martin Albertus Pontius.**(46)** They were married on 4 July 1905 in First Reformed Church, Miamisburg, Montgomery County, Ohio.**(47)** She died on 11 August 1973 at Bethany Lutheran Village. She is buried at Hillgrove Cemetery with husband Bert Pontius.**(48)**

REFERENCES

1. Fox, Daniel Gebhart, *The Fox Genealogy including the Metherd, Benner and Leiter Descendants* (n.p., 1914), p. 146.

2. Marriage Records, Montgomery County Court, Miami Township, Ohio, page131, Frederick Leighder and Anna Maria Gephart, 11 February 1836, Rev. Henry Heinecke, MG; *Gebhart, Gephart, and Related Families 1609-1996*, page 268; *Fox Genealogy*, p. 146

3. Ibid.

4. *Miamisburg - The First 150 Years from Historical Essays of Esther Light*, pages 42 and 95-98.

5. Fox, *Fox Genealogy*, p. 146.

6. Fox, *Fox Genealogy*, p. 146; *German Church Records*, Montgomery County, Ohio, published by the Ohio Genealogical Society, 2000, page 197, St. John's Lutheran Church, Gebhart Cemetery, Frederick Leiter.

7. Documentation presented in the December 1, 2008, *News from Fox's Gap* article by Carole Troup; *Fox Genealogy*, pages 138-9, 146-8; Estate of John Lighter, Case #709, Vol. G-1, page 44, Montgomery County, Ohio, names Daniel Booker Fox and Elizabeth Leiter administrators; references to John Leiter in *Gebhart, Gephart and Related Families* by Julia Shupert Hagwood, 1996, pages 268-271; St. John's Lutheran Church Archives, Miamisburg, Ohio; death record, Gebhart Cemetery, St. John's Church Records, published 2000 by Montgomery County, Ohio, Cemetery Inscriptions Genealogical Society, page 197.

8. Genealogical Data and Charts created by Ralph Leis and his sister, Anna Leis Loesch.

9. Montgomery County, Ohio, Marriage Records, Mary Leiter and William Shepherd Houk.

9A. *German Church Records*, Montgomery County, Ohio, published by the Ohio Genealogical Society, 2000, St. John's Lutheran Church, Gebhart Cemetery.

10. Parke County, Indiana, Marriage Records, Emanuel L. Leiter and Malissa A. More.

11. Death Certificate, Elizabeth Leiter Leis, Ohio Department of Vital Statistics, Montgomery County, Ohio, Certificate Index #48828, Vol. #2327, File #176.

12. Marriage Records, John Adam Leis and Elizabeth Leiter, Montgomery County, Ohio.

13. Montgomery County, Ohio, Death Certificate#30826, Vol. #4750, Ohio Reg. District, #907, Registration #37; tombstone photograph, John A. and Elizabeth Leis, Hillgrove Cemetery, Miamisburg, Montgomery County, Ohio.

14. Genealogical Data, Charts, created by Ralph Leis, sister Anna Leis Loesch.

15. *German Church Records*, Montgomery County, Ohio, published by the Ohio Genealogical Society, 2000, St. John's Lutheran Church, Gebhart Cemetery.
16. Fox, *Fox Genealogy*, p. 146;

17. Leis Family Bible Records.

18. *Montogmery County, Ohio, German Church Records*, Volume II, Transcripts of the Records of First Reformed Church of Miamisburg, Ohio including Membership, Marriages, Baptisms, and Deaths & Funerals, Extracted, Edited and Indexed by Anne Walker Johnson and Robert Eugene Johnson, Published by Montgomery County Chapter Ohio Genealogical Society, 1999, page 65; 1870 US Federal Census, Faberville, Butler Township, St. Clair County, Missouri; 1880 US Federal Census, Jackson Township, Montgomery County, Ohio, page 555b.

19. *Montogmery County, Ohio, German Church Records*, Volume II, Transcripts of the Records of First Reformed Church of Miamisburg, Ohio, page 87.

20. Ibid, page 88.

21. Ibid, page 61.

22. Genealogical Data, Charts, created by Ralph Leis, sister Anna Leis Loesch; 1870 US Federal Census, Faberville, Butler Township, St. Clair County, Missouri; 1880 US Federal Census, Jackson Township, Montgomery County, Ohio, page 555b.

23. *Montogmery County, Ohio, German Church Records*, Volume II, Transcripts of the Records of First Reformed Church of Miamisburg, Ohio, page 126; *Gebhart, Gephart, and Related Families 1609-1996*, Herman's Registers, diptheria, croup.

24. *Montogmery County, Ohio, German Church Records*, Volume II, Transcripts of the Records of First Reformed Church of Miamisburg, Ohio, page 89.

25. Leis Family Bible Records.

26. *Montgomery County, Ohio, Cemetery Inscriptions*, Volume V - Jefferson Township, Book B, All Except Dayton National Cemetery, Published by Montgomery County Chapter of the Ohio Genealogical Society, Compiled and Edited by Anne & Robert Johnson, Co-Chairs, Cemetery Committee, 2002, page 191; 1870 US Federal Census, Faberville, Butler Township, St. Clair County, Missouri; 1880 US Federal Census, Jackson Township, Montgomery County, Ohio, page 555b; 1870 US Federal Census, Sedalia, Pettis County, Missouri, page 56.

27. *Montogmery County, Ohio, German Church Records*, Volume II, Transcripts of the Records of First Reformed Church of Miamisburg, Ohio, page 89.

28. Leis Family Bible Records.

29. Ibid, 1880 US Federal Census, Jackson Township, Montgomery County, Ohio, page 555b.

30. *Montogmery County, Ohio, German Church Records*, Volume II, Transcripts of the Records of First Reformed Church of Miamisburg, Ohio, page 89.

31. Leis Family Bible Records.

32. *Hillgrove Cemetery Inscriptions, Records, Miamisburg, Ohio*, published by Miamisburg Historical Society, page 312.

33. Ibid, 1880 US Federal Census, Jackson Township, Montgomery County, Ohio, page 555b.

34. *Slifer's Church Birth and Baptismal Records*, Reverend Milton Frank, Reading Suella Leis-Fenton - Other children of John Adam Leis and Elizabeth Leiter; Obituary of Ambert Myers, 21 July 1933, *Dayton Daily News*.

35. Ibid.

36. *Montogmery County, Ohio, German Church Records*, Volume II, Transcripts of the Records of First Reformed Church of Miamisburg, Ohio, page 68.

37. *Hillgrove Cemetery Inscriptions, Records, Miamisburg, Ohio*, published by Miamisburg Historical Society, page 163; 1880 US Federal Census, Jackson Township, Montgomery County, Ohio, page 555b; 1900 US Federal Census, Miami Township, Montgomery County, Ohio.

38. Noah Adam Leis Baptismal Certificate, Slifer Reformed Church, #171, Register of Baptism by Rev. Milton J. Frank, Farmersville, Montgomery County, Ohio.

39. Marriage Record, Noah Adam Leis & Edith Mary Beck, Montgomery County, Ohio, File #23318; Noah Leis and Edith Beck church marriage record, 1st Reformed Church, *German Church Records*, Montgomery County, Ohio, page 72.

40. Ibid.

41. *Montogmery County, Ohio, German Church Records*, Volume II, Transcripts of the Records of First Reformed Church of Miamisburg, Ohio, page 72.

42. Edith Mary Beck Leis death certificate, Dallas, Dallas County, Texas, File #10903; Death Certificate, Noah Leis, Lee County, Florida.

43. *Montgomery County, Ohio, Cemetery Inscriptions*, Volume V - Jefferson Township, Book B, All Except Dayton National Cemetery, Published by Montgomery County Chapter of the Ohio Genealogical Society, Compiled and Edited by Anne & Robert

Johnson, Co-Chairs, Cemetery Committee, 2002, page 92; Photograph of tombstone, Noah Leis and Edith M. Beck Leis, Ellerton Cemetery, Jefferson Township, Montgomery County, Ohio.

44. Death Certificate, Noah Leis, Lee County, Florida; will of Noah A. Leis, Lee County, Florida; 1880 US Federal Census, Jackson Township, Montgomery County, Ohio, page 555b; 1900 US Federal Census, Miami Township, Montgomery County, Ohio; 1910 US Federal Census, Miami Township, Montgomery County, Ohio; 1920 US Federal Census, Miami Township, Montgomery County, Ohio; 1930 US Federal Census, Miami Township, Montgomery County, Ohio.

45. *Montogmery County, Ohio, German Church Records*, Volume II, Transcripts of the Records of First Reformed Church of Miamisburg, Ohio, page 72; *Slifer's Church Birth and Baptismal Records*, Reverend Milton Frank, Reading Suella Leis-Fenton - Other children of John Adam Leis and Elizabeth Leiter.

46. *Montogmery County, Ohio, German Church Records*, Volume II, Transcripts of the Records of First Reformed Church of Miamisburg, Ohio, page 72.

47. Ibid.

48. *Hillgrove Cemetery Inscriptions, Records, Miamisburg, Ohio*, page 242.

October 15, 1916, Miamisburg, Ohio
Back Row: Urvin George Leis, Bessie Leis Pontius, Earl John Henry Leis, Clara Leis Myers, Noah Adam Leis, Elva Leis Carey
Front Row: Cora Leis Myers, John Adam Leis, Elizabeth Leiter Leis, Amelia Leis George, Peter Frederick Leis

Genealogy Documentation Section
by Curtis L. Older

A feature of each Fox Society Newsletter that began with the December 1, 2004, newsletter is the inclusion of an article that documents or genealogically proves a descendant or spouse of a descendant of John Fox of Fox's Gap in Maryland. The article will present a written description about the individual and his or her family as well as a listing of the related genealogical source records that support the written description. This newsletter contains documentation for two individuals.

The tenth individual to be presented in this section of the newsletter is John Frederick Fox, the father of Frederick Fox and the man for whom Fox's Gap in Maryland was named.

Previous issues of the Fox Society Newsletter contained documentation for the following individuals:

December 1, 2004 - Frederick Fox
December 1, 2005 - John L. Fox
December 1, 2006 - Elizabeth Jane Ricketts
December 1, 2007 - Susannah Hiligass
December 1, 2008 - Jane Ogle
June 1, 2005 - George Fox
June 1, 2006 - Daniel Alexander Fox
December 1, 2007 - Elizabeth Ann Link
December 1, 2008 - John Adam Link II
December 1, 2009 - John Frederick Fox

Documentation for John Frederick Fox
(before 1735 to after Jan 17, 1784, and before Dec 4, 1784) father of Frederick Fox (May 10, 1751 to Feb 27, 1837)

John Frederick Fox was born before 1735. This seems certain because his oldest son, Daniel, who is identified as such in the will of John Fox, was born before 1751.**(1)** Another son of John Fox, Frederick, was born May 10, 1751.**(2)** Surely John Fox was more than fifteen or sixteen years old when he became the father of Daniel Fox.

Before coming to America, John Fox probably lived in Hesse-Cassel, Germany. According to Daniel Gebhart Fox, author of *The Fox Genealogy* which was compiled in 1914 and published in 1924, "Frederick Fox, 1, was born May 10, 1751, in Hesse-Cassel, Germany, (a former Electorate of Germany, now forming the district of Cassel in the Prussian Province of Hesse-Nassau)."**(3)** There is, however, a statement in The *History of Vermillion County, Indiana* that indicates Frederick Fox was born at sea. "The father (i.e., George Fox) of our subject (i.e., John L. Fox) was a native of Maryland, and a son of Frederick Fox, who was born on the ocean while his parents were immigrating to America."**(4)**

Daniel Gebhart Fox gives the middle name of John Fox as Frederick.**(5)** The sources D. G. Fox gives for the middle name of Frederick are: 1) "records of the port of Philadelphia, show that John Frederick Fox landed at the port" in 1752, and 2) "Mrs. Christiana (Fox) Allison, who was the surviving great-granddaughter of John Frederick Fox, stated to the writer during an interview about two years prior to her death, that 'the old man Fox's name was John Frederick'."**(6)**

The father of John Fox might have been named Daniel Fox, since John Fox named his oldest son Daniel. Frederick Fox, a son of John Fox, also named one of his sons Daniel.**(7)**

Daniel G. Fox in the *Fox Genealogy* indicates John Fox and his family came to America in 1752. A John Fox appeared in the state house in Philadelphia the day of his arrival and "took and subscribed the usual Qualifications."**(8)** There is no conclusive proof however that this John Fox was the father of Daniel and Frederick Fox mentioned above.

John Fox and his family may have settled for a period of time in the Pennsylvania German community before coming to Maryland. On the other hand, they might have settled at the location that became known as Fox's Gap shortly after arriving in Philadelphia. Many Germans followed the Great Philadelphia Wagon Road out of Pennsylvania and into Maryland and Virginia.

The gap in the South Mountain at which John Fox chose to settle, was on a wagon road known as the Great Philadelphia Wagon Road. The road also was known as the Road from Conestoga to Opequon, the Monocacy Road, the main road leading from Frederick Town to Sharpsburg, the Old Sharpsburg Road, the German Monocacy Road, and the Main Road that leads from Frederick Town to Swearingen's Ferry and near to John Foxes House.**(9)**

Fox's Gap in Maryland lies about midway between Frederick and Hagerstown, Maryland, and about two miles from Boonsboro, Maryland. Sharpsburg, the site of the Battle of Antietam during the Civil War, lies approximately five miles west. Fox's Gap in Maryland was destined to become not only the home for John Fox and his family, but an historical landmark due to the events of the Braddock Expedition of 1755 and the Battle of South Mountain, called the Battle of Boonsboro in the South, on September 14, 1862.**(10)** It is unknown if John Fox and his family resided at the gap when General Braddock, George Washington, and Maryland Governor Sharp passed through there on May 2, 1755. It is entirely possibly they did. We can only speculate if the reason or reasons John Fox chose to settle at Fox's Gap were similar or like-minded to those of the Confederate Army on September 13 and 14, 1862.

There is strong evidence the gap was named for John Fox by no later than the mid 1760s. The primary support for the arrival of the John Fox family at Fox's Gap by the mid 1760s is a land record for a tract named Grim's Fancy.**(11)** Land tracts in Maryland in the 1600s and 1700s were given names. The Grim's Fancy land record states, "for and in the name of him the said Alexander Trim all that tract of land called Grims Fancy lying in the County aforesaid beginning at a bounded Black Oak tree standing on the north side of the Main Road that leads from Frederick Town to Swearingen's Ferry and near to John Foxes House on the West side of the South Mountain and running thence". The Grim's Fancy tract of land is approximately one-half mile west of Fox's Gap. For purposes of identifying the location of Fox's Gap, we consider the Reno Monument, dedicated to Union Major General Jesse Lee Reno who was killed there on September 14, 1862, as being at the heart of Fox's Gap.

There is no record for a tract of land owned by John Fox in the vicinity of Fox's Gap. Perhaps John Fox, coming from Germany, was not able to purchase land in Maryland and simply became a squatter at Fox's Gap. Frederick Fox, a son of John Fox, patented a tract of land that includes the areas of both Fox's Gap and Turner's Gap in the South Mountain, not far from Boonsboro.**(12)** A tract named Friendship for 231 and 1/2 acres was the subject of an unpatented certificate, #228, on June 8, 1795. On May 9, 1797, Frederick Fox patented Addition to Friendship for 202 acres. The Reno Monument stands on the southern portion of Addition to Friendship.**(13)**

Frederick Fox was a farmer and perhaps a tavern keeper.**(14)** He married Catherine Booker on March 1, 1773, probably at or near Middletown, Maryland.**(15)** Catherine was a daughter of Bartholomew Booker and Margaret.**(16)** She was born May 1, 1748.**(17)**

It does not seem viable to the author that the John Fox family could be any nationality other than German. Several historical records support this conclusion. First, upon the death of Catherine Fox, the wife of Frederick Fox, the death register of Zion Lutheran Church indicated "Catarin, wife of Friedrich Fuchs, bur. 4 Nov. 1800. Heb. 4:9."**(18)** Fox is spelled Fuchs in this church record and is clearly a German spelling. Second, the services of this church were only held in the German language for many years. George Fox, the oldest son of Frederick Fox, was a member of this church, the Zion Lutheran Church of Middletown, Maryland.**(19)** Third, Zion Lutheran Church records indicate, "Samuel, son of Jacob and Magdelena Benner was born April 14, 1801. Baptised June 21, 1801. Sponsored by George Fox, a single person". (Mary) Magdelena Benner was a daughter of Frederick Fox and a sister of George Fox. Fourth, Daniel Gebhart Fox in *The Fox Genealogy* indicates Frederick Fox was born in Hesse-Cassel, Germany.

John Fox was a skin-dresser by trade.**(20)** There is mention in his will, "that my Son **Frederick** shall have the Clocke and one half of the skin dressing tools used my son Michael is to have the Young Mare with the Other half of the Aforesaid tools and also my Wearing Apearel Except my fine fure hat which I leave to **Frederick".(21)** The Birely Tannery Report gives an excellent description of what the tannery business was like in the area surrounding Frederick, Maryland, in the 1700s.**(22)**

The name of John Fox may be found in the Moses Chapline Sr. Administration Account papers submitted by the executors of the estate, bearing a date of June 19, 1766.**(23)** Moses Chapline Senior lived about two miles west of Fox's Gap towards Sharpsburg.**(24)**

Little is known of the wife of John Fox or if he might have had more than one wife during his lifetime. His will states, " First I give and Bequeath unto **my beloved Wife Christina** all that I do possess of during her Natural life".**(25)** John Fox apparently married his first wife before they came to America. We cannot be certain his first and only wife was Christiana. The letter of Jacob Reel does seem to indicate or imply that Christiana Fox was the mother of Frederick and Michael Fox. Christiana Fox died August 6, 1812, probably in Sharpsburg, Maryland.**(26)**

John and Christina Fox apparently lived in Sharpsburg, Maryland, by the mid 1760s since we find a record of Lot #143 purchased August 23, 1766, by John Fox from Joseph Chapline.**(27)** Joseph Chapline was the founder of Sharpsburg in 1763, having named the town after Maryland Governor Sharpe.**(28)**

We can only speculate that Frederick Fox continued to live at or near Fox's Gap, after his parents moved to Sharpsburg, due to the fact that Frederick patented the Addition to Friendship land tract at Fox's and Turner's gaps in 1795.**(29)** *The Fox Genealogy* by Daniel Gebhart Fox indicates that Frederick Fox owned the Fox Inn at one time.**(30)** Daniel G. Fox identifies a land tract named Turkeyfoot, land records in Maryland were given names in the 1700s, where the Fox Inn stood. However, from analysis of land records by Curtis L. Older, the Fox Inn was owned by George Fox, oldest son of Frederick Fox, for a period of only a few years until all the Frederick Fox family clan moved to the area that became Miamisburg, Ohio, near present day Dayton, Ohio, in 1807.**(31)**

The Fox Inn is located about two miles from Fox's Gap towards Middletown, Maryland. Since Frederick Fox never owned the property and George Fox only owned the property for a few years up to 1807, it is somewhat mysterious why the property would continue to be known as the Fox Inn right up to present day in 2009. The only reason the building has been know for over 200 years as the Fox Inn might be that the old tavern or inn was the first place a traveler through Fox's Gap from the west might stay for the night after passing through Fox's Gap.

John Fox died in 1784. He wrote his will on January 17, 1784 and it was probated December 4, 1784, in Washington County, where Sharpsburg is located.**(32)** Since John Fox died in 1784, you will not find him listed in the first United States census of 1790.

Christiana Fox died August 6, 1812, in Sharpsburg. The support for this date of death and location comes from a letter or copy of a letter that was in the possession of Robert H. Fox of Cincinnati, Ohio, in the late 1990s.**(33)** The letter, from Jacob Reel of Sharpsburg to Michael and Frederick Fox of Franklin Township, Warren County, Ohio, about the death of their mother Christiana, was dated August 9, 1812, at Sharpsburg. The letter indicated that "we inform you that our aged Mother departed this life the 6th of Aug after a sickness of four weeks". Why he indicated "our aged Mother" is not known. There is no record of a Jacob Reel marrying a woman with the last name of Fox. Christina Fox was buried at the Lutheran Church lot in Sharpsburg, Maryland.**(34)**

Michael Fox, a brother of Frederick Fox, was born January 6, 1760, and died in Franklin, Warren County, Ohio, on August 23, 1837, aged 77 years, 7 months, and 17 days. He and his wife Susannah Fox, 1761 - 1836, are both buried in Woodhill Cemetery in Franklin, Warren County, Ohio. Michael and Susannah Fox were the parents of Elizabeth, Eve, Jacob, Daniel, and Michael.**(35)**

See **APPENDIX ONE** for the full text of the will of John Fox; **APPENDIX TWO** has a list of the John Fox Land Records in Frederick County, Maryland; **APPENDIX THREE** has a list of the Christiana Fox Land Records in Washington County, Maryland; **APPENDIX FOUR** has the September 8, 1812, Letter from Jacob Reel of Sharpsburg, Maryland, to Frederick and Michael Fox of Warren County, Ohio; **APPENDIX FIVE** has a Map of *The Road from Swearingen's Ferry on the Potomac River through Sharpsburgh to the Top of the South Mountain at Fox's Gap*. August 23, 1792; **APPENDIX SIX** has an article on the Occupations of Residents along the Old Sharpsburg Road in the 1700s; and **APPENDIX SEVEN** discusses John Fox's House mentioned in the Grim's Fancy Land Record.

A Kodak Photo CD-Rom disc entitled "Fox's Gap in Maryland" by Curtis L. Older contains photos of many documents and items related to the descendants of John Fox through his son Frederick Fox, as well as material related to Fox's Gap in Maryland, the Braddock Expedition, and the Battle of South Mountain. A copy of the CD-Rom is at the Washington County Free Library, Hagerstown, Maryland.

Children (**Fox**) :

i. **Daniel**, born before 1751, died after 1783

ii. **Frederick**, born May 10, 1751, died Feb 27, 1837

iii. **Rachel**, died after 1783

iv. **Magdelin**, died after 1783

v. **Unknown daughter**, died before 1784

vii. **Michael**, born January 6, 1760, died August 23, 1837**(35)**

REFERENCES

1. Will of John Fox, Court House, Washington County, Maryland, Book A, Liber 102, January 17, 1784. See **APPENDIX ONE** for the full text of the will of John Fox.

2. *The Fox Genealogy including Metherd, Benner and Leiter descendants, giving biographies of the first and second generations, with sketches of the third generation*, compiled by D. G. Fox, 1914. (n.p.) 1924 . 1 p. 1., (5)-172 p. 20 cm. 37-9439, CS71.F79, 1924, page 12; tombstone of Frederick Fox, Gebhart or St. John Cemetery, Miamisburg, Ohio.

3. *Fox Genealogy*, page 12.

4. *History of Vermillion County, Indiana*, page 491.

5. I. Daniel Rupp, *Thirty-Thousand Names of Immigrants* (Baltimore: Genealogical Publishing Co., 1971), 280-1.

6. *Fox Genealogy*, page 169, APPENDIX NO. 1.

7. Will of Frederick Fox, Will Book C, case #1444, Montgomery County, Ohio;;

tombstone of Daniel Booker Fox, Gebhart or St. John Cemetery, Miamisburg, OH; *Fox Genealogy*, pages 101 through 103.

8. I. Daniel Rupp, *Thirty-Thousand Names of Immigrants* (Baltimore: Genealogical Publishing Co., 1971), 280-1. The name "Johan Friederich Fuchs" appears; also R. B. Strassburger and W. J. Hinke, *Pennsylvania German Pioneers, Lists of Arrivals* (Norristown, Pa.: Pennsylvania German Society, 1934), 488-9. John Fox took the oath on arrival.

9. Curtis L. Older, *The Land Tracts of the Battlefield of South Mountain* (Westminster, Md.: Heritage Books, 1999), pages 41-42; *The Braddock Expedition and Fox's Gap in Maryland*, (Westminster, Md: Heritage Books, 1995) pages 78-104.

10. *Braddock Expedition*, Introduction and Afterword.

11. Grim's Fancy, Maryland State Archives, BC & GS 40, p. 114, Alexander Trim's certificate of survey, examined and passed 5 June 1765, [MdHR 17,451, 1-23-4-5]. "On the North Side of the Main Road that leads from Frederick Town to Swearingen's Ferry and near to John Foxes House".

12. MdHR, 17,478, 1-23-4-34, Frederick Fox, patent for Addition to Friendship, May 27, 1805, 202 ac. Maryland State Archives, IC #P, 672-3.

13. *Braddock Expedition*, pages 103 and 189-190; also *Land Tracts of the Battlefield of South Mountain*, pages 206-210.

14. FCLR, WR-19-206, Mortgage from Christian Benner to Frederick Fox, recorded April 11, 1799, Shaffs Purchase and Mount Sinai. "Between Christian Benner Sen. of Frederick County farmer of the one part; and Frederick Fox of the same county farmer of the other part."; Lemoine Cree, *A Brief History of the South Mountain House* (Boonsboro, Md.: Dodson, 1963); Ohio D.A.R. Soldiers Rosters, 2 Vols., 1:146; *Fox Genealogy*, pp. 13-14.

15. *Fox Genealogy*, page 12; will of Bartholomew Booker, Frederick County, Maryland, Register of Wills Records, GM-2-431; will of Margaret Book (Booker) Frederick County, Maryland, Register of Wills Records GM-3-126.

16. Frederick S. Weiser, ed., Maryland German Church Records Vol. 2, *Zion Lutheran Church 1781-1826* (Manchester, Md.: Noodle-Doosey Press, 1987), 77. The Death Register of Zion Lutheran Church indicates "Catarin, wife of Friedrich Fuchs, bur. 4 Nov. 1800. Heb. 4:9."; *Fox Genealogy*, page 12; will of Bartholomew Booker; will of Margaret Book (Booker).

17. Fox, *Fox Genealogy*, page 12.

18. Frederick S. Weiser, ed., *Maryland German Church Records* Vol. 2, *Zion Lutheran Church 1781-1826* (Manchester, Md.: Noodle-Doosey Press, 1987), 77. The Death Register of Zion Lutheran Church indicates "Catarin, wife of Friedrich Fuchs, bur. 4 Nov. 1800. Heb. 4:9."; *Fox Genealogy*, p. 12.

19. Frederick S. Weiser, ed., *Zion Lutheran Church 1781-1826*, Maryland German Church Records, Vol. 2, (Manchester, Md.: Noodle-Doosey Press, 1987), 25; "Samuel, son of Jacob and Magdelena Benner was born April 14, 1801. Baptised June 21, 1801. Sponsored by George Fox, a single person". (Mary) Magdelena Benner was a daughter of Frederick Fox and sister of George Fox.

20. Will of John Fox; *Fox Genealogy*, page 12.

21. Ibid.

22. See *The Birely Tannery Report*, held by the Frederick, Maryland, library, a report on the tannery business in and about Frederick, Maryland. The Birely Tannery began operation in Frederick, Maryland, in the 1760s and remained in business until the 1920s. Archaeological Data Recover at the Birely Tannery (18FR575) City of Frederick, Maryland, prepared by M.A.A.R. Associates,

Inc. of Newark, Delaware, 1991.

23. The Moses Chapline Senior Administration Account papers submitted by the executors of the estate, bearing a date of Jun 19, 1766, mention the name of John Fox. See Frederick County, Maryland, The Account of Joseph and Jennett Chapline, executors of Moses Chapline, late of Frederick County deceased.

24. *Braddock Expedition*, pages 76-77, 79-80, 86, 123-124; *Land Tracts of the Battlefield of South Mountain*, pages 42 and 226. See page 226 of the *Land Tracts* book for a discussion of The Moses Chapline Senior Cemetery and references to other material on the subject.

25. Will of John Fox.

26. Letter from Jacob Reel to Michael and Frederick Fox, dated at Sharpsburg, Aug. 9, 1812, from a copy obtained from Robert H. Fox of Cincinnati, Ohio. "The following letter received and forwarded from Lebanon, Warren County, Ohio, Sept. 8, 1812, addressed to Msrs. Fredric(k) & Michael Fox, Franklin Township, Warren Co. Ohio"; *Fox Genealogy*, page 12.

27. Frederick County, Maryland, land records, to John Fox, K-703, August 23, 1766, from Joseph Chapline, Lot #143, Sharpsburg.

28. Aubrey C. Land, *The Dulanys of Maryland* (Baltimore: Maryland Historical Society, 1955), 180. *Braddock Expedition*, page 4; *Fox Genealogy*, page 12.

29. Arthur G. Tracey Collection, The Historical Society of Carroll County, Maryland, 210 East Main Street, Westminster, Maryland, Friendship, 231 and 1/2 acres, June 8, 1795, unpatented certificate #228; Maryland State Archives, IC #P 672-3, May 9, 1797, Frederick Fox, Addition to Friendship, 202 acres; *Land Tracts*, page 210. Addition to Friendship was a resurvey obtained by Frederick Fox out of the western shore land office by a special warrant of proclamation to resurvey and affect the vacancy included in a resurvey made for him on the eight day of June seventeen hundred and ninety five by the name of Friendship, the caution money for which had not been paid within the time limited by law. In pursuance whereof, a resurvey was made and a certificate thereof returned containing two hundred and two acres lying in the county aforesaid and called Addition to Friendship.

30. *Fox Genealogy*, page 13.

31. *Braddock Expedition*, Appendix D, pages 200-205; *Land Tracts*, pages 211-213.

32. Will of John Fox.

33. Letter from Jacob Reel to Michael and Frederick Fox, dated at Sharpsburg, August 9, 1812; *Fox Genealogy*, page 12.

34. *Fox Genealogy*, page 12.

35. *News from Fox's Gap*, Issue 3, Volume 2, June 1, 2002, published by The Society of the Descendants of Frederick Fox of Fox's Gap in Maryland, "Michael Fox of Fox's Gap in Maryland" by Lois Ann Baker. Also see Issue 4, Volume 2, "Michael Fox, a brother of Frederick, and The Fox - Beard Connection in Ohio" by Lois Ann Baker.

APPENDIX ONE

will of John Fox

Book A Liber 102, will of John Fox, January 17, 1784

Washington County, Maryland (probated December 4, 1784)

In the name of God Amen I John Fox of Sharpsburg Washington County and State of Maryland being very sick and weak in body but of perfect mind and memory thanks be given to God calling to mind the mortality of my body and knowing that it is appointed for all men once to die do make and ordain this my last Will and Testament, that is to say principally & first of all I give and Recommend my Soul unto the Earth to be buried in decent Christian burial at the discretion of my Executors nothing doubting but at the General Resurrection I shall receive the same again by the Almighty power of God. And as touching such worldly Estate as it has pleased God to bless me with in this life. I give devise and dispose of the same in the following manner and form.

First I give and bequeath unto **my beloved Wife Christina** all that I do possess of during her Natural life and at her Death it is well that **my Son Frederick** shall have the Clock and one half of the skin-dressing tools used.

My son Michael is to have the Young Mare with the Other half of the Aforesaid tools and also my Wearing Apparel Except my fine fur hat which I leave to **Frederick**, and the remaining and Residue of my Estate I leave and bequeath unto my Children and Grand Children viz. as follows, **Frederick, Magdelin & Michael is to have three fourth of it divided Equally amongst them** and the remaining fourth part I give and Bequeath unto **my live Grand Children, Elizabeth & Catherine Furtnay (?Fortney?)**, and also I leave and bequeath unto **my Oldest Son Daniel** and **my Daughter Rachel** five shillings each to be paid when demanded And also I Constitute and **appoint my Wife Christina and my Son Frederick to be the Executors** of this my last Will and Testament and I do hereby utterly disallow revoke and dis(?) all and every Other Testaments Wills Legacies bequests and Executors by me in any wise before named Willed and bequeathed Ratifying and Confirming this and no other to be my last Will and Testament

In Witness whereof I have hereunto set my hand and seal this 17 day of January in the Year of our Lord Seventeen Hundred & Eighty Four.

Signed Sealed published & delivered before the Said John Fox as his last Will and Testament in the presence of us who in his presence and in the presence of each other have hereto subscribed our names

John X Fox (seal)
his mark

Peter Dick Mathias Coons Christopher Cruse

APPENDIX TWO

John Fox Land Records in Frederick County

(Note: Washington County was formed on October 1, 1776 by the splitting of Frederick County.)

Ref No.	Date	From or To	Other party	Name of Tract/Item
K-703	Aug. 23, 1766	From	Joseph Chapline	Lot #143, Sharpsburg
K-1231	May 12, 1767	From	Joseph Chapline	Lot #16, Sharpsburg
J-1400	Aug. 18, 1767	From	John Barroughs	Judgement*
K-1278	June 2, 1769	From	Henry Joel	Lot #7, Sharpsburg
K-1279	June 2, 1769	From	Henry Joel	1/2 Lot #6, Sharpsburg
Probably **not** John Fox of Fox's Gap in Maryland:				
J-504	June 2, 1764	From	Daniel Dulany	Lot #269, Frederick Town*
K-499	May 22, 1766	To	Elias Bruner	Lot #269, Frederick Town*

* It is the author's opinion Lot #269 was bought and sold by a John Fox other than the father of Frederick Fox. It is not known which John Fox was the one in the Judgment record. It is the author's opinion all of the Sharpsburg lots above were owned by John Fox, the father of Frederick Fox.

APPENDIX THREE

Christiana Fox Land Records in Washington County, Maryland

Reference No.	Date	From or To	Other Party	Name of Tract/Other
G-754	1792	From	Joseph Shock	Lot #145, Jerusalem Town
WR-11-414	3-26-1793	n/a	Various	Boundaries of Spring Garden*
WR-22-418	5-31-1802	To	John Harmon	Spring Garden*
P-581	1804	To	Peter Crise	1/2 Lot #145, Sharpsburg
P-583	1804	To	Jacob Reel	1/2 Lot #145, Sharpsburg

*It is the author's opinion the Spring Garden tract was owned by a Christiana Fox other than the mother of Frederick Fox. This Christiana Fox was the widow of Adam Morningstar and married a John Fox after the death of her first husband.

APPENDIX FOUR

Letter from Jacob Reel of Sharpsburg to Frederick and Michael Fox of Ohio

A copy of the following letter from Jacob Reel of Sharpsburg to Michael and Frederick Fox about the death of their mother Christiana was obtained from Robert H. Fox of Cincinnati, Ohio:

> Received and forwarded from Lebanon. Warren Co. Ohio Sept. 8, 1812. Addressed to Msrs. Fredric & Michael Fox, Franklin Township Warren Co. Ohio.
>
> Sharpsburg Aug 9 1812.
>
> Dear. Brothers and Sisters by these few lines we let you know that we are in considerable good state of health at the present time. Thanks be to God for all his blessings. But we inform you that our aged Mother departed this life the 6th of Aug after a sickness of four weeks and was decently buried on the 7th and hope she is now at her rest. We had a physician who attended her regular. She did not complain of very severe pains in the time of her sickness. We suppose on account of her much sleeping. Mr. Widmeyer and wife were down to see her in time of her sickness and gave advice in some cases it seemed to give her some relief but according to the decree of God "dust thou art to dust return" stands good against all of the human family to which period we all hasten as fast as the wheels of time can carry us and may it please the Great Author our being to grant and give us all that true wisdom from above that we may consider our in most soul to meet the great Redeemer of Mankind who is the great Judge of quick and dead therefore let us all seriously and with good earnest consider the great importance of these things to our souls salvation. So we conclude by remembering our love and esteem for you all Yours Truly. Jacob Reel.

Jacob Reel died in 1844 in Sharpsburg. His Will is found in ?, pages 547-552, in Washington County Records. He mentions Christiana Fox twice in his Will, both times in reference to the 1/2 of Lot #6 in Sharpsburg which he purchased from her. He gives his wife's name in the Will as Elizabeth. On an 1877 Map of Sharpsburg, 1/2 of Lot #6 was owned by a D. Reel. Although this property was left by Jacob Reel to his daughter, ? ? , it could have come into the hands of one of his sons, David Reel.

"Item. To my daughter Nancy Michael, Wife of Adam Michael, I give and devise the half lot and premises in the town of Sharpsburg Washington County Maryland adjoining Crise and Beard and which was purchased of Christina Fox etc."

"To my beloved Wife Elizabeth I give, bequeath and devise for and during her natural life the following property viz. half a lot of ground in the town of Sharpsburg Washington County Maryland adjoining Crise and Beard which was purchased of Christian Fox, also the house and lot on which I now live situate in the said town of Sharpsburg and which I purchased from Jacob Houser etc."

APPENDIX FIVE

John Fox's House mentioned in Land Records

The following information is contained on a Surname Card and a Land Plat Card in the The Arthur G. Tracey Collection in the Historical Society of Carroll County, Md., 210 East Main Street, Westminster, MD. 21157)

Surname Card:

Fox, John
2-27-1764 Grims Fancy - 50 A. - CFW: u-40
Near John Fox's House

Land Plat Card:

OFW: u-40 Wash. Co.
GRIMS FANCY
2-27-1764 50 A.
6-12-1769 Alexander Grim
BC & GS 40-114
N.S. Main Road that leads from Fredericktown to Swainingens (Swearingens) Ferry & near to John Fox's house.
On the west side of South Mtn.
On this land is 2 log cabbins 27 x 12 & 14 x 12 & 15 A. cultivated land.
Next to Mt. Atlas.
Wash. Co. near Foxes Gap.
F. C. 1743 Sheet 392

[**Note:** Name spelled Trim in deeds, not Grim. This tract is located where the name Andrew Bash is found on the 1792 map of the road from Foxes Gap to Swearingens Ferry. This tract was subsequently owned by Michael Bash, probably having inherited it from Andrew Bash, who might have been his father. Michael Bash and his wife Catharine sold the property to Mathias Hutzel and Jacob Hutzel on May 8, 1813. This deed is recorded in Book Y, pages 723-725, Washington County Land Records.]

Daniel Gebhart Tavern

News from Fox's Gap

Published December 1 of each year by:

The Society of the Descendants of Frederick Fox of Fox's Gap in Maryland

Membership dues are $3.00 per year. President of the Society is Curtis L. Older.

Make Society inquiries by the following means:

Curtis L. Older
2417 Kinmere Road
Gastonia, NC 28056-7818

e-mail: curtolder@earthlink.net
cell: 704-685-2760
phone: 704-864-3879

President's Message

by Curtis Lynn Older

Please visit the new genealogy website of Curtis L. Older at:

http://www.cloldergen.com

The website lists original source records and other documentation for most of the ancestors of Curtis L. Older. Images of many of these original source documents are available for download.

* **Membership in the Society will be $3.00 for the 2010 calendar year.**

* ***News from Fox's Gap* is published once per year, December 1st.**

* ***News from Fox's Gap* is seeking articles by Fox Society members about their family genealogy, primarily as it relates to their descent from Frederick Fox. I hope to publish a number of articles in the future that were contributed by Society members.**

* **There were no new Society members for calendar year 2009.**

* **The Fox Inn property and the 175 acres on which it stands has been sold to Dominion Transmission. For the latest developments on the effort to save the Fox Inn near Middletown, Maryland, please view the following website of the Citizens for the Preservation of Middletown Valley at:**

http://www.cpmv.org/

* My book, ***The Braddock Expedition and Fox's Gap in Maryland*** has been reprinted and is available from Heritage Books. Their website is:

http://www.heritagebooks.com/

News from Fox's Gap

The Society of the Descendants of Frederick Fox of Fox's Gap in Maryland

December 8, 2010

Dear Fox Society Friend,

First of all I would like to wish you a happy holiday season and to thank you for your support of **The Society of the Descendants of Frederick Fox of Fox's Gap in Maryland**. The purpose of this letter is to inform you that I am no longer going to publish *News from Fox's Gap.* The simple fact is that I have run out of things to say related to the society and I have turned to other genealogical and historical pursuits.

In the future, I intend to update you from time to time on any developments related to The Fox Inn and Fox's Gap in Maryland that are of high significance. I would be happy to send anyone a free copy of my latest Fox Master CD-rom I created on March 15, 2010, which contains virtually all the information I have and everything I know about the Fox family, Fox's Gap in Maryland, the Fox Society, the Braddock Expedition, the land tracts of the battlefield of South Mountain, etc.

I will attempt to keep my website operational at www.cloldergen.com. My intent is to display the most up to date genealogical and historical information I have on that website.

Thank you once again for your support over the years and I hope you have received some enjoyment from the information on the Fox family and Fox's Gap that I have dug out and made available to you and the public. Please don't hesitate to contact me anytime you wish.

Sincerely,

Curt Older

2417 Kinmere Road
Gastonia, NC 28056

curtolder@earthlink.net
704-864-3879
www.cloldergen.com

News from Fox's Gap

The Society of the Descendants of Frederick Fox of Fox's Gap in Maryland

Issue 1, Volume 4 **Remember Freedom!** December 1, 2010

Courageous Life of Mary LaRose Gebhart Houk

(7 Oct 1815 to 5 Jan 1877)

by Carole Leis Troup

[Note: Numbers in parentheses are Reference numbers. Reference number section is at end of this article.] **Mary LaRose Gebhart** was born on 7 October 1815 in Miamisburg, Miami Township, Montgomery County, Ohio. She died 5 January 1877 in Beulah, Gerard Township, Crawford County, Kansas. Her father was Colonel **Emanuel Gebhart**, born 31 March 1788, in Tulpehochen Township, Berks County, Pennsylvania. He was baptized 2 April 1789 in the same place. He served in the War of 1812 in Pennsylvania. Emanuel died 22 January 1868 in Miamisburg, Montgomery County, Ohio. He was buried 24 January 1868 in Hillgrove Cemetery in Miamisburg, Ohio. Mary's mother was **Elizabeth LaRose**, born 22 October 1785, in Guilford County, North Carolina. She died 26 December 1867 in Miamisburg, Montgomery County, Ohio, and was buried with her husband, Emanuel Gebhart. Emanuel Gebhart and Elizabeth LaRose were married in 1809.

The progenitor of this Gebhart family was **Joachim Gebhart**, who was born in 1609 in Abtweiler, Germany, and died in 1689 in Desloch, Rhineland Pfalz, Germany. Originally, four Gebhart brothers came to America from Abtweiler and Desloch, Germany. Members of the Gebhart clan emigrated in the early 1730s and 40s into Pennsylvania, USA. Many of them who emigrated to Miamisburg are buried there in Hillgrove Cemetery.**(1)**

Mary had the distinct honor of having two grandfathers who served in the Revolutionary War. The first was **Johann Nichlaus Gebhart** born 23 June 1751 in Lancaster County, Pennsylvania.**(2)**

The second was Reverend **John Jacob LaRose** born in Magunshy Township, Pennsylvania. Both grandfathers are buried atop a hill within sight of each other in Hillgrove Cemetery, Miamisburg.**(3)**

Reverend LaRose and Barbara Gift, his wife, and family came to Ohio in 1804 where they raised a family of eight children. He was the first German Reformed Minister of Montgomery County. He founded four churches in the area. He had 160 acres on the Miamisburg-Springboro Pike, west side upon which Emanuel Gebhart built his white brick house standing near Maue Road. This road was called a "turnpike" at the time. Emanuel Gebhart was president of the Southeaster Turnpike Company. The Gebhart and LaRose families have distinguished rich histories in the settling and planning of the tiny village of Miamisburg, Ohio. All three of these gentelmen's graves are marked with the DAR, SAR, and the military honors deserving of their was one of four men who laid out the village which was originally named Hole's Station, changing the name to Miamisburg. The cities in those days sprung up along the rivers due to being the main course of navigation. Miamisburg lies to the east of the Great Miami River which flows into the mighty Ohio River at Cincinnati being the division between Ohio, Indiana, and Kentucky near this juncture.**(4)**

The marriage of **Mary LaRose Gebhart** to **Frederick Leiter** took place 11 February 1836--in Miami Township, Montgomery County, Ohio.**(5)**

The Reverend Henry Heineke, M.G. presided over the ceremony.**(5A)**

Frederick Leiter was born 22 March 1813 in Miami Township, Montgomery County, Ohio. He died 14 October 1838 in Miami Township, Montgomery County, Ohio. Frederick was the son of John Leiter and Elizabeth Fox. **(6)**

Family sources described Mary as being a nurse.**(7)**

After her husband, Frederick Leiter died in 1838, Mary returned to her parents' home with her two young children, Emanuel, and Elizabeth, in Miami Township, she lived with them until she married her second husband, William Shepherd Houk in 1845.**(8)**

The Reverend Henry Heineke led a rigourous and interesting life. He was born 15 December 1793 at Carlshaven, Schleswig Holstein, Germany to Franz and Maria (Schumann) Heineke. He had an excellent literary education; his father had been a merchant at Bergstadt. Henry Heineke served with Napoleon's army until the battle of Waterloo in 1815. He came from Germany to Baltimore, Maryland. He then emigrated to the Miami Valley where he studied theology under the Reverend John Caspar Dill of Germantown, Ohio, who also became minister to the Lutheran congregation in Miamisburg, having organized it in 1821. In 1820 Reverend Heineke was licensed to preach by the Ohio Synod and was with the Hetzel congregation in Moraine, Ohio. He married Catherine Hetzel, daughter of Peter Hetzel. In 1825 he became an ordained minister at Lancaster, Ohio, and on January 15, 1826, he assumed charge of the Lutheran congregation of Miamisburg. Mary La Rose and other family members of the Gebhart family were in his first confirmation class in May 1825. He served the Miamisburg congregation for 33 years until his death in July 1859.**(9)**

Two children, Emanuel and Elizabeth, were born to Mary LaRose Gebhart and Frederick Leiter:

1. **Emanuel Leiter** born 1837 in Miami Township, Montgomery County, Ohio. Emanuel married Malissa A. More. They were married on 4 December 1859 in Parke County, Indiana.**(10)**

Emanuel L. Leiter and Malissa A. More had 5 children:

I - Lewis Leiter. He was born between 1865-1870. He married Mamie Libecap. They were married on 31 December 1899 in Stetiler Lutheran Church.

II - George Leiter. He was born 1865 in Missouri.

III - Leroy Leiter. He was born 1870 in Missiouri.

IV - Sadie Leiter. She was born 1875 in Indiana.

V - Melissa Leiter. She was born 1876 in Indiana.

2. **Elizabeth Leiter** was born 5 February 1839 in Miamisburg, Montgomery County, Ohio and died 21 July 1917 in Miami Township, Montgomery County, Ohio.**(11)**

Elizabeth Leiter married **John Adam Leis** who was born 11 October 1836 and died 16 Mary 1925, also in Miami Township, Montgomery County, Ohio.**(12)**

They were married on 4 July 1861 in Montgomery County, Ohio. She died 19 July 1917 in Miamisburg, Montgomery County, Ohio. **John Adam Leis** was the son of **George Leiss** and **Salome Leiss**, both born in Berks County, Pennsylvania. They came to Miamisburg, Ohio, in 1836 shortly after their marriage.**(13)**

George and Salome Leiss are buried at Gebhart Church Cemetery (St. John's Lutheran Church), Miamisburg, Ohio.**(14)**

According to my father, Ralph Leis, John Adam Leis lost his left eye when he was a small child growing up in Miami Township, Ohio, when he fell by accident on a stick. My father indicated that John Adam Leis never seemed to have felt that the loss of his eye was of great consequence.

The following is a family story as told to me by my father, Ralph Leis, in 1999.**(15)**

John Adam Leis and Elizabeth Leiter Leis decided to move from Ohio to Missouri in the spring of 1970 in order to be near Elizabeth Leiter Leis's mother, Mary LaRose Leiter Houk. The railroads were offering free passage to the western frontier at this time so the women and children rode on the train, the men and boys old enough to do so traveled by river on flatboats. The men carried supplies, produce and farm animals on the flatboats. They left Miamisburg in wagons to travel the approximately 50 miles south to Cincinnati, Ohio, to board the train and river flatboats. Exactly the length of time traveled is not known. There were about ten families who made this journey. The times were had in Missouri when the families arrived. They had a difficult time farming and at times did not have enough food to eat. My Leis Family stayed approximately six years. For many generations the three families - John Adam, Noah Adam, all the children and grandchildren lived in the same household, consequently my Dad heard many stories about the trip to Sedalia, Missouri, and the return to Jackson and Miami Township, Ohio, where the family remained their entire lives. These stories were legend in our family, repeated through the years

John Adam Leis and Elizabeth Leiter Leis were the parents of eleven children:**(16)**

1 - **Urvin George William Leis** was born November 1862 in Montgomery County, Ohio, and died 23 April 1853 in Ohio.**(17)**

He married (1) **Phoebe Slaughman.**

He married (2) **Sarah Bell Breen** 7 June 1898, at First Reformed Church Pasonage.**(18)**

2 - **Clement Emanuel Leis** was born 11 February 1865 in Montgomery County, Ohio. He was baptized 12 February 1867 and died 17 October 1865 in Montgomery County, Ohio. Tombstone reads "Lyce".**(19)**

3 - **Peter Frederick Leis** was born on 14 October 1866, He was baptized 16 February 1867.**(20)** He married (1) **Phoebe Slaughman**. He married (2) **Rosa Berger-Hannah**. They were married on 17 April 1892. He died 1945 in Dayton, Montgomery County, Ohio. They were buried in Dayton Memorial Park Cemetery, Montgomery County, Ohio.

4. **Eva Anna Leis** was born on 5 June 1868 in Montgomery County, Ohio. She died on 1 March 1869 in Montgomery County, Ohio.

5. **Amelia Ella Leis** was born 8 December 1869 and was baptized 6 February 1870. She married **Abraham George** in 1888 in Preble County, Ohio. She died 26 September 1954 in Darke County, Ohio. They are both buried at Lower Miami Cemetery, Jefferson Township, Montgomery County, Ohio.

6. **Cora Belle Leis** was born on 8 January 1872 in Sedalia, Pettis County, Missouri, and was baptized 3 January 1875 in Ohio by Reverend William McCaughey. She married Charles E. Myers. They were married on 14 January 1897 in Preble County, Ohio, She died in 1957.

7. **Elva Alzonia Leis** was born on 21 October 1873 in Sedalia, Pettis County, Missouri. She married Charles Carrey. They were married on 2 February 1899. She died in 1955 in Ohio.

8. **Clara Elizabeth Leis** was born on 1 July 1876 in Ohio. She was baptized on 2 February 1877. She married Ambert M. Myers. They were married in 1895. She died in 1973 in Ohio.

9. **Early John Henry Leis** was born on 7 March 1878 in Ohio. He married Maud Elizabeth Smith on 30 December 1900 at First Reformed Church Parsonage. He died 30 January 1951 in Montgomery County, Ohio. They are buried in Hillgrove Cemetery.

10. **Noah Adam Leis** was born 10 April 1880 in Miami Township, Montgomery County, Ohio. and he was baptized 14 August 1881 at Slifer's Church in Farmersville by Reverend Milton Frank.**(NM)**

Noah Adam Leis married **Edith Mary Beck** on 18 January 1904.**(NN)**

Edith was only 17 at the time of marriage.

Her father, **Samuel Beck**, signed the marriage license with permission for her to marry Noah Adam Leis.**(JJ)**

Edith's mother was **Martha Houser**.
Noah and Edith were married by Reverend H. M. Herman, Minister, First Reformed Church, Miamisburg, Ohio.

After Edith died in 1947, Noah married Louise Stamin's widow in 1951. They moved to Lee County, Florida, and lived there until he died 16 October 1966.

Noah was buried beside his first wife at Ellerton Cemetery.

His last will and testament appointed his son, Ralph Leis, executor of his estate.

Noah Adam Leis, the youngest son of John Adam Leis and Elizabeth Leiter, was the grandfather of Carole Leis Troupe. **Ralph Leis**, the father of Carole Leis Troupe, was the son of Noah Leis.

11. **Bessie Catherine Leis** was born on 26 December 1882 in Montgomery County, Ohio. She married Martin Albertus Pontius. They were married on 4 July 1905 in First Reformed Church, Miamisburg, Montgomery County, Ohio. She died on 11 August 1973 at Bethany Lutheran Village. She is buried at Hillgrove Cemetery with husband Bert Pontius.

Story to be continued in the December 1, 2010, *News from Fox's Gap* newsletter.

REFERENCES

1. *Gebhart, Gephart, and Related Families 1609-1996,* by Julia Shupert Hagwood, Prologue and pages 268-270.

2. *Hillgrove Cemetery Inscriptions and Records, Miamisburg, Ohio,* Published by Miamisburg Historical Society, 2005, page 37.

3. Ibid; *Miamisburg - The First 150 Years from Historical Essays of Esther Light,* Published by Miamsiburg Lions Club in connection with the Miamisburg Sesquicentennial Celebration, pages 42 and 71.

4. *Miamisburg - The First 150 Years from Historical Essays of Esther Light,* page 72; *Gebhart, Gephart, and Related Families 1609-1996,* pages 268-270.

5. Marriage Records, Montgomery County, Ohio, Doc. #131 - Rev. Henry Heinecke, MG; *Gebhart, Gephart, and Related Families 1609-1996,* page 268.

5A. Marriage Records, Montgomery County, Ohio, Doc. #131 - Rev. Henry Heinecke, MG

6. Documentation presented in the December 1, 2008, *News from Fox's Gap* article by Carole Troup.

7. Genealogical Data, Charts created by Ralph Leis, sister Anna Leis Loesch.

8. Ibid; 1840 US Federal Census, Miami Township, Montgomery County, Ohio; 1850 US Federal Census, Miami Township, Montgomery County, Ohio.

9. *Miamisburg - The First 150 Years from Historical Essays of Esther Light,* pages 42 and 95-98.

10. *Gebhart, Gephart, and Related Families 1609-1996,* page 268.

11. Death Certificate - Elizabeth Leiter Leis - Ohio Department of Vital Statistics, Montgomery County, Ohio.

12. Marriage Applications and License - John Adam Leis and Elizabeth Leiter Leis - Montgomery County, Ohio; Death Certificate - John Adam Leis - Ohio Department of Vital Statistics, Montgomery County, Ohio.

13. *Gebhart, Gephart, and Related Families 1609-1996,* page 270; *Montgomery County, Ohio Cemetery Inscriptions*, Volume VI - Miami Township, Book A, All Except Hillgrove Cemetery, Published by Montgomery County Chapter Ohio Genealogical Society, Compiled and Edited by Anne & Robert

Johnson, Co-Chairs, Cemetery Committee, 2000.

14. Nita Petticrrew, Archivist, Gebhart Church (St. John's Lutheran): Historian, Miamisburg Historical Society records of Church and Cemetery.

15. Genealogical Data, Charts, created by Ralph Leis, sister Anna Leis Loesch.

16.

17.

18.

19.

20.

NM. Noah Leis Baptismal Certificate Slifer Church, Farmersville, Montgomery County, Ohio.

NN. Noah Adam Leis & Edith Mary Beck Marriage Application and License.

2. *Montogmery County, Ohio, German Church Records*, Volume II, Transcripts of the Records of First Reformed Church of Miamisburg, Ohio including Membership, Marriages, Baptisms, and Deaths & Funerals, Extracted, Edited and Indexed by Anne Walker Johnson and Robert Eugene Johnson, Published by Montgomery County Chapter Ohio Genealogical Society, 1999.

19. *Montgomery County, Ohio Cemetery Inscriptions*, Volume VI - Miami Township, Book A, All Except Hillgrove Cemetery, Published by Montgomery County Chapter Ohio Genealogical Society, Compiled and Edited by Anne & Robert Johnson, Co-Chairs, Cemetery Committee, 2000.

20. *Montgomery County, Ohio, Cemetery Inscriptions*, Volume V - Jefferson Township, Book B, All Except Dayton National Cemetery, Published by Montgomery County Chapter of the Ohio Genealogical Society, Compiled and Edited by Anne & Robert Johnson, Co-Chairs, Cemetery Committee, 2002

REFERENCES for Above Article

1. *Gebhart, Gephart and Related Families 1609-1996*, Julia Shupert Hagwood.
2. Montgomery County, Ohio, German Church Records Vol. II, Transcripts of Records of First Reformed German Church Book of Miamisburg, Ohio.
3. *The Fox Genealogy* by Daniel Gebhart Fox, Compiled 1914, Published 1924.

4. Leis Family Bible Records, Charts, Genealogy Data created by Ralph Leis, Anna Leis Loesch.
5. Miamisburg - The First 150 Years from Hitorical Essays of Esther Light, Published by Miamsiburg Lions Club in Connectcion With the Miamisburg Sesquicentennial Celebration.
6. Death Certificate - Elizabeth Leiter Leis - Ohio Department of Vital Statistics, Montgomery County, Ohio.
7. Death Certificate - John Adam Leis - Ohio Department of Vital Statistics, Montgomery County, Ohio.
8. Marriage Applications and License - John Adam Leis and Elizabeth Leiter Leis - Montgomery County, Ohio.
9. Baptismal Certificate - Noah Leis - Slifer Church, Farmersville, Montgomery County, Ohio, Reading 1992 Suella Leis-Fenton.
10. Marriage Application and License - Noah Leis and Edith M. Beck - Montgomery County, Ohio.
11. Death Certificate - Noah Leis - Lee County, Florida.
12. Will - Noah A. Leis, Lee County, Florida
13. Photo - Tombstone - Noah Leis and Edith M. Beck Leis, Ellerton Cemetery, Jefferson Township, Montgomery County, Ohio.
14. Photo - Daniel Gebhart Tavern - Miamisburg, Ohio, Historical Society, Diane Forbes Warrick, Editor, Tavern Log
15. Photo - Elizabeth Leiter Leis - Charles Leis
16. Photo - John Adam Leis Family - Charles Leis
17. Hillgrove Cemetery Inscriptions and Records, Miamisburg, Ohio, Published by Miamisburg Historical Society, 2005.
18. Nita Petticrrew, Archivist, Gebhart Church (St. John's Lutheran): Historian, Miamisburg Historical Society records of Church and Cemetery.
19. Montgomery County, Ohio, German Church Records, Volume II, Transcripts of Records of First Reformed German Church, including membership, Marriages, Baptisms, Deaths, Funerals, Edited and Indexed by Anne and Bob Johnson, Published by Montgomery County, Ohio, Genealogical Society 1999.
20. Montgomery County Cemetery Inscriptions, Volume V, Jefferson Township, Book B, All Except Dayton National Cemetery, Published by Montgomery County, Chapter OGS, Compiled and Edited by Bob and Anne Johnson.

US Census Records Citations for Above Article

A. 1850 US Federal Census, Miami Township, Montgomery County, Ohio.
B. 1860 US Federal Census, Winchester Township, Randolph County, IN, page 144.
C. 1870 US Federal Census, Faberville, Butler Township, St. Clair County, Missouri.
D. 1870 US Federal Census, Sedalia, Pettis County, Missouri, page 56.
E. 1880 US Federal Census, Jackson Township, Montgomery County, Ohio, page 555b.
F. 1900 US Federal Census, Miami Township, Montgomery County, Ohio.
G. 1910 US Federal Census, Miami Township, Montgomery County, Ohio.
H. 1920 US Federal Census, Miami Township, Montgomery County, Ohio.
I. 1920 US Federal Census, Miami Township, Montgomery County, Ohio.

J. 1930 US Federal Census, Miami Township, Montgomery County, Ohio.
K. 1860 US Federal Census, Parke County, Indiana.
L. 1880 US Federal Census, Penne Township, Parke County, Indiana.
M. 1840 US Federal Census, Miami Township, Montgomery County, Ohio.

Butler Twp., St. Clair, MO
#Montgomery Co., OH Cemetery Inscriptions Vol. VI, Miami Twp., Book A--Except Hillgrove Cemetery, Published by Montgomery Co. Chapter OGS Compiled and Edited by Anne & Robert Johnson 2000
#Death Certificate - Elizabeth Leis - Ohio Dept. of Vital Statistics
#Death Certificate - John Adam Leis - Ohio Dept. of Vital Statistics
#Marriage Application & License - John Adam Leis & Elizabeth Leiter - Montgomery Co., OH
#1870 US Census, Sedalia, Pettis Co., MO, pg56
#1880 US Census, Jackson Twp., Montgomery Co., OH, pg555b
#1900 US Census, Miami Twp., Montgomery Co., OH
#1910 US Census, Miami Twp., Montgomery Co., OH
#1920 US Census, Miami Twp., Montgomery Co., OH
#1930 US Census, Miami Twp., Montgomery Co., OH
#1930 US Census, Miami Twp., Montgomery Co., OH
#1860 US Census, Parke Co., IN

#Noah Leis Baptismal Certificate Slifer Church, Farmersville, Montgomery Co., OH

#Noah Adam Leis & Edith Mary Beck Marriage Application & License

#Noah Adam Leis Death Certificate - Florida Dept. of Vital Statistics, Lee Co.

#Last Will & Testament of Noah Adam Leis - Appointed Ralph Leis, son, Executor

#Tombstone Noah Adam Leis & Edith Mary Beck - Ellerton Cemetery, Jefferson Twp., Montgomery Co., OH

#Montgomery Co., OH Cemetery Inscriptions Vol V, Jefferson Twp., Book B All Except Dayton National Cemetery, Published by Montgomery Co. Chapter of OGS, Compiled and Edited by Bob and Anne Johnson, 2002.

#31 Leis Family Bible Records & Genealogy created by father Ralph Leis & his sister, Anna Rose Leis Loesch, 1970□ s

#1880 US Census, Penn Twp., Parke Co., IN

#1840 US Census, Miami Twp., Montgomery Co., OH, pg& ..

#Nita Petticrew, Archivist Gebhart Church (St. John□ s Lutheran)
Historian, Miamisburg Historical Society, Miamisburg, Ohio

#Montgomery County, Ohio German Church Records Vol. II Transcripts of Records of First Reformed German Church Book of Miamisburg, Ohio, Including: Membership, Marriages, Baptisms and Deaths and Funerals Extracted Edited and Indexed by Anne & Bob Johnson Published by Montgomery Co. Chapter Genealogical Society 1999.

#D.G. Fox, The Fox Genealogy Book by D.G. Fox, Compiled 1914 Published 1924 Including the Metherd Benner & Leiter Descendants Giving Biographies of the First & Second Generatiosn with Sketches of the Third Generation.

#Hillgrove Cemetery Inscriptions & Records Miamisburg, Ohio, Miamisburg Historical Society Historic Resource & Research Committee, 2005

#Microfiche of St. Jacob□ s Lutheran Church from 1821 forward showing marriages, births, deaths, funerals

#Gebhart Gephart And Related Families 1609-1996 by Julia Shupert Hagwood

#Miamisburg The First One Hundred Fifty Years From Historical Essays of Mrs. Esther Light Published by the Miamisburg Lions Club In Connection With the Miamisburg Sesquicentennial Celebration

#Marriage Record, Montgomery Co., Court, Dayton, Ohio, pg. 131, Frederick Leiter & Mary LaRose Gebhart 11 February 1836, Miami Twp., Montgomery Co., OH

1850 US Federal Census, Miami Twp., Montgomery Co., OH

#A Register of Marriage Certificates Recorded in Montgomery Co., OH July 26, 1803 to July 20, 1851, Transcribed by Lindsay M. Brien from Montgomery Common Pleas Record of Marriage Certificates Book A, B, A2 and B2.1850 US Federal Census, Miami Twp., Montgomery Co., OH

#1860 US Federal Census, Winchester Twp., Randolph Co., IN, pg144

#1870 US Federal Census, FabervilK□b□d□\□÷□ä□öl

1850 US Census, Miami Township, Montgomery County, Ohio, page 33b, Book 1, Roll 713.
Emanuel, 12, w, m, OH, (living with mother and stepfather and siblings)

1860 US Census, Sugar Creek Township, Parke County, Indiana
Leiter, Emanuel, 23, m, w, Selling Lightning Rods, 1,000 300 OH
Melissa Leiter, wife, f, w, 20, Keeping house, IN

1880 US Census, Penn Township, Parke County, Indiana
Lighter, Emanuel, w, m, 43, farmer OH MD OH
Melissa A, w, f, 40, wife, keeping house, IN PA OH
George, w, m 15, son, farm hand MO OH IN
Leroy, w, m, 10, son MO OH IN
Sallie, w, f, 5, daughter, IN OH IN

1850 US Census, Miami Township, Montgomery County, Ohio
Leiter, Elizabeth, 11, 2, f, OH (living with stepfather, mother and siblings)

1870 US Census, page 56, Sedalia, Pettis County, Missouri
Liee, John, 33, m, w, Carptenter, 450/200 Ohio
Elizabeth, 31, f, w, Ohio
Irvin, 8, m, w, Ohio
Peter, 4, m, w, Ohio
Amelia, 7/12, f, w, Ohio

1880 US Census, page 55b, Jackson Township, Montgomery County, Ohio, 8th June 1880
Lies, John, w, m, 43 Head, Farmer, OH PA PA
Elizabeth, w, f, 40, wife, Housekeeper, OH OH OH
Urvin George, w, m, 17, son, Farmer, OH OH OH
Peter Frederick, w, m, 14, son, Farmer, OH OH OH
Amelia, w, f, 10, daughter, helps in house, OH OH OH
Cora Belle, w, f, 8, daughter, school, MO OH OH
Elva E., 6, daughter, school, MO OH OH
Clara E. w, f, 4, daughter, OH OH OH
Early John, w, m, 2, son, OH OH OH
Noah Adam, w, m, 3/12, son OH OH OH

1900 US Census, Miami Township, Montgomery County, Ohio, 3 August 1900:
Leis, John Adam, head, w, m, Oct 1836, 63, married 38 yrs, OH PA PA Farmer
Elizabeth, wife, w, f, Feb 1839, 61, married 38 yrs, 12 children, born 12 children living OH OH OH
Early J. H. son, w, m, Mar 1878, 22, s, Ticket Agent Railroad
Noah A. son, w, m, April 188, 20, s, Farm Laborer
Bessie Catherine, daughter, w, f, 17, s, Dec 1882

1910 US Census, Miami Township, Montgomery County, Ohio, Roll 1218 Book 2:
Leis, John A. head, m, w, 73, married, 1, 49 yrs, OH OH OH, Farmer, General Farming
Elizabeth, wife, f, w, 71, married, 1, 49 yrs, 12 children born, 9 children living, OH OH OH
Noah A., son, m, w, 30, married, 1, 5 years, OH OH OH, Farmer
Edith, daughter-in-law, f, w, 22, married, 1, 5 years, 3 children born, 2 children living, OH OH OH
Mildred, granddaughter, f, w, 4, 8, OH OH OH
Margaret, granddaughter, f, w, 1 1/2, s, OH OH OH

1920 US Census, Miami Township, Montgomery County, Ohio, Roll 1423, Book 2, page 533:

Leis, Noah, Head, r, m, w, 39, OH OH OH Farmer General Farming
Edith M., wife, f, w, 34, m, OH OH OH
Mildred V., daughter, f, w, 14, OH OH OH
Margaret E., daughter, f, w, 11, OH OH OH
Ralph C., son, m, w, 9, OH OH OH
Ruth M., daughter, f, w, 6, OH OH OH
Leis, John A., Father, m, w, 83, widowed, OH OH OH

<u>1930 US Census, Miami Township, Montgomery County, Ohio, Roll 1857, Book 1, page 207:</u>
Leis, Noah Adam, head, r, 17, n, O, M, no, 49, married, 24, OH OH OH, Machine Hand, Paper Mill
Edith, wife, f, no, 42, married, 17, 100, yes, OH OH OH
Ruth, daughter, f, no, 16, s, Y, Y, OH OH OH, typist
Anna, daughter, f, 9, s, y, y, OH OH OH
Mary, daughter, 5, s, y, y, OH OH OH

October 15, 1916, Miamisburg, Ohio
Back Row: Urvin Leis, Bessie Leis Pontius, Earl Leis Myers, Noah Leis, Elva Leis Carey Front Row: Cora Leis Myers, John Adam Leis, Elizabeth Leiter Leis, Amelia Leis George, Peter Leis

Daniel Gebhart Tavern

Next Issue of News from Fox's Gap

???? ???? ????

Genealogy Documentation Section
by Curtis L. Older

A feature of each Fox Society Newsletter that began with the December 1, 2004, newsletter is the inclusion of an article that documents or genealogically proves a descendant or spouse of a descendant of John Fox of Fox's Gap in Maryland. The article will present a written description about the individual and his or her family as well as a listing of the related genealogical source records that support the written description. This newsletter contains documentation for two individuals.

The tenth individual to be presented in this section of the newsletter is John Frederick Fox, the father of Frederick Fox and the man for whom Fox's Gap in Maryland was named.

Previous issues of the Fox Society Newsletter contained documentation for the following individuals:

December 1, 2004 - Frederick Fox
December 1, 2005 - John L. Fox
December 1, 2006 - Elizabeth Jane Ricketts
December 1, 2007 - Susannah Hiligass
December 1, 2008 - Jane Ogle
June 1, 2005 - George Fox
June 1, 2006 - Daniel Alexander Fox
December 1, 2007 - Elizabeth Ann Link
December 1, 2008 - John Adam Link II
December 1, 2009 - John Frederick Fox

Documentation for John Frederick Fox
(before 1735 to after Jan 17, 1784, and before Dec 4, 1784)
father of Frederick Fox
(May 10, 1751 to Feb 27, 1837)

John Frederick Fox was born before 1735. This seems certain because his oldest son, Daniel, who is identified as such in the will of John Fox, was born before 1751.**(1)** Another son of John Fox, Frederick, was born May 10, 1751.**(2)** Surely John Fox was more than fifteen or sixteen years old when he became the father of Daniel Fox.

Before coming to America, John Fox probably lived in Hesse-Cassel, Germany. According to Daniel Gebhart Fox, author of *The Fox Genealogy* which was compiled in 1914 and published in 1924, "Frederick Fox, 1, was born May 10, 1751, in Hesse-Cassel, Germany, (a former Electorate of Germany, now forming the district of Cassel in the Prussian Province of Hesse-Nassau)."**(3)** There is, however, a statement in The *History of Vermillion County, Indiana* that indicates Frederick Fox was born at sea. "The father (i.e., George Fox) of our subject (i.e., John L. Fox) was a native of Maryland, and a son of Frederick Fox, who was born on the ocean while his parents were immigrating to America."**(4)**

Daniel Gebhart Fox gives the middle name of John Fox as Frederick.**(5)** The sources D. G. Fox gives for the middle name of Frederick are: 1) "records of the port of Philadelphia, show that John Frederick Fox landed at the port" in 1752, and 2) "Mrs. Christiana (Fox) Allison, who was the surviving great-granddaughter of John Frederick Fox, stated to the writer during an interview about two years prior to her death, that 'the old man Fox's name was John Frederick'."**(6)**

The father of John Fox might have been named Daniel Fox, since John Fox named his oldest son Daniel. Frederick Fox, a son of John Fox, also named one of his sons Daniel.**(7)**

Daniel G. Fox in the *Fox Genealogy* indicates John Fox and his family came to America in 1752. A John Fox appeared in the state house in Philadelphia the day of his arrival and "took and subscribed the usual Qualifications."**(8)** There is no conclusive proof however that this John Fox was the father of Daniel and Frederick Fox mentioned above.

John Fox and his family may have settled for a period of time in the Pennsylvania German community before coming to Maryland. On the other hand, they might have settled at the location that became known as Fox's Gap shortly after arriving in Philadelphia. Many Germans followed the Great Philadelphia Wagon Road out of Pennsylvania and into Maryland and Virginia.

The gap in the South Mountain at which John Fox chose to settle, was on a wagon road known as the Great Philadelphia Wagon Road. The road also was known as the Road from Conestoga to Opequon, the Monocacy Road, the main road leading from Frederick Town to Sharpsburg, the Old Sharpsburg Road, the German Monocacy Road, and the Main Road that leads from Frederick Town to Swearingen's Ferry and near to John Foxes House.**(9)**

Fox's Gap in Maryland lies about midway between Frederick and Hagerstown, Maryland, and about two miles from Boonsboro, Maryland. Sharpsburg, the site of the Battle of Antietam during the Civil War, lies approximately five miles west. Fox's Gap in Maryland was destined to become not only the home for John Fox and his family, but an historical landmark due to the events of the Braddock Expedition of 1755 and the Battle of South Mountain, called the Battle of Boonsboro in the South, on September 14, 1862.**(10)** It is unknown if John Fox and his family resided at the gap when General Braddock, George Washington, and Maryland Governor Sharp passed through there on May 2, 1755. It is entirely possibly they did. We can only speculate if the reason or reasons John Fox chose to settle at Fox's Gap were similar or like-minded to those of the Confederate Army on September 13 and 14, 1862.

There is strong evidence the gap was named for John Fox by no later than the mid 1760s. The primary support for the arrival of the John Fox family at Fox's Gap by the mid 1760s is a land record for a tract named Grim's Fancy.**(11)** Land tracts in Maryland in the 1600s and 1700s were given names. The Grim's Fancy land record states, "for and in the name of him the said Alexander Trim all that tract of land called Grims Fancy lying in the County aforesaid beginning at a bounded Black Oak tree standing on the north side of the Main Road that leads from Frederick Town to Swearingen's Ferry and near to John Foxes House on the West side of the South Mountain and running thence". The Grim's Fancy tract of land is approximately one-half mile west of Fox's Gap. For purposes of identifying the location of Fox's Gap, we consider the Reno Monument, dedicated to Union Major General Jesse Lee Reno who was killed there on September 14, 1862, as being at the heart of Fox's Gap.

There is no record for a tract of land owned by John Fox in the vicinity of Fox's Gap. Perhaps John Fox, coming from Germany, was not able to purchase land in Maryland and simply became a squatter at Fox's Gap. Frederick Fox, a son of John Fox, patented a tract of land that includes the areas of both Fox's Gap and Turner's Gap in the South Mountain, not far from Boonsboro.**(12)** A tract named Friendship for 231 and 1/2 acres was the subject of an unpatented certificate, #228, on June 8, 1795. On May 9, 1797, Frederick Fox patented Addition to Friendship for 202 acres. The Reno Monument stands on the southern portion of Addition to Friendship.**(13)**

Frederick Fox was a farmer and perhaps a tavern keeper.**(14)** He married Catherine Booker on March 1, 1773, probably at or near Middletown, Maryland.**(15)** Catherine was a daughter of Bartholomew Booker and Margaret.**(16)** She was born May 1, 1748.**(17)**

It does not seem viable to the author that the John Fox family could be any nationality other than German. Several historical records support this conclusion. First, upon the death of Catherine Fox, the wife of Frederick Fox, the death register of Zion Lutheran Church indicated "Catarin, wife of Friedrich Fuchs, bur. 4 Nov. 1800. Heb. 4:9."**(18)** Fox is spelled Fuchs in this church record and is clearly a German spelling. Second, the services of this church were only held in the German language for many years. George Fox, the oldest son of Frederick Fox, was a member of this church, the Zion Lutheran Church of Middletown, Maryland.**(19)** Third, Zion Lutheran Church records indicate, "Samuel, son of Jacob and Magdelena Benner was born April 14, 1801. Baptised June 21, 1801. Sponsored by George Fox, a single person". (Mary) Magdelena Benner was a daughter of Frederick Fox and a sister of George Fox. Fourth, Daniel Gebhart Fox in *The Fox Genealogy* indicates Frederick Fox was born in Hesse-Cassel, Germany.

John Fox was a skin-dresser by trade.**(20)** There is mention in his will, "that my Son **Frederick** shall have the Clocke and one half of the skin dressing tools used my son Michael is to have the Young Mare with the Other half of the Aforesaid tools and also my Wearing Apearel Except my fine fure hat which I leave to **Frederick".(21)** The Birely Tannery Report gives an excellent description of what the tannery business was like in the area surrounding Frederick, Maryland, in the 1700s.**(22)**

The name of John Fox may be found in the Moses Chapline Sr. Administration Account papers submitted by the executors of the estate, bearing a date of June 19, 1766.**(23)** Moses Chapline Senior lived about two miles west of Fox's Gap towards Sharpsburg.**(24)**

Little is known of the wife of John Fox or if he might have had more than one wife during his lifetime. His will states, " First I give and Bequeath unto **my beloved Wife Christina** all that I do possess of during her Natural life".**(25)** John Fox apparently married his first wife before they came to America. We cannot be certain his first and only wife was Christiana. The letter of Jacob Reel does seem to indicate or imply that Christiana Fox was the mother of Frederick and Michael Fox. Christiana Fox died August 6, 1812, probably in Sharpsburg, Maryland.**(26)**

John and Christina Fox apparently lived in Sharpsburg, Maryland, by the mid 1760s since we find a record of Lot #143 purchased August 23, 1766, by John Fox from Joseph Chapline.**(27)** Joseph Chapline was the founder of Sharpsburg in 1763, having named the town after Maryland Governor Sharpe.**(28)**

We can only speculate that Frederick Fox continued to live at or near Fox's Gap, after his parents moved to Sharpsburg, due to the fact that Frederick patented the Addition to Friendship land tract at Fox's and Turner's gaps in 1795.**(29)** *The Fox Genealogy* by Daniel Gebhart Fox indicates that Frederick Fox owned the Fox Inn at one time.**(30)** Daniel G. Fox identifies a land tract named Turkeyfoot, land records in Maryland were given names in the 1700s, where the Fox Inn stood. However, from analysis of land records by Curtis L. Older, the Fox Inn was owned by George Fox, oldest son of Frederick Fox, for a period of only a few years until all the Frederick Fox family clan moved to the area that became Miamisburg, Ohio, near present day Dayton, Ohio, in 1807.**(31)**

The Fox Inn is located about two miles from Fox's Gap towards Middletown, Maryland. Since Frederick Fox never owned the property and George Fox only owned the property for a few years up to 1807, it is somewhat mysterious why the property would continue to be known as the Fox Inn right up to present day in 2009. The only reason the building has been know for over 200 years as the Fox Inn might be that the old tavern or inn was the first place a traveler through Fox's Gap from the west might stay for the night after passing through Fox's Gap.

John Fox died in 1784. He wrote his will on January 17, 1784 and it was probated December 4, 1784, in Washington County, where Sharpsburg is located.**(32)** Since John Fox died in 1784, you will not find him listed in the first United States census of 1790.

Christiana Fox died August 6, 1812, in Sharpsburg. The support for this date of death and location comes from a letter or copy of a letter that was in the possession of Robert H. Fox of Cincinnati, Ohio, in the late 1990s.**(33)** The letter, from Jacob Reel of Sharpsburg to Michael and Frederick Fox of Franklin Township, Warren County, Ohio, about the death of their mother Christiana, was dated August 9, 1812, at Sharpsburg. The letter indicated that "we inform you that our aged Mother departed this life the 6th of Aug after a sickness of four weeks". Why he indicated "our aged Mother" is not known. There is no record of a Jacob Reel marrying a woman with the last name of Fox. Christina Fox was buried at the Lutheran Church lot in Sharpsburg, Maryland.**(34)**

Michael Fox, a brother of Frederick Fox, was born January 6, 1760, and died in Franklin, Warren County, Ohio, on August 23, 1837, aged 77 years, 7 months, and 17 days. He and his wife Susannah Fox, 1761 - 1836, are both buried in Woodhill Cemetery in Franklin, Warren County, Ohio. Michael and Susannah Fox were the parents of Elizabeth, Eve, Jacob, Daniel, and Michael.**(35)**

See **APPENDIX ONE** for the full text of the will of John Fox; **APPENDIX TWO** has a list of the John Fox Land Records in Frederick County, Maryland; **APPENDIX THREE** has a list of the Christiana Fox Land Records in Washington County, Maryland; **APPENDIX FOUR** has the September 8, 1812, Letter from Jacob Reel of Sharpsburg, Maryland, to Frederick and Michael Fox of Warren County, Ohio; **APPENDIX FIVE** has a Map of *The Road from Swearingen's Ferry on the Potomac River through Sharpsburgh to the Top of the South Mountain at Fox's Gap.* August 23, 1792; **APPENDIX SIX** has an article on the Occupations of Residents along the Old Sharpsburg Road in the 1700s; and **APPENDIX SEVEN** discusses John Fox's House mentioned in the Grim's Fancy Land Record.

A Kodak Photo CD-Rom disc entitled "Fox's Gap in Maryland" by Curtis L. Older contains photos of many documents and items related to the descendants of John Fox through his son Frederick Fox, as well as material related to Fox's Gap in Maryland, the Braddock Expedition, and the Battle of South Mountain. A copy of the CD-Rom is at the Washington County Free Library, Hagerstown, Maryland.

Children (**Fox**) :

i. **Daniel**, born before 1751, died after 1783
ii. **Frederick**, born May 10, 1751, died Feb 27, 1837
iii. **Rachel**, died after 1783
iv. **Magdelin**, died after 1783
v. **Unknown daughter**, died before 1784
vii. **Michael**, born January 6, 1760, died August 23, 1837**(35)**

REFERENCES

1. Will of John Fox, Court House, Washington County, Maryland, Book A, Liber 102, January 17, 1784. See **APPENDIX ONE** for the full text of the will of John Fox.

2. *The Fox Genealogy including Metherd, Benner and Leiter descendants, giving biographies of the first and second generations, with sketches of the third generation,* compiled by D. G. Fox, 1914. (n.p.) 1924 . 1 p. 1., (5)-172 p. 20 cm. 37-9439, CS71.F79, 1924, page 12; tombstone of Frederick Fox, Gebhart or St. John Cemetery, Miamisburg, Ohio.

3. *Fox Genealogy,* page 12.

4. *History of Vermillion County, Indiana,* page 491.

5. I. Daniel Rupp, *Thirty-Thousand Names of Immigrants* (Baltimore: Genealogical Publishing Co., 1971), 280-1.

6. *Fox Genealogy,* page 169, APPENDIX NO. 1.

7. Will of Frederick Fox, Will Book C, case #1444, Montgomery County, Ohio;; tombstone of Daniel Booker Fox, Gebhart or St. John Cemetery, Miamisburg, OH; *Fox Genealogy,* pages 101 through 103.

8. I. Daniel Rupp, *Thirty-Thousand Names of Immigrants* (Baltimore: Genealogical Publishing Co., 1971), 280-1. The name "Johan Friederich Fuchs" appears; also R. B. Strassburger and W. J. Hinke, *Pennsylvania German Pioneers, Lists of Arrivals* (Norristown, Pa.: Pennsylvania German Society, 1934), 488-9. John Fox took the oath on arrival.

9. Curtis L. Older, *The Land Tracts of the Battlefield of South Mountain* (Westminster, Md.: Heritage Books, 1999), pages 41-42; *The Braddock Expedition and Fox's Gap in Maryland,* (Westminster, Md: Heritage Books, 1995) pages 78-104.

10. *Braddock Expedition*, Introduction and Afterword.

11. Grim's Fancy, Maryland State Archives, BC & GS 40, p. 114, Alexander Trim's certificate of survey, examined and passed 5 June 1765, [MdHR 17,451, 1-23-4-5]. "On the North Side of the Main Road that leads from Frederick Town to Swearingen's Ferry and near to John Foxes House".

12. MdHR, 17,478, 1-23-4-34, Frederick Fox, patent for Addition to Friendship, May 27, 1805, 202 ac. Maryland State Archives, IC #P, 672-3.

13. *Braddock Expedition*, pages 103 and 189-190; also *Land Tracts of the Battlefield of South Mountain*, pages 206-210.

14. FCLR, WR-19-206, Mortgage from Christian Benner to Frederick Fox, recorded April 11, 1799, Shaffs Purchase and Mount Sinai. "Between Christian Benner Sen. of Frederick County farmer of the one part; and Frederick Fox of the same county farmer of the other part."; Lemoine Cree, *A Brief History of the South Mountain House* (Boonsboro, Md.: Dodson, 1963); Ohio D.A.R. Soldiers Rosters, 2 Vols., 1:146; *Fox Genealogy*, pp. 13-14.

15. *Fox Genealogy*, page 12; will of Bartholomew Booker, Frederick County, Maryland, Register of Wills Records, GM-2-431; will of Margaret Book (Booker) Frederick County, Maryland, Register of Wills Records GM-3-126.

16. Frederick S. Weiser, ed., Maryland German Church Records Vol. 2, *Zion Lutheran Church 1781-1826* (Manchester, Md.: Noodle-Doosey Press, 1987), 77. The Death Register of Zion Lutheran Church indicates "Catarin, wife of Friedrich Fuchs, bur. 4 Nov. 1800. Heb. 4:9."; *Fox Genealogy*, page 12; will of Bartholomew Booker; will of Margaret Book (Booker).

17. Fox Genealogy, page 12.

18. Frederick S. Weiser, ed., *Maryland German Church Records* Vol. 2, *Zion Lutheran Church 1781-1826* (Manchester, Md.: Noodle-Doosey Press, 1987), 77. The Death Register of Zion Lutheran Church indicates "Catarin, wife of Friedrich Fuchs, bur. 4 Nov. 1800. Heb. 4:9."; *Fox Genealogy*, p. 12.

19. Frederick S. Weiser, ed., *Zion Lutheran Church 1781-1826*, Maryland German Church Records, Vol. 2, (Manchester, Md.: Noodle-Doosey Press, 1987), 25; "Samuel, son of Jacob and Magdelena Benner was born April 14, 1801. Baptised June 21, 1801. Sponsored by George Fox, a single person". (Mary) Magdelena Benner was a daughter of Frederick Fox and sister of George Fox.

20. Will of John Fox; *Fox Genealogy*, page 12.

21. Ibid.

22. See *The Birely Tannery Report*, held by the Frederick, Maryland, library, a report on the tannery business in and about Frederick, Maryland. The Birely Tannery began operation in Frederick, Maryland, in the 1760s and remained in business until the 1920s. Archaeological Data Recover at the Birely Tannery (18FR575) City of Frederick, Maryland, prepared by M.A.A.R. Associates, Inc. of Newark, Delaware, 1991.

23. The Moses Chapline Senior Administration Account papers submitted by the executors of the estate, bearing a date of Jun 19, 1766, mention the name of John Fox. See Frederick County, Maryland, The Account of Joseph and Jennett Chapline, executors of Moses Chapline, late of Frederick County deceased.

24. *Braddock Expedition*, pages 76-77, 79-80, 86, 123-124; *Land Tracts of the Battlefield of South Mountain*, pages 42 and 226. See page 226 of the *Land Tracts* book for a discussion of The Moses Chapline Senior Cemetery and references to other material on the subject.

25. Will of John Fox.

26. Letter from Jacob Reel to Michael and Frederick Fox, dated at Sharpsburg, Aug. 9, 1812, from a copy obtained from Robert H. Fox of Cincinnati, Ohio. "The following letter received and forwarded from Lebanon, Warren County, Ohio, Sept. 8, 1812, addressed to Msrs. Fredric(k) & Michael Fox, Franklin Township, Warren Co. Ohio"; *Fox Genealogy*, page 12.

27. Frederick County, Maryland, land records, to John Fox, K-703, August 23, 1766, from Joseph Chapline, Lot #143, Sharpsburg.

28. Aubrey C. Land, *The Dulanys of Maryland* (Baltimore: Maryland Historical Society, 1955), 180. *Braddock Expedition*, page 4; *Fox Genealogy*, page 12.

29. Arthur G. Tracey Collection, The Historical Society of Carroll County, Maryland, 210 East Main Street, Westminster, Maryland, Friendship, 231 and 1/2 acres, June 8, 1795, unpatented certificate #228; Maryland State Archives, IC #P 672-3, May 9, 1797, Frederick Fox, Addition to Friendship, 202 acres; *Land Tracts*, page 210. Addition to Friendship was a resurvey obtained by Frederick Fox out of the western shore land office by a special warrant of proclamation to resurvey and affect the vacancy included in a resurvey made for him on the eight day of June seventeen hundred and ninety five by the name of Friendship, the caution money for which had not been paid within the time limited by law. In pursuance whereof, a resurvey was made and a certificate thereof returned containing two hundred and two acres lying in the county aforesaid and called Addition to Friendship.

30. *Fox Genealogy*, page 13.

31. *Braddock Expedition*, Appendix D, pages 200-205; *Land Tracts*, pages 211-213.

32. Will of John Fox.

33. Letter from Jacob Reel to Michael and Frederick Fox, dated at Sharpsburg, August 9, 1812; *Fox Genealogy*, page 12.

34. *Fox Genealogy*, page 12.

35. *News from Fox's Gap*, Issue 3, Volume 2, June 1, 2002, published by The Society of the Descendants of Frederick Fox of Fox's Gap in Maryland, "Michael Fox of Fox's Gap in Maryland" by Lois Ann Baker. Also see Issue 4, Volume 2, "Michael Fox, a brother of Frederick, and The Fox - Beard Connection in Ohio" by Lois Ann Baker.

APPENDIX ONE

will of John Fox

Book A Liber 102, will of John Fox, January 17, 1784
Washington County, Maryland (probated December 4, 1784)

In the name of God Amen I John Fox of Sharpsburg Washington County and State of Maryland being very sick and weak in body but of perfect mind and memory thanks be given to God calling to mind the mortality of my body and knowing that it is appointed for all men once to die do make and ordain this my last Will and Testament, that is to say principally & first of all I give and Recommend my Soul unto the Earth to be buried in decent Christian burial at the discretion of my Executors nothing doubting but at the General Resurrection I shall receive the same again by the Almighty power of God. And as touching such worldly Estate as it has pleased God to bless me with in this life. I give devise and dispose of the same in the following manner and form.

First I give and bequeath unto **my beloved Wife Christina** all that I do possess of during her Natural life and at her Death it is well that **my Son Frederick** shall have the Clock and one half of the skin-dressing tools used.

My son Michael is to have the Young Mare with the Other half of the Aforesaid tools and also my Wearing Apparel Except my fine fur hat which I leave to **Frederick**, and the remaining and Residue of my Estate I leave and bequeath unto my Children and Grand Children viz. as follows, **Frederick, Magdelin & Michael is to have three fourth of it divided Equally amongst them** and the remaining fourth part I give and Bequeath unto **my live Grand Children, Elizabeth & Catherine Furtnay (?Fortney?)**, and also I leave and bequeath unto **my Oldest Son Daniel** and **my Daughter Rachel** five shillings each to be paid when demanded And also I Constitute and **appoint my Wife Christina and my Son Frederick to be the Executors** of this my last Will and Testament and I do hereby utterly disallow revoke and dis(?) all and every Other Testaments Wills Legacies bequests and Executors by me in any wise before named Willed and bequeathed Ratifying and Confirming this and no other to be my last Will and Testament

In Witness whereof I have hereunto set my hand and seal this 17 day of January in the Year of our Lord Seventeen Hundred & Eighty Four.

Signed Sealed published & delivered before the Said John Fox as his last Will and Testament in the presence of us who in his presence and in the presence of each other have hereto subscribed our names

John X Fox (seal)
his mark

Peter Dick Mathias Coons Christopher Cruse

APPENDIX TWO

John Fox Land Records in Frederick County

(Note: Washington County was formed on October 1, 1776 by the splitting of Frederick County.)

Ref No.	Date	From or To	Other party	Name of Tract/Item
K-703	Aug. 23, 1766	From	Joseph Chapline	Lot #143, Sharpsburg
K-1231	May 12, 1767	From	Joseph Chapline	Lot #16, Sharpsburg
J-1400	Aug. 18, 1767	From	John Barroughs	Judgement*
K-1278	June 2, 1769	From	Henry Joel	Lot #7, Sharpsburg
K-1279	June 2, 1769	From	Henry Joel	1/2 Lot #6, Sharpsburg
Probably **not** John Fox of Fox's Gap in Maryland:				
J-504	June 2, 1764	From	Daniel Dulany	Lot #269, Frederick Town*
K-499	May 22, 1766	To	Elias Bruner	Lot #269, Frederick Town*

* It is the author's opinion Lot #269 was bought and sold by a John Fox other than the father of Frederick Fox. It is not known which John Fox was the one in the Judgment record. It is the author's opinion all of the Sharpsburg lots above were owned by John Fox, the father of Frederick Fox.

APPENDIX THREE

Christiana Fox Land Records in Washington County, Maryland

Reference No.	Date	From or To	Other Party	Name of Tract/Other
G-754	1792	From	Joseph Shock	Lot #145, Jerusalem Town
WR-11-414	3-26-1793	n/a	Various	Boundaries of Spring Garden*
WR-22-418	5-31-1802	To	John Harmon	Spring Garden*
P-581	1804	To	Peter Crise	1/2 Lot #145, Sharpsburg
P-583	1804	To	Jacob Reel	1/2 Lot #145, Sharpsburg

*It is the author's opinion the Spring Garden tract was owned by a Christiana Fox other than the mother of Frederick Fox. This Christiana Fox was the widow of Adam Morningstar and married a John Fox after the death of her first husband.

APPENDIX FOUR

Letter from Jacob Reel of Sharpsburg to Frederick and Michael Fox of Ohio

A copy of the following letter from Jacob Reel of Sharpsburg to Michael and Frederick Fox about the death of their mother Christiana was obtained from Robert H. Fox of Cincinnati, Ohio:

> Received and forwarded from Lebanon. Warren Co. Ohio Sept. 8, 1812. Addressed to Msrs. Fredric & Michael Fox, Franklin Township Warren Co. Ohio.
>
> Sharpsburg Aug 9 1812.
>
> Dear. Brothers and Sisters by these few lines we let you know that we are in considerable good state of health at the present time. Thanks be to God for all his blessings. But we inform you that our aged Mother departed this life the 6th of Aug after a sickness of four weeks and was decently buried on the 7th and hope she is now at her rest. We had a physician who attended her regular. She did not complain of very severe pains in the time of her sickness. We suppose on account of her much sleeping. Mr. Widmeyer and wife were down to see her in time of her sickness and gave advice in some cases it seemed to give her some relief but according to the decree of God "dust thou art to dust return" stands good against all of the human family to which period we all hasten as fast as the wheels of time can carry us and may it please the Great Author our being to grant and give us all that true wisdom from above that we may consider our in most soul to meet the great Redeemer of Mankind who is the great Judge of quick and dead therefore let us all seriously and with good earnest consider the great importance of these things to our souls salvation. So we conclude by remembering our love and esteem for you all Yours Truly. Jacob Reel.

Jacob Reel died in 1844 in Sharpsburg. His Will is found in ?, pages 547-552, in Washington County Records. He mentions Christiana Fox twice in his Will, both times in reference to the 1/2 of Lot #6 in Sharpsburg which he purchased from her. He gives his wife's name in the Will as Elizabeth. On an 1877 Map of Sharpsburg, 1/2 of Lot #6 was owned by a D. Reel. Although this property was left by Jacob Reel to his daughter, ? ? , it could have come into the hands of one of his sons, David Reel.

"Item. To my daughter Nancy Michael, Wife of Adam Michael, I give and devise the half lot and premises in the town of Sharpsburg Washington County Maryland adjoining Crise and Beard and which was purchased of Christina Fox etc."

"To my beloved Wife Elizabeth I give, bequeath and devise for and during her natural life the following property viz. half a lot of ground in the town of Sharpsburg Washington County Maryland adjoining Crise and Beard which was purchased of Christian Fox, also the house and lot on which I now live situate in the said town of Sharpsburg and which I purchased from Jacob Houser etc."

APPENDIX FIVE

John Fox's House mentioned in Land Records

The following information is contained on a Surname Card and a Land Plat Card in the The Arthur G. Tracey Collection in the Historical Society of Carroll County, Md., 210 East Main Street, Westminster, MD. 21157)

Surname Card:

Fox, John
2-27-1764 Grims Fancy - 50 A. - CFW: u-40

Near John Fox's House

Land Plat Card:

OFW: u-40   Wash. Co.
GRIMS FANCY
2-27-1764 50 A.
6-12-1769 Alexander Grim
   BC & GS 40-114
N.S. Main Road that leads from Fredericktown to Swainingens (Swearingens) Ferry & near to John Fox's house.
On the west side of South Mtn.
On this land is 2 log cabbins 27 x 12 & 14 x 12 & 15 A. cultivated land.
Next to Mt. Atlas.
Wash. Co. near Foxes Gap.
F. C. 1743 Sheet 392

[**Note:** Name spelled Trim in deeds, not Grim. This tract is located where the name Andrew Bash is found on the 1792 map of the road from Foxes Gap to Swearingens Ferry. This tract was subsequently owned by Michael Bash, probably having inherited it from Andrew Bash, who might have been his father. Michael Bash and his wife Catharine sold the property to Mathias Hutzel and Jacob Hutzel on May 8, 1813. This deed is recorded in Book Y, pages 723-725, Washington County Land Records.]

News from Fox's Gap

Published December 1 of each year by:

The Society of the Descendants of Frederick Fox of Fox's Gap in Maryland

Membership dues are $3.00 per year. President of the Society is Curtis L. Older.

Make Society inquiries by the following means:

Curtis L. Older
2417 Kinmere Road
Gastonia, NC 28056-7818

e-mail: curtolder@earthlink.net
cell: 704-685-2760
phone: 704-864-3879

Please visit the Indiana University of Pennsylvania website for Fox's Gap in Maryland at:

http://www.iuparchaeology.iup.edu/FoxGap/

President's Message

by Curtis Lynn Older

* Membership in the Society will be $3.00 for the 2010 calendar year.

* News from Fox's Gap is published only once per year, on each December 1st.

* *News from Fox's Gap* is seeking articles by Fox Society members about their family genealogy, primarily as it relates to their descent from Frederick Fox. I hope to publish a number of articles in the future that were contributed by Society members.

* There were no new Society members for the calendar year 2009.

* Update on The Fox Inn near Middletown, Maryland.

* New Website - www.cloldergen.com

* **Reprint of The Braddock Expedition and Fox's Gap in Maryland by Heritage Books**

Some Photos from September 14, 2012 by Curtis Lynn Older

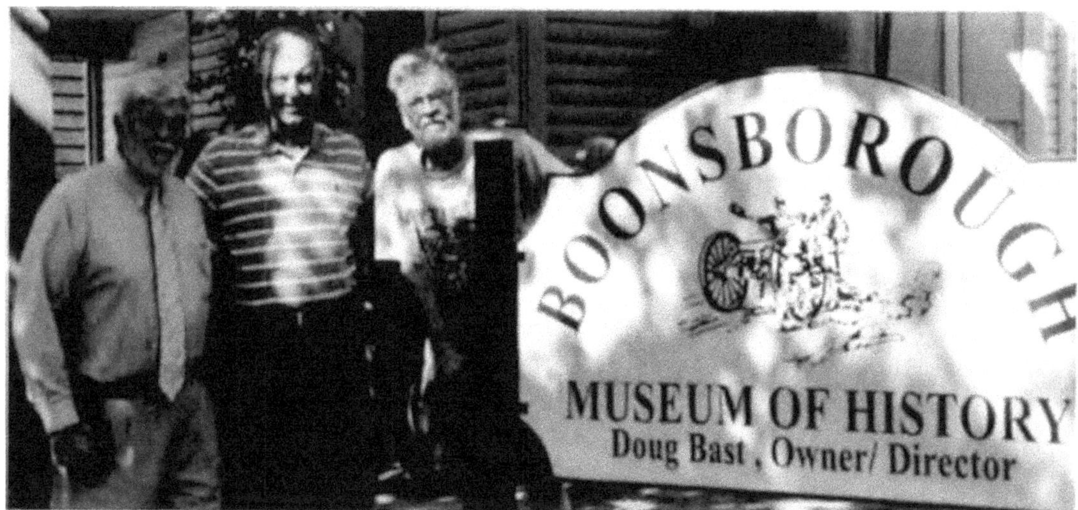

Allan Powell, Curt Older, and Doug Bast in Boonsboro

Preparing to fire cannon near Fox's Gap

Fire!

The North Carolina South Mountain Monument at Fox's Gap

The Battle of South Mountain started in this area about one half mile south of Fox's Gap at 9:00 AM on a Sunday morning

About the Author

Curtis Lynn Older earned a master's degree in Accountancy from Northern Illinois University after serving in the United States Navy as a Spanish interpreter. His professional career included practicing and teaching accounting and working as a computer programmer. His avocation for the past twenty-five plus years has been as a history and genealogy buff.

He is the author of ***The Braddock Expedition and Fox's Gap in Maryland***, ***The Land Tracts of the Battlefield of South Mountain***, and many related e-books on the Apple iBooks Store. He created The Society of the Descendants of Frederick Fox of Fox's Gap in Maryland in 1995 and served as its President until the organization stopped accepting members and ceased publishing the ***News from Fox's Gap*** newsletter in 2011.

Books by Curtis Lynn Older on the Apple iBooks Store

The Land Records, Roads, and People of the Battlefield of South Mountain

News from Fox's Gap

The Land Tracts of the Battlefield of South Mountain

My Relatives, My Heroes – A Documented Genealogy of American History

The Fox Genealogy by Daniel Gebhart Fox Reprinted, Expanded, and Illustrated

The Braddock Expedition and Fox's Gap in Maryland

Articles by Curtis Lynn Older

John Kerr, Founder of Kerrstown and Soldier in the American Revolution
(published in A Journal of Franklin County (PA) History, Vol. XXVIII, 2016)

17th Michigan Monument
at Fox's Gap

Marker for General Samuel Garland
at Fox's Gap

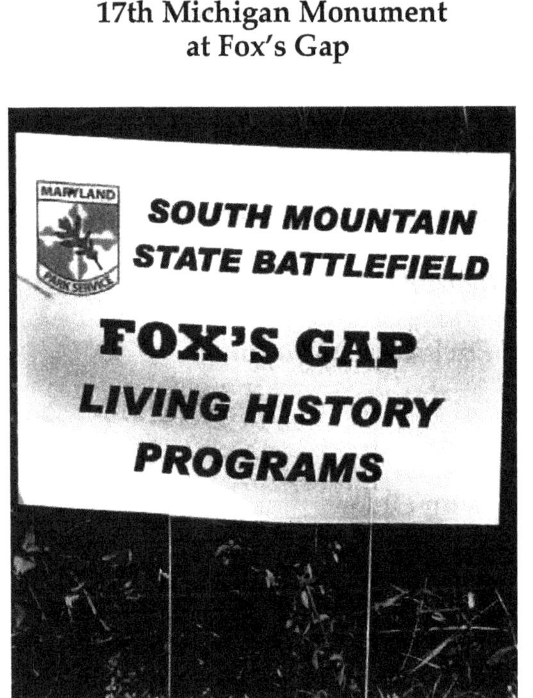

Sign at 150th Anniversary of the
Battle of South Mountain

Stone wall about a half mile south
of Fox's Gap

www.ingramcontent.com/pod-product-compliance
Lightning Source LLC
Chambersburg PA
CBHW081425270326
41932CB00019B/3102
* 9 7 8 0 7 8 8 4 5 8 4 2 2 *